Faithfully recalled and well told, this story of growing up during World War II and in East Germany is a treasure. Gisela's personal history brings the reader into a rare place in her homeland during the war.

Nina Foran Gee
Author, *Springer's Quest, Life of a Pacific Chinook Salmon*

In this story of courage, Gisela Wicks shows us what war is like for a child, what loss—of love, of country, of freedom—means, and what strength abides in families.

Sally Harrold, Ph.D.

Among today's collection of memoirs, **Born into Hitler's War** is a fascinating story of a child living through Hitler's War. Then growing into a young woman behind the "Iron Curtain" in communist East Germany until her escape to West Germany in 1953.

Recommended reading for those desiring to know, what life and survival were like before, during, and after WWII in Germany.

Charles J, Sharps, Ph.D.
Author of: *One More Wake-Up, Where Memories Were Made, Still More Memories* and *One More Wake-Up Revisited.*

This is an extremely well written and moving story. Gisela has conveyed her emotions extremely well, which is remarkable when considering how her emotions were so cruelly repressed when she was very young. This is truly an amazing and far-reaching story. She is an excellent writer, constantly drawing her readers in.

Patricia Flitcroft
Librarian

What a wonderful, heart warming, poignant story . . .

Shinan Barclay.
Author of "Arctic Heart"

BORN INTO
HITLER'S WAR

BORN INTO HITLER'S WAR

A Memoir
by Gisela Wicks

Library of Congress Control Number:		2014901848
ISBN:	Hardcover	978-1-4931-6947-4
	Softcover	978-1-4931-6948-1
	eBook	978-1-4931-6945-0

Rev. date: 04/21/2014

To order additional copies of this book, contact:
Xlibris LLC
1-888-795-4274
www.Xlibris.com
Orders@Xlibris.com
541307

Book One

My Early Years of Survival and Heartbreak

Oma and I

"Are your little eyes open already?" *Oma*, my grandmother, turned and, cuddling me, whispered, "It's early yet, so let's close them for a little while longer." But my eyes didn't want to close, so I traced my finger along my grandmother's closed eyes and brows, then down her nose. When I got near her mouth, Oma tried to gobble my finger. Shrieking with laughter, I pulled my finger away. Oma hugged me and said, "You're just a little wiggle worm."

"What's a wiggle worm, Oma?"

"It's a little worm that can't lie still; it has to wiggle." Oma's tickling made me wiggle and laugh, "See how you wiggle? That's what a wiggle worm does." Stopping her tickling, she turned away. "It's time for me to get up."

"No, Oma, not yet, we haven't played the mouse game!" I clung to Oma's back.

"And now, you're a little pest, and before you ask, a pest is someone like you who doesn't want to give up. I promise we'll play the mouse game tomorrow morning, but not now. It's time for me to get up. Your father has to go to work and Christa to school, and I need to fix their breakfast."

The mouse game was my favorite. Then Oma recited the mouse poem,

> *Kommt ein Maeuschen kriecht in's Haeuschen*
> *Was tut's suchen Kaffee and Kuchen.*

Here comes a little mouse, sneaking into the house
    What does it seek? Coffee and sweets!

As she spoke two of her fingers pretended to be the mouse and walked up my outstretched arm, ending with a tickle under my chin. I giggled with delight begging, "Do it again, Oma!"

Oma and I played the mouse-game nearly every morning while *Vati*, my father, my eight-year old sister Christa, and I, Gisela, lived with Oma in Goerlitz, Germany, before WWII began.

Vati, my sister, and I lived with Oma on the top floor of a three-story apartment building. I only remember the living room, a long room furnished with an ornate, high-backed sofa against one wall, a table in front of it, with chairs grouped around it. On the opposite wall was a bed where Oma and I slept. At the far end of the living room was a window, and out that window was a flat roof, overgrown with thick green moss that felt like a soft pillow to our feet whenever Christa and I walked on it. It was a pretty big roof with no fencing. My sister and I were allowed to sit on the roof right next to the window, where Oma would lay out a blanked for us to sit and too play on, with strict orders, "Do not go near the edge." But one day, we were sitting just outside the window playing when curiosity got the better of Christa and going near the edge of the roof she called, "Gisela, come over here and look down." She motioned with her outstretched arm to come to her. Frightened, I shook my head "no!"

"Christa, what do you think you're doing?" Oma called from the apartment. My sister was in trouble. "You're old enough to know better," Oma told her when Christa and I came in from the roof. After that, Oma kept watch on us.

At dinner I never wanted to eat with Oma and Christa. Instead, I waited for Vati to get home so I could sit on his knee and eat with him no matter what time it was. Vati had spoiled me.

While I lived with Oma, our mother was never mentioned, or did I see her. I didn't remember ever having a mother. She didn't exist to me. Therefore I didn't miss not having a mother. I was happy living with Oma, Vati, and Christa.

Then one day, late in the afternoon, Vati came with a woman I had never seen before. Her plump body almost filled the doorframe, where she stood waiting and watching. Her eyes were cold like steel when she looked at me—she frightened me and I felt uneasy. But the doll the woman brought me was a pretty doll with movable arm and legs. She wore a red and white polka dotted dress, a white apron, white socks and black shiny shoes. On her back she carried a tiny *Tornister*, a school bag, made of brown leather—just like real school children had. I named her Roswitha and she became my favorite doll.

Oma didn't look at the woman. Silently, with tears in her eyes, Oma put on my coat; then she hugged and kissed me. Fearful, I threw my arms around Oma, hanging on to her, but Vati loosened my grip, took my hand, picked up the suitcase Oma had packed earlier, and the woman, Vati and I left, leaving Oma and my sister behind.

While Vati, the woman, and I were riding in the streetcar, it had gotten dark. When I discovered I had lost the doll's school bag, I started to cry. Vati, the woman, and other passengers looked, but found no schoolbag. Drying my tears, Vati said. "I promise, we'll get off at the next stop and walk back to where we got on and see if we can find the missing school bag." But we found no school bag, so I started crying all over again. I could feel the dislike the woman had for me, so when she reached for my hand, I pulled away from her. Holding my new doll close to me, I clung to Vati's hand and begged to be taken back to Oma, but in an unusual firm voice he said, "No, from now on you'll be with us."

Little did I knew how those words would change my life. My loving Oma would become a distant memory. Heartache and sorrow would follow.

Shortly there after in summer of 1939 when I was still four, my father and the woman got married at a church in Kohlfurt, a small town where her parents lived. I was dressed in a light blue short silk dress, black patent leather shoes, and white socks. In my blond hair, curled for the occasion, I had a wreath of tiny pink roses. I carried a small white basket filled with rose petals and trimmed with a satin ribbon, the color of my dress.

The bride, dressed in white, carried a spray of flowers that hung over her right arm. As the church bells rang, the groom and bride, followed by her veil carrier, led the procession of family members and guests along the sidewalk to the nearby church—with a photographer ahead. Just before we left, the bride, hovering over me large as a puffed up white cloud, her eyes glaring, told me, "On the way to the church, you will walk ahead of us, holding the white flower basket in front of you. Then, at the church you scatter the rose petals down the aisle to the altar." But the bride had made the arrangement without consulting me. It was not what I had in mind. *If she could hang onto Vati, so could I.* I heard her tell me to walk ahead, but I ignored her and clung even tighter to Vati's hand—he didn't tell me to walk ahead. So, my father, a handsome, tall, slim figure, dressed in a tux, his plump bride, her white gloved hand resting on his arm, and me, a little sprig of a girl holding his hand, walked to church together.

At the church entrance, Vati let go of my hand, bent down to me, and whispered, "I want you to slowly walk ahead of us and scatter the rose petals down the aisle." And I did just what he told me.

She never forgave me. Every time she looked at her wedding pictures, there I was, holding my father's hand. When no one was around, furious, her eyes spewing hate, almost screaming, she'd say while hitting me across the face, "You ruined my wedding pictures. You're a spoiled child and I will take that out of you. I promise you!"

Shortly thereafter we settled in *Liegnitz*, a city further east of Kohlfurt and Goerlitz. There we lived in a suburb called *Neuhof, on Aurikelweg 9*, a new development of white four plex stucco houses. Ours was a downstairs three-room apartment, which consisted of a combined living room and kitchen, a bedroom, and a formal dining room. All the rooms, just like the kitchen where airy, clean, and inviting with crisp white lace curtains on the windows.

Sitting on the sofa in the kitchen with me beside her, holding my hand, the woman my father had married, in a sweet voice said, "The people you lived with in Goerlitz are no relatives, only babysitters who took care of you while Vati and I were working. The old woman you called Oma is not your grandmother, and the girl, Christa, is not your sister, only a relative of the old woman. Your grandmother and grandfather live in Kohlfurt. I am your mother and you will call me *Mutti*." I believed her and, so, I called her Mutti, the endearment for mother.

Taking a deep breath, Mutti continued in a much firmer tone. "I forbid you to talk about those people again or to tell anyone about them or talk to your father of what I have just told you." Feeling her steel-blue eyes on me I shrank and said, "I won't." But her explanation left me wondering, *if she was my mother, why had I not seen her before Vati and she took me away from the 'old woman' as Mutti called her*. So, I didn't ask, not even Vati, because I was forbidden to talk about them.

I learned quickly that my life had undergone a drastic change. I was confused. I had been taken from a loving, warm environment to a cold unloving one. I missed the love and care that had been given me from the old woman and silently wished I could be there again. The only thing that had not changed was Vati. I felt safe when I was around him, for I could feel that he loved me. I almost glued myself to him when he was home, and I think he enjoyed that, too. He never tired of my chatter, and chatter I did.

I don't recall having received a spanking in my first four years, so I remember that first one well. I was spoiled. I wanted my eating pattern to continue, to get my way, but Mutti's mind was made up. She was the boss, not I.

And I soon found out that she was indeed the boss. I don't remember the reason for our first confrontation. Possibly, I wanted to sit on Vati's lap at dinner, as I always did. But Mutti had decided to end that. I screamed and fought, and hit at her when she tried to pull me off Vati's lap. I tried to hide behind Vati so he could protect me, but she dragged me out from behind him. She laid me over her knee. Then with one hand she pulled down my panties and beat me with her wicker rug beater. I tried to cover my bare bottom with my hands, while I screamed "Vati! Vati!" but it was no use—I got the beating. After she was done with me, I could barely sit, and my hands were swollen and red. *Why had Vati not helped me? What happened to him?* But I learned sitting on Vati's lap at dinner was out! I feared Mutti, so I tried not to get her mad, if at all possible.

Things were pretty quiet for a while after that, and Mutti didn't touch me. She'd only glare at me and I would shrink. One thing I was sure of; I loved Vati and always anxious to please him.

Not long after that beating, I heard Vati say, "Well, I'd better go." The next thing I knew, Vati had a uniform on and was hugging and kissing me good-bye, telling me that he had to go to war. Then he was gone—leaving me to Mutti and an empty feeling of loss.

After Vati had gone, Christa came to Liegnitz for a visit. Oma, the old woman as Mutti called her, who loved me and had cared for me, came with Christa to drop her off. I was so happy to see Oma. I wanted to hug her, but Mutti held me tight by the hand and didn't allow me to hug her, only to shake her hand and a curtsy. Oma had brought gifts for me, but Mutti took them by saying, "I will put them up, so, that, later you can open them." But I never saw them again. Oma had her other daughter Elfriede with her and Elfriede's daughter Uschi, short for Ursula, who was my age. Uschi and I played and, then, they were gone.

Christa stayed with us for a very short time. Her dislike for me had not changed. But Christa disliked Mutti even more. "I hate that fat woman!" she'd tell me. Christa sassed Mutti the whole time she was with us, but Mutti never touched her. *Why isn't Mutti spanking her?* Whenever Mutti was not nearby Christa would whisper, "I will not call her Mutti. She is not your real mother or mine; she is a mean, fat stepmother. I'm your sister. I'm living with our real mother and Oma in Goerlitz."

"Mutti is too my real mother," I protested out loud.

"Sshh, do you want her to hear you?"

"She told me so." I persisted.

But I was confused and asked Mutti. "Christa is lying to you," was her answer. Soon Christa was gone—never to visit again. I don't know if I was happy or not, but Mutti was relieved.

After Christa was gone, Mutti again, gave me strict orders never to speak of Christa or about the people who had been here. "I'd better not hear you talk about them. No one needs to know anything about our past. I am your mother, no one else. Is that clear to you?" Then, she added in a softer voice, "You do believe that I am your mother?"

"Yes, Mutti, I believe you." I felt uneasy. *Why does Mutti keep telling me she was my mother? Why is she so mean to me? Oma, the old woman was never like that.*

I missed Vati and wished he were home.

Soon after Christa had left, Mutti said, "Vati is coming home on leave from France." I was overjoyed when Mutti and I, me in my prettiest dress, went to the train station to pick him up.

The train station, called *Bahnhof* in German, was an enormous extensive passageway with a high rounded ceiling. Large chandelier-like lamps hung from the ceiling illuminating the area. On one side were big glass windows with people behind them in dark blue uniforms trimmed with red piping and red shoulder bars and matching caps. People stood in line to buy tickets for their train trip. Flower and candy shops were on the opposite side, as well as a restaurant at the far end. Straight across from the entrance were four gates or booths that looked like miniature boats to me. The lower part was of wood and the upper, of glass with a half-door in the center. In that booth as the people went through the uniformed official took the tickets and punched a hole in them with a hole-puncher hanging from his waist on a bright shiny chain. After their tickets were validated, the people went into a tunnel-like wide walkway and up the steps to the designated platform where the train was waiting.

From above I heard the rumble of trains, the screeching of the wheels, and a loud voice announcing "Liegnitz, Liegnitz"! Others were calling out, *"Alle Einsteigen,"* all aboard, followed by two short whistles from the locomotive, telling everyone of its leaving the station with its passengers. The steam engine started with a loud hiss followed by the slow and even rolling of the wheels as it left the train station. The Bahnhof was filled with the excitement of people and trains coming and going.

Vati was coming on one of those trains, and I could hardly wait. People with children were standing at the gate, including Mutti and me, everyone had come to pick up someone. People were hugging and crying, and children were calling out to their fathers.

Mutti picked me up so I was able to see among all those people. I saw men dressed in green uniforms coming through the gate, but none looked like Vati.

Mutti said, "There is Vati. Do you see him?" My eyes strained. I looked and looked, but I did not see him. A man in uniform with suitcases slung over his shoulder stood in front of me smiling and laughing. He had a mustache, but my Vati didn't have one. I was sure of that. I kept looking past that man, but I didn't see Vati anywhere.

"*Spatz*,'" the man said, putting his face close to mine, "don't you remember me anymore?" I looked at him, but he wasn't my Vati! My Vati didn't have a mustache! The man did know my nickname "Spatz", the name Vati always called me. He took me from Mutti, hugged me, and wanted to kiss me, but not with that mustache! I pushed him away! I knew it was my father, but that was not how I remembered him. My excitement turned into disappointment. I kept looking at him, and he just laughed, thinking I was funny, but to me it was not funny at all. It was a serious matter. In the trolley going home, he tried to get me to kiss him, but I wouldn't do it. Not with a mustache!

With me sitting on his knees while riding in the trolley, Vati finally said, "Let's make an agreement. You give me a hug and a kiss, and when we get home, I'll shave the mustache off."

"You promise?"

"Ja, I promise." So I gave him a hug and a kiss and wiped my lips afterward because Vati's mustache had tickled me. He just laughed, and when we got home, he shaved the mustache off. Then I hugged and kissed him. I felt as if I had Vati back. He was home, I was happy, and my world once more was complete. Mutti was the only unhappy person. She was mad because I got my way. "You got home just a short while ago and already you're spoiling her," she told Vati. Vati only smiled and ruffled my hair.

Vati had brought silk from France for me for dresses, solid sky blue material and a soft pink with red pinstripes that made little squares. He also had brought a small silver statue of the Eiffel Tower and a dollhouse. The dollhouse was in a suitcase form, not bigger than an overnight case with the outside covered in blue material. After the lock in front was opened, it unfolded into a dollhouse with the furnishings of a living room inside. I was so proud of it and played with it every day—for hours. When it was folded up, I carried it like a suitcase, making me feel important, like I was going on a trip.

I was happy. Vati was home and Mutti never got mad at me. But my happy time was short. I watched as Vati, with Mutti's help, packed his suitcase. All my crying and begging wouldn't stop him from leaving again. Bending down and hugging me, he said, "Spatz, I don't want to leave you, but I have to go. I'm a soldier and soldiers go to war. I promise to come back, and then I'll never leave you again; I promise." I didn't know what a war was. I only knew that Vati was leaving.

Mutti and I didn't go to the train station with Vati as we had when he'd come home. Tears ran down my cheeks as I watched Vati in his uniform walking down the street, carrying his suitcase, waving at me. I waved back as he disappeared around the corner, leaving me clinging to his words, "I promise to came back and then I'll never leave you again." I thought it was the saddest day, but I didn't know then how wrong I was.

After Vati left, Mutti's rules applied once more. All the yards in our subdivision had low wooden fences with matching gates. One of Mutti's rules was that I was not allowed to leave the yard, so I had no playmates. Only five and not very tall, I draped myself over our gate, my feet on the cross bar, my arms clamped over the top of the gate with my head resting on my arms. As I watched the kids running and playing, I wanted to be out on the gravel street too—having fun. The boys were playing ball: the girl's, hopscotch and jump rope when I saw a little girl pushing her doll buggy up and down the street. Watching her, I realized I, too, had a doll buggy. Forgetting Mutti's orders, I decided to join the little girl. I ran in the house to get my doll buggy, telling my doll, "We're going for a walk." I pushed the doll buggy through the kitchen where Mutti was cooking.

She turned, "And just where do you think you're going with that doll buggy?"

I froze. "I was going to play with a girl who's walking with her doll buggy up and down the street."

"Have I not told you, you're not to go out of the yard?"

"Yes, Mutti, but I want to play with her."

"You put that buggy right back where you got it from!"

Head down so Mutti couldn't see my tears; I put the buggy back, wiping my tears on my apron before returning. When I came back out, Mutti's cold voice continued. "How many times must I tell you the kids don't want to play with you! You're too ugly! They don't want you, and, besides, you don't know how to play."

So, hanging on the gate, I continued to watch the kids. Sometimes they'd come up and ask me, "Why don't you play with us?" Backing away, I'd shake my head; afraid, Mutti might see me talk to the kids. After a while, they stopped asking.

Two sisters about my age lived in the house next to us. I could see them play in their yard, having fun. Since they were playing in the yard and not on the street, I asked Mutti, "Can I go and play with the girls in their yard?"

But again Mutti told me, "No, the girls don't want to play with you. Don't you remember what I told you? You're ugly and nobody wants to play with you. You stay in the yard and play alone."

So I got used to not having playmates and learned to entertain myself. My favorite toy was my tricycle. While riding it, I'd sing and hum, in my own fantasy world, where it's bright and cheerful. Then, one day when I went to get my tricycle, it was gone. Always when I finished riding it, I put it in the storeroom, but it wasn't there. I looked everywhere. I couldn't find it. I was close to tears. *It had to be here! Where could it have gone?* I stood, not knowing where else to look, when I saw the girls in their yard, riding a tricycle. My tricycle! They had my tricycle! Excited to have found it, I ran into the house. "Mutti, I found my tricycle! The girls have my tricycle! They're riding it in their yard. Please hurry, Mutti, we have to get it back."

Mutti, the newspaper in her hands, just sat and shrugged her shoulders. "No, we will not take it back. I gave it to the girls because you have been bad and that's your punishment. Now you can watch the girls have fun with your tricycle."

What had I done? I sat on the doorsteps and sobbed. Mutti came out, grabbed my arm and took me in the house where I got a spanking for crying. I hated the girls from then on, and whenever I saw them ride my bike, it felt as if they were laughing at me. I swallowed my tears, because if Mutti knew I was crying, she'd spank me again. I wished someone would help me get my bike back, but there was no one. I felt an ache inside me that I couldn't explain, and I longed for Vati to come home. *He wouldn't tell me that I was ugly. Or was I as ugly as Mutti said?*

Time passed. The seamstress came and sewed dresses for Mutti and I, mine of the material Vati had brought for me from France. I was so proud of the dresses but was allowed to wear them only on Sundays or special occasions. The seamstress came twice a year in early spring and fall, sewing new clothes for Mutti and me. People dressed when going out in public. Mutti wanted us to look good, so I was dressed well when we went somewhere and Mutti was always nice to me in public. But I had to be alert not to make a mistake, because if I did, I felt it when we got home.

Whenever Mutti and I took the streetcar to down town Liegnitz we always dressed up; I, in one of my favorite dresses made of the materials Vati had brought from France.

I don't remember much of Liegnitz, the city, except that there was an ice cream parlor with the best ice cream. This parlor had white and black marble tiled floor. Its big folding glass doors opened wide to the warm summer breeze, creating a large and airy entry. Small round marble topped tables and dainty chairs were placed throughout. Mirrors covered the walls, giving the sensation of a bigger parlor. Stretching all the way across the back was the counter of white and black marble. It looked cool and clean. Servers were busy dishing up ice cream, satisfying the wishes of their guests, big and small, and making steaming coffee, it's aroma filling the air. Silver and glass dishes sat neatly lined up in rows on glass shelves, on the wall behind them. Little silver coffeepots, looking like toys to me, sat next to the silver trays. The huge mirror centered above the shelves was tipped slightly forward, reflecting the ice cream containers with their shiny conical lids in the holes of the marble-topped counter. Black trousered waiters with ties and white shirts lent the parlor an air of elegance. Palm trees, in large decorative containers were placed here and there. The ice cream itself was served in a small silver dish on a silver tray lined with a white, lace paper doily. Two small waffles decorated the ice cream. Placed on the tray was a tiny silver spoon that was flat in front for easy and delicate eating.

I loved watching myself in those mirrors while eating my favorite ice cream, a scoop each of vanilla and chocolate. When Mutti noticed what I was doing, she said, "Eat and don't look at yourself—it's bad manners." But I could not resist and sneaked a little glance every now and then. It was a nice place, and I felt extra special to be there. Of course, I had to mind my manners. It was expected of me without question.

Germans were strict disciplinarians in table manners and respect. Children were always expected to be on their best behavior showing courtesy and respect for their superiors and elders. From an early age, children were taught to be seen only, not heard, and to talk only when they were spoken to. When greeting grown-ups, girls curtsied; boys removed their hats and bowed. Children became very proficient in this, because no matter how many people they had to greet, everyone received the same courtesy.

S tarting school in 1941 was a big event for me and all other first graders. The girls dressed in their best dresses with ribbons in their hair; the boys, in suits and ties. Everyone was on his or her best behavior. The first session was short, mainly for students to get acquainted with the teachers and the teachers with their future pupils. The teacher assigned to each class stayed with the children throughout their school years, including eighth grade. Everyone was eager for class to be dismissed because a surprise was waiting for each child outside the classroom. Godparents, grandparents, or family members had arrived and brought the surprise with them. It was a big cone made of cardboard, in different sizes, from two to three feet high. The outside is wrapped in shiny aluminum foil, each a different color. Colorful pictures decorated the cone, depending whether the cone was for a boy or a girl. Crepe paper of matching color, tied together with a ribbon, closed the cone, making a big tuft on top. Inside each cone were chocolates, cookies, and maybe a small gift.

For my first day of school, and with Vati in the war, only Mutti was waiting for me outside the classroom, holding my cone because there were no other family members attending. And when after class Mutti gave me my cone I was so proud of it. I felt as if everyone was looking and smiling at me as Mutti and I rode the streetcar back home. I knew I had started another part of my life.

Living in the suburb of Liegnitz, I attended the city school with several other children. Every day we rode the streetcar to town, a half hour trip. To catch the streetcar we had to walk a short distance to the stop and never be late. The streetcar stopped right in front of the school called *Dornbusch Schule*. The school was a new four-story building. It's outside of grayish red and dark blue shining rock, gave it a majestic look. Inside wide staircases lead to each floor and the classrooms. On each floor was a spacious sitting area with polished tables and benches for eating and rest periods. And in the center for drinking, stood a large round running water fountain made of the same grayish red and dark blue shining rocks as the outside. The classrooms were bright and sunny with big windows, and desks lined up in three precise rows. Everyday before classes, all students and teachers had to assemble for the hoisting and saluting of the big red flag with a white circle in the middle that held the black swastika. When saluting, we had to raise the right arm stretched forward, and in a clear, strong voices say, *"Heil Hitler."* This salute and greeting were also required when passing the teachers in the hallways or when entering the classroom. If the salutation was not correct or sincere enough, we were called back to repeat it until it was satisfactory.

My teacher was *Fraeulein Kaetzler*, a short round lady with gray hair and a kind face. All the kids in the class loved her. To me she was like an angel, and I have never forgotten her. Never did she make me feel that I was not smart enough or that I was ugly, as Mutti told me I was. It was just the opposite. She encouraged me, and I loved going to school.

To ride the streetcar was lots of fun. The older kids put pennies on the track, and when the trolley ran over them, they were flattened into funny shapes. Of course, when the conductor saw that, the kids got in trouble. When the streetcar was speeding across the farmland, the bigger kids stood in back of the open platform in the second car jumping up and down, making that car bounce a little. That, too, came to a quick stop, but they still tried it when the conductor wasn't watching. The older ones ignored us younger kids, but we enjoyed watching them.

I liked to ride the trolley for other reasons. First, I got away from Mutti, and I could daydream. Sitting in the trolley, I saw all the pretty, slim ladies, in fashionable dresses, hats, leather gloves, matching purses, and high-heeled shoes. In my mind, I talked to them as if they were my mothers, and they looked at me and smiled. Maybe I was just staring at them, or they could read my thoughts, or maybe it was just my imagination. *Why could I not have a mother who was slim and trim?* I saw children sitting close to their mothers, holding hands, and I could see the affection they had for each other. Right then and there I had one wish, that I'd be just as pretty and slim when I grew up. I was sure fat ladies were mean, and I would never daydream on the trolley about them.

With Vati gone, I was left to Mutti's care, to do with me as she saw fit. Homework from school was a horror for me. We carried all our school supplies in brown leather bag, a *Tornister*, strapped on our back. We had slate boards the size of a large writing pad and slate pencils to write with in the first grade. When I pressed too hard with the slate pencil it made the most awful screeching sound and Mutti would get mad at me. The whole board was framed in wood. Through a small hole on one side was a string with an attached sponge and a cloth to clean the slate with. One side of the slate, had lines for letters, and the other side had squares for math. I don't know how many times Mutti wiped off the board with the attached sponge for one thing and another. Whenever I started to cry, she got the rug beater. Then, she closed the windows so the neighbors could not hear and gave me a spanking. Sometimes she even put the rug beater on the table right in front of me, scaring me even more, making me unable to read or do the math.

My first grade-reading book had two pages permanently stained red from the bloody nose she gave me. When reading and learning the alphabet, I found the letter "e" my enemy. I simply could not get it into my head, and I stumbled every time. It just sat there on the page staring at me. Mutti always grabbed my for-finger and pointed it to the "e", and screamed at me "e . . . e . . . e", taking my head, pushing it on the page until my nosebleed all over the page. Those sessions so scared me that I was unable to concentrate, making things harder. With her screaming at me, "You're just to dumb and ugly!"

In a firm tone of voice Mutti told me, "When the teacher asks you why you have a bloody page in your reading book, you'll tell her it's none of her business. Is that understood?" Her eyes glaring, she added, "You know what will happen to you if you don't do as I tell you?"

"I will tell her just as you said, Mutti." I said, but thinking, *I will never say that to my teacher because what Mutti told me to say is rude.*

As it happened the next day, a mother came past my desk in school and saw my book. Concerned, she called the teacher to make sure I was all right. When the *Fraeulein Kaetzler* came to check on me, I lied and said, "I had a nosebleed at home." *That was not really a lie, just not the whole story.* Leaning down and stroking my head, the teacher in a soft and caring voice said, "I'm sorry to hear that. Are you feeling better again?" Aware of her caring hand, I just nodded my head because I had to stop myself from crying or telling her what really had happened. I knew Mutti would be furious and I was afraid of her reaction. Oh, how I wished Vati would come home from wherever he was.

Sometimes Mutti rode the trolley to downtown Liegnitz, leaving me at home—alone, "You are almost seven, old enough to stay home alone." With a stern look in her gray cold eyes, her finger pointing, and her voice firm, she gave me her orders, "Do not play with matches, knives or scissors; do not open the window; do not make any noise, and do not turn on the radio. Should someone knock at the door, do not answer; keep quiet and away from the window, they will leave again. Do not touch the stove or build a fire. You can color, with crayons only, or play with your dolls or read a book, or play with your building blocks. Most of all, do not open the door or, answer if someone knocks and do not go outside while I'm gone. Do you understand me?"

I nodded my head. "Yes."

Then, with the bread machine Mutti sliced a piece of bread for me, placed it on a sandwich board, put jelly on it, and repeating her orders once more, she was gone, but not before she heard me lock the door from the inside. I was left alone, and it didn't scare me at all. Although I was told what to do and not to do, my toys did not interest me. I had my own imagination for entertainment without crossing the line of her "do-not orders". It was an invisible border, laid out by Mutti, and I wouldn't cross it. I knew the consequences.

Whenever alone, my favorite thing to do was to use the couch in front of the window as a trampoline. I watched Mutti walk down the road to the streetcar station as I bounced up and down. After bouncing and seeing her disappear in the distance, my interest turned to Mutti and Vati's bedroom. There, attached to a low vanity in a natural wood color was a large mirror with wings on each side. It's top was covered with thick plate glass with smooth, round edges. Pale green doilies of different sizes lay underneath the glass, matching the placement of items on top. Mutti had a set of pale green crystal, engraved with tiny flowers: a shallow, narrow, oblong platter for combs; a covered round container for powder; and a perfume atomizer with a green tassel of the silky thread that covered the rubber ball for squeezing. The atomizer had perfume in it that I loved to smell, but I did not dare squeeze the ball. I knew from past experience that, Mutti would smell it right away when she returned. The invisible barrier stopped me, including the punishment sure to follow. I knew everything was for show only and not to be touched by me. Turning the wings of the mirror, I could see myself from all directions. Contrary to Mutti's teaching that looking at myself in the mirror was inappropriate and could make me even uglier—I loved it. I tied a scarf around my head to make a turban, as I had seen ladies do. I put on my red coral necklace, placed the silver hoop engraved with flowers on my lower arm. I was allowed to wear these items only on special occasions, usually the lay in my own small jewelry box lined in red velvet, it's outside covered with tiny, shiny seashells. Nodding my head in a friendly greeting, I talked to the person in the mirror, pretending she was a lady riding in the trolley with me. When I asked her where she was going, her answer was always the ice cream parlor, my favorite place.

Dancing and swirling, I sang in front of the mirror, forgetting my surroundings for a short time. I was in my own world of bright and happy make-belief. I was beautiful. With all this whirl of activity my stomach started to talk to me. So, I put back the jewelry, folded the scarf and returned it to its proper place. I pushed the wings of the mirror back to their original position, said good-bye to the lady in the mirror, and returned to reality.

Having been made earlier, the jelly sandwich edges had started to roll up. On close examination I could tell that the jelly, once on top of the bread, had sunk in. My stomach made funny little leaps as the sandwich glared at me from the breadboard like a big red blob. I had to fix that somehow, make it more tasteful looking, and I just happened to know how.

I got the butter from its cool storage place, unwrapped it, and cut a thin slice, carefully re-wrapping it again so that it looked untouched. I gently rounded the edges and returned the butter to its original location. The butter, creamy and sweet, improved the looks and taste of my dried jelly bread immensely. It disappeared in a hurry as I was hungry from my trip to the land of make believe.

To fix up my sandwich was not that easy because I had to run to the window once in awhile to make sure Mutti was not on her way home. I could not be found out; that would have been big trouble for me. Everything returned to its normal place, and with book in hand, I watched at the window for Mutti's return. I waved at Mutti, outwardly glad that she was home again. *Would Mutti notice the carving on the butter?* But luck was with me, she never did. That puzzled me. *Maybe I was not as dumb as Mutti said I was.*

Often, in summer, Mutti and I took the train to Kohlfurt to visit her parents. Kohlfurt, halfway between Liegnitz and Goerlitz was the town where Mutti came from and where she and Vati got married. Her parents lived in a big red brick apartment building across from the Bahnhof, the train station. All the people living in those red brick apartment buildings, and there were about five of them, were employed by *Der Deutschen Eisenbahn,* the German train system. Mutti's father, a mechanic, worked on the engines.

While playing in front of Mutti's parents' apartment building, I heard clearly the whistle of the trains as I jumped rope or jumped off the entrance steps three and four at a time. I was unable to see the trains because the station was below street level, but I saw the white steam from the engines rising in the air like big puffs of cotton floating up into the blue sky.

Just a little ways across the street was the pedestrian bridge that crossed over to the train station. Since the station was lower than the street, people had to walk up the steps on the street side of the bridge, then, over and down on the other side to the station and platforms below. The bridge, of black iron and high above the train tracks had a banister and a high fence for safety on both sides. Although I was not allowed, I loved to stand on that bridge looking down as the trains rolled in and out underneath me. The huge black engine strained, the big wheels began to turn slowly, not knowing if they really wanted to go. While blowing the whistle, the engine kept pressing on, turning the wheels faster and faster. Steam, in big white puffs, was coming out of the chimney, and down by the huge, black wheels. I stood in that white steam as it came up and over the bridge engulfing me momentarily, giving me an eerie feeling, like having a cloud of my own that I was floating in. It felt airless. I saw nothing. I was in a white, soft, clean cloud that hugged. There was no scent, just cuddly, suspended, humid warmth. Within minutes my white cuddly cloud was gone, and I was on the bridge again. Like a long snake the train was on its way, rolling underneath the bridge and me, slowly winding out of sight. But sometimes the engine gave up clouds of thick black smoke. That is when I ran as fast as I could off that bridge. I knew what that smoke could do.

Trains came and stopped, doors opened, people got off, and new passengers got on. The stationmaster in his dark blue, red trimmed uniform with a red cap and polished black shoes walked along the train. He closed all open doors with a bang and, looking in the direction of the engineer, blew his shiny whistle. Then, he raised his arm high, and with the red signal in his hand that looked like a flyswatter, gave the command that the train was ready to depart. The engineer answered with a short whistle, and the locomotive started with a puff-puff and a hiss-hiss to pull out of the station. Passengers waved goodbyes out the windows with their hankies, and others left behind wiped their tears.

But there were other things I saw that left me puzzled. Standing on the bridge, I saw a long train of cattle cars stopped three tracks over from the main train, isolated from the rest. A long line of people with children and small suitcases in their hands were getting into those cars. On their coats, marked in white, they had big stars. Gestapo stood watch, stern faced, their helmets reflecting the sun, their uniforms fitted, their black boots up to their knees, demanding respect without saying a word and invoking fear in others. German shepherd dogs on the leash were sitting at attention and on guard beside the Gestapo. Soldiers with rifles over their shoulders patrolled up and down the throng of people as they climbed into the railroad cars. Up high out of the slit windows faces appeared; no one spoke a word, no conversation at all. They looked sad and faced the ground as they walked along the train with the Gestapo and their dogs on guard. *Where were they going? And why in a cattle car? And not like me in a regular train?* But there was no answer to my question. When grownups came over the bridge, I was told to leave and stop watching. The whole thing felt strange and scary to me, and I was glad to leave. When I was with Mutti, she, too, told me in a low voice, "Don't watch! Look straight ahead!" *Why was I not to look?*

I could hear fear, too, when Mutti and her parents whispered in low voices, saying that this or that store is closed; that they, the store owners, were taken away during in the night; or that so and so was arrested last night. When they realized I was present, their conversation stopped, and they told me, "Go outside and play, what we're talking about is not for little ears to hear. We'll call you when you can come back in." *Why send me outside? What is so secret?* I didn't ask and did what I was told.

Mutti told me that although her parents were like strangers to me, they were my grandparents and I was to call them Oma and Opa. Oma was a cold and unloving person, much like Mutti. No matter how hard I tried to please her, she did not like me. I jumped to pick up things that she'd dropped. I helped with the dishes. I set the table. I ran errands to the store. But no matter how hard I tried, she did not like me. I could not figure it out. *Why?* Sometimes when Oma was busy doing things, I sat quietly and watched her, but it didn't help. She was like an iceberg, cold and sharp. Unlike Mutti, she was not fat, but skinny with gray hair combed straight back, braided and put in a knot like a snail house at the nape of her neck. Her face was always puckered and stern, and very seldom if ever did I see her laugh.

Opa, Mutti's father, was a small person, quiet and kind of mousy looking. Oma fought with him all the time, and it scared me. Sometimes she would hit him right in front of me. She'd scream at him something about a woman that he had looked at who lived in the same building. I felt sorry for him and wanted to hug him, but I knew that was not a good thing to do. There was never any hugging at all. It was best for me to find a corner and quietly make myself invisible.

Opa was my favorite person. I felt drawn to him, and when I was able to go with him, I was happy. While walking, we talked, small children talk, and I chatted all the time until we got back home. We picked *Huflattich*, a tea, along the banks of the railroad tracks. It grows low to the ground, looking like a spider, spreading its long green legs. In the center on short stems it has yellow flowers, like a star or a dandelion, real bright and shiny. We picked only the bloom, and when we got home, Oma dried them in the sun on the windowsill. After that she put the dried flowers in an airtight container to be used for medical usages. To go with Opa was fun. He held my hand, making sure that I didn't fall. We stopped, sat down and ate our sandwiches. The sun was shining. It was warm and cozy, and the air was filled with the sweet, fragrant smell of wild flowers all around us. The birds were singing in the branches of the tree we rested under. I sat close to Opa, feeling relaxed and secure, and I enjoyed every minute. I knew he liked me without even saying so. Other times we collected mushrooms in the forest and put them in the basket that we carried. "You must watch," he said. "Every mushroom has a neighbor, so when you find one, there is a second one nearby." It was a game, and I had fun looking, seeing who would find the neighbor first. At home the mushrooms were sliced, put on a cookie sheet, covered with a dishtowel, and dried in the sun on the windowsill. It was my job to turn them every so often so they dried evenly. Once big smooth pieces, they shriveled down to small wrinkled ones. Then, they were stored for winter.

Sometimes I asked Opa to take me to see the big black engines in the *Schuppen*, the repair building. The half round building was stained black from the dark smoke of the locomotives. Inside the building were several big stalls that had tracks. Directly in front of the building, made of black steel, was a large turntable with tracks that crisscrossed. I liked watching the man who sat in another small house controlling the turning of the carousel when the engine in need of repair sat on one of those tracks. When the engine was lined up with the tracks of the stall for its repairs, the man stopped the carousel. Then, another man drove the engine into the stall. The men working on the engine, covered with black soot and grease looked like chimney sweeps. The locomotives stood big and powerless, no whistling, no steam, motionless and quiet. It was as if all the energy had gone out of them. They were looming like monsters, empty, like a huge round black iron pipe with wheels.

When I got close, the big, black sturdy wheels were almost twice my size. Although they were not moving, it was intimidating to stand that close. I knew they blew steam from down low, too, and I was just the right height to feel it, but I held onto Opa's hand tight. Looking down he said, "Don't be scared. They're here to be repaired so they can pull the trains, maybe even the one you will be on when you go home to Liegnitz." With a smile he added, "They will not hurt you." I believed him, but still, I kept a watchful eye on them while Opa was visiting with his coworkers. Opa and I always had fun together, but when we returned home, he changed. He kept his distance and would never say much to me, and I stayed out of his way.

Each resident in the red brick apartment buildings had a garden in back of the building, and I liked to go to the garden with Opa. I watched as he planted vegetables and flowers, and I got to water all of them with the watering can. Sometimes Oma, when she was mad about one thing or another, would not allow me to go with Opa in the garden or for a hike. I cried silently because I did not want her to know just how much I wanted to go. I was afraid if she realized just how much I liked Opa, she would use that to stop me from going with him whenever she was mad.

Another reason Mutti and I went to Kohlfurt was to pick blueberries in the woods. I liked the outdoors and the forest with its birds, squirrels, butterflies and flowers. *Heidekraut,* or heather, colored the ground of the woods lavender with the green from the blueberry bushes dotted in between. It looked like a giant puzzle in greens and lavender with the added red of the tree trunks. There was no undergrowth, just flat ground, so I could see a long way. The sun coming up made the prettiest rays in all colors between the trees and branches, settling on the soft ground. I wished that I could walk up on those rays and go to a new and different place, like the dolls in my storybook.

But I was not a doll, but a person, and was here to pick blueberries and not to daydream. I had my own basket to fill, with strict orders from Oma and Mutti, "No berries, no sandwich." I loved blueberries, and my basket seemed never to get full. If I was unlucky, I spilled the berries on the ground, and had to start all over again. Then big tears ran down my face, and I got a tongue lashing from Oma and Mutti who said I was clumsy and too dumb to pick berries. "You are never going to be good for anything," was always the final sentence. At day's end, Oma and Mutti filled my basket reluctantly, "It would be a waste to go home with an empty basket," was their explanation.

But when Opa was along, he'd sneak past me and dump some berries into my basket. I gave him a quiet smile as he walked away. If anyone had asked me, "What do you like best in Kohlfurt?" I would have said that I liked the walks with Opa, gardening with him, and feeling that he cared. I liked going in the forest, watching Mother Nature put on her show. Most of all, I liked the bridge of the train station and the trains coming and goings. Clasping the wire with my hands, my face pressed close, watching the train disappear in the distance, I dreamed of being on it, taking me to faraway places. *Could one take me to Vati?*

W hen at home, not in school or in Kohlfurt, I entertained myself with my toys. A new one was my swing.

When Vati had been home on furlough from France, he had made me a detachable swing. In the yard behind the house stood two tall cement poles topped with a heavy wooden crossbar—making it look like an upside down 'U'. Rugs were hung on this 'U' then beaten with a rug beater to get rid of dust. Into that crossbar Vati screwed two big steel hooks that looked like cork screws. "Vati, why are the hooks twisted?" I asked him.

"That's so when you swing, the steel rings attached to the swing's ropes won't slip out. It keeps you safe." To finish my swing, Vati attached a big heavy ring to one end of the rope, then measured the length so that when I sat on the swing, my feet would touch the ground. Then, he attached the second ring to the other end. I watched as Vati next took the swing seat a smooth wooden board, and cut a "V" on each end. "Why are you doing that?"

"That's to hold the board in place when you swing." Bending down he showed me how it worked. "See the rope fits right in here." As long as Vati was home and the neighbors weren't beating or airing out their rugs, Vati hooked the swing up, but when he was gone, I had to ask Mutti, and she often wouldn't do it, telling me "You don't need to swing."

I loved the swing and swinging. Slowly I'd swing back and forth, singing and humming, happy that Vati had made a swing for me. Sometimes while swinging, I watched the girls in their yard as they played with my tricycle. I still hated the girls and wanted to cry when I saw my tricycle, but I knew it would only cause trouble for me. So I'd swing and watch.

I had a *Mundharmonika*, a mouth organ. I couldn't play any songs, but that didn't stop me from playing, because I liked the sound of different chords. Draped over the garden gate, I'd swing back and forth, playing the

Mundharmonika to my heart's content. I watched the kids play, but I was not allowed to play with them, no matter how many times I asked Mutti, "Please, can I play with the kids?"

Her answer was always the same, "The kids don't want to play with an ugly girl. I have told you that before; now stop asking."

I couldn't understand. *Was I so ugly that they didn't want to play with me? It must be so if Mutti said so.* So I watched and played my music and daydreamed. I had books for reading and coloring, as well as blocks for building towns, but I mostly liked coloring on rainy days, in particular with watercolors. I mixed them with other colors to get different shades.

Whatever I did, Mutti watched me and I had to do it to her specifications. She said, "If you don't treat your toys right, I will take them away from you and give them to some other little girl to play with, and you'll never see your toys again!" Then, looking straight at me, she added, "Just remember your tricycle!" Oh yes, I remembered. I see it every day. I learned to be very careful with my toys and tried not to make Mutti mad at me so I didn't lose any more of my toys.

I liked my doll buggy, a replica of a real baby buggy, creamy white. Just about every little girl had one. The buggy had a real mattress with a feather cover for bedding. The sham pillow with matching spread was made of soft green silk knit with tiny embroidered flowers and a ruffle edge. The baby for my buggy was made of skin colored porcelain with eyes that closed. It looked just like a baby with movable head, arms, and legs. Mutti had crocheted a baby outfit for it that I was not allowed to take it off. She said, "You're too clumsy and will drop the doll, so leave it in the buggy." I didn't play much with the doll because I was scared I might break it, being clumsy, as Mutti said I was. She also said it was a showpiece for the buggy.

Sitting on my bed beside Roswitha, my best loved doll in her red and white dotted dress I had received from Mutti when Vati and she had picked me up, was Fritz, my well-used teddy bear that Oma had packed in my suite case. He was golden with brown with glass button eyes and movable arms and legs. Brown wool marked his little nose and mouth. When I turned him on his tummy, he gave a pleasant little bear-growl. Fritz, dressed in brown shorts with suspenders and a green sweater, knitted by Mutti, looked like a *Seppel,* a Bavarian boy. He was just the right size for holding close and cuddling in my arms.

My buggy had an extra narrow upholstered seat Vati had made that could be laid over the top at the foot end, just like a real baby buggy where smaller children could ride. When I took Roswitha and Fritz for a walk, they sat side by side and rode on the buggy like real children. Of course, I could only walk in our yard with it because Mutti did not allow me to leave. I was a loving Mutti to Roswitha and Fritz, and never spanked my children.

On some sunny Sundays, Mutti and I, all dressed up, went walking with my buggy in the city park. Strolling in parks on the weekends was a pastime for young and old. We took the trolley to the park, and I felt like a real grownup riding the trolley with my baby. The only bad thing was that Mutti did not allow me to take Fritz and Roswitha along. She'd say, "Putting the seat on top of the buggy makes the buggy looks ugly. You can do that at home but not in the park." So Fritz and Roswitha had to stay home, and I felt sad. Pushing my doll buggy, however, I soon forgot all about my teddy and doll because there was so much to see.

There were ponds with water fountains shooting high into the air, reflecting color from the sun like a rainbow. Water lilies in a beautiful array of colors displayed their splendor. Some were open like stars, and others were about to open, looking like colored eggs sitting upright on green leafs. Shimmering goldfish of all sizes swam in the ponds, making ripples or rings on top of the water with their movements. Walkways followed around the ponds and flowerbeds, well-dressed people were strolling about. Others were sitting in the sunshine relaxing and visiting on benches placed here and there. For some, shadows from big tall trees provided comfortable, cool air while they were resting. And, yes, there were other little girls with their doll buggies going for a stroll with their families.

Flowers exploded in the warm summer air, their scent sweet, fresh, and new with every gentle breeze. I did not know where to look first. I wanted to see, smell, and remember it all, to plant it deep in my memory. We stopped at a garden restaurant. Mutti had coffee served on a silver tray, and I had a vanilla and chocolate ice cream served in a silver dish with a waffle cookie. All too soon the afternoon ended, and we took the trolley back home. Mutti never got mad at me on those outings, they were quiet and fun days. That night, flowers danced in my dreams, accompanied by the scent of summer sunshine.

I loved the summer. Birds were singing their happy songs, celebrating the summer sunshine. Rain showers came and went in no time, allowing the sun and blue sky to reappear, refreshing the air. Flowers gave new meaning to color and fragrance. Butterflies glided from flower to flower in search of the last drop of summer rain. The ground was warm and damp after a summer shower so walking barefoot was fun. I felt connected to the earth's energy. I wanted to sing and swoop like the birds.

Yes, summer was my favorite time when the air was warm, and even when it was hot. On extra hot days we had thunderstorms with lightning that Mutti didn't like. When the storms came at night, she got me up and we dressed, including raincoat and boots then we sat in the kitchen waiting for the storm to pass. Vati had made a wooden attaché case of polished natural wood with a lock and handle in which all our important papers were kept. Mutti sat holding the case and purse in her lap, ready to run. I was scared, but only because of her fear. "Mutti, why do we have to get up?"

Looking at me she said, "We need to be ready to run in case the lightning strikes the house." So we sat in silence with the candle flickering on the kitchen table, making eerie shadows on the walls and ceiling.

Watching the candle flicker, I had to ask, "Mutti, why aren't you turning on the light?"

"The lightning may strike the house if the light is on. So, be still and ready to run, just in case." And so we sat as every flash of lightning and crash of thunder made Mutti and me jump. I was frightened, thinking that our house was the only one in danger. When the storm was gone, we went back to bed. I was glad the lightning had spared our house, and soon I was sound asleep again.

After Vati had gone to war, Mutti did not want to sleep alone in the bedroom, so I had to sleep on Vati's side of the bed next to the window. Mutti said to me, "I need you to protect me in case someone climbs in the window during the night!" I had no idea who it was that was supposed to climb in the window, and I never did find out. I slept on Vati's side from then on, and I didn't mind because I felt close to him there.

One of my other jobs was to pick up things for her that fell on the floor or to take the dustpan and scoop up the dust from her sweeping the floor. Mutti explained, "I have bones in my stomach, and it is painful when I have to bend down; therefore, I need you to do the bending down for me. You are so much younger and quicker than I." I felt sorry for Mutti, but when I felt my tummy, I couldn't feel any bones, and it didn't hurt when I bend down. I always hurried to help Mutti. I didn't want her to harm herself and I feared she might fall when she bent down, and I wouldn't be able to help her.

This fear made me think of the story of "The Wolf and the Seven Little Goats" in which the wolf ate six little goats while their mother was out shopping. He could not find the seventh because it was hiding and he was full. After eating the six baby goats, he got thirsty. It was hard for the wolf to walk because his stomach was full of bones from the little goats. When he went to the well for a drink of water, he fell in—his stomach was just too heavy. Luckily, Mama Goat got home in time. The seventh little goat told her what happened. Mama Goat pulled the wolf out of the well, then she cut the wolf's stomach open and six happy little goats re-appeared. Then, mama goat, with the help of her little goats filled the wolf's stomach with rocks and threw him back into the well.

That summer, Mutti started to work in the factory near where we lived. The factory was a light colored, four-story stucco building with high, boxy looking windows. I did not know what kind of factory it was or what they made there. Right across from the factory was a *Kinderhort,* a daycare. The ladies working there were trained childcare nurses and wore blue and white striped dresses, white aprons and white caps that sat on the backs of their heads. Those caps were stiff and had a Red Cross on them. I loved to go there when Mutti was at work. We played games and made things for our mothers. Soon Mutti would not allow me to go there, saying, "You do not need that. It's not for you. They don't like you. You'll stay home and amuse yourself." And that was that.

Still it puzzled me. *Why did she say, they don't like you?* They were nice to me, and I didn't think I had done something wrong. *Was it Mutti who didn't want me to go there?* There was no answer to my question, and I didn't dare ask Mutti. Her answer was always the same, "You're ugly and no one likes you!" And I didn't want to hear, that I was ugly.

Mutti would fix a sandwich for me, before she went to work but she didn't lock me in, leaving me free to play in the yard.

One day, Mutti had baked on the weekend and when she went to work she told me I could have some of the cake. It was *Streuselkuchen,* made with yeast dough rolled flat on a cookie sheet with butter crumbs on top, my favorite cake.

The sun was shining, it was warm, and the neighborhood kids were out playing. Vati had built a sitting area out in the yard with a bench and table where the vines of green beans grew all around. Feeling alone and wanting company and friends, I set the garden table with tablecloth, dishes, and silverware. I made lemonade with water, vinegar, and sugar, the way Mutti always made it. Then I took the platter with the already cut cake and set it in the middle of the table and invited the kids in. I was so happy that everyone came. The cake was eaten in a hurry, so only a very few small pieces remained. The friends I had so hoped for ate and left. While I was cleaning and putting back the dishes, tablecloth, silverware, and the few remaining pieces of cake, I worried, *how can I explain to Mutti about the nearly gone cake when she gets home?* I knew I had done wrong, and I had an idea of what was in store for me. One thing she had told me before she left, "No children in the house."

Well, I didn't have them in the house, and she didn't say anything about the outside. I was allowed to have cake, but I just hadn't thought the kids would eat that much. Then they left me and never played with me anyway. Oh, I had lots of thinking to do about how I could possibly talk myself out of trouble. The closer it got to Mutti's homecoming, the more scared I got. Time was running out.

When Mutti got home, she asked, "What happened to all the cake?"

I answered timidly, "I was real hungry and ate it." She looked at me in disbelief. Looming over me, she shouted, "Don't you lie to me? Never did you eat all that cake by yourself! Who did you have in the house?"

"No one, Mutti."

"I'm asking you once more," she persisted, "Who did you have in the house and who ate that cake?"

Tears of fear welled up, and I knew I was in trouble with no way out. I started to cry, but neither my tears nor my confession swayed Mutti. I knew what was to come. I begged her, "Please, Mutti, I will never do it again. I had the kids in the yard. I fixed the table, set out the cake, and invited the kids because I wanted to play with them. Please, Mutti, don't spank me!"

But she just closed the windows so the neighbors could not hear and gave me a spanking, sending me to bed afterward. The next day I was locked in the house with a jelly sandwich. "If you can't behave while I'm at work, then I have to lock you in and if you have to go, use the bucket."

I did not play in front of the mirror or use the couch as a trampoline or re-fix the sandwich. I felt sad and lonesome. *Why had I such a severe punishment?* I knew I had done wrong. All I wanted was to have someone to play with! *Was that so bad?* I saw the blue sky and the sunshine, but I could not stop crying, wishing only for Vati to be here.

The next day, I was allowed outside again with strict orders from Mutti, "Do not invite the kids in the yard again. You play alone. Is that clear to you?"

"Yes Mutti, I'll be good. I promise." That was the end of my trying to make friends.

When I was seven in the summer of 1942, Mutti and I rode the train to visit my grandparents in *Pfaffendorf* by Lauban. A visit that stayed in my memory.

Those grandparents were the parents of my father. My grandfather, a bricklayer by trade, built the house. My father and all of his siblings were born in that house. And so were my two cousins, the children of my father's brother and his wife. They still lived in the house with our grandparents, because their father, just like mine, was in the war.

Mutti and I rode the train to a small town called *Nicklausdorf*. From there we had a short walk to Pfaffendorf, as Pfaffendorf did not have a train station. We walked along the *Landstrasse,* a country road, lined with fruit trees. Fields of wheat, golden in the summer sunshine, waved back and forth in the gentle breeze. Along the Landstrasse, under trees and at the edges of the fields, grew wildflowers of scarlet red called *Mohnblumen,* or poppies. Competing with the sky, were the blue *Kornblumen* or bachelor buttons, intermingled with white and yellow *Margareten* or daisies. Fields of potatoes with their lush green leaves and white flowers scattered the countryside. Cabbages of red and soft greenish white stretched like ribbons across the farm fields. Lush green pastures were dotted with black and white cows. I saw horses, shiny brown and black playful galloping inside their corral. All this kept me occupied, looking and absorbing the surroundings. The air was filled with warm sunshine, birds were singing, and butterflies were winging from flower to flower. Feeling like the butterflies, I wanted to skip and sing like the birds, but I knew Mutti wouldn't approve. "It's not how a girl should behave," she would say, so I just watched as the birds and butterflies skipped about.

Halfway there, Mutti and I set down our suitcases and rested. There was not much talk between us, just the usual instructions from her to me. "Do not tell them anything that goes on at home; it is none of their business. If they ask a lot of questions, tell them not to be so nosey, and most of all, don't talk so much. Keep your mouth shut! I will keep an eye on you! If I hear that you don't abide by my rules, we will discuss it when we get back home. Is that clear to you?"

"Yes, Mutti," was my only reply because in the distance I could see the town with its red and brown roofs, and towering above them the steeple of the church its cross reflecting the sun. I heard the rooster's crow. As we passed their farms, the geese, stretching their necks hissed at us, and the dogs barked, making their presence known.

The closer I got, the more excited I became. I remembered and loved that house with its occupants, but most of all I looked forward to seeing the *Pfaffendorfer-Oma* as she was called. Crossing the small bridge that led over a little babbling creek, I saw the gray two-story stucco house, with its tiny windows and white curtains, the large yard encircled by a picket fence. Filling the air with their sweet, fragrant blossom, two *Lindenbaeume* or linden trees huge and dignified, abuzz with the sound of bees, stood guard in front of the house. When we arrived, I hurried to open the garden gate, pulling down the handle, listening to its squeaking hinges. Oma came out of the house, and tears came to her eyes when she saw me. She hugged me and said, "I'm so glad to see you, little one; let me have a good look at you. My, how pretty you are, and how you remind me of your father. Well, come on in and say hello to Tante Grete and the children Walter and Christa."

Tante Grete came and she, too, hugged me and gave me compliments. Tante Grete was a tall lady with black hair combed back in a twist behind her head. She had brown eyes and a happy welcoming smile. Her son Walter was much older than I, almost a young man, and his sister Christa, four older than I, had blond her and blue eyes.

Opa came, shaking my hand, and said in his gravelly low voice, "So, there you are!" I curtsied, but gave no hugs. There isn't much to tell about my Knebel grandfather; he was just there, a tall slender man with a moustache. When he looked down at me, it gave me the feeling that he was looking deep inside me. He seemed grumpy to me with his gravelly, low voice, so I stayed out of his way. He scared me a little, although Oma said, "You never mind him; he is not going to do anything to you."

Oma, always referred to as the *Pfaffendorfer Oma*, was a tiny, fragile looking woman. Her gray hair was braided tight, neatly rolled into a round mound held together at the nape of her neck with pins that looked like long-legged U's. Underneath her apron, she wore a dark linen dress that went to her ankles. Her feet in husky leatherwork shoes showed her black knit wool stockings. She was a hard-working little woman, running here and there, tending to her kitchen and house, including her goats.

I followed Oma everywhere. When entering the house, there was a square hall, its floor covered with tile in a blue, green, and white design and a staircase that led to several bedrooms. To the left was a door leading into the *gute Stube,* the good room where company was welcomed. To the right of the hall was another door leading into two rooms connected to one another. Continuing down the hall, to the left was Oma's domain, the kitchen, and on through the kitchen was the day room, a long room. It had a sofa-like bench against one wall the same length as the table placed in front of it, with additional chairs around it. It was made for a large family. That is where Oma served her meals and where the family gathered. Here, too, crisp white curtains covered the sparkling clean windows. Across the hall from Oma's kitchen was a staircase leading upstairs to several bedrooms. Just before going upstairs was the door to the washhouse, toilette, and the stalls with the goats. Next to Oma's kitchen was the *Keller,* the cellar and the door that lead into the back yard, where immediately on the left a huge cherry tree laden with big black cherries, made a paradise for the bees located in a wooden house underneath. All around the house was a huge area, partly a garden with flowers and vegetables, and a large lawn. It was a little girl's dream of grandma's house come true.

I followed Oma around wherever she was, talking about anything and nothing in particular. Oma seemed never to tire of my chattering. We went to the butcher shop adjacent to my grandparents' home. When we got there, Oma said to the woman behind the counter, "Look who's with me! It's Alfred's daughter Gisela; she came for a visit." The woman turned around and called to her husband, "Come and have a look; Alfred's daughter is here." I felt like a special person, as they shook my hand and I curtsied.

"Well," said the butcher, as he was walking behind the glass-encased counter displaying the different meats and sausages he had made. He reached inside that counter and pulled a sausage out. Cutting off a big piece and leaning over the counter, he handed it to me, saying, "Here, this is for you!" My eyes got big in disbelief, and I looked at Oma for an answer.

Nodding her head, she said, "Go ahead and take it." What a large piece of sausage! Never had anyone given me anything like that before! It was as big as my hand and smelled of smoke and spices. I didn't want to seem greedy, but I couldn't stop myself from taking big bites and just eating it up.

The butcher, still leaning over his counter, said, "Looks like you're enjoying yourself!" I could only nod my head in agreement because my mouth was full of sausage. The butcher smiled, turned, and walked away. Oma finished her visiting and shopping; then she cleaned my face and hands with her hankie, and we went on our way. I thanked the lady once more for the sausage and curtsied. Smiling, she said, "You are welcome. Anytime you want a piece of sausage you come and see me, daughter of Alfred."

Outside I asked, "Oma, how come they know Vati?"

She laughed, "That is because they saw your father grow up right here, and he used to go with me, and sometimes I would send him to the butcher. He, too, received a piece of sausage whenever I shopped, but not as big as you had today. That was just for you."

Oh, I felt special; they knew Vati and now they knew me, his daughter. The invitation she gave me I could not resist; whenever Mutti was not watching, I slipped under the wire fence and visited the shop. The butcher lady just handed me a slice of sausage, I curtsied, and out the door I hurried, back under the fence, eating my prized possession. Oma knew where I had been and smiled, but she never said a word to Mutti.

Oma warned me when I was going out in the back yard to stay away from the bees and their house, "They don't know you and might sting you."

How can bees know someone? How does Oma know about that? I had to see for myself, only to scream seconds later, holding my chin. "Oma, Oma, I got stung and it hurts!"

Wordlessly, she went into the kitchen, reappearing with a raw onion sliced in half, saying, "Now, sit here and rub the onion on your chin; it will help the sting and pain." Looking at me, she continued, "Don't go so close to the bees again; they don't know you." The bees never saw me close up again. Oma's onion remedy took care of my pain, so soon I was myself again.

Opa had cut the grass to make hay for the goats, and every evening Oma would rake the grass into piles. Christa, my cousin, and I had fun throwing ourselves into the hay piles Oma had raked so neatly. Without a word, Oma raked the piles again, only to have us destroy them once more. Our fun came to a sudden stop when Opa appeared in the yard, his gravelly voice booming, "Now you two stop that, right now!" Christa and I hopped to attention like soldiers called to order. We shook the hay from our hair and clothes and went, heads bent into the house, passing Opa standing guard to make sure we left Oma in peace to finish her chores.

In Oma's guter Stube stood a beautiful china hutch. Oma saw me standing there looking and admiring it. She said, "Do you like it?"

"Oh, yes," I said. "I like it very much."

With pride in her voice she replied, "Your father made that hutch; it was for his final exam as a carpenter, and afterward he gave it to me as a gift." It was beautiful and special, because Vati had made it. The top of the hutch was in part made with glass, and the whole hutch was finished in intricate blonde woodwork. I let my fingers touch and glide over the smooth wood, and a feeling of connection with Vati went through me. My father had made that hutch, and it filled me with pride.

In that hutch, Oma kept her special dinner dishes, but down below she also had a plate of honeycomb. She gave Christa and me a piece to suck the honey out of with the sticky golden syrup dripping from our chins. One time, Christa got a spoon for us, and we slipped upstairs to a room where Oma had several brown crocks filled with honey that she sold to people in the area. We dipped the spoon in it and ate honey until we got sick and could not eat dinner. Christa and I got in trouble, and Mutti wanted to spank me, but Oma and Opa would not allow it. Instead, Christa got a talking to since she knew the rules of the house.

Walter paid no attention to me at all. He had black hair like his mother and deep blue eyes. I thought him so handsome and so grown up. Whenever he was around, I'd just stare at him, but it made no impression on him; after all, he was seven years my senior and I was just a little goggle-eyed girl, staring.

I liked Tante Grete a lot. The two children and she had two rooms to the right of the big hall at the front of the house with their bedrooms upstairs. The first room was the kitchen with a table, chairs, a hutch, and the stove. Adjacent to it was the living room furnished with a couch, easy chairs, and coffee table, and an upright piano with golden candleholders on each side. I liked the sound of pianos and loved listening to Tante Grete. Whenever I came to see her, after knocking, waiting for her to say, "*Herein*"! or come in, she stopped what she was doing to play songs I knew on her piano. Then, I stood next to her and together we sang. Afterward turning to me, she said, "You have a wonderful voice." Embarrassed I hugged her and hurried out of the room. I adored Tante Grete because she was so nice to me, and I wished that she were my mother.

But soon Mutti forbade me to visit with Tante Grete. She took me where she thought no one could hear her and started questioning me, "What has she been asking you? What have you been telling her? Have I not told you not to tell anything and to keep your mouth shut?"

"I have not told anything, and Tante Grete did not ask me anything,"

"You are a liar, and I should spank you here and now!"

Suddenly, a low voice growled, "There will be no spanking her; she didn't do anything! You'll find yourself out of here if I hear anymore about spanking." Mutti looked shocked, and I could have kissed Opa for rescuing me, but he still scared me. I had the feeling Mutti was not liked or welcomed. After that Mutti walked around with a sour look, and, all too soon for me, we left.

The day we left, Oma stood by the garden gate, a corner of her apron in her hand, wiping her eyes. Hugging me and telling me to take care, she gave me a small paper cone filled with my favorite candy. They looked like real coffee beans, only made of chocolate and were filled with a sweet liquid. I thanked Oma, hugged her, and told her I would take care. Everyone else came and gave me hugs and said goodbye. They shook Mutti's hand, but their goodbyes were cold and impersonal. Walking away, I turned around several times and waved at Oma. She was still standing at the garden gate, the one corner of her apron still in her hand, waving.

A voice brought me back, "Stop that right now and let's go!" I turned, and we walked away. After while, I pulled out the small bag with the candy, when Mutti reached over and said, "Let me see that!" She took the candy and with a mighty fling scattered the candy into the ditch. "You don't need anything from them; besides they're not good for your teeth!" I was back in Mutti's grip again.

The wonderful visit had come to an end, but I took the memory with me.

That was the last time I saw the *Pfaffendorfer-Oma*. She passed away in December of 1942.

After Mutti and I returned home, and she was again in control, I thought about the nice time I had had visiting with the Pfaffendorfer-Oma and with everyone in that house. I missed them and the care and love they had given me. I liked and loved that tiny little Pfaffendorfer-Oma.

The year was 1942, I was seven, and fall had started. I went back to school, and Mutti to work in the factory nearby. Sometimes on the way home from school, I got off the trolley at a garden nursery and bought Mutti flowers. Then, taking the next trolley, I hurried home, to do the dishes and sweep the floor. I finished my tasks by putting the tablecloth on the table, then the vase with the flowers. I hoped Mutti would be pleased with me. I had learned to do things for her, hoping it would make her happy.

Then, there were times when Mutti did nice things with me. She'd take me to the movie to see a fairytale whenever there was one playing. Mutti was on the trolley that came past the school at the exact time that school let out. I got on, and we continued further to the city and the movie. In her handbag Mutti carried a sandwich and in a thermos she had warm cocoa. Hungrily I ate the sandwich and drank the cocoa while watching the movie.

I recall that over the years I lived in Liegnitz and while Vati was in the war, I had the measles, whooping cough, and diphtheria. My sickbed was always on the couch in the kitchen, and Mutti took care of me. When I had the measles, Mutti kept the kitchen dark, and in the evening she had a cover over the ceiling lamp so I could not look into the light. "It is bad for your eyes," Mutti told me.

The whooping cough was pretty bad. I coughed and coughed, and Mutti had some stuff that she cooked all day long on the stove that smelled like menthol. Diphtheria I do not recall too much. I was just sick with a high fever, which I eventually recovered from.

Mutti was busy knitting. I asked her, "Mutti, what are you knitting and for whom?"

She answered without stopping or interrupting the click-clack of her knitting needles, "I'm knitting socks for your father. Winter is coming, and he needs warm socks while fighting the war."

We also baked cookies, and I helped. Then, we made a package with the cookies and several pairs of socks, all knitted by Mutti, and several other items and sent it all to Vati. I was so glad that Mutti let me help; it made me feel close to him. I also wrote Vati a note but Mutti told me what to write. After that we took the package to the post office.

When Mutti was knitting or mending, she always had the radio on, and I could hear the man who was called *Hitler* talking in a forceful voice. People would shout, *"Heil Hitler."* Then, they played the national anthem. I was familiar with that because we sang it in school, too, and said, "Heil Hitler," when passing teachers or entering a room.

Our neighbors living above us had one child, a boy, the same age as I. His mother was a scared and fragile looking tiny woman. She wouldn't stop to talk to anyone; she'd only acknowledge daily greetings and hurried on. Her husband was a short, ugly, hunchbacked man. He beat his wife almost every day when he came home from work. Over the screams of his mother, we could hear their son cry out to stop, but his father didn't stop. Mutti would take the broom and knock on the ceiling, but not before she locked the door. That is when I noticed that there was someone Mutti was afraid of.

Cold winds were blowing the leaves of gold and dark red all around. One morning when I got up, there was a hushed calm in the air, and when I looked out the window, everything was covered in white. The leaves that had danced and whirled days before now lay quiet under the white blanket of snow. Mister Winter had moved in. White flakes, big and small, like frozen crystal stars, were steadily, silently, and gently falling to earth; covering my world in a silver white blanket. The roofs of houses turned white. Fence posts wore white hats, and the trees bowed their branches from the snowflakes settling on them. People hurried to get into their houses, and I could see curious faces at windows watching the snowy show, just like me.

That winter was cold and long. Sometimes we couldn't get out the front door of the house; the blizzard had blown the snow against the door. Mutti took the broom and pushed the snow out. The shoveled snow from the walks and streets was piled high into big mountains. We kids used them for hills to sled on or just to scoot on with no sled at all. The windows froze over with layers of ice, making crystal flowers sparkling in the cold sunshine, its rays unable to defrost the windows. But school continued; we bundled up with only our eyes showing as we made our way through the snow and cold.

On nice days, however, the children came out with their sleds, and some went shopping with their mothers. Mutti pulled me on the sled to the store, but on the way back I had to help pull the sled because we had the groceries packed on it.

I was still sleeping in the bedroom with Mutti in Vati's bed on the window side. Sometimes at night when I had to get up, I was disoriented because the room was so dark, and I, half sleep, bumped into things and woke up Mutti, making her mad at me for disturbing her sleep. For punishment, she did not allow me to return to bed. Instead, I had to stand in the middle of the cold bedroom in only my nightgown with nothing on my feet. Her icy voice matching the cold of the room, she said, "If you don't want to sleep, then you stand there until you get tired and are ready to go back to bed and sleep." With that she covered herself and went back to sleep. I stood there with the cold creeping up on me like a snake. It wound itself around me, and I got colder and colder until my body started to shake.

After what seemed like forever, "Mutti," I called out, "please let me go back to bed. I'm so cold, and I promise I will go to sleep. Please, Mutti!" After several minutes of pleading, Mutti allowed me to go back to bed. I lay very still and did not move, my body stiff from the cold. I could not feel my feet. I pulled the feather bed over my head, my breath warming my body. Soon I had a cold, and then my coughing would wake her up. Mutti warned me, "If you don't stop that coughing and stop keeping me awake, I will spank you."

I tried to suppress the cough, but that did not work. It would come up into my throat; first a tickle, then it progressed to a choking until I could not hold it anymore. I coughed and coughed, until it choked me. Tears came to my eyes and my throat felt sore, but Mutti had no mercy. Silently, she got up, went to the kitchen and got the wicker woven rug beater. I knew what was going to happen to me. "Mutti, please don't spank me!" I begged.

"I have warned you to stop that coughing, and you are not minding me," she snapped, and I got a spanking. Then I had to stand again in the cold until Mutti decided I was ready for bed.

One of my jobs was to clean her feet and clip her toenails. Mutti told me she was unable to bend down, saying, "Anyway, you do such a good job." I clipped her nails, removed any calluses that had collected on her heels, and massaged her feet. That job remained mine for a long time.

Sometimes while Mutti was knitting a winter pullover for me, because she always dressed me in the best clothes, I'd comb her hair, making different styles with fancy combs and ribbons. Mutti sat on the couch that stood in front of the window, with me standing behind her combing her hair. But I had to be very careful not to pull her hair because that would make her mad and I would have to sit on the chair for punishment.

I also had to learn how to knit, crochet, sew buttons on, and darn socks. With the ruler as the teacher, my hands turned red, and I could hardly concentrate, tears blocking my view. I learned how to iron handkerchiefs and dishtowels. Mutti showed me how to fold them in precise squares so only the top corner showed, with the others lined up underneath to match the top. Not a wrinkle was allowed, or I had to do it over until it was right. Mutti watched me do the work, repeating, "You are just too stupid and clumsy to do anything right. You will never learn and will stay stupid all your life! You will never amount to anything!"

Did we have a Christmas? I really don't know; I do not recall having a tree. The winter passed, and the snow started to melt, making little holes, where little tiny delicate white snowbells showed themselves, giving the promise of spring to come. Easter came and then Mother's Day, and spring had arrived, with violets, crocuses, tulips, narcissus, and hyacinth. Mutti showed me what flowers I could pick for her Mothers' Day bouquet. I followed her orders and picked only what she allowed me to pick. When presenting the flowers to her, I had to hug her and tell her she was the best mother in the world and would never leave her.

Then, one day in the spring of 1943, something strange happened. Mutti and I got up as usual and had our breakfast. The morning sky was deep blue, the sun was shining, and it was nice and warm outside. But Mutti did not open the windows or the front door as she did every morning, instead she did the opposite, she kept them locked. When I asked Mutti if I could go outside, she told me, "No, you stay in for today." She also gave me further instructions with that strict, cold look in her eyes, "When there is a knock at the door, we will not answer and whatever happens, there will not be a sound out of you. Is that clear?"

Mystified, I replied, "Yes."

"Now, you sit down, keep still, and don't move until I tell you, you can. Is that clear?" With that she pointed at the chair next to the table, and I sat down. *Why was I not to go outside and play, but sit on a chair instead? Had I done something wrong?* As I was sitting, I watched Mutti. She had binoculars and was standing by the couch in front of the window, and she kept looking out with them.

"Mutti, could I look, too?"

Turning to me she said, "Did I not tell you just to sit and be quiet? Do you understand me?" I looked down and said nothing, as it was always best not to make Mutti mad. After what seemed a long time, Mutti suddenly put down the binoculars. Stopping before me, her eyes, cold and staring, in a very low voice she said, "You will keep still, make no noise, and do not, I repeat, do not answer if your name is called or to the knock on the door, if you do, you will be sorry. That I promise you!" *Why was she talking like that? Why was she acting as if we're not home? What was outside?* Mutti had me scared, thinking that something outside was going to hurt us.

Mutti took one more glance out the window and stepped away as if she didn't want to be seen. Then, she, too, seated herself at the far end of the table glaring at me, giving me a stern look. I heard voices, but saw only what looked like the top of ladies hats going past the window. Then, came a knock at the front door, a pause and another knock. A voice called out, "*Hallo*," and someone called, "Gisela, are you in there?" I listened to the sound of that voice. It was a voice I knew but had not heard for a long time. I heard them talk, but I could not hear what they were saying. They knocked several more times, even called out my name again, but Mutti did not move or make any attempt to open the door, all she did was glare at me. I wanted to see who was out there and whose voice it was that was calling my name. *Who was calling me?* I wanted to jump out of that chair, run and open the door, but I remembered the warning. I looked at Mutti but she gave me a look that needed no words. So I sat immobile and did nothing. The top of the ladies hats went past the window again as they were leaving. I stretched a little, but I could see only the hats going by, no faces. Mutti, with a look of satisfaction, took up her station at the window again—watching. "Come look and see who has came to visit you. Here, use the binoculars so you can see close up. It's the old woman from Goerlitz, the one who took care of you! Do you recognize her?" *I knew who that was! And now I knew who had called my name. It was Oma; she had come with Christa, Uschi and Uschi's mother. They had come to see me.* Looking through the binoculars, they were so close. *I wanted to reach out to them, yet they were so far away. I wanted to cry out, don't go away! I'm here! Don't leave! Please, come back!* But my fear of Mutti stopped me. Silently I cried.

The rest of the day I had to stay in, and Mutti kept watching, but nothing happened. Oma from Goerlitz did not come back.

After they were gone, Mutti said, "Good, we don't need them to snoop around here, and they have no business at all to come. They are no relatives of ours, only people that took care of you when we lived in Goerlitz before we moved to Liegnitz." I wanted to tell her I did not feel that way and I would have loved to see them again, but that would have made her mad. That I could not risk and there was no one else to talk to, so I kept it to myself. I tried to play, but my heart was not in it. Mutti watched and noticed my despondency. She said I was ungrateful and needed a spanking to set me straight. And that is what I got. That day has always stayed in my memory.

Oh, how I longed for Vati, but he was nowhere near. All I heard was that he was in the war, and I didn't understand what that meant.

Not long after the mysterious visit in summer of 1943, Mutti and I took the streetcar to the city to go shopping for new clothes for me. Mutti bought, white shoes, socks, a dress, a new summer coat and hat to match, and some other items. Going shopping for new clothes was always exciting. Although Mutti made all the choices, trying new clothes on was fun for me.

That day, her actions were rather short, but I had no idea what her problem was.

The following day, Mutti took out our suitcases and started to pack. I watched her as she packed in silence. *Where we going on a trip? To Kohlfurt? But, no, to go to Kohlfurt Mutti would not buy new clothes or look so upset. Then why is Mutti packing my little black shiny suitcase with my new clothes?* Grim faced, with that cold expression in her eyes, Mutti continued packing. The atmosphere was uncomfortable, filled with anger about to explode. I wanted to ask, "Mutti, why are you packing suitcases?" But I knew Mutti did not like to be questioned. Finally, after what seemed like forever, she closed them and set them next to the couch. Then, she put a clean, white-laced, hanky, comb, mirror and a tiny bottle of cologne in my new purse and set it next to my suitcase with my new clothes.

"There," Mutti said, "you're ready for your trip."

"My trip? Where am I going? Am I going to Kohlfurt?" I asked.

"No," she said, "I'll stay in Kohlfurt while you're going to Goerlitz, visiting those people that you used to know, the babysitters." Her voice sounded angry, indicating to me that she was not happy. Now I knew what the new clothes and all that packing were for. I was going to see the Goerlitzer Oma. I wanted to jump up and down, sing and dance, laugh and cry all at the same time. But I kept my composure because I didn't want Mutti to know how excited I was when I thought about going to Goerlitz and seeing Oma.

Mutti watched me and after awhile, pointing to a chair, said, "Sit down. We will have a talk." I hurried to follow her command. She continued, shaking her finger at me to underline the importance of her statements, "I want you to pay close attention and remember what I'm going to say to you." She took a deep breath and looked straight at me, eyes like steel, finger still pointing, "These people you're going to see, and I have told you that before, are no relatives to you or us, no matter what they say. They will tell you that Christa is your sister, that the woman who is a nurse, your mother, and that old woman your grandmother—those are all lies." My mind went blank. I was mystified. *What nurse? I didn't know any nurse!* Leaning towards me, she asked, "Is that clear to you? Do you understand what I'm telling you?"

My head was whirling. *What was she telling me?* I wanted to say, "No, I don't understand." Instead I nodded my head and said, "Yes, I know they're not my family, whatever they say."

I was lying. I did not understand what she was telling me. I didn't even know what she was talking about, and I was afraid to ask her any questions because I could sense she did not like them—but I did. My excitement was overpowering me and I didn't care about anything, only that I was going to Oma, that old woman, as Mutti called her.

With a stern face and tone Mutti continued, "I am your real mother, and you belong to me and your father and no one else. Oma in Kohlfurt is your real grandmother. So don't let them tell you otherwise, because they will and they're liars. I'm telling you once more, they were your caretakers for a short time, as your father and I were working while we lived in Goerlitz. You will stay with them for two weeks and not any longer. I hope I made that clear enough and I want you to repeat what I just said."

Looking at Mutti, I concentrated real hard and repeated, "I can visit them for two weeks, they are not my family, and Christa is not my sister, the nurse is not my mother, and the old woman not my grandmother. You are my real mother and Vati is my father. Oma and Opa in Kohlfurt are my real grandparents."

"And what else?" she demanded. "The rest, what was the rest?"

"And, uh, ah, if they tell me, ah, if the tell me that, then they're liars."

With emphasis in her tone she added, "And you make sure that you tell them that they're liars, all of them, and that I said so!"

Nodding my head in agreement, but knowing I would never repeat her harsh words, I said, "Oh, yes, Mutti, I will tell them you said so."

"Well then, if this is clear to you, I expect you to follow my orders." With that she got up and said, "It will be a long day tomorrow, so get ready for a bath and then go to bed. We will finish our conversation tomorrow."

I took my bath and hurried to bed. Lying there I could not go to sleep because I was so excited and confused. *Why am I allowed to visit Oma in Goerlitz when Mutti wouldn't open the door for her, when she was here? And the nurse? I don't remember a nurse when I lived with Oma. What does she look like? Is she fat like Mutti, mean and cold? Oh, but Oma will be there protecting me from that nurse. No matter what Mutti said, Oma is a nice old woman, and I love her. Will I recognize Oma when I got there? Will Christa be at the train station, too?* I had so many unanswered questions, but the Sandman took over, and I went to sleep.

The next morning we got up early and ate breakfast. While she supervised my dressing, Mutti continued with her drill. "If they ask you how you're doing and how I am treating you, you tell them nothing and I mean absolutely nothing. It is none of their business what goes on here. Do you hear me?"

Trying to dress myself and keep my excitement under control, I answered, "Yes, Mutti, I will tell them nothing." She was standing before me, her hands on her hips, her elbows sticking out like handles on a large, round pot, looking down at me. She added, "If I find out you have been telling them what goes on around here, well, I don't need to explain to you what is in store for you when you get back. And there is one more thing," she continued, "you are not to come home with gifts from them. If you do, they will go in the garbage, so don't bother to bring anything back!"

I dressed as fast as I could to keep her voice away from me but it was loud, demanding, and mean. Her words were like a hammer that pounded on me. I wanted to cry out, "Stop, please stop!" But I knew better. It would have been the end of my trip, and that I could not risk.

Finally, I was dressed in the new white shoes, knee socks, dress and blue summer coat and matching hat. I was ready to travel, so excited that I could burst. Mutti carrying her suitcase and purse, and I mine we made our way to the trolley. After what seemed a long ride, we arrived at the Bahnhof.

Mutti walked over to the window where the tickets were sold while I stayed with the suitcases. We proceeded through the gate where the man punched the tickets. After that, we walked in the tunnel with trains rolling overhead making a thunderous sound, then to one of the sets of stairs that led to the platform where our train was to arrive. The Bahnhof in Liegnitz had many platforms. People already were waiting for the train to come. Some were sitting on benches with their suitcases next to them. Others came to pick up friends or family members, and some even had flowers for a welcome greeting. It was a busy place and I was part of all that happy activity.

The announcement was made over the loudspeakers that the train would be rolling in and everyone was to step back. And there it came. The engine was bellowing out white steam as it slowly pulled the train next to the platform. Its whistle blew to give warning once more to step back. I covered my ears as the wheels screeched to a halt. The conductor called out loudly, "Liegnitz! . . . Liegnitz! . . ." Doors opened, people spilled out, and the platform was humming with greetings and goodbyes. All that hugging and shouting had me in a trance.

"Gisela, Gisela, don't just stand there and gaze. Get on the train or you'll be left behind," Mutti, already in the train called out to me. Grabbing my suitcase I scrambled as fast as I could up the steps and in. "Why are you always standing around daydreaming? People will say you're retarded, and they might be right. You look stupid when you do that," Mutti chided me. But her icy words did not bother me.

The conductor walked along the train and closed all doors, then, blew his whistle, held up the flyswatter-looking sign, and the train moved slowly out of the Bahnhof, giving its own final whistle. The people stepped back and waved goodbye with their hankies. At last, we were on our way to Goerlitz. What an exciting and fearful day! Mutti sat on the isle seat. Sitting next to the window kept my mind occupied as the train made its way through the countryside, rolling through towns and villages with people on bikes or foot, some in horse drawn wagons. I saw children playing. Animals were grazing in the green pastures. High on rooftops *Stoerche*, or storks, stood in their nests, flapping and waving their huge white and black wings, as if in farewell. *Were they waving at me? Did they know I was going to Goerlitz?*

Storks, so I had been told, were smart. A stork brings little brothers or sisters. The way that was done was really simple. All a child had to do before going to bed is, place a slice of bread with cream cheese on the opened window—on the sill. If the wish was for a girl, the cream cheese should be sprinkled with a little sugar, and if for a boy, sprinkled with salt. Then, the stork would come and pick it up during the night. When the stork delivered the baby, it bit the mother in the leg, so she had to stay in bed after the baby arrived. I had tried to lure the stork under Mutti's supervision, with a cream cheese sandwich sprinkled with salt, but nothing had happened. Only our neighbor lady got bit by a stork and received a baby. I was allowed a short visit to take a look at the wonder the stork had brought.

Afterward I asked Mutti, "Why did the stork not come to our house? Did he not like the sandwich I put out?"

"Well, I'm sure he liked the sandwich you put out, but maybe he has not found the right baby yet."

"Mutti, did he pick up the sandwich?"

"Yes, he did. You just have to wait."

I gave up hope, but I still liked storks. They looked so majestic and elegant with their red long beaks and equally long fragile red legs. They would bend their slender necks way back, making clapping noises with their long red beaks that could be heard far away. They built large round nests on the roofs of barns or stalls, returning every spring to the same place. Many farmers put old wagon wheels on the roofs for the storks so they could build sturdy homes for their young. Other than cream cheese sandwiches, they liked frogs that they hunted around ponds and creeks. In flight they looked like a large white glider swooping and dipping, their wings swooshing high up in the blue summer sky. Children were always excited to see storks because there was a mystical aura about them.

Mutti sitting silently next to me, my mind started to drift as the train brought me closer to my destination. The wheels rolled, singing a song, "She's coming, she's coming, she's coming!"

But other wheels were saying, "She is scared, she is scared, she is scared!" My imagination was playing tricks on me. *How could the wheels sing about how I feel?*

"Yes, I was coming! Yes, I was excited! And, yes, I was scared!" I thought while the wheels rolled singing their chorus. It had been a very long time since I last saw Oma. *Would I still recognize her? Would Oma still like me? Will she hug me? And Christa does she still dislike me?*

Mutti also said something about a nurse. What nurse? And why is Mutti telling me over and over that she is my mother and no one else! Why? Why is she putting such fear into me?"

The whole thing had me scared. I thought of asking Mutti not to take me there, but I wanted to see Oma. I felt warm and cuddly inside, just thinking of her. *No, I'm going and I will be fine.*

After some time that seemed forever the train rolled into Kohlfurt. Then, after a short stop, we were rolling underneath my favorite bridge. The speeding train got closer to our destination, my anxiety got bigger.

"Now, I will tell what you do when we get to Goerlitz." The unexpected sound of her voice sent a shiver through me, and I sat straight up. *Could Mutti tell what I was thinking?* I looked at her and she continued, "When we get off the train, you will hold my hand. You will not, I mean will not, run and greet those people until I let go of your hand. You will shake their hands and curtsy, like you do for any other stranger. You will give me a hug and kiss and tell me that you love me." Her eyes were demanding, as was her voice, and I nodded my head. "I can't hear you, repeat what I said!"

"I'm to hold your hand until you let go; I'm to shake their hands and curtsy; I'm to give you a hug and kiss and tell you that I love you."

"That's right, and you say you love me loud enough so they can hear it, too."

"Yes, Mutti, I will."

The train entered the *Goerlitzer Bahnhof.* My heart was pounding louder than the screeching of the wheels as we came to a stop. The Station master in his dark uniform called," Goerlitz, Goerlitz!" Doors flung open, people poured out, going this and that way, shouting greetings, hugging. Mutti was holding me close with her hand. And then, in all that chaos, I saw Oma, standing there, looking and waving. Underneath her brimmed dark blue hat, her blue eyes shone, and I saw a bright, loving and welcoming smile. My heart was jumping for joy. All my fears were forgotten. I recognized Oma and she me. It was as if we were the only ones on the platform. All I saw was Oma. I wanted to run and throw my arms around her, but an iron grip held me back. Mutti walked slowly toward Oma, and coolly nodded her head. Mutti still holding my hand, I did my impersonal greeting of *Guten Tag,* with the customary curtsy. Then, Mutti turned me toward her, her eyes commanding me. I gave her the hug she demanded, a kiss, and a loud, "I love you, Mutti." But all I wanted was to get away.

That done, I grabbed Oma's hand. She took my suitcase, and we turned to leave.

Tugging on her hand, I wanted Oma to go faster, but she said, "Don't worry, relax, you'll be fine. Absolutely nothing will happen to you." She squeezed my hand for reassurance. I wanted to believe her, but I knew Mutti was watching, and I feared she might grab me and take me back. Oma, I think, knew what my problem was. She looked down at me, still holding my hand in hers, and said, "You're fine and safe; just relax. You're with us now."

With us? In all my hurry and excitement I had not realized that Christa was there, too, and Uschi with her mother. I got hugs from all of them, except Christa, she shook only my hand. *Where was the nurse? There was no nurse.* Quietly I looked around. No nurse anywhere. *Why did Mutti talk about a nurse when there was none?* My vacation in Goerlitz began, and, for that moment in the whirl of doings, I even forgot about Vati. I knew one thing; it felt good being there, as if I belonged.

We went to Oma's apartment. After I was unpacked and had eaten, Oma said, "Now we have to go someplace. Someone very special is waiting for you." I looked at Oma in surprise. *Who could that be?* "Oma? Is Vati here?"

She just looked at me with a smile all over her face, her eyes misting, and said, "Well, if I tell you, then it is not a surprise anymore, now is it?" Putting on her dark blue hat, holding her purse in one hand and taking mine in her other, we were off with Christa following. We crossed the steel bridge that spanned the *Neisse River*, passed a church high above us; a towering giant built on top a hill, supported by a high gray rock wall. It looked powerful with its two tall steeples pointing and stretching to heaven, majestic and dignified, overlooking its people, demanding submission from anyone.

"What is the name of that church, Oma?"

"That's the *Peters Kirche*, one of the oldest churches in Goerlitz," she answered with pride in her voice. Turning left, leaving the gray giant behind us, we walked along the banks of the Neisse River, where white swans and ducks swam. Looking across the river, I could see Oma's apartment.

The sky was blue, the sun was shining, the birds were singing in the trees, and I felt that warm sensation come all over me, that I only had when I was around Vati. I wanted to sing, skip, jump, and tell Oma that I was glad to be here and that I loved her, but I felt unsure of her reaction. *Maybe Oma would think I was foolish and stupid, as Mutti said. So, I decided to just enjoy the sunny warm day with my hand in Oma's, walking along feeling secure and happy.* It was a long walk. We walked along the city park with the Neisse River following us. We walked up a wide street, a promenade, lined with trees and benches where people were sitting, talking, and resting.

After while we crossed the street and went through a wide wrought iron gate into a park like setting of green lawns, flowers, shrubs, fountains, and white benches beyond. People sat there, mostly men, some in wheelchairs with nurses in attendance. *What kind of place is this? What are we doing here? Who are we going to see?* I saw a huge red brick building with big shiny windows opened wide, white curtains were swaying in a gentle breeze. A glass veranda ran the length of the building with rows of rocking wicker chairs—people resting in them. They had bandages on their legs, their arms, or around their heads. Some had their legs in a white cast resting on another chair with a cane next to them. I saw nurses walking among them, bending down here and there to talk to the people sitting in chairs. As we got closer, I could tell the people were men. "Oma," I whispered, tugging on her hand, "Oma, what kind of a place is this?"

"It's a *Lazarett,* a military hospital, where our soldiers come to heal the wounds they received in the war," she replied in a low voice.

The war? I heard people talk about it, and knew, that is where Vati was. But people got hurt there?

"Oma, is Vati here? Did he get hurt?" I asked with a mixed fear and excitement.

"No," she said, "no, he is not hurt. He is in the war with other soldiers, fighting."

I was sad that Vati was not here but relieved to hear Oma say, "He was not hurt."

Entering the lobby, we saw more men, even some in uniforms like Vati's, sitting under large palms and potted trees. Nurses were everywhere. Oma walked over to the desk and asked to see *Schwester Helene,* Sister Helene, but before I knew what had happened, someone called out, "Gisela, Gisela," and started to hug and kiss me. *Who was that?* I loosened myself from the loving embrace, for I knew that is what it was, and took a look to see who was hugging me, so familiar with me.

It was a nurse!

I looked at Oma. She had a big smile on her face as she said, "This is your mother, your real Mutti!" I couldn't grasp what Oma had just said. My *mother? My real Mutti? A nurse?* Before me stood a woman, smiling at me as if I were no stranger to her. She wore a uniform, a blue and white striped dress with a crisp white apron over it. On her head, a white cap with a Red Cross in the center sat like a crown on her black hair. White stockings and shoes finished her look. *There really was a nurse! Is that the nurse Mutti had warned me about?* I was totally confused. But I let her hug me. She smelled so fresh and clean, sort of like medicine, and I soaked up the love she gave me. She was just what I had always dreamed of to have as a mother. She was pretty, slender, not too tall, with black hair, shining brown eyes, and a face full of love and laughter.

Soon there was a circle of nurses and people around us. Everyone said, "Oh, your daughter got here! And what a pretty girl!" They shook my hand, and I was busy with curtsying and the proper greetings. But what I heard most among the greetings was "What a pretty girl!" I wished the Mutti waiting for my return in Kohlfurt could hear that.

The nurse and I went out in the park and sat down on a bench among the flowers and trees. My "newfound" mother sat next to me, holding my hand. She just looked at me, and I at her. Her brown eyes looked teary. As I felt the love pouring from her to me, the feeling of real belonging engulfed me. Then, taking hold of my chin and looking straight at me, she said, "I know you don't remember me. You were much too small when you went away with your father. I'm glad I finally get to see my daughter, for I have missed you so." I just sat and listened to her. I didn't know what to say. I could not grasp what I was hearing. *My mother?* Somehow I felt she was telling me the truth. *How could that be? I had a mother already! I would not mind having this one for a mother. She was pretty and slender and looked kind.* And I felt as if I knew her, yet she was a stranger to me. She gave me one more hug and a kiss and said, "I have to go back to work, but I'll see you this evening."

I curtsied to her. Then Oma, Christa, and I walked back through the Iron Gate and into town, where Oma did some shopping.

Every evening and sometimes during the day I would see that nurse, always in uniform. I felt special, so proud to walk next to her. We met acquaintances on the street, and she told everyone with pride, "This is my youngest daughter Gisela." I got hugged and heard over and over, "You look just like your father," or "She looks like Alfred," or "Oh, look how big you have grown and so pretty, too!" *How come those people knew Vati? And why did they say I was pretty when the other Mutti, says I'm ugly?* But I liked what I heard, and it made me feel good. The nurse said, if I wanted to, I could, call her Mutti. I wanted to, so I did, but it felt awkward, knowing that the other Mutti would not like it all. I sat on Mutti's lap; she cuddled me and I was happy to call her Mutti. I slept with Oma, but we didn't play the mouse game. I felt I was too big for it, but I cuddled with her. She smelled of lavender and was so cuddly, like a fluffy pillow. We visited lots of people, who I was told, were part of my family. I played with Uschi and was told that Uschi s mother Elfriede, and my new Mutti were sisters. Everyone was so nice and it felt so good; naturally, I didn't want it to end. But it did.

Christa and I sat on the bank of the Neisse River in the grass right across the street from where Oma's apartment was, feeding the ducks and swans. It was my last day in Goerlitz. She was not much of a talker, not like me, but rather short sometimes. We sat side by side, throwing bread into the water. Christa had been told by Oma to watch out for me because of the river. Christa started to talk, "You do know that I'm your real sister and the nurse is our mother. Oma is our real Oma, yours and mine. Do you understand that? We both have the same father. They were married once, but now they're not, and no matter what that fat lady you call Mutti is telling you, she is not your mother." Looking at me solid as steel and in a voice showing all her hatred, she said, "I'm telling you, she is a big fat liar! And I mean fat!" She named some other people I'd met while visiting who were related to me.

Reflecting on what I had heard, I felt relief come over me. My mind was racing. *That's it! I don't have to go back!* Excited and overflowing with happiness, I looked at my sister, exclaiming, "If Mutti, the nurse, is my real mother, and Oma, is also my real Oma and you my sister, then I don't have to go back. I can stay and Vati can come here!" I was bubbling with excitement. *How lucky could I be!*

But Christa, throwing bread to the ducks, shook her head. "No, that is not how it is. You have to go back!"

Her words fell on me like a thunderclap, and her voice seemed to echo, "You have to go back, back, back!"

How could that be? Maybe Mutti, the fat lady, as Christa called her, was right. Maybe they were just friends and Christa was a liar as Mutti had told me.

Christa interrupted my thoughts. "Our mother and father were married once, but, then, they divorced, and you went with him."

"But why?"

"That was set by the court, and there is nothing you or I can do about it. That is the way it is."

"But why are you not with us?"

"I hate that fat lady he is married to, and they could not make me!" She stood up. This matter was closed to her. "Come on, let's go back in the house. Soon we have to take you to the train station."

Oh, I did not want to hear that. I wanted to stay, even if they were only friends. They were nice, loving people, but Oma was my favorite. I liked the nurse a lot, but she was like a stranger to me although she said she was my mother. I wanted to cry, throw my arms around Oma, and beg her not to send me back. I wanted to tell her I would be a good girl and that I loved her, but I didn't. I was afraid of what she would say, and, anyway, they probably didn't want me. I kept up a brave front, but I cried inside.

My suitcase was packed, and forgetting Mutti's warning I even had a second one. That one was shiny red and smaller then my other one. It was filled with gifts I had received from Oma, Mutti the nurse and the family. I had a new dress; tiny dolls, Uschi and I had played with, books to color and read, and other toys, things to remind me of Goerlitz and the people I loved.

My cousin Uschi and her mother Tante Elfriede came, and soon we walked to the train station together. I walked silently, not chattering. Oma looked at me and gave me a smile, but her eyes said she was sad, too. She squeezed my hand to assure me all would be fine, but I knew better.

We arrived at the train station, but all the excitement of traveling had left me. I felt nothing. All I wanted to do was cry. I received hugs and goodbyes from everyone, including my sister. I kept looking to see if Mutti the nurse had come to say goodbye, but she did not come. *She didn't like you after all because you were not pretty enough!* A voice inside told me.

The train came. Oma gave me a big hug and kiss, telling me, "Be brave. "Someday" you will come back to us, you'll see." I could see the tears in her eyes, too, and her sad face under the brim of that dark blue hat of hers.

The conductor was informed that I was traveling alone and my destination was Kohlfurt where I was to be picked up. He agreed to check on me during the two-hour trip. He walked along the train shutting the doors, blew his whistle, and with the flyswatter looking signal raised high, told the engineer that the train was ready to leave. The engineer answered with a whistle and slowly the train began to roll out of the Goerlitzer train station. I stood by the window, waving at the family, but mainly at Oma, and my tears came as I watched her disappear from my view. I couldn't stop my tears no matter how hard I tried and still weeping, I sat down. A kind-hearted woman sitting across from me leaned over and touched my knee, "Are you alright?"

I nodded. "Yes." With my tear soaked handkerchief in my hands, I sat, Christa's words echoing in my head, "You've got to go back, you've got to go back, you've got to go back!" After a two-week visit filled with warmth and love, I went back home, sad and alone. Oh, how I wanted Vati, but he was not anywhere near.

The train kept moving, bringing me to where I didn't want to be. My tears had flowed until there was none left; only the uncontrollable heaving sighs remained. I knew I had to stop and pull myself together because Mutti was going to look me over very closely, and I had to be as normal as possible. It was hard to leave caring, warm, surroundings, knowing what awaited me in Mutti's care. My heart and soul cried out, and I wanted to stop that train and run back. But the train moved on. The scenery that once excited me passed before my eyes, unnoticed. Instead, I leaned back and let the past days wash over me. I wanted to imprint them on my mind so I would never forget them. I saw Oma in her blue hat smiling as her gentle, reassuring voice told me, "You'll come back to us someday. You'll see." *But when is someday.* I saw the nurse, my mother, a familiar stranger, holding and loving me. I recalled her fresh smell, her blue and white nurse's uniform. Then, I heard Christa's voice telling me, "We're your family, but you have to go back!"

Confused I asked, *but who is my family? And why do I have to go back?* I heard only Christa's words, "You have to go back! You have to go back!" I sat crouched in the corner of the train seat—confused. Soon the train arrived in Kohlfurt, going underneath the bridge I liked so much, but even that did not cheer me up. I knew I had better straighten up before the train came to a stop.

Cold crept over my body as I saw Mutti standing on the platform, grim faced, watching for me to get off the train. There was no hugging, no warm greeting. Mutti just stood, looking down at me and said icily, "I hope you enjoyed your visit, because this will be your last one—if I have anything to say about it. You're back to reality, my reality, and it's time for you to stop dreaming and forget all the lies you've been fed." She reached for my suitcase, and then stopped abruptly, "Why do you have a second suitcase? Was yours not good enough? Did you beg them for a new one and red no less! Did I not tell you not to bring anything back from them?" I tried to answer that it was a gift, but she just kept on walking and talking, "Well, we'll see what we can do with that one!" *What did she mean by that?* With me in tow, Mutti walked over the bridge to her parents' apartment, carrying my suitcase. I carried the new one. Although the sky was blue and the sun warm, my hands were like ice. Oh, I was lonely, with only a cloud of doom following me.

When we arrived at the apartment, the other Oma was there. But what a different Oma! This one was skinny, tall, uncaring, and unsmiling, staring at me with her cold eyes. I wanted to turn, to run and scream, "No, no, no! I don't want to be here!" But where could I run?

Mutti told me to unpack the suitcases. When I unpacked the red suitcase, Mutti and Oma, murmuring to each other, looked it all over, paying special attention to the dress and the gifts I got. Then Mutti put it all back into the suitcase and closed it. Quietly I watched her, relieved. *She was going to let me keep my gifts.* I almost wanted to hug Mutti I was so happy. But, reaching for my hand, pointing at the red suitcase with my treasures in it, Mutti said in a calm voice, "Come, get your suitcase and we'll take a walk."

"Where are we going?" I wanted to ask, "Why take the red suitcase?" But I could not question her authority.

I picked up the suitcase, took Mutti's hand, and we walked outside. We went around the corner of the apartment building to a big square garbage dumpster. The top was covered with heavy metal and had a trap door opening on top near the front. Mutti, with me in tow, my possessions in hand, walked to the dumpster, lifted the door, and said, "Hand me your suitcase!" I knew what she was going to do!

"Mutti please let me keep the suitcase." She took my suitcase, treasures and all, and flung it into the dumpster. With a look of satisfaction she turned to me, "And that will be the end of that, and I don't want to hear, ever, a word said about this. Am I making myself clear to you?" Her steel eyes bored deep into me. Horrified by her action, I heard nothing at that moment. All I knew was that my beautiful suitcase with all my treasures was lying among the stinky trash. My mind was in a whirl. I wanted to climb in there and dig it out again. I wanted to scream at her, "No! Pull it back out! It is mine, not yours!" But I knew that would only get me severely punished.

I knew what she could do when she was aroused, so I stayed frozen in place, staring. Suddenly she had me by the shoulders, her face before me. Like a monster, she was shaking me and shouting, "Did you hear what I just said!"

Scared, and shaken, I was unable to repeat her words, but answered, "Yes, Mutti, I heard what you said," hoping she would not demand for me to repeat them because I had not heard a word. I was lucky; she took me by the hand again, and we marched back inside.

Oma looked up as we came back, nodded her head toward Mutti and spoke not a word. Only Opa, taking his jacket from the hook on the back of the door, said in a low voice, "What a cruel thing to do!" and walked out. The evening meal was served, but I was unable to swallow; my throat felt as if someone was holding it closed. Mutti and Oma watched me with sharp eyes, as I tried to eat. Tears wanted to spring up, but I had to fight them back the best I could. Pictures of my red shiny suitcase lying among all that nasty stuff kept coming into my head, and my heart was there with it. Quick and without warning Mutti sprang from her chair, grabbed my arm and pulled me away from the table, saying, "If you don't want to eat then you can go to bed. We don't want to see your ungrateful face." And, under Mutti's watchful eye, I undressed and went to bed. Quietly I cried under the covers. I wished with all my heart that Vati or someone would come and get me, but no one came.

Suddenly the covers were pulled back. Mutti and Oma stood there, and without a word, I got a spanking from Mutti. After that she yanked me out of bed, and while pulling me behind her, said, "If you want to cry for *them*, you can do that somewhere else." Out the door we went and up the wide wooden stairs in the hallway of the building, past the second floor; then, opening a second door into additional but smaller wooden steps, we continued. I knew where I was going, and I tried to pull in the opposite direction, begging, "Please, Mutti, don't put me upstairs! I'll be good! I'll stop crying! Please!" But she paid no attention to my pleading. At the top of that floor there were several doors, and she stopped in front of one of them and opened it with a key. Mutti turned on the light and pushed me inside. There was a bed with the *Nachttopf*, the chamber pot underneath, a nightstand, and a closet. Walking over to the bed, she pulled back the covers and pointed wordlessly to the bed and me. I got into bed; she turned off the light and left the room, locking the door behind her. I was petrified to sleep upstairs, alone, in the dark.

It was the attic of the house, and everyone who lived in the building had a room upstairs. Also, there was a huge space where in bad weather the tenants could hang their wash to dry. From past experience I knew how creepy it was to sleep in the attic. There were all sorts of noises, like creaking, squeaking, and fluttering. One day going upstairs with Oma I had seen a dead bat lying on the steps. Oma told me they lived here, under the roof. I slid under the covers and sweated, but I would not come out. What always amazed me was that in the morning I was still there and unharmed. The furniture had also remained in the same place, and in the daylight it didn't look that scary.

This night, I lay there, crying and calling, "Vati, Vati, please come and get me. I want you!" No one came, except Mutti. She came through the door, flying over to where I was lying. She bent over me with her finger pointing in my face, saying, "If you don't stop that crying and calling for your father, you will sleep outside, there is no one who will come for you. No one! Not even your father!" And out she went, relocking it behind her.

I fell asleep, exhausted, my body hurting inside and out. I didn't even have the energy to be scared. The next morning Mutti came and got me. Silently we went downstairs, silently I dressed, and silently I ate my breakfast. Oma, Christa, and the nurse in Goerlitz were never mentioned again. The red suitcase, although it was gone, I never forgot. That was something Mutti could not control, and I knew it.

From then on a loving face in a blue hat was following me, saying to me with a smile, "Someday you'll come back to us; you'll see!" I had a secret from Mutti, and she could not do anything about it. I clung to those words. Only when was, *someday? And was the Mutti, here, really my stepmother?*

S ummer vacation was over and with memories of Goerlitz still in my mind; the school year of 1943/1944 had begun, when shortly thereafter Mutti packed our suitcases again. I was wondering why. So with all my courage I asked, and she answered, "I have to go away to see your father."

I wanted to go with her and said, "Mutti, can I go with you and see Vati, too?"

"No! You cannot! I need to see your father alone. I'm leaving you in Kohlfurt with Oma. You'll go to school there until I come back from seeing your father. I do not want any tears from you; it will do you no good. You know I'll spank you!" With that she turned and continued packing.

I didn't want a spanking, so I sat and watched Mutti packing our suitcases. *Why can't I go with her to see Vati? And why had she referred in such an icy tone to as "your father,"* she had never done that before. It made me feel uneasy. *What was wrong with Vati?* I didn't like going to Kohlfurt to Oma's and to the school that was unknown to me. But soon I experienced the *Kohlfurter Schule,* and I have never forgotten it.

On the day following our arrival in Kohlfurt, Mutti and I went to the school to sign me up. The school was a gray, two-story square stucco building with tall high windows, a steep tiled roof—all enclosed by a stout wire fence with a gate. The entrance to the school building had an imposing wooden door. This door was locked. When Mutti rang the bell, the school custodian, stiff and stern faced, answered the door. He escorted us to an open waiting area, then went to notify the principal. When Mutti was called in to see the principal, I sat on a bench waiting, looking at my future surroundings.

The floor was made of small black and white mosaic tiles. The walls and the rounded, ornate ceiling were painted white. Right in front of me was a wide staircase, leading to the upper floor. The atmosphere was impersonal;

the plain surroundings demanded respect. On my far right sat was a small open foyer area with freestanding coat racks and doors leading to two classrooms. All I heard were the teachers' loud and forceful voices. I was terrified I would never escape from here.

After a while, I too was called, so the principal could meet the new student. I do not recall the principal at all, only that I was scared. I was to report for class the next morning at eight. On our way out, the custodian showed me which door was to my classroom. I had a creepy feeling about that school, so I was so glad to leave. It was not at all like my school bright, shiny, and friendly in Liegnitz. I hoped that Mutti would soon return with Vati, and we all would go home together.

On the way back to Oma's I asked, "Mutti, will you be gone long and will you bring Vati back with you?"

"I don't know. All you have to do is go to school; all other things do not concern you."

Oh, I wished she would tell me what was wrong with Vati and when he was coming home. I longed for him and his caring for me, but I was not allowed to ask any more questions. At Oma's, Mutti gave me her final instructions; then, she was gone.

My first day of school arrived too soon. Oma fixed me breakfast and a sandwich for school and off I went. I was scared, but I knew I had to go. My stomach felt prickly as if little butterflies were fluttering around inside, and I could not stop them. When I got to school, the teacher was not in the room, so I waited in front of the classroom door. And then I saw him approaching.

He was skinny, tall and old, his short hair parted in the middle. He wore an immaculate tailored dark suit with a stiff white collar almost up to his ears and a tiny black bow tie. Books under his arm, he was down to his black shiny shoes a figure of respect. What little courage I had abandoned me. My stomach churned. I was petrified. Stopping in front of me, from the upper pocket of his waistcoat he pulled a monocle attached to a silver chain. He clamped it in one of his eyes, looking me over coldly. Timidly, I curtsied and said, *"Guten Morgen, Herr Lehrer,* Good morning, Mister Teacher.

In a voice as skinny as his body, he said, "So you're the new one. Follow me." And we entered the classroom. What was previously a noisy room turned into total silence. Everyone was standing at attention at their desks, eyes forward, like wooden marionettes. There were four rows of wide wooden desks, each desk wide enough for two children. The rows were split; the boys' occupied two rows on the inner side of the room, while the girls had the other two rows at the window side.

I could feel all eyes on me. I wanted to hide, but I had to stand until he had made his announcement, "This is Gisela Knebel, she is a temporary student." There was silence. He pointed at a desk way in the back and said, "That will be your place for the time you'll here." I hurried to get there so I could sit down and get away from those staring eyes. I was the only occupant of the desk assigned to me.

The teacher's *pult, a* desk, stood on a podium and was almost the same as the children's, only much bigger. Its chair was separated, where as our desks were all one piece and smaller. Standing on the podium, the teacher stood straight up, his monocle still clamped in his eye, looking down at the class. "*Fraeulein Knebel*, I believe you were not given permission to sit down, were you?" he demanded.

I jumped up, my face flushing. Some of the kids started to laugh, and I said a faint, "No, *Herr Lehrer.*"

"Speak up, we can't hear you!"

Clearing my throat, I repeated, "No, Herr Lehrer."

"Then, please be so kind to stand up with the rest of the class."

The laughter got a little louder. He reached into his desk, pulled out a willow switch, and slapped the top of the desk, "Silence!" he bellowed in his skinny voice. Instant silence! His eyes roamed over his pupils. "Be seated!"

On the left of the teacher podium was the blackboard. It was free-standing, on rollers, with a revolving board that could be flipped over from a writing side to a math side. As class began, the teacher called the name of a boy and with chalk in hand he stood next to the blackboard. During class, he looked over us kids with a watchful eye. Sometimes he stepped behind the blackboard to do something, then he watched again.

What was he doing? I leaned to the girl in front of me and whispered, "What is he doing behind that board?" But she gave me no answer; she sat unmoving. Class continued. But every time a new session began, he called on a new student to stand there.

My curiosity was soon to be stilled. The bell rang, announcing the end of the school day, but no one made a move to get up and walk out of the class. The last person standing behind the blackboard announced the names of kids, and everyone called came to the front, lining up facing the teacher. There was quite a long line, and my name was called, too. I hurried to join the line, happy to be included. The teacher, willow stick in hand, looked the line over. "Hands out!" "Palms up!" The kids put both hands out, palms up. "How many?" he asked the person behind the board. Whatever number given was the number of times the switch made contact with the hands of the offenders.

What did I do? Why did I get the switch? He stopped in front of me; my hands were shaking. As the switch was about to come down, I pulled my hands away, blurting out, "I didn't do anything!" He stiffened; his face turned to stone. I knew I had made an unspeakable blunder. I had defended myself, questioning his authority in front of the class.

"You," he said, pointing his willow switch at me, "were talking during class, and that is not allowed. Hands out!" The switch came down hard, "And one extra one, so you will remember never ever to question my authority again."

It stung! My hands got welts, and they burned. While I attended the school, my name was called every day. I cried on the way home, but I did not tell Oma. She would not have defended me, thought I deserved it. I was a stranger in that school; therefore, I was treated like one.

One day in school between classes I wanted to see the teacher about something. He was standing in the hallway talking to another teacher. I approached him and started to tell him my problem; he turned and without a word hit me across my face. My head was humming, my cheek, burning like fire. "You will not interrupt grown-ups when they're in a conversation. Go and sit down!"

Humiliated, feeling the stares, and hearing the sniggers of the kids, I went back to my desk. Tears rolled down my burning cheeks, but I did not care. *What kind of school was this? Where did Mutti put me? How long did I have to stay here?* I wanted to leave, but that was impossible. I had to stay.

Then one day I was late for school, for the second time. Lucky for me the door had not been locked yet. The first time I was late and after knocking had entered the classroom, making my excuse why I was late, I got the switch on my hands and had to stay after class to write for one hour, "I will not be late again," over and over.

But here I was again, late. I stood in front of the door, ready to knock, my knees weak. I was afraid of that man called teacher and the kids. My hand sank back down, and I stood motionless. I heard his voice and that of another teacher in the room next door, but I could not bring myself to knock. I can't go home because Oma will send me back and I'll be even later. Although the front door is still unlocked, I can't walk out of here. Someone might see me leave. But I am not going to knock.

As I stood there, I heard steps coming. *I have to find a place to hide! But where?* As the steps got closer, I looked around, but all I saw were two freestanding coat racks filled with coats against the walls in the hall. I dove as fast as I could behind one of the racks, crouched down in the corner, and stopped breathing. Had they seen me? I peeked through the coats. No, it's a girl who's been to the bathroom and is returning to class. There I was, stuck in the corner; hiding, scared that someone would find me. I tried to think what I should do, but no answer came. My final decision was just to stay and not move until school let out. What worried me next were the kids. If they came and collected their coats, they would see me. I would be exposed!

I was trapped, but I would rather risk that than go into the classroom to face that awful teacher. I could hear the teachers' voices as they echoed in the otherwise quiet school building. Some kids came for their coats, but they did not see me or did not care and paid no attention to me. When the opportunity came, I slipped to the rack that had more coats on it so I would be hidden better. I don't know how long I stayed hidden, but when I thought it was time for class to be over, I hurried from my hideaway and ran all the way home.

Oma said, "Aren't you home from school early?"

"Oh, I ran all the way home," I said with as calm a voice as possible.

"So you did," is all Oma ever said about it.

Mutti returned to Kohlfurt alone. She was irate. Her face and eyes had that icy look. But I had to ask, "Mutti, why isn't Vati with you? Isn't he coming?"

"No, he is not!" she answered with an angry voice. "He will be coming later." Emphasizing "he". My spirits sank. *Where was Vati? Why did Mutti come home mad, and annoyed?*

Oma and Mutti kept whispering in heated voices to each other. I tried to hear what the whispering was about, but they realized I was listening, and sent me outside. "Go and play, and stop trying to listen to us." I went outside and sat on the stairs at the entrance. My disappointment was big; I had wanted Vati so much for so long, and now I still had to wait.

Before we returned to Liegnitz, Mutti went to school to sign me out.

I was sure she'd be told about my skipping school, but she never said anything at all. Maybe they had not missed me, or I was just not important enough to bother with. In any case, I counted myself very lucky. Mutti and I took the train back home without Vati. I wanted to cry, but Mutti would have only gotten mad at me and she was that already. I felt alone without Vati, and I sat on the train thinking and hoping of *someday*?

I was glad to be back at my school in Liegnitz, with the kids I knew and my favorite teacher, Fraeulein Kaetzler. Although busy with school, many times my thoughts went back to Goerlitz, still vivid in my mind. I thought about that nurse I had called Mutti, and the conversation Christa and I had had. But mostly I thought of Oma in her blue hat, reassuring me that someday I would return. *When would "someday" come?* But, someday echoed like a never, never day in my mind. No beginning. Far away. High as the blue sky above. I wanted to ask Mutti, but I dared not.

Sometimes Mutti and I on hot days sat by the river called *Katzbach* that flowed through Liegnitz. With water, vinegar, and sugar, Mutti made lemonade and packed sandwiches for us to eat. Then we sat on our blanket under a shade tree and watched people, mainly mothers, play with their children in the water. Mutti not wearing a bathing suite didn't want me in the water and I didn't mind because I was scared of large bodies of water. So, I just sat and watched.

That summer I also learned to ride Vati's bike. I wanted a bike of my own, but Mutti said, "You do not need one." But Vati had a bike. It was a big, heavy dark blue one, a man's bike with the crossbar. I watched other kids, in particular boys, riding their father's bikes. Some too were not big enough to ride the man-sized one, but they rode it sideways by crouching under the crossbar so their feet could reach the pedal on the opposite side of the bike. I thought I could try that with Vati's since I was not getting a bike of my own. So, I ask Mutti, "I'd like to learn how to ride a bike; please, could I take Vati's?"

"No, you will not!" She immediately answered. But after much asking and begging, she finally gave in, and I was allowed to use it. Her final words of warning were, "If you're crying because you hurt yourself, don't bother telling me. It will be the end of your playing with your father's bike!"

I started by walking the bike back and forth along the side of the house, needing to get the feel of how to balance the bike. Then, I put my right foot on the left pedal and used my left foot to push off the ground. Standing on the left pedal, with my right foot I let the bike roll, holding it steady. This practice kept me busy for some time until I got really good at balancing the bike.

After I had mastered the balancing, I switched legs and worked on putting my right leg underneath the crossbar and on the right pedal. But that was a real challenge. The right pedal had to be in the up position so I could place my right foot on that pedal as the lower half of my body twisted underneath the crossbar. My shoulders were above the crossbar with my hands holding on to the handlebars. Then, with my right foot I pushed the right pedal downward and as the bike started to roll, I put my left foot on the left pedal and started to pedal. The bike fell to the left and I was underneath. I untwisted myself from the wreck, dusted off my clothes and picked up the bike. Crying was out of the question since I did not want to lose my bike privileges. After many tries, crashes, and bruised knees, I did master Vati's bike quite well. Sometimes, I could even take it on small errands for Mutti, like to our neighborhood grocery store. And so time passed with play and responsibility.

Then, one day, I was sitting in my usual chair, next to the kitchen table—but really Vati's before he went to war—daydreaming. When out of the corner of my eye I saw the top of a green, ship like looking cap, passing underneath the kitchen window. That could only mean one thing: Vati had come home. Jumping off the chair and calling out, "Mutti, Mutti, Vati is home! He is here!" I ran for the door and opened it. There he was, standing in front of me. I stood frozen, just looking. I could not believe that he was really standing here, before me! He had a cane and wore a funny looking big shoe on his right foot. His tall slender figure was dressed in the green uniform that soldiers wore. The suitcase he carried was next to him on the ground. As I looked up at his face, I saw two blue eyes filled with love looking down at me. His big bright smile showed white, pearl-like teeth. It really was Vati. I wanted to burst with joy. *Had Goerlitzer's Oma "someday" really come?*

He let go of his cane, removed his uniform cap, and I threw myself at him, saying over and over, "Oh, Vati, you're home! You're home! Will you stay?"

He scooped me up and hugged me tight as if he never wanted to let me go. "Spatz, I will never, never leave you again." Those words, like music filled my heart. I wrapped my arms around him, kissing, hugging, laughing, and clinging to him. Vati was home, and, most of all, he promised never, never to leave me again. It felt as if someone had turned a warm light on inside me, and a feeling of unbounded happiness washed over me.

Mutti came. To my amazement, there was only a cool, "Hello," from her. But I didn't care. Vati was home, and I was happy. After while, and when things had settled down, Mutti told me to go outside. She said they had to talk, and Vati nodded in agreement. As I waited outside, I heard Mutti talk in a loud voice. She kept saying something about *that whore in Goerlitz* and the time he had spent there; that he had himself transferred to Goerlitz and into that Lazarett, where that whore was working just so he could be near that whore and her family; that it would be best for him not to think he could go back to her again. She said she would put him in jail first and then he could not even see his precious little girl anymore. Vati did not say much at all, if anything. Mostly Mutti was accusing him.

When I heard her say, "Goerlitz, Lazarett, and jail," a picture appeared in my mind. *I know Goerlitz and the Lazarett. I know the nurse who works there, the one I was told was my real mother! Vati has seen her? Has he seen Oma and Christa also? Why is Mutti so mad, and why does she call the nurse a "whore"? What kind of a name is that?* It sounded so mean and I didn't like Mutti to say such mean-sounding things. *I really like that nurse. What about the jail? Can she put Vati in jail just because he went to Goerlitz? She can't do that; I won't let her. I didn't go to jail when I was there. Why would Vati?*

One thing I understood; Mutti did not like it that Vati had been in Goerlitz. I had been there, too, and what a nice time I had had. But I also remembered what had happened to my gifts when I returned from Goerlitz. Mutti hated those people. That was why, when they had come to visit a long time ago, she would not answer the door. That's why she threw my suitcase in the garbage. Fear gripped me that Vati would leave again, and deep inside me, I began to hate Mutti. She was mean. I wanted to go in, push her away, and tell her, "Stop that! You leave Vati alone or he'll go away again. He is my Vati! You stop! I don't like you anymore!" I wanted to put my arms around Vati and tell him, "Don't listen to her; she is mean, but I love you. Please, don't leave me!"

But I was not allowed to go in, so I waited. When Vati came out, I looked at him, afraid of what he might tell me. Did he know I was scared he might leave again without me? He put his hand on my shoulder and tipping my face up to his with the other, he said, "Don't worry, Spatz. I'm not going anywhere, and, most of all, not ever without you." Relief swept over me. My world felt secure, and I stayed close to Vati. When I was out playing, I would stop and check to see that he was still there.

But always there he was, with his sometimes-cold pipe clamped in the space in the lower left corner of his mouth where there used to be a tooth. He knew what I was doing and smiled, reassuring me, "I'm still here, Spatz." Something else changed; Vati told Mutti there would be no more spankings.

Vati kept busy working in the yard getting part of it ready to plant potatoes the following spring. He readied beds for vegetables and put in an area for strawberries just for me, since they were my favorite. All got fertilized with natural fertilizer so it could work into the ground over the winter, he explained to me as I was holding my nose.

He busied himself building a garden house and lined the inside with rabbit hutches, filling them with young rabbits and one he called *Meister Lampe*, a nickname for male rabbits. He was pretty mean, so I was not allowed to touch him. "He will bite," Vati warned. Every time we had new baby rabbits, Vati showed them to me, and when they were big enough, I could hold them.

He cooked potatoes for the rabbits then mixed them with wheat. Sometimes the neighbors would bring potato peelings and carrot greens for the rabbits. I think he had a small rabbit business because Vati butchered quite often. He would not allow me to watch when he killed them, but I watched when he skinned them. Wherever Vati was, that's where I was, much to Mutti's distaste. He talked to me, and showed me how to do things. I never stopped talking or asking questions. He always said, "You're just like the Spatz, a tiny bird, always chattering," and with that he pointed up in the tree where there was a gray brown speckled little bird, hopping from branch to branch, chirping. It made me feel special to be compared to and nicknamed after a real bird because I liked birds.

In the stairwell of the house, halfway up the stairs was a small oblong storage room. In that room Vati had his carpenter's workbench with all his tools. That place was my favorite. I sniffed the fresh-planed wood, wet paint, and stain. This aroma had attached itself to Vati, so whenever I hugged him, I could smell it. Wood chips littered the floor and stuck to our socks and shoes. They made a rustling sound when I kicked them around, like the fallen leaves I enjoyed kicking outside.

Vati stopped me from doing that, saying, "You're making dust and that will settle on the wet items I have just painted sitting on the bench." He gave me leftover wood, a hammer and nails, and I hammered and built, all the while chatting, chatting, and chatting. Vati, wearing his light-colored carpenter's apron with pockets to hold his small tools, his well worn and dusty cap sitting square on his head, a flat carpenter's pencil pressed behind his ear, just kept on working. He never interrupted me or told me to stop; he just patiently listened.

Our neighbor upstairs, Herr Schulz, was still beating his wife, so Vati went upstairs with his cane in hand. I heard him tell the man, "If you have too much energy, maybe you need to be sent out to the *Russian front*. There you will forget about beating your wife. You'll be to busy trying to stay alive. As long as I live here, I do not want to hear anymore beatings in this house or I will do something about it." Herr Schulz never answered Vati. After that, there was never a beating anytime we were at home. I think Vati scared the little man, and I was glad and proud of him.

Christmas of 1943 we spent in Kohlfurt. Mutti had knitted me a new pullover. I had a new navy blue pleated skirt with matching tights, and since it was winter, black, patent leather looking high rubber boots that fit over my new shoes. A red coat and hat, both trimmed in black fur, finished my ensemble. I was proud of my new clothes, and didn't even mind going to Kohlfurt, because Vati was with me.

I was sitting on the couch all dressed, except for my coat, watching Vati shave. That was the first time I saw him lose his temper. I don't know exactly what started the fight, but I think he didn't want to go. I felt that he, as I, did not like Oma in Kohlfurt. Mutti kept talking about this that and other things, and pretty soon up came Goerlitz and that whore again. Vati told Mutti to stop talking like that in front of me, but she ignored him and kept right on talking. Watching Vati, I could see that he was getting mad. I noticed the vein popping up from his hairline, going straight down to the bridge of his nose and it was throbbing. Before I knew it, he threw his razor clear across the kitchen! It bounced off the wall and slid underneath the stove. I, wanting to please him, jumped off the couch and belly-landed, new clothes and all, underneath the stove to retrieve that razor. Vati chased after me to stop me, "No, Spatz, don't touch that razor! You'll cut yourself!" But I already had captured the wayward razor and handed it to him like a trophy. I wanted Vati to know, I loved him. "Never touch a razor again, Gisela, you will hurt yourself." Then, he patted me on the head and said, "Thank you, Spatz." Her face pinched, Mutti silently checked my clothes, but since she was a spotless housekeeper, even under the stove, my clothes did not show any dirt. The journey in the train to Kohlfurt was made in silence. Vati met some soldiers on the train and they were talking about the war. I do not remember anything about that Christmas in Kohlfurt; I had Vati, and I was happy. While in Kohlfurt, I slept with Oma and Opa but Mutti and Vati slept in that dreaded room in the attic. After our return home, I went back to school. Vati worked in his shop, took care of his rabbits, and life took its place.

Oh, yes, with Vati home, I was able to sleep in my own bed again in the other room. But when the opportunity presented itself, after Mutti was up, but Vati still in bed, I crawled in bed with him and snuggled up close to him. My world was secure.

Winter had passed, spring was on the way, and the year was 1944. Vati was working a lot in his carpenter shop upstairs, and I was with him. He made wooden toys, like scooters, dachshunds with movable parts, airplanes with propellers, doll strollers, and many more items, all hand made and painted. But my favorite was the doll stroller made of wood, its wheels had a narrow rubber strip around them for quiet rolling. The back of the stroller was movable so the doll could be laid down. The side panels were oval with a narrow rounded wooden strip of over the top. Then the stroller was painted a soft light creamy yellow, the strips including the handle bar, and the wheels were trimmed in red. As a final touch the back and side panels of each stroller was decorated with decals picturing bouquet of flowers. Vati always let me pick out the decal he was to apply. It was not an easy job because he had so many pretty decals to choose from. There were yellow roses with daisies; or red poppies and blue cornflowers mixed with daisies. Then there were decals of lilies of the valley with blue forget-me-notes. But mostly I chose the decals that showed a bouquet of daisies, with blue cornflowers and red poppies. I like them, because in summer they grow wild along the farmer's wheat fields.

Vati also made airplanes that had propellers. He painted them gray adding the emblem of the German Luftwaffe. He placed one on a pole in our front yard, and when the wind was blowing, the propellers turned and so did the airplane.

I played outside with the toys Vati had made, and soon he had requests from the people in the neighborhood to make some for them. The airplane and the stroller were much in demand. Vati had to tell the people that he could not make any promises because he also had a job. The toy-making was a hobby of his.

Every time Vati finished a new stroller, I liked the new one better. Sometimes I had not had a chance to play with the last one, so we traded. Vati usually let me exchange it, much to Mutti's disapproval. She put an end to it by saying, "That will have to stop. No more! She is getting spoiled!"

I didn't like her interfering or her decision and Vati told me when we were in his shop alone, "Just wait until the time comes; we will do one more exchange." Then, he added, "But it will have to be the last time. You will have to keep what you got from then on." We made one last final exchange, and Mutti never noticed. We had a secret and that made me feel special.

Vati started getting the garden ready for planting, as the natural fertilizer had soaked into the ground over the winter, just as he said it would. He was busy every day, never stopping. He was either at work, in the yard, in his shop, or tending to the rabbits, and I followed right behind him. I had no friends; Vati filled that void. I felt safe being near him. On hot days when he was working in the yard, he would wear a shirt that had tiny small holes, like a net. When Mutti saw what Vati was wearing, she called him in, and I could hear her demanding voice telling him, "You take that shirt off! The woman across from us is staring at you. It's embarrassing that you present yourself in that shirt."

Vati only laughed and told her," You're only jealous, and I will not change; it's hot out there, and she is not looking at me!" He didn't change, but continued to wear that shirt whenever it was hot. I never heard Mutti again tell him to take off that shirt.

He also had a job as a carpenter at the nearby *Flughafen*, the Air Base of the German Luftwaffe, and he rode his bike to work every day. But on weekends he allowed me to ride his bike, so one day when I went to get his bike, there was a girl's bike leaning on his. Looking at it, I got all excited with hope. I ran to find Vati. "Vati, Vati, did you know there is a girl's bike leaning on yours?"

"Yes, I know. Do you like it?"

Did I like it? It was not a new one, but I didn't care. It was a pretty bike, and I could ride it like a girl should. "Yes, I like it. Is it for me Vati? A bike all my own? And no one can take it away from me?"

With a smile on his face, his cold pipe hanging from his mouth, he said, "Yes, it is for you and only for you. And no one will take it away from you."

"What if Mutti is going to give it away like she did my tricycle? She will do that when she finds out you gave me a bike," I asked.

"No, she won't do that. It's yours, and she knows that. It is for you! Don't worry, just have fun with it."

"Oh, thank you Vati!" I was hugging and kissing him, smelling his special aroma of wood and paint.

"Go on, Spatz, and ride your bike," was his reply, but I could tell he liked my hugging and loving him.

The bike removed me even further from Mutti. It gave me freedom and space from her. I was out in our neighborhood riding and meeting the kids I rode the streetcar to school with. Mutti would complain that I was running in the neighborhood with the kids, but Vati told her to leave me be. Usually she gave me that stony look when Vati told her that. Almost every day when I got home from school, I hurried with my homework, and then rode my bike to the airbase where Vati was working. Then, together, we rode our bikes back home. I had no problem getting past the guard at the base.

"Ach, das Fraeulein Knebel ist hier!" the guards greeted me waving me through with a gesture befitting a queen.

I gave them my best smile with a royal nod of my head, *"Danke schoen."* I felt pretty important being called *Fraeulein Knebel,* and I noticed how handsome those young men were in their fitted uniforms.

Vati's carpenter shop was in a wooden building with carpenter benches and tools, as well as wood chips on the floor. He had two men, *Auslaender, foreigners,* working with him. They were friendly and always talked to me. Vati helped translate what they said. Only when we were riding our bikes home, Vati warned me not to be too friendly with his workers because the base commander would not like it, and it might create a problem for him.

"Why, Vati? Those men are nice people."

"Yes, they are." Is all he said giving me the feeling that Vati didn't want to talk about it and I didn't probe any further.

Vati also went to people's homes to do carpenter work. One of those families I really liked, so I went with him whenever possible. They had a daughter the same age as I, but she did not attend my school. Their business made things out of wicker, like baskets, big footlockers, footstools, and chairs. The place looked like a farm with barns where the employees wove the wicker and where the finished products were stored, ready for sale. In another barn facing the large wooden entrance gate were horses, some cows, chickens, and geese. I didn't mind the chickens, but I was afraid of the horses, cows, and geese. I had seen horses on the street their eyes big, kicking, snorting, and running uncontrollably while harnessed to wagons. They also had a big German shepherd; even though he was tied to a chain, I still watched him.

With the family house across from the building where the wicker was worked, the animal barn facing the large wooden gate big enough for a horse drawn wagon to go through, that formed the courtyard in to a big square.

But I loved best the oblong concrete pits behind the house that is where the wicker branches soaked in murky green water. In those pits were frogs whose ribbiting and squawking made a concert. The family's daughter and I chased the frogs around. Then when one jumped out of the pit, we ran as fast as we could, squealing, only to return and tease them some more. But we didn't hurt the frogs. On rainy days we played inside the house. The people, especially her mother and grandmother, were really nice to me, and I liked them a lot.

But I made a mistake that I will never forget. It was on such a rainy day that we played inside. In one of their rooms, among other furnishings, was a high chest of drawers. As I passed that chest of drawers, I saw the most beautiful ring lying there. It was gold with a big red stone in the center. It shone so that every time I passed it I had to stop and admire it. This ring was like magic, and it drew me to it. It was tantalizing and alluring, enticing me to pass it every opportunity I had. Finally, I had to reach up and touch it. Then it was in my hands. It had me totally captivated, like a spell had come over me. I heard someone coming, and instead of putting it back, I slipped it in the pocket of my apron.

What had I done? What should I do? Fear gripped me. I was afraid to put it back scared for someone might see me. Good behavior said, no one is to touch someone else's property without permission of the owner, and I had violated that law. I couldn't say, "Here is your ring. I had it in my pocket. I'm sorry." I could not just put it someplace else; they would know that I had touched it. What was I to do? I didn't want to play anymore, and I sat down, waiting for Vati to get through with his job. The ring in my pocket began to burn like fire, and I felt its heat going through me.

Everyone in the house asked me if I was feeling well, telling me I looked flushed. I had to assure everyone I was fine. But I was not fine. I was unable to look at them, so I kept my eyes down. I did not want anyone to see the lie in my eyes.

They called Vati, who said, "What is the matter, Spatz. Are you not well?"

"I'm fine, Vati; I just want to go home." He finished his work, and the mother and grandmother wished me well and lovingly stroked my cheeks before we left. We rode home, Vati on his bike and me on mine. I was holding the handlebar with one hand and with the other I was holding on to the ring in the pocket of my apron. I knew that I could not lose it. It would make things worse. I also knew that somehow I had to return the ring soon, but I just did not know how.

As we were riding, Vati said," You'd better use both hands on the handlebar, or you will fall."

But I replied as calmly as possible, "Oh, I'm fine, I do that all the time." How I hated to lie to him. How I wanted to tell him what I had done. But I couldn't. He loved me and I had disappointed him, and I did not want to see the hurt and sorrow in his eyes. And Mutti, she would beat me; that I knew. Even Vati would be unable to protect me. I knew I had done wrong and it hovered over me like a giant ugly monster. I wanted to shake it off, make it go away, but it would not leave me.

When we got home, I went into the room where my bed was and frantically looked around. Where could I put the ring? I had to decide fast. Mutti could come in at any moment, and she would sense there was something wrong. It had to be someplace where no one would find it, but where? My doll buggy? Yes, that would be the place. I was the only one who played with it. I could put it underneath the mattress; it would be safe there. I took the ring out of my pocket and looked at it. It had lost its luster, its glow. It was not pretty anymore. It lay in my hand cold, yet burning, laughing and sneering at me, "I do not belong to you; you stole me; and now you have to return me to my rightful owner." I lifted the mattress of my buggy and threw it in there. I did not want to see it anymore; it had become ugly, and I wanted to forget it.

Days passed. I went to school, and every day when I returned home, I checked the buggy to see if the ring was still there. And there it was, grimacing at me saying, "Are you ready to take me home yet?"

And then that big ugly monster that had followed me around came crashing down on me! When I got home from school, the ring was lying on the kitchen table in plain sight. My heart stopped; then it began to beat as if it was about to jump out of my throat. All strength left me; I felt weak standing there, frozen, the ring looking at me saying, "See, here I am. You did not hide me well enough; they found me." Mutti was standing there, her bosom heaving, her hands on her hips, her cold eyes staring down at me, looking like that gigantic ugly monster that had been following me around. "Tell me what this is," she said, pointing at the ring.

"It's a ring," I replied timidly.

"Yes, I know that, and where did you get this ring?" Her voice rose to a higher pitch.

"I took it from those people's house where Vati is working sometimes," I admitted.

"I want to know why you did that, what possessed you to do that. You'd better have a good explanation for it."

"I don't know. I just took it," was my measly answer.

A look of loathing came to her face and eyes. Her voice changed to a sneer. "You did not take it; you stole it. Do you hear me? You stole it! You're a thief! I always knew no good would come of you! And now you are a thief!" There was that horrible disgraceful word, which I knew was used for people who took things that didn't belong to them. I was a thief, and that monster that had followed me got even bigger and uglier.

"I don't know what your father is going to say about his precious little girl stealing when he gets home!"

Oh, Vati, what is he going to say? He will never like or love me again! In my mind I got smaller and smaller. I felt horrid and I wanted to cry, but no tears came.

"I want you to sit right here on this chair and wait for your father. I want to hear how his little girl is going to explain this to her doting Vati," she gloated.

"Yes, Mutti," I said, and I sat down to wait for Vati to come home from work. It was the hardest stool I had ever sat on in my short life. When Vati got home, Mutti told him what his precious little girl had done. Mutti told Vati that she had seen the woman who had asked her how I was doing because I had not felt good when I was there last and had suddenly wanted to go home. "Well," Mutti continued "I told her there was nothing wrong with Gisela. Then, she told me that she is missing her ring and can't find it, having last seen it lying on her chest of drawers when the girls were playing in the house. So I did some checking in your daughter's toys and here we are, I found the ring in her buggy." Mutti was gloating.

Vati never said a word; he just stood and listened to her. I was afraid to look at him and kept my eyes to the floor. "Gisela," he said, not Spatz, "look at me. Did you take that ring?"

"Yes, of course she did!" Mutti shouted.

Vati just gave her one of his stern looks and turned back to me.

"Yes, I did, but I didn't mean to. I'm sorry and I didn't even want it. I didn't mean to steal it!" It just happened!" I blurted out.

"Well, what should we do with it?" was his question to me.

"Give it back to them?" I asked timidly.

"She needs a spanking that she will never forget," Mutti demanded.

But Vati said, "No! That will not be necessary." I wanted to jump off the chair, hug him and tell him just how sorry I was over what I had done. Instead he took me by the hand and said, "Come, Gisela, take the ring. There is something you have to take care of." He got his bike out and, since it had gotten dark, I had to ride in front of him on the crossbar. The battery charger on Vati's bike that supplied the power for light hummed low as he peddled us toward our destination. Vati never said a word; he just peddled and the charger hummed, lighting our way. *Why doesn't Vati scold me? Has he stopped loving me? I wish he'd get mad. I wouldn't even have minded if he had spanked me. Don't stop loving me.* But, never saying a word, he just peddled and the charger hummed low.

When we got there, he let me off the bike and said, "You go in, return the ring, and tell them what you did. It is up to the people if you ever are welcome in their house again or not." I had the hardest walk in front of me. I stood at the door, looking back at Vati, but he just said, "Go on."

I knocked, and the woman whose ring I had in my hand answered the door. She asked me to come in. I opened my hand for her to take the ring, but she just looked at it and then at me, saying, "Why did you take my ring? This ring is very valuable to me. You're a nice, well-behaved little girl. Tell me why did you take it?"

I had no answer for her. All I could say was, "I'm so sorry and I never ever will do that again." Tears were choking me.

"Now, now don't cry. I'm glad that I did not lose the ring, but you did wrong and you gave me days of anxiety looking for it. You must never ever do that again to anyone. Do you hear me?"

"I'm very sorry. I will never do that again. I promise." I solemnly nodded my head in earnest agreement with her. My tears flowed with sorrow and relief. I had returned what did not belong to me. The great big ugly monster that had followed me was gone, lifted from my shoulders and disappeared. A sense of calm came over me. The lady shook my hand and I curtsied, and then she said, "You are still welcome in our house anytime, Gisela. I know you are not a thief and I believe you have learned a lesson."

I curtsied again and said, "Thank you," and went out to Vati, tears still rolling down my cheek.

"So did you take care of everything?" he asked me, as he wiped my tears away.

"Yes, Vati, I did."

"Then let's go home, Spatz." *Spatz! That was what I wanted to hear. He still loves me.* My tears stopped rolling, and my world was whole again. I asked him if that charger didn't have a nice humming sound as I hummed along with it while Vati peddled.

When we got home, Mutti wanted to start all over again, but Vati said, "Enough, there will be no more talk of the incident again. It is all over and done." I could tell, Mutti did not like that answer. She never forgot it, reminding me, telling others, every chance she had, that I was a thief.

Vati never mentioned the ring incident again, and I was glad. It was something I desperately wanted to forget, but Mutti would use every opportunity, when Vati was not around, to remind me that I was a thief. More and more I attached myself to Vati, and I stayed as far away from Mutti as possible. When she gave me orders, I checked with Vati first, but that created a problem between them. I sensed she did not like losing control over me. Vati saw the problem I was creating, telling me, "You must do what Mutti asks you to do." Looking at him a little disbelieving, I heard him continue, "That's the way it is, Spatz." I assured him I would do as he asked, but I didn't like it. She was mean.

Not always was I the perfect daughter. I pushed Vati just to see how much he would let go by. He had me spoiled, not that I was allowed to be sassy or disrespectful, but spoiled with love. Sometimes I would not heed his request. Maybe I was not feeling like it, or I was just testing him. I recall such an incident when he made it clear to me that he was the boss, not I. I don't remember what it was about, but we were in the yard, Vati was working and he asked me to do something. Not thinking, I replied, "Not now."

He straightened up to his full height. Looking up at Vati, I realized what I had said. His face was stern, his loving eyes sharp as needles, boring in to me. The vein appeared on his forehead and was throbbing. I knew I had gone too far. "When I tell you to do something, you will not talk back to me. I will not ever hear you say again, 'Not now!' Do you understand me and what I'm saying?"

I knew what he was saying, and I understood perfectly. Miserable over my misbehavior, I peeped, "Yes, Vati, I won't do it again." He went back to his gardening and I to my chattering. I slipped sometimes, but all Vati did was either give me the "You-know-better-look," the stern look out of his blue eyes, or he called me "Gisela". When he called me that I knew I was in trouble. He never once spanked me because his method of correcting me was working. I also tried my best not to upset him, and I felt Vati knew that. Afterward he would always say, "I know you don't mean it, Spatz, but try to do better." I was his Spatz again and that was important to me.

Fall of 1944 had arrived and School had resumed. As winter approached, snow started to cover the land. People with worried faces and low voices talked of the war. Throngs of covered wagons, pulled by horse or oxen, passed through our small suburb on the main thoroughfare.

Every day when returning from school, getting off the trolley and walking home alongside the road, I saw wagons filled with people and their belongings passing me. One day as I walked home, it was snowing hard, the icy wind attacking human and animal alike, when a big man whose oxen-pulled wagon was stopped to one side of the road approached me. The oxen whip in his hand, a blanket slung around his shoulder, his cap pulled over his ears and forehead, all I could see was his unshaven face. Although he was big and scary looking, I was not afraid of him because his dark eyes were gentle as he asked politely, "Do you know of a place where my family could cook a warm meal? We have all the food with us." I looked over toward his wagon, and I saw faces looking out from underneath the canvas. They had sad eyes, their faces were begging, and I felt sorry for them. I just stood there not knowing what to do or say. "Where do you live? Do you think your parents would mind if we cooked something good to eat for your family and us? We'll do the cooking, and we have plenty of food in the wagon. Your mother wouldn't have anything to do. We will do it all."

"We live right down the street from here, around the corner, the third house on the right," I said.

"Do you think we can come to your house and cook?"

"I suppose so," I answered, not too sure of myself anymore, realizing that maybe I had already done too much talking, worrying about what Mutti and Vati would say or do when this family pulled up with their oxen wagon in front of the house. Wanting to end the conversation, I said, "I've got to be going." I ran, hoping that he would not see the way I went, forgetting that I had already told him where I lived.

After a while, I heard a knock at the door, and Vati answered it. I peeked to see who it was, and my fear was justified. It was the man from the street. He was holding his cap in his hand and, a smiling and sincere face was greeting Vati. "My family and I were coming from the east, fleeing from the *Russian front* advancing further into Germany." He looked past Vati and saw me, "Oh, there is that nice little girl. She said we could come and cook dinner at your house."

I wanted to sink into a hole. I did not really say that, but I knew I was in trouble. The man continued, "We have all the food. We just need a place to cook. My family has not eaten a warm meal in days."

Vati, looking back at me, said, "If my daughter invited your family, then you are welcome."

I looked at Mutti's stone face, and I could tell she was upset with me, and I was sure I would hear about it later.

The people came in, filling Mutti's small kitchen with cold and clammy unwashed bodies. Their two children, about my age, sat on the sofa and never said a word. The man and the young women went outside, only to return with arms full of food. And just as he had claimed, they had food, from sausage, ham, and other meat to bread and more. The younger woman and the grandmother did all the cooking. The man brought in a bottle of schnapps, and the grandfather, Vati, and he had a lively conversation about the war. They were from Pommern, a province located to the far northeast of us, where they had a farm. They were refugees, fleeing from the advancing *Russian front* and had already spent days on the cold and blustery road. All that did not make much sense to me. I was only glad that Vati got along with the men and that he had pulled me out of the hole I had made for myself. Everybody ate; then, they cleaned up. It had gotten dark and even colder outside as the night had come. Vati told them they could stay and sleep in the kitchen. The man gratefully accepted, and said, "the women can sleep in the house but my father and I we'll sleep in the wagon to keep watch on the oxen's." Then, from the wagon they brought in beddings and blankets, and although the woman and children had to sleep on the floor, they were glad of a warm place to spend the night.

I felt pretty confident that I had done the right thing after all, but Mutti kept quiet throughout the whole thing. Once in a while she would look disgusted at me, waiting for her opportunity to pounce on me once they were gone. After eating breakfast, they packed up their food, but not before leaving some for us as a thank you for our hospitality extended to them. After thanking all of us, the grandmother prayed to God to protect and to keep us safe. We said "Amen" and they made the sign of the cross and with best wishes and handshakes they were gone.

Mutti looked around at her once clean kitchen and, with anger and disgust, looked at me and said, "I hope you will never offer this place to total strangers again. I will not have it, do you hear me?"

But before I could answer her, Vati cut in and said, "These people needed a place to rest up. And let's not forget that someday, probably very soon, we will be in the same situation." Mutti never said a word and kept quiet.

As usual, I didn't know what Vati was talking about. "Why should we be out traveling on that cold and blustery road when we have a place to live?"

He turned to me and said, "What you did was nice, Spatz, but try not to bring people you see on the road home again. Our place is really not big enough to hold lots of people." The throngs of covered wagons continued day after day, but I kept my eyes on the ground, hoping that people would not approach me again.

The big frozen crystal stars continued to fall, covering everything with a white glistening blanket. The icy cold felt like sharp knives cutting through the air. The strong blowing winds made high snowdrifts everywhere. The windows had solid ice-covered designs of stars and flowers. Winter had taken possession of the land. People stayed in their houses, the chimneys blowing out smoke. Mutti and Vati said it was the coldest winter we had had for several years. Talk of *Weihnachten,* Christmas, became louder but with careful statements such as, "We might as well enjoy Weihnachten; it may be the last one in our homes."

People got busy with their projects and so did Vati.

"Spatz, what is your wish for Weihnachten? What do you want the *Weihnachtsmann,* Santa Claus, to bring you?"

I knew what I wanted, and I had been waiting for him to ask me.

"I want *eine Puppenstube,* a dollhouse, Vati, a real dollhouse, two stories high, with lights, windows, furniture, and tiny dolls. Do you think the Weihnachtsmann will bring me a dollhouse made the way I would like?"

"Well, that is a pretty tall order, but it is possible; of course, he will be watching how you behave. Then, he will be judging if you should have a two-story dollhouse with all the extras you are asking for." Vati spoke sincerely but his eyes were shining as if he knew something I didn't.

Soon after our conversation, I noticed something. In the room where I slept was a china hutch, and one day there was something on top of the hutch covered by a sheet. Every night after I had gone to bed, Vati came in very quietly so as not to wake me and took that something off the hutch. Every morning when I woke up, it was back again. And then one morning when I woke up, it was not covered at all. My sleepy eyes got big. I could not believe what I saw. Up there on the hutch was a half-built dollhouse, and from what I could see, it had two stories and windows. The outside was covered with paper of a small brick pattern. My heart jumped. *Is that for me? Can it be that I'll get a dollhouse?* I hurried out of bed, hoping that Vati had not gone to work yet because I had to ask a very important question. But he was gone. Mutti was there, but I was not going to ask her.

I went to school, but could hardly wait to get home, to see Vati so I could ask him, "Vati, Vati, there is a dollhouse on top of the hutch in my room. Is it for me, Vati?" He was in his shop upstairs working. Stopping his work and looking at me in surprise, he said, "What are you talking about?"

"The Puppenstube, Vati, on the hutch. I saw it; it was not covered!"

"Oh, that one," he said slowly, turning back to his work. "That is not for you. I'm making it for someone special for Christmas. You just have to wait and see what the Weihnachtsmann will bring you." My disappointment was big. It was not for me but for someone else. I wanted to cry. Vati turned back to me and said, "Na, na, Spatz, don't be sad; maybe you will get your wish yet." Patting me on the head, he added, "Now be a good girl and go. I have work to do." I went, but I was sad. All I kept hearing was, "It is not for you!" When I went to bed that night, I looked up, and there it was all covered again. Every evening Vati came in and got the dollhouse. I could hear him working in the kitchen, filing and tapping until I went to sleep. And in the morning it was there again, but never without the cover. Christmas got closer and closer, and that dollhouse never left the hutch. I hoped that maybe it was for me after all, and I wanted Weihnachten to come soon.

One day before Weihnachten, Vati and I got all dressed up. He was in a suit and tie; I, in my best dress and winter coat. I knew it had to be something special because he seldom got dressed up; he was always working.

We rode the trolley into town, and while in the trolley, I asked, "Where are we going, Vati?"

"Just wait. It is a surprise for you." After getting off the trolley down town Liegnitz, he took me by the hand, and, after a short walk, we entered the opera house.

"Oh, Vati, what are we doing here?" I asked in a hushed voice. We had entered the huge lobby, its interior trimmed in red velvet and gold. A dark red carpet with a floral design covered the floor. The big crystal chandelier was shimmering and glistening below the ornate ceiling. Men and boys were dressed in suits and ties, ladies in gowns and furs, and the young girls, like I, in their best dresses. The atmosphere was quiet and dignified, and a low murmur of voices filled the vestibule. After checking our coats, Vati and I continued up the wide staircase, which then branched in two directions. The stairs, like the vestibule, were covered with the same carpet, and statues of cherubs, reminding me of angels, adorned the staircase. I was so excited because never had I been in such rich surroundings and grandeur. I did not know where to look first and just held onto Vati's hand. It was so special, and I was so proud to be here with him. As we came to the top of the stairs, a page in a red outfit with gold trim showed us to our red velvet seats framed in gold. I was almost afraid to sit down. "Sit down, Spatz," Vati told me.

Directly in front and below us was the stage. The deep red velvet curtain with gold tassels was closed. A giant Christmas tree decorated with lights and tinsel stood to one side on the stage. The orchestra in a hole below the stage was quietly tuning their instruments.

The balconies trimmed in red and gold were filling with people. Another even bigger chandelier illuminated the theater, reflecting the red and gold in its crystals. I was unable to speak. All I could do was look and put it into my mind so I would remember it forever.

Vati gave me the program, and then I knew what I was about to see; "*Schneewittchen und die sieben Zwerge,*" Snow White and the Seven Dwarves.

In much too loud a voice, I turned and said, "Vati, its Schneewittchen und die sieben Zwerge!"

"Shush," he said as he put his finger to his lips. The orchestra started to play, the chandelier dimmed, the curtain opened, and I was in a different world. Captivated, I was hardly able to breathe in that world of make believe. I hated Snow White's stepmother who was so mean to her, when Snow White had no one to protect her. When she died, I cried along with the sad dwarves, although I knew the prince would come and kiss Snow White awake and they would live happily ever after. When it was all over, Snow White received a big bouquet of dark red roses. She bowed in front of the audience, and everyone applauded her. I, too, applauded her, and I was glad she was alive again. She was so beautiful in her long dress of shimmering white, with a crown that sparkled on top her long black hair. In his cream and gold color pants and top, the prince was holding her hand. I was dreaming, wishing I was standing there with the prince holding my hand, not wanting the show to end, but it did. On the way home in the trolley, I chattered non-stop, and everyone knew where we had been. I thanked Vati for taking me, for making it the best Christmas, ever, promising never to forget it.

As *Heilig Abend*, Christmas Eve, approached, the dollhouse disappeared, and my heart sank, as I realized it was not for me. On Christmas Eve I went to late afternoon church service. Vati and Mutti stayed home, Mutti to cook the dinner, and Vati to do other things, like helping the Weihnachtsmann, so he said. When I returned from church, I was told not to enter the room where I slept until *das Weihnachtsgloeckchen*, the Christmas bell was rung, because while I was in church the Weihnachtsmann and the *Christkind*, the Christmas Angel, had come to decorate the tree and to lie out the gifts. We ate our meal of *Ruehrkartoffel*, mashed potatoes, *Sauerkraut, and Bratwurst*, a traditional Christmas Eve dinner in *Schlesien*. The dishes were washed, and my face and hands were cleaned. Then I waited anxiously for that little Christmas bell to ring to invite me into the so secret room.

Entering it, I saw the tree aglow with lights, Vati standing to one side smiling, Mutti watching me with a peaceful expression on her face. I stood there not able to take it all in at once. I did not know where to look first. Mutti started to sing *"Stille Nacht, Heilige Nacht"*, Holy Night, and I joined her and so did Vati. While standing and singing, I kept looking at what was underneath the tree, as gifts were not wrapped, but openly laid out. Then my eyes got big and lit up, just like the candles on the tree. My hands flew to my face; I stopped singing and instead laughed and cried out, "A dollhouse, I got a dollhouse. Look Vati! Mutti, look! Meine Puppenstube, I got a dollhouse!" Hugging Vati, never wanting to let go of him, I knew he had helped to make my Christmas wish come true. I went over to Mutti, gave her a hug and a kiss, and thanked her with a warm feeling in my heart.

I had my very own dollhouse, two stories high, with lights, windows, furniture, and tiny dolls. Downstairs were the kitchen and living room, and upstairs two bedrooms. The dollhouse and its furnishing were handmade by Vati. There were switches for turning the lights on and off in each room, and Mutti had made all the bedding, curtains, and the rugs on the floors. It was truly a little girl's dream come true and all because of the love from my father for me. I passed the days with the wind blowing the icy air outside, happily inside playing with my dollhouse in a world of make believe, made just for me.

Little did I know what was ahead of me, how often I would think of that wonderful Weihnachten of 1944 with Vati, the little-girl promise to him never to forget it, not realizing just how much it would stay in my memory, forever.

The New Year of 1945 continued with lots of ice and snow. It was bitter cold, the winds, blowing, mean and furious. The snowflakes were whirling around as if in a big funnel, clinging to everything, including the people hurrying to their homes. They made high snowdrifts that were like big cotton walls, so soft that children could sink into them.

The throngs of covered wagons pulled by horses, cows, and oxen got longer and longer, a steady stream, slow moving along the thoroughfare. People with their children sat in the wagons, clumped together for warmth. Their bodies and heads were heavily wrapped, leaving only a slit for their eyes, to keep the cutting wind at bay. Their scarves had turned white, frozen stiff when their breaths met the icy air. Men and women walked, whip in hand, alongside the wagons to keep the animals moving. The animals had icicles hanging from their mouths; their breaths made puffs of white clouds, their eyelashes heavy with frozen snow. Their hooves were encrusted with ice, some with cloths wrapped around them. Every step showed the agony of man and beast alike, fighting against the deep snow and the blowing, bitter cold winds. Everyday going to and from school I saw them. I knew not to look for fear they would want to come home with me. There were just too many of them. I felt sorry for them because they looked so forlorn. Sad and worried faces were all around me.

Do they not have a home? Why is the throng of wagons getting longer and longer, never ending? Where are they going? But there was no answer from the grown-ups.

The *front* is coming. The word front was familiar to me, but it had no meaning. I heard it everywhere. The grownups, including Vati, had concern in their voices and stopped talking when children were around. I tried not to worry; I knew Vati would take care of us. I wanted to ask him, "Why all that talk of the front? What does it mean?" But I knew the answer he would give me: "Never mind, Spatz, you just go and play. There is nothing for you to know or to worry about." But I did. I could sense *the front* was something that frightened and terrified people; something that made them powerless; something they were unable to stop. It must be incredible, big and scary. My mind painted a picture of a monstrous massive wind or a wall, something big and ugly that was coming, pushing and sweeping on top of us, hurting us all. *Is that what the people with their covered wagons were trying to get away from?* They were *fluechten,* fleeing as the grown-ups called it. And the words fluechten and *Fluechtlinge,* refugees, were new words I heard repeated by many voices many times over.

Soon there were other sounds in the air, sounds unfamiliar to me. When I first heard them, I thought they were thunder, but in the winter? The thundering left a rolling vibration in the air, like waves. The earth was trembling. It was night, and I heard Vati and Mutti get up. They were really quiet so as not to wake me, but I was already alert to that strange sound. My heart was pounding. I knew what was coming! The front! That wall! That ugly thing! I jumped out of bed, "Vati, Vati, take me with you! I'm scared! Don't leave me here." But he didn't hear me. Mutti and he were already outside.

I went to the iced up window, blew my breath on it to make a hole to see through. They were talking to the neighbors who had also gone outside. They were pointing, and then I saw it, too. The clear cold winter night sky was glistening with starlight, a starlit dome, serene and majestic, the snow reflecting the moon, but in the distance there was a fire red glow, in a huge half circle extending high into the sky. Explosions flashed in red and yellow that lit the sky continuously, followed by rolling, thundering rumbles.

Unable to open the window, I started to cry and called even louder. I did not want to be left alone. I wanted Vati. I needed my hand in his to feel safe. I put on my slippers, and ran outside calling at the top of my voice. "Vati, Vati!" He came running, scooped me up, and said, "Spatz, what are you doing out in the cold night? You belong in bed." Holding me, he limped into the house and put me back to bed, telling me, "Go back to sleep and don't worry. I'm not going anywhere without you, ever!"

"*Ja*, but, Vati, the front is coming, and I can't go to bed!"

"No, the front is not coming, and, yes, you can go to bed. I'm just outside and soon I'll go to bed, too," he assured me.

He put me back to bed, but I could not sleep until I heard he and Mutti come in, listened to their voices as they were talking in bed. My last thoughts were, maybe it was not the front, and maybe it was not coming, but I still could hear the rumbling sounds as I drifted of to sleep.

The next morning, Vati and Mutti were talking, and I heard them say that *Breslau*, a city to the east and nearby, had been attacked by the advancing *Russian front*, and what we had seen in the night was, the German artillery making their stand, but with no success. The explosions and rumblings continued throughout the day and into the night. "We'd better get out of here before we get overrun by the Russians," Vati said to Mutti on one of those mornings. He also told me I was not going to school, and after breakfast they started to pack our suitcases.

"Where are we going, Vati?" I asked.

"Well, we have to leave for a little while."

"Will we be gone for a long time?"

"It could be for some time," he patiently replied.

"Will we be coming back, Vati?"

"I hope we will, but let's not worry about that right now. Most of all, don't you worry, Spatz; let me take care of that. You are just a little girl and should not worry about such things. Now, be good and let us tend to the packing."

I just nodded my head. I was already thinking of what I should pack. Going to my room, I got my doll buggy and took out the pillows and mattress and placed some of my favorite books and toys in the bottom of it. Then I replaced the mattress and pillows, adding Roswitha and Fritz, my teddy bear, to the porcelain baby doll already in the buggy. I covered them all up and told them to be real quiet. "We're going on a trip and may not come back." When I was done, I came out of the room with my buggy laden to the top.

Mutti had the most surprised look on her face that I had ever seen. "What do you think you're doing?" was her sharp question to me.

"I packed my toys and my dolls; I have to take them with me; I can't leave them here alone."

"You can just take that stuff back where you got it; it will not leave the house. Do you hear me?"

"Please, I want to take my toys. I can't leave them!" Tears started to come as I pictured my toys and dolls left alone in a cold, empty house. "Vati said he was not sure when we would come back. I can't leave without them! I'll push the buggy; I promise, please, Mutti?"

"Did you hear me? "No!"

"Yes, Mutti." But all was not lost yet. I still had Vati; he would not tell me I had to leave my toys. I put the buggy back and went to find him, but his answer was the same. "Spatz, you can't take your toys; we'll be going far from here. Take a look outside at the frost and snow. It is impossible for you to push your buggy for a long way."

What was I to do? I couldn't leave all my things. Tears were rolling down my cheek, as I looked pleadingly at Vati.

"What do you like the most of your toys?"

"My doll Roswitha and Fritz, my teddy," I said with no hesitation.

"You can take them with you, but no more!" That was a firm reply and I knew not to pursue it further.

When I gave Mutti the doll and my teddy to pack in the suitcase, she said, "Did I not tell you, no toys?"

"Yes, but Vati said I could take my most favorite and here they are."

"So you went to your father behind my back, did you?" She was ready to pounce on me, but just then Vati came in and told her it would be all right; they would not take that much room in the suitcase. Silently and with a disgusted look in my direction, she packed them. We went to bed early because we had to get up early the next morning, Vati explained. During our last night at home, I heard that thunder and the vibration; it sounded as if it was louder and closer than the night before, but Vati didn't go outside this time.

The next morning, it wasn't even light yet when, after our breakfast, Vati went outside to the rabbit hutch, and I went with him. He took the baby rabbits, all black and cute, their little ears sticking up, their noses twitching, and turned them loose in the basement. He gave them water and placed hay and feed on the floor. Then he went back and got the rest, except Meister Lampe; Vati set him free to run, leaving hay and feed in the hutch for him.

"Why are you doing this, Vati?" I asked, puzzled.

"We will not be here to feed the little ones and their mother. They will be just fine down here. It's too cold to leave them outside." I stood looking at the little rabbits; they were so cute hopping about, and they did not seem bothered by their move at all. Vati took me by the hand, "We have to go, Spatz."

Back outside, he took our suitcases and my leather school bag and loaded them all on the sled, tying them down with a rope. He left a space for me to sit, "For when you get tired of walking," he said. Mutti did not like that, but Vati paid no attention to her. Teary eyed, I said goodbye to my buggy and the porcelain doll, promising I would be back soon. Daybreak had come; it was icy cold and windy but not snowy. I was bundled up to keep warm, leaving a slit for my eyes, but making it hard for me to walk. Mutti locked our apartment door, with Vati asking her, "Why do you lock the door?" The Russians will only break it down when they get here." But Mutti locked it anyway and put the key in her purse. We were on the way. Where to I had no idea; all I had to do was walk, walk, and walk.

Soon we, too, became part of the throng I had seen for some time. I remembered Vati's words when those people had followed me home, "Someday we will be in the same situation." He was right, but how did he know that? There were people, just like us, who had their suitcases on sleds with their children walking beside them. It seemed as if the whole world was turned upside down and in chaos. Nothing seemed normal anymore.

It started to snow, slowly at first, but soon, harder and harder. The hard, icy wind cut through my clothes and body, freezing me. The air was full of snowflakes whirling wildly around us, as the sharp wind whipped them here and there. It was impossible to see far ahead; we saw only thick flakes in front of us, settling on our clothes. My scarf got hard from my breath, the frost, and snow. My eyes started to water from the sharp wind. It hurt to breathe, and walking seemed almost impossible. My hands and feet felt frozen, as if they were not attached to me, and I wanted to cry. But Vati, pulling the sled, with Mutti pushing, the rope slung around his body like a horse, his cane supporting him as he fought the wind and snow, tapped me on the shoulder and gave me an encouraging look, saying, "You must be brave!" And so I walked on.

We got away from the throng of wagons to a wide street where soldiers were driving trucks. The trucks had swastikas painted on them, like big black crosses with feet, the German emblem, that was in the center of the German flag. Those trucks were pulling huge long pipe like looking guns, heading in the same direction as we were. Vati flagged them down, and they gave us a ride for a distance and gave me something to drink. It was only a swallow but it burned all the way down into my stomach. It made me cough, but Vati said, "It will warm you up some." But before long, we were walking again.

Soon we met up with the throng of wagons again that seemed to coming from all directions, and I saw some strange sights. Dead cows and horses were lying stiff on both sides of the road. People were sitting in their wagons with nothing to pull them. Some wagons had broken wheels; others had slid in the ditch and fallen over. Women and old people were sitting, crying, and rocking something in their arms. There were bodies lying in the snow, still and unmoving, covered with blankets. Children like me looked scared, unable to comprehend what was happening. I turned to Vati, but before I was able to ask him, he just said, "Keep walking; don't stop, and try not to look. There is nothing anyone can do; just keep walking and don't look." I guess he saw and knew what I wanted to ask him, and I had the feeling he did not have an answer for me.

I don't know how many days or how long we walked or where we slept, but at one point Vati found the house of an elderly couple who let us come in and made something to eat for us. The lady moved a chair close to her stove and put my feet in the warm part of the oven to defrost them and to dry out my shoes. They were nice people, and the old gray haired lady kept stroking my head with sorrow in her eyes, shaking her head, repeating, "All those poor children and their families."

After some time we ended up in Kohlfurt at Mutti's parents, Oma and Opa. I do not recall any particulars about our time there. Vati was there, so the treatment from Oma and Mutti was good. I continued reading and doing math from my schoolbooks under Vati's supervision, glad that I didn't have to go to that awful school and teacher. Mutti wanted me to go to school there, but Vati told her, "We won't be here that long. We have to move on to get away from the Russians." *The Russians, what's that?* But I didn't ask. I knew what Vati would say to me, "It's nothing for you to worry about."

I shared the bed with Oma and Opa, but Vati and Mutti slept in that dreaded room upstairs in the attic where Mutti had locked me in many times. I don't know just how long we stayed in Kohlfurt, but the snow was starting to melt. The talk about the war continued. The front and fleeing were still on everyone's mind. The radio was on, and I heard Hitler's speeches and people cheering, shouting, "Heil Hitler!" But I didn't understand his talk of siege and victory. There was talk that Hitler had something, something that was a secret; something that will win the war, therefore, all was not lost. But others were saying that he had nothing, that the end was near and that people will have to pay for that war many times over. All that talk was whispered as if people were afraid to speak out loud. I would hear Oma and Opa talk of people they knew who had been arrested by the Gestapo because they were Jewish or someone had made remarks that were offensive against Hitler.

I could not; no matter how hard I tried to understand what was happening. Then one day, Mutti sent me to the store, and as I was on my way, the sirens began to howl with their low to high whine. Surrounded by that awful wailing sound, I stopped walking, and holding my hands over my ears I looked up to the sky. Airplanes were flying in a low, steady hum with a leader out in front, like geese. I didn't think anything about it since we had lived near the airbase of the German Luftwaffe in Liegnitz. I had seen airplanes flying many times before, but before I knew it, the leader broke loose, followed by the other planes and they dove to the earth. My mouth open, I stood as if I was nailed to the ground. *What is happening?* While the sirens still howled; the airplanes fell from the sky with a whistling sound that got louder and louder, ending in earth-shattering explosions, shaking me, sending vibrations through my body. I grabbed for the wooden fence near me, fearing I was going to be blown away. I just stood there, hanging on to the fence, unable to move as the explosions continued.

As if from a far distance I heard someone call my name, "Gisela, Gisela, where are you?" It was Vati; he was running and limping, without his cane, coming for me. He pried my hands off the fence and pulled me away; then we ran for the house wall, pressing our bodies against it, with Vati laying his arm across me. My mind was churning. All I wanted was to feel Vati, to be next to him and to feel safe. The planes were gone as fast as they had appeared, leaving behind a smell of fire, gases and smoke. The air was mixed with something I had never smelled before that stung my eyes and nose and made breathing hard. Vati pulled out his hanky, put it over my mouth and nose, and told me to breathe easy and slow. "They're gone for now; they dumped their load, but that will not be the last one. They will come back. What were you doing out here?"

"Mutti sent me to the store; then, the sirens started, and the airplanes came. Vati, what was that and what does it mean?"

"You are too small to think about that; you let me take care of that. Are you all right?"

"Yes, Vati, I'm better." We went in the house while the sirens were blowing in a long and steady pitch, letting everyone know the danger was over and the planes were gone. When we came back in, Vati got in an argument with Mutti about sending me to the store. Oma or she should have gone, not me, knowing there could be air raids anytime. Vati had happened to be in the shed when the air raid had started and had run in the house to get the family in the basement, but he hadn't been able to find me, so he had gone outside looking for me.

After the air raid, I overheard Opa and Vati saying that the airplanes had come to bomb the railroad cars loaded with fuel for the German troops fighting the Russian Army, but had missed them. Opa said, "Ja, that's because they didn't know that the tankers were already on there way east. It's a good thing the fuel transport was gone. If it had been at the station, we would've been blown up too. Instead they bombed the railroad cars loaded with supplies for the troops, and the train tracks, stopping all east going train transports through Kohlfurt."

Vati nodded in agreement. "Ja, and with the train station just across the street from us, we're lucky that none of the apartments houses got hit by their bombs too."

As I listened, I wondered if my favorite bridge was still standing, where I had stood engulfed in that white cloud of smoke from the engine as it rolled beneath me. Vati did not allow me to leave his side, and I didn't want to ask if he would take me so I could see if the bridge was still standing. I knew what his answer would be, "You don't need to see that."

Vati announced to everyone we were leaving, heading toward Zittau, a city south of Kohlfurt. Suitcases were packed once more, and I handed Mutti my doll and teddy to be packed, too. "Do we have to drag those things with us? I think we need that space for more important items."

"Yes, they will be packed; they are the only things Gisela has left from home. It will give her some comfort away from all her surroundings," was Vati's answer, but I could see she did not like it at all. We went to bed, only to be awakened by that howling siren in the middle of the night. Vati hurried us, me in pajamas with a blanket wrapped around me into the basement. We heard the planes overhead with their low heavy hum; and the other tenants, some in their nightclothes, said, "They're loaded and ready to drop it on us." But they flew past, their heavy hums slowly fading in the distance. Everyone sighed, saying, "I wonder were they are headed. They were loaded with bombs; you could hear it by the sound of the planes engines." The siren called that all was clear, and we went back to bed. I wanted to ask Vati, "Why are the planes loaded with bombs? Why do they want to drop them on us or someplace else? The planes I saw in Liegnitz didn't do that. Why here? Is that what the people mean by the front? I was full of questions, but I always got the same answer, "You're too small to understand; don't worry!" But slowly I learned.

The next morning Vati took the handcart that belonged to Oma and Opa and loaded our suitcases on it. I said goodbye to them both, but I didn't cry; Mutti did when she said goodbye to her parents who wished us good luck, waving, hoping for a safe reunion. I asked Vati, "Are Oma and Opa not coming with us?"

"No, they wanted to stay."

"Then why are we leaving?"

"I want to keep you safe and out of harm's way. Walking is hard on old people, so some prefer to stay home, taking their chances, hoping that they will not be harmed when the Russian Army and their soldiers get here." I wanted to ask, "What are Russian soldiers and why are they coming and what are they going to do?" But I knew what Vati's answer would be, "Never mind, Spatz, it is nothing for you to know about." And so we were on the road again, this time not with a sled but a hand-pulled wagon loaded with our meager possessions.

We were fleeing like so many others. The streets and thoroughfares were filled with people, their children, wagons, and handcarts. The snow had melted, the air was warm, and spring was on the way. It was easier for the refugees who came from the east, like us, to flee from the advancing

Russian front. I do not recall any particulars from that portion of the trek, but eventually we arrived in Zittau, a city southwest of Kohlfurt. We were lucky Vati was able to find a place for us to stay, one room, furnished, on the top floor of an apartment building. It combined all in one, a living room, bedroom, with a small corner for cooking. I liked it because from four stories up I could view the entire area and all the activities below on the street. It was a busy street with stores and people walking, shopping, and tending to their daily activities. Children, carefree, were playing ball and hopscotch on the sidewalks.

When we arrived in our little room, Mutti started to unpack the suitcases. I waited patiently for Roswitha and Fritz to reappear. The closer Mutti got to the end of her unpacking, the more concerned I got, recalling her words in Kohlfurt at Oma's, "Do we have to drag those things around with us?" My eyes got teary. I wanted to call out, "Where are Roswitha and Fritz?" as she was storing the suitcases beneath the bed. But I just stood there unmoving, watching her.

"So that is done and I hope it will stay done for a little while," she remarked as she straightened up from storing the suitcases. My mouth went dry; my stomach started to flutter as my watery eyes swept the small room. I did not see my doll or Fritz anywhere. "What is the matter with you? Why are you standing there like a statue with a dumb look on your face? What are you looking for?"

"My doll and my teddy? Where are they? Where did you put them?"

"Oh, *them,*" she said with a hateful laugh, "well; they're not here, as you can see. I did not pack them; I left them in Kohlfurt. I decided you do not need them anymore. You will have other important things to do, and it is time for you to grow up!"

"But Vati said I could have them and you were to pack them!" That was the wrong approach. She walked over and slapped me in the face so that my ears popped and my head felt as if it was about to come off.

"Don't you ever talk to me like that again! I'm your mother, and I know what is best for you, not your father! And you'd better remember that!" My stomach was heaving, and I felt sick as a voice inside me said, "Oh, how I dislike you! You're not my mother! I don't want you for my mother, and you never will be my mother! I have a mother, and it is not you, and someday I will be with her—Oma in Goerlitz told me so!" More and more I clung to believing that I had another mother, a real mother and always the picture of the nurse came into my memory. But I never asked Vati, because I was afraid he'd tell me that that isn't so. I never uttered a sound or shed a tear when she slapped me. Still my heart ached for my doll Roswitha and Fritz, my teddy, my friends. When Vati came home, he saw I was unhappy and sad, and he asked me, "What's the matter?"

But before I could answer, Mutti chimed in, "I left her doll and Fritz in Kohlfurt; I have decided she does not need them anymore! And now she is pouting." He looked at me, tired, his blue eyes drained and sad.

"Maybe Mutti is right; we need other things more; and you will be fine without them." I was astonished to hear Vati say that. *What was the matter with him? How could he say that?* He's never talked like that before. *Does he not love me anymore?* Watching him sitting there looking tired and exhausted, I went and sat next to him. Taking my hand, he said, "Don't worry; things will be all right again. And maybe when we return to Kohlfurt, your doll and Fritz will still be there." But my feelings told me I would never see them again.

Mutti was anxious to put me back in school, but Vati, much to her disapproval would not allow it because of air raids and unexpected bombings. So, I never went to school as many parents kept their children close by. Vati also said that most of the schools were closed and used to house the refugees.

In the later part of April, Mutti decided it was time I join the Nazi Club of the German Youth. The girls were called *BDM, Bund Deutscher Maedchen,* and the *Hitler Jugend* for boys was called *HJ.* The girls wore regulation black skirts, white blouses, and light brown scarves held together with brown leather knots. Black shoes and white knee socks for the younger ones and silk stockings for the older group finished the uniformed look. The boys wore khaki uniforms with swastika armbands and were trained and treated like soldiers. The *Nazi* organization was strict, and every young person had to join; it was a requirement of the Hitler Regime. Although my tenth birthday was not until July, Mutti was anxious to sign me up. They had an argument over that. Vati asked, "What for? The war will be over soon and there is not going to be a Hitler or his regime anymore. We will be lucky to survive what is yet to come and not get killed in the process."

Mutti told him, "This kind of talk coming from you is uncalled for, and you'd better be careful with your opinion. Hitler is not done yet; he will save us from disaster; you'll see".

But Vati just said, "*Ja,* we will see!" I don't know what Mutti was doing, but it sounded threatening to me. I could tell because Vati did not say anything else, but kept quiet. Why was she doing that?

Losing no time, I had to wash and put on clean clothes. Taking my hand, Mutti took me to sign up. On the way there she told me, "They will teach you a thing or two. Vati's little girl will be straightened up in a hurry. And wait until they hear you're a thief! They have their ways of taking care of thieves, teaching you not to steal. And your father won't be able to help his little girl! You will be at their mercy," she added, satisfaction in her voice. *So she never forgot it! Will she always tell people about my mistake? Although Vati said it would not be mentioned again. Will the dark cloud I thought had left always hang over me?*

I was scared of what they would do to me once I was signed up. When we got there, we had to greet the uniformed group leaders, much older than I, sitting at desks with a *"Heil Hitler"* by raising our right arm and standing at attention. Then, we were asked to step closer and to state our name.

Mutti pushed me in front of her and said, "Tell them your name."

A uniformed BDM matron took my name and date of birth and other information. I was given a date in July for my first meeting or assembly. I was ready to leave, glad that Mutti was not going to mention my foolishness. "Isn't there something else you need to tell so it can be noted on your records?" Mutti asked me. Embarrassed, I stood there; I felt a hot flush creeping all over my face. I didn't think Mutti would really make me tell. My eyes were downcast and I could feel the Matron looking at me, questioning, waiting to hear what else there was that needed recording. "Now, go on and tell her," Mutti said, shoving me on the shoulder. "Tell her!" she insisted.

"I'm a thief," I said in a low fearful inaudible voice.

The matron, not understanding, was looking at Mutti for help, who promptly blurted out loud enough so everyone could hear, "She is a thief! She steals!"

I stood there, dumbfounded and embarrassed, feeling very small. The matron asked me, "Is that true?"

"Yes," I answered as I felt my face turning red.

The matron, looking at Mutti, but never replying, raised her arm and said, *"Heil Hitler."* We were excused.

Although cut short by the matron, Mutti had accomplished her goal, so we returned the salute and left. On the way home, she kept saying how glad she was I finally would learn something; and when I got called into service as a maid, they would watch my long stealing fingers. She continued, "And I'm telling you, wherever you go, people will know you're a thief, now and forever, because it is in your file! You also will not tell your father that they have been told of your shameful habit. Is that understood? If you do, you will live to regret it. I promise you that!"

I nodded in agreement, knowing I could not do anything about it, and I didn't tell. I knew she would never let me forget it. She'd always make sure to tell people about my slip-up. I wanted to get away from her, but I had to hold her hand and walk next to her like an obedient little girl. My dislike for her grew and I detested her. *Why was she so mean to Vati and me at every opportunity? What was the reason for that?* I had the feeling Vati was losing his grip and she was running our lives. Many times I heard her say to him, "Don't get any idea that you can run to your whore in Goerlitz when the war is over. I'll make you regret it. Mark my words!" He did not answer her. He looked sad and defeated. It scared me when I saw him like that. But Mutti walked around with a smug, satisfied look on her face. I wanted to scream at her, "Leave him alone. I hate you!" But I didn't, and couldn't.

Since all the schools were closed, used for refugees to sleep in, my job, among others, was the shopping. Climbing to the fourth floor was a chore for Mutti because of her size, so I did the shopping for her. On a bright sunny day, I was on my way to the butcher shop with list and money in my hand. People were going here and there; the street was buzzing with activity. Unexpectedly, the sirens started to howl loudly. I stopped walking and put my hands over my ears. Chaos broke out on the street. People ran and scattered in all directions, screaming, *Tief-Flieger!* Tief-Flieger! The were Dive-bombers with the airplanes already above us flying close to the rooftops, shooting at people on the street. Someone grabbed me by my arm, saying, "What are you doing out there? Get in here!" I was pulled inside an apartment building into the basement. People with children from the apartment house came running down the stairway to the basement. Some were already sitting on benches along the wall and in the center with suitcases beside them. Mothers were holding their children close to their bodies, some with babies in their arms. The woman who got me off the street sat next to me and saw the money in my hand.

"Where were you going?" she asked.

"To the butcher shop," I replied. Then I started to cry because I was scared and wanted to leave. We heard the planes flying overhead; then the whistling of something that was falling fast, exploding as it hit the ground, shaking everything around us. The apartment building made the most eerie, crunching, grinding noise, that hung in the air of the dust-filled basement. The bricks and mortar were crumbling; some people had dampened cloths they put over their mouths and nose. Others used their scarves or whatever they had to cover their children faces, keeping them from breathing in the dust. The building kept shaking with the explosions near us. Children screamed. I ducked, covering my head with my hands and arms for protection. The lights flickered then went out. Someone lit a candle, only to be told to put it out; it was too dangerous because there could be leaking or broken gas lines in the building.

I cried for Vati, wanting to get out of there. I knew he was looking for me. But the woman was held me back, not allowing me to leave, saying, "You cannot leave. You will be hurt, maybe killed, if you go out there now!"

Suddenly there was silence, the sound of the airplanes disappeared, the bombing and explosions had stopped; sirens blew, declaring that the air raid was over. As fast and quick the planes had come, they disappeared. Everyone in the cellar was relieved, glad to be alive, glad that the building was still standing. The tenants went back to their apartments and others back out on the street. The woman took my hand, and we went outside. To our surprise the apartment buildings in our close neighborhood were still standing. We had been spared, except for ruined facades and balconies, broken windows, toppled chimneys. Bricks and glass were strewn all over sidewalk and street; even flower boxes from balconies and windows were scattered all over. Roof tiles, loosened from the explosions broken into bits were everywhere. The woman, bending down and facing me, said, "We've been lucky, the falling bombs didn't hit us—this time. I want you to go straight home. Your mother must be worried." Grabbing my arm she leaned closer, "Do you hear me? And walk more in the middle of the street because there might be more roof tiles sliding off."

"But I have to go to the butcher's first before I go home. Mutti gave me a list and I have to do it," I told her.

"You go home now, and go quick! Let your mother do the shopping!" was her firm reply, "I'm sure the butcher is not going to be open after what just happened. Go home!"

I went home, and once again Vati was beside himself with worry that I was out there again in an air raid—unable to find me. He forbade Mutti to send me out shopping ever again, telling her in a firm voice, "From now on, you will do the shopping!" Mutti turned away, but her backward glance told me she was not done with me, that her time would come, but I tried not to let it bother me. The air raid had taken place at mid-morning and talk was that many people who were shopping at the *Marktplatz* were killed, gunned down by the dive-bombers. And more, including children, were killed in buildings that had been hit by bombs.

Something else happened about that time that made me breathe with relief. The talk was that Hitler was dead and the war would soon be over. But some said he was not dead; that his death was a rumor. But the flags were flying at half-mast with a black veil attached to the tip of the poles. I didn't understand all that, but I knew something was happening and there would be changes.

I asked Vati about it. "I don't exactly know, but I think he is dead meaning that the war will soon be over, and if it's true, then there will be no more BDM for you."

"*Ja*, but how is that?" was my next question.

"Let's not get too far ahead of ourselves, Spatz; everything is so unsure, and I can't explain it all to you. You wouldn't understand. Right now it is only a rumor even though the flags are flying half-mast."

I was hoping I didn't have to go, and I think it was showing in my face. Mutti piped up and said, "Don't be too thrilled about it; it may not be true that Hitler is dead and you will have to go to the meeting. Want to or not!"

Neither one of us, Vati nor I, answered her. I knew she was trying to put fear into me.

The same day but in the afternoon, while I was standing at the window, looking out and enjoying the sunshine, the sirens started up again. We hurried with all the other tenants into the basement. The planes with their low drone were overhead. We listened and waited for the bombs to fall, but slowly their humming drone faded into the distance. It was a false alert, a fly-over to a different destination, so I heard Vati say. Shortly, the sirens called an all clear and the end of that air raid.

Coming out of the cellar, Vati said, "The air alerts are coming too often and the bombing is getting much more severe. We are packing. They will be back, and we will not be waiting for them. We are getting out of here, now!"

I always heard about *they*, so I asked Vati, "Who is *they*?" Looking at me, wondering if he would tell me, I said, "Please, Vati, tell me who is *they*?"

"Well, *they*, are our *Feind*, our enemy. They're the ones that bomb us and they're the reason why we keep fleeing, getting further and further away from our home. No more questions. You're too young to understand all that." We packed in a hurry, and Vati found a handcart, since ours had disappeared, and we were on our way again. We were not alone; there was an exodus of people and children fleeing from the city of Zittau, pulling handcarts, pushing buggies or carrying their belongings.

Trying to keep up the walking pace, my mind wandered. I became aware of our surroundings with a strange feeling of mystery. Here we were, away from our homes and our familiar surroundings with only suitcases holding our possessions. But when I looked and listened, the sky was blue, the sun was shining, flowers were starting to bloom, the trees were showing their fresh green leaves, and the birds were singing and swooping in the soft afternoon air. Everything was continuing, nothing had changed, except our lives. *I wish we could go home. I missed my bed, and my toys. I want to go back to Kohlfurt and get Fritz and Roswitha. What about the little bunnies in the basement? How are they doing?* I had all those questions and no answers. I must have slowed down, for Vati called, bringing me back to reality, "Gisela, come on, keep up the pace!" And so I kept up the pace, still wondering and wishing for what I couldn't have.

We had walked into the night when we heard the sirens in the city we had left behind, a warning of an air raid. The droning planes were high above us, flying toward Zittau. Several earth shattering booms illuminated the surrounding area with a green hue. I looked up at the sky where four big bright, shiny green fiery balls were hanging in the air. It was as if daylight had come.

Vati, grabbing me, threw a blanket around me and slipped me into the ditch beside the street and said, "Don't look up there; *they* can see your face. Lie down on the ground; keep your face covered, and stay there." Then he called out to the people, "Everybody in the ditch and cover up!" Vati's voice was so forceful and demanding, they followed his orders. Then, he lay next to me, putting his arms around me, protecting me.

Vati was right; *they* had come back in the night, with their planes bombing and destroying Zittau. I was so glad we were gone from the city and proud of Vati because he knew how to safeguard us. The lights in the sky went dim, and we started to walk again. We hadn't gone far when, with the same power and ear-deafening boom, a second set of lights appeared in the sky. Everyone went for the ditch and covered their faces once more, quietly listening to the bombing of Zittau. Lying there, I could feel the tremors as the bombs hit the ground, exploding. When the planes had disappeared and the bombing stopped, we got up from the ditch and stood, watching, too stunned to move. Where the sky had been green, it was now mixed with red and yellow. Everyone exclaimed, "Oh my God, the city is on fire!" and "Those poor, poor people!" Although the planes were gone, the explosions continued and the air, warm from the heat of the fire, was filled with the odors of burning gases. I heard people talk. "Why the bombing of Zittau? Nothing is there! Why are *they* still bombing? Is Hitler not dead?" No one knew for sure. Others were saying that Hitler had left the country and it was for us, the people, to take the brunt of rage against his regime of ruin and disaster. Yet others asked, "When is the bombing going to stop? Is the war not over?" It seemed that no one had the answer. Vati, taking our wagon, said, "Let's get away from here. The air is full of gases and smoke and there is nothing we can do to help."

Just how long we walked, I have no recollection, but eventually we ended up in a small farm town. Vati said we would be safer in a small town than in the city with the bombing. He found a place with an elderly couple who had a two-story house and a room for us to sleep in. There was already another refugee family living there, whose home was further east of Liegnitz. Their family name was Hoffman. Mutti, *Frau* Hoffman, and the elderly couple who owned the house shared the kitchen. I liked the house, the huge garden for playing, and the old people who lived there.

On May 8, 1945, the war was declared over and lost. People were relieved, but there was no jubilation, only apprehension and gloom. "Yes, it is over, but our problems have just begun!" were their words.

Little did I know what lay ahead of us.

The war had ended. People walked about with forlorn looks, unsure what to do next, afraid of what the future would bring. Vati and *Herr Hoffman* were talking about going back home. Excited I asked Vati, "Will we stop in Kohlfurt?"

"I'm sure we will. We have to see if Oma and Opa are still there."

"Oh, I hope we will, then I'll have my doll and teddy back."

But Vati warned, "Don't get too excited. We're not there yet. We have a long way ahead of us."

The old people we stayed with were nice to me, and I liked to visit with them, much to Mutti's disapproval. She'd often asked me, "What are you telling these people? Don't you tell them our family affairs; it is none of their business."

Why does she always think I am talking about us? "I'm not telling them anything, Mutti; we are just talking about nothing important at all."

"Well, I'd better not find out you are talking too much of things that are nobody's business."

I kept visiting with the couple. I especially liked visiting with the old man. Most of the time I would find him at the back of the house splitting wood. "For the winter," he said, "when it gets cold again." For me, winter was a long way off since we had just been through it. He stacked the wood in a circle, which looked like a roundhouse and topped it in a slant so it looked like a pointed hat. I wanted to help, but he said, "No, you might get hurt." So I just kept him company and chatted about whatever came to my mind. I guess he didn't mind because he never sent me away or got annoyed with me.

One morning, Vati and I were standing at the garden gate in front of the house when, a man walking along the street came straight toward us. He looked scary. He was grubby and unkempt with a long ruddy beard. He had small slanted slits for eyes. He was so dirty that his striped raggedy pants and shirt were almost black from dirt. Holding a revolver in his hand, he radiated hate and anger. Vati shoved me behind him and said, "Go in back of the house and hide behind the wood stack. Don't come out until I call you. Now!"

I ran behind the house, but only far enough so that I still could see what the man wanted and why Vati had told me to hide. Pointing the revolver at Vati, the man said something. Then, Vati opened the garden gate and they went into the house. After some time, I sneaked out from my hiding place to see what was happening. When I got close to the house entrance, I peeked inside and saw Mutti and everyone else standing in the entrance hall. No one was talking or moving. They all looked worried and frightened. *Were they listening for sounds from upstairs where the stranger and Vati must have gone?* But there was no sound. I wanted to run upstairs to see what the man with his revolver wanted with Vati, but something told me not to, so I waited, unnoticed, fearing for Vati.

After what seemed forever to me, I heard a door open. Then, I saw the man coming down the stairs, alone. I ran back around the corner of the house to watch him leave. I could not believe what I saw! That man, that dirty, hateful looking man, had Vati's clothes on. *What is he doing with his clothes?* I ran back into the house, just as Vati, stiff legged, arms away from his body, came down the stairs with that man's clothes on, those dirty grimy, stinky old clothes.

I ran to hug Vati because I was glad to see that he was not hurt, but he held out his hand to stop me and said, "Don't touch me!" "Stay away!" I stopped. Then, Vati and the old man I liked went behind the house, the old man carrying clean clothes for Vati under his arm. Vati washed, redressed, then they burned the clothes full of fleas and lice. Only then did Vati explain that the man with the revolver was from Mongolia and had been a prisoner of war. He wanted only the clothes Vati wore and he wanted to trade. That was why Vati had ended up wearing the man's prison clothes. Also, Vati knew not to make that fellow mad because he had a gun. Vati just said to all to us, "All is done, I am washed off, and we are still alive." I had known he would make it all right again.

Vati and Herr Hoffman still talked about the trip back home, to Liegnitz for us and somewhere in the same vicinity for the Hoffman family. But how to do it? We were all a long way from home and the Hoffmans had a lot of stuff to take back home. Where they got it or how they got here I don't know. We had only our suitcases. They also had two children, a girl and a boy, about my age, but I do not recall their names.

Early the next morning Vati left on foot, telling me, "I'm going to find someone with a horse and wagon going in our direction and perhaps we could travel home together, making it look like a family. So you be good, and I'll be back soon." He hugged me, then, he was gone. I stood and waved as he limped down the street and out of sight. I felt sad, but the old man consoled me, saying not to worry, that my father would be back and soon. So I occupied myself with other things while I waited for his return. I believed Vati when he told me he'd be back because he had promised he would never leave me. But he was gone for what seemed a long time, the longest wait for me, ever.

Finally, after being gone overnight he got back with good news. I was overjoyed to have him back, and I think he was also glad. Apparently, he had had to hide out several times, so it had taken him a long time to get back. Why he had to hide or from whom, I never knew. Vati had been lucky to find two former soldiers who were hiding out in the woods. They too were from the eastern part of Germany and they had horses and wagons and wanted to go home. Vati said that the soldiers had to hide out because they couldn't travel with horses and empty wagons because the Russians or released prisoners would take the horses and wagons away from them. Because we had lost the war, we could do nothing about it and were lucky not to be killed in the process. We were hated and had to take what was handed out to us. I did not understand, but I saw that people lived in fear. I had to stay close to Vati ever since that man had appeared and was not allowed out by myself, except in the back of the house where the old man was always working on something or smoking his pipe and sitting on the wood chopping stump.

The soldiers in civilian clothing arrived in the early morning hours with their wagons. One wagon had a big, husky brown horse, and the other had two black cute ponies. Vati and the men loaded the wagons. We had only our suitcases, but the Hoffman family's belongings filled both wagons. Our belongings, plus some of the Hoffman's, were stowed in the wagon with the two horses. Vati made a place in the back for Mutti and me to sit when we got tired of walking. The former soldier and he sat up front. The Hoffman family and the rest of their belongings were stowed in the wagon pulled by the big horse, where Herr Hoffman sat with the driver.

Again we were saying goodbye, thanking the old couple for their hospitality. Once more we were on the move, but this time our destination was home, or so I thought.

At the beginning, Vati, Mutti, and I were walked behind the wagons. Looking all around me, I saw men sitting in ditches alongside the road, looking like the man who took Vati's clothes. Seeing that I was staring at them, Vati leaned over, whispering to me, "Don't stare at those men; they don't like that and could get real mad at us." He didn't have to warn me twice.

Lots of people were moving about, people like us who had fled from the east and the Russian front wanting to return home again. The throngs of wagons that had gone in one direction were now going back in the other—homeward. Although sullen, people had a glimmer of hope on their faces. The war was over, and they wanted to get home to start rebuilding what had been lost or destroyed.

The weather was sunny and warm, so traveling was pleasant. Vati sat in front with the driver of our wagon, and Mutti and I walked behind or sometimes rode in the wagon. The other wagon with the big horse and the Hoffman family one was ahead of us. Mutti got tired of walking, so we decided to ride for a while. Vati stopped the wagon and we climbed up. Mutti didn't want to sit down so we stood hanging onto the rear gate that closed the back of the wagon. Mutti stood on the right side and I on the left. We were going downhill at a pretty fast speed when the wagon jumped and Mutti lost her balance, rolling into the ditch. I hollered, "Vati, Vati, Mutti fell off and rolled in the ditch!"

By the time he heard me and was able to stop the little ponies and wagon, we were quite a ways from where Mutti had fallen off. We ran back and saw Mutti, lying in the ditch, unable to move and her right leg was bleeding. When she'd fallen, her leg had been caught by the fast turning wheel, cutting the whole length of her inner calf severely as if with a knife. Other wagons behind us stopped, and people tried to help Mutti and fixed her up the best they could. It took several people to load her back into the wagon to be taken to the nearest hospital.

Standing there watching, I noticed two men sitting in that same ditch, not far from Mutti, eating and watching. They were not Germans that I was sure of, but they didn't have that mean look in their eyes and faces. They had a loaf of hard dark bread, a can of white fat that looked like bacon grease, and a large bottle filled with clear liquid that they were drinking from—heartily. The bread looked so good that my stomach started to growl. To my surprise, they smiled and offered me a thick slice of bread with an even thicker amount of fat that looked like whipping cream plunked on it. Afraid to accept it I shook my head. Vati came over and talked to the two men. Then he, too, took a hearty drink out of their bottle. The men were still holding the bread out, with Vati telling me, "Go on, you can take it!" I thanked them with the customary curtsy. Then, I bit into the bread so hungrily that some of the grease hung on my nose. They laughed, nodding and saying something that I didn't understood as I wiped it off.

I waved goodbye to them, and we were on the way to the hospital. Mutti's leg was stitched and bandaged from her ankle clear past her knee. Again, with help, she was deposited back on the wagon.

Toward evening, Vati and the men looked for a place to stay overnight. They found a farmer who allowed us to sleep in the barn. The wagons were pulled into the barn to keep our belongings safe, and the horses were turned loose in the pasture. The farmer's wife brought soup for us made with flour and water and we ate hungrily. Then, with blankets, Vati made us a comfortable bed in the hay, so soft, like a cloud. I slept with the bouquet of sweet dry grass wrapped around me.

When I awoke the next morning, there was excitement. The men had gone out to the pasture to get the horses, and found that the two black ponies had been stolen during the night. Vati and the men went looking for the ponies and found them in someone's stall. Since it had taken all day to find the two ponies, we stayed over for another night. Although the soldiers slept near their horses, somehow when they awoke the next morning, one pony was gone again, this time for good. We traveled on with one pony. When a hill was too steep for the little pony to pull the wagon, the big horse was brought back down to help the little one up the hill. It was slow going, but it worked.

When we got to the outskirts of Zittau where the bombing had taken place, all wagons came to a halt. There was a long row of wagons, some without their drivers, others with women sitting on them, looking lost and crying. Our wagons also came to a stop and the men walked forward to see what was happening. Mutti was lying in the wagon unable to walk. Vati came to tell Mutti and me, "I'm going to see what's happening in front and why we're being stopped. You stay with Mutti. I'll be right back."

"I will, Vati, but please hurry." Then he limped off. I looked around, taking in the surroundings. I could tell something was not right. I walked out in the middle of the street to see where Vati was, but I could not see him. Then, I noticed a little ways up to the left was a partially destroyed farm. This farm had a high wire fence attached to two corners of the barn, like a big square. Russian guards with rifles over their shoulders, stationed along the outside of the fence, were guarding the men behind the fence. Women were standing at the edge of the street crying, their children clutching them, as they tried to talk to their fenced-in husbands or family members. Mean looking Russian guards chased the men away from the fence by slamming their rifles against the fence, not allowing the men to talk to anyone. I went back to Mutti and told her what I had seen.

"Where is your father?" she asked.

"I don't know where he is. I can't see him."

"Then you'd better find him, now."

Scared, I ran off to find him. When I looked closer at the imprisoned men, I saw with horror our two soldiers and Herr Hoffman there too. Then, I saw Frau Hoffman sitting in the wagon with her children. She, too, was crying. My heart was racing, my eyes straining, looking for Vati, and expecting to see him, too, behind that fence. Then I saw him, standing in the middle of the street, near the entrance of the farm and the fence. A Russian soldier was standing there confronting him. The soldier wore a mustard green uniform, black heavy shoes, his trouser legs wrapped to his knees in the same color as his uniform, making his trousers look like knickers. His jacket was long and loose over his pants, held together with a black belt. The blouse buttoned on one side up to his shoulder. A cap with the hammer and sickle insignia was sitting squarely on his head. He stood there, solid, his face stern, his legs slightly spread, rifle over his shoulder, motioning Vati toward the fence. Vati, walking cane in his hand, was pointing to his oversized bulky shoe, but that seemed to make no impression on the Russian.

Terror gripped me. *He wants Vati! He can't have him! He can't make him go behind that fence! I will not allow it!* Racing up there, my mind in turmoil, before anyone knew what was happening, I shoved that Russian in the stomach with both hands as hard as I could so he almost lost his balance. Before he could get his composure back, I kicked him in the leg, screaming, "You leave Vati alone! He is not going in there! You can't make him! You go away! I hate you!" All the while, my fists were pounding him.

Vati grabbed me, lifting me, shaking me; his eyes were like steel and his voice ice-cold with fear, "What do you think you're doing? Do you want us to get shot right here? Do you know the danger you put us in with your behavior?" My anger and frustration left me. I hung in the air like a beat puppy.

"But, Vati, I just wanted to help you! I don't want you to go behind that fence," I peeped. My tears rolled because Vati was mad. All I wanted was to help him. The Russian just stared as Vati scolded me. Then, he put me down and said something to the Russian, who, tired of all the commotion, waved us away.

I grabbed Vati's hand, "Let's go, Vati, quick. Let's get away from him!" On the way back to our wagon, he explained to me that although I had saved him from being imprisoned, what I did was a dangerous thing. The Russian could have shot both of us right then, and no one could have helped us. I was glad, Vati was not really mad at me; he was only afraid for our safety. After that I stayed glued to Vati, I would not let him out of my sight for fear I would lose him. That's when I realized that the soldiers called

Russians where in charge, because, not only had we lost the war we had lost our freedom too.

Vati was planning to take all of us to the next town. The wife of Herr Hoffman was to take the reins of the wagon with the big horse. He told her the big horse was a quiet, gentle-tempered animal, easy to handle, but before we started moving, her husband came and took over the reins. I heard him tell Vati because he wore a corset and could not do any hard labor, they let him go. Our wagons moved on. The same guard I had attacked waved us through, but I didn't look at him for fear he might grab me.

We went to the nearest town to stay overnight. Herr Hoffman said, that the Russians wanted the Germans to clear the debris of the streets in Zittau left from the bombings. He also said, for us stay to stay close by because the other two men would try to escape during the night and catch up with us. The next morning they were back, so we were on our way again, with Mutti propped up in the back of the wagon. How long it took us I don't know, but our final stop was *Pfaffendorf*, a small farm community by Goerlitz.

This Pfaffendorf by Goerlitz is not the Pfaffendorf by Lauban where Vati's family was from and where he was born. That Pfaffendorf however is now in the Polish territory.

The soldiers dropped Vati, Mutti, and me off at a deserted, partially destroyed farm in Pfaffendorf, where we spend the night. All the windows were torn almost off their hinges and hanging on the outside of the building. The furniture was now lying in pieces all over the floor. Broken dishes crunched under our feet. Mattresses were sliced and feathers scattered like snowflakes. Bullet holes had pierced the framed pictures of people still hung on the wall; others lay on the floor. Boot prints smudging the pictures. The bathtub reeked from having been used as a toilet. Thinking the people who had lived here had done that, I asked Vati, "Why is everything broken up? Why did they use the bathtub like that? Where are the people that lived here?

"Well, the owners of that farm must have fled and have not returned yet. Because, the lowly Russian fighters and released prisoners hate us, they destroy whatever is in their path. Most likely they had not seen a toilet or a bathtub before, and didn't know what to do with it."

"And the torn beds and the scattered feathers?"

"That is also unknown to some of them. They probably had fun scattering the feathers."

That seemed strange to me, but if Vati said so, it must be so. We found a room far from that smell and by shoving the debris to one side of the room;

Vati and I swept the floor as clean as we could with a couple of old brooms he had found. Then after Vati had spread out our blankets, for us to sleep on, he and I went to get Mutti sitting on the floor leaning against the wall in another room where the soldiers and Vati had put her. Since Mutti was to heavy for us to lift, we pulled her backward by her arms across the hall into the room we had cleaned, with her whimpering in pain. After Mutti was deposit on the blanket Vati told me, "You stay with Mutti and do not, I mean do not, come after me! I will be back! I also don't want anyone to know we're spending the night here." Then he left. When he returned, he had some cheese, bread, and milk. Where he got it, I don't know, and I didn't care; it was food, and I was hungry!

The next morning, Vati left again and returned with the town nurse, another man, and a flat handcart to transfer Mutti to the nurse's house, across the farm we had spent the night.

After Mutti was settled in one of the upstairs bedrooms in the nurse's house, I heard Vati and the grown-ups say that because we had lost the war, Germany had been divided between the four conquerors. The Americans, the English, and the French governed the western region of Germany while Russia governed the eastern.

Then, Russia divided their part of Germany again and gave the region east of the rivers Oder and Neisse to Poland as their territory and using the rivers for a border they immediately closed it, guarding it on both sides, thus preventing refugees from retuning to their homes and farms east of the rivers.

Unable to go to our home in Liegnitz because it was in the Polish occupied territory, Vati said we had to stay under Russian occupation in East Germany. And so with Mutti needing care and no home to go to, we stayed in Pfaffendorf by Goerlitz for the next several weeks in the home of the *Dorf-Krankenschwester*, a town-nurse who took care of minor illnesses and injuries.

Although Mutti had good care, the wound on her leg didn't heal quickly. Not allowed to walk, Mutti had to stay in bed with her leg up, and I had to wait on her. But whenever I could I went outside to look around without Mutti's watchful eye. It was a nice house with a garden and fruit trees. There were no animals anywhere because the Russians had confiscated them all. Vati was busy working, doing repairs for the farmers as word got around that he was a carpenter. I don't know if he got paid, but we had foot to eat.

I also had a playmate. She was a family member of the nurse, and we played in that wonderful garden overgrown with grass underneath the blossoming fruit trees. The sky was blue, the sun was shining, the air was warm, and the birds whistled in the trees above. I felt free like the birds.

Only Mutti kept a close eye on me, always afraid I might tell something about our family, but with Vati's love wrapped around me like a soft blanket, I was content.

On one of those days, when Vati was busy cutting grass behind the house with a scythe in big wide swathes, and had stopped to sharpen the blade with a wet stone, I asked him, "When are we going home?"

Vati stopped sharpening the scythe. Shaking his head, he said, "I don't know. Nobody knows. Maybe never. The Russians and the Polish are not allowing us to go home. No one is allowed near the border." Looking at me, he then asked, "Don't you like it here, Spatz?"

My hands behind my back, my eyes looking nowhere, I said, "I just want to go home, Vati."

"Yes, I know you want to go home and so do I. No one knows what will happen but for now we have a place to stay. You go and play and don't worry about things that are not for you to worry about." Then, patting my head, he returned to cutting the grass. My hands still folded behind me, I slowly walked away, still hearing Vati's words, "Maybe never" then I realized I would never see my doll Roswitha and Fritz, my teddy again. I didn't know they were not the most important possessions I was to lose.

Many times along the road I saw groups of refugees who had fled and now wanted to return to their homes and farms, but they had come to a stop just as we had. They slept in barns or deserted houses. They were telling that East Germany was in turmoil because the conquering Russian troops, did whatever they wanted, like a wild herd turned loose with no orders to restrain their looting, killing and raping. The Russians enforced a compulsory curfew, no Germans were allowed out after nine in the evening. If the patrolling Russian soldier saw Germans after curfew and called out *stoi*, stop, and the Germans didn't stop, the Russian shot them.

Rape, a new word to me, and was spoken about by the grown-ups with terror and panic in their voices and eyes. When the nurse got home from a call, she would tell about women who were dragged outside and raped in the middle of the night by drunken Russian soldiers, sometimes raped by several. Then, if someone came to the women's rescue, they were shot. There were women who'd gone out of their heads with fright and some had died. I heard those shots and frantic screams during the night but I didn't understand it. All I understood and knew that the men, called Russians, were cruel.

One thing puzzled me. Although the Russian soldiers were able to put fear into people, they were not very smart. They didn't know what to do with a bicycle. It was comical to watch a uniformed Russian soldier, rifle over his shoulder, trying to ride a bicycle, wobbling and falling. Then, when he saw a child or others riding a bike, he'd throw his bike on the ground and demand that person's bike, thinking that that bike was a better. Vati warned me, "Whenever you see a soldier, don't watch or laugh at him, no matter how funny it looks to you. He'll get mad, and no one knows what he'll do if provoked."

I saw more houses where the owners had fled, where the Russian soldiers had destroyed and demolished everything, just as I had seen in the farmhouse where we had slept for one night. Unfamiliar with water faucets and how they worked, the Russian soldiers ripped them from the wall and attached them to another wall, expecting water, while the broken water line was flooding the house. Every house where the owner was absent was destroyed.

The Russian soldiers wore many watches, all the way up to their elbows, rolling up their sleeves so everyone could see them. They shot at ringing alarm clocks. They washed their socks in toilets, then, flushed the toilets, and when the socks disappeared, they cussed the Germanskies, the Germans, saying their machines did zapzerap, it stole. Then, they shot the toilets to pieces. I could not figure out how they could be so stupid and mean at the same time, but I was careful not to laugh when I saw them trying to ride a bike.

Everyone feared them, including me. What scared me the most and everyone else in the house: the Russian soldiers making their nightly drunken rounds in town. However, they were expected to respect the big Red Cross on the Dorf-Nurses house, but sometimes they didn't. Then, I heard them, banging their rifles butts against the downstairs house door. Vati, the only man in the house, had to let them in. Although this was almost a nightly occurrence, I'd hide under my covers, knees pulled up to my stomach, my heart racing as I listened to their heavy clumping footsteps on the creaking wooden stairs. Then, I'd hear them move about, mumbling, getting closer to where I slept. A hand would pull my covers aside and, bending over me, flash a light into my eyes. Their breaths stunk of alcohol, the hand smelled of chewing tobacco, sweat, and dirt, but I was a child, so they walked away, clumping back down the stairs. After locking the door behind them Vati always came to check on me, and silently, with a kiss on my forehead, he'd tuck me back in. Even though they were drunk, they never dragged the nurse or anyone else sleeping in her house outside. On one after such night, I heard the nurse say, "They were looking for women. I always keep another Red Cross symbol near my bed just in case they don't respect the sign of the Red Cross on the front door. So far it has worked. I just hope it will keep on working."

Some time later, when no one was near, I asked Vati, "How does a Red Cross work?"

"A Red Cross means there is a medical person present who has to be respected by all military personal in war or peace, no mater what country or enemy."

"Then why aren't the Russians soldiers respecting the Red Cross on our door?"

But before Vati answered me, he looked, at what seemed to me, at an unseen distant object. Then, he shrugged his shoulders. "Well," he said, "some of them do and others don't." As always he ended by patting my head. "Spatz, it's nothing for you to worry about."

The Russian commando in charge of Pfaffendorf confiscated the biggest ranch in town, called a *Rittergut*. Then, guarded by Russian soldiers carrying rifles, the farmers were ordered to herd their livestock to that ranch. There, the farmers had to either butcher or care for the livestock, and the women from town had to do the milking, cooking and cleaning. Every day after the Russians took what they wanted, the children from town were allowed to come in the late afternoon to collect the leftover milk. Having heard stories about the beating and raping of the people working there, I hated going there for the milk.

Whenever I had to go for milk, I'd see the Russian soldiers sitting on the ground near the gate, leaning against the wall, rolling their cigarettes with paper, drinking vodka from bottles clamped between their legs, scrutinizing everyone that passed. I knew they didn't harm children, but I was scared just the same. I saw them as ugly, nasty, stinking, and dirty, out to hurt people whenever they felt like it. I hated them and felt powerless, but that was the only place where we could get milk.

Before the new school year began in fall of 1945, we moved to a small house next to the schoolhouse. Mutti's leg was better, and she was able to walk with a cane, because the wound was still not closed. Our new house was a whitewashed duplex cottage with a low thatched roof, brown crisscross beams on the outside and tiny windows. The cottage was built and owned by the farmer who lived across the street. The old couple who lived in the other half of the cottage were the parents of the farmer. They had once worked the farm but were now retired and had handed the farm to their son. The old couple moved to what is called das *Altenhaus*, the old folks house, to live out their days—a standard practice.

To one side of the front lawn of our new house was a well. A small building made of rocks and cement covered the well and looked like an igloo cut in half with a front door added. Opening that door, I saw the water was at ground level. A low, narrow rim kept the sand from falling into the well, but did little to protect the person who had to dip for water. The inside of the well house was painted white, which made the water glisten and shimmer a beautiful emerald green as it reflected the white from above. I was mesmerized by the well house, frightened of being pulled into its soft green, watery, never-ending depth. I remembered the story of the Frog Prince with the golden ball. He lived in a beautiful water fountain in the park near the castle where the princess was living. But I was no princess and there was no Frog Prince with a golden ball for me, so I stayed as far away as I could. Vati saw my fear and said, "Don't go near the well house; you might fall in, so stay away." Maybe Vati was my prince who protected me.

Between the school and the cottage was a clean, narrow, shallow, murmuring creek. It snaked along near our side of the cottage, flowed into a big concrete pipe underneath the street, then meandered on through the farmers yard and pasture.

Our half of the cottage had a tiled entrance, a small kitchen/living room downstairs and one bedroom upstairs and was partly furnished. The kitchen had a hutch for pots and dishes, a table with three chairs, a small stove for cooking, and a washstand that stood in the far corner of the kitchen. The kitchen also had several small windows where I could see in three directions, the street out front, the little creek on our side of the duplex and, across from it, the schoolhouse. Then, out the back window, I could see the lawn, covered with wildflowers and the shrubs that grew along the creek. The toilet was in back of the hallway with a holding tank that the farmer emptied every so often using its contents as fertilizer on his fields. The upstairs bedroom had three beds and a *Kleiderschrank*, a wardrobe with our suitcases stored on top.

With the schoolhouse next door, I did not have far to walk. The school, a two-story stucco building, had the living quarters upstairs for the *Schulmeister/Lehrer*, schoolmaster/teacher, and two classrooms downstairs, first through fourth grades in one room and the higher four grades in the other. I didn't mind going to that school because I was not a stranger. Having arrived in Pfaffendorf before school started, and Vati having worked on most of the local farms, I was well acquainted with the children.

By the time school started, about six months after the war had ended, the Russians' horrifying behavior was somewhat under control. The raping and killing had slowed considerably. Although the farmers received some of their livestock back, they now had to supply the Russian command post with food from their farms. The curfew for the Germans remained in effect.

Vati had started going to work for a *Tischlerei*, a carpenter/furniture firm, in Goerlitz. He got up early in the mornings and came home late in the evenings. It was about an hour's walk from the last streetcar stop in

Goerlitz at the *Landeskrone*, and then he had to walk along the foot of the Landeskrone, on a field road into Pfaffendorf. Although he was working during the week in Goerlitz, he continued working for the farmers on weekends for food. I didn't get to see him very much, so sometimes I would meet him on his way home. I would ask Mutti, "Can I meet Vati along the way?" Most of the time her answer was, "no," and she'd say I had not finished the chores, or she'd find something for me to do about that time. Many times, not giving her the chance to stop me, I called out, "Mutti, I'm going to meet Vati!" as I ran off. I could see him limping in the distance using his cane to support him, walking slowly. He looked so tired. I carried his briefcase, and we walked hand-in-hand back home. We talked about school and things from the day, and he always asked, "Did you sneak out again?"

I looked at him with a grin and said, "Well, not really, I told Mutti on my way out the door and ran before she could stop me."

"I see. You ran, hmm?"

"Aha, Vati, I wanted to meet you."

Returning home, Mutti just looked at me, not saying a word, but I knew that she was waiting for her chance to get even.

Time passed and soon October arrived, when strange things were happening that left me wondering and worrying. I heard Vati say to Mutti, "I'd better finish making the bed frames and headboards before time runs out."

"Before what time runs out, Vati?"

But he only said, "Never mind, Spatz, nothing at all."

Then one day a short time later, after he had come home from work, tired and exhausted, he saw the fake sweet peas Mutti had in a vase on the kitchen table. He was standing there, the aroma of wood and paint on him like perfume, his pants showing bits of wood dust, leaning on his cane looking drained and pale, asking Mutti, "Did you already buy the flowers for my wreath? Can't you wait?" Wait for what? What did he mean by that? What wreath? Mutti ignored him and never said a word. I looked at Vati, a big question mark in my eyes. Realizing that I was standing near him, hearing him questioning Mutti, he stroked me on the head, smiled and said, "It's all right, Spatz." But I knew everything was not all right.

He brought home the beds that he had made and set them up upstairs, returning the beds we had used to the farmer. The only things of the farmer's we still had were the Kleiderschrank and the bed I slept in, and Vati never said he would make a bed for me.

It was the end of October, and Vati was still walking every day to Goerlitz. When they got into arguments, Mutti would say to him, "You can look all you want to for that whore in Goerlitz. You'll never find her; there is not enough time left." Time left for what?

The winds started to blow ice cold, forecasting the coming of winter. But every day Vati walked to Goerlitz, no matter the weather. He would come home from work cold, tired, and exhausted, but he did not stop.

He kept on going, until one day he stayed in bed. When I went upstairs to see him before leaving for school, he said, "I'm only a little tired, Spatz. Tomorrow I will be fine. You'll see!" But tomorrow came, and he was not fine. Every day when I got home from school, he was still upstairs in bed. Why isn't he getting up as usual? Why is he so tired? Why is Vati not telling me what is wrong with him? Why was everyone, in town, asking me with concern in their voices, how is your father? Why? Why? Why?

I wanted to stay upstairs with him, but Mutti gave me all kinds of things to do, saying, "You don't need to stay with your father. He is fine; he doesn't need you." Was she keeping me away from him? What for?

Whenever Mutti was not watching, I would sneak upstairs to see him, and his comment was always the same when he saw me, "Don't worry about me, Spatz I will be fine. You'll see."

Then, one day Mutti was cooking a big pot of soup, and I wondered what that was for. But I didn't have long to wait. She told me, "That soup is for your father and you. All you have to do is make a fire and heat it up. It will hold the both of you until I return. I have just found out where Oma and Opa are, and I'm going to see them." Hearing that Mutti had found her parents did not excite me. I didn't care. Mutti's sharp voice continued, "I'll only be gone for a couple days. Do you understand me? "I nodded my head in agreement; I knew how to build a fire. "And this cup here with the spout is for your father to drink from, including the soup. Your father will be all right while you're in school, and you can run home on breaks and check on him!"

"I can't leave him alone!"

Grabbing me by my shoulder, her face cold and close to mine, she threatened, "You will go to school! You will not stay home! I'd better not find out you skipped school to stay with your father! He does not need you! Is that clear?" All I wanted was for her to let go of me and leave, so I agreed to her demands. Giving me her orders on housework, she soon was gone.

The next day I went to school, but when I came home to check on Vati, he was really sick. I made him tea as he asked and put it in the cup with the spout. He was so weak he could not hold it himself, so I held it for him. That is when I made up my mind I was not going to school even if she beat me for it. For the next two days I tended to Vati with all the care my ten-year-old self knew. At night he would call me for water to drink, but sometimes I did not hear him right away, so he had to call my name. He was so weak he could not hold a spoon, so I fed him in the mornings with a thick soup I made of flour and milk.

I put the glass bottle men use to urinate in between his legs, and Vati was careful to stay covered and decent, knowing I was embarrassed. But I could see he was in great pain. On the third day, the schoolmaster came over to check on me. Vati and he sent me out of the bedroom, and they talked. Then, the town nurse was called, and before I knew it the ambulance was there. They had Vati on a stretcher in the hallway downstairs, and I was saying goodbye to him. Again he reassured me he would be fine and he would soon be home with me again. Bending to kiss him, my tears flowing, I saw Mutti like a big black shadow filling the doorway. "What's going on here?" she demanded. Seeing me bending over Vati and not in school, she lashed out, "Did I not tell you not to skip school?" Not knowing what to say, I stared at Mutti while the two men carried Vati to the waiting ambulance—and drove off. He was gone! I had no chance for another kiss. No chance to tell him that I loved him. No chance to tell him to come home soon. Oh, how I feared and hated her! Mutti was going to slap me, but the schoolmaster and the nurse protested, saying that Vati had gotten worse and needed professional care.

The next morning before I went to school, Mutti, sitting in the kitchen, the cat in her lap, said, "Make a phone call to the *Korolus Krankenhaus*, a Catholic hospital from the school's telephone the only one close by, and ask how your father is doing and report back to me. All you have to do is ask how Alfred Knebel is, and they will tell you."

I went to the phone, anxious to find out about Vati. The principal got the number and dialed it, then, he handed me the phone. After several rings a woman answered, "Korolus Krankenhaus, Sister So-and-so is speaking."

"I want to know how Herr Alfred Knebel is."

"Oh, he died!" Said that matter of fact voice.

"He what?"

"He died last night!" Came from that indifferent voice again.

"No, he didn't! I know he didn't! I saw him yesterday afternoon. He was alive when they took him to the hospital. He didn't die! You're lying to me!"

"No, I'm not! He died last night!" There was a hesitation. Then, with a slightly softer voice, she asked, "Whom am I speaking with?"

"This is his daughter Gisela!" Once again there was a short silence on the other end of the line. With a glimmer of hope, I was waiting for her to say that she was wrong and Vati was fine. But her voice continued, "You need to tell your mother she has to come to the hospital to take care of things."

"I'll tell her," was all I could say before hanging up. I stood there like a statue, staring at the phone, my emotions on a roller coaster, my ears hearing over and over, "He died! He died last night!" I was empty, not able to move. My eyes were open but they saw nothing. My body was severed in half and I couldn't even feel the pain of it. Someone was putting an arm around my shoulder, asking me something, but I didn't hear. All I was able to say in an empty, broken voice of no hope, "He left me! He died! He's dead! Vati is dead! Gone!"

The date was November 9, 1945.

I was unable to grasp the enormity of what had happened and what I was told, early the following morning. I was heard the words, but my mind did not want to accept them. It can't be true! They're wrong! He is not dead! They have the wrong person. Vati would not leave; he promised that he would never ever leave me again. I have to hurry home and tell Mutti so she can tell them they're wrong. I ran home, and before I had the door all the way open, I called out, "Mutti, Mutti, they told me Vati is dead. You have to do something; you have to tell them they're wrong. He is not dead! Please, Mutti!"

She was still sitting in the kitchen, holding the cat, looking at me, and with no emotion in her voice said, "So he died, did he?" I could tell she was not going to do anything. I wanted to scream at her and pull her out of the chair, "You have to do something, go and get him! He is not dead!" I was waiting for her to move from the chair, to say something, to tell me they were wrong. But she didn't move, never said a word; she just looked at me with a cold and indifferent stare and continued to pet the cat. My last hope fell on the floor and with a thud my heart fell beside it. Then and only then did I know Vati was gone; he was lost to me forever. I was drained of feeling and emotion. My soul and the child in me were crying, calling for Vati, but there was no sound, and no tears came from my eyes.

I just stood there, unbelieving, glued to the floor.

"What are you standing around for, like a statue? Get your coat so we can go to the hospital and take care of your father and make arrangements." Mutti's voice echoed from a distance. I got my coat and hat, and Mutti and I left for the hospital in Goerlitz. It was a long silent walk with not a word spoken. My mind was a blank. I wanted to do something, but what? I felt alone, and it frightened me.

117

We came to the hospital and after Mutti rang the bell, a nun let us in. She directed us to a bench and asked us to be seated. "I will announce that you are here," she said, and with that she left us soundlessly.

Another nun appeared, but she was older and had a kind face. It was framed in a white stiff hat that spread out like wings with a veil that hung down her back. Her habit was long and black, and she wore a big cross hanging from a shiny chain. She had a soft smile and a gentle voice and greeted us with, "*Gruess Gott.*" Praise God, shaking Mutti's hand and turning to me. I curtsied to her, casting my eyes downward in profound respect. The nun, taking my hand into her soft one, looked at me and said, "You must be Gisela; your father spoke of you last night." I would have liked to ask her what he had said, but it was not for me to ask.

The nun released my hand and turned to Mutti. Mutti asked how he had died, and the nun said, "Very peacefully, he just went to sleep." They talked a little more, and then I was told to sit down again and wait for Mutti's return.

Sitting there alone, my feet dangling, I was absorbing the surroundings. It was a big hospital, all of red stone on the outside with shiny marble floors and white painted doors and windows with white curtains on the inside. The nuns in their long habits looked as if they didn't have any feet as they soundlessly glided along, coming out of one door and going in another. Some were carrying small trays, and others, nothing. Their long habits swayed, barely touching the floor. They, too, had crosses, but they hung from their waists and bounced when they walked. Their heads were also adorned with the winged white hats, and some had their hands tucked into the wide sleeves of their habits. Every time they passed me, they nodded their heads with an ever-so-slight smile and whispered, "*Gruess Gott,*" looking like angels to me, coming from heaven to care for people. I was thinking of Vati, and in my mind I saw them sitting by his bed, talking, and maybe even holding his hand while he was telling them of me. I felt his presence as I sat there, and I was glad he was in a place so close to heaven. And I was thinking that had I come with him to this place, maybe Vati would have taken me, too, and I would be with him now.

Mutti and the nun returned. Again she said, "*Gruess Gott,*" I curtsied, and we left with Mutti holding a small package. We took the trolley further into Goerlitz; Mutti went to several places, "Taking care of things," she said. Then we stopped at *Onkel* Alfred's, Mutti's cousin. He and his wife *Tante* Marie were living in Goerlitz. They hugged me, told me how sorry they were, and said if ever I needed something, I could always come to them. Mutti, not liking it very much, told them that I'd be fine. Shortly after, we left to go back home again.

A couple days later we dressed Mutti in black and me in my regular clothes with black ribbons in my hair. It was a cold winter day; the sky was gray; and a dusting of snow covered the ground. We walked the frozen field road, through the forest at the foot of the Landeskrone; then, we caught the trolley into town. Mutti stopped at a flower shop, "to pick up the wreath and flowers for your father," she told me.

But, when the lady brought out the wreath from the back, my eyes got big in astonishment. I could not believe what I saw. The flowers, the ones Vati had asked her about on the kitchen table, were in the wreath. How could that be? It was the ugliest wreath ever, those bright red, blue, and white wax flowers with a ribbon that had her and my names on it, saying, "Rest in Peace." I didn't want Vati to rest; I wanted him here with me! I wanted her to throw that ugly thing away, to get Vati instead. But I knew deep down that was impossible. He was gone, and all the yearning inside me would not bring him back.

We had come to the church at the foot of the cemetery. Encircling the church and part of the cemetery was a black ornate wrought iron fence, it's gate already open. There were dark marble and old iron crosses and small buildings, called a *Gruft* that marked the graves from a long time ago. It was an old church that had stood for hundreds of years, tall and proud, guarding its inhabitants who were laid to rest. The building stones, once gray, had turned dark over the years. A huge ornate heavy wooden door with cast iron hinges and handle opened into the large interior of the church. Mutti pushed me inside the church's cold musty air, the closing door behind us echoing through the interior. I stood there, in the strange smelling air, too timid to walk, unsure of what I saw. There were no benches, no pews, just caskets. Rows and rows of plain caskets, long wooden boxes neatly lined up like an exhibit with walkways between them.

Mutti took me by the shoulder, steering me a couple rows down toward the wall where a man was waiting to open Vati's casket for us. I looked at Vati and froze. His head rested on a paper pillow, and he was covered with a paper blanket that matched the pillow. He was lying there so still, his loving blue eyes closed, never looking at me again. His once working and always-caring hands were still and folded, never to touch me again. I saw the cut on his thumb where he had cut himself chopping wood. Why was that still there when Vati was not? I was holding the flowers and looking at that still body that once was my loving, walking, talking father, asking him silently, "Why did you leave me, Vati? Why?" But there was no answer and just as silently, tears rolled down my cheeks. Mutti once more nudged me, "Lay your flowers on your father's chest."

I hesitated at first, scared to touch him. I bent down close to Vati to lay the flowers on his chest when a strand of his hair fell across his forehead. It was the same strand of hair that always hung across his forehead when he was working. I was startled and stood up in a hurry, the flowers still in my hands. Was he alive? But he didn't move. Mutti tried to put the strand back in place, only to have it fall right back down again. Placing the flowers in the coffin, I touched Vati's hands. They were ice cold, sending a shiver through me.

My eyes swept over the ocean of caskets, and I saw a few other people standing at coffins. A woman, alone, on the far side of us was on her knees, her body draped over the casket, crying, and I could hear and feel her pain and sorrow. At the front of the church a funeral service was in progress with a couple pews for the people to sit. The pastor's words mingled with the cries of the woman echoing from the high domed ceilings. None of the many caskets had flowers. It was as if they were all alone in this big church. There was no color anywhere. I saw tall narrow windows that reached way up to the ceiling, but they were dim because there was no sunshine coming through the plain glass windowpanes.

A man was coming with a cart. Mutti tapped me on the shoulder, saying, "They're going to close the casket now. Kiss your father goodbye." She started to push me forward, but I stiffened.

I didn't want to kiss Vati's cold body. "No, please, Mutti, I can't do it; don't make me, please!" I begged in fear as my body started to revolt. I heard someone say, "Grete, don't force her; she is frightened and has had enough of an ordeal the last several days to work through." I don't know who my savior was; neither do I remember all who attended Vati's funeral, but I was glad they spoke in my defense, which made Mutti loosen her grip.

I watched the men close the casket. I clamped my mouth tight to keep from screaming. I wanted to throw myself onto the casket, to save Vati from being shut in. But I knew I could not stop it, so I just stood there, unmoving, watching the men seal Vati in that coffin forever.

The coffin was wheeled in front where the pastor, finished with the last service, stood waiting for us. We sat with the coffin in front of us. Mutti had placed that ugly wreath with those waxy, bright-colored flowers on top of the casket. I looked at them in loathing, hearing Vati say, "Are those for me? Can't you wait?"

"Oh, Vati, I wish I could take them off you. I hate them, too; they're ugly, but I can't. Mutti will not allow it." The pastor was talking, saying what a nice man and father he had been and how much his family would miss him. Sitting on the bench looking at Vati's casket, remembering, I had my own conversation with him. *What does he know Vati? He doesn't even know you. He doesn't know how much you loved me and I, you. He doesn't have to tell me that I will miss you. I will always miss you. I will always love you and never will I forget you. Mutti didn't even cry once for you, the whole time. She doesn't care. So, who is going to love and miss you? Not Mutti!*

After a short sermon the pastor came and shook hands and said he was sorry and conveyed his condolences. I felt like a puppet on a string. Mutti pulled and I followed in that direction, and when she pulled again, I followed another way. My mind could not hold any more.

We walked outside, and I noticed Onkel Alfred and Tante Marie were talking to Mutti. A black hearse with two horses was waiting outside the church. Men pulling a cart with a casket on it stopped at the hearse, loading it on. Then they brought Vati's coffin and placed it next to the first one, then two more caskets were stacked, one on top of Vati's and the other on top the first one. The driver took the reins, and the horses started to pull the hearse up the hill. Mutti and I were the only ones who followed behind the hearse, Mutti carrying that ugly wreath.

My head was bent down, protecting myself from the icy winds that had started to blow. I was frozen, from the inside out and my mind could not think anymore.

I just walked behind the hearse, not knowing what was to come next. As the hearse went up the old cemetery hill road, rolling over the cobblestones, it shook and rattled the caskets. After we got on top, we walked a short distance, and then the driver of the hearse stopped by a field that had new graves with sparse flowers, mainly bare mounds. The men pointed, telling Mutti something. Taking me by the hand, she walked between those graves until I saw four dug out graves.

The men brought the first casket, set it down and like taking the lid off butter dish took the top off. A body wrapped in heavy dark paper, tied with a rope to keep the paper from opening, was lying on a board. Picking up the heavy rope that was lying on the ground, they lowered the body on the board into the grave. Then they went back and got the second casket and followed the same procedure, each time returning the lid to the hearse. *What are they doing? Why do they take the lid off? Why are these people wrapped in paper and tied with a rope? Where are their families?*

And then they came with Vati's casket. My heart stood still as I started to shiver from cold and fear. Will they take his casket apart, too? But to my relief, without stopping they lowered Vati into the ground. Looking down at the casket beholding what had been most important to me in my life, my tears rolled, as my body shook, and I cried. I knew it was final. Never would I be so close to Vati again, never ever. He had left me, never to return, and part of me went into that grave with him. Mutti scooped dirt and threw it on top of the coffin. It made the worst hollow sound I had ever heard. Then, she told me to do the same. Not wanting to scare Vati with that horrible sound, I took a little dirt, crumbled it in my hand and let it fall softly on the coffin.

Then, Mutti laid that ugly wreath down, for the men to put on top of the grave later on. Once more Mutti pulled my string, and I followed, wiping my tears with a final look at Vati, promising never to forget him and always to love him. We left the cemetery and stopped at Onkel Alfred and Tante Marie's. They had something warm for us to eat. Soon we were on our way home, to Pfaffendorf. It was the hardest and saddest walk home because there was no one waiting there for me—I was alone.

My life took a drastic turn again. Mutti was in charge to do as she saw fit with no one to challenge her. Soon I learned that the cleaning of the house was my job because she claimed she was unable to bend down.

Every Friday after school, on my hands and knees, I scrubbed the floors from upstairs to downstairs with ice-cold soapy water. By the time I was done, my hands were red and so cold that I was unable to feel them. Mutti, the cat in her arms, watched me to make sure I was doing this job right. If not, I had to do it over. I hated her standing there, watching, scolding, "You are too dumb and stupid for that job. But that is what you will be doing when you are hired as maid, scrubbing floors and pulling weeds in the fields. So get used to it!"

The scariest job of all was to get the water from the well. I was sure Mutti knew I was scared of the well. She did not allow me to use a dipper. "You can do without one." I could hear Vati's words, "Don't go near the well. You might fall in." But there was nothing I could do. Mutti wanted me to get the water, so I had to do it. I took the bucket and dipped it in the water, holding onto the handle and letting the bucket fill up until the weight was about to pull me down. I braced myself against the low rim in front of the well. Then, I pulled the heavy bucket full of water from the well. If the bucket was not full to the brim, I had to go back, dipping it back into the well, filling it up. While I was carrying the water in to the house, spilling it on the floor was not allowed. It usually ended with Mutti hitting me in the face, saying, "You can't even carry water right; you're just too clumsy, dumb, and stupid." Sometimes, when the water level was low and I had to bend deep into the well, the old man from next door would come and help me. Attaching his pole to my bucket and dipping it deep into the water, he'd fill the bucket for me.

One of my past jobs returned to me: cleaning and washing Mutti's feet and clipping her toenails. While Vati was alive and at home, she never had me do it; but with him gone, it became my regular duty again. I also did the darning and mending of my socks and clothes, and if it was not right, I had to do it over until it was to her satisfaction. Always, Mutti told me I was stupid, ugly, and clumsy. "You will never amount to anything, you will only be good enough to work on a farm as a maid in the fields plowing and pulling weeds." Often she reminded me that I was a thief and always would be, saying, "I'm not sure if anybody would want you once they know that you're a thief."

Vati was never mentioned at all. It was as if he had never existed, but he was in my thoughts every day. In the evenings, alone upstairs in my bed, I cried because I missed him so much. I felt lonely and forgotten and wished many times that he had taken me with him. There were times I even got mad at him for leaving me when he had promised never to leave without me again. But he had, so I questioned him, "Vati, why did you leave me here? I want to be with you!" My body shook with grief and sorrow as tears rolled onto my pillow. The person I loved the most was gone, and never again would I hear his voice call me Spatz. Way deep in my heart I knew he could not help it, that he would never have left me, and I consoled myself with that. I knew he was watching over me from heaven, sending his love and care. It helped me to go on alone whenever I was sad and wanted and needed him. I had to be strong; he wanted me to be.

It was December 1945, Christmas had arrived, and Vati had been gone for six weeks. It is the custom when a close relative passes away, that the family not celebrate any holidays for a year; therefore, we did not have a Christmas tree. Instead, we went to a friend of Mutti's in Goerlitz for Christmas Eve. I had never seen her or children before. In fact, Mutti had never mentioned her before. When we got there, I met the children, a boy my age and a girl younger.

After the greetings I was going to sit down, but Mutti pulled out a chair and declared to everyone, "It is best we let Gisela sit by herself, away from everyone, because she steals and has to be watched. But not only is she a thief, she is also stupid, dumb, and ugly." She placed my chair away from everyone, not allowing me to leave it. She told them how I had stolen a ring and my father hadn't even spanked me. She said, "I have to tell everyone what kind of a child Vati's little girl really is. After all, I'm responsible for her and it is my duty to warn people about her." Sitting there, listening to her making me look bad, I despised her—no, I began to hate her. I was sorry I had stolen, and really hadn't meant to. I'd returned the ring and apologized to that lady, and she had forgiven me. I had never stolen from anyone before and I never would again. I was not a thief; I knew I was not!

Mutti's girlfriend and her children were looking at me as if I were dirty. I hung my head and wished Vati were here; I knew he would not have allowed her to say those things. But Mutti pointed at me and said, "Look at her! She can't even lift her head and look at us because she knows that she's a thief." The children had their small Christmas gifts, and I sat there unmoving, watching. I knew what they had received was not much but I would have liked to see it, but Mutti said, "No, you stay where you are; we can't trust you!" We went back home that same day. But I knew I would never forget or forgive her for what she'd said about me. I feared and hated her!

Soon after that visit we went back again, and at the first opportunity I told the boy, knowing that Mutti couldn't hear me, "You know that she is not my real mother, and no matter what she says, I'm not a thief. I have a real mother, a sister and Oma, and they would never say ugly things about me. And someday my real mother will come to take me away from her; then, I will be so happy." Although I was not sure of my own story, it felt so good to tell something I thought I knew and something Mutti did not want anyone to know about. She wanted everyone to think I was her daughter, but all of my feelings unsure as they were, were fighting against it. I didn't want to be *her* daughter, and I didn't want *her* to be my mother! I had wanted to get even with her and to hurt her for a change. But I hadn't thought that he might repeat what I had said, telling his mother, who eventually told Mutti.

On our next trip to Goerlitz, it was cold and snowing. Mutti stopped at Tante Marie's to leave me there while she was running errands. Tante Marie's husband, Onkel Alfred, was Mutti's cousin. When Mutti returned, they asked us to stay and have a bowl of soup before going home. Mutti accepted. We were sitting around the table, me on the sofa where their baby was lying. The baby was gurgling and laughing, and everyone was looking and talking to the baby, including me. Before I knew it, Mutti hit me in the face, yelling, "You put your face in the bowl and eat! I don't want to see you turn away from it. Do you hear me?"

I said, "Yes, Mutti." Starting to cry, I could not hold the soup in my mouth, and it ran back into the bowl. Mutti grabbed me by my upper arm, yanked me from the sofa, and pulled me out of the apartment into the hall of the apartment building. Then, with her icy cold eyes she told me, "You will stay here until you learn to behave, and even if you freeze out here, you will not come into the apartment until I give you my permission." Turning away, she left me in that cold hallway. When I heard people coming, I pressed myself in the corner, embarrassed to be found standing in the cold, crying. *Why wasn't I allowed to look at the baby? Everyone else did, including Mutti.* Again I cried, but not because of her. I cried for Vati, wishing he had taken me with him. I wanted to be dead just like him.

After a while Onkel Alfred came and got me, but I was afraid to go back in because I hadn't been given permission from Mutti. He said, "You come in now; it is too cold for you to stand out here." Against Mutti's wishes, Tante Marie had heated soup for me, but my stomach fought it all the way. Tante Marie hugged me goodbye, Onkel Alfred shook my hand, I curtsied, and we were on our way home. While we rode the trolley to the Landeskrone, Mutti never said a word. After getting off at the last stop and walking along at the foot of the mountain to Pfaffendorf, Mutti stopped abruptly. I stopped, too, looking up at her to see what was the matter. She hit me in the face, first on one side and then on the other. My head was flying in two different directions. My eyes got big and I started to cry. "Do you know what that is for?"

Shocked, in tears, I said, "No."

"Well, I'll tell you! You said that I was not your mother, that the whore in Goerlitz is your mother, and that she will come and get you! Think again! They're dead! Do you hear me? They're all dead; all of them! They are not coming. Never will they come for you! Never! Do you hear me? You're staying with me, and I do not want to hear again that you're telling people I'm not your mother. I'm all you've got, and you're lucky I don't throw you out on the street!"

Once again, in an instant, all my hopes and dreams were crushed by the word *dead*. Mutti's words, like knives, cut deep, each cut, saying, "They're dead, dead, dead!" She continued walking, leaving me standing, not knowing in what direction I should be go, but what direction was there? So I followed Mutti, thinking about what she had just said. *Had that woman, the nurse, Mutti called a whore, really been my mother? And was she dead too?*

When we got home, Mutti started again. "Let me tell you, you've hurt me. After all I've done for you, I'm not sure I can go on living with you. I'll hang myself, and you will have to watch me hang here on that hook." She pointed to a small hook in the ceiling meant for the *Adventkranz*, the Christmas wreath. Then, she went to the drawer and pulled out a short rope. I started to cry, begging her not to do it, but she paid no attention to me. "Look, this is how I will do it," she said as she wrapped the rope around her throat and reached, without a chair, up to the hook in the ceiling and put the rope through it. "I will hang there until I'm dead, cold dead, like your father and that whore, your mother."

The image of her hanging there terrified me. I felt responsible for it; my mind was about to snap. Wherever I turned and looked, I heard the word *dead*. I threw myself on my knees before her, tears streaming, my hands folded upward, as in prayer, begging, "Please, Mutti, please don't hang yourself. I will never say again that you're not my mother. You're my mother, no one else. Please, Mutti, I beg you."

Taking the rope out of the hook, with the other end still wrapped around her throat, she looked down at me. "Say that you love me, that you will never say it again, and that you will never leave me! Say it!"

"Mutti, I love you, I will never say it again! I will never leave you! Please, Mutti, I'll be good!"

She took the rope off her throat and said, "If you ever say again that I'm not your mother, then if I don't hang myself, I'll drown myself in the creek outside."

"I will never say that again, Mutti. I promise! Don't go in the creek." I went to bed after that, I couldn't stop crying, my heart felt heavy, my head was aching, I was exhausted. Silently, between sobs, I called for Vati, "Why didn't you take me with you? Why did you leave me here alone? Mutti and Oma in Goerlitz are all dead, too. Vati, please come back and get me!" But I knew he was not coming, he couldn't. I also knew that I could not be with him, that I had to go on living and I had to accept it.

From then on, my life took a turn for the worse. It got bitter cold. My meals were the same, three times a day; in a small aluminum pot the size of a coffee mug, Mutti kept soup warm for me. When I went to bed, I only took off my shoes, coat, mittens, and hat, for I had only a blanket to cover me—but Mutti had a featherbed to cover with. I washed my face in the mornings with cold water, combed my hair, ate the soup, and put the rest of my clothes back on. I was ready for school.

I had another job added to my chores: pick the lice out of Mutti's hair. Oh, I was good at it. I knew how to catch those guys and squish them and their eggs between my thumbnails so they popped. I was allowed to wash my hair and take a sponge bath on Saturdays with a change of clothes. Mutti would sit and watch me, making sure I washed behind my ears. If it was not right, she would scrub them until they burned. Since I couldn't wash my back and Mutti didn't help me, my back started to itch, feeling as if little feet were crawling all over it. I would rub against doorframes and trees to scratch my back; it felt so good, but the all-over itching did not go away. My head was itching, too, from the lice biting and crawling, and my feet had blisters from not taking my socks off for a week.

But one thing was good. I don't know how, but whenever Mutti sent me on errands in town, some women, in particular the wife of the farmer from whom we rented, called me in and gave me something to eat and milk to drink. Some kids in school gave me part of their sandwiches or brought an extra one for me. The principal's wife also brought me a sandwich, too. How did they know? I never told them anything.

I knew I could not go on living like that. I had to do something. I had to get away from her, but how? Daily I tried to think of some way. The only solution I came up with was to run away. I heard of orphanages where children were kept whose parents were lost or had been killed in the war. I didn't have any parents either, so why could I not go there? The curfew was still in force, so I thought if I sneaked out at night, the Russians would catch me and when they asked for my name, I would give them some other and tell them my parents were dead. The more I thought about it, the more reasonable it sounded. But before I set my plan in action, something or someone stopped me from doing it. Was I afraid to go out into the unknown? Was it Vati, or a guardian angel that protects and guides children? Was it both?

It was February 1946. Mutti and I went to Goerlitz, and she dropped me off at Tante Marie's. After Mutti had left for town, Tante Marie approached me asking, "How are you doing, and how does Grete, treat you?"

Oh, I thought, no, not again; I'm not going to tell her anything, so I answered, "Fine."

But she continued, her hand on my shoulder, "Gisela, tell me the truth; I can see she is not good to you."

But I answered, "Oh, but she is," not willing to give in.

"Did you know that I knew your father for a long, long time and your whole family, too, including your mother?"

Forgetting I was not going to talk, my head popped up, my ears perked, and I said, "You know my mother? My real mother, Oma and my sister, too? You know all of them?"

"Yes, I know all of them. Now, one more time, and you tell me the truth, how is she treating you?"

I broke down, and between tears and sobs; the words fell out of my mouth without my thinking.

"We have to do something about that. You see, your father knew he was sick and was going to die. He asked me to look after you. He tried to find your mother until he got too sick and passed away."

Oh! I had someone I could talk to, but then my fears came. What if she is just trying to make me talk so she can tell Mutti, who will drown herself or worse, hang herself because I talked? Oh, what have I done? I'm in trouble again!

But Tante Marie went on talking, "Did you hear what I said?"

I looked at her in amazement. Just what had she said?

"You didn't hear a word I said did you? I said I would get your mother's address and write to her. I will tell her that Alfred, your father, has passed away and she needs to come home and take care of you."

"I don't think she can come and take care of me.

"And just why not?"

"Because they're all dead."

"And who told you that?" Tante Marie asked.

"Mutti said they were all dead, and no one was coming to get me."

"Don't you believe it! I would know that!" I wanted to believe her, but I knew it was not so; Mutti had said they were dead. "This evening I'll go to a cousin of your mother's, I know where she lives and get her address. I think all of them, your mother, your aunt and your cousin Uschi, as well as your Oma Anna, fled to *Erfurt*, a city not to far from and west of Goerlitz, to your Oma Anna's brother's house. He is a blacksmith. After I have the answer, and the next time you're here, I will show you the letter. You and I will go to the basement where you can read it for yourself. In the meantime, this will remain our secret."

I was so happy I could not speak; tears choked me.

"You have to stop your crying or we will be found out when Grete returns. So dry your tears." And I did.

When Mutti returned, we went home. I was bursting. It was all I could do not to tell her I knew she had lied to me, that it was possible my mother and family were not dead. I wanted to believe it with all my heart and soul, but I was afraid it was not true.

I could hardly sleep that night, and the next day I was in a hurry to get to school. The day seemed to be electrified with hope that something was going to happen. I was in high spirits, but I didn't know why. It felt as if something important was going to happen; or was it the excitement of having someone who cared for me? All my plans to run away were forgotten, and I couldn't concentrate. I wanted to tell somebody, but I couldn't and didn't.

When I came home at noon from school and walked into the house, I looked around as if I was looking for something or someone. Mutti, sitting with her cat, asked, "What are you looking for? Are you expecting someone? There is no one here!"

My spirit sank. Mutti is right. *What is the matter with me? Who am I expecting? There is no one and probably never will be.*

While eating my meager lunch, Mutti said, "You have to go back to school this afternoon for the weekly protestant bible class, and while you're in school I'll have my leg re-bandaged by the nurse. After you're through with your class, you come and pick me up at the nurse's house." I nodded my head in agreement and returned to school for the two-hour afternoon bible study, given by a lady from the protestant church. We had to learn a new verse from the hymnbook. At the end of class I was busy copying the verse, because I didn't have a hymnbook of my own.

A boy came to me, saying, "Gisela, there is someone who wants to see you."

I told him, "In a minute."

But he came back, "She wants to see you now!"

"Yes, in a minute. I have to copy this first," I said.

The principal came and said, "Gisela, you'd better stop and take a look at who wants to see you," he pointed toward the door.

I turned around, a little annoyed at the interruption. My heart started to skip beats; my mouth fell open; my eyes were looking but my mind would not believe what they saw. I just sat, staring.

My *someday* was here, standing in the doorway, in a nurse's uniform, smiling and laughing at me while I stared in disbelief. Then, she spoke and called my name, "Gisela, aren't you going to say *hallo*?"

"Mutti?" I asked in disbelief. "Mutti, is it really you?"

"It is none other!" Then I flew into the arms of my mother, my real Mutti. She was hugging me and I her, never wanting to let go. Tears came as they had done so often, but they were happy tears. All the kids gathered around us, watching and listening.

"Please, Mutti, take me with you. Don't leave me here, please," I begged.

"That is what I'm here for, to take you home where you belong. You will go with me!"

"Then let's go and get my clothes. We need to be gone before the other Mutti gets home."

"Before we do anything, I think there is someone you need to acknowledge." Pointing at a lady standing beside her, Mutti said, "This is your Tante Hilde; she is the wife of my brother, your Onkel Heinz."

Noticing only now that there was someone standing next to Mutti, I shook her hand I curtsied and said, "Guten Tag, Tante Hilde." Turning to Mutti again, I said, "It's all right; I can pack my clothes while she is not at home."

But Mutti said, "No, we can't do that. She will have to be called home."

"But, Mutti, you don't understand; she is going to drown herself if I leave her. I had to promise never to leave her."

"Well, that is one promise you will have to break. And where is it that she is going to drown herself? I don't see a river anywhere."

"In the creek next to the house where we live," I replied.

My mother started to laugh out loud, "In that little creek? It will run over its banks if she goes in there!" I couldn't understand why Mutti thought it was so funny when it scared me so. Mutti must have seen my distress because she said, "Don't worry. She will not drown herself in the creek; of that I'm sure."

"But, Mutti, what if she won't let me go with you? I don't want to stay with her anymore."

"You'll go with me. Don't worry. Your father is gone and you belong with me. I'm your rightful and legal mother, and there is nothing she can do about it!"

Word had passed fast in the small town because when we approached the house, the other Mutti was already standing in front of it, blocking the doorway. She had her arms on her hips, her expression daring us to come near her. My mother, with me in tow and Tante Hilde following, told my stepmother that she had come to reclaim her daughter.

"You don't have a daughter; you gave her up years ago," my stepmother snarled.

"That was then and this is now. Don't think you can stop me or do anything about it. Alfred is dead, Gisela is my rightful daughter, and she belongs with me," my mother said.

Gripping Mutti's hand, facing my stepmother, listening to her refusal to let me go, my heart raced, and my stomach flip-flapped. *Please Mutti, don't let her scare you! Please don't leave me here!*

"Well," my stepmother retorted, "we will see about that. Let's go to the *Gendarme*. the sheriff, and have him make that decision."

Holding my mother's hand, we walked to the sheriff's office. "What do you want?" he asked me.

Fearful of the outcome, I said timidly, "I want to be with my sister."

"Well, there you have it. She will go with her mother to her sister. That's what she wants."

"That's not good enough; we will talk to the Buergermeister!" my stepmother demanded.

"We can do that, too," my mother said, "but I don't think it will make any difference. I'm her mother."

The Buergermeister asked the same question, and I gave the same answer. "You have to let her go," he said. "The child's father has passed away, and the rightful mother is here to take her back. She belongs with her mother."

We went back to the house. I packed my few belongings, and then said goodbye with a wave of my hand. Afraid the other Mutti would reach out and grab me, I hung on tight to my real mother while Tante Hilde carried my small suitcase. As we walked through town, people came and gave us food to take home and told Mutti they were glad she had come to take me away.

Oma's promise, *someday you will come back to us*, had come true. Then, I thought of Vati, wishing that he, too, could be with us. I silently thanked him and the guardian angel for their guidance, and silently I said, "Rest in Peace, Vati. I'm going home."

W alking with my real Mutti, holding onto her hand, feeling her warmth and care flowing through me, were a gift to make me well again. The day's events had happened so fast that I was dazed, unable to comprehend my good luck and destiny.

I had entered a new world within hours. Walking next to Mutti, I kept looking up to make sure I was not dreaming, but it was real. Mutti looked down at me, smiled; squeezed my hand, but said not a word. I knew she was telling me I was safe, a feeling I hadn't had for some time.

I was not alone anymore. Vati was gone, and part of me had gone with him that gloomy day on the telephone. I would always love him and miss him, keep him in my heart and memory, but I knew a new chapter of my life had begun.

Late in the evening we arrived at the apartment in Goerlitz where Onkel Heinz and Tante Hilde lived with their three-year-old son Reiner. Onkel Heinz, a tall, muscular, very handsome man, he had dark hair and gray eyes that twinkled with laughter and life. I liked him right away, but I did not show my feelings; it was all too new for me. He was a stranger to me, and I was frightened by my feelings.

As soon as we got there, Mutti und Tante Hilde heated pots of water. A round metal tub, big enough for a person to sit in, was placed in front of the stove where it was warm. Then Mutti took of my clothes, and exclaimed, "Hilde, come and look at this! Just look at her back! It is covered with festering sores!" I started to cry, not because I felt bad but because someone was taking care of me. I had known my back itched and burned when I'd rubbed it hard against trees or doorframes, but festering sores?

"Don't cry. This is not your fault," Mutti consoled me. "That fat slob of a woman did not take care of you, and if we had normal times, her big fat so-and-so would end up in jail, charged with child neglect."

"And her hair! The lice are stacked on top of one another. Didn't she know you had lice?" Mutti asked.

"I don't know. She never checked my hair. I only killed the lice on her head."

"Unbelievable!" And your feet, how were you able to walk? It had to be misery! But don't worry, it will clear up in no time. It was high time I came to get you. No telling what you would have looked like a little later on."

I got my bath. Mutti washed my hair and wrapped it tight with gauze, saying "so the lice can't escape during the night." Looking in the mirror, my head all bandaged, I thought I looked like the soldiers I'd had seen in the hospital where Mutti worked when I visited them in Goerlitz.

Mutti continued, "Tomorrow morning I'll go to the hospital and get lice killer and ointment for your feet and back. Before you know it, you'll be feeling good again. But we can't tell anyone you have lice, or your hair will be shorn clean to your scalp."

"Why, Mutti?"

"Lice cause illness, and lots of people and children are ill, and medication is scarce. Shaving the head and burning the hair get rid of the problem. But don't worry; you will not lose your hair. I can get applications to take care of that problem." All that sounded gruesome to me. I was just glad Mutti was a nurse and able to take care of me.

I was so exhausted that after my bath and Mutti's care, I fell into bed. Mutti tucked me in, kissed me good night, and said, "You sleep well. I'll be joining you shortly." Mutti and I slept together in a small room big enough for only one bed and a Kleiderschrank for wardrobe, but I didn't care. The bed felt nice, clean and cuddly, so I dropped off to sleep immediately. But I did feel Mutti come to bed, and we snuggled. Mutti's light scent of medicine reminded me of Vati and the hospital. I tucked myself next to Mutti, relaxing and feeling secure, and I slept, slept, and slept.

"Hey, sleepy head, how long are you going to sleep? I have already been to the hospital to get the medications for you," a voice called to me. When I opened my eyes, there was Mutti. I stretched out my arms, hugging her, so glad the day before had not been a dream but reality.

"Come, Gisela, get up! It is almost noon! I need to take care of you and your hair. Then I have to go to work." Cleaning and creaming my back, soaking my feet in a solution, applying lice killer to my hair, wrapping it again with new gauze—all this after a wonderful night's sleep and Mutti's loving care made me feel like a new person. Mutti followed this procedure for the next several days until the lice were killed and my hair was clean once more. With Mutti's nursing, my back and feet healed and soon I felt better than I had in a long time. I was coming out from underneath a dark heavy cloud, seeing a ray of sunshine for the first time. The past months of agony faded. Only the loss of Vati stayed with me. Although I was with my real mother and family, I knew the emptiness in my heart would never be filled. Part of me was gone, dead and buried with Vati.

Mutti was a happy person, and laughter came easily to her. She encouraged me, telling me, "Chin up, life goes on. You cannot change the past. You're back where you belong, so let's be happy. Your father would have wanted you to be happy again." Soon her zest for life and her approach to living influenced me, too, and laughter came back—slowly and in small doses at the beginning, but soon I was happy and contented.

Since there had been an epidemic of typhoid and other contagious illnesses, the schools in the city were closed, and the hospitals, were under quarantine. Every day I met Mutti at the hospital, but because no one was allowed to enter, I waited for her outside the locked gate. The hospital, a complex of several red brick buildings, was four stories with balconies and tall white-framed windows. In the center was a small park with benches for the patients. A wrought iron and brick fence enclosed the complex with a large gate at the front entrance. The catholic hospital where Vati had died was on the outskirts of Goerlitz. Mutti's hospital mainly protestant, was simply named *Stadtkrankenhaus*, city Hospital, but both treated anyone of either belief.

Food was in short supply, so we ate lots of soups made with flour and water, sometimes with milk. If we had a potato or two, Tante Hilde or Mutti without peeling they grate them with the hand grader, then add a little flour and salt and fried them like pancakes on top of the stove—stopping the gnawing hunger for a short while.

Even hunger didn't keep Mutti from being happy and cheerful and I fell right in with her. I had my real Mutti and life was good. When we walked in town—Mutti, slim and pretty in her nurse's uniform, and I in clean clothes, my hair braided with curls and ribbons, I felt ten feet tall. We walked arm in arm, laughing and talking, and I was on top of the world. When we met people on the street, Mutti, with pride, said, "This is Alfred's and my youngest daughter Gisela. Alfred passed away, and she is back with me again." If they had known Vati, I felt extra special. They shook my hand, saying, "You look just like your father, I'm sorry to hear he has passed away. He was a fine man." I was elated to hear them say he was a fine man.

I curtsied and thanked them. Then, Mutti and I were on our way again with Mutti explaining to me why and how these people happened to know Vati and her. I even met the midwife who'd delivered me. Mutti told her, "This is Gisela, the little girl who was not going to live. Do you remember?"

She looked at me and said, "So I see, quite a pretty girl at that."

But mostly we met distant relatives and cousins to my mother, as well as longtime friends living in and around Goerlitz. They, too, had come back after fleeing from the front and the Russians, only to be stopped from going any further.

One day, Mutti and I were walking along the main street called *Berliner Strasse*, when, to my horror I saw my stepmother in the distance coming down the street toward us. "Mutti, quick, let's cross the street; the other one is coming toward us!" I pulled Mutti's arm to cross the street with me, but she would not budge.

"What other one?" she asked.

"You know, the other one, the fat one."

"Oh, that one. Well, let her come!"

"Please, Mutti! Quick, before she gets too close to us!"

"Just stay next to me. She can't do a thing to you!"

That was easy for Mutti to say. My fear of that woman grabbing me and taking me back with her was bigger than Mutti's reassurance; it over-powered me. I was not going to take that chance! Why did Mutti not understand my panic? I let go of Mutti and ran across the street to get as far away as possible. Watching Mutti from across the street, I saw her walking with her head held high past the other Mutti as if she had the world in her pocket, a smile of total satisfaction on her face.

When they had passed each other, I crossed the street to be back at Mutti's side. Mutti said, "Why didn't you stay with me? Do you think I would have allowed her to take you?" Mutti really didn't understand the terror I had of the other one whom I never wanted to see again. We never talked much of things that had taken place after Vati had passed away, so Mutti didn't understand or know of my fears and terrors.

After a short stay with Tante Hilde and Onkel Heinz, Mutti found us a place to live. Oma and Christa, still living in *Erfurt*, were planning to come back to Goerlitz, so we needed our own apartment. The Housing Authority gave Mutti three rooms in a house, located on the *Langenstrasse*.

Mutti told me that the house belonged to the Protestant church, located *am Obermarkt*. The *Pfarrer, a* preacher, had fled to West Germany and had left the furniture behind. The house and its furnishings had been confiscated from the church by the East German government and were rented to people in need of housing. Mutti got three rooms: the formal dining room and the pastor's study on the second floor, and a room on the top or third floor. The large formal dining room contained an oak buffet filled with expensive china, crystal and silverware. The matching credenza was filled with linens and centered in the room stood the matching oak dining table and chairs. Then to one side of the room were two oversized beige and brown easy chairs and a coffee table with a teacart next to it and oil paintings on the wall. The oblong study was empty except for a bed with bedding and a tiny cooking stove that stood on four skinny legs in the far corner. It looked as if someone had lived there and had to leave in a hurry. With the chairs and a small table that Mutti found in the room upstairs, and items that Tante Hilde shared with us, Mutti made the study a cozy place of for us two to live. The living room she left alone because, with Oma and Christa still in *Erfurt* we didn't need that room.

Because the school buildings were used to house refugees, there was no school, so every morning when Mutti went to work, I walked to Tante Hilde's and spent the day playing with Reiner, their three-year-old son. Then, later in the day, I met Mutti at the hospital, and we went to our little place. Mutti sometimes brought food home from the hospital. When I asked how she got it, she told me, "It's from patient's that passed away today, sometimes they have food in their night stands, and we nurses share it." Food from dead people sounded a little strange, but it was food to eat, and no one cared where it came from. One day, Mutti came home with cream cheese and mashed potatoes. She built the fire, mixed the cream cheese with a little flour and sugar, and fried it on top the stove since we had no fat or a frying pan. It stuck to the stovetop, but we ate it, and it tasted good. Licking our fingers clean, Mutti and I laughed over that sticky gooey mass that stuck to our fingers.

Mutti also had a longtime girlfriend named Annie, but I called her Tante Annie, because children were not allowed to call grownups by their first name only. We visited her often, and on one occasion, Tante Annie and Mutti cooked oatmeal mush. The oats had not been processed, they were kernels and need to be cooked for quite a while to soften so they pop open. When we finally sat down to eat, we had to chew slowly to sort out the oats from the husks, which we spit out. Tante Annie, Mutti and I laughed, spitting the husks back into our spoon and then into a bowl on the table. We nicknamed that dish *Spucksuppe,* spit soup. It was not good table manners, but it was fun and filled our stomachs.

Although it was March, it was still very cold and with utilities like power and gas strictly rationed, Mutti and I went to bed early, saving the wood or coal for our meager cooking. We snuggled in bed to keep warm, and Mutti and I talked. I had lots of questions, and she tried to answer them all. However, the old rule had not changed; children do not need to know all grownup business. I asked Mutti, "How come you came for me the day after I'd talked to Tante Marie? The other Mutti told me all of you were dead, but Tante Marie said you were in Erfurt with Oma and Christa! Please tell me how come!"

"Well, first of all, you know she lied to you—we were not dead. She wanted you under her control and scared. But luckily that didn't work. Also, when your father was wounded in 1943, he was here in *Goerlitz* with me. We agreed that after the war we would look for each other here in Goerlitz."

"But how come you didn't find him? He worked every day in Goerlitz."

"That is what Tante Marie told me, but I was too late. By the time I returned to Goerlitz and looked for your father, he had already passed away. That is why I couldn't find him, no matter how much I looked. I never dreamed that he had died. We had planed for your father to divorce the fat one, so he and I could marry again." Mutti's telling me that made me feel good and sad at the same time—good that my parents had loved each other, and sad because they didn't find each other. It was like a fairy tale to me, but one that never came true.

"Tell me more, Mutti. How did you find me so fast?"

"The same day Tante Marie talked to you, she went to my cousin Helene here in Goerlitz, to get my address in Erfurt. But Helene told Marie I was already in Goerlitz working in the hospital, looking for Alfred and living with my brother, Heinz and his wife Hilde on the *Kottbusser Strasse*. Then, Marie immediately went to see them. Because I was at work, Marie left a message with them telling me to come and see her right away; it was urgent. When I got home and got the message, I hurried to see Marie, thinking that finally I had found your father and you, only to be told that Alfred had died and I needed to get you, immediately. The next morning I went to the hospital to tell them what I needed to do. They gave me the time off to get you. That is how Tante Hilde and I arrived the next day in Pfaffendorf to claim you."

"How did you know where to find me? How did you know I was in school and where the school was?"

"First, I went to the Buergermeister and then to the sheriff and told them who I was and what I intended to do. They knew of you and your father and told me where I would find you." I also had a letter from your father before he went in the war saying, you should be returned to me if something happened to him.

"So they knew you were going to take me away?"

"Yes, they knew, so when we made our rounds, they were ready for us. They were aware of the circumstances and of how you were treated, so they were glad that I had come to take you away. Now, go to sleep, no more questions for tonight."

"One more question, please, Mutti? How come I was allowed to come to Goerlitz for a visit?"

"Well, when Oma, Christa, and Tante Elfriede with Uschi came to Liegnitz and she wouldn't let them see you, I wrote to your father and told him what had happened. He wrote to her and told her to bring you to Goerlitz."

"So, that's why she was so mad. She didn't want me to come to Goerlitz. She didn't want me to find out that I had a real family and that you were my real mother, not her." I hugged Mutti and cuddled close to her, as I used to do with Vati. I never wanted to lose her, and I went to sleep.

Not long after our conversation, Mutti came home from the hospital, complaining of headaches, earaches, a sore throat, and stiff neck. She went to work the next day only to feel worse. That night she perspired so much that the bedding got damp, and she shivered with chill. I changed the sheets with a set I had found in the credenza and her gown, but she was not any better in the morning. Mutti told me, "Gisela, I can't get up; I'm too weak. You need to get the doctor for me."

Looking at Mutti, I could tell she was not feeling well and that made me afraid. Her face was red, her eyes, glassy. She could not turn her head at all. She gave me directions to find the doctor, and I ran as fast as I could because I did not want her to be alone. I remembered what had happened with Vati when he was left alone.

I returned home before the doctor arrived. When he arrived, he came into the room and, with his hand still resting on the door handle, he took one look at Mutti and declared, "You, *Schwester Helenchen*, have typhoid and need to go in the hospital. There is nothing I can do for you here."

"Hospital?" I repeated, "No, Mutti can't go there! I'll take care of you! I can do it! Please don't go in the hospital, please!"

But *Doctor Dietrich*, a small, stout man said, "That is where your mother will have to go. You can't take care of her! Your mother is ill, very ill."

I started to cry, forgetting my manners, and shouted at him, "But you don't understand. She can't go to the hospital. Vati went there and he died there, and Mutti will die there, too! I know it! You can't take her there! You just can't! I won't let you!" I shouted even louder at him. But he paid no attention to me. He was the doctor and I was a child.

Mutti told him, "She just lost her father and she is scared." He said he was sorry, but it would not change what had to be done. I threw myself across Mutti, and begged her not to go.

"I'll be fine; don't worry. I'll be back in a couple days." She tried to console me, but I knew better.

"Vati said the same thing, and he died in the hospital, and you will die, too! Why did you come and get me when you're going to leave me, too? Why? Why did you come for me at all?" I was filled with fury. Tears were streaming down my face. I had finally found what was dear to me, only to lose it again. "I'm going back to that other Mutti! You don't care about me! I don't want to be here when you die! Never do I want to see you again! The doctor pulled me off Mutti. Men came in and took Mutti out of the bed, sheets and all, carrying her downstairs and putting her in the wheelchair. All the while I was screaming, "No, please, Mutti, don't let them take you! You won't come back! Get out of that chair! I hate it! I won't leave you! Please stay with me!" The men wearing a red cross on their cap, wrapped a blanket around Mutti and pushed her down the street with me left behind screaming, "Mutti, please, come back!"

Tenants from the house came and took me inside. Sitting on the stairs that lead upstairs to our apartment, I cried. My world had ended once more. I was sure of that. Tante Hilde came and sat on the stairs with me and cradled me, but I did not want her. All I could say over and over was, "Mutti will die just like Vati. I know it!"

"No, she will not die; your mother is strong. You must have faith," Tante Hilde consoled me.

I told her with sobs and tears, "I'm going back where I came from."

"No, you will not! I have already sent a telegram to Erfurt, and Oma and Christa will arrive in two days. Oma will take care of you until Mutti comes home again. Until then, you will stay with us, so dry your tears, and let's go home."

Because all my past experiences were coming back to me, I was so scared and angry that I wanted to lash out at anything or anybody. I was glad that Tante Hilde had me in hand. Drying my tears, I looked forward to seeing Oma again. But at night I missed Mutti, alone now in the same bed where I had slept with her for the first time.

The next morning I awoke with fear and apprehension. My secure life with Mutti had turned in an uncertain direction. Mutti was in the hospital, and I was with Tante Hilde. Today, Oma and my sister Christa were arriving from Erfurt, returning to Goerlitz to take care of me. *Will Oma still recognize me? Will I recognize her? Will Christa be glad to see me?* Thoughts and unanswered questions whirled in my head.

"What are you thinking so hard about?" Tante Hilde's voice interrupted my thoughts. "You look so worried."

"I was just wondering if Oma would recognize me and I'd know her," I answered, a little surprised she recognized my distress.

"And why do you think she wouldn't?"

"I don't know. She's not seen me for a long time and I haven't seen her."

"Oh, don't worry; she'll recognize you, and you'll know her, too. She has not changed; she still looks the same. You know when your mother and

I came to Pfaffendorf to get you, I recognized you right away. You haven't changed much either. You've grown some and right now you look more like your father than your mother."

"You've seen me before and you knew Vati, too?"

"Yes, of course. When you were here the last time visiting in Goerlitz, I was already married to your Onkel Heinz, your mother's brother."

"I don't remember!"

"There were too many people for you to remember all of them. I met your father when he was wounded and spent time here in Goerlitz." I was looking at Tante Hilde; she was pretty, of medium height, slim, with greenish gray eyes, her dark blond hair loosely combed about her soft and smiling face. I was beginning to like her a lot. Her mentioning of Mutti brought other worries into my head. "Tante Hilde?"

"Yes!"

"Is Mutti going to die?"

"Your mother is not going to die. She will get well again and come home. She is a strong person who has had many ups and downs in her life. She'll win this one too. We all have to believe that."

I wanted to believe that, too, but I could not shake off my own fears. "I think Mutti will be mad at me when she comes home."

"Why would she be mad at you?"

"I said some awful things to her when the doctor said she had to go to the hospital. I screamed at her that I was not going to be here when she dies, that I was going back to the other one. I even said that I hated her. But I really didn't mean it. I would never go back to the other one. Never! I would not leave Mutti. She is my mother, I love her, and I wanted her for a long time."

"Well, I think you were just too scared, afraid of a repeat of your recent experience. Your mother will understand that. I will go so far as to say that she will not say a word about it when she gets home. She knows how you felt at that moment, so don't worry any more." Looking at the clock, she said, "It's time for us to go to the train station. Oma and Christa will be arriving shortly."

She put Reiner in the stroller, and we walked to the Bahnhof. What a change had taken place from the time I had visited Goerlitz in 1943. The big main entrance of the train station was barricaded with heavy wooden beams crossed over the doors. German police with dogs and Russian soldiers were patrolling the front of the train station, preventing anyone from coming too close. On the far side of the train station was another door, and leading from it was a fenced in wooden boardwalk that led into a small crudely built wooden building. Guards patrolled the walk, making sure every person coming out off the train station went through that temporary wooden building. People from inside the city were not allowed to come close to their family members and could only wave at them from a distance. Dark green trucks that showed a faint but still visible swastika were parked in front of that wooden building. People who had come and gone through the building were now being loaded into those trucks.

"Tante Hilde, why are the people being loaded into the trucks?"

"They're being taken to a camp and quarantined for two weeks."

"Quarantined for what?"

"To make sure they don't bring any contagious diseases with them. The city already has a huge problem with that. Your mother and many others have fallen ill."

"Will Oma and Christa be quarantined, too?"

"Yes, they have to, but Oma will try to get out of it because she has to take care of you. Because you were so close to your mother, it's possible, that you, too, may be infected and contagious. Reiner is small, and we have to protect him." Before I could ask any more questions, Tante Hilde called out, "There is your grandmother!"

I saw her, too, in her blue hat, stopping, waving and smiling, calling out to us, "Hallo, hallo!" Only Christa stood there, unsmiling, not waving, as if she did not know us. I called out to her, but she just looked at me.

Excited, I wanted to run toward Oma, but Tante Hilde held me back. "Stay here; you can't go!" Ushered by the guard they disappeared into the building.

"Why didn't Christa wave at us?" I asked Tante Hilde.

"Don't concern yourself about that too much. She sometimes acts that way."

Oma came out of the building and motioned to us that I was to come to her. She hugged me quickly and took my hand. Then, we went inside the building. There she talked with a man in charge who seemed to know Mutti, saying, "Yes, I know Schwester Helene is in the hospital, but I can't take her," pointing at me, "from inside the city and put her into the quarantine camp meant for incoming travelers only."

But Oma was not about to give up. "Look here," she said in a firm voice, "I came to take care of my granddaughter Gisela. She has had to stay with my daughter-in-law and son until my arrival and they have a three-year-old child. If Gisela is contagious, she should not be around that boy, and my other granddaughter and I have to go into your camp. Don't you think the camp is the best place for Gisela to be watched in case she's infected from her mother? If you can't do that, then we need to be excused from going to camp!"

The man looked puzzled, thought for a while, then said, "I guess you're right. I can't let you in the city without being quarantined and there is no better place to watch her than in camp."

Oma in her sure voice replied, "I knew you would see it that way, and I thank you." I could tell Oma was not a person who easily gave up. She knew what she wanted. Satisfied, she took Christa and me out to the truck and shouted to Tante Hilde, "I'm taking Gisela to the camp with me! Can you bring her some clothes to wear?"

Tante Hilde shouted back, "I will tend to it!"

We climbed into the people-filled truck, and off I went to a camp adventure. In the truck Oma pulled me next to her. "Let me have a look at you; it's been a long time since I have seen you!" She looked me straight in the face and I looked at her. *She looked just as I remember her. Tante Hilde is right; Oma has not changed.* I gave her a big hug, and Oma reassured me, "All will be fine from now on. I'm so glad that you're back with us, although under sad circumstances, but I'm here now to take care of you." Her words settled my anxiety, and I leaned on her with relief. Oma put her arm around me and pulled me close, letting me know she meant what she said.

After a short ride, the truck stopped. Men came and opened the back of the truck, and everyone got out. We were told to go into the wooden building and wait. As we waited, I went to the window to see where we were. Looking out, I saw a large complex of long, low wooden buildings with walkways between them. These buildings had several small windows, high up, almost close to the roof. One of the buildings had a big Red Cross painted on it. Another building had signs for showers and restrooms; another said *Kueche,* kitchen, in big black letters. Then I spotted one that said *Kinder-Hort,* a Daycare. To my surprise the whole complex was enclosed with a high chain link fence with barbed wire on top. *What kind of a funny quarantine is that? Why that high fence? Do we have to stay here forever? Are we not allowed to go home?* It scared me a little.

Just then Oma called me, and I returned to her. People were taking our names and other information. We were given the barracks number where we were to stay as well as metal bowls, cups and flat wares. With Oma and Christa carrying their suitcases, we found our barracks and entered a small cubicle where a person gave each of us two blankets and a pillow, telling us to continue through the door and to make ourselves at home.

I started to worry about all that stuff they gave us being told to make ourselves at home. But Oma took it, ushering my sister and me through the second door. It was an oblong room with a small path for walking down the middle, marked by narrow strips of wood the length of the room. From one end of the room to the other thick layers of straw covered the floor on each side of the pathway. Placed in intervals and crosswise from the walking path were small boards that divided the spaces for beds. Oma found us three spaces next to each other near the end of the room, and we put our blankets down, one to lie on and the other for cover. People were already there, some with children. I didn't like it very much. I felt uncomfortable with all those people watching us as we made a place for us to sleep. "Oma, how long do we have to stay here?"

"For about two weeks, just long enough for them to know that we're not sick."

Crooking my finger at her, indicating that I wanted her to lean down to me, I whispered in her ear, "Will all those people watching us. will they be here, too, all day and all night?"

"Yes, they will." Oma whispered, "but don't pay any attention to that. They probably don't like it any better than you and I do." I could tell Oma was not able to change that, so I made up my mind that that was the way it was. Looking at my fifteen-year-old sister, I saw she was not happy at all. She just sat there, not saying a word. I wanted to talk to her, but I decided not to because she was cool to me. I had been looking forward to having a big sister, so I was disappointed.

Soon we fell into a routine of eating our meals from the containers given to us in a big hall, after standing in line and waiting our turn. For breakfast the kitchen staff ladled big plops of oatmeal or cream of wheat on our dishes. The children received milk, and the grownups had something that looked like coffee, but smelled awful. Lunch was noodle soup with little meat at all, but lots of noodles.

One day, Oma, with me trailing behind her, went out along the fence where the first green of spring was showing. She walked along, looking and bending down, picking the tiny new green sprouts, like picking parsley. "Oma, what are you doing? Why are you picking grass?"

Looking at me with a twinkle in her eyes, knowing she had me puzzled, she said, "I'm not picking grass. I'm picking *Brennessel,* fire nettles!"

"Brennessel?" Now I was really puzzled. "Why? What for? Oma, seeing the question mark written all over my face, seemed to have fun, for she didn't volunteer any more information, but waited for me. She didn't have to wait long. My curiosity was awakened; I wanted to know.

"Oma," I said, my head cocked to one side, looking and smiling at her, knowing she was telling me a story, "tell me for real, what are you doing?"

The game continued, "I'm picking fire nettles for real!"

"Ja, but why and what are you going to do with them?"

"For our soup today!"

"For our soup? Today?" My eyes flew open, and I was not sure what I just heard. Brennessel? I knew that when touching the Brennessel, it burns, itches, and blisters the skin. I was already feeling a burning and itching sensation on my tongue. "Oma, you're not really putting that in our soup, are you?"

"Yes, that's what I'm picking them for. Young fire nettles, chopped and added to soup, taste very good, like parsley, only better and they contain lots of iron which is healthy for all of us." Pointing at me, she said, "You, most of all, you look like you could use a little iron."

How does she know that I need iron? She must be a smart Oma. "But I'm not going to touch them; they'll sting and burn me!"

"No, they don't, not when they're young, only when they get big and tall. See, touch one!" Timidly I touched those green little sprigs, and Oma was right; they didn't sting at all. Now I knew she was smart! The chopped soft green nettles gave our soup flavor and smelled of spring freshness. Every day I helped Oma find and pick nettles for our soup.

Some days I went to the Kinder-Hort where we played games, sang songs, and did little projects. It was fun, and it passed the time. Only at night did I feel uncomfortable with all those people in one place. Trying to avoid the board separating us, I snuggled close to Oma; she made me feel secure, so sleep came easily to me.

Because the whole complex was fenced-in with a high wire fence and with no one being allowed to enter the complex, Oma had a meeting place along the fence where every day Tante Hilde came with Rainer in the stroller and reported on how Mutti was doing. Oma looked worried, but when I asked her about Mutti, she said, "She is doing all right; we just have to have patience." I knew she wouldn't say that unless she was sure about it.

While in camp, I never felt pain or was ill. It seemed that I had not been infected by Mutti, so with all of us feeling fine, we were finally released to go to the place Mutti had rented, where we'd stayed before she got so sick. And so, Oma, Christa and I, were back at our allotted rooms at the Langenstrasse.

When Oma, Christa, and I went home Mutti was still hospitalized, and every time I heard Oma and Tante Hilde talking in low voices, their faces were grim and I heard them talk that Mutti was in a coma ever since she'd been hospitalized, three weeks ago. I closed my mind. I didn't ask Oma any questions about Mutti because I was scared whenever my mind recalled what I wanted to keep hidden. Oma did not volunteer to talk about Mutti's condition. Did she know how scared I was? How I tried to ignore how ill Mutti was? I don't know. All I wanted was not to be told, so I kept busy and helped Oma to arrange our living quarters.

Oma rearranged the once formal dining room, with the items available to her. It was decided that Christa would sleep in the adjacent room, the study, in the bed where Mutti and I had slept. Then, with Onkel Heinz's help, Oma moved the bed from the upstairs room downstairs and placed it underneath one of the large windows in the living room, for her to sleep on. For me, the only bed available was a solid wooden white giant baby crib, with the front folded down for getting in and out. It was meant to be a bed for a young child, but since I was rather small, it fit me just fine. Oma placed it on the wall opposite her bed between the china hutch and the brown gold tiled *Kachelofen* used for heating, but it was cold because we had no coals. Oma placed the credenza that matched the china hutch on the narrow wall between the two windows. Because the credenza was right next to her bed, Oma used it as her nightstand.

Then, she moved the two overstuffed chairs and the round coffee table in the center of the room and the big table and chairs against another wall, and that's where we ate. The small two-flame gas burner for cooking was placed on a narrow stand. Using solid wooden crates for additional storage, Oma stacked them next to the two-burner gas stove. Next to them, Oma placed the table Mutti and I had brought down from the upstairs room, and that's where Oma prepared our meager meals. The once formal dining room now looked bizarre, with oil paintings, fancy overstuffed chairs, oak coffee table, a credenza, and matching hutch displaying crystal and silver with the chandelier sparkling from the ceiling.

The rubble of the bombing was being cleared away, so Oma and I went daily, along with many others, to check the dump for usable items. I loved to dig in the rubble to see what treasures I would find. Mostly we looked for pots, pans and any other usable kitchen items. It was a mad scramble with everybody digging and looking. Being small and pretty agile, I got right down to things and hollered at Oma when I found something good. I learned to hold the pots up against the sky to make sure they had no holes. I found odds and ends of silverware and kitchen utensils, buckets, a stainless steel washbasin with a few dents, and a chair with the back partially broken off, but still usable. My sister used it as a nightstand after Oma took the back support off and covered it with a cloth. The dump was like a giant for—free department store, only everything was piled together. Some people gathered bricks and carried them away, probably for rebuilding their damaged homes.

Then, one day Oma announced with great excitement, "There are going to be fireworks, and we will go and watch them." Listening to Oma telling me just how pretty they were going to be and how much fun it would be to watch them, I got excited, too, full of anticipation. Why there were fireworks, I don't know. Maybe it was the one-year anniversary of the end of war. When it got dark, Oma, my sister and I, and many others gathered at the *Postplatz*, the center of Goerlitz. Everyone was eager to see the display, as well as the children, who were told to watch and look up at the sky because at any minute the fire works would start. It started with a loud boom and an explosion of glittering and shimmering color that seemed to rain on us. Another explosion just as powerful followed with a boom that echoed in my mind. Holding my ears and burying my face in Oma's coat, I started to cry, pressing my head deeper into her with every new explosion. Oma said, "Look up and see the pretty colors! It's not going to hurt you!"

"No, Oma, no, I'm afraid. Please take me home, please?"

"Take a look. It's really pretty and it will not hurt you. You're right next to me!" Feeling her arms tightening around me.

"No, Oma, please, I want to go away from here," I begged, crying and ducking my head with each exploding boom. Oma gave in and we walked, she holding me close to her, consoling me and telling me I was all right. The further we got away from it, the more relieved I was.

I was not the only one who was scared and cried. Many children were taken away, crying, just like me. My sister was unhappy, not because of the noise but because she wanted to stay and watch, but Oma did not allow her to be there alone—it was not safe, so Oma told her.

Not long after the fireworks—it was a Sunday—when I awoke, I was not feeling too well. I told Oma who said, "You will be fine. I'll make you a nice warm dish of soup made with water, flour, and a little milk. You will feel better after you have eaten it. That sounded good to me, but after eating it, I didn't feel much better. My head started to hurt; my ears ached and it felt as if needles were being jammed into them. As the day went on, I got hot and then cold. My neck felt stiff and I ached all over. Oma tended to me lovingly, telling me, "You'll be just fine. It will pass." But I got worse. My head ached and my ears were attacked by thousands of sharp needles. My neck and shoulders stiffened, so that I was unable to move. My lungs hurt when I took a breath. Chills ran up and down my spine.

"Oma, I want to go to bed and lie down."

"No, you can't go to bed, not today."

"Why not Oma? I don't feel good and I want to lie down."

"I can't let you go to bed, not on a Sunday!"

"But, Oma, why can't I?" I looked longingly toward my bed.

"It's because of the omen that says never put sick people to bed on a Sunday. It's believed they'll never get up. I can't let you go to bed, just yet." It sounded strange to me, because my stepmother never said that when I was sick. But Oma was firm, she loved me and I felt she knew what she was talking about. "I'll make you a comfortable place where you can rest until the evening comes and then you can go to bed." She pushed the two big overstuffed chairs together, put a blanket down, got my pillow and covers out off bed and bedded me down. "There," she said, "you will be fine here, and by evening I will put you in your bed, and tomorrow you will feel better." She made tea, and catered to me but there was nothing I wanted except my bed, and I was relieved when evening came.

The next morning I was not better. I was worse and weak. Oma gathered me up and out of bed while I protested, "Please, Oma, I don't want to get up. Don't take me out of my bed." But she continued to get me dressed while I cried in pain when she moved me about. My whole body felt stiff. Any movement caused stabbing pains through me.

"I have to get you to the doctor. I know you're in pain, but I have to get you there. So be good, let me get you dressed, and as soon as we get home, I will put you back to bed." With me whimpering, she bundled me up. Then, putting one arm around me under my shoulder, her other arm in front of my chest, she clasped her hands together to hold me up, while she dragged me to the doctor. My legs were weak, hardly able to support me.

———

She rang the bell and a nurse came out, looked at me and asked Oma questions, advised us to use the back door as she suspected I was highly contagious and did not want us in the main waiting room with the other children. As soon as we entered, the doctor came, a lady. She took one look at me, and said, "This little girl has typhoid. How has she been exposed to typhoid? And by whom?"

"My daughter, Schwester Helene, do you know her? She is in the hospital right now with typhoid and has been for the last four weeks."

"Oh, *ja*, I know her. She is very ill, and . . ." Looking at me, the doctor stopped herself from talking about it any further. "The best thing to do is to put this little girl in the hospital also. It would be safer for you if she was isolated from everyone."

But Oma would not hear of it. "No, I don't think we will do that. I do not want her hospitalized; she has had bad experiences in recent months and does not need more. I will take care of her." Her arms were still wrapped around me, daring anyone to reach for me.

"Who else is living with you?"

"My other granddaughter, Gisela's sister. She is fifteen."

"If you take care of Gisela, then her sister cannot stay in the same place. We have to quarantine the apartment with only you attending. No one can come and visit. Am I making myself clear?" Oma nodded her head in agreement.

"You made it clear. Thank you for your understanding. I will see to it that Christa can stay somewhere else."

"Now, I will stop and check Gisela on a daily basis. Keep her in bed, use cold compresses around the clock, as much as possible. Since we have no medication available, the disease has to run its course." Oma had other discussions with her, but I didn't care. I just sat there, with Oma supporting me like a wilting flower, wanting my bed. Oma dragged me back home with her arms around me again.

Soon, I was in my bed, and from then on I do not recall much. The fever took over, and I was delirious. I heard myself cry out and saw Oma standing over me, trying to settle me down. I could feel her lifting me out of bed, putting dry clothes on me. I heard myself whimpering for her to leave me alone, but everything was a haze. All I knew was that Oma was there. I don't think I would be alive today were it not for her keeping me out of the hospital and giving me her tender love and care.

When I finally got a little better and regained consciousness, my recovery was slow. Oma allowed me to get out of bed for only a short time. I was weak and had lost weight. She put the big chairs in front of the open window and covered me up. "There, the sun is nice and warm, and the fresh air will be good for you. After a while I'll put you back in bed." Oma was right. The sun felt nice and warm, and I could smell the fresh spring air.

While I was sick Tante Hilde would come and call up to the window to ask Oma how I was doing. Tante Elfriede, Mutti's sister, also came, standing on the street, calling up to Oma to find out how I was progressing.

After I had passed the worst stage of the typhoid and was on the mend, the doctor came every two days to check on my recovery. She was the motherly kind, and I liked her.

With Oma's care, I got well. The skull that had been put on the outside of our apartment door was taken off and Christa came home again. Soon I was allowed to walk outside with Oma beside me. As I got stronger, we went to the hospital to visit Mutti. We were not allowed to go inside, but walked behind the hospital on a small gravel road and waved at Mutti standing on the balcony. I was so glad to see her and to know she also was getting well again and would be coming home soon.

I had Oma and I was happy and content. But whenever I went to bed, I remembered Vati and how much I missed him. My heart ached for him with a sorrow I was unable to share with anyone, even Oma.

Recovered from typhoid, Mutti came home from the hospital and was soon herself and on the go again. First, Mutti rearranged our living room. I was moved in the room with my sister, the same room Mutti and I had shared before she got ill. Mutti exchanged the youth-bed I had slept in for the regular bed Onkel Heinz and Tante Hilde had, because the youth bed was a better size for Reiner.

Oma and Mutti took the bed apart, then, loaded it on the *Leiterwagen,* a hand cart, in the downstairs hall, there, so all five families in the house could use it. The Leiterwagen was the only way to transport belongings, so it was common to see people pulling it around the city when they were moving things. We didn't have a rope, so Oma and I held the bed parts to keep them from sliding off. Then, through the city we went with Mutti and Onkel Heinz pulling the Leiterwagen to the Koblenzer Strasse, where Mutti and I had stayed when I first returned to the family. My sister, now fifteen and not about to be caught pulling a handcart in public, refused to help.

We had to carry the bed parts up four flights of stairs to Onkel Heinz and Tante Hilde's top floor apartment. After that, Mutti helped Onkel Heinz set it up. Then, carting the other bed the same way, we returned home.

Oma's bed went back upstairs into her room because Mutti got a bed from a friend and placed it where Oma's bed had been. In the daytime, Mutti made her bed into a couch or daybed. She rolled the bedding lengthwise, placing it like a bolster along the wall with her pillow at the headboard; then, she covered the bedding it with a blanket.

The credenza stayed at the narrow wall where Oma had moved it. On the credenza Mutti placed a radio she had found in the attic, our storage space. In order to improve the reception, Mutti used her metal bed as an antenna, running a wire from her bed to the radio. It worked! But, when we had a thunderstorm, Mutti, would not go near it, thinking lightning could strike and electrify the bed.

The big china hutch filled with porcelain, crystal, and silver belonged to the Pastor who'd left it behind when he'd fled with his family. It was centered on the opposite wall from Mutti's bed and covered the wide double door that led to the *Musikzimmer*, the music room, occupied by another family. Mutti said the china cabinet would muffle the sounds of conversations on both sides.

The oak china hutch was heavy to move. Even I, slight as I was, had to help Mutti and Oma push it into place. Mutti guided the buffet on one end while Oma and I pushed with our backs against the other end. Before we moved the china hutch, we took out its fragile contents because Mutti didn't want them broken. "They do not belong to us. The Pastor may return someday to take them back for his wife. So be careful." Everything was so pretty and delicate. There were hand carved tall-stemmed crystal wine glasses in different colors called *Roemer*, liqueur glasses, decanters, heavy crystal bowls and vases. In the lower part of the hutch was a full set of exquisite dinnerware, including a brown leather box lined in velvet and filled with silverware. I admired it all, and knew the lady who owned all this must miss her things, just as I missed my doll Roswitha and my teddy Fritz.

After the hutch was centered, Mutti moved the two overstuffed chairs and coffee table to the space between the hutch and the Kachelofen, where my sick bed had stood, making it a nice cozy area for sitting and visiting. Mutti moved the dining table and chairs; Oma had shoved against one of the bare the walls, in the middle of the room underneath the chandelier.

The small cook stove, the size of an end table, with its skinny legs was moved from my sister's and my bedroom, to the living room next to the gas burners. The two-burner gas stove Mutti couldn't move because of the only gas connection in the room. In the attic Mutti found a wooden ironing board. She took off its legs, and laid it over the stacked crates, to use as her kitchen counter and for ironing clothes. To conceal our odds and ends of dishes, pots, and pants stored in the crates, Mutti covered them and the board with a big tablecloth. I don't know where Mutti or Oma got the crates. Everyone was scrounging for useful items, throwing nothing away as it might be useful later.

With hammer and chisel and Oma's help, Mutti made a hole in the brick wall near the ceiling above the small cook stove one big enough to run the stovepipe through into our bedroom. With additional piping she extended the stovepipe along the ceiling into the chimney across from my bed. On either side of the stove pipe, Mutti screwed big hooks in the ceiling, wrapping wire around the pipe and the hooks to support the extension and to keep it from falling on my bed, thus heating our bedroom in the winter when the little stove was used.

The best place to me was, my corner, next to the second window, a space left from when Mutti moved the china hutch. Into that space Mutti moved the wooden *Pult* that looked like a big school desk, painted white with storage beneath its lid and the attached bench. Mutti angled it so I could see either the living room or glance out the window. That is where I did my homework, and spent hours of drawing, painting, and doodling. It became my world, my special place. Gazing out the window at the sky—sometimes blue and sometimes gray—I'd dream, and my dreams and thoughts would fly out the window, over the roof tops, right up into heaven to Vati, telling him that I missed him so and wished he could be here with us.

With the furniture placed the way she liked it, Mutti gave our two rooms her final stamp of approval. She cleaned them once more, and as a final finishing touch, placed doilies she had found in the credenza here and there. Everything looked so pretty, cozy and inviting; it gave me a feeling of security, belonging, and warmth. Watching Mutti, not too tall, slim, with shiny black hair, lively brown eyes—I could tell she'd enjoyed moving the furniture around. Our new living quarters looked presentable, even cozy, a result of Mutti's motto, "Make the best of a bad situation, and make it look good."

Oma moved to a room of her own. A half flight up from us was a big landing with a window. On this landing were two separate living quarters where the servants used to live. Oma's midsize room was built partially underneath the roof, known as the *Mansarde,* an attic room. All the walls were straight except one, which had a slight slant. Oma's room was furnished with the bed that Mutti had moved back upstairs. Her room also had a *Kommode* a dresser, a Kleiderschrank, a well-used small wooden table with three un-matched chairs, a homemade open three-shelf sideboard, as well as a Singer sewing machine.

The room had a large window with a step below it, like a small podium. Looking out over rooftops and into the far distance, I could see the cemetery on the hillside covered by trees. Extending above the trees were the towers of the crematorium, a gray church-like majestic structure, where services were held for people who wanted to be cremated. I could also see our back yard. That is how Oma always knew what was going on when we kids played in the back yard. All the tenants in the house were refugees moving into furnished rooms, bringing only a suitcase, just like us. Thus, moving Oma didn't take long; because she had only a suitcase. I asked her, "Do you like your room?"

"*Oh ja*, it's a nice little room, and with the view out the window, what more can we ask for? I like it very much! It is small but comfortable; I will make it my home, and we're lucky to have a place to live." I didn't know what she meant by that because I had lived in many different places after Vati, my stepmother, and I had left Liegnitz. So, to me this house was just another place to live and to explore. I nodded in agreement because I liked Oma's room a lot. It became my favorite place, and I spent lots of time with Oma there.

The schools in the city were still closed and I hadn't gone to school ever since Mutti picked me up in Pfaffendorf. I didn't miss it, but I was curious. "Why are the schools still closed, Oma?"

"They're being used to house refugees, people like us."

"But, Oma, Mutti found a place for us to live! How come they can't?"

"Your mother was one of the lucky ones. She left Erfurt early, soon after the war ended, and returned to Goerlitz. Remember, she was looking for you and your father."

"I remember Mutti telling me she'd come back too late to find Vati and me. She didn't know he'd died, but she found me."

"That's right, so when your mother applied for a place for us to live, she got part of this house; otherwise, we'd have had to live in a school, too." Oma stopped moving around in her little room and sat down. Leaning back, her left arm resting on the table, she looked at me. "I have the feeling this is going to be a long question and answer session coming up."

"How can you tell, Oma?"

She laughed. "Because it's written all over your face."

"Oma, why can't we go home?"

"Well, all our family—my brothers, sisters, and I all have homes on the other side of the *Neisse River* too. And like us, many people who fled from the Russian front want to return home, but can't, because Poland is keeping us out. They're using the rivers as their border, banning everyone from returning to our properties."

"Vati was talking about that with other people in Pfaffendorf."

"Oh I'm sure he did, and it's still on everyone's mind. We're not only banned from going home but the bridges have been destroyed also."

"Is that why they were destroyed? To keep us from going home, Oma?"

"No. Hitler ordered *die Deutsche Wehrmacht,* the German Armed Forces to destroy them to stop the Russian Army from coming further into Germany."

"But, Oma, the Russians are here. It didn't stop them."

"No, it didn't stop the Russians. They marched all the way to *Berlin.*" Shrugging her shoulders Oma continued, "Maybe some bridges were still passable, time had run out because our soldiers were overrun by the Russian troops, it was one of Hitler's last orders to destroy the bridges. Shortly thereafter the war ended. Then, with the defeat of Germany, World War II ended on May 8. 1945. After that, the conquering powers—the Americans, the French, the British, and the Russians—met in Berlin and divided Germany among themselves."

"Oma, Vati was talking about that too in Pfaffendorf."

"Well, then, you know Germany got split down the middle. Russia was to govern the eastern part of Germany, while the Americans, the French and the British governed the western part. Now you know why there is an East Germany as well as a West Germany. Then, Russia split East Germany again and gave Poland all the German provinces east of the *Oder and Neisse Rivers.* Russia and Poland are now using the two rivers as their border line."

"But Oma, how can Russia divide between two rivers?"

"No, not between two rivers. It's like this: The Neisse originates in Czechoslovakia, south of Germany. The Oder also comes from Czechoslovakia, but further south. Eventually the two rivers meet and flow into the Baltic Sea, forming a straight line from south to north, dividing Germany along what is called the *Oder-Neisse Linie* the Oder-Neisse Border. If we had an atlas, I'd show it to you."

"Are the Poles always going to keep that part of Germany, Oma?"

"I really don't know. It might be a long time before we are allowed to go home again, if ever."

"I asked Vati that same question in Pfaffendorf, and he said the same thing as you, Oma."

"Yes. Hitler devastated Germany. He brought chaos and despair to our land and its people and to other countries he invaded. I can say it now; I never liked what Hitler was doing. Neither did our family nor many others, but no one voiced their disagreement for fear of being imprisoned to hard labor or worse. People who did were labeled traitors to *Das Deutsche Reich,* the German Empire, and were shot."

"Oma, I had heard Vati say that too, before he put on the uniform to go to war."

"Yes, if a man refused to put in a uniform, he was called a traitor and was shot. Like so many Germans, your father really didn't want to go to war either. He too didn't like what Hitler was doing. Hitler was a dictator."

"A dictator? What's a dictator Oma?"

Oma nodded her head. "A dictator is a person who dictates his country and to the people in it. He doesn't like for anyone to oppose him. If they do, they're traitors. Then, by his law the traitor is imprisoned to hard labor or shot." Oma took a deep breath, "So, where was I? Oh ja, then, after the Russia and Poland closed the border, they built watchtowers on both sides up and down the Oder-Neisse Rivers to stop anyone from trying to cross. Since the Neisse also flows through Goerlitz, former soldiers, husbands, fathers, and brothers, desperate to get home to look for their loved ones, try to cross the river here in Goerlitz either by swimming or rowing in small boats. Some drowned trying to cross because the Neisse is wide with undercurrents and there was the danger of being shot by Russian or Polish border guards. But even if the bridges had not been destroyed, we still couldn't go home because Poland has the land east of the rivers. And so as the returning refugees keep coming, but can't go any further, they have to stay in the schools, big halls or hotels. Villas and big apartments have been divided, with owners ordered to share their homes with refugee families. The housing authority moved refugees into the unoccupied houses or apartments of people who had fled. They moved us and our co-tenants in here the same way."

"Oma, Goerlitz wasn't bombed much, was it?"

"No, the people in Goerlitz were lucky. The war was almost over when Goerlitz was bombed. The Russian did most of the destruction when they marched through the city on their way to Berlin."

"Do we have to move if the pastor comes back, Oma?"

"Well, this house belongs to the church, called *Dreifaltigkeits Kirche* and is *Am Obermarkt*, (the name of one of the town squares). She was the owner until the housing authority took over, so we may not have to move anytime soon."

"And the furniture, Oma, is it ours now?"

"I don't know. The Pastor fled, supposedly to West Germany."

"Oma, what about the people from Goerlitz, who fled and are now returning? Do they get their places back?"

"I don't know that either, but some people find strangers in their apartments and homes—using their belongings. It will take a long time before all the stranded refugees with their families find places to live." Oma stopped and looked at me. "Do you understand what I'm telling you?"

I nodded my head, "Ja, sort of. But not really. I like listening to you. Oma, do you know people who drowned or were shot trying to cross the Neisse?"

Oma shook her head, "No, I don't, but people whisper when shots are heard in the night or a body is found along the banks of the river."

I felt sad for those people. "Oma, even though the war is over, some children can still lose their fathers?"

"Yes, that is very possible." Oma's answer made me sad, but I had more questions. "Are we Russians now?"

"No, we are not! We have to live under Russian jurisdiction. That means we have to do what they tell us because we lost the war. They dictate to us and we have to live by it. Now go and play or see if your mother needs you. I'm all talked out."

"But, Oma, just one more question, please?"

"That will be the last one."

Do you remember that bridge we walked on when I visited here in Goerlitz? Do you remember, Oma? Is that bridge destroyed too?"

"Yes it is. Someday when we're allowed to walk along the river, I will show it to you and my apartment I lived in when you were here—on the other side of the Neisse. But right now no Germans are allowed near the Neisse because the Russians barricaded all streets leading to it." Oma got up and gave me a love smack on my back-end and gently shoved me out the door. "I'm tired and all talked out. I've never seen any one who can ask more questions than you."

Going downstairs I was thinking how confusing every thing had gotten. People looked unhappy. Everyone was looking for someone. Notes asking if people knew the whereabouts of family members were attached to house doors and trees or put under rocks at bombed out houses. It felt as if a dark cloud was covering the city and its people.

Every time when Oma and I went for a walk, I would see a boarded up section, so I asked, "Oma, why is this boarded up? Who lives behind it?"

"It's the Russian military. They have taken part of Goerlitz all the way down to the Neisse for their military installation, including a portion of the city park. They ordered the owners out of their villas and large homes bordering the park, allowing them to take only what they could carry. The rest of their possessions were confiscated for the higher ranking Russians and their officers."

"But why did they build a high wooden fence with extra barbed wire on top all around the area where they live?"

"They did that so no eyes can watch them and to make sure no one will jump or climb over the fence to sabotage their installation."

"Oma, what is sabotage?"

"That is when you purposely destroy someone's property or try to hurt them. Apparently, the Russians do not trust us."

"Are they afraid of us?"

"Could be. We are strong people, fighters, and although we lost the war, they don't trust us. They're living in our land now, telling us what we can and cannot do and what we can eat and how much."

"Why don't they go home?"

Oma kind of chuckled, "That would be nice, but they're the conquerors and we're the losers, and that is why they have part of our land. We're like a trophy. Do you understand that?"

I nodded my head as though I understood, but it was really difficult. I was not finished asking questions because it scared me as we walked past the part where the Russians lived behind that high wooden fence and where the soldiers stood with rifles and dogs. I still remembered them from before and what they did. "Oma," I asked in a low tone, afraid the grim-faced Russian standing there might hear me as we crossed the street, "Why is there a guard house in the middle of the street, and a Russian with rifle and a German shepherd dog beside him standing there?"

"That is to make sure no one goes in, other than the Russians themselves. They will shoot when anyone comes too close after they give a warning call of *stoi*. They also patrol the inner area along the fence of their compound with German shepherd dogs."

"But, Oma, they're not going to shoot us when we walk on the other side of the street on the sidewalk, are they?"

Oma shook her head, "No, they won't as long as we're not too close and on the other side of the street. We just don't go along the fence." Oma was looking down at me, saying, "Now, be quiet for a little while. I'm all talked out answering your never ending questions." So that is what I did because I had a lot to think about.

With no school, I had lots of time to explore the house and our co-tenants. It was a big house. On the *Parterre*, bottom floor, there was a hallway with a room on each side. A single lady occupied the room to the right, and a young couple occupied the room to the left. The husband was an invalid who had lost one of his legs in the war and was seldom seen outside. Further down, the hallway opened into a square foyer. Just before the kitchen on the left side was the door to the cellar, across from that door was a wide wooden staircase leading upstairs. The lady and the young couple shared the large kitchen beyond the cellar door. Straight on from the kitchen was the door to the back yard. The floor of the foyer was made of white and black tiny mosaic tiles kind of sprinkled in no particular pattern, except for a strip along the walls that was darker, giving it a framed look.

The *erste Etage* or second floor was where we lived. It also had a landing that we shared with a war widow, her son *Siegfried*, and her daughter. *Frau Schmitt* was assigned the master bedroom and the music room that bordered our living room, sharing the nice-sized bathroom with us. It had a tub and tank/stove for heating the water, and the water closet was separate from the bathroom. The only problem was that when we used the bathing facilities, the Schmitt's could not leave their two rooms because to do so they had to pass through the bathroom. Oma and Mutti always made arrangements with Frau Schmitt, so we could take our baths undisturbed. Our floor had a large kitchen right off the landing, and though Mutti was allowed to use that kitchen with Frau Schmitt, Mutti had made her own private cooking corner in our living quarters.

A short flight up from our floor was the *Zweite Etage* or third floor; it had another landing with two separate private rooms, and that is where Oma had her space. The small attic assigned to us was also on that floor. It was filled with all kinds of interesting things stored by the Pfarrer, and Mutti found some useful items. The room next to Oma's was occupied by another young war widow *Frau Hartman* and her two small children.

Across from Frau Hartman's room and through another door were steps leading up to a large attic where the wash was hung to dry in the winter. I had lots of fun exploring the house, meeting the tenants and Siegfried, my age, with red hair and freckles all over his face.

There were strict rules enforced by Oma and Mutti: be polite at all times; always greet the tenant according to the time of day, don't forget to curtsy, hold the door open; help Frau Hartman up the stairs with her children; and no excessive noise at any time.

Oma reminded me, "Children should only be seen, not heard,"

S pring arrived with its glorious colors. Tulips, hyacinths, and daffodils, even little white snowbells, waved in the soft breeze, filling the air with their sweet aroma. Birds hopped from branch to branch, their beaks wide open, whistling and singing a chorus of tunes. Walking in the back yard, taking in the aromas, sights and sounds, smelling, touching, and examining the flowers that came out of nowhere. The sun sent its warm rays from heaven, awakening the earth, kissing the flowers and all living things. I could not help but wonder how nature carried on, ignoring our hurt and pain. Or was this spring a sign of hope, a new beginning?

Had it only been three months since my return to my real family?

So much had happened. Daily I reminded myself that I didn't have to go back to that woman who had claimed to be my mother. I was free from her and the unseen cage that had been around me for many years. But whatever my thoughts were and however happy I felt to be free, I carried an empty place in my heart of sadness and sorrow I could not fill with happy feelings. Whenever I thought of Vati, the picture of him in the casket appeared in my mind as clear as if it had been only yesterday, and I had to control my tears. I asked myself, "Why did he leave me? Why did he have to die? What was wrong with him?" Mutti and Oma never talked with me about his death and I never brought it up. Maybe they did not want to open a subject they knew would bring back only sad memories. *Was what happened in the past? Closed? Another chapter added to the book of my life?*

For Mutti, spring had to be a sign of a new beginning. A happy, always laughing person, Mutti didn't like brooding, looking back, or feeling sorry for herself. When she rearranged the furniture in our apartment, she had the radio playing, singing, dancing, grabbing and whirling me around, laughing, telling me, "Be happy!" She often said, "We have enough of a hard time just finding food for us to eat. Moping around is just going to make it harder, so no moping!"

I knew Mutti was right, at least about the food. It was scarce. I asked Mutti, "How come we don't have any food?"

"We are allowed a limited amount of life's necessities for our survival. Food is rationed, and every household must claim the number of persons in it to receive *Lebensmittelkarten*, food stamps, allocated for daily living. They provide barely enough for us to survive for the month. On the last day of the month we pick up our Lebensmittelkarten for the next month at a special office."

"Is that the office called *Lebensmittel-Amt*, the food stamp office, where Oma and I have gone?"

"Yes, that's where we all have to go."

"They have windows set up alphabetically to speed up the long lines, but sometimes Oma and I are gone for hours."

To prove how many are living in the household, Oma has to have identification papers with her. One day when Oma was sitting at the table in her room, me standing next to her, watching as she checked Lebensmittelkarten over, she showed them to me. Printed on cream-colored sheets of paper, each sheet had the name and address of a family member on it. One sheet had my name on it. These sheets were divided into lots of small squares, each showing just how many grams of particular items we were allowed to buy. There were squares for milk, eggs, flour, sugar, bread, wheat-like flour, margarine, meat, lard, as well other items. "See here," Oma, pointing at the sheet with my name. "Children, get a little more food than grown ups because they're still growing."

"Do we have to pay for the food when we shop, Oma?"

"Yes, we do. These stamps are not for a free supply of food. They're strictly for the rationing of food."

"Is that why the stores don't have many foods, only what's on the card?"

"Hmm," Oma continued, nodding her head, "The shelves once laden with goods that were provided by privately-owned neighborhood stores, are empty. The stores, too, are rationed in their supply of food for sale."

"How do you know when they have food to sell?" I sat down across from Oma and continued with my usual line of questioning.

"They inform their customers when a delivery is to arrive. Then I get up early while you're still sleeping to stand in line with the rest of the early shoppers before the store opens. It means I'll be one of the first ones in the store, so I'll be able to get the food should the grocer not get a full delivery," Oma patiently answered. It all sounded so strange to me that I had to ask again, "Why do you have to do that Oma? We have stamps, so he has to sell us food."

"Ja, that's right, he does and would like to, but sometimes the delivery is delayed and the grocer doesn't know when it is arriving. Then, I come back with no food."

"Is that why you send me several times during the day to the store to see if he has received a delivery?"

"Yes, that's right. We have to watch and be on the alert, so we're right there when he has a delivery. And you're doing a good job running home to get me." I was so happy Oma had praised me.

When I went shopping with Oma, I'd watch the grocers, bakers, and butchers cut out the number of stamps needed from our sheet, so I'd asked Oma, "What are they doing with the food stamps they cut out?"

"They paste them on sheets of paper needed for ordering the new supply of food. The number of food stamps turned in is what they receive for the next delivery."

"Oma, how come we have so little food to eat and have to eat stuff that doesn't taste good?"

"Well, remember we lost the war, and the Russian troops living in our land come first. They don't care about you or me."

The more I asked, the more complicated it seemed. Reaching across the table, Oma gave my hand a squeeze. "Don't worry. I'll make sure you don't die of hunger. I promise."

Power and gas were rationed as well, two hours during the morning, noon, and evening to cook meals. Oma and Mutti planned their cooking ahead, but because of the scarcity of food, they rarely planned big meals. We mainly ate soups. Oma did the cooking most of the time because Mutti went back to work.

The only item sold but not rationed with food stamps, and only one or two per customer, was *Runkelrueben,* a turnip the size of a baby's head, oblong and a pale orange. In better times, it had been used as feed for livestock. After scrubbing it well, Oma cut the Runkelruebe in small cubes to make soup with it adding a grated raw potato for thickness. Sometimes, she'd slice the Runkelruebe into one-half inch slices that she sprinkled lightly with salt and fried them in cooking grease. If she didn't have cooking grease, then Oma used left over coffee, made from roasted wheat. As long as the turnips were fresh, they were edible, but sometimes when the Runkelruebe had grown too big, they were woody, hard to chew and even harder to swallow. Then, I spit the pieces out and hid them under the rim of my plate, hoping Oma wouldn't see them. She did, but she never said a word.

The salt, too, was for livestock; it was unpaged in rough, jagged pieces of many sizes—all painted orange. When Oma came home with the odd colored rocks in her shopping bag and laid them on the table, not knowing what they were, I had to ask, "What are those rocks for, Oma? What are you going to do with them?"

"That's our salt for cooking."

"That is salt? It's so big and that awful color?"

"The color will come off when I soak it overnight; after that, I'll smash it into small pieces."

"Why is it painted, Oma?"

"I really don't know. It's meant for livestock."

"Why do we have to eat it?"

"It's the only salt we can get. It's safe and better than none."

So Oma soaked it overnight to get the paint off. Then, she smashed it with a hammer and crushed it into smaller pieces with the rolling pin. To keep the salt from jumping all over, she put the smashed rocks in a small sack she had sewn. I never asked Oma where she got the salt. It could have been at a store where it was handed out to the people because no other salt was available.

Oma also made what she called *Karnickelbutter*, like rabbit butter, a spread to put on a slice of bread for lack of anything else. Why Oma called it Karnickelbutter I don't know. The name had nothing to do with a rabbit. Maybe the name was of her own making. To make the Karnickelbutter, Oma chopped onions and browned them in her homemade coffee. Then, she added water and salt and gave the mixture a short simmer. When she added the flour mixed with water to the simmering brown onions, it formed a thick paste. The Karnickelbutter. When it was freshly made, it was not too bad, but after a couple days sitting covered up on the sideboard, it looked pretty gray. "It will stick to your ribs and fill your tummy," Oma said, and as usual Oma was right, but it took a lot of extra swallowing to keep it down.

Merchants had irregular deliveries of food, so it was common to see people standing in long lines in front of stores along the sidewalk, sometimes for hours, with family members relieving them for a short time. The women with scarves around their heads, their faces drawn, no emotion in their eyes, their clothes worn, they stood unmoving, waiting to get inside the store, hoping the merchant wasn't sold out. Oma would stop and ask what the line was for and what the merchant had to sell. Then, she too, would stand in line. At times, when their turn came or just shortly before they got inside the store, the grocer sold out and closed the store for the day. Empty handed, people walked back home to wait in another line the next day.

Also when a merchant, like a baker, butcher, or grocer, had something for sale, the news spread quickly throughout the neighborhood. People raced to the store, hoping to get there before everything was sold out. When Oma knew there was a supply of food, she would send me ahead to stand in line, saying, "You're so much faster. Run along ahead of me and hold a place in line for us. But don't let anyone push you out of the way. You know they like to do that to children."

"I won't let them, Oma. I'll hold a place for you. I won't let them push me out," I assured her, running off to secure a place. I never knew what the store had to sell. I just knew it was food and we needed it.

Then, one sunny morning Oma handed me the shopping bag. "What's the shopping bag for Oma? What are we going to do?"

"We're going Brennessel or fire nettle picking."

"Brennessel picking? Why?"

"They'll be our meal today." With Oma in the lead, still in her apron, not taking it off as she usually did when she went someplace, we walked to where Brennessels grew, like among weeds, against rock walls, fences, and along the wall by the cemetery in the old part of Goerlitz. They were not spring green and tiny anymore as they had been when Oma had picked them while we'd been in camp. They had grown almost as tall as I and had long stringy white blooms on them. The big leaves had turned dark green. I had gloves to protect my hands, but since I wore a short-sleeved dress, the nettles touched my arms and legs when I got too close, giving me huge, itchy red blisters that burned. "Oma, why do they itch and burn like fire? I hate them!"

"They have tiny, short, almost invisible hairs on their leaves and along their edges. That is what causes the blisters, burning, and itching when they touch you. That's why they're called fire nettle, because they burn like fire on the skin."

I hated picking them, but Oma, always trying to find something good in everything, said, "Don't worry; they're good for rheumatism."

So what's rheumatism? With no gloves or arm protection Oma reached right in the middle of the patch to pick them. It looked so easy. Watching Oma, I could see that her arms were full of blisters, but she paid no attention to them. *Maybe she had what Oma called rheumatism.*

Oma always amazed me with her sayings for everything, and I wondered where she learned them all. I guessed that when you were an Oma, you knew a lot.

Always, every day, Oma wore black. Even her wool stockings were black, and over her ankle-length dress she tied a dark apron, taking it off only when she went shopping or visited family members. "Why do you always wear black, Oma?"

"I am a widow, and widows always wear black."

"But, Oma, your husband, my Opa, died a long time ago, didn't he?"

"Yes, he was killed in Russia in 1914 during World War I, only six months after he had joined the Service."

"So you never married again?"

"No, my children were small when he was killed and a widow, no matter how young, has to wear black and it's not proper for her to marry again." Oma took a deep breath, "let's stop talking and get back to our job. Once you start asking questions, you never stop; you just talk, talk, talk." I knew Oma was not being mean to me. She was right; I did ask a lot of questions, but I had to know because everything was new to me.

We picked a bunch of nettles that day, and when we got home, Oma washed and chopped them, then cooked them in water like spinach. After that, she added an unpeeled, grated raw potato to the nettle mixture to thicken it. That was our soup. It tasted bitter and grassy, and I expected it to sting my tongue and set my mouth on fire, but it didn't. It looked awful in the bowl, dark green, almost black like cow poop. I had a hard time swallowing it, rolling it around in my mouth, trying not to look at my bowl, trying to control my imagination. Looking at Oma, watching her eat it as if it were the best ever, trying to encourage me to do the same, I heard her gentle voice say, "You'd better eat. It's better than nothing!"

To my dismay Oma kept the leftover soup for the evening meal. I tried to wriggle out of it, claiming no hunger while my stomach was telling me otherwise, but Oma knew better. "I know it is not the best, but I will let you have a slice of bread along with the soup and maybe it won't taste so bad." When Oma reheated the soup, it was even more bitter. I was so glad I had a slice of bread to cover some of its bitterness. That soup was the worst I ever had to eat, and I was glad Oma didn't make it too often, even though the nettles grew all summer long.

But when Oma was lucky enough to get bones from the butcher without food stamps, she would boil them, and then, she'd add the vegetables and a grated raw potato. I watcher her as she chopped the short greens that grew close to the carrots like parsley and added them to the soup. "Why do you do that Oma?"

"Well, it gives the soup a little color and the eye wants to eat, too, don't you think?" I gave her a look of disbelief, and Oma smirked as if she had said something really funny. I also asked Oma why she never peeled the potato when she made soup. She said, "there are lots of vitamins underneath the skin and we needed them." That soup tasted so good! I didn't even mind the leftover soup.

On special days like Sundays, we counted ourselves lucky when we had mashed potatoes with gravy made from *Leberwurst*, liverwurst. Oma would buy a small piece of liverwurst at the butcher's with our stamps. Then, she'd make gravy with the liverwurst thinned out with water and a cold mixture of flour and water added to thicken it again. It was so good. We felt like kings. Other times, Oma boiled potatoes with their skins on. Then, while they were still hot, we peeled them and she put onions that were browned in her home made coffee over the boiled potatoes. My favorite dish was mashed potatoes with onions browned in bacon bits, then added to the mashed potatoes with buttermilk to drink. We only had that whenever bacon was available at the butcher's and we had the food stamps for it. The buttermilk, too, was from our milk stamps, but it was seldom available. With meals like that, I had no difficulty eating, making up for lost time, and Oma, smiling, would say, "I see you have no problem eating today, do you?" I just nodded in agreement as I was busy eating.

When Mutti and the family planned to have a Sunday coffee get-together, they each contributed ingredients for a cake. It was Oma's job to prepare the dough and mine to take it to the baker for baking because our small stove had no baking space. It was a common practice, for as long as I can remember, for the baker to bake cakes for his customers. A couple days before our family get-together, Oma sent me to the baker to ask when it would be convenient for him to bake our cake. Most of the time, it was right after he got done with the baking of bread and *Broetchen*, rolls, because the oven was still hot enough to bake cakes for his customers. Oma made a pound cake and stuck a short flat wooden peg in the dough with our name on it. I paid the baker when I picked up the cake. Depending on his supply of flour, the baker did not bake daily, so people, adjusted their baking schedule accordingly, which was not a problem because people were not baking as much.

Mutti's job was to make the *Schlagsahne*, whipped cream, from a raw, peeled, and grated potato that she first cooked with water and a small amount of milk. Then, she let this rubbery, glassy looking mass cool; then everyone present, laughing and joking, helped with the beating of the Schlagsahne. It took about an hour, but after a while, still heavy, it turned sort of fluffy and white. It was kind of slimy, rubbery, and tasteless, but with a little sugar added, it still was a treat.

Coffee was a different matter. Since real coffee was not available, Oma got long dark kernels of wheat with our stamps, and dry-roasted the kernels in a frying pan. To cool them, she spread them out on a board, and, when they were dry, she put them in a tightly covered container. Oma ground the kernels with the *Kaffeemuehle, the* coffee mill, a small square wooden box that had an opening on top for the kernels to be poured into. Then she turned the handle on top and the ground kernels were caught in the little drawer below.

I asked Oma if I could do the grinding and she agreed, but not before she gave me instructions. "Sit down and put the coffee mill between your knees with its drawer against your leg so it can't fall out. With one hand, hold the mill, and with the other turn the crank." It was one of my favorite things to do, so I always asked if I could work the mill for her. Oma always had a metal pot with leftover home-made wheat coffee standing on the back of the stove to be used when she needed some for cooking or frying. It added "a little flavor to the food," another of her favorite sayings.

Although food was in short supply and everyone was scrounging for it, Mutti and everyone else had fun whenever they got together at our place. It was mostly our family: Onkel Heinz, his wife Tante Hilde, their son Reiner, Tante Elfriede, her husband Onkel Richard, their daughter Uschi (Ursula), Oma, my sister Christa if she was not out with her friends, and me. With everyone sitting around the table, set with the china that didn't belong to us, laughter filled our living room, and for a short time all problems were forgotten. It was a lively, cheerful, happy time. Everyone enjoyed gathering around Mutti, forgetting the misery, the daily fight for survival, being oppressed—just living in the moment.

I enjoyed watching Mutti. She was filled with laughter. Sometimes she'd laugh so hard tears ran down her cheeks. Soon her free, happy spirit was sending out its rays, touching me with her zest for life. My own personality started to appear as if it had been sleeping like Cinderella, with Mutti the good fairy awakening me with her kiss of happiness.

She'd say, "Laugh a little; have fun. You can't bring your father back. No one can. He wouldn't want you to be sad. Love him and think of him, but try to cheer up. Living is great if you just allow it." It was not easy for me to change. But thanks to Mutti's and Oma's love, their care and encouragement, I began a young life filled with singing, laughter, and fun. Yes, what had happened, were pages of the past, closed chapters. Ahead of me were new chapters in the book of life. Never did I forget Vati, but the spring of 1946 was a fresh beginning for me.

Although many schools reopened in May of 1946, some were still closed used to house returning refugees. I had to go to school for only two or three hours a day, one week in the morning and the following week in the afternoon. Books were so scarce that we shared, one book for two students. All our work was done in school, leaving the schoolbooks for other classes to use. Although it was almost time for summer vacation, the schools were opened to get us kids to think again and to get us used to the routine of going to school.

After Oma had a discussion with the school principal, they decided because I had missed the last six months of fourth grade in 1945 and all of fifth, I was to repeat fifth grade. I'd gone to school only here and there while fleeing, and schools had been closed because of bombings and because teachers, too, were fleeing with their families. Even when I'd returned to Mutti, I'd been sick and the schools in Goerlitz had been used for housing refugees. Lots of children had the same problem. I knew I was not in the right grade, but Oma and the school principal made that decision, and I never questioned Oma about it but went back to fifth grade.

Mutti, totally recovered from typhoid, went back to work as a nurse, so Oma took care of my sister and me. I noticed that when Mutti left for work, she didn't come home for quite a while, and I missed her. One day as Oma and I were sitting in the back yard underneath the old cherry tree that protected us from the hot summer sun, I asked Oma questions. Oma had a basket filled with clothes, mainly socks for darning. Next to her was a wooden bench where she had her scissors and yarn spread out. I watched Oma pulling the needle with the heavy yarn in, out, and over, skillfully filling the hole in the sock so that it looked like a basket weave. "Someday you need to learn how to do this so you can darn your family's socks." Oma talked without stopping the in, out, and over movement of her deft hands and the threaded needle.

"I know, Oma. I already kind of know how," I said, not wanting to think of the former Mutti and the way she'd tried to teach me. Putting her out of my mind, I turned to Oma, "Can I ask you a question?"

Stopping her darning, she looked at me and laughed. "When is there a time that you don't have a question? What is it you want to know?"

"Oma, I like being with you, but why is Mutti always gone for such a long time? She never comes home in the evening."

"Well, your mother works on a transport train with other nurses and doctors to escort after-war refugees, deported by the Polish government into East Germany."

"I know we're refugees, but what are after-war refugees?

"I'll try to explain it to you. Some Germans didn't flee from the approaching Russian Army. They stayed home, believing they were safe on their land—hoping to protect their farms and homes from the Russian Army. Then, after the war ended and Russia gave Poland that land, those people were left at the mercy of the Polish government. Now the Polish government is throwing out all Germans who lived in the provinces known as *Nieder-Schlesien, Ober-Schlesien, Pommern and Preussen*—all German territories east of the Oder-Neisse Rivers. Because the war is over, those Germans who are being evacuated are called the after-war refugees."

"Why did Russia give Poland part of Germany?"

"We talked about that before. Remember?"

"Ja, I know. But why did Russia do that?"

Oma shook her head. "I really don't know. The rumor is that in 1945 when Russia was given control of all of eastern Germany all the way to the borders of Poland, Russia and Poland did a land trade. After that trade, Russia and Poland declared the Oder-Neisse Rivers, as their borderline, closed it, and placed it under strict observation from both sides. Because we Germans had lost the war, we had no say so in the matter."

"But, why did they close the border?"

"Well, as I said before, Poland does not want any Germans to cross the border into their newly acquired German territory. You might say, with Polish guards on their side of the rivers and Russian guards on this side, the Pole's keep us out and the Russian's keep us in. After that Stalin . . . ."

"Oma, who is Stalin?"

"He is Russia's leader."

"Like we had Hitler?"

"Yes, Stalin is a dictator, just as Hitler was. Stalin ordered all the borders around East Germany closed and guarded. To the west is West Germany, to the south is Czechoslovakia, to the east is Poland, and to the north is the Baltic Sea. Those borders lock in all of us living in East Germany on all four sides, leaving us nowhere to go. Russia's leader Stalin and his communist regime is controlling us now, isolating us from the rest of the world."

"Why is Russia's Stalin doing that, Oma?"

"They're the . . . ."

"I know, Oma. They're the winners of the war."

"Do you want me to finish telling you the rest?"

"Hmm, hmm," I nodded.

"Then, stop interrupting! So where were we? Oh, ja, the Polish in control are forcing every German citizen out. The homes, farms, and lands once belonging to the Germans became the property of the Polish government."

"Can they do that?"

"Yes, they can. They can do whatever they want. It's their land now. So, to answer your first question, your mother is working with doctors and other nurses transporting these after-war refugees, relocating them elsewhere, either in East Germany or in West Germany. That is why she is not home every night. And, now, it's best not to talk about it anymore."

But I had one more question. "Does that mean Liegnitz and the house I lived in with Vati and uhhh, you know, the fat one, does all that belong to the Polish? The toys Vati made for me, everything is theirs, not mine anymore? Polish kids are playing with my baby buggy and the baby doll made from porcelain? All my toys are theirs?"

"Yes, it's all theirs. No more questions. You tired me out, and it's all that I can safely tell you." Oma returned to her darning.

I had another question, but Oma shook her head, stopping me before it came out of my mouth. *What did she mean by "Safely?"*

Oma went back to her socks and mending, leaving me to think about what she'd just told me. In my mind I saw my doll buggy with the baby doll in it, all covered with the matching pillow and cover left in the dining room in the corner right behind the door; the wooden stroller Vati had made me; the dollhouse Vati had made for me for Christmas, covered up on top of the hutch in the dining room; the big box sitting next to Vati's work bench with all kinds of wooden toys, every one made for me by Vati. *All gone? Not mine any more?* I had never thought that far back because too many other things had taken place, like fleeing, Vati's death, my life after his death, my return to Mutti and Oma, getting to know the whole family—all that had kept my mind busy.

But now it all came back to me. *I have a home on the other side, too! I thought when we left Liegnitz on that icy-cold day, fleeing from the invading Russian Army, that when my stepmother locked our front door that everything would be waiting for us, that the door would still be locked and no one would have gone in. But that's not so!! That's why Vati told my stepmother not to bother to lock the door; it would only be broken down or kicked in when the Russians got there.*

I thought about the farm house where Vati and my stepmother had spent the night in and other houses I had seen in Pfaffendorf where the owners had fled; everything had been smashed; nothing had been in one piece; their poop had been in the bathtubs; feathers had been everywhere because they'd sliced the bedding open; even windows and doors had been ripped out. *Is that what's happened to my toys? The dollhouse, destroyed; the buggy and doll, destroyed; the stroller, destroyed; everything I loved, destroyed! And what about Kohlfurt? It's on the other side, too. That's where my stepmother purposely left Roswitha and Fritz at her parents' house. Are they destroyed, too?*

"Why are you so quiet all of a sudden?" Oma's voice brought me back to the yard and the cherry tree.

"I was thinking about my toys in Liegnitz and my doll Roswitha and Fritz, my Teddy. They're all lost."

"You have to forget about that, and be happy and thankful we're still alive and you're back with us. Although you're sad about losing those things you cherished, remember they're only material things."

"I know, Oma, but I can't help but miss them," I answered as tears welled in my eyes.

"You'll be fine. As time goes by, it will become easier to think about losses without the pain." Oma put her arm around me and gave me a squeeze as if to say, "I know how you feel."

"I feel so sad at times, Oma. So much has happened. But one thing will never become easier as time goes by—the loss of Vati."

"That is a real loss, one you will never forget. Neither will we. Thinking about it will become easier for you, but you'll never forget. He was a fine man, and we loved him, too. He never had the chance to set things right between himself and your mother, and that is sad."

When Mutti did get home and then only for a very short time, she had a lot to say about what the refugees were saying on the train. I was sitting at the pult doodling and listening to Mutti and Oma sitting around the table talking in whispers. "People coming from the other side," Mutti said, "were given no time at all, only thirty minutes, to gather a few belongings, leaving only with what they could carry. No more than *Zwanzig Pfund*, about 22 pounds. Guarded by the Polish militia, they had to gather in their town centers to be brought in cattle cars under the worst conditions to train stations closest to an East German city along the Russian border of East

Germany. From there, they had to walk into the Russian sector of East Germany.

In Goerlitz, the after war refugees had to cross over the only bridge there was, one inside the Russian perimeter and crudely reconstructed after the war.

Then, these refugees—families, young and old—carrying their meager belongings were immediately loaded into trucks guarded by Russian soldiers and driven to the same camp you, Christa, and Gisela once stayed in. No one is allowed near the camp to look for a familiar face among the refugees although many people are still frantically hoping and searching for family members or for any knowledge of their whereabouts."

I could see Oma shaking her head, saying, "How sad," or, "Those poor people."

Nodding her head, Mutti continued. "These people were given three choices: stay in the cities where they had crossed over, stay some-where in the Russian sector of East Germany or go on to West Germany. A few of the people who crossed over in Goerlitz decided to stay here. All others were put on trains in Goerlitz to be relocated to other cities in East Germany or further on to West Germany. But the ones that chose West Germany, they made the smartest choice." Now I knew why Mutti sometimes was gone for weeks. These were long trips. As a nurse, she was escorting these people to whatever destination they had chosen.

Whenever Mutti returned from one of her trips, I would hear her tell more stories to Oma or her sister and brother. They always talked in low voices so they could not be heard outside our rooms. Pretending to read, I'd listen to Mutti saying, "The trains have to move slowly, passing through damaged and bombed-out train stations, causing long delays, because only one track is repaired and usable."

That's why doctors and nurses are needed to care for the after-war refugees, I thought.

"Trains," Mutti continued, "stopped at designated train stations where the refugees were fed hot soup by the Red Cross. Also, additional needed supplies, like medicine and food, had to be replenished but that didn't take long because there was not much to be had. Some people, including entire families, had to be taken off the train because they were ill and could not go on. Others, mainly the very old, babies, and young children had died on the train from starvation on the long journey from Poland, because they were given so little food or none at all." I heard Oma say over and over, "Oh, those poor, poor people."

Mutti nodded her head in agreement. "Others died because they were unable to cope with the pain of being forced to leave their life's work, their homeland passed from generation to generation being confiscated by the Polish government. They were treated worse than animals, and women of all ages were misused. Their husbands, even the old, were forced into labor camps and shot if they didn't cooperate. It is heartbreaking to see these people broken, their faces blank, with no will to live or die."

Mutti explained that the trains were not allowed to leave the Russian sector. To insure they did not, the railroad tracks were taken up, then, blocked with big boulders. Russian guards boarded the trains at the last stop in East Germany to insure that no one was crossing the border other than those refugees wanting to go to West Germany. When the trains stopped at the end of its tracks, the refugees then walked under the watchful eyes of Russian soldiers across the border into West Germany where they received food and were loaded onto a waiting train that carried them further into West Germany. Mutti told us there were many delays because the trains had to stop or be moved to a sidetrack so trains transporting Russian troops could pass. It took days for the refugee trains to get to the border and back due to damages from the war. She added that it would take many months to relocate these people because they're coming by the thousands, all stripped of their dignity, ripped from their homes, land, and belongings.

Several days later when we were alone, I asked Oma. "Why are Mutti and everyone else whispering when she talks about the people on the train?"

Oma, straightened to her full height, pointed her index finger at me, and warned me, "Whatever you heard or will hear within these walls, you will not repeat to no one, not anyone. I'll tell you again! Do not repeat what you hear; I want you to forget it. Do you hear me?"

Oma really scared me. She had never pointed her finger at me before and spoken that sternly to me. She reminded me of someone I didn't want to think of. Oma must have seen my fear because she continued in a more gentle voice. "Your mother is not allowed to talk of what she sees or hears on those train trips with the refugees. She will be in danger if it is discovered that she is repeating what she has been told. No one working on those trains is allowed to talk about it. They could arrest her and take her to a work camp in Russia, or even worse, to a work camp in Siberia. Now, you don't want that to happen, do you? And your mother is not the only one; our whole family would be in trouble, too."

I remembered the time when Vati had been standing by that Russian who'd pointed and told him to go behind the fence with all the other men. I'd been so scared. Oma's words scared me all over again. In my mind I saw Mutti behind that fence, knowing that it was my fault because I had carelessly talked and not listened to Oma. "I promise, Oma! I will never, never tell! I promise!"

"I believe you. Just remember your promise and what I said." After that, whenever grownups started to whisper, I always disappeared, not wanting to hear and accidentally let slip something that could put Mutti and all of us in danger.

When Mutti returned, she sometimes brought real chocolate back and a small amount of real coffee beans for Oma. Those things she saved. Oma would brew only a cup at a time, grinding the beans herself, savoring the smell of the freshly ground coffee beans. After the first brew, she'd cook the grounds several times over. "Oma, why do you cook the coffee grounds over and over," I asked.

"To get the entire flavor, because after just one brewing there is still some good left in the coffee ground." Then, when she was done, she put the grounds in the flowerbox outside her window, filled with blooming geraniums. Saying, "The coffee grounds are good for the flowers. They keep the dirt moist."

I ate the chocolate Mutti had smuggled in from West Germany in small bites, sharing it with Oma though she mostly declined, telling me to eat it because I needed it for nourishment so I would grow. I made it last for a long time and kept it in my pult with all my other possessions. Real coffee or chocolate could not be bought in stores because there was none anywhere. Mutti said that in the West sector of Germany, people had all kinds of food to eat; only we in the East sector had none.

When Oma was brewing a cup of that smuggled-in good coffee, the aroma went through the whole house. She said, "Brewing the coffee is risky because the people working on the train are forbidden to accept gifts or buy things from the people in the West."

Everyone in the house knew where it had come from. No one said a word because everyone scrambled for food one-way or the other.

There was a single attractive lady about Mutti's age who lived on the bottom floor of the house and dressed in the best clothes with her blonde hair combed to perfection. She never talked to anyone in the house. It seemed as though she didn't care. She always brewed the good smelling coffee, and when she cooked her dinner in the kitchen she shared with the couple living across the hall from her, the aroma of her cooking engulfed the whole house. My stomach growling, I sat on the steps on the second landing, taking in the wonderful smell, wishing to have some of that good food, too. When she hung out her undergarments, they were of the finest and laciest I had ever seen. I could not help but marvel at them. Sometimes she was gone for a while, and, when she returned, the good smell and the washing of her lingerie started all over again. I heard Oma and Mutti talking in low voices about her possibly dealing in the black market and smuggling goods. Mutti said she wouldn't mind doing that, too, because it would give us food to eat, but with her luck she would get caught and shot for sure.

Black market! What's that? Does it mean to shop at night? Is that why it's so dangerous? I knew there was a strictly enforced curfew. No one was allowed out on the street after eleven in the evening, except those who carried a pass. I wanted to ask Oma, but I knew she would not tell me. She'd just say, "That is nothing for you to know, and it is best you forget it."

So I did, but every time I saw the lady I could not help but wonder why she had all that good smelling food and wonderful clothes while we didn't. Whatever this Fraeulein did, she was never found out while she lived in the same house with us.

Mutti was only home until the next train was ready to leave Goerlitz. She traveled back and forth between the eastern and western borders, escorting transport after transport of Germans who kept coming and coming, a never ending throng of after-war refugees, channeled through Goerlitz and other cities along the border.

Oma was pretty strict when Mutti was gone, so I enjoyed my freedom when Mutti was home. When Oma asked Mutti, "Should Gisela be allowed too do that?" Mutti always answered, "Oh, let her be. She has had enough sorrow and restrictions in her short life. Let her have some freedom. She is not going to do anything bad." And I never did; I never wanted to disappoint Mutti because she trusted me, and I wanted Oma to know she could trust me, too.

But when Mutti was not home, Oma was in charge and she restricted me although she was not mean. Oma believed there were certain things a girl should not do, like being in front of the house on the street just before dark visiting with the neighborhood kids. That was not seemly for a girl. Sometimes I would complain to Mutti when she was home, but she just told me, "Oma is from the old school. That is how she raised my sister, my two brothers, and me and that is what she is doing with you. So just do as she asks. She is responsible for you when I'm not here, and she wants to keep you safe even if you don't agree with her way of doing it." So Oma continued in her ways, and I followed.

When I was not allowed out on the street in the evening, I spent lots of time in the back yard, and a nice yard it was. To me it was like a park at our back door. Out that door and on its right, a wing was attached to the house where the *Waschkueche,* a laundry room was located. It was a large square room with painted white walls, a window, washtubs, and scrub boards. The smooth concrete floor sloped toward the center where the drain was. In one corner was the wash kettle, enclosed with red bricks, making it look like a big square block. A cast iron door in front covered the firing hole near the floor. The wash kitchen was used only for washing and was always locked to keep it clean. A little ways across from there was the garbage bin, also made of red brick and covered with a heavy metal plate—reminding me of the one my suitcase had been flung into. The immediate surrounding area was covered in red bricks, too.

Then came the yard; on the right was a big old cherry tree; along the neighboring high red brick wall were individual oblong beds for planting. Centered toward the back was a wooden garden house with an open front and wood flooring. Its sidewalls were half high and open, like big windows with a floor to ceiling back wall. A grapevine's big green leaves grew all around it, covering the roof, hanging over the sides—looking like the castle of Sleeping Beauty. Attached on one side of the garden house was a trellis as high and as long as the garden house, also covered with grapevine, it tendrils thick and strong twining around the trellis.

Across from the garden house and the trellis was a huge hedge of tiny, sweet-smelling pink roses. They reached across to the trellis, making an arch over the walkway, enhancing the fairy tale look of the garden house in my imagination. Beyond the garden house and the hedge of roses stood a high wooden fence that bordered the street. Hedges of gooseberry and currants grew along the fence with more beds for planting in front of it. In the center of the yard was a round lawn encircled by the walkway.

To me it was a beautiful garden, and I spent lots of time in it. Standing at the back door, I could see the whole yard. In my mind I saw the Pastor who had lived here, dressed in his long black robe, an open Bible in his hands, walking around and around, past the garden house, then under the arch of roses, past the planting beds with the fence where the berry hedges grew, studying for his next sermon.

Everyone in the house took a weekly turn to clean that area, except for the single Fraeulein and the young couple; neither had children and made very little use of the yard. The young husband who had lost his leg in the war never came outside or in the yard and had no conversation with anyone in the house. Siegfried and I, and sometimes our friends, used the yard the most, so we had to clean it. Oma made sure of that.

The planting beds in the yard were divided among the occupants of the house. Except for the Fraeulein and the young couple, they declined. Oma, of course, planted. On a spring Saturday morning we got up early and went to the farmers' market at the *Elizabeth Platz*, covered with old oak trees and right in front of my school. Oma bought bedding plants, like carrots, butter lettuce, beans, peas, and other vegetables. But she also put a few flowers in between the vegetables. I think she liked asters of all colors the most. And when they bloomed she'd carefully cut a few, here and there, for her table, making sure not to disturb the rest of the flowers and the vegetable.

Oma did the planting and I was her helper. With instruction from her, I carefully watered the newly planted seedlings. Taking the watering can, Oma showed me how to water, saying, "Don't water too much or you'll wash the seedling right back out of the ground." As she was watering, she continued, "You make a small circle around the plant, like so, water gently, and not on top of the plant or it will fall over because it has not rooted yet."

Eagerly I took the watering can from Oma, saying, "Oma, I know how to do that. Watch me!" And out of the ground came the seedling!

"Now, do you see what I mean?" Putting the seedling back in the ground, she reminded me once again, "Be careful and while watering, bend down a little."

"I will, Oma."

Oma never said that I was too dumb or too stupid to do anything, and I was so glad. She just continued planting her seedlings, and I was right behind her, watering carefully. As the summer went on, I enjoyed watching the seedlings grow into vegetables and helped Oma with the watering. I would carry the water, bucket by bucket, to Oma, refilling her watering can so she could continue watering.

Slowly I got to know some of the neighborhood children. There was Siegfried, the son of Frau Schmitt. They lived in the room next to us, the room where Mutti had moved the china buffet in front of the door to muffle the sounds. Siegfried was skinny, with red hair and freckles.

In school I became friends with a girl whose name was also Gisela. She lived on the other side of the street, a little further down from me. The house that was attached to hers had been hit by a bomb and was all crumpled in, so part of her stairway was exposed from the explosion, but the apartment was livable. She was not in my class, but we walked to school together. Every morning she stood on the other side of the street in front of my house and hollered, "Giii-se-laaa, Giii-se-laaa, are you ready?" Oma just hated it. "Why can't she just wait until you come down? Does she have to holler so that the whole neighborhood can hear her?"

Other times she'd call to see if I could come down to play. I always hurried to the window, motioning with my finger on my lips, stopping her from hollering, signing that I'd be right down. I liked her a lot and she was a nice girl, but Oma didn't care for her.

Around the corner from us lived Jochen and his younger sister Regina. The kids from down the street were mainly boys with another Siegfried. Some of them knew each other from school. The second Siegfried was blonde and skinny, but I guess we all were skinny. He had buckteeth. The kids claimed that he liked me. He'd smile at me or stand right next to me every opportunity he had, and that embarrassed me because when he was not around, the kids would tease me, saying, *"Wo ist Dein Freund heute?* Where is your boyfriend today?* That is when I would leave and go in the back yard or upstairs. Siegfried, the one with the red hair, would come after me, "Oh, come on. We're only teasing you. Come back out."

Gisela, Regina, Inge, and I were the only girls. The place Inge lived was partially bombed out, too, and bordered our back yard, right behind the garden house. Inge was loud and forward, and Oma did not approve of her at all, much less the rest of the kids. I do think Gisela was in better graces with Oma than Inge. We were all around eleven and twelve, and Regina was the youngest. In the daytime Oma allowed me to be in front of the house, but not after dinner. But sometimes when I begged just right, she would allow me to be in front of the house where she could see me at all times. We'd be sitting on the doorsteps talking and laughing, and Oma would look down from the window to check on me and to quiet us down. The kids would whisper to me, "Your *Grossmutter,* your grandmother, is watching us!" They were a little leery of her because Oma looked real stern. They always greeted her with respect, but Oma just gave a kind of grumble.

"Why do you do that, Oma?" I asked her.

Laughingly she replied. "That's to keep your friends in line."

Helping Oma on her washday was a new experience for me. First, a week before washday Oma signed up on the roster so our tenant knew that she was going to use the Waschkueche. Then, Oma wrote an excuse to my teacher, saying I was needed at home to help on washday—common practice then.

When washday morning came, Oma got me up to my usual whining, "Oma, it's too early. I'm still tired!" But Oma, her hair combed and braided in a bun, dressed in her dark clothes with a big apron over them paid no attention to me. "Just roll out of bed, wash your face in cold water, and you'll wake up." Seeing that I would get no sympathy and Oma was not falling for my whining, I got up, washed my face, and brushed my teeth. "Are you awake now?" Oma asked while I ate breakfast, a thick soup made of flour and water with a little milk poured over the top. "The warm soup will give you a good start. We have a long workday ahead of us, so I am making a sandwich for our mid-morning break." I guess she could see by the look on my face that I was not too eager to eat a sandwich made with her famous mushy spread. "It's fresh. I just made it yesterday. The sandwiches will taste good when we get hungry and, believe me, you and I will be hungry a little later on." We had no refrigeration, so Oma kept all our food on the shelves Mutti had made for food storage. Oma's spread was made with no oil or butter, only coffee from roasted wheat kernels to brown the onions with, then, water, flour, and salt. There must not have been a danger of getting sick from it because we never did. For all the other foods, Oma always claimed, "As long as you bring the food to a boil, it will kill everything that could make you sick." Exactly what she meant by that, I didn't know. I just believed Oma, for she was the grown up who knew, not me.

Our big wash was done every three months with small washes in between. The day before a big washday, Oma cooked a big pot of soup from a grated raw potato and a few carrots, including the tops for color. At the same time, she laid sheets and towels on the lawn in the back yard in the sun to bleach. With Oma's luck, the sun was always shining. When I got home from school, I had to keep them wet with the watering can, left sitting on the lawn, ready for me to use. Oma told me, "I spread the wash out on the lawn, and I want you to keep it wet, practically soaked, with the watering can, so don't forget to water it often. I don't want the wash to dry out."

I asked Oma, "Why do you do that?"

"The sun will bleach out all stains and the wash will get bright and white."

"But why water everything?"

"They have to stay wet because if they dry they'll turn yellow from the sun. It is your job not to let them get dry, so stay in the back yard, use the watering can often, and keep them soaking wet."

I busied myself to do what Oma had asked me to do. At the beginning it was fun, but after a while I got bored because I was unable to visit with the kids in front of the house. Soon I forgot the watering because I was playing with the tennis ball I had gotten from Onkel Heinz, using the outside wall of the laundry room as a backboard. It was another of my favorite things to do, a game, and a challenge to see how far I could get before making a mistake or dropping the ball and having to start all over again. Oma called to me from a small balcony that overlooked the back yard, "Gisela, have you checked the wash on the lawn? It looks pretty dry from up here!" Oma was right. I had forgotten all about the wash, so I hurried to get the watering can.

Early the next morning, before Oma got me up, she had built the fire under the wash kettle. The wash that had lain on the lawn the day before had been soaking overnight in soapy water in the tubs in the laundry room. I helped Oma wring out the sheets from the soaking water, Oma on one end of the sheets and I on the opposite end, twisting in different directions, making the sheets into thick twisted ropes. "Hang on and twist as hard as you can," she told me.

"I'm hanging on," I told her. And I was because I wanted her to know that I could do it. Then, she put the sheets in the kettle already filled with clean water, added the soap, and brought them all to a boil as she kept stoking the fire. "Do you want to sit on the bricked rim of the kettle and stir the sheets around?" Oma asked me. Looking at the round kettle lined in white enamel with the sheets in it, I could see the kettle was enclosed with a wide brick rim, wide enough to sit on it.

"Do what?" I looked at Oma in disbelief. "Stir the sheets? Why?" I was sure Oma was kidding, but she was not.

"You sure have lots of why's and what for's for such a little person," she said, starting to stir the sheets in the kettle with a wooden paddle. "The sheets need to be move around so they doesn't turn brown at the bottom of the kettle where all the heat is. What's on top also needs to be pushed down so it, too, gets a hot bath."

It didn't make much sense to me, but I sat on the warm brick rim and moved the sheets around with a big flat wooden paddle, like the ones used on small boats.

"Now watch what you're doing so you don't fall in," she warned me. "The water is boiling hot."

"I'm fine, Oma. I'll be careful." Sometimes Oma added cold water to the kettle to slow down the intense boiling, making bubbles, sending them floating up in the air in brilliant colors, like beautiful glass marbles. I tried to burst them, but Oma told me not to do that because I could loose my balance, fall in and get badly burned.

Then Oma took the big yellow rubber apron from a hook on the wall, put it on, and tied it in front of her. It totally covered her front, from above her chest almost down to her feet. "That sure is a big apron, Oma!"

"*Ja*, it's big; it's supposed to be big. It keeps me dry while I scrub the wash in the tub." When Oma thought the sheets had boiled enough, she took the paddle and pulled each sheet out of the hot bath. She told me to stay out of the way because the sheets were dripping with hot water, splattering all over the floor, the steam engulfing her. Oma transferred them to an oval tub sitting on a wooden bench. In the tub she had a scrub board, a big glassy looking bar of soap, and a scrub brush.

"Oma, that soap you're using smells awful."

"That soap is for washing clothes only, not for your face or bathing. We're lucky even to have soap to wash with." Up to her elbows in the water, she scrubbed, then soaped, then scrubbed again, up and down over the metal board's waves, pushing and pulling the sheets in and out of the soapy water. Then, she used more of that stinky soap, more hot water from the kettle, and plunged the sheets into the water while pressing them hard on the scrubbing board until she was satisfied. I watched Oma, her face glistened with tiny pearls of perspiration as the steam rose from the tub. She was so intense, so forceful that I almost felt sorry for those sheets.

Next, she wrung each sheet out, twisting it slowly, the sheet winding around her arm like a snake. "I can help you do that, Oma!"

"No, better not; the water is hot and it will burn your hands."

"But your hands are in the water."

"Yes, mine are old and tough and used to hot water, not like your tender young hands." After that she put the sheets into another tub, a larger oblong aluminum tub sitting on the floor, already filled with cold water from a hose attached to the faucet above the tub for rinsing. With the hose in the tub, Oma turned on the water to let it run slowly. Turning toward me, she said, "Now you can help again. Use the paddle and swish the wash around, letting the water run over the top into the drain at the center of the floor." That was the most fun of the whole washday. I took off my wooden sandals and because I wore a dress, Oma used a big safety pin and pinned the back of my skirt on to the front of my dress, making my dress look like large blousy bloomers. I swished, I splattered, my elbows deep in the water, pulling the sheets up as far as I could, then plunging them down again with the water running over the edge of the tub, and my feet disappearing in the run off. I felt so important. I was able to wash, too, just like Oma. "Looks like you're having fun," Oma said.

"*Oh, ja*, Oma, this is lots of fun!" I didn't stop to look at Oma.

"I can see that, but move over. We have to get the sheets out so we can put them on the line in the sun to dry." Oma did more rinsing. Then, she and I wrung out the sheets with her on one end and me on the other, twisting in opposite directions, and together we hung them on the line. I held the sheets so they didn't touch the ground and handed Oma *die Waescheklammern*, the clothespins to pin the sheets on the line.

Then, it was the towels turn. They had also soaked overnight and now needed to be cooked in the kettle. Oma told me to go upstairs and get our sandwiches and the cold coffee. We ate outside on the bench next to the laundry room while the towels were heating up, Oma keeping a close eye on them. The sandwich tasted pretty good because we were hungry. Then, I sat on the rim and kept the towels moving in the kettle, and when the time came, I got to swish them around in the tub. By the time noon came, Oma had washed the sheets, towels, and all the white items. They were now hanging on the clothes line we'd strung from post to post: the sheets with the sheets, the towels with the towels, the tablecloths with the tablecloths, and the undergarments with the undergarments, all in order, hanging in the nice warm sunshine. All the time Oma had been washing, I hadn't asked her any questions. She was humming or even whistling a tune or two.

"Oma, do you always sing and whistle a lot?"

"*Ja*, I do. Singing makes me happy. It is good for the well being of mind and body. It also makes the job go faster. You should try it sometime."

I decided to hum along with her. I didn't know what she was humming or whistling so I had to pay close attention. I wanted to learn what Oma was singing, but this was not the time to ask her to teach me.

The fire had died down and gave just enough warmth to keep the colored clothes soaking in warm water. That is when Oma and I had our

Mittagessen, noon dinner, with the soup I'd already heated, ready for us to eat. I was hungry and the soup tasted good. Oma even cut an extra slice of rationed bread for me. Surprised for the bread, I heard her say, "You've earned it, you worked hard, and we're not done yet." Although the bread was dry, it tasted so good.

I loved Oma more every day. Never was there a mean or bad word from her to me. She was strict and demanded respect, but she was also a very loving grandmother. Sometimes I was not too happy about her restrictions, but I gave her no sass because I knew it wouldn't do me any good. I had never been allowed to talk back to the former Mutti, so it was not part of my behavior.

Oma set the soup pot in the back of the stove for the evening meal, with me giving it a disgusted look—I hated leftover food. Then, while I did the dishes, Oma took a rather loud short nap. When Oma got up, we returned to the washhouse to finish the washing. After we had hung all the wash on the line, then it was time to clean the washhouse. Oma rinsed the tubs, cleaned out the fire hole with the hand broom, scrubbed and rinsed the floor so it was ready for the next tenant. For me washday had been fun.

When the sheets were dry, Oma called, "Gisela, come help me stretch the sheets back into shape and pull some of the wrinkles out!"

"But, I don't know how!"

"There is no better time than the present to learn. Come here, watch and follow me!" Oma took a corner of the sheet in each of her hands, and I did the same. "Now, you gather the sheet until your hands meet, like so!" The sheet looked like a big fat rope again, only not twisted. "Now hang on and pull as hard as you can, while I do the same!" I had to laugh! It felt like playing a game of tug of war with Oma. Sometimes Oma pulled so hard that the ends of the sheet slipped right out of my hands while I was laughing and Oma was grinning, saying, "You've got to hang on tight!" To put the towels back into their shape again, Oma and I pulled them catty corner. When we had all the clothes off the line and the line hung back in the washhouse, I helped Oma carry the full wash basket upstairs where she sorted it out. Sheets, pillowcases, towels, and tablecloths went in one pile, and all the rest in another.

"Why do you doing that, Oma?"

"What?" she asked.

"Sort out the wash?"

"This stack needs mending and ironing and that stack," she said, pointing at the sheets and things, "you and I will take to the *Waeschemangel* tomorrow."

"The *Waeschemangel?* What's that?"

"A machine that presses all flat wash, like sheets and tablecloths and so on. But you'll see tomorrow. We have an appointment. You need to come straight home from school so you can help me carry the wash basket."

I was eager to go because I wanted to know just what that machine was, so I hurried home from school the next day. A clean apron over her dark dress, Oma and I carried the wash basket as we walked across the *Obermarkt*, past the *Reichenbacher Turm,* past the *Stadttheater,* the city opera house, up *Luisenstrasse,* and on to the *Karl Liebknecht Strasse.* There, on the corner of the *Leipziger Strasse,* was the store with the Waeschemangel. And soon I had the answer.

Oma went into the small grocery store to tell the owner that she was here. They gave her a key to a clean white-walled room in a daylight basement where the Waeschemangel stood. Never had I seen such a thing so massive and scary. It was sitting against the back wall of the small room. It was big, wide, oblong, squatty, made of light colored wood and polished to a sleek shine. It took up the whole back wall and ran almost to the ceiling, dominating half the room.

My eyes wide, I whispered to Oma, afraid that thing might hear me. "Aren't you scared of that thing? I am!"

"Oh, it is not going to hurt you. Nevertheless, it's heavy, made of oak and you can't be careless about it. You could lose an arm or hand if you reach in at the wrong time while it is working."

Across from the machine was a table of the same sleek polished wood as the Waeschemangel, all smooth and shiny. Resting on a pedestal was a wooden roll that looked like a rolling pin, as long is I was tall, also smooth and shiny. Underneath the table was an attached shelf that looked like a basket with white blankets in it. Oma and I set the basket on the bench next to the table. Then, she took one of the blankets, laid it on the table, set the pin on the blanket and rolled it once. Then, she took a sheet, folded it in half, laid it on the blanket, smoothed out any wrinkles, and then rolled that pin real tight inside the blanket and the sheet. She moved her hand back and forth over the sheet and the blanket to make sure the pin was rolled even, straight, and, most of all, tight with no wrinkles. With space left, she added another sheet, stopping just before she ran out of blanket.

As I watched, Oma used all of her strength, leaning into the table, her upper body leaning forward. With both arms and hands, she worked the sheets like rolling dough around a rolling pin. I hesitated to ask a question because I could see she was concentrating on what she was doing, but finally I just had to ask, "What are you doing Oma?"

"Just wait and see," she answered as she continued working, rolling the sheets with the blanket around the pin.

When Oma had finished rolling that pin, she went over to the Waeschemangel, took the crank located in it's middle and turned it. Oma had to work hard with that crank to get it moving. The upper part, a big box, the same size as the base of the Waeschemangel, started to move slowly over to the far side. When it got to a certain point, close to the opposite wall, it stopped, tipping the box slightly upward. With the box tilted, the gate in front of that side dropped down, and Oma reached in to take the empty pin out and replaced it with the already covered pin. Making sure it was straight, she snapped the gate back into place. Then, she rolled the new pin like the first one. Again she used the crank, making the box move to the opposite side, until it tilted and the gate on that side dropped down. Oma took the empty pin and replaced it with the rolled one, making sure that it, too, was straight. Then, she pulled the gate up, making sure it clicked into place, and pushed the red button in the center of the Waeschemangel.

My eyes grew big. I could not believe the hugeness, the heaviness of that thing as it started to moan and groan, not wanting to start but forced to move by an unseen power. It sat heavy on the pins, moving back and forth over the pins with our newly cleaned wash. As it moved, it unrolled the pin on one side, while the pin on the other side was rolled up. In the center and above the wooden box was a strong heavy black iron wheel with teeth. Powered by electricity, the wheel turned, and the toothed steel bar attached to the whole length of the box worked in unison with the wheel, making the box move back and forth, rolling and unrolling the pins, pressing our sheets, pillowcases, tablecloths, and towels while I watched in amazement. Finally, I could not wait any longer, I had to ask, "Oma, what is in that big box that makes it moan and groan so much?"

"It has rocks in it, so it is very heavy. As the box moves back and forth, rolling and unrolling the pins, the weight of the box filled with rocks presses the sheets and whatever else is rolled up in those blankets. You have to be careful not to put your hands underneath the box when it is in motion. You could lose them for good." Oma continued, "You also have to make sure when rolling the pins that they are rolled up tight and straight with no bulges." That sounded like a lot of work to me. Oma kept talking. "When the pins roll back and forth if there not tight and even, they will roll sideways, and that will cause a problem. Then, you have to stop and re-work the pins all over again. You can't have any clothes with buttons because they get crushed." Oma finished her explanation, and after several runs over the pins, the first gate automatically dropped open. Oma took out the rolled up pin and replaced it with another readied pin, then closed the gate with a snap.

Again she pushed the button, and the box rolled over the pin to the other side. The gate fell open with the box tilted upward looking like a big open mouth saying, "It's all right to reach in. I won't move." Oma replaced that pin, pushed the red button, and, with its moving sounds, the machine slowly started to move, rolling back and forth. While it was working, Oma unrolled the pin she had taken out from underneath. The sheets, just like magic had no wrinkles at all and looked so nice, like new. When Oma was all done with the wash, she put the empty pins under the box, closed the gates, and centered the box with the crank. The extra pin went back in its holder on the table. All our wash was back in the basket, nice and neat. With one last look around, making sure all was back in order, Oma turned off the light and locked the door. She returned the key and paid the owner fifty pfennigs for the use of the Waeschemangel. With the basket between us, we walked back home. "So, now you know how to wash clothes and how to work the Waeschemangel. When you're married, you'll know how to do that."

I knew washing clothes was not that bad, but I was sure I was never going near that "thing" alone. I didn't want Oma to know just how much it scared me, so I said with a conviction in my voice, "I'm not going to do that, Oma."

"And why not?"

"Because I will have people do that for me."

Oma only smiled and with a twinkle in her eyes, said, "Oh, is that so?" It made me wonder if Oma knew something that I didn't.

With Mutti gone for her job, my life revolved around Oma. I enjoyed spending time with her, being with her. She was not like the Oma in Kohlfurt, my stepmother's mother, who was skinny and mean. That Oma never talked to me in a nice way, so I didn't miss her at all. This Oma, my real Oma, was nice, and most of all, she loved me. I could feel it when she talked to me.

How sad I had been when Oma and other family members had come to Liegnitz to visit me, and my stepmother hadn't let them in. When I'd gone by train to Goerlitz for a visit, Oma had been at the train station in Goerlitz, wearing her blue hat and smiling at me. She still has that blue hat and wears it on Sundays or special occasions. Every time I see Oma wearing her blue hat I think of that day at the train station—a lot has happened since then.

I remembered Oma from when I was really little, when I lived with her before Vati took me away. Oma had played that mouse game with me in bed. It was a long time ago, but I remembered that. I loved her then and now, my warm and caring Oma.

Sitting in my favorite place, the stoop in Oma's room, watching her never-idle hands busy mending clothes and darning socks, I asked, "Oma would you tell me about the time when I was born, Vati, and why he took only me and not Christa?"

Oma looked up from her mending with a puzzled look, "what brought that on?"

"I was just thinking about when I lived with you and you played the mouse game with me and how afraid I was when Vati took me from you."

"Yes, that was a sad day for me too."

"Oma, tell me about it, all the way back to the beginning, please?"

Oma laid her mending in her lap. "Let's see! You were born here in Goerlitz in July of 1935—right into Hitler's war. Your father was born in Pfaffendorf, Kreis Lauban"

"I went to that Pfaffendorf with my stepmother once and saw the house where Vati was born and the tiny Pfaffendorfer Oma and the tall, burly Opa with his gravely voice, Vati's parents." Oma nodded. "Your mother was born in Nieder Schoenbrunn and that's were they got married. Your sister was also born in Nieder Schoenbrunn. Did your mother ever told you she was a twin?"

"No Oma. Is Tante Elfriede her twin?"

"No, Tante Elfriede is two years older. Your mother's twin was a boy. He weight six pounds and died right after he was born. Your mother weight two pounds and survived."

Resting my elbows on my knees my hands supporting my head, I listened eagerly to Oma's story.

"Back to you, at the time of your arrival, your parents lived in a three-story apartment building in the Zittauer Strasse where your father was not only the maintenance person for the apartment building but also a carpenter for a furniture manufacturer. One day, your mother, seven months pregnant with you, had to cut short your sister's play at the playground and hurry home because you had decided to arrive two months early."

"I was born too early?" I was mesmerized to hear about me.

"Yes, you couldn't wait. But your early birth was not unexpected because your mother had lost a baby boy in her six month of pregnancy two years before you were born."

My eyes got big. "I could've had a bigger brother besides my sister?" Then I got sad. I felt as if had known and lost at the same time.

Oma nodded again. "Yes, there was a baby brother before you. So on with the story you wanted to hear. Your father's *Skatabend*, a poker evening with his friends, was cancelled so he could take your sister to Tante Elfriede, because children are not allowed to be nearby when the stork is on his way. At the same time he also brought your sister a doll, customary with the arrival of new babies."

"Oma, what would he bring to a boy?"

"Maybe a car, a teddy bear or some kind of a boys toy."

"Let's move on. The midwife who delivered you told us . . . ."

"You were there too when I was born?"

"Of course I was. So, the midwife . . . ."

"Oma I met the midwife when I was with Mutti out shopping right after Mutti had gotten me."

"If you keep interrupting I'll never get done telling what you want to hear, so hush. So," Oma swallowed to clear her voice, "the midwife told us that you would be dead within two hours. Sadly and silently I agreed with her because you were a sorry sight to see. Your closed eyes had to be opened with drops. Your head was hanging. You looked like a little wet rag, and you cried and cried. You were so fragile we were afraid to pick you up. But we were not ready to let you die, most of all not your father. So he, your mother, and I took turns walking the floor, nearly day and night. Cuddling you was the only way to stop your crying.

At the beginning you couldn't eat and got vitamin shots to stay alive. Then, finally, little by little you began to settle down, and nursed in small amounts, but your crying continued. You were not a happy baby, because you were born so early. Then, after two months when you were stronger, you were baptized in the *Kreuz Kirche,* a Lutheran church not far from the apartment. You were a tiny baby but you had eight godparents, all family members, who attended the baptism."

For your baptism your mother had a very fashionable black baby buggy, but anyone looking in the buggy could hardly find you among the pillows. Before we went to the church your father had hid a bottle of cognac in the buggy for after your baptism. Your mother didn't want a bottle in that fashionable buggy at a baptism, and the bottle was bigger than you."

"You mean I was that tiny?"

"You were not far from it."

"Why did Vati do that?"

"Well, your father celebrated with the family right after the baptism. He had good reasons to celebrate. It was two months after your birth, and you were still alive. It's also customary that after a baptism and before the godparents bring the baby in the house, the father, wearing an apron, has to be in front of the house and serve the godparent's cognac or schnapps, toasting the baby's health and happiness. Should there be passersby, they too join in the toast."

Your crying and our holding you continued, but your daily shots lessened as you began to eat. When you cried, your sister would say, "Throw that boy in the garbage." We had to watch her when she came near you."

Is that the reason why my sister doesn't like me? She hated my crying and getting all the attention? Is that why she disliked our father?

"Then in 1938, when you were three, your parents divorced."

"Why, Oma?"

Oma shrugged her shoulders, "You're too young to hear all the details. Let's just say, a divorce is not easy to get, infidelity . . . ."

"Infidelity?"

"Yes, infidelity had to be proven. Your mother was unjustly accused of that because your father and his future wife swore in court that they were not guilty of infidelity."

"Why did they do that?"

"I don't know if you'll understand all that."

"Please Oma, I'm almost eleven. Please tell me."

Oma squinted her eyes and looked at me, as if she was thinking how best she could tell me. Then she continued, "We, our family, we like to think that that woman had your father so browbeaten, so controlled that before he knew it he was in so deep that he couldn't back out of marrying her. Also, because the woman was close to being a thirty-year-old maid and grossly overweight, she saw in your father her only chance to get married, and she wasn't going to turn him loose, but instead threatened him with perjury. He knew the mistake he had made, but it was too late. He couldn't back out because of perjury."

"Perjury?"

"It's perjury when you lie in court. People go to jail for it."

My mind was spinning. *So that's why my stepmother threatened Vati with jail. It had something to do with the court.*

"Your father also wanted custody of both of you girls, but your sister, then age seven, refused to go with him. She hated the woman and your father too, so only you were awarded to him. After the divorce and the court's custody decision, your mother left Goerlitz and no one knew where she was. That's when I took care of you and your sister."

"Why did she leave? Did Mutti ever come back?"

"Yes, she did a long time after you were gone. She just couldn't stand by and watch when you were taken away. It's a sad thing when a mother loses her child to another woman. Then, a couple of days before he was to get married in Kohlfurt, your father came to Goerlitz to see me, to tell me of his mistake and to tell your mother that somehow he would come back and for her to wait for him."

"Did you tell Mutti when she came back to Goerlitz?"

"Of course I did. But then came the war and the whole world turned upside down. That woman never wanted you, but she had to accept you if she wanted to be married."

"I remember when they picked me up."

"Yes, I do too. It was a sad day when your father came to pick you up and you didn't want to leave. But now you're here, and all is well."

"Oma!"

"Another story?"

"Who named me Gisela?"

"That was your mother and Tante Elfriede. Both your mother and Tante Elfriede were pregnant with babies due about the same time. They each liked the names Gisela and Ursula, Uschi for short. Gisela was first choice and Ursula, second. They decided that if the first baby born was a girl, it would be named Gisela. Three months after you were born, your cousin Ursula was born." With a twinkle her eye, Oma said, "But she waited, not like you, in such a hurry."

Sitting in Oma's room, thinking about what I just had heard, I looked at Oma, now only a head taller than I, but still that cuddly, round, fluffy, loving person I remembered. Her face was more wrinkled, but her blue eyes still twinkled when I looked at her.

"Oma, what a story that was!" I got up and gave her a hug. "I'm so glad you told me."

Oma smiled. "Good. Now, you go and play and I'll do some more mending before I have to start fixing our evening meal."

With Mutti gone to work so much, Oma was the person I clung to. Oma had her own way of doing things, things that fascinated me. Sometimes she wore her teeth, and other times they rested in a glass filled with water. I'd ask, "How come you're not wearing your teeth, Oma?"

"They bother me sometimes."

"Can you eat without them?"

"*Oh, ja,* I can. We have mostly soup anyway, and other times I just soak the bread or mash the food some."

"Can't you get new ones made at the dentist's?"

"We have dentist's, but they don't have the means to make new teeth. It could be a long while before that happens. So I wear the old ones when I go visiting. They will do me just fine."

I couldn't imagine not having any teeth at all, but Oma seemed to do just fine without them. I could tell when Oma had them in; she sounded clearer when she spoke to me. She looked different, even younger. But not wearing them didn't stop her from talking or laughing. When I looked at other older people, they seemed to have the same problem, no teeth. With or without them, she was my Oma and I went to town with her, even, when she had left them accidentally at home, safe in the glass. We went for walks, and talked, and I could ask questions. She patiently answered, explaining to me whatever I wanted to know. I always liked to be with her, either walking or just sitting in her room while she did mending and sewing.

When Mutti re-arranged our living quarters, and Oma moved upstairs, she spent most of her time in her room, coming downstairs around dinnertime. When Mutti was gone, Oma would stay with my sister and me, sleeping in Mutti's bed, doing the cooking and cleaning. Sometimes I'd help. But whenever she had time, she'd go up to her room to sew or to take a little nap. She'd always let me know, warning me she was taking a nap so I would not burst into her room, startling her as I had been known to do. When she was in her room, Oma opened the window wide, revealing the attached flower box she had filled with geraniums, which were now blooming in brilliant reds. The warm summer air filled her comfortable little room and I liked spending time with Oma there.

A couple of days, and after the wash was done, I sat on the stoop—my favorite place to sit—and watched Oma do the necessary mending on the Singer sewing machine already in her room when she moved in. Oma always had a basket of mending to do, either on the machine or by hand. She gave me things that needed buttons sewn on or some that were close to falling off. "Here," she would say, "you can do this; it's good practice for you." At first I'd be nervous and afraid, knowing I was not that good at it, fearful of her getting mad at me for being clumsy. But Oma calmly showed me how, and after a while I liked doing it. *Did she know I was afraid of being scolded and yelled at? Is that why she always talked so quietly to me?* Whatever the reason, I was glad she didn't do it.

Other times, I sat on the stoop and watched Oma as she ripped the seams on the men's shirts and turned the collar over so the frayed side was underneath and the nice clean looking part was on top. She also did that with the cuffs of the shirt. I wondered whose dress and work shirts they were, as we had no men in our household, so I asked Oma, "Whose shirts are those? We don't have any men here."

"We don't have any men in our house, but we do in our family."

"*Oh,* I forgot, Onkel Heinz and Onkel Richard." Oma's son, and her son-in-law, my uncles.

"That's right, and neither of their wives knows how to do this and neither has a sewing machine."

Of course, I had to ask, "Why are you ripping the collars and cuffs off the shirts?"

"Well," she said, "the collar and cuffs are frayed and worn. The rest of the shirt is still good. Since there are no new shirts in the stores to buy, we have to mend them."

"Oma, where did you learn to do that?"

"Nowhere, necessity is the teacher," she replied, looking down at me over the top of her glasses with a twinkle in her eyes, knowing she had me puzzled once more. I had never heard of *necessity* being a teacher, "Oma, who and what is necessity?"

"It's not a person. It is something you have to do out of necessity. Like it is necessary that I fix the shirts so they can be worn again. When you don't have the means or the possibility to purchase new, then, you learn to invent and to help yourself, and that is why I say *necessity* is a teacher. Maybe you need to learn this also. So you know how to mend your husband's shirts."

"Oh, I don't think I'm going to do that. It looks too hard, Oma."

"You're not? It's not that hard; it just takes time and patience," she explained, again looking at me over the top of her glasses.

"No, I think I'll have someone do it for me." Then my eyes lit up, and looking at Oma, I said, "I know! I'll have you do that for me!"

Oma slightly shook her head as if she knew that was not going to happen anytime soon. "I'm not so sure about that. By the time you need sewing done, I may not be able to do it anymore. I'm getting old, and my hands are, too, and are not what they used to be."

"Oma, you can do it! You're not old, and your hands are fine."

"I'm not so sure."

I thought of how in Liegnitz my stepmother had a seamstress come to sew our clothes. Then I got all excited; I knew what I was going to do. "Oma," I shouted, "I know! I'll marry a rich man and have a seamstress sew for us both!" But Oma was not convinced.

"That's a good plan for you to keep in mind, but what'll happen if you don't marry rich and can't afford it?" Her blue eyes smiled at me.

"I'm sure the man I marry will be rich, Oma." But Oma still looked skeptical. I had the feeling she was not convinced about my future plans.

"Well, I do hope so. That is what every young girl dreams of, and I hope it will come true for you, but just in case, I still think you need to pay attention."

I did watch her, but I was not too interested. I knew I was not going to do that because it looked way too difficult to me, poor or not. Oma turned back to her sewing machine and started to sing and hum as she pedaled which made the needle race up and down at a fast click clack.

Her singing made me smile and feel at ease. The Mutti in my former life had never sung. I wanted to get up and give Oma a hug to show her just how much I had loved her, but I was afraid to do that. Content and happy, I just sat there watching, listening to her singing as her feet worked the pedal of her sewing machine. I tried to catch the words until finally I had to ask again, "What are the songs you're singing, Oma?"

"They're old traditional folk songs," she answered, not stopping her sewing and pedaling.

"You sure know a lot of them, Oma."

"Yes, I do. Why don't you sing with me?"

"I don't know any of them."

"I like to sing. It makes me happy. Do you want me to teach them to you?"

"Oh, would you, Oma, please?" Oma taught me lots of the old German folk songs and that's how Oma and I started to sing together; she would sing alto and I, soprano.

"You have a wonderful clear voice. You need to join the school choir. But, don't ever sing alto you'll lose your soprano voice." Oma didn't know just how much it meant to me to hear her say that. Her praise was an unseen gift to me. Only one other time had I been told that and that was Tante Grete when I visited my grand parents in Pfaffendorf by Lauban. Oma had a huge knowledge of songs, so I asked her, "How come you know so many songs?"

She leaned back, resting her hands in her lap. "When I lived in my little house in *Schoenbrunn*, a small farming community, now on the Polish side, where your mother and all my children were born, there was a group of townspeople of all ages. We had a choir and put on plays. At times I even wrote words to an existing song to match it to the play, and I helped with the sewing of costumes for everyone. We sang a lot of songs. All four of my children took part in the plays when they were young. That was so much fun. You would have liked it, too."

"I would have liked it, Oma. It sounds like a lot of fun."

"It was."

"But, Oma, where are those people and why can't we do it here and now?"

"You're asking too many questions at one time. Question number one, Elfriede, Heinz, and your mother are here, but Rudi is missing in action." I could tell from her voice that she was sad when she mentioned her eldest son Rudi. I had never met him. I had heard many times that short phrase *missing in action*, but never asked what it meant.

"Oma, what does 'missing in action' mean?"

"In a war, and when communication is lost and no one knows what happened to a soldier, the family gets notified that the soldier is *missing in action*. My son Rudi was listed as that when the Deutsche Wehrmacht, notified his wife and me."

"But, Oma, if they don't know what happened to him, he still could be coming home, couldn't he?"

"Yes, he could. He is listed as missing from the Russian front, and we don't know where he is, or if he still is alive, but I hope and pray that he will come home to his blind wife and his two sons."

"He has a blind wife and children?"

"Yes. She, too, was an after-war refugee, evicted from my house in Schoenbrunn where she was living with her two boys and family. Your mother spoke to her when she saw her on the transport train. She made a wise choice to go to West Germany. We don't know where she is living now and we have no way of locating her. It is impossible for people in East Germany to trace loved ones and family members in West Germany. And as for your second question, the singing and playacting in Schoenbrunn was before and during the war. Then, in early1945, many fled to get away from the approaching Russian front. I don't know where these people are or if they're still alive. If they never fled from the Russian front then they were evicted by the Poles, chased out, like all the Germans were. Who knows what happened to them, where they are. Times have changed. I can't go to Schoenbrunn anymore and if my house is not destroyed, then, Polish people are living in it now. The border is closed, maybe even for good, it's all part of the past, never to return." Oma sounded sad, looking back, recalling a time and place she had loved that was not so long ago but was now and forever only a memory.

Like so many times before, I wanted to hug Oma and tell her I loved her, but I was unsure and too shy. The only person I had been able to freely through my arm around was Vati but he was gone—taking my free feeling of loving with him. I had learned, mostly when Vati was in the war and when he had passed away, to control my feelings, and I was still unable to let go.

Shaking her head as if to get it out of her mind and to let go of her memories, Oma said, "That's enough of that. Let's get back to our task. We can't change what's happened." She continued her sewing and teaching me songs. Some of the happiest hours I ever spent with Oma were singing with her. Every time she'd sew or cook our miserable soup, Oma was singing and I, right along with her. Sometimes she would whistle. Maybe that's what made her life bearable, for Oma never complained.

Because of Oma, singing came easily to me now. In the attic next to Oma's room, I found a gramophone and a stack of records. The gramophone was made of blonde wood and was kind of boxy looking. It had two small doors in front where the speakers were located. Underneath the lid was the actual player, and on the side was a removable crank to wind it up. The records I found were operas and instrumentals, and I loved them. On rainy days I would sit by the hour next to Oma's room on the steps to the attic and listen to the operas. Eventually, I was able to sing along, imagining that I was the opera singer dressed in a beautiful shimmering long gown. The square landing that led to Oma and Frau Hartman's doors was my imaginary stage, like in a big opera house. I would act out the movement with the song, swirling and smiling flirtatiously. The people would look up, admiring me as they applauded.

I would bow my head graciously at the end of my performance, holding my imaginary long gown, sweeping it behind me with flair as I curtsied; accepting a bouquet of red roses as I had seen Snow White do a long time ago in Liegnitz when I was with Vati at the Opera House.

Once in a while Oma would catch me as I made my bows and swirls, but she just gave me a smile and went about her chores. Because the house was three stories, when I was standing on the second landing, the open foyer below gave my voice a strong, full sound. I loved to stand there and sing. It was the same landing I had sat on just a short while back, screaming when they took Mutti to the hospital. The neighbors told me, they always knew when I was around and enjoyed listening to my singing. Although I liked the compliments, their comments embarrassed me, and I would not sing when I knew someone was nearby or listening.

I was not the only one in our family who could sing. My sister Christa also had a beautiful voice. When she was in one of her good moods, she would sing in the evening with me when we were in bed. That didn't happen too often. She was busy with her friends. She was sixteen, working, going to high school twice a week and out with her childhood girlfriend Rosel, dancing and dating. Christa still didn't like me and was uncaring. At times she'd say unkind things, like I really didn't belong to them, or that they felt sorry for me when they found me under a rock or in the mailbox screaming. I would sit and cry. Looking at me with glee in her eyes, she'd say, "That's how you cried when we found you. We should have left you!" Then she'd laugh, pleased she could make me cry.

When her girlfriend Rosel was there, she'd laugh and make fun of me, too. I hated Rosel. I hated her for being friends with my sister. I hated her for laughing at me. I wanted to scratch her with claws like a cat. I wanted to hurt her. I wanted to fight back at both at them. Then, tears stopped, and I exploded, yelling at my sister, pointing at Rosel, "Your girlfriend is ugly! She has a nose like a witch! She is bowlegged and pisses her pants all over our floor! She did it right here in our living room! I saw it and I'm going to tell everyone!" That made my sister mad, and she started to chase me around the living room table. I ran, and as soon as I reached the door, out I went down the stairs, jumping three at a time, laughing because neither my sister nor Rosel could catch me.

Standing on the upper landing, my sister yelled, "You just wait until I get hold of you!"

"You've got to catch me first!"

When my sister and Rosel were laughing hard, it was true that Rosel could not control her bladder. When that happened, they both made me promise almost swear; never to tell anyone, but I wouldn't promise or swear to anything. Although I would never have told anyone, I believed I had some kind of power over them, but mostly Rosel. I knew both of them took great care in their appearance and Rosel didn't want anything embarrassing told about her. Rosel was not ugly, nor did she have a nose like a witch, nor was she bowlegged; but she'd lose control of her bladder sometimes.

When Mutti was home and my sister was saying these things about my not really belonging to the family, Mutti didn't stop her. "Don't pay attention to your sister. You know what she's saying isn't true." But I cried, saying I wished I was dead like Vati and that no one loved me. Then, Mutti would get mad, threatening to spank me for saying those things and wishing to be dead.

Coming from a strict upbringing with no sass, I couldn't understand why Christa always got her way. One time when she was nasty, Onkel Heinz threatened to lay her over his knee, but Mutti stopped him. From then on my sister was very careful when he was around.

Sometimes she had two dates or she changed her mind and didn't want to go out with her date. Then, it was my job to go to her date and deliver her excuses.

I hated when she approached me so sweetly, saying, "Gisela, would you do me a big favor?" *My sister wants a favor from me?* My first reaction was to tell her, "No!" But I knew when Mutti heard her asking me, she'd tell me to do it.

"What kind of a favor?"

"Deliver a message to a date who is waiting for me?"

"How far do I have to go?"

"Not far. He'll be waiting at the corner of *Langenstrasse* und *Breitestrasse.*"

"And then what do you want me to do?"

"Give him a message from me. If you do, I'll give you fifty Pfennings."

"And what do I say?"

"You tell him that you're my sister and I'm breaking the date because I'm not feeling well. Deliver the message, and I'll pay you when you come back." So I delivered the message to her date waiting for her on the corner only a little ways from where we lived. I felt embarrassed about lying and sorry for the young man. He was really nice looking, well dressed in suit and tie, ready for the date. What I really wanted to tell him was that it was a lie and that my sister was not sick at all, but that would have gotten me in trouble. When I returned home, my sister had left already, and so had my money. When I reminded her that she owed me money, she said, "I'll pay you as soon as I get my next pay from work." But her promises to pay rarely happened.

Soon I refused to go and hid where she couldn't find me. It filled me with great satisfaction. Because I couldn't fight her, that was my way to get even. Sometimes my friends would help me. They watched when my sister left the house because she had to go to the date herself. Then I came out of hiding, happy about a job well done. When Mutti or Oma saw me, they'd ask, "Where were you? Your sister was looking for you."

I wanted to say, "Yes, I know!" But I shook my head and said, "Oh, I didn't know!"

Christa was aware I was hiding from her and the others kids knew where I was but only shrugged their shoulders, saying, "We don't know where she is. We haven't seen her." That made her furious, so she called my friends brats. After a while she stopped asking me to deliver her messages, and I was glad. Christa had to admit her dates and friends thought her little sister was cute, only too young for a date.

I continued to stand my ground whenever possible, but our fighting continued for many years.

Mutti always asked, "Why can't you two get along like sisters? It's a good thing your father can't see you two!" Christa would shrug her shoulders, saying, "And what could he do about it?"

Oh, I thought he could do a lot, remembering when I had sassed him, only that one time. Then his face and eyes had gotten stern, with his vein throbbing on his forehead, scaring me. Another time, because his wife made him mad, he threw his razor in a fit of temper and it landed underneath the stove. I wondered if my sister would have been so smug then. We were truly never sisters. We only tolerated each other. We grew up like strangers. I hated and loved her, but I don't know which was stronger.

Hunger was a constant companion. The rationing of food continued. Oma's soups made with the nettle, the soup made with one potato, the soup made from dark flour, the Runkelrueben fried by Oma in the leftover coffee made from roasted wheat kernels, her famous spread of Karnickelbutter, and whatever else Oma came up with—all kept the hunger away for a little while. One time, Oma made a soup with butter lettuce. She added a grated potato, some carrots, and parsley she had raised in the garden for *color for the soup*, Oma's favorite saying. The lettuce went limp from cooking, so the soup was a glassy, slimy-looking mass in my dish. It sat in my mouth like a blob of tasteless glue, my throat closed up, wanting no part of the soup. My stomach started to make gentle heaving motions. With my head low, I looked across the table at Oma to see if she was watching me as my stepmother always had watched me, ready to spank when I had a hard time swallowing foods like spinach. But Oma, seeing that I was looking fearfully at her, tried to encourage me by saying, "Don't look at it so much; just eat. It's better than nothing at all." But sometimes I wondered, if *nothing at all wasn't better.*

Oma, like others, strictly rationed our daily food, especially bread. We had only three slices a day: one in the morning with our soup made of dark flour and water, then, two slices in the evening. Sometimes we had to eat the leftover soup from noon in the evening with only one slice of bread. For school I had a sandwich made with Oma's Karnickelbutter spread. Oma sliced the bread better with her kitchen knife, than any bread machine.

Oma kept the rationed food—bread, marmalade, margarine, sugar, and flour—locked away, or so she thought, in a small home made cabinet that set next to the door in her room. Sometimes when Oma had to run an errand, I stayed home. Then I stood in front of the cabinet, trying to figure out to get a slice of bread to still my growling stomach. This time hunger

195

was *the necessity* so I checked the cabinet. It had a non-lockable drawer, so by taking the drawer out I could reach through the empty space to the shelf below and pull out the bread. I felt guilty. I knew Oma was not purposely letting me go hungry—sometimes she gave me part of her slice of bread—so I put the bread back and the top drawer back in place. But there were times when hunger got the best of me and I carved a slice from the bread. Although it was dry and often hard, I savored every bite. Oma never said a word, but I'm sure she could tell from my carving that I had found a way to get to the bread.

Then, one day the cabinet was not locked. The bread and the other rationed food were gone. By watching Oma, I learned where she had moved the bread. The new place was a dresser with five drawers. In the second drawer from the top is where Oma locked the bread away, but she didn't lock the top drawer, and by pulling out that drawer I was able to get to the bread. I was sure Oma knew, but she never got angry—as my stepmother had done—so I felt guilty and stopped carving.

Then came my eleventh birthday, the first one after I had been reunited with my family. Mutti was home, and Oma baked a cake with ingredients she had saved from the rations. Mutti had brought home the good coffee. From the china hutch she took the special coffee service and tablecloth and set a pretty table with it. Tante Elfriede, Tante Hilde, and my cousin Uschi came for the afternoon birthday coffee. Uschi had a colorful bouquet of aromatic sweet peas for me. She and I were allowed to have milk coffee with the cake Oma had baked especially for me. I do not recall if there were gifts. It was my best birthday ever, and I felt I was the most important girl in the world. The only person missing was Vati. The year before, although there'd been no birthday celebration, he had been alive. Sometimes I was so busy that I forgot about him; then, I felt sad and guilty, and I promised him and myself that I would not forget him, ever, just like the promise never to forget our last Christmas at the opera house in Liegnitz.

With Mutti home and then gone again, still working on the train, I attached myself more and more to Oma. School was out for the summer, and on Saturday mornings when the sun was shining Oma and I went to the cemetery, carrying a watering can and flowers for Vati's grave. Oma liked to water the graves of family members and people she had once known. Our walk took us through the old part of Goerlitz and to the cemetery, past the church and up the hill where I had followed the hearse that carried Vati's casket. My thoughts went back to that sad, cold day in November. Only nine months had passed, yet it seemed a lifetime ago to me, divided into *then* and *now*. My memories were like a framed picture with me on the outside, standing there, looking at it. For once I was silent, quiet, my head down, trying not to look up for fear I would see that picture. Oma took my hand and squeezed it, letting me know she was there and I was not alone.

But before we walked up the hill of the old cemetery, Oma stopped and pointed to an ancient tree, at the entrance and across from the church where Vati's service had been held. "Gisela, do you know what that tree over there is all about and why the crown has an odd shape?"

Looking where Oma was pointing, I saw only an old knotted tree with a thick wide iron ring around its trunk to keep it from breaking apart. What had been a grave was now a mound of dirt overgrown with grass and weeds. The rusted low wrought iron fence that encircled the grave was crooked and had a plaque attached, but its engraved words were blurred. "No," I said, as my eyes wandered up the trunk to the crown.

"There is a story about that tree. Do you want me to tell you about it?"

"Oh, yes, Oma." Oma was a great storyteller.

"The tree's name is *Moller-Linde*."

"Moller-Linde?"

"Yes, Martin Moller was a theologian, a Pastor of the Lutheran faith who lived and died in 1606, right here in Goerlitz, and was in charge of the Peterskirche. He was accused by the Goerlitzer Councilmen of not teaching the Lutheran word, as he should. They claimed that Moller secretly was preaching Cripto-Calvanismus, against Luther's word. A highly educated person, Moller wrote poems and songs for the church and was smarter and kinder than any of the councilmen. Until the year of his death he ignored their cruel accusations. Before he died, he asked to have a seed from the Lindenbaum, a Linden tree, placed on top of his grave and said, "When the roots grow leaves and the crown grows roots, it will prove that I'm innocent of all accusations." Oma stopped talking. "Now, look at the crown. What do you see? Doesn't look that the roots stretch outward? Not upward like the crown of a tree should be?"

Looking at the old and gnarled tree, I said, "*Ja*, Oma, I can see. The top looks like an umbrella, flat, with twisting long branches that reach out."

"It proves his innocence. Now you know why it is called the *Moller-Linde*, and if you're asked about it, you can tell the story."

That got me thinking, "Oma, do you think the top of the tree is growing inside his grave?"

"No one can say for sure. The only thing we know is, what we see."

Oma took me by the hand again, and we continued walking up the hill of the old cemetery with tombs, statues of angels with broken off wings and arms, big crosses carved out of gray stone, leaning, their names unreadable. It was a cemetery from a long time ago. On top of the hill, just beside the road, was a round building made of red brick with colored windows like a church. "Oma, what is that building and what's inside?"

"It's the *Leichenhalle*, a mortuary with caskets, where family members and friends come. They bring flowers and say their goodbyes to the deceased."

"How come Vati was not in there? Why was he down there in the church with all those other people? Why, Oma?"

"Because there were lots of sick people who died at nearly the same time. Lots of room was needed for all the caskets." Oma was right. I remembered all the caskets, a sea of them.

Walking through another big, wide wrought iron gate, leaving the old cemetery behind us, we entered the newer addition. Oma knew so many stories of people who were buried here, but the grave that interested me the most, where I always had to stop, was an older one, overgrown with neatly trimmed ivy. In the center it had a green painted metal heart with a picture of a bride inside. "Oma, look! Here is a picture of a bride!"

"Shhh, not so loud. Yes, she died just before her wedding day," Oma said in a low voice.

"*Ja*, but why did she die? What was the matter with her? Is she really in her wedding gown?" I tried to be quiet, but I got so excited over the picture of the bride that my voice was not low.

"Yes, she is. I knew her. She would have been a beautiful bride, but she got sick and died shortly before her wedding day. It was very, very sad."

"You knew her? How?"

"We were not friends but we knew each other when we were young."

"I feel sorry for her, Oma. It's like Snow White. She was lying in a glass casket all in white with everyone feeling sad. Only she came back to life. But this bride? That is sad, Oma."

"You sure have a fascination with that grave, Gisela." Oma was right. I was fascinated with the bride and the idea of being buried in her wedding gown. "Come, let's go." Oma took my hand and pulled me away.

We went to Vati's grave. He had a brown painted wooden cross with his name on it. I was surprised to see it. Maybe my stepmother had it made. His was almost the only marker in the whole field of graves. Many were overgrown already with weeds. Oma and I weeded the ones next to Vati's. Then, we planted the flowers we had brought. Touching the earth, it felt as if I were touching Vati. I told him silently that I missed him and loved him, that I would never forget him.

Slowly we made our way back home through the cemetery. Oma stopped here and there, resting on a bench underneath old trees, enjoying the warm sunshine. The graves around us—older then Vati's—were covered in flowers and the birds were singing their never-ending songs. People walking by, mainly women dressed in dark clothes, carrying flowers and watering cans, nodded their heads in silent greeting to Oma. I wanted to do some more talking, but Oma said, "Shhh," putting her finger on her pursed lips. "In respect for the dead and the people walking by, when you're at the cemetery, you can't talk a lot. You have to be extra quiet."

But I had one more question. Leaning into Oma, I asked, "Oma, can I whisper in your ear then?"

Oma just smiled and whispered, "I guess you can."

When Oma had no need of me, I was allowed to be with my friends, even though Oma didn't think they were the right company for me to keep. She wanted me to be more demure and quiet like my cousin Uschi, Tante Elfriede's and Onkel Richard's daughter. "Why don't you go and visit Uschi for the afternoon?" Oma would ask me, "Brigitte, here girlfriend is there, too, and you three could play together."

"I just don't feel good right now, Oma. Do I have to go?" I wanted to make a good excuse.

But Oma looked at me with her I-know-what-you're-thinking look, saying, "Oh, you don't look sick to me. You'll forget all about it and have a nice time when you get there. Besides, it's better than being out on the street with those neighborhood kids."

But I liked the kids and we had lots of fun, not doing much, just talking, teasing, and laughing. I went to Uschi's, but with a slow wandering walk, the longer my walk—the less time I had to spend there. I didn't want Oma to know that I felt uncomfortable when Uschi's girl friend came to play with her. She was not my friend and only accepted me because I was Uschi's cousin. Uschi and her have known each other since they were toddlers because the parents were long time friends. They, too, had returned, but unable to go to their home, they'd settled in the Russian sector of Goerlitz.

Uschi and her girl friend's way of playing was stupid or it just felt stupid, because I didn't want to be there. I liked playing out-doors and they didn't. Playing store was their favorite thing. They had made paper money by laying a sheet of paper on top of coins and rubbing it with the blunt end of a wooden pencil, showing the imprint of the coins on the paper and cutting them out. Also drawn on paper, then colored, and cut out were the store's goods, like red apples, tomatoes, green cucumbers, salad leaves, orange colored carrots, and loaves of brown bread. These colored and cut-out paper goods were laid out on the table for the shopper. For a counter, Uschi and her friend put a flat board over the back of two chairs. When the shopper paid, the sales lady acted out the tapping of keys on the cash register, sounding off in a clear voice, *ring, ring*. The shopper paid with the money that had been divided up three ways. We were to take turns as sales lady.

Uschi and her friend had a rule that if you ran out of money, you could not play, but I always felt that rule was more her girl friend's than Uschi's. Somehow, I ran out of money pretty fast and had to wait until they changed from shopper to saleslady. Being the saleslady was fun. But when it was my turn to be the saleslady, it usually was time for me go home, because my turn was always last.

When I got home, Oma would ask, "*Na*, how was it? Did you have fun?" Not wanting to disappoint Oma, I just nodded my head, "Oh, ja, it was fun." I liked Uschi a lot. We were very different from each other. Uschi was dark haired with dark brown eyes and a natural tan. I was blonde with blue eyes and pale skin. At family get-togethers, Uschi was always quiet and only spoke when spoken to. I was always talking. Once in awhile Oma would say, "Why can't you be like Uschi, a little quieter?"

Then, Mutti would say, "She is fine. Let her be, she is Gisela, not Uschi." It never bothered me that Oma would ask me to be more like Uschi. I knew Oma loved me, and I was around her a lot more than Uschi was.

Sometimes, coming home from Uschi's, my girlfriend Gisela was waiting for me, and she shouted from the street below, "Gisela, Gisela, are you home?"

"You just got home! Doesn't she have any other friends? Tell her you can't come down right now," Oma would tell me.

Leaning out the window, loud enough for Oma to hear me, I would call out, "I can't come down right now," while pointing at the *Haustuere*, the house door below. Gisela would nod her head to show she understood my signal. After a short while I would tell Oma I had to go to the bathroom, even if I didn't. Then, I flushed the toilet, hoping that Oma would hear it. I tiptoed down the stairs, trying to miss the squeaky ones, and went out. The house door had an alcove and I would stand there while, across the street, Gisela would watch the window above the house door, to see if Oma was looking out. When Gisela slowly walked away, that meant Oma was at the window. But when the coast was clear, she would come over and we would sit on the doorsteps and talk. Soon the gang showed up. But sometimes our approach didn't work and Oma was watching, so I went back upstairs. I don't think Oma knew that Gisela and I had our signals, but maybe she did.

Then one day in the early afternoon, the two Siegfried's, as well as Jochen, and Franz showed up to tell us girls, "We're going apple picking."

"Apple picking?" Where are you going to pick them? There are no apple trees in the city."

The boys were smug, telling each other, "You tell the girls!"

"So tell us! What's the big secret?"

"It's boy stuff, and you girls don't want to do that anyway!"

"You tell us or we're going to follow you. We'll find out! Come on! Tell us! Where are you going to pick apples?"

The boys looked around, gathered in a huddle and motioned to us to come closer, whispering, "We're going to the outskirts, where apple trees line the *Landstrasse,* the farm road. That is where we pick the apples."

"You can't do that! That's stealing. Those apple trees belong to the farmers nearby. You'll get in trouble."

"Keep your voices down," they cautioned, their hands making downward motions. "We're not going to steal; we're just taking the ones on the ground. If you don't want any apples, then just forget it. We know girls are afraid of everything." They turned, leaving us standing there.

"Wait," I called. "How long are you boys going to be gone?" Gisela, Inge, and Regina nodded their heads.

"Not long, maybe an hour or so! If you girls go with us, you can't tell anyone, not until we get back!" The whole thing sounded iffy to me because I was not allowed to leave unless I asked Oma first. Apples were something we did not have on a daily basis, and it sounded exciting. Getting apples would surprise Oma, and she wouldn't be too mad at me. Besides, it was only for an hour, and Oma would not miss me. Sometimes she got busy and forgot all about time and me. With one last glance up at the window, ignoring all caution, only thinking of the adventure, we set out.

We went along Weberstrasse, past the Stadtkrankenhaus where Mutti had been hospitalized when she was sick, and into the farmland on the blacktopped road lined with apple trees. We looked under many trees on both sides of the road, but most of the apples on the ground were full of holes and maggots. "Well," we girls piped up, "you boys had a real nice idea, dragging us all the way out here to no apples, only maggots. That's the last time we'll ever listen to you!"

"Oh, ja, no apples you say! Watch this!" Before we knew it, the boys were up in the tree, shaking it hard until the apples fell. We girls shrieked with laughter. I was sure Oma was going to be glad I was bringing apples home to her. But before I could put my thoughts back on our adventure, the boys jumped out of the tree and started to run, leaving us girls standing there. "What are you kids doing?" An angry voice shouted behind us. "Who said you could steal apples off my apple tree?"

As if by an unseen command, we turned around to see the farmer, coming out of his field where he had been working, and watching us. He was not very big, but his voice made up for it. We tried to explain that it was the boys who shook the tree and all we wanted was to pick up the apples that had fallen off, but that didn't make any difference to the farmer. Paying no attention to our stammering and tear-soaked faces, he continued, "So the boys ran out on you girls, leaving you standing here!"

He motioned to us to follow him. He started to walk when he realized we were still standing there, four statues with wet faces, unable to move or run like the boys, so he bellowed once more, "Let's go!"

"Go where?" was our timid question.

"To the *Gendarm* the sheriff, where else? You know the rule, "*Mit gegangen, mit gefangen, mit gehangen,*" meaning, "went together, caught together, hung together." It was a familiar phrase. "So let's go!" he shouted. We walked behind him carrying the pitchfork over his shoulder, muddy boots and dirty clothes from the field; we with faces smeared with tears and dust, looking down at the pavement, scared of what would happen to us. He stopped and turned to see if we were still following him. "Why are you stealing apples? Don't you know stealing is against the law, food or otherwise? Do your parents know what you're doing?" We shook our heads. There was that word *stealing* that I had heard in my life with the other Mutti. Had she been right? Was I really a thief?

"We just wanted some apples for eating," we answered, our heads down.

"But you can't just go and take them. Do you girls understand that?"

"Yes, we do! We are really sorry, and we promise never to do it again if you just let us go home, please," we begged, looking at him with remorseful, wet faces.

"I'll let you go, but if I ever see any of you again, I will take you to the Gendarm. Is that clear?"

"Oh, yes, it is, thank you very much." We curtsied over and over again, then wiped our faces and ran home as fast as we could.

I knew I was in trouble because we'd been gone longer than an hour, and Oma was looking for me. She already knew where I had been. She had asked Siegfried, who got home long before we girls did, if he had seen me, and he'd told her what I was doing and where. I got a short lecture from Oma, telling me how worried she was and that she would have not enjoyed the apples at all. For a while I was not allowed to see my friends. I could leave the house only with Oma. When finally she loosened up and I was able to see my friends, we girls gave the boys the cold shoulder, but that didn't last too long. Soon we started to talk, tease, and laugh again. But I never did I go to an adventure like that again.

It was late in August and Oma was sewing and humming. "What are you sewing, Oma?" I asked, looking at the rough brown material she was working with.

"I'm making pouches for us of old potato sacks."

"What for?"

"So we can go *Aehren lesen,* wheat gleaning tomorrow."

"Aehren lesen?" That sounded like another lesson. "What is it?"

"Well," she answered, never interrupting the rhythmic sound of her sewing machine, "when the farmer is through harvesting his wheat field and after he has raked it several times with his team of horses pulling a big rake to get the excess of husks of wheat lying on the ground, he then allows people to glean the field and take what they find home."

I had to think about. "You mean like a field mouse looking for grain and then taking it to his house below the ground, storing it for the winter?"

"Something like it."

"But what are the pouches for?"

"They're for you and me to use in the field gleaning. We'll collect the ears of wheat in our pouches, and when there full we'll empty them into a bigger sack and keep gleaning until we fill the bigger sack—hopefully."

Oma had finished the larger pouch and was now working on the smaller one, "Is the small one for me?"

"Ja, it is. I had to shorten it so you wouldn't stumble with it, since you're a tiny person, but you do make up for that with all the talking and asking a thousand questions, keeping me from getting the sewing done." Her eyes smiled. I knew Oma didn't mind my continuous chatting because she always answered in her gentle loving voice.

Standing next to Oma, I watched as she sewed a wide seam around the opening. After that, she pulled an extra long rope through half the seam of the sack that made it look like a pouch.

"Why the long rope?"

"Come here. I'll show you." Oma took the pouch and put it in front of me, fastening it with the rope around my waist. The pouch covered me like an apron with a huge pocket, but hung past my knees. "Oma, it is too long; it's past my knees!"

"That's fine. It's supposed to be like that. Mine is the same, only bigger."

I could see that Oma's pouch was much bigger and her rope was even longer. Oma was round, like a soft, fluffy cotton ball, and I loved to *kuschel*, or snuggle with her when she was sitting and relaxing. But I was not done asking questions.

"How and when are we going to do that?"

"Early tomorrow morning. We need to be there when the farmer is done with his last raking and allows the people to glean, so bedtime will be early tonight. We need to be fresh and ready to go." Oma was not teasing. Early, before the sun was up she called, "Time to get up, Gisela,"

"But I'm still tired and it's so early and the sun is not even up yet, Oma," I moaned.

"Well, for a change, maybe you can beat the sun out of bed," she responded cheerfully.

"Why so early, Oma?" Squinting my eyes, I saw Oma, wearing her dark work dress, covered by an apron, black wool stockings, and black high top shoes, moving about. "We need to be at the field early in order to have a good start. So get up!"

"But I'm still tired."

"Yes, I know, but get up and wash your face in cold water. It'll wake you up." I stumbled out of bed to the water faucet, using only two fingers, and just enough cold water to wet my eyes. Steaming on the table was our soup made of flour and water, topped with a small amount of milk. When my bowl was half empty, Oma added more soup, saying, "Better fill your stomach now. It will be a long day!" While Oma cleaned the dishes, I dressed in an old weekday dress, brushed my teeth, braided my hair and, yes, washed my face again.

Oma picked up the big shopping bag containing the water bottles and sandwiches for us. She made a bundle with our pouches, including an extra sack. "Oma, what's the sack for?"

"I guess you are awake and already asking questions. I told you yesterday, the sack is for us to carry the wheat home in." Handing me the bundle, she continued, "Here, you can carry that, and I'll carry the bag with our food."

Then, she handed me a scarf "A scarf? What for?"

Oma, sighed, "It's to keep the dust out of your hair and the sun from burning the top of your head. Tie it loosely around your neck for now."

That's when I saw that Oma had her head covered with a beat up looking straw hat with a black scarf tied over the top squashing the hat into an egg-like looking thing. "Oma, where did you get that hat? You look sooo funny." Looking at Oma and her silly hat, I started to giggle.

"Never mind my hat! We need to go! We can't stand around here and talk about my hat!" I think she was a little perturbed with my giggling.

"But, Oma, you look so funny. Where did you get it?"

"I found it in the attic, so now can we go?" Not to wake the neighbors, we went quietly, down the stairs and out the front door.

Although the sun had started to rise, it was still cold. I wanted to take a sweater, but Oma stopped me, saying, "It will get warm as the day goes on, even hot, and hopefully we'll have wheat to carry home. Let's just walk a little faster. That'll warm you up." We walked the same route we kids had taken on our apple adventure. When we got to our destination, people already lined the field, encircling it like a black ribbon, waiting for the farmer to leave and give permission to go on his field. The ribbon started to move and broke as people walked on the field. Everyone, including children had pouches tied to their waists.

We, too, walked onto the field. "I'll show you what we're looking for and what to put in our pouches," Oma said, slowly walking, looking at the ground, bending down to pick up an ear of wheat. "Now, this is what you and I will watch for. You need to be looking down and not watching the rest of the people." *How does she know I am watching the people?* "So, keep your eyes to the ground. The more you find, the better for us. It will give us bread in the winter, so try not to miss any ears of grain." That sounded pretty easy. The sun was shining, its warm rays filling the air. Birds were swarming all around us, looking for kernels of grain. But I soon found out it was not that easy at all. The stubbles left from the stalks of grains were stiff, like short poles sticking straight up, poking and scratching. Some had water in them that sprayed up my legs. With only wooden sandals on my bare feet, every step meant my ankles and legs got stabbed, scratched, and sprayed. "Oma, when I walk, the stubbles hurt my ankles and have water in them,"

"Don't walk like you usually do: brush your feet along the ground; to push the stubbles down, and you won't get scratched or sprayed. The water is only dew and will be gone when the sun gets a little higher and warmer." I tried Oma's advice, but it didn't help much. The stubbles I stepped on were under my sandal, but the ones next to my feet were still straight up, poking and scratching around my ankles and legs. Also every time I wanted to pick up an ear of wheat, the stubbles scratched my hands. *Why are we doing this?* Standing up, looking over the field, I saw nothing but bent backs, dark moving humps slowly walking, with pouches swinging back and forth. "Do we have to do this, Oma?" I finally asked.

"Yes, we do, if we want to eat this winter. It's not that bad. Just think of something nice, or hum a little. I know it's not what you like to do, but we have to, and sometimes we have to do things we don't like. It's part of life. You will find out as you grow up. Now, let's get busy filling our sack with wheat so we have some to take home." And with that Oma walked slowly, back bent, head down, eyes sweeping, picking up ears. I walked close to her, head low, looking and looking. "You missed one, Oma," I shouted with excitement, finding one she had missed, picking it up, and showing it to her like a trophy.

"That's the way to do it, Gisela! Keep your eyes open and on the ground, making sure we put them in our pouches and not walk past so others will find them." That made sense to me, so we walked and walked, up and down the field, eyes glued to the ground.

Once in while I'd see a field mouse scurrying by. "Did you see that mouse, Oma?"

Straightening up and placing her hand behind her back and stretching, she answered, "Oh, ja, I saw it; they, too, want to eat." I could tell Oma was not too impressed with my mouse sighting. The sun's rays were settling on us, penetrating our clothes, burning our exposed skin. It was hot. People stretched by putting their hands on their hips, wiping their faces, then, bending down again, looking and searching intently to not miss one ear of wheat. Sometimes we almost bumped into other people because everyone had their heads down.

When noon came, Oma and I sat at the edge of the field under a tree, taking a short break from the sun's unrelenting heat, eating our sandwiches with the spread Oma had made the day before, and drinking the now warm water made with vinegar and a little sugar added. Oma, wanting to close her eyes, said, "I will rest my eyes, just for a little while, and then we need to do more gleaning." She leaned against the tree, using her gleaning pouch to support her tired back. I was tired and hot and didn't want to continue. My knees were sore and red as the pouch rubbed against them when I walked. My ankles scratches, were burning and bleeding, but after Oma's short rest, she tied a handkerchief around them, saying, "Don't worry. When we get home, you can bathe your feet. I have ointment for your feet and knees, and all will be better. Only a little while longer, then, we'll go home." I wished we would go now, but Oma wanted to do more gleaning to fill the sack. We carried the sack filled with wheat husks between us; stopping now and then to rest our tired arms and Oma's sore back from walking stooped all day. "We sure have a lot of wheat, Oma. It will last us a long time," I said.

"That's not much once the kernels are out of the husks; we'll have more husks than kernels. We need to go again, several times," was her tired reply. I tried to ignore her comment, hoping she would forget. But I knew she wouldn't.

The next day in the back yard was a fun day, the *dreschen* or threshing of the wheat. Oma dumped some of the ears in a washtub, leaving some in the sack. Laying it on the ground, we beat or threshed the sack with the wash paddles. Every so often, Oma would take the sack and shake it. "Why are you doing that, Oma?"

"To shake the husks around so all of the kernels will fall out when you beat them." After a while, Oma caught my hand, "Let's stop and check to see if all the kernels are out of their husks." Oma opened the sack and took a handful out, saying, "We have to beat just a little longer. We need every kernel out of the husks. We can't waste any." When Oma was satisfied, she dumped the now separated kernels and husks into another tub, and filled the sack again to thresh the rest of the husks.

After that was done, then, came the separating or cleaning of the kernels from the husks. Since there was very little wind, we had to make our own by blowing with full cheeks. We scooped up the wheat with a bowl and let it fall out like a waterfall, all the while blowing with all the air we could squeeze out of our lungs. The tiny husks, catching the sun, floated like miniature golden stars before settling on the ground while the kernels fell back in the tub. Oma had to stop and rest, "I'm getting dizzy from all that blowing." But it didn't bother me at all, so I told Oma, "I'll do that." It was like playing in water, only it was bumpy and prickly on my hands and a lot more fun than being out in the field gleaning.

When we were done, Oma gathered the kernels in a clean white linen sack.

"So, every time we need extra bread or flour, we'll exchange the kernels at our baker," she said, satisfaction in her voice.

"What's the baker going to do with it?"

"After he weighs the kernels, he'll exchange them for bread, rolls, or flour. And when he has enough kernels, he'll grind them to bake bread and rolls again for his customers. We need no food stamps and pay him only for his work, the baking and grinding."

"The people who were on the field with us, are they taking their kernels to their baker, too?"

"Yes, they exchange their kernels at the baker too."

Looking at the clean white sack and its contents, I realized Oma is been right. For all the gleaning we'd done, there was not much left of the big sack we had carried home.

Glancing at the evening sky, Oma said, "I've heard there will be another field ready for gleaning tomorrow, and it looks as if it will be a nice day for it." My heart sank at that remark, and I wondered how Oma knew about it. But I didn't ask. That's what Oma had decided, so we went many more times, Oma in her funny egg-shaped hat and I with ankles wrapped, a scarf on my head, gleaning.

With the wheat gleaning done, Oma and I moved on to the gleaning of potatoes. Potato gleaning was another new adventure for me, so I asked Oma, "What do we have to do?"

"Well, when the farmer is done harvesting the potatoes, and just like the wheat gleaning, people are allowed to dig for potatoes he has missed. It will take a lot of digging with a hoe, and hopefully we'll get some potatoes."

"Aren't they lying on top of the ground, like the ears of wheat?"

"That would be nice, but we have to dig for them, they're buried deep; that's why the farmer misses some of them. It will take muscle power to swing the hoe, and I know you have lots of it."

Stretching my arms and looking at them, I told Oma, "But my arms are skinny; I don't see any muscles."

But Oma in her confident way just said, "You'll get them. You'll see."

Again we got up early, with Oma having to pry me out of bed by reciting her favorite phrase, "*Morgenstund hat Gold im Mund* or morning hour is golden. Now, get up before you miss it!"

I enjoyed going with Oma. I just hated to get up early and didn't see anything golden that early in the morning. While I was eating my soup, I watched Oma making our sandwiches with her special spread, as well as the water with vinegar and sugar added for drinking. It was a thirst quenching and I liked it.

We took the Leiterwagen that was in the house because Oma and I couldn't carry the potatoes home as we had the wheat. Oma put a couple of brown potato sacks, two buckets, two hoes, and our lunch in the cart. "Why two buckets and hoes?" I asked.

"A bucket and hoe for each of us."

"Oma, can I sit in the cart and you pull me, please?"

"I don't know, maybe you should pull me," she answered, that funny twinkle in her eye.

"You're too big, Oma! You'd look funny, and people would laugh."

Oma always liked to tease by saying funny things. "Well, if you think so. We don't want to be laughed at, so hop in and let's go!" And we were on our way, Oma in her funny hat, and I with the scarf to protect my hair and head from dirt and the sun. But not without Oma reminding me that on a hill, I'd have to walk. Taking the handlebar, and looking up at the sky, Oma remarked, "It will be a beautiful day today."

As the cart rolled and rattled over the blue and gray cobblestones, my voice quivered when I talked. I made funny noises just so I could hear and feel that wobbly bubble in my throat making short gurgling sounds. After a while I told Oma I wanted to walk and pull the wagon. "You can pull it. It's not heavy," said Oma, handing me the handlebar.

When we got to the field, people were already encircling the field, ready to move as soon as the farmer gave the signal. Many, like Oma and I, came with carts. Some had flat carts with wheels from baby buggies, and others used baby buggies—anything, just as long as it had wheels. Oma found a place on the edge of the field where she left the cart. Handing me the hoe and bucket, she said, "We need to keep an eye on our stuff, but most of all on the Leiterwagen." I knew what she meant. Times were hard and people took things that were not theirs. In the field Oma showed me what to do and how to handle a hoe. "First of all, you need to be careful when you swing the hoe. People are around you, and you don't want to hit them. Also, watch that no one has their hand in the way when you come down with the hoe. Keep space between you and the person next to you and be very, very careful." Oma also said, "try not to damage the potatoes with the hoe, they'd rot and we needed every one of them for our winter supply."

"I'll be careful Oma."

"Now, move over a little. It's not like when we were gathering wheat. Here we need room between us. Also, don't forget you have to dig deep, and where there is one potato, sometimes you find more, so keep digging."

Listening to Oma, I could tell this was a lot harder than gleaning for wheat—so many dos and don'ts. Oma and I worked for a while, but we didn't have any luck, only a potato here and there. "Everybody is digging in the center. Let's go closer to the edge of the field. Sometimes you can find more potatoes there," Oma decided. Looking around, I could see the field was filled with people, black silhouettes against the blue sky, swinging their hoes in irregular arcs. Some had pouches hanging from their waists; others buckets; yet others had sacks, dragging them as they moved, searching for the spot to find a potato or two. The sun's hot rays settled on the field and the people.

"Oma, why is the edge better?"

"When the farmer works back and forth with his team of horses making turns, he sometimes misses the far edge, so that is where we'll dig."

"How come you know all that?"

"Remember, I used to live in the country and worked in the field at harvest time. My children had to helped, just like you."

Swinging the hoe was hard work. The potatoes grew deep in the ground, so I had to dig. My arms got tired and began to hurt. My hands were red, and I could see blisters forming. I watched Oma as she was vigorously swinging the hoe so that it dug deep into the ground. "How come your hands don't blister, Oma?"

"My hands have done lots of hard work and are used to it; yours are still tender. Why don't I do the hoeing and you do the digging for the potatoes? Then, I won't have to stoop. Besides, you're closer to the ground." I looked at Oma. Was she joking? But she just smiled. Oma worked the hoe, and I was the potato spotter. I was on my knees, digging with my hands, checking for more. Sometimes four or five would hang together, connected by the roots, and that was a real find, encouraging me to dig a little harder not to miss one.

At noon we drank our vinegar water and ate our sandwiches, and although made with Oma's Karnickelbutter they tasted good. After Oma took a short rest, we continued working, Oma with the hoe and me with the digging.

We felt so lucky at the end of the day when we had both sacks filled with potatoes. Dirty from head to toe, I pushed the cart while Oma pulled. When we stopped to rest, Oma said, "Gisela, don't push so hard; I can't walk that fast. I'm too tired."

"I want to make it easy on you, Oma, so you don't have to pull so hard."

"That's nice. Just ease off a little and don't push quite that hard. We'll make it home. Don't worry."

In the back yard the following day, Oma spread the potatoes out in the sun, then, with a broom she cleaned the soil off. Watching Oma and looking at our harvest it gave me a feeling of pride that I, too, had helped to glean. "Why are you cleaning the potatoes?"

"Before we put them in the cellar, they need to be dry and clean, or they rot and our work would have been for nothing. You can help me carry the potatoes to the cellar."

Going in the cellar was not my favorite thing to do. The cellar and stairs were made of big rocks cemented together with the stairs smoothed out, but the wall was bumpy. The cellar, too, was divided between the tenants.

I didn't like going in the cellar. I was afraid of spiders. Although the basement had electricity, all the light bulbs were removed to save electricity so we had to use candles. When I held the candle, it fluttered, reflecting my bumpy shadow on the wall, giving me an eerie feeling that a ghost, was walking behind me.

But Oma, flicking her hand, told me, "The spiders don't do anything. They run when they sense strange movements, and the shadow is your own. So what is there to be afraid of?"

The running of those fat spiders and the skinny long-legged ones frightened me. In my imagination I could feel their dusty webs on my face. I feel them run over my bare feet and up my legs or land on my head. I had to help carry our harvest into the cellar, but I always stayed behind Oma, just in case. Oma knew what I was doing and said as she turned around, shaking her head, "For someone who can ask a thousand whys and what for's, you're sure a scaredy cat." And she was right.

Soon Oma heard of another potato field coming due for gleaning, so we started out again.

When the wheat and potatoes gleaning was over, it was time to glean for *Zuckerrueben* or sugar beets. I never asked Oma how she knew where there were fields ready for gleaning. She rarely talked to the neighbors other than in casual conversation or with a *Guten Tag!* But she always knew where and when to glean. As before, Oma and I got up early, me whining which Oma ignored. "Just get up; forget the fussing! It's not going change anything, so get up." While she prepared our sandwiches and our drinks, she added, "Come and eat your soup, then get dressed, wash your face, brush your teeth, comb your hair, and lets ready so we can go. It will take an hour to get to the sugar beet field."

Oma in her egg-shaped straw hat and me in a scarf, we took the hand cart which contained our lunch, the hoes, buckets, and sacks and walked toward the country road, leaving the city behind, passing fields we had gleaned, now deserted. But no matter how early we were, people were already standing at the edge of the field, waiting for the farmer to get through. When his hand signaled the go-ahead, before the last wheel of his equipment had left the field, an onslaught of people moved to the field with hoe and pick; looking for food for survival.

Oma instructed me, "When you're digging and you find just a piece of a *Zuckerruebe* keep it, because they'll get cut up when we cook them. So take whatever you find." We spent all day digging and hoeing. At noon, we sat under a tree to eat our sandwich and drink vinegar water. Then, Oma took a short nap, sounding like a duck her lips quivering, as she blew out air. I lay in the grass looking up at the deep blue sky, wondering what it looked like on the other side.

I thought about when I had lived in Liegnitz and Vati was alive. I'd gone to church to the *Kinder Gottes Dienst* or children's sermon where the *Pfarrer* taught us that *Gott*, God lived *im Himmel*, in heaven and He has *Engel, or* angels who watch and protect us. I wondered if one Engel was watching me right now, and what it looked like. I imagined it with curly blonde hair, a small round face, blue eyes, and tiny shimmering wings, just like the angel statues I'd seen at the cemetery. I wondered if Vati could see me. I knew he was with God and the angels. I missed Vati. I knew his memory would never leave me. He would always be in my heart. As I lay there, I saw birds soar way up into the sky, spreading their wings, swooping up and down, playing in the soft warm breeze, chasing one another, like children running. Then, I felt the soft breeze, too. I smelled the air, the earth, and the musty odor of the field. The sweet delicate scents of wild flowers warmed by the sun, floating around me, tickling my nose.

I could hear the words of my stepmother in my mind, "You will never amount to anything, you're too dumb and ugly and the only thing you're good for is to work in the field for a farmer when you grow up." *Is that what she meant? Me, right now, working in a field? But I'm not working for a farmer, and Oma is here, too.* I must ask Oma about that. She will tell me. I was glad not to be with my stepmother anymore, happy to be with Oma. When Oma woke up, I asked her right away, "Oma, with us gleaning, does it mean I'm working in the field?"

"What do you mean? What kind of a question is that?" Oma asked trying to wake up.

"I was told many times that when you're working in the field for a farmer that you're dumb and ugly, and we're working in the field, aren't we?"

"Yes, we are, but why are you asking such silly questions? What brought that on?" Oma looked at me and took a swallow of vinegar water.

"Well, you know, the fat one always said that's what I will be doing when I grow up."

Oma, realizing what I was asking, said, "No, you're not working in the field for a farmer. And no, you're not dumb or ugly. You were never ugly, so put it out of your head. We're doing this so we have food to eat. She is just a mean, nasty woman and will be punished someday for all the cruel things she has said and done." With that, our conversation ended and we went back to hoeing for sugar beets.

By the time we went home, dirty, tired, and sunburned, Oma and I had two sacks filled with sugar beets. "Oma, what are you going to do with them now?"

"We'll store them in the basement until we have more. It looks like a lot, but when they get boiled, there won't be much left. We need to go every day while the harvesting is on."

"Every day, Oma," I said, hoping I'd misunderstood her.

"Oh, ja, every day."

No, I hadn't misunderstood her, so we continued gleaning sugar beets until Oma was satisfied.

Processing the sugar beets took two days. First, Oma and I cleaned the sugar beets with a scrub brush and water until they were so clean they almost shined. Then, Oma chopped them into small pieces with a hatchet. The next day Oma and I got up early. "We have work to do, and I need your help." After our morning ritual, we went downstairs into the laundry room where Oma built a fire under the wash kettle, after that she filled the kettle with chopped beets and covered them with water.

"What are you making, Oma?"

"We're cooking the *Zuckerrueben* to make *Zuckerrueben-Sirup.*"

"*Zuckerrueben-Sirup?* How?"

"Just watch and see. First, we have to boil the beets, making sure they don't burn in the bottom of the kettle by stirring the beets with the wash paddle. You can do that." She explained, setting a footstool next to the kettle and me.

"What's the footstool for?"

"For you to stand on, so you can stir the beets in the kettle."

"Why, Oma? I can sit on the edge of the kettle, like when you do the wash."

"I'd rather you use the stool. The beets will get soupy and hot. They'll even spit a bubble ever now and than. Just use the stool!"

As usual, Oma was right. The beets got soupy and started to boil, spitting little bubbles. The steam rising into the air made the washhouse smell like a candy shop. I stood on the stool and stirred the beets with Oma closely watching the cooking process.

When the sugar beets were cooked soft and mushy, Oma took the hot coals out of the fire hole, dumping them into a metal bucket. I was going to ask why she was doing that, but I could see she was too busy. After she'd removed the coals, she scooped the hot beets and the liquid from the kettle with a clean bucket, transferring them to a leased wooden press the size of a chair without a back. Lined with aluminum the press had a spout under which she'd placed another clean bucket. When the press was filled with parts of the cooked sugar beets, Oma put the metal lid on the press and fastened the cast iron bar with a hole in the center over the top of the lid. Then, she screwed what looked like a big cast iron screw with a wheel on top into the hole of the iron bar. Then, Oma took hold of the wheel, gave it a turn or two and said, "Here, Gisela, you can do this. As you turn the wheel, it pushes the lid down, squeezing the beets dry so the juice runs from the spout into the bucket. Watch the bucket so it doesn't run over. While you do this, I'll get the next batch ready for cooking."

I followed Oma's instructions. When I turned the wheel, the big screw moved through the hole of the bar, pushing the lid down, pressing the sugar beets with the juice running from the spout. "Oma, the press is hard to turn, and the bucket is getting full," I announced.

"Let me empty the bucket into a clean tub, and then I'll turn it some more."

Oma turned the wheel until there was not another drop left in the beets. When she emptied the press the dried pulp fell out like a hart square block. Then, Oma refilled the press with the rest of the beets from the kettle. "Now you can turn again, and I'll refill the kettle because we have a lot more beets to cook today. So, we need to stay with it." Oma built another fire with the leftover coals from the bucket and added more wood. When the press was getting hard for me to turn, Oma took over once more. "I'll do the press, and you can watch the kettle and stir."

Standing on the footstool and stirring the beets, I just had to ask, "Oma, why are you doing all this?"

"The sugar beet syrup will give us extra food and help us to get through the winter."

"But how do you do that, Oma?"

"Well, we already cooked the beets. Now we extract the juice; after that, we'll cook the juice into syrup."

"But Oma, that's just clear water we're pressing out of the sugar beets."

"It might look like clear water to you, but it isn't. Dip your finger into the bucket and taste it."

So I did. "You're going to cook that? I don't like the taste; it tastes kind of sweet and earthy, like the smell of the field where we dug them."

"You're right! It's the taste of nature, nothing else. But you will see. When we get done, it will be good. Believe me."

After all the sugar beets were cooked and pressed dry, Oma scrubbed the kettle, so not the smallest piece of beet was left. Then she poured all the juice we had extracted into the clean kettle, filling it almost to the top. "Oma, what are you doing now?"

"Now, it's time to make syrup." Again she was building a new fire under the kettle. "Cooking the juice into syrup is a critical job. We have to watch the fire and the cooking of the syrup very closely. The juice needs to be stirred all the time so it doesn't sit still in the bottom of the kettle, because the sugar in the juice will burn quickly, and that will make the syrup taste bitter." So we both stood by the kettle, me on the footstool, and Oma standing next to me each of us stirring with a wash paddle, watching the contents. Every so often Oma checked the fire. "Why are you checking the fire, Oma?"

"We have to keep an even heat under the kettle, so I check it. If the fire gets too hot, the juice will boil too fast and that's not good."

I don't know how Oma knew all that stuff. To me she was like a book filled with wisdom and information. When the juice started to boil, Oma pulled some of the hot fire out from underneath the kettle, saying, "Now we have to let it simmer ever so gently and stir, stir, stir. This is the most critical time of our cooking. If it burns, all our labor was for nothing. We'll have to eat bitter, burned syrup on our bread because we can't toss it out. So, stir with all your strength, clear down to the bottom." Oma used her business-like voice, so I knew not to ask questions.

The juice began a soft rolling and bubbling, turning from a clear water to gold, then brown, and eventually black, all the while getting thicker until Oma tossed water on the fire and immediately removed it from under the kettle.

What began as a wash kettle full of clear, watery juice, was now half as much black sweet-smelling syrup. The syrup was a success. Oma handed me a spoon of that black, thick, sweet-smelling syrup to taste. "Be careful! It's hot!"

"Hmm." I licked and smacked my lips in surprise. "That's so good, Oma!"

"Yes, I knew you would like it!"

This black, thick, sweet-tasting syrup was truly a honey of the earth. I just had to dip the spoon once more, hoping Oma would not see it, but I heard her say, in her jovial way, "If you keep licking, pretty soon the spoon will be gone, too!" I guess she saw me dip after all.

The day before, Oma had readied and gathered all the containers she could find, like pots, big pitchers, or anything that would hold the syrup until it cooled. After we had scooped out all the syrup and the kettle was empty, not a drop left. Oma built a small fire so she could clean the kettle with hot water, making it a wash kettle again. We filled many glass jars with that dark, thick syrup. It was golden and precious to us. With careful rationing, it kept us supplied all winter long. And so, because of the strict food rationing by the East German communist regime, Oma and I continued to glean for the next two summers.

The gleaning for this summer had ended and after Oma finished the processing of the syrup, now, it was time to do the harvesting in the back yard. The old cherry tree was laden with sweet black cherries, and the red currants and grapes needed to be picked. Because several families shared the house, everyone living there had a right to the fruit. Oma set the harvest date so everyone had an equal share of the harvest. The only person not interested was the blonde Fraeulein with the delicate lingerie who cooked that good smelling food, brewed real coffee, and lived on the bottom floor. Onkel Heinz, Oma's son, my favorite Onkel, came to help. Siegfried, Frau Schmitt's son, and Onkel Heinz climbed the ladder to get up into the tree to pick the cherries. Or to shake branches so the cherries fall to the ground.

I wanted to be in the tree, too, but Oma was firm, "No, you will not do that!"

"But, Oma, Siegfried is up there, and he's just as old as I am, so why can't I?"

"It has nothing to do with age; girls do not climb trees!" I knew Oma was firm, probably tree climbing was not for girls, but I sure wanted to.

While helping to pick up the fallen cherries, I ate some; then, I hung a pair of cherries still hooked together, over my ears, like earrings. Our neighbors watched me, and when Oma realized that, she told me, "You can't eat as many cherries as you want because they are not only ours. They have to be shared with our neighbors. If you keep eating, we'll have less to divide." It didn't make much sense to me because there were lots of cherries, but once in while I slipped one in my mouth. Siegfried, too, had the same rule told by his mother as there were more cherry pits falling from the tree then cherries. Finally, using a scale, Oma divided the cherries equally among the families. The same process was applied to the red currants that grew along the fence after Oma and Siegfried's mother finished picking them.

The gathering and dividing of the grapes that grew over the garden house and the arbor was lots of fun because I was able to climb to the roof of the garden house to pick the blue grapes with Siegfried, while the grown-ups picked the grapes on the lower vines that grew on the trellises. At first, Oma didn't want me to be up there, but I begged, "Oma, please, can I be up there and help? It's not a tree and I know how to climb. I've done it before, please?"

"I know you have, and I didn't approve of it then or now; it is not for girls to climb into high places; only boys do that."

"But Oma, why not? Why only boys?"

"Well, boys wear pants. Girls wear dresses and don't climb because it is not seemly." I was not going to give up, so I moved a little closer to Oma, so close I could touch her arm. Looking up at her, I pleaded, "Oma, please, I'll be really careful so no one can see under my dress. Please, can I?"

"All right, I really don't like it, but you be careful, and don't fall off."

Before Oma had finished speaking, I was climbing on the sturdy vines that grew like a stepladder behind the garden house wall. Siegfried's freckled face appeared over me, "What are you doing? Did your grandmother let you come up here?"

"You're not the only one that can come up here! Oma said I could, so here I am!"

"I was only asking because you always had to sneak up here so your grandmother wouldn't see you!"

The roof of the garden house overgrown with the grapevine was our favorite hide and seek place. At times when Oma looked out the window from her room and saw us, she'd tell us to get of the roof and out of the grapevine. "All you kids do is destroy the growing grapes."

When Mutti was home, Oma talked to her about the grapes and the kids climbing in them, but Mutti only said, "Those old sour things—who wants them?"

But Oma, was the firm person in our household, and retorted, "They might be sour things to you, but people here want them and it doesn't help when the kids destroy in them."

Mutti just shrugged her shoulders. "They won't hurt them much." Turning to me she said, "For peace in the house, you stay out of the grapevine and off the garden house until they're harvested."

That was the end of that, although every now and then Siegfried and I climbed up on the garden house. But when the grapes turned color, I stayed away because they left blue stains on my dress and underwear, a give-away to Oma when she saw my clothes.

Onkel Heinz and Tante Hilde, sometimes come to visit with Oma and Mutti when she was home. Onkel Heinz was so handsome, tall and slender, his chiseled face, lively eyes and a full mouth that could fill the room with laughter. I adored him. He was like a remembrance of Vati. I would hug him and sit on his lap, or I'd tickle him and the teasing would start. He'd threaten to lay me over his knees, though he never did, because I could move fast and he never tried very hard to catch me.

Then one day he almost laid me over his knees. He got really mad at me, and I guess I had it coming. He was talking to Oma and Mutti, and I was standing behind his chair playing with his hair, which I had done before. Since he was almost bald, instead of braiding his hair into a real thin short braid, I decided to knot it with one knot atop another so that when he tried to comb it out, he couldn't. I was laughing, thinking it was funny that he could not comb his hair and had played a real trick on him. But he didn't think it was very funny at all. He was mad. "That is not a nice thing you've done! You deserve a spanking!" I stopped laughing, embarrassed that he had talked to me like that.

Mutti, trying not to laugh at her brother for being so mad, told him, "Well you always spoil her and let her do what she wants, and now she made a mess of your hair." Later, when Onkel Heinz had left, she scolded me and told me to apologize, which I did. He was kind of cool towards me for a while, and I tried hard to have him see how sorry I was. Eventually, all was forgotten, but he would not let me touch his hair again.

At the first opportunity I asked Oma, "How come, Onkel Heinz has so little hair? What happened to it? He's not an old man, is he?"

"No, he is not old. He had lots of hair, all black, but lost most of it during his active war duty. He was a *Panzer Fuehrer*, a tank driver. The stress of war and having to wear a helmet made him lose most of his hair."

"Oh, Oma, he must have been really nice looking then."

"That he was, but I think he still is nice looking, don't you?"

All I could do was nod. I had a picture of a handsome, tall, good-looking Onkel in my mind with lots of black hair. I never told anyone because it was my innermost secret, but I had a real girlish crush on him. From that day on I dreamingly wished and hoped for a dark haired, tall, good-looking man just like Onkel Heinz to marry some day.

Fall was approaching; it was getting cold; 1946 was ending. School had started again, and, with my usual peck on Oma's cheek, I went to school. Much to my dismay, I was still a year behind, because Oma or Mutti never went to school to correct it. Also Oma said, "That I missed to much schooling to jump a whole year ahead. Gisela continued calling from downstairs because Oma did not allow children to visit in the house.

Oma and I went back to doing our trips to the cemetery and, according to her; it was also time to cover the graves with the fir branches Oma had bought at the weekly farmers market. When she and I took the handcart to the cemetery with the branches in it, I asked, "Why are we doing this?"

"The flowers we planted on the grave this summer will bloom next year again, so we cover them up to protect them from the frost and snow. Also, the grave looks nice and clean, and when the snow gets high, we can't come to the cemetery. It has been a practice for ages, and now you know why we're doing it."

We covered Vati's grave, and it felt to me as if we tucked him in for the winter. Silently I told Vati we would not be coming often for a while, promising that I would think of him with all my heart.

On November 9, 1946, Oma and I did go to the cemetery once more to place a spray on Vati's grave because it had been a year since he had passed away.

Three months after Vati's death—nine months ago—I'd returned to my loving and caring family. This is where I belonged. I held onto Oma's hand really tight as we silently walked home from the cemetery in the cold, crisp air.

Winter came in all its fury, howling around every corner in Goerlitz, its sharp teeth biting deep. People hurried to get home, their bodies bent forward, braced against the wind. Others wrapped in shawls and scarves put their heads down to keep the icy air away from their faces. We children, our caps pulled low, hurried home from school to where it was warm. "That wind is so cold, Oma. It's like ice."

"I know. It's blowing straight from Siberia. It doesn't even want to snow it's so cold."

"Why Siberia?"

"Siberia is way east from here. It's part of Russia, a cold and icy place. People living there don't have much of a summer. When the wind blows from that direction, it brings freezing air with it. It will be a long, hard winter."

The rationing of electricity and gas continued, two hours, three times a day. Oma and I made several trips with the handcart, first, to the *Kartoffelhaendler* a potato merchant, to buy our winter's ration of potatoes, based on the number of household members; then, to the *Kohlenhaendler* a coal merchant, to buy coal, also rationed. We got pressed coal the size of building bricks called *Briketts,* and loose coals, like small rocks, called *Koks.* It looked like a lot to me, but Oma said it would hardly get us through the winter. Had we not gone gleaning for wheat and potatoes and made syrup from sugar beets, we would be starving.

On some weekends when it was not too cold, Oma and I took the handcart to the forest outside Goerlitz to collect sturdy branches and small tree trunks to start the fire with. We had an ax and a hand saw that looked like a bow. If the trees were skinny and not too tall, Oma felled them with the ax. I could not believe how quickly she chopped them down. A half dozen were chopped and lying on the ground. We both sawed, but only

Oma chopped, "I don't want you to do the chopping. You might miss and hit your leg or cut off a finger. You can load the cart or look for more wood for us to take home."

It was hard work, but I didn't mind. I liked being in the woods. I marveled at how the big trees reached for the sky, stretching out their branches like giant umbrellas, protecting the creatures living on the forest floor. But there was no time for dreaming. We had work to do, and it took all day. We ate our sandwiches sitting on a stump, and there was no nap for Oma. "It's too cold to lie on the ground. We'll get sick." We loaded the cart clear over the top. Then, Oma tied the wood down with a rope. She pulled the cart and I pushed. Sometimes we traded places because Oma got tired and her back hurt; then, I'd pulled.

Uphill I had to push hard, but downhill I always liked to take the cart. I'd hold the handle with both hands against my lower back, and, with the cart pushing, down the hill we went, Oma shouting after me, "Be careful! Watch for the farmer's wagon on the road with his horses or oxen!" I couldn't answer because I was too busy holding back the cart when it went too fast.

When Oma finally caught up, she told me, "You're going way too fast with that old cart. It's heavily loaded, and we don't want it to break down. We need it." I continued pulling on the flat road with Oma walking beside me, but when a hill came, I still did my downward dash, but a bit more carefully to satisfy Oma. Her smile said, "You just can't stop yourself!"

When we got home, Oma chapped the wood into smaller pieces then, it was stacked in the cellar. It was useless for me to be scared or complain of spiders or try to get out of going into the cellar. "If you want to be warm this winter, you need to help." Oma was firm and I knew it.

I wanted to ask, "Why isn't Christa helping? Doesn't she want to be warm this winter?" But I didn't ask. She was never home and would've had some excuse anyway.

And so our lives moved from November into December of 1946. From the stamps Oma had saved sugar, flour, margarine, and eggs. With some of our extra wheat she planned the baking of the *Weihnachts Stollen* the Christmas bread. We were given an allowance for raisins, a vanilla substitute that smelled like vanilla and yeast for baking. Oma had gotten the vanilla and raisins weeks earlier by standing, as usual, in line at the grocer's. The baker sold yeast only on certain days, so Oma had put her name on the list to make sure she had the needed yeast.

When it was time, Oma gave me *zehn Pfenning,* ten Penny's, to pick up the yeast and to make the appointment with the baker to bake the Stollen. *Why was Oma baking so early?* I knew Christmas was still several weeks away. "Why are you baking already? It's not Christmas yet, Oma."

"The Stollen has to be baked early and stored so the flavor can mature. You'll see."

And, so, baking day came. I was home from school, eager to watch and help as Oma had promised. As usual, Oma had gotten up early, so when I got up, the fire was already going in our small stove, the room, warm and cozy. Placed in front of the stove were two chairs, side by side; on them sat an aluminum tub, like a small washtub, covered by a cloth. I was curious, although I ate my morning soup made of flour, water and some milk without asking.

"Aren't we in a hurry this morning! I've never seen you eat so fast."

"I want to help, Oma."

"That you can, but first get dressed, brush your teeth and comb and braid your hair. I want no hair in our Stollen. Looking at Oma, I saw that her teeth were missing. *Why? Is she afraid her teeth will fall into the Stollen like my hair? Is that why?* For once I didn't ask because sometimes Oma didn't like me asking her too many personal questions. Oma always dressed, her hair combed, braided, then fastened in a round knot on the back of her head, wore a clean apron that covered her dress and a scarf that wrapped around her head. She looked ready to do her baking. "Go to the bathroom," she told me, "because later on no one is allowed to walk in or out of this room."

"Why can't we walk in or out, Oma?"

"Because the room has to stay warm while we're baking."

"Why?"

"First, the yeast in the tub has to rise, and, later on, the dough has to rise." I decided to be quiet and wait to see what Oma was going to do next. When I finished dressing, combing my hair, and brushing my teeth, Oma tied a kitchen towel around me. "That is to keep your dress clean,"

After she tied my headscarf, I, too, was ready to help Oma with the baking.

When she removed the cloth, I peeked in the tub and saw a mound of flour like a hill. In that hill was a hole containing a bubbly gray mass that smelled of yeast. "Oma, what's that? It smells like yeast."

"That's what it is, yeast. It bubbles when it rises."

"Yeast rising?"

"It's the yeast from the baker; it is rising for the Stollen." Oma washed and scrubbed her hands up to her elbows in the washbasin. Now things got really interesting for me. *What is Oma going to do?*

"Why do you scrub your hands and arms?"

"When I bake, I use my hands and they have to be clean."

Oma dried her hands and arms, then, walked over to the tub to pour warm milk around the outside of the hill. From a small dish she poured the already beaten eggs, then the sugar, then the melted margarine. Last came the vanilla. Finally she put her hands into the gray bubbling yeast and mixed it all up. The hill fell and became a sticky, gooey mass on her hands and fingers.

On Mutti's makeshift counter Oma had lined up the sugar, flour, and raisins. "As I work the dough, it's your job to pour the additional sugar and flour for me and, in time, the raisins. I'll tell you when and how much. Do you think you can do that?"

"That's not hard; I can do that, but, Oma, can I have just one raisin?"

"Count yourself out five, but no more. That is all we have. I need all of them for the Stollen."

Slowly, I ate the raisins one by one, and they tasted so good. "Now, pay attention. I need more flour and sugar; pour both right on the dough but slowly, and put some flour on my hands." I poured the sugar, then the flour, and last of all the raisins. As Oma kneaded, the dough stopped clinging to her hands. The thicker the dough got, the harder Oma had to knead it. Her arms worked like pistons. The tub started to jump, wanting to leave the chairs. "Hold onto the tub so I can knead!"

I braced my knees against the sides of the tub to keep it from jumping off, all the while holding it down, while Oma slapped the dough with one splat, then another, tossing the dough around and around in the tub. Then, with both hands, Oma lifted the dough, a big creamy mound with raisins peeking out here and there. With two fingers I pinched a piece of that yummy looking dough and stuck it in my mouth. "Mmmm, that tastes good, Oma, so sweet and creamy!" I said as I licked my fingers.

Still holding the dough, Oma told me, "When you get done licking your fingers, put a little flour over the bottom of the tub." I watched as she laid the dough carefully and rather lovingly back into the tub, then powdered the top with flour. I didn't quite understand. First, Oma had smacked the dough so hard that the tub wanted to jump off the chairs, and now she was so tender with it. "Why did you slap the dough so hard, Oma?"

"The dough has to make bubbles, so, letting out the air makes for a good solid Stollen."

Oma covered the tub once more. Then, she placed the two chairs with the tub near the cozy warm stove. "While the dough is rising, there will be no going in or out; we need to keep the door closed, the warm air in, and the cold air out." She busied herself with cleaning and putting away the things she'd used.

Then, she brought out a big, square board, scrubbed almost pure white, and placed it on the table, covering it with a thin dusting of flour. Next, Oma laid clean towels and a blanket next to it. *What is that for? Oma does the funniest things.* I waited, knowing in time I'd find out. And I did.

After what seemed to be a long time, Oma carefully lifted the towel and looked in the tub. "Now, look at that! Doesn't that look nice?" I hurried to look, too, and couldn't believe what I saw. The dough Oma had slapped around had grown big, almost filling the whole tub.

"Oma, what are you going to do with all that dough?"

"I'll form it into several loaves of Stollen. Just watch." Oma kneaded the dough once more, then made several mounds all the same size. She took the rolling pin, a clean glass bottle because we didn't have a rolling pin, and rolled the dough square. Then, she folded it in half so it looked like a loaf of bread. She placed these loaves on the floured board, brushing each with warm milk, and covered them with the clean towels. "When it is time to take them to the baker, you'll help with the carrying. But for right now, they can rest and rise some." Oma sounded satisfied.

Her hands and arms washed, she took off the scarf and changed her baking apron for a clean one. She was ready for the baker. One final thing needed to be done: stick small picks with our name on it into the dough, identifying our Stollen from all the others. When it was time, we bundled up. Oma took the blanket and put it over the top of the towels that covered the loaves. "That should keep them from getting too cold. We have to hurry so they stay warm."

Oma and I carried our loaves like jewels to the baker. At the baker's, were many people, all with their traditional *Weihnachts-Stollen* for baking. The air was laden with the aroma of warm baked goods, interwoven with sugar and vanilla. All those sweet aromas—I couldn't breathe fast or deep enough to take in all, those aromas so seldom enjoyed. "Oma, it smelled so good at the bakery."

"It sure did. It's something we can't enjoy very often. These days no one has the goods for baking, and it's not getting better anytime soon. We need to eat our Stollen slowly and enjoy it while it lasts."

When we picked up our baked Stollen and while it was cooling, our living room had that same aroma. Every once in a while I lifted one corner of the towel and sniffed the loaves, my mouth ready for the first bite. After they cooled, Oma took them upstairs to her room and stored them, covered with towels, in the drawer of her commode. That's where they stayed until Christmas morning.

After the baking was done, Oma took care of the washing. There was no spreading of sheets out on the lawn as in the summer. Oma and I carried the wash up to the attic for drying, but as soon it was on the line, it froze. It was so cold that I wore gloves and a coat as we hung up the wash. "Aren't you cold, Oma?"

"No, I have more meat on me than you. If I was a skinny little thing like you, I'd be cold, too." We had a rhythm. Oma told me what piece she wanted next, and I'd get it from the basket, handing it to her with a clothespin so she didn't have to bend down. "You're closer to the ground."

Where have I heard that before? Oh, my stepmother used that a lot. Maybe it's something that all grownups say to their children. By the time we'd hung up the last of the laundry, it was frozen stiff. "Oma, look, our clothes are frozen!"

"It's below freezing outside, so it will freeze even inside." I was touching the frozen clothes when Oma warned me, "Don't touch the frozen clothes. They will break!" Oh, I was tempted to try it, just to see if they would, but Oma would not have been happy with me.

"Why would they break?"

"Because they're frozen, and if you fold or bend them, they will break."

"Oma, can't you wash when it's not so cold?"

"In the winter, we don't have much choice. It's always cold and I don't like the wash to be around over the holidays; everything has to be clean to start the new year with."

"Maybe you could wash between Christmas and New Year. Maybe it won't be so cold?"

"No, I cannot and will not wash at that time at all!" Oma's tone told me she was not going to discuss it any further. But her answer didn't satisfy me, so I pushed on, "But why not?"

"Because you're not to wash in between the holidays."

"But why not, Oma?"

Oma looked a little impatient, but knowing I was not going to give up, with a sigh she explained, "If you wash clothes between Christmas and New Years, it is said that the people whose clothes you wash will get sick and die in the new year."

"Is that true? Do you believe that, Oma?"

"Oh, I really don't know. I have heard it all my life. It's an old wives' tale, a superstition, but I never put it to the test." Then, with a shrug of her shoulders, she added, "It's just as easy to do the washing now and to start the new year all clean."

"You mean no one washes on those days, Oma?"

"It's a superstition, and I don't know what other people do. I just know that I don't." Oma took the empty wash basket and we went downstairs. I had the feeling she was done answering my questions.

When the wash was ironed, mended, and put away, it was time to clean the house for the holidays. Mutti was home, cleaning our rooms from one end to the other. No corner was safe from her. On her hands and knees she scrubbed, waxed, and polished. The windows were cleaned with vinegar water. The curtains and sheers were washed and ironed by Oma, then hung up again. I could hardly wait for Christmas Eve to arrive!

But before Christmas there was another very important event, *Sankt Nikolaus Tag* or Saint Nicholas Day. Sankt Nikolaus, also known as *Knecht Ruprecht* is a big, burly man, with a bushy white beard. He wears a long, dark hooded coat, pants that puff out from his high black boots, a wide black belt that encircles his round tummy, and dark green shirt. Slung over his shoulder is a sack filled with ginger cookies, apples, nuts, and candy, only for the good children. For the bad and unruly ones, he carries a switch made from several small branches sticking out from the top of his sack. The children worry because Knecht Ruprecht is aware of everyone's behavior. To receive a switch is bad because everyone would know where it came from and why. He makes his appearance the night of December fifth when the children are asleep. He carries a lantern and checks that they are in their beds sleeping. If not, he goes unseen, leaving their shoes empty. "Don't forget to put your shoes out," Oma reminded me. "You know who is coming tonight." Oma didn't have to remind me. I knew what night it was and who was coming, and so did every other child.

"I won't, Oma!"

"Are your shoes clean? You know what happens if they're not; you get nothing." So, I made sure my shoes were polished and shining, ready and waiting outside our door for Knecht Ruprecht.

In the evening when the power and gas were turned off all over the city, Oma built a fire in our small stove. She left the oven door open for us to see the flames and hear the crackling and snapping of the wood. Sitting by the fire, huddled next to Oma, I felt the warmth radiating through the darkened room, illuminated only by the flames that made shadows on the walls. We sang Christmas songs, accompanied by the crackling and popping of the hot coals and wood. "Oma, let's sing *Stille Nacht Heilige Nacht*, Silent Night Holy Night."

"No, not yet."

"Why not, Oma?"

"Because it's not Christmas Eve yet. We'll sing it when it's Christmas Eve. That's when Jesus was born and not before." I wanted to sing it so badly, but Oma was firm, not until Christmas. So we sang other Christmas songs.

Sometimes I thought I heard some rumbling and stomping like heavy boots outside our door, but it could not have been Knecht Ruprecht, I was not asleep yet. I was so excited I thought I could not sleep at all, but I did, and as soon as I awoke the next morning, I jumped out of bed and with bare feet ran to the door to see if Knecht Ruprecht had come and what he had left for me. Yes, he had come! He had filled my shoes with *Pfeffernuesse*, ginger bread cookies, apple, and sweets. "Oma, Mutti, look what I got! He did come! He did not forget me like last year."

"He has not forgotten you or any other child. Last year was a sad year. The war just ended, so I suppose he couldn't even find the children because they had left their homes behind, just like you," Mutti explained with Oma adding, "I think he was not able to see or find any children at all. Also he didn't have sweets to give. And shortly after the war, your father passed away. It was a sad and unhappy year for everyone."

"Did you even put your shoes out last year," Mutti asked.

"No, I didn't." But I remembered that last Christmas with my stepmother, and her telling everyone that I was not to be trusted, that I was a thief. I did remember. It all came back to me, and I started to hang my head. Oma gave me a squeeze, kissing the top of my head.

"Na, na, no sad faces this morning. All is well and you're home with us." I, too, was glad, but I always wished for Vati to be there with us, and most of all to be with me.

With our rooms clean and shining, Christmas came nearer and nearer. On Christmas Eve morning, we took our baths in the shared bathroom. Mutti scrubbed me from head to toe. She washed my hair, pouring water like a waterfall all over me, while I sputtered. Mutti had me shining, just as she did the floor. After I dressed, she combed and braided my hair, adding a small ribbon at the end of each braid. "There now, don't you look nice and squeaky clean!"

I don't know if I was squeaking, but I was clean and happy.

Oma and I planned to go to the late afternoon Christmas Eve Service at church. Thanks to Oma and her saving of stamps, we ate the Schlesien traditional Christmas Eve dinner of mashed potatoes, *Sauerkraut*, with a *Bratwurst* for each of us. It was a feast. I was so excited about Christmas that I could hardly sit still while we ate our special dinner.

After dinner I had to help with the dishes, mainly drying, because they, too, had to be put away and our room tidied once more for the Weihnachtsmann to come. Then, it started to snow, little tiny white flakes, sparkling as they gently fell from heaven. "Look, it's snowing!" I danced around the table shouting, "It's snowing! It's snowing! Now it's really Christmas!" When Oma and I got ready to go to church, Oma in her blue hat, I asked Mutti, "How come you and Christa are not going to church with us?"

"Somebody has to stay home because the Weihnachtsmann with the Christkind will come to decorate our Christbaum while you're with Oma in church." Mutti looked so festive in her long-sleeved black dress trimmed in blue, a kind of satiny dress. Her black hair, done up by her hairdresser, just like that Fraeulein who lived below us. And once more I realized that I, too, had the slim, pretty, caring, and loving mother I had always wished for. All of us were dressed for that special event, including my sister who, at the moment was in a good mood. In my excitement I had forgotten about the tree, decorated like magic by the Weihnachtsmann and the Christkind. Children weren't allowed to see the tree until Christmas Eve. "Oma, let's hurry to church so the Weihnachtsmann can come," I shouted.

"Slow down a little or you'll wear me out. We'll go in a minute. It's early yet."

Finally, it was time! When we got outside, church bells were ringing, calling everyone to church with a sound so wonderful, so heavenly, weaving through the cold brisk air mixing with softly falling snowflakes, moving over snow-covered roof tops, touching our hearts with their brilliant sound. I held onto Oma's hand, listening to the bells telling us that Christmas had come. "Oma, I can hear more than just one church ringing its bells."

"Our city has more than just one church. We have five Protestant churches and two Catholic Churches. That's why you hear more than one."

"How come only two Catholic Churches?"

"The eastern portion of Germany for many, many years has been mostly Protestant, while the western part has been mostly Catholic."

"The bells sound so nice, so special for Christmas. What church are we going to, Oma?"

"To the *Peterskirche*. It's the oldest church in Goerlitz."

"How old is it, Oma?"

"It was started in 1200 and finished from 1423 to 1497 to its present look."

"That's pretty old."

"Yes, Goerlitz is an old city with new added to it, making it a nice city to live in."

"I will always live here, Oma. I like it here."

I could hardly wait to enter the church, to see what it looked like inside because I liked churches. They were so majestic, and the organ, so powerful. The closer we got to the church, the louder the bells, and I could hear the organ. Oma and I walked up the wide steps leading to the arched portal and heavy ornamental wooden door. Stepping inside, I heard the organ thundering, filling the church with its force, its sounds bouncing off the walls, spilling outside into the clear winter air.

The church was filled with people, but Oma and I found a seat, and I snuggled close to her. Way up underneath the church's many arches, I could see the organ with pipes all big round, tall pipes all the way down to small short ones. When the organist played the low keys, the big thick pipes droned, sending their vibrations right into my tummy with the little ones' whistling mixing with the middle and small-sized ones. I could see the man who played the organ. With his back turned to the people, his body and shoulders moving, he reached from one side of the organ to the other, working, forcing the most beautiful notes, high and low, out of those pipes. I had never seen such a huge organ. The little church I used to go to when we lived in the suburb of Liegnitz didn't have such a big organ. "Oma, listen! I know that song he's playing. It's *Ave Maria,* the same one that's on one of the records I play at home. It's my most favorite song."

I knew right then and there that when I was a bride I wanted that song played at my church wedding. "Oma, I want to . . . ."

"Shhh, you need to be quiet. People around you want to meditate and listen to the music."

"What's meditate?" I wanted to ask, but I didn't.

So I looked around. People looked sad. Some were quietly crying. Others just sat there listening, motionless, staring into the distance with an empty look in their eyes. Others, hands folded in their laps, their heads low, moved their lips as in prayer. Is that what Oma meant by meditate?

But soon other things got my interest. I marveled at the tall high pillars, big and strong, standing like soldiers, supporting many arches throughout the church. All around the walls of the church, extending to the high ceiling, were narrow windows made of individual small ones with some colored ones as trim. I noticed it had gotten dark outside. I tried to whisper, but the organ was too loud, so I had to speak up a little louder, "Oma, why are some of the small windows broken?"

Oma bent down so I could hear her. "Just before the end of the war, the big iron bridge below the church that spanned the Neisse River to the other side of Goerlitz was blown up, and the pressure from the explosion broke the window panes."

"I can see snowflakes coming in. Can you?"

"Shhh, time to stop talking and put your nose to the front." When I looked at the altar, there was a Christmas tree, but it had no lights, no decorations at all. It stood there, bare and erect, as if to say, "Here I am and always will be." I was going to ask Oma why it had no lights, but the organ started again and everyone stood up, holding their hymn books, and sang,

"*Oh Du Froehliche, Oh Du Selige Weihnachtszeit*" ("Oh Happy and Blessed Christmas").

Then the Pastor appeared, dressed in a black robe with a white collar extending from his shoulders, looking like a long wide shawl. His sleeves made me think of butterfly wings when he lifted his hand while talking and reading from a book. I wasn't really listening to what he was saying, but I heard him tell the story of Jesus and his birth, though I didn't understand everything. He talked for a long time, only stopping for a song every now and then.

I began to get cold. I could see my breath and everyone else's, too. That's when I looked at the people. They were all bundled up and huddled together. And just as I could tell who was with whom, people could tell that I had come with Oma. She had her arm around me, keeping me from shivering. At the end, the Pastor asked us to join him in prayer, "*Das Vater Unser*" ("The Lord's Prayer"). I lowered my head and prayed with Oma.

After we finished praying, the organ started to play, and as if by magic, the bells started ringing so that the whole church seemed to vibrate. The people stood up and with joy in their voices sang "*Stille Nacht, Heilige Nacht*" ("Silent Night, Holy Night"). It was as if everyone was relieved of an unseen burden. They sang with hope in their voices; they sang for a new beginning. I, too, while the Pastor was giving his sermon, folded my hands, and thought of Vati and the last Christmas we had together, the opera house he had taken me to, the love he had for me. I felt no one would ever love me more than he did.

But for some reason I had no tears. It was as if I had locked Vati and the loss of him away in a place in my heart that no one could reach—only me. I knew that for me a new life had started, and that I had to let go of the past, but never of Vati.

After we sang "Silent Night," the pastor made the sign of the cross, blessed and wished all of us a *Frohes Weihnachtsfest* a Merry Christmas. The organist kept on playing as people quietly filed out of the church. I had enjoyed being there and listening to the organ music, but I was glad it was over because I had gotten so cold sitting still. Oma had put her arm around me and pulled me close, but I was still cold. Outside was cold, too, but I could move and slowly got warm again.

I took Oma's gloved hand, and we walked home with the sound of the church bells following us. Because the ground was covered with newly fallen snow, we walked slowly so Oma wouldn't slip on the round cobblestones or when she stepped off or onto the sidewalks. It had stopped snowing. The dark clear sky illuminated by the Milky Way arched over us like a long almost white ribbon. Stars sparkled like diamonds on dark velvet. They felt so close I wanted to reach up and touch one. "Oma, look at the stars. They are sparkling and glistening extra special tonight."

"That's because tonight is a special night. It's the night that Jesus was born."

"And, Oma, look at that great big star, it has rays; it really sparkles."

"That's the Christmas star. It shines especially bright tonight."

The newly fallen snow had covered the ground like a blanket, so not a sound was heard except the bells and the crunching of the snow as Oma and I walked home. There were no horses or wagons rattling over cobblestone streets, no running or shouting children. Everyone was walking quietly. "It is such a beautiful evening, Oma, so quiet, no noise at all."

"Yes, it's nice. I like it quiet and serene."

Serene? "What's serene Oma?"

"Serene is a calm, quiet kind of a hush, like when you're not asking a lot of questions."

I had to think about that for a minute. "Do you mean you don't want me to talk and ask you questions, Oma?" Oma smiled at me from underneath her blue hat and squeezed my hand. "I was only teasing you. You can ask all you want, but sometimes it is nice when you're quiet and don't ask a lot of questions."

"You had me scared, Oma."

She laughed. "But not for long, I'm sure." When I looked up at Oma, I saw that she wore her teeth. It must be a special day. Oma, underneath her coat, was wearing her Sunday dress and her best shoes, the ones she only wore on special occasions.

I wanted to say something nice to her, and it popped out before I realized what I was saying, "Oma, you look so nice today with your teeth."

Oops! That came out wrong. Oma stopped walking. Looking at me, she laughed, "Are you saying I don't look nice any other time?"

Embarrassed, I answered, "You know what I mean, Oma, your teeth and all."

"Yes, I know what you mean, but they don't fit right anymore and I don't like to wear them much, only on special occasions, and Christmas is special."

"You're always my Oma no matter what you look like."

"Now I'm glad to hear that. It's like a Christmas present from you."

I really had never told Oma just how much I loved her and I guessed that was just what I had done, just then. I think I always loved Oma, even when I lived in Liegnitz with my stepmother and Vati was in the war. I remembered someone loving and caring, but it was a hazy memory, so I didn't know why I had this feeling. In 1943 when I visited in Goerlitz, I hadn't recognized Oma was that memory of love because I was so happy to see her again that I forgot all about it. But now I knew who that loving someone was. It was Oma! That cold evening, walking along with Oma, holding her hand, feeling her warmth through my gloves, I felt secure and happy. Little by little, pieces of my earlier life started to come together like a puzzle.

As we walked, I realized we were not walking in the dark. Usually, when the electricity and gas got turned off in houses and over the city, the gas lanterns on the streets were off, too, so people walked in the dark. "Oma, the gas lanterns are still on! They're not off! How come?"

"It was in the newspaper that over Christmas and New Years the gas and electricity will stay on."

"Does that mean we have both of them on all day? Like tomorrow and the next day? They're not going to shut it off?"

"No, they're not. We have electricity and gas all day for the next two days. It started this morning. It will be shut off only after midnight and turned back on at six in the morning."

"We don't have to sit in the dark for the next two days?"

"No, we don't! And by the time it's turned off, we'll be in bed. It will be a nice Christmas with gas to cook with and electricity all day and part of the night."

While we walked, I looked up at the apartment houses. I could see Christmas trees in some windows, light in some and darkness in others. Maybe the people living there were not going to have a Christmas, or maybe they were sad like I was last year when Vati had passed away just before Christmas. "Oma, I can see Christmas trees in some windows and in others only light or all darkness."

"Maybe some people are not home yet, like you and I, or some are not celebrating Christmas. Maybe they've lost their family, or they don't know where they are, or they can't get over the border to them. There are all kinds of reasons why people are not celebrating. Let's not forget, it's just a year and a half since the war ended. People are still hurting, trying to heal, to rebuild their lives, trying to make a new home away from their homes. If it weren't for you, I think we might not celebrate either."

"Why is that?"

"We, too, have losses from the war, like your father and my son and our homes on the other side, but you're our youngest, a child, and children like Christmas. So we're celebrating Christmas."

"Are Onkel Heinz and Tante Elfriede celebrating, too?"

"Yes, they are. Onkel Heinz and his wife have Rainer; Tante Elfriede and her husband have Uschi. Not too many people celebrate at the moment because these are not happy times. Families will do what they can, and we, too, do the best we can." Listening to Oma, I knew we would have a nice Christmas, and I was looking forward to it.

By the time we got home, the bells from the Peterskirche had stopped, but in the distance I could hear other bells ringing. When Oma and I came upstairs, Mutti greeted us in front of our door in the hallway, telling me, "I want you to cover your eyes with your hands as you go through the living room into your room to take off your coat and things. The Weihnachtsmann was here with his Christkind, and they decorated the tree, leaving small gifts for you. You have to wait and come out when you hear the ringing of the little Weihnachtsgloeckchen."

"She'll peek through her fingers. Close your eyes," my sister insisted. She tied a scarf so tight over my eyes that even if I had wanted to, I would have been unable to open them. Mutti told her that was not necessary, but my sister, as always, did what she wanted, ignoring others. She guided me into our bedroom, removed the scarf without saying a word, and left, closing the door behind her. I took off my coat, hat, gloves, and shoes, and while putting on my house shoes I thought again about why my sister always got her way and nobody told her to mind her own business. *Why does she always treat me this way? She's not the boss of me! She is only my sister! She's not going to make me sad or unhappy. No, she won't!*

Then I heard the tinkling of the bell, my cue to come out. When I came out of my room, Mutti and Oma were standing to one side of the Christmas tree with Christa behind them. Mutti or Oma had turned off the lights and, oh, what a sight! The small tree was standing on the credenza, it's fresh scent weaving through the air, it lights shining bright, illuminating the room with joy and cheer. It was decorated with colored ornaments. Small colored sugar rings, called *Fondant,* were hanging attached to ribbons on branches here and there. Candles, placed in holders, were attached near the tips of branches to keep the tree from catching fire. Tinsels reflecting the lights of the candles were hung over the branches. The tree was sparkling, the most wonderful tree I had seen! I stood unmoving, looking, my eyes shining. All I could say was, "What a beautiful Weihnachtsbaum!"

Then, Oma stepped forward and started to sing *Stille Nacht Heilige Nacht* with Mutti, Christa, and me following her. My mind was whirling with such happiness and sadness that I started to choke up. Oma, without interrupting her singing, put her arm around me, assuring me that all was well. After we were done singing, Mutti told me, "Why don't you go over to the table? I believe the Weihnachtsmann has left some small gifts for you."

And he had! There was the traditional Christmas plate filled with Pfefferkuchen, nuts, and candy, a book for young adults, pencils and notebooks for school, and a pretty hand-knitted pullover. Its long sleeves and back were knitted in a solid brown, but the front was knitted in diagonal stripes in colors of red, blue, green, and beige. I was so happy I didn't care it was partly knitted from wool of an old brown pullover or sweater I had helped Oma to unravel. Christa, my sister, had made me a *Taschentuchhalter* a handkerchief holder, out of green material, embroidered on top with my initials "GK" in the center.

I went to Mutti and Oma and gave them the customary thank you hug and a kiss. I also went to my sister to give her a big hug and to thank her for that wonderful gift, but she stood stiff, not returning my hug, and said nothing!

The next morning Mutti called us, "Sleepy heads, get up, clean up, and get dressed for breakfast." I didn't have to be called twice, not like when I had to work with Oma. This was fun time, and I knew what would be served this morning for breakfast, no soup! Already dressed, Mutti had set the table using the china and linen from the Pastor's wife. In the center of the table she'd placed a three-armed porcelain candleholder trimmed in gold, its candles already burning. Oma, also dressed in her best, was busy lighting the candles on the Christmas tree. The radio was playing Christmas songs intermingled with the sounds of church bells. The room was warm and so cozy. The smell of that "good coffee" perfumed the air. It was an atmosphere of peace and love. Even my sister was mellow.

On the table and to one side of the candleholder, the Weihnachts-Stollen was sliced and arranged on a cake plate. On the other side of the candleholder was another cake plate filled with Streuselkuchen, sliced in strips and stacked, like a pyramid. It was the same kind I'd shared with the neighborhood kids in Liegnitz, and got me in trouble with my stepmother, but it still was one of my favorites. "Oma, did you bake the *Streuselkuchen*?"

"Now, what do you think?"

"How come I didn't know?"

"Well, you don't know everything, do you?"

I turned to Mutti, "Did you know that Oma baked a Streuselkuchen for us?"

"Yes, I knew she was going to do it, but I, too, was not here when she was baking."

"When did you bake it, Oma?"

"While you were in school and your mother at work. Now, hush, eat and enjoy. A feast like this does not happen very often." And Oma was right.

Mutti allowed me to have some of that good coffee with an equal amount of milk, and I ate until I was about to pop. Every bite was so good! "Oma, this is so good. You are the best baker."

"Well, I should be. I have done lots of baking in my time. I'm glad you like it. I can tell that you do by the way you're eating."

When breakfast was done, I blew out all the candles and helped with the dishes. Christa had left to go somewhere. Despite her unfriendliness at home, she had lots of friends. Then Mutti and Oma started to prepare our dinner, and it smelled so good. The day before Mutti had cooked the *Rotkraut*, red cabbage; Mutti always claimed letting it sit overnight made it taste better the next day. Our dinner at noon consisted of *Rotkraut, Fleisch-Braten* and *Kartoffel-Kloesse,* red cabbage, roast and potato dumplings, made by Oma. The aroma of good food cooking filled our room, but I knew it would not last forever. Christa came home and helped set the table, again with the china, the silverware, and the candleholder. The day was a reminder of good times past, a small room filled with contentment and tummies full of wonderful good-tasting food.

In the afternoon Onkel Heinz and Tante Hilde came with Rainer and Tante Elfriede and Onkel Richard with my cousin Uschi. Everyone brought something to share at the table, filling our room with laughter again.

Mutti and my aunts made sandwiches for the evening. There were even *Wienerle*, hot dogs, for my cousins and me. The grown ups had beer, while we kids had tea.

The next day, also a Christmas holiday (Germany has two holidays each Christmas, Easter, and Pfingsten), was quiet and relaxing. We ate leftovers without setting a fancy table. The room was warm and cozy, and we had eaten all we wanted for once. Mutti had company in the afternoon, co-workers from the train. Oma and I went to visit her sister Ida who also lived in Goerlitz. And before we knew it, the Christmas holidays were over. The gas and electricity were off again until the New Year holidays.

All the Christmas excitement had passed and the tree, still standing on the credenza, was waiting for the New Year holidays to pass and only then to be taken down. The sugar rings on the tree were almost gone. Although I was allowed to eat them, I picked them so no bare spots would show. Mutti had bought four paper garlands that she was trying to hang. I watched Mutti standing on a chair trying to attach one end of the garlands to a hook in the corner of the ceiling. Over her shoulder, she called, "Gisela, I need your help. While I try to hook up my end of the paper garland, you take the other end and walk to the middle of the room. Hold the garland as high as you can, and slowly let it fall apart. But be careful. Don't lose the end of the string. We can't restring it." Glad to help Mutti, I took the end she handed me, walked to the middle of the room, my arm high, the garland made of thin paper slowly falling apart like an accordion, it's zigzag pattern changing colors, red to green, yellow, and blue.

When Mutti had fastened her end, she took my end and fastened it to the chandelier. Then we fastened the other garlands the same way, from the four corners to the chandelier. Finally I asked, "Mutti that looks so nice, but why are you doing this?"

"It's a tradition. After Christmas we decorate for our New Year's Eve party with colored paper garlands, hats, horns, confetti, and streamers."

"Does everyone decorate like that?"

"Yes, most people do or used to. I don't know if they do now. I suppose some won't because they're not with their families. They're alone, but in time they will celebrate again. We're lucky, because most of our family is here, so we'll celebrate!"

"We're celebrating New Year's Eve? We're having a party? A real party with our family? Here?"

"Yes, right here."

"When Vati was alive and we lived in Liegnitz, we never had a party."

"Your father didn't have much to party about being married to that woman. He was in the war. During the war people were getting killed or fleeing, so, no one celebrated. But the war is over now, and life is slowly returning to normal again."

"Did Vati like to party?"

"Oh ja, he liked family gatherings and a good time. When he was wounded in 1943, he came to Goerlitz, his leg still in a cast, for a visit. The whole family got together and we had a nice time. He was so happy and relaxed, but there was one little person missing that we both wanted to be here with us, and that was you."

"And now I am here and Vati is not. It's as if we traded places."

Mutti's words made me think back. *So Vati had been in Goerlitz and had spent time with Mutti and the family. Somehow my stepmother had found out. Then she and I had ridden the train to Kohlfurt where she'd dropped me off at her parents' while she continued on to Goerlitz. She'd planned to find Vati! That's why she hadn't wanted me to go with her. Furious and alone, she'd returned to Kohlfurt. When I'd asked her where Vati was, she'd said in her icy voice, "He will come later." What had happened, I didn't know but I could tell she was mad!*

Soon after that, Vati came home to Liegnitz. Then, my stepmother had told me to go outside because they needed to talk. But they'd had a fight. My stepmother had yelled and called my real mother a whore because Vati's been here in Goerlitz with Mutti and her family. Why had she called my mother a whore? What had she meant by that? I knew it was something ugly because she'd spat out that word with such hate. Had she known that Vati was going to leave her after the end of the war? She'd hated my mother! Why, she'd hated me, too! I was the daughter of the woman she called a whore. She'd hated me all along, even when Vati and she had come to pick me up at the apartment where I'd lived with Oma and my sister. She'd always hated me, and that's why she'd been so mean to me, like an evil stepmother! She knew that she was losing her husband to my mother, and she knew she couldn't stop it. Now, no one had him, not even I.

"What are you thinking so deeply about?" Mutti interrupted me.

"Oh, nothing much." I knew all that was in the past, so I asked, "Who's coming to the party, Mutti?"

"Onkel Heinz, Tante Hilde, Onkel Richard, Tante Elfriede, Tante Annie, my girlfriend, and her husband, and another couple who are good friends of mine."

"Is Uschi coming, too? Can we stay up until midnight?"

"Yes, Uschi is coming, too, and, yes, you two can stay up 'til midnight."

"It's going to be so much fun! I can hardly wait!"

"What is it that you can hardly wait for?" Oma came into the room decorated with the garlands, then asked Mutti, "And what are you doing, *Lenchen,* short for Helene?"

"Getting ready for our New Year's Eve celebration."

"Ja, and, Oma, we will have so much fun! Everyone is coming,"

But, Oma, unsure about that, said, "Do you think that is a good idea considering the circumstances we're living under?"

"That isn't going to change anytime soon. We might as well enjoy life, and be glad that we're still among the living. Soon enough we have to go back to our daily drudgery, but in the meantime, we will celebrate and have a good time."

Oma just nodded her head. I think she knew Mutti liked having parties and good times whenever possible. I was glad Oma's remarks didn't make Mutti change her mind about the party because I was looking forward to it! *It sounded like lots of fun. Maybe I, too, liked to party like Mutti?*

On New Year's Eve day Mutti set the table once again with the things that didn't belong to us, like the tablecloth, the porcelain dishes, and the crystal beer glasses. As a final touch, again Mutti placed the porcelain candleholder in the center of the table. Then she threw confetti all over the table and laid paper streamers that unwound like snakes down the center, with paper horns and hats between them. She handed the leftover confetti to me and said, "Scatter it all over the floor. Then, throw the streamers everywhere, even over chairs and over the garlands so they hang down." It was a party room filled with color and fun. The radio was playing and I danced around the beautifully set table, underneath the up-side-down arches of garlands crisscrossing our living room. "Oh, it's going to be so much fun!"

"We can see one person who is going to have fun!" Mutti and Oma laughed.

Mutti and Oma had made a big bowl of potato salad. I heard Mutti tell Oma that everyone gave her potatoes to make the salad. And in the evening when the guests arrived, they brought *Bier*, beer and *Knackwurst*, smoked sausage to be heated in water along with ours. Everyone was dressed up: the men in suits and ties, and the ladies, in their best dresses. Oma, Uschi, and I also dressed for the occasion, sat in the cozy corner next to the Kachelofen eating our dinner. Oma had made tea for us, and served it in the china teapot that matched our dinner plates, cups, and saucers. It was so much fun.

After dinner, Uschi and I played games, called *Mensch aeger Dich nicht*, Aggravation, with our New Year's hats and the paper horns next to us, waiting for midnight to come. Oma leaned against the warm *Kachelofen* resting her busy hands in her lap. The grownups at the table talked and laughed, leaning toward Oma to include her in their conversation. On the radio different brass bands played *polkas, waltzes, and beer drinking songs* everyone knew. Mutti joined in the singing, holding her beer glass up, and everyone else around the table followed. They sang and *schunkelt*, a sideways motion to the music, and arms intertwined with your neighbor on each side of you.

Time passed fast and midnight came before we knew it. Through out the city all church bells rang, to welcome in the New Year of 1947. Mutti opened the windows to let in the sounds of the bells from the Dreifaltigkeitkirche. Our street came alive with people shouting *"Frohes neues Jahr!"* Happy New Year! Others, like Mutti and our family, looked out the windows, shouting and blowing their horns.

With our New Year's hats on, Uschi and I went downstairs, blowing our paper horns, shouting *Frohes Neues Jahr!* Uschi held back a little, but I shouted and blew the horn. It was so much fun. Fun I never had before.

When the church bells stopped ringing, people closed their windows. Uschi and I went back upstairs. 1947 had arrived. The family wished each other a "Happy New Year," hoping it would be better than the last. But their faces and voices told me, they were not so sure about it. Soon everyone said, "Auf Wiedersehen," thanked Mutti and Oma for the nice time, and went home.

Mutti opened the windows to air out the smoke from the room. Then, she cleared the table. Ready with hot water, Oma washed the dishes. Mutti turned to me. "Gisela, you turn the chairs upside down on the table. Then, take the broom and sweep the floor. Make sure you get all the confetti,"

Then, while Oma washes the dishes and I dry, you put them away, but be careful not to break them."

I really wanted to go to bed. "Mutti, do I have to?"

"You had a nice time, and now it's time to help with the clean up. It won't take long, and you can sleep in tomorrow morning as long as you want." So I took the broom and swept the floor, then set the chairs back down and put the dishes away, and it didn't take long at all. Just as we got done, my sister came home. Mutti and Oma listened as she told about her evening of partying. I was so tired that I kissed Mutti and Oma *Gute Nacht*, goodnight, but not my sister. I just told her goodnight and went to bed. When I laid my head on the pillow just before I fell asleep, I had one last happy thought—it was a wonderful party.

The next morning when I awoke, I smelled that good coffee Mutti was brewing for our breakfast and I knew we were not having soup. The clatter of dishes told me someone was setting the table, and the sound of the voices said Oma was up, too. Because it was the New Year's holiday, I knew what was on our breakfast table this morning. I sat up in my bed to see if my sister was still sleeping, and she was. So I took my clothes, and then sneaked out of our room to dress where it was warm. Mutti and Oma looked at me in surprise. Mutti said, "*Guten Morgen*. Good morning. I thought you were going to sleep in?"

"I was. But I smelled the coffee and got hungry."

"Ja, Oma and I know what you're hungry for."

"So wash up for breakfast, we'll wait for you." I was right, no soup. On the table were two cake plates filled with Oma's baking. Mutti gave me half coffee and half milk to drink, and I had the most wonderful New Year's morning breakfast. Mutti opened the window just a crack so we could hear the church bells ringing, a reminder that services would start soon, but Oma and I didn't go to church.

Instead, Mutti and Oma cooked the noon dinner while I went outside to play in the snow with my friends. With no horse carts on the street, we had a snowball fight, so when I came upstairs, my cheeks were glowing from the cold winter air. Oma didn't quite approve of me romping in the snow on the street. Some if my friends were boys, and that was just not right. But Mutti said, "She is having fun and the clothes will dry."

After the noon meal, Mutti took a short nap, and Oma went upstairs to her room to nap. I sat in the corner, leaning against the warm Kachelofen reading the book I had gotten for Christmas. My coat, hanging over the back of the chair by the stove, was still damp, so I could not go outside to play in the snow again. Besides, my friends were not outside. It was a holiday, and in the afternoon families had company, so the children had to stay in, too.

After Mutti and Oma had gotten up, Mutti made coffee and Oma set the table with the leftover Christmas Stollen and the Streuselkuchen for the afternoon coffee. Onkel Heinz and Tante Elfriede with their families came, bringing some of their baked goods, and we had a pretty lively afternoon.

After the Christmas and New Year's holidays, our life went back to its daily routine: power and gas again were turned off at their regularly scheduled times; our eating of meat and baked goods ended, our breakfast again was soup made from flour and water, with a little milk; Oma cooked soups from Runkelrueben with a grated potato to thicken it.

It was a cold winter with lots of snow, and I had to go back to school. Everyone walked around with scarves over their noses as protection from the icy wind. There was no snowplow to clean the street, so storeowners and people living in apartments shoveled the snow off the sidewalks into the street, leaving openings between piles of snow so people could cross the street. Schools were never closed, and at times we had to leave our coats on because there was no heat. On those days school was short; we got our assignments and went home. Then bundled up to our noses, we played in the snow and didn't mind the cold at all.

Oma found a sled in the attic and I went sledding every day, a thirty-minute walk from where I lived, a section of the city park that the Russians had not enclosed. That portion of the park was on a slope extending close to the Neisse River. In the winter the park was filled with kids and sleds. We all liked a particular walkway and gathered on it. We'd start sledding down the upper walkway; then halfway down, using our right heels and leaning to the right, we'd maneuver the sled into a right turn onto another walkway. Bouncing over several dips made by the runoff from rain, we sledded straight down, stopping just short of the river. It was the best hill for sledding. After several days the slope got so slick from the sleds, we would just fly down.

Gisela didn't have a sled, so she went with me whenever she was allowed to go. She always sat behind me, and when we were not alert, we'd miss the curve, ending face first in the snow. We'd laugh, wipe our faces, brush off the snow, and hike back to the start again while I instructed Gisela, "You need to work the curve with me; lean the same way I do because both of us need to use our right heels to steer the sled to the right. Or I can do the steering while you keep your feet on the sled and lean into the curve with me."

"I wasn't watching," she said. "The turn came so fast and I leaned the wrong way. I'll watch next time." After several tries we worked in sync. We'd fly down the hill, hollering *Auf passen,* watch out or *Achtung* because so many of the kids, pulling their sleds up the slope, were not watching. Also, when we were sledding down, we had to watch for sleds in front of us in case they crashed. There were many crashes, so some kids always were crying and going home. After I got several bruises on my legs, I learned to pull my legs up on my sled when crashing into other kids. Sometimes the boys got into fights because they were bullies and thought they owned the downward course.

Oma set a time that I had to be home, always before dark. Even without a watch, I knew by the darkness of the sky that it was time to go home. But sometimes I waited until it got a little darker because below the city park was a football field that became an ice rink in the winter. It was fenced in and had a wooden booth to one side where the skaters paid, then entered the ice rink. Colored lights were strung all around, crisscrossing, reflecting on the ice. A loudspeaker played *waltzes* for the skaters. While the power was on for two hours in the evening, people came to skate. It looked like so much fun that I stood on the fence watching, wishing that I, too, had skates.

So the winter passed with school, sledding, and just being out in the snow with my friends. We had snowball fights or slid on the sidewalk. With a running start, we slid in the snow, eventually turning the snow into a long slick slide. When Oma saw what we were doing, she stopped us. "You kids stop sliding on the sidewalk. You make it so slick people will fall and get hurt. Gisela, you get some ashes and cover it. And when you're done with that, you'd better come up." As usual, my friends dissolved into thin air. Oma had ruined the fun, and I knew when I got upstairs, I was going to get another talking to. "Stop sliding! You know those are your only winter shoes. When you have a hole in the sole, they can't be repaired. The shoemaker has no leather to resole them, so you'd better stop sliding."

"Yes, Oma, I know, but it's so much fun!"

"I realize that, but it's also dangerous for people when the sidewalk is slick. By the way, I don't know what you're doing when you're sledding, but the heels of your shoes, in particular the right one, are starting to wear. Try not to use your heels when you're sledding downhill." I listened to Oma, but when I got outside, Oma's words were forgotten.

Sometimes when Oma and I went somewhere and we were on a sidewalk where the kids had been sliding, she reminded me. "Now you can see how dangerous it is when the sidewalk is icy from kids sliding." Inwardly, I agreed with Oma as I helped her go around those places so she wouldn't fall. But it still was hard not to slide because it was so much fun.

Then, Mutti came home from one of her trips with the flu and had to stay in bed. She was so cold she was unable to stop shaking. Because we had to watch our coal rations, the room was not very warm, so Oma piled bedding and blankets over Mutti, but they didn't stop her shaking. Then, Oma took the big pot of hot soup she had made in the morning, covered it with a lid, and wrapped it in newspapers. Putting a towel over the top, she placed it as a bed warmer near Mutti's feet.

"So," Oma said, tucking the pot in, making sure that Mutti's feet were only touching the towel, "That will do two things: keep our soup and your mother's feet warm." I was unsure what the soup would taste like after being in bed with Mutti's cold feet on the pot, but it didn't taste any different at all. It still tasted awful. Mutti recovered and went back to work, but Oma's foot warming with a pot of hot soup became the joke of the family for a long time.

It's 1947, another year of struggle for survival. The good food had come to an end. Mutti, recovered from the flu and returned to her job escorting after-war refugees on the trains. My sister, too, was working and going to school and Oma was busy taking care of us. When I was not in school, I was sledding in the park with Gisela. Since it was winter and cold, I didn't meet my friends very often, and that made Oma happy. But sometimes Gisela and I did see them in the park with their sleds. Then, we'd fasten our sleds together and, like a long snake, we'd sled downhill. We'd scream for everyone to get out of the way because the tied-together sleds needed lots of room. Speeding downhill, the rider on the last sled had to hang on tight to not fall off, while maneuvering the curve, the bumps, and the weaving back and forth of the sleds. At the bottom of the slope we untied the sleds, only to retie them on top, laughing over the ones we had lost on the way down. At times my sled was the last on and I, too, fell off. Then, it wasn't funny, and even less funny with everyone laughing at me.

When the weather was really bad and the snow was piled high, nobody was sledding. Then I'd spend the day with Oma, or run errands for her. I didn't want Oma to fall and get hurt, and it didn't bother me when I fell. But one day I fell with the milk can, spilling milk all over the sidewalk, which froze immediately. Then, we didn't have any milk for two days, due to the rationing. I worried about what Oma would say when I came home with the nearly empty milk can, but she just said, "The next time you need to be more careful." I was so glad she didn't get mad at me, but when we ate our morning soup, I felt guilty. In the evenings when the power and gas were turned off, we sat by the stove with the oven door open, watching the flames, singing, or listening to Oma's stories. On snowy days I could hardly wait for it to get dark so I could sit next to Oma to sing or listen to her, or just spend the winter evening with her.

With the rationing and short supply of food, people were hungry and walked for hours to farm communities. Then, they go from farmhouse to farmhouse to beg for food, called *hamstern,* or hoarding. They took their children with them, sending them to houses and farms—begging. On brake from her job, Mutti and I did the same thing. We went to Pfaffendorf where I had lived and where Vati had died. I really didn't want to go, but Mutti thought since they had been so nice to us when Tante Hilde and she had come to take me back, maybe they would be glad to see me and give us some food—like potatoes, cheese, bread or some meat—anything to eat. So Mutti and I took the trolley to the Landeskrone and walked an hour on a field road to Pfaffendorf, the same road my stepmother and I had taken many times before when going to Goerlitz; the very same road where she had told me my mother was dead; the very same road where I used to meet Vati walking home from work in Goerlitz, tired and exhausted. It was a road of memory for me.

That day was cold and the wind was blowing the snow sideways. But we needed food, so Mutti and I walked, scarves over our faces, our heads down, dark figures like mummies pushing through the flying snow. But when we got to Pfaffendorf, we didn't have much luck. Some people were glad to see that I was well. Some gave us a few potatoes, others, a couple slices of bread or a little cheese. I felt embarrassed, but Mutti encouraged me to knock on doors and to ask for food. It was Mutti's hope that the farmers' wives still would be sympathetic and not have forgotten what had taken place almost a year before. But they had. Some didn't even open their doors. Frozen, Mutti and I walked back the way we had come, lucky to have something to eat in our bag, however little. It had stopped snowing but the wind was still icy cold.

Not understanding why the farmers were so unfriendly to the people from the city, I asked Mutti, "How come the farmers don't like us or want to give us food? Don't they know we're hungry? They have so much and we have nothing."

"They have food, but they also have to give most of their crop to feed the Russian Army living in Germany and is controlled by the East German government."

"How do they know how much the farmers have?"

"There are Germans who work for the communist regime. It's their job to check on all farmers to see how much land and livestock each has and how much his land and livestock produce. Then, according to their findings, they tell the farmers what they can keep for their own living. The rest they have to give up."

"You mean the farmer goes hungry, too, just like we do in the city?"

"No, he has more food than you and I. He's not going hungry. But so many people come from the city begging for food that the farmers can't give to everyone. Some don't want to give nor do they want people knocking on their door, begging. I had hoped since your father had done work for them and they knew you, they would give us something. I guess there are just too many people begging for food," Mutti concluded.

"Mutti, does the farmer get money for the food he has to give up?"

"No, his pay is the food he can keep. He gets money, but that's to buy more seeds and feed for his livestock."

"How much does he get? And where does he get all that stuff?"

"I don't really know. I'm sure there are places where he gets his supply. And I'm sure it's according to how big his farm is. I'm not a farmer, and you're asking too many questions again. Let's stop talking. The wind is cold and we'll get sore throats. So, mouth closed."

We were gone all day, and it was almost dark before we got home, and I was glad to be where it was warm. That was our last trip to Pfaffendorf. Mutti didn't like begging either.

Oma's neighbor, *Frau Hartman*, was a young war widow with two small children. She shared the same landing, which at times was also my "stage". Her room, like Oma's, had slanted walls, but it faced the street. Frau Hartman was a slender, always smiling, friendly lady. She'd stop and talk to Oma when they saw each other on the landing. Sometimes, when Mutti was home, she'd invited her to come and visit.

I liked her and the two children, and whenever Frau Hartman had to do her shopping, and, because it was too cold for the children to be outside, I'd watch them for her. Oma also told me, "It's polite and courteous to help someone who's all alone with no family."

One day I overheard Mutti and Oma saying that the baby had a Russian father. They said Frau Hartman had told them she had befriended a Russian officer, who had brought food for her and the little girl. Also, he protected her from getting raped by ruthless Russians soldiers, as so many other women had been. I had heard before, when grownups were talking, that when a woman said the word *Kommandant*, sometimes the Russian soldiers would back off, afraid to touch a woman they thought knows an officer. But some women still were raped. When Russia finally controlled their armies, no Russian soldiers or officers were allowed to communicate with the German people, so Frau Hartman and he lost contact.

Frau Hartman, her children, and the Russian officer became a mystery to me after I overheard Mutti and Oma talk about them. But mainly I looked at her baby to see if there was anything different about it. But this baby looked just like any other baby I had seen. In my imagination it was as if it had come from another world.

I had never known a Russian baby before, and this baby was Russian, but it was tiny and sweet, but I knew what the real Russians were like. I remembered in Pfaffendorf how scared I was when the drunken soldiers came in the middle of the night, banging on the house door, going from bed to bed with flashlights, drunk, stinking of sweat, their dirty hands near my face, flashing the light into my eyes, looking for women to rape. I remembered how ugly and horrible they were, how the German women screamed and the men got shot trying to protect their wives, mothers, and sisters.

But this was a small baby of a Russian officer, and I tried to picture him as a nice Russian, like the two men who'd given me a slice of bread to eat. I did ask Oma, "How come Frau Hartman had a Russian baby?"

Oma, surprised to hear my question, looked at me, "You're not to listened when grown-ups talk!" Then, unsure how she should answer me, Oma said, "women had to protect themselves when Russia's Armee was marching into Germany with their uncontrolled soldiers. To protect your sister, only fourteen, your mother and I hid her in the attic at my brother's house in Erfurt where we had fled. But your mother was safe. She could walk anywhere and they didn't bother her because she was a nurse and wore her nurses cap with the Red Cross and the band of the Red Cross on her arm at all times. So, you see, everyone tried their best not to get raped, to stay out of their way, and that is how Frau Hartman survived. She has a baby, but that does not make her a bad woman. It was all for survival. Also, some women who were raped ended up sick and . . . ." Oma interrupted herself as if she had said too much, and continued in a low voice, "I think you should not concern yourself with that. You're too young to understand."

"Oma you're saying the same thing Vati always said."

"Yes, and he was right."

I didn't ask any more questions, but I understood what Oma was talking about. I was afraid of the Russians, I hated them, and I was glad they stayed behind the fence they'd built around their perimeter in our city.

As Frau Hartman became friends with us, Christa and she got along well, and they, too, decided to go *hamstern*. People took whatever they had, from jewelry to clothing, to the farmers to bargain for food, so my sister looked around for something she could take to bargain with. We had no jewelry or extra clothing, so she decided to take my only good pair of shoes, the only nice pair I had left that I wore on Sundays only. No matter how much I fought and hung on to my shoes, they went with my sister. "They don't fit you anymore," she said.

"But they're my shoes!"

"Right now you have your high tops, and in spring you'll get sandals," Mutti said. I knew I had lost the battle. Yes, they were getting a little too small for me, but those shoes were bought just before my last Christmas in Liegnitz. I had worn them when Vati and I had gone to the theater, and they were special to me. My sister packed a few other things, even small items like a crystal vase that had belonged to the Preacher. You had to have something to bargain with the farmers. Mutti told Oma, "The farmers are getting rich with the goods the city people bring to exchange for food."

"Yes," Oma replied, "it's a shame. People have lost so much and now what little they have left they have to bargain away for food. I'm glad Gisela and I did gleaning this fall. It helped a lot, but even that is slowly coming to an end, no matter how hard I try to save and scrimp."

Hearing Mutti and Oma talk, I was hoping that with my shoes and the other things that Christa took, she'd return with some food. While Frau Hartman and Christa were gone, I watched her children, with Oma checking on me once in awhile. I liked playing with Monika the little girl. She had dark hair and big brown eyes and was a chubby little thing. The baby had real fine blonde hair and blue eyes.

Late in the afternoon Christa and Frau Hartman returned, with potatoes, some bread, even a small piece of ham. They laughed and talked, telling of things that had happened to them. But the funniest story of all was when they had been at a farmer's trying to bargain with him, but the farmer had stood firm. He practically threw my sister and Frau Hartman out. When they were back on the street, Frau Hartman, just as proud as could be, told my sister, "Maybe he didn't give us any food, but I got a nice pair of hand knitted Norwegian-design gloves."

She pulled the gloves out of her bag to show them to my sister, who, looking at the gloves, exclaimed, "Those are my gloves!"

Embarrassed, Frau Hartman tried to apologize, "Oh, I'm sorry; I feel really bad. I thought I was getting even with that nasty old farmer."

Standing in the street, both of them laughed uncontrollably, my sister assuring her, "I'm so glad you stole my gloves back from the farmer. I had laid them down on the bench when we tried to bargain with him, and I forgot all about my gloves when he threw us out. They farmer never would have given them back to me. Thank you! That was nice of you."

That day when they thought about that little episode, they laughed. And when they got home, the laughing started all over again.

The eastern cold winter winds kept blowing bringing snow and ice. Everyone stayed inside as much as possible. I went to school, but on pleasant days, I went sledding, glad to be free of the boredom from staying inside.

Those days ended when I got the mumps on both sides at once with never ending headaches, earaches and eating was impossible. Oma, again pushed the two overstuffed chairs together like a bed, and that's where I spent the day curled up, covered with my bedding. Taking care of me kept Oma busy because I was in pain and not a good patient. "I want the pain to stop, Oma, now!" I whined.

"Yes, I know." Oma, believing that warmth helps healing, stuffed cotton with drops of warm oil in my ears, then, wrapped a warm dry towel around my neck, which she replaces with another she kept warm on top of the lid of a pot filled with hot water. She also folded a big handkerchief oblong, dipped it in vinegar water, and placed it on my forehead. "It will ease your headache." Ever so often, Oma re-dipped the hanky in the vinegar water, then, placed it on my forehead again. She also made herb tea, but it hurt to swallow. "Oma, it hurts when I swallow and the tea is too hot."

"I know. Take little sips and keep stirring the tea, so it will cool. You'll get better, but it will take time."

"I want it to stop, Oma."

"It depends on how well you drink the tea. You'll make your throat hurt more if you keep whining. I can do nothing to take the hurt away. You have the mumps and they have to take their course. But you will get well, and never again will you have the mumps. That I can promise you." What Oma was telling me sounded good, but it didn't do much for the pain. Her cuddling did. In the evenings when we sat near the stove, me in a blanket, Oma wrapped her arms around me, cradling me, rocking and humming.

The nights were the worst, and my sister complained, "I can't sleep with her whining like a baby all night."

"You, too, had the mumps once and didn't behave any differently." Oma reminded her. After that my sister didn't say another word. But, she'd stick out her tongue at me. After several weeks, as Oma had promised, I recovered and was like new again.

Then, we had the first sign of spring. Snowbells green stems broke through the partly frozen ground, their little white bells swaying in the warm breeze, ringing in the spring. With the sun's rays, color exploded: the crocuses vibrant blues, yellows and lavenders; the daffodils' bright yellow; the tulips', teacups of red, yellow, and white; and the hyacinth's pinks, blues, and whites—all filling the air with their sweet smell. Spring, my favorite time of year, had come, a promise of beginning.

Oma and I walked in the park, breathing in the clean, fresh air. Coming out of a winter's sleep, others enjoyed the blue sky and smiled at us as they walked by. New tree buds emerged, soft green. My favorite birches, white and graceful, swayed their fragile green foliage whispering in the air. Birds sang and whistled. Winter was over. Spring had begun. The Easter holidays were approaching.

One day, a rainy day, shortly before Easter I went up to Oma's room to visit. There, Oma had a shelving unit that looked like a bookshelf. On top sat her two-burner gas stove with the coffee pot; below, concealed by a curtain, Oma stored leftover food, some dishes, a frying pan, and silverware in a small wooden box. That day the curtain was not drawn all the way, so I noticed an almost empty glass bottle of what looked like clear water. "What's in the bottle Oma?"

"That's my holy water." Rather abruptly Oma got up, took the bottle from me, placed it back on the shelf, and closed the curtain. I could tell she was going to say no more.

"Holy water? What for?" I persisted.

"I use it whenever I need it."

"Need it for what, Oma?"

"I rub it on my joints when they hurt."

"Does it help?"

"Only if you believe in it."

I looked at Oma to see if she was serious. "Where do you get holy water?"

"At a creek," Oma answered hesitantly.

"A creek? Where is the creek, Oma?"

"Any small creek out in the farm country."

Although I knew Oma didn't want to talk about it, I did.

"How do you do that?"

"Well, I can see you're not going to let it rest until you know everything. People who believe in the holy water get up early on *Karfreitag,* Good Friday, morning—it must be before the sun rises—and walk to where a clean creek flows. Then, they gather the holy water when the sun's first rays appear on the horizon."

I pictured myself walking with Oma in the fresh morning air, so I burst out, "Oma, that sounds like fun! I want to go with you!"

Oma shook her head, "No, you can't."

"Why can't I go?"

Shaking her head, smiling, she said, "Because you talk too much! You can't stop yourself. You like to talk. Going for holy water means you can't talk. You have to be silent or the holy water will lose its power. You can't talk until you have scooped the holy water and are on the way home."

"Oma, please, I'll be real quiet. I promise I won't say a word."

"I know you think you can be still, but I know better. This is something I need to do alone." Oma was firm.

Later, thinking about Oma's words, "you like to talk", I wondered if that's why my stepmother had never wanted me to be alone with people. *Maybe she feared I would tell family things, so she kept me away from people. Was she afraid I would tell that I had another Mutti, Oma, and a sister in Goerlitz? But then, I thought she was my mother, and having another family in Goerlitz was something I really didn't understand. But now I understood why she'd been afraid. She didn't want people to know that I had another mother and family living in Goerlitz, then, people would know she had married a divorced man with children. She'd wanted no one to know that she was my stepmother. Was it bad to have married a divorced man? I remembered after Vati had passed away, how angry my stepmother had been with me when her girlfriend told her that I had talked to her son, telling him that the woman I called Mutti was my stepmother; that I had a real mother; and that someday I would go and find her. At that time I didn't talked because I liked to talk. I'd talked because I'd wanted to tell on her—I'd hated her.*

Although all holidays in Germany are made up of two days of celebration, a first and second holiday, Easter passed quietly. I never asked Oma if she had gone for her holy water. The week before Easter, Mutti did big spring cleaning from corner to corner, including Oma's room. Furniture were moved from the walls so Mutti could clean behind them. Windows were washed with vinegar water, then polished with newspaper. Oma washed and ironed the curtains and sheers, and Mutti hung them back up. After that Oma did the baking, but not as much as she had for Christmas. Our family spent the first Easter holiday together. Mutti had only a large bouquet of tulips and daffodils in a vase because Easter was a time to be quiet and to enjoy each other. Oma, Uschi, and I went for a walk in the city park in the warm sunshine.

The next day, the second Easter holiday, we relaxed at home, doing nothing. I could not meet with my friends because all kids had to be at home. The street had only quiet walkers here and there. I had my one and only Sunday dress on, the deep sky blue one—the one the seamstress had made for me when my stepmother had hired her to come to the house and sew dresses for us in Liegnitz. This dress had special meaning for me, because it was made from the material Vati had brought from France when he'd come home on his furlough. Because I had not grown very much, it still fit me; all Oma did let the big hem out a bit.

Our next holiday, is *Pfingsten,* celebrated on the seventh Sunday after Easter, at the beginning of June, depending on the date of Easter. Pfingsten also has a first and second holiday. It brought the Easter season to a close, so it's a big church holiday. Although Oma and I went to church on Christmas, we never went to church on Easter or Pfingsten even though Oma believed in the Easter holy water. To me Pfingsten was the end of spring and the beginning of summer. I liked Easter and Pfingsten because church bells rang almost all day, the sun was warm, flowers and trees bloomed, the birds sang, and so did I.

One more thing that made me so happy: all Germans had been transported out of the Polish territory, so Mutti's traveling with the refugee trains had stopped. I was able to enjoy Mutti as well as Oma. Mutti found a nursing job, with a lady Russian doctor who spoke German. She told Mutti that her ancestors had been from Germany. The doctor's office was in a villa, part of the enclosed perimeter of the Russian compound. The Russian patients entered the villa from the inside of their compound, while Mutti entered from the street. She'd ring the bell at the front door receiving permission from a Russian guard to enter. Mutti said the doctor's patients were from the upper Russian ranks. Her job was to give shots, do lab work, and help the doctor with the patients. Mutti liked her job and the doctor.

Oma continued taking care of the household, my sister, and me, dividing her time between downstairs and upstairs. When the weather was rainy, I too was upstairs with Oma in her room or sitting on the landing outside her room, playing the gramophone, dancing and singing the bad weather away.

After one week of spring vacation, school, much to my dislike, continued. I was not a very good student, so I saw school as something required of me, a daily chore. We had math, writing, reading, history, geography, social studies, drawing, music, needlework, sports, and Russian. All classes taught by the same teacher, except for the Russian.

I absolutely did not like Russian. The grades I received proved it, but it was mandatory. The Russian teacher was a German man who spoke perfect Russian. The letters of the Russian alphabet differ from the letters in our alphabet. We had to learn to read and write the letters before we were taught anything else. All through school, Russian was required, but I didn't want to master that language. We were taught that Russia needed to teach us Germans culture since we didn't have any of our own. When I told Mutti and Oma that, they both exclaimed, "What? The Russians? Teach us culture? Where did you hear this?"

"In school! Our teacher said that." I could tell they strongly disagreed with the teacher.

"Ja, your teacher, she's young, a believer, and doesn't know much. She has lots to learn. But culture? That is something we need to teach the Russians! We saw the culture they had when they marched into Germany! Or have you forgotten?" No, I had not forgotten. I remembered, but I was not going to say anything about that in school.

Thus, I scooted through school with above average grades. The classes I did well in were not the most important ones. Oma would ask if I had done my homework, and when I said "yes," she was satisfied. I knew if I didn't do my homework, Oma would not allow me to see my friends. Mutti seldom asked, so it was up to me to get it done. To Oma it was more important for me to learn the "female" aspects of life, like cleaning, sewing, darning socks, and doing tasked of a future housewife and mother. To teach cooking to me was not on top of Oma's list because we had barely enough food for Oma's cooking. That was all right with me, I wasn't ready for any of that.

Our classroom teacher was a petit, blonde, young woman we all liked. For music she brought her violin. Although I enjoyed listening to records of operas, the violin, alone, sounded whiny, serious, and too squeaky. I got goose bumps when she took her violin out of the case. She also taught choir, that I liked because I enjoyed singing. We also learned to read poetry. At Christmas or at the end of each school year when the parents were invited for an evening of entertainment, I not only sang in the choir, I was almost always chosen to recite a poem.

For the needlework class, Oma found knitting needles, but she had to unravel an old sweater for its wool. The old sweater was dusty, so Oma sat in the back yard to unravel it. She wound the yarn on a flat board the length of her lower arm. Then she washed the wool, letting it dry on the board. When the wool had dried, she wound it into a ball, and that was my yarn. It was easy to see that my worn gray wool was used. Oma also sewed a pouch with drawstrings for me to carry the wool and needles. I was glad I was not the only one with used wool and a drawstring bag made of old material because some girls in my class had nice yarn and pretty round knitting baskets with drawstrings and tassels for closure. Not all the school kids were refugees. Some had never fled with their parents, so they still had all their belongings. Not many of those children made friends with us refugee kids. It was as if we had refugee written on our foreheads. Although I had been born in Goerlitz, we were living in makeshift refugee quarters. Once I tried to made friends with a girl I really liked and, as it turned out, she was the daughter of the doctor who knew Mutti, the same one I had run to get when Mutti was so sick. This girl had invited me to her home, but the next day in school she would hardly talk to me, and our friendship ended before it even began.

When I was not with my friends, either in the yard or in front of the house, my other favorite thing was drawing. I'd sit at my pult and with pencils of red, blue, green, yellow, and brown; I'd draw. For black, I used the pencil. I loved to do our school drawing assignments. I also made birthday and Mother's Day cards for Mutti and Oma. Sometimes I used real flower petals. I'd paste them with a mixture of water and a little flour into heart shaped designs, then, with a color pencil, I write "My best wishes" and "Love."

In summer, Oma and I again made our trips to the cemetery every other Saturday, with me stopping at the grave where the bride was buried. We planted pansies and forget-me-nots on Vati's grave because, as Oma said, "They're the most thankful plants; they'll bloom all through the summer."

Oma, again planted her garden of carrots, kohlrabies, lettuce, cucumbers, beans, and asters, her favorite flowers.

I loved gardening, so I helped Oma with the watering, and watched the plants grow. When we harvested our vegetables, they tasted especially good.

It was on one of those warm summer evenings when Oma said, "Let's go for a walk. I want to show you something." Going for walks with Oma was always fun, so I was eager, wondering what Oma wanted to show me. We walked down a hilly, narrow cobblestone street in the old part of Goerlitz, called the *Neisse Strasse,* named after the Neisse River. Having not been down that street before, I asked, "Where are we going?"

"Remember when you were in my room and had all those questions why we couldn't go home and you asked me about the bridge? Do you remember me telling you that when we were allowed to go near the river, I would show the bridge to you?"

"I remember."

"That is where we're going, down to the Neisse River and the bridge."

"Is it safe Oma?"

"Yes, its safe. We're finally allowed to walk along the street that follows the Neisse, but just for a short way."

"Why just a short way?"

"That's because, further down along the river, the Russians have their military compound, barricaded like you saw in the city."

"But we're not going close to them, Oma, are we?"

"Don't worry; we're not."

When we got to where the *Neisse Strasse* met the *Ufer Strasse,* I saw it. Once spacious and majestic, the black heavy iron bridge that had spanned the Neisse River for many, many years now was in ruins, lying in the water of the *Neisse.* It looked as if someone had cut through the center with a giant saw, crashing it into the water below—like a "V"—its iron pillars bent, but still partly attached on both sides of the river's edges. It was a sad reminder of what had been, as the water of the Neisse with it's steady, never ending flow, keeps rambling through its broken rafters, turrets, and arches. "Oh Oma, that poor bridge!"

"Yes, it's a sorry sight to see. Like many others, I used to walk almost daily across that bridge to go shopping and visiting."

Looking across the river I saw the apartment house Oma used to live in. "Look Oma, isn't that the apartment house you lived in when I was here visiting!" But her old apartment house, empty of life, now had broken windows hanging from their hinges on the outside of the building. What once were sheer curtains now were shreds, plastered against the outside frame of the black hole that had been a window. The main entry door, partly ripped out, hung sideways. Through a hole in the roof a tree had started to grow. Oma's apartment, the one where I'd stayed when I visited in Goerlitz in 1943, had been on the bottom floor. I saw the grassy riverbank where my sister Christa and I had sat feeding the ducks and swans. There, Christa had told me that this was my family, but that I had to go back to Vati and my stepmother in Liegnitz.

Oma stood looking at what once was her apartment, her home, among the row of vandalized apartment houses, thinking of something that was but never would be again. "Oma?"

"Hmm?"

"What about your furnishing? Do you think it's still in there?"

"I suppose so. But seeing what these buildings look like, I'm sure it got demolished when the Russian troops went through here. With rats and mice making it their home now. I wouldn't want to see it."

Yes, Oma shouldn't see it. It would only maker her sadder. In Pfaffendorf, I saw what had been done to houses.

After a while she turned, sighed, and said, "Let's go! I can't look at it any more."

Holding Oma's hand and while we walked away, I took another look at the bridge, lying in its watery grave. "Oma, this bridge was so beautiful. I remember when I walked across it with Christa and you when I was visiting. Now it's in the water."

"Yes, this bridge and all the others in Goerlitz were demolished, including the viaduct, our railway link to the east."

"But, Oma, it didn't stop the Russians from crossing the Neisse River."

"No, it didn't, because early in May of 1945 the Russian attached from two different fronts. One front came fighting from the north on this side of the rivers Oder and Neisse towards Goerlitz. The second Russian front advanced from the east, fighting our Wehrmacht on the east side of the Neisse near Goerlitz. That's when Hitler ordered all bridges in Goerlitz blown up, so the second Russian front couldn't march across them." Oma shook her head, as if she still could not believe it. "It was such useless, dumb thing. All Hitler accomplished was trapping the Wehrmacht and the German people trying to flee from the Russians and the ground fighting. Now this bridge and others lie in the rivers they once spanned.

War is not a good thing. It kills people, destroys homes, and uproots lives." Oma sounded sad, so I decided not to ask any more questions. Slowly and quietly we walked back up the narrow, small cobble stoned street, crossed the *Untermarkt,* the Lower Marketplace, then went underneath the arches of the *Rathaus,* and walked on to our home, away from home.

In the fall Oma and I went gleaning again for potatoes and wheat. We gleaned for sugar beets and made syrup for the winter. We harvested the cherries, grapes, and berries in the back yard, sharing it with the tenants. It had been over two years, since the war had ended and we still had little food to speak of. Specialty items like bananas, oranges, chocolate, spices, and real coffee beans, as well as simple things like oatmeal and cream of wheat were all unavailable in stores. The rationing of food and stamps was as strict as ever, with only the absolute necessities for survival available to us. Although we had stamps, the grocer did not always have a supply and when he did, people rushed to get there before he sold out again. As always, Oma told me to run ahead and hold a place in line for her. Lines of people in front of stores all over the city had become part of the landscape for the living. Nothing had changed. No improvements. Knowing they were defeated and powerless, people became more solemn, their faces gloomy, with a look of sadness in their eyes.

Just before the first snowfall, Oma and I covered Vati's grave with boughs of pine for the winter. Then on November 9th, Oma and I laid a spray on his grave decorated with pinecones and holly because it had been two years since his passing—but never ugly waxy-looking sweet peas. I missed Vati terribly.

Christmas came and went. Oma and I went to church, but this time we walked to the red brick *Luther Kirche,* with a tall bell tower. Mutti had her New Year's Eve party with streamers and strung garlands. Before we knew it, 1947 had ended and 1948 had begun. That winter brought snow and sledding and ice-skating. Onkel Heinz had found a pair of rusted ice skates that he restored enough so I could go ice-skating, much to Oma's disapproval. I had worn out my only pair of winter shoes the year before, but because my feet had not grown and the tops of the shoes were still usable, Oma had taken them to the shoemaker for repair. He took the worn leather soles off and replaced them with a thick one-piece wooden sole, nailing the top of the shoe to the wooden sole. This was a common type of shoe repair since the shoemakers didn't have the leather to resole worn out shoes. I had no other shoes because Christa had taken my only other pair to the farmer for food, and new shoes weren't available in stores. Lots of children wore shoes with wooden soles. It took time to learn to walk with stiff soles, but after a while, sounding like a clubfoot, I got used to walking in them. To ice-skate, I would clamp the ice skates with a special key onto my shoes. After doing so several times the skates made a dent in the wooden sole that eventually started to splinter. Then, even Mutti agreed with Oma and told me to stop ice-skating. Luckily the shoes made it through the winter ending eventually in the garbage.

Spring returned with its wonderful colors and smells. Mutti was still working for the Russian doctor, and Oma continued to take care of the household and me.

One day, around noon, I was upstairs in Oma's room making potato pancakes on her small gas burner. Oma had set the table with plates and silverware, and the small sugar dish decorated with roses, with a tiny spoon in it. She had made applesauce to complement our potato pancakes. Then, there was a knock at the door. I looked at Oma. "Are you expecting someone, Oma?"

"No, not that I know."

"*Herein,* come in," I called out. To my surprise, a policeman opened the door. With cap in hand, smiling, he said, "I'm *Martin Hentschke.* I'm a friend of *Helenchen,* your daughter," he told Oma, shaking her hand. Turning to me he said, "And you're Gisela." He shook my hand too as I curtsied, but I wondered how he knew my name.

"Please, come in," Oma said finally, offering him a chair and inviting him to sit down. Soon they were deep in conversation while I continued frying the potato pancakes. I wondered if he was Mutti's boyfriend. She had talked about meeting someone, but she hadn't talked about it much. And now, he just showed up. While I busied myself with frying the potato pancakes, I glanced at him and decided that in his blue uniform he was not a bad looking man. He was, I think, Mutti's age, tall, slender, with a rather narrow lean face, but a lot of people had lean faces in those days. He was a friendly, smiling man, but his uniform made me feel uneasy. I kept looking to see if he had a gun or handcuffs on him, but I didn't see them. In his police uniform he looked so authoritative, like a law book. Taking my heart in my hands, trying to be friendly, I asked, "Would you like a potato pancake?"

"Yes, I would. They smell awfully good. You must be a good cook." I could feel my face getting hot, turning from red to purple. Quickly I turned to the frying pan, hoping he had not seen the rush of color in my face. I was never sure if compliments were sincere. The words of my stepmother always echoed in my ears, "You're ugly. People don't like you." But here was a man, a stranger, giving me a compliment.

Not realizing my embarrassment, Oma continued, "Yes, Gisela likes to make potato pancakes. It's her specialty."

"I can tell. They smell and taste good." After a while he thanked Oma and me for the excellent pancakes, said goodbye and left.

I turned to Oma and asked, "Oma, did you know that Mutti had a boyfriend?"

Oma, as puzzled as I, answered, "Your mother has mentioned that she met someone, but it seems odd that he would come here alone." When we told Mutti about the unexpected visit of her "boyfriend," she laughed and said, "He told me he was going to visit you one of these days, but I didn't believe him."

After many more of my potato pancakes, the best he had ever eaten so he claimed, Martin Hentschke became a regular figure in our family. Everyone liked him, including me. As it turned out, he was not a policeman but a border guard. His job was to patrol the perimeter assigned to him, out in the country along the Neisse River, even at night. He was to watch for smugglers because the black market was so strong. When he was on watch, he carried a rifle and handcuffs, neither of which he ever used. He said, "I never see any smugglers or have to use the rifle or hand cuffs. I just don't see anybody."

Mutti laughed, "That's because he turns his back and doesn't want to see anyone. The smugglers know when Officer Hentschke is on patrol." Mutti made a motion with her open hand indicating Officer Hentschke was getting something in return.

"Don't say that too loud. It'll get me in trouble. Smugglers or not, I can't shoot at people, and besides, I haven't seen many." But in fall when the potato and vegetable fields were ready for harvesting, Mutti would say, "I'm taking a walk to *Ludwigsdorf*." To walk to Ludwigsdorf, a small farm community outside Goerlitz was like walking to Pfaffendorf, about an hour, only in the opposite direction. Mutti would take a big shopping bag with another small one tucked inside it. She'd be gone all day. When Mutti came back, she had both bags filled with potatoes and vegetables. Mutti made many trips to see Martin Hentschke when he was on duty, always bringing food back home. Oma would warn her that someday the farmers was going to catch up with her, but Mutti laughingly replied, "As long as Officer Hentschke is patrolling in his uniform, the rifle over his shoulder, the farmers don't suspect that someone is lying on the ground digging for a few potatoes and vegetables. Besides, it beats begging for food and being turned down or having the door shut in my face by the farmers."

Then, something sad happened to one of our friends. When in the afternoon we parted, all of us were healthy and well. Oma and I went for our evening walk. When we got back, the kids were in front of the house, sitting on the steps, waiting for me. When Oma saw them sitting there, she grumbled, "Haven't they gone home yet? You can't stay out, so just make it short." As soon as they saw me, they came running, shouting, "Have you heard about Siegfried?" With all of them talking at once I couldn't understand them. Then, I heard, "Siegfried is dead! He died this evening!"

"Don't make jokes like that! That's not funny!" The word "dead" brought Vati's memories back and gave me a shiver. When I looked in their faces, I saw they were sincere.

"It's true! He died," they repeated. I couldn't believe it! Siegfried, the one who liked me, is gone, dead. A cold crept into my body and it felt as if I had made that phone call again, hearing a cold voice telling me "He is dead!" But now I understood what dead meant, never to return. Siegfried would never laugh with us. He was gone, forever.

"What happened?"

"He was playing ball, and when he went to catch the ball, he ran into a tree, and it killed him."

When I came upstairs, I told Oma. She nodded her head. "That is sad. He was way too young to die."

"But, Oma, how can someone die from running into a tree?"

"Well, he must have been running fast to catch the ball and wasn't looking where he was running, so when he hit the tree, he hit it hard. It must have broken his neck or given him a severe concussion. I feel sorry for his family."

The next day we gathered—Gisela from down the street, Regina, Inge, Jochen, Franz, and the other Siegfried who lived with his widowed mother and older sister in the same house as I. Each of us carried a small bouquet of flowers. When I told Oma we were going to the cemetery to say goodbye to Siegfried, she nodded her head in agreement. Still in shock, we walked quietly, not wanting to believe that Siegfried was gone when he had just been there with us the day before, laughing. Hardly anyone spoke and then only in a subdued voice. We walked past the church where Vati's casket had been and where his service had taken place and up the hill of the old cemetery. I didn't want to think about that. Instead, I thought about Siegfried and how his mother, father, sisters, and brothers must feel. How sad they must be for losing him as Oma had said, "So young."

When we got to the top of the hill and before we entered the mortuary, a red brick round building with a heavy wooden door, we stopped and looked at each other as if we were taking strength from one another. Then, we went in. Huddled close, we looked around. There were caskets placed all around with divider walls between each of the caskets for privacy. It was cold and clammy. It smelled of death mixed with the scent of flowers and burning candles, placed in the individual sections with the caskets. Gisela and I reached for each other's hands.

One of the boys asked the attendant, a man dressed in a black suite, a white shirt and black tie, which one was Siegfried's coffin. Showing us, he asked in a low voice, "Should I open the casket for you children?" We nodded our heads, afraid to talk in that still, soundless place. We walked over to the opened coffin. My heart skipped a beat, then, wanted to stop. Siegfried was lying with his head on a pillow, his body covered by a blanket of heavy off-white paper like a comforter that matched his pillow. He had flowers all around him, but some had started to droop. Siegfried's mouth had fallen wide open, like a huge cavity in his face, which made his buckteeth stick out. I laid my flowers in the casket, said my silent goodbye, and told him I would miss him, then turned and walked out. I could not look at Siegfried any longer. My whole body and self were in turmoil.

When I got outside, I took a deep breath, smelled the warm fresh air. I was glad to be alive, but sad to have lost a friend. That day, standing in front of the mortuary overlooking the old cemetery and church, I made a silent vow to myself. Never, never again will I go to see a dead body, never, never again. Siegfried's pale face and open mouth stayed in my memory just as I still remember Vati's strand of hair falling over his face as I was bending down to touch him and put my flowers in his folded cold hands.

I have kept my solemn vow.

Siegfried's death dampened our spirits and left a gap in our circle. No matter what we did, we always ended up talking about how much we missed Siegfried and, so, our little circle slowly drifted apart. Gisela from down the street befriended other kids. Her hollering for me had stopped, making Oma happy. Siegfried I saw daily, but then we lived in the same house. Jochen, his sister Regina and Inge lived within shouting distance from Siegfried and me, so we'd meet occasionally.

That summer of 1948, I was thirteen and all five of us kids were about the same age. Sometimes we played marbles in the backyard or ball using the outside wall of the washhouse as our backboard. Other times we sat on the lawn and just talked.

To play marbles, we had to dig a small hole for the marbles to be maneuvered into. Glass marbles were prized possessions and not available in stores, only colored clay marbles, but when they hit each other hard, they split apart. I always lost, so my marble collection dwindled fast, but I never traded my one and only glass marble for clay ones. After we were done playing, Oma made sure, that we refilled the hole. "If someone steps into that hole they break an ankle." Often I heard Oma tell Mutti, "I don't know why the neighborhood kids have to play in our back yard."

Mutti just said, "Well, they don't have one and the kids have to play somewhere. They don't hurt anything, and Gisela is not on the street."

Sometimes on warm summer evenings Oma and I sat in the back yard, looking at the almost darkened sky and its stars. Oma would tell me who was who and what was what, but I could never remember. The only thing I could identify was *der grosse Wagen*, the big bear, *der kleine Wagen*, the little bear, *die Milchstrasse*, the Milky Way, and the brilliantly shimmering *Abendstern*, the evening star.

One of those summer evenings, Jochen, Regina, Inge, Siegfried and I, were sitting on the lawn, talking. Mutti had a date with Martin Hentschke, her now steady boyfriend. My sister Christa and I were left to ourselves because Oma was gone, too. Before Mutti left, she told me I had to be upstairs by eight, in bed by nine, and told Christa to make sure I was in bed on time. No sooner had Mutti left than my sister, thinking she was my boss, stood on the balcony overlooking the back yard and called for me to come upstairs, "Now!"

"No, Mutti said eight and the *Rathaus Turm* hasn't chimed eight yet."

"You come up now!"

"No, I'm not! Mutti said eight and you're not the boss of me!"

"You come up now! Or I'll come down and get you!"

"Yeah, why don't you?" I hollered as we grinned at my sister. That made her mad. She came running down the stairs, chasing me around the yard. The kids and I were laughing. My sister was fuming. Finally she gave up, warning me, "You have to come upstairs sooner or later, and I'll get you for this!"

"Oh, well, that will be later!" We went back to talking as if nothing had happened. When the *Rathaus Turm,* the city-hall-tower, chimed eight, I went upstairs. My sister was waiting for me and again the chase was on, around and around the table, but she couldn't catch me. She was so mad that she began throwing spoons, forks, and knives at me. Laughing and taunting I dodged behind one of the big chairs as silverware flew over and around me. "You missed me, you missed me!" When the throwing stopped, I slowly came out from behind my cover. The floor was littered with silverware and utensils.

"Now, you pick it all up!" Christa demanded.

"No! You threw it, you pick it up!" Looking at Mutti's clean but now with silverware and utensils littered floor, I started to snigger. To my surprise Christa started to laugh, and I was glad. I didn't know how it would have ended, but I knew I wasn't going to give in. I went to bed.

A couple of days later when Mutti was mopping the floor, she found a spoon my sister had missed underneath the china buffet. "What's this doing under here?"

"Ask Christa. She was throwing the silverware at me."

"Why?"

"Because I wouldn't jump to her demands." I wanted to add, "Like everybody else does," but I didn't.

Oma and Mutti, both shook their heads. "Why can't you two get along?" Then, sighing Mutti added, "I wish Alfred were here."

I, too, wished Vati were here. I could have told Mutti and Oma why Christa and I didn't get along. Christa was always right and no one contra dictated her. I thought about why that was so. After our parents divorced, Oma had raised Christa; she grew up to be demanding, used to getting her way. Also, Christa didn't go with Vati, and had always lived with the family. Where as I had lost seven years of growing and bonding with Oma and Mutti. Many times I wished my sister would be a little caring towards me, but she was unbending, unapproachable, so our relationship was always on the edge of war.

Summer passed into fall and before school started, Oma and I did gleaning for wheat, potatoes, and sugar beets. We beat the wheat, stored the potatoes in the cellar, and made syrup from the sugar beets.

Then, the school year of 1948/1949 started again. I joined the choir and a non-school *Volks-Tanz-Gruppe*, a traditional dance group. We had to wear red skirts, black vests, white blouses, and white knee socks. The boys wore short dark pants and white shirts and knee socks. Oma sewed the red skirt with a black ribbon around the bottom, a black vest, and a plain white blouse from scraps she'd found. We performed at fests throughout the city and I enjoyed it very much.

Next, I asked Mutti, "Can I take ballet lessons?"

When Oma heard me ask Mutti, she said, "Why do you want to do that? You're already in the Volks-Tanz-Gruppe!"

"I'm still dancing in the group, but I'd like to take ballet lessons. Ballet looks so graceful."

"That's fine," Mutti told Oma. "It can't be that expensive. There isn't much else to spend our money on, with only what is rationed to us in stores. We can't go anywhere or do anything." So Mutti and I went to enroll me at the school for ballet. *What a different walk this is from the one with my stepmother in Zittau just before the end of the war. Then, in early spring in 1945 she'd insisted on signing me up for the BDM, telling me I was good for nothing, a thief. Now Mutti is enrolling me for ballet lessons. I wonder what my stepmother would say now?*

The long established Ballet School was in a two-story older villa across the street from the Russian compound. A somewhat damaged square gold sign attached to the black cast iron garden gate stated in bold letters, *Ballet Schule*. Walking up to the front entrance, Mutti rang the doorbell.

A young woman answered the door and invited us in.

"One moment, please. I will let Madam know that someone is here." The parlor she had ushered us into had big pictures in ornate frames of a ballerina in different poses hanging on the walls. Petite chairs covered in a faded floral print were positioned in front of an antique white desk, with an armchair to match. A well-worn carpet in soft shades covered the center of the floor, leaving a rim of polished parquet. A potted palm stood in one corner almost reaching the high ornate ceiling. White fluffy sheers covering a partly opened window moved gently in the warm summer breeze.

An older lady, holding a silver cane, looking like a fairy that has just stepped out of a storybook, entered the parlor. She was tall, slim as a willow, her graying hair pinned on top of her head like a bird's nest, with tendrils hanging about her face. She wore a cream-colored mid-length satin dress and in the same color as the satin, she wore a loose fitting layer of chiffon over it, trailing behind her like a cloud when she moved. White stockings, ballerina slippers, and a long pearl necklace completed her attire.

Walking towards her desk, she nodded her head in greeting to us, motioning Mutti to have a seat in front of her desk. "I have come to enroll my daughter in your School of Ballet," Mutti stated, seating herself as I curtsied.

The lady, still standing, didn't answer but looked at me. Then, pointing with her silver cane, she said, "Walk over there. I want to have a look at you." Her gray eyes never blinking, she looked me over. With a circular motion of her cane, she commanded, "Turn slowly!"

"Yes, I think she has potential," she said, talking more to herself than to Mutti. "Now," she said as she seated herself behind her desk, "I'll tell you the house policy. I expect you, like all my students, to follow it."

"First, I'm *Madam* to you. Second, you will be in class on time. If you're late, you will have to miss class. If it happens more than three times, you're dismissed. Third, you'll need a short bib skirt, not too tight, with straps over your shoulders, and matching undergarment. Finally, I will not allow disrespect or misbehavior." Looking at me with cool, strict eyes, she asked, "Do I make myself clear?"

Standing next to Mutti in front of Madam's desk, I curtsied and murmured, "Yes, *Madam*." I was enrolled in the beginner's class once a week for two hours after school, the first hour for gymnastics and the second for ballet. After Mutti bought my ballet slippers from Madam, and paid for my first month of lessons, we were excused. The same young woman guided us to the door and smiling, said, "Auf Wiedersehn," closing the door behind us.

Outside on the sidewalk, Mutti stopped, "Are you sure you want to do this? That is one strict woman!"

"Yes I do." But I was scared. "Do you think the pictures on the wall was Madam when she was a ballerina?"

"I believe so. They looked like her. In order for her to teach and to have a business, she had to have been a ballerina. Otherwise, she could not teach."

Elated I thought *a real ballerina and she'll be my teacher.*

Oma once more came to my rescue. She found some blue silky material and sewed the ballet outfit according to Madam's specifications. As a finishing touch, Oma added a white ribbon around the bottom of the short skirt and the attached bib. She also made me a bag for carrying my slippers, skirt, and matching panties.

With pounding heart, I went for my first ballet lesson. The school was filled with subdued activity, as tights and tutus flitted around me. To my surprise, the young woman who had answered the door was our gymnastics teacher. Then, a slim man, younger than *Madam,* wearing a body suit, was our ballet teacher. At the ballet hour, *Madam,* wearing tights and a softly flared chiffon dress, her silver cane in hand, positioned herself near the black grand piano and the ballet teacher counting the beats of the piano player, "One, two, three, and one, two, three." As her cane tapped the floor, her sharp eyes roamed, watching our reflections in the mirrors that covered the walls. Then, when our legs on the bar were not straight, or our backs and shoulders slumped, knees buckled, or arms were not gracefully stretched far enough, she'd take her cane and tap us in the incorrect places and positions. Madam never smiled but we respected her and her silver cane, so we tried hard not to be tapped. Although gymnastics and ballet were hard, I enjoyed going to my classes.

The most fun was at home on Oma's landing, playing records, dancing and practicing what I had learned. The banister was the same height as the working bars we used in class to do the leg exercises. When my cousin Uschi heard of my ballet lessons, she too enrolled for ballet and was assigned to my class. Then, whenever she came, we would practice together on the landing, proudly showing Oma what we had learned. Neither Uschi nor I could do the splits. We always ended up four or five inches above the floor, saying, "That hurts!" I continued with my lessons until shortly before I left school in the summer of 1949.

At the beginning of 1949, I was not quite fourteen and in seventh grade, when the *Jungen Pioniere,* the Young Pioneers of the Free East German Youth were established. A communist organization mandatory for young children under the age of fourteen. There, we again were taught the communist way: be patriotic, believe in social equality and Stalin because he will lead us to prosperity through hard work and unity. We were taught Russian folk songs and patriotic songs, such as, "Go Home, Ami, Ami, go home . . ." *(Ami is short for American)* We marched on special occasions, like May first, Stalin's birthday, or on the birthdays of East Germans communist leaders. Because of Mutti and Oma's influence I had no real interest in anything Russian or communist and did only what was expected.

All Pioneers were required to wear the Pioneer uniform, a blue scarf on a white blouse, dark blue skirt, and knee socks, for meetings, marches, and choir performances. The scarf was given to us, but not the rest of the required uniform. We could buy it from our leader or have someone sew it.

I asked Mutti for money to buy the uniform, but Mutti told me, "No, I'm not spending our money on any communist uniform. I have no use for their organizations or their communist teachings. How can you believe all that communist preaching when your stomach is empty? Their preaching isn't filling your stomach. All they do is fill your heads with lies and false promises." Mutti's arms flailed the air as if to underline her statement. "I wish you could see how the children in the West live, how much food they have while here the children have none. So, don't ask me for money to support the communists!"

As always, Oma came through and made me a dark skirt from an old one she had gotten somewhere. Then, after much begging and Oma telling Mutti, "There is no way around it. Gisela needs that uniform. If she doesn't have it, it will show that her family is anti-communist and you know what that means." Mutti gave in and I bought the white uniform blouse from my troop leader.

Hearing Mutti and Oma's talk, again, I realized they weren't supporters or believer of the communist regime or in love with Stalin and Russia. I never repeated what was said at home, for I'd heard that some people in Goerlitz had been arrested for talking against communism, Stalin and our East German leaders. As in Hitler's time, the people living in East Germany were not allowed to voice their opinions. Those who did, disappeared, never to be heard of again, turned in by their own countrymen who believe in Stalin and the communist regime.

All the communist speeches and teachings didn't still the people's hunger for food and freedom. They grumbled quietly that the people in the West had all the food they wanted, but nearly four years after the war, we still went without. Food, like spices for baking and cooking, coffee, cacao, chocolate, food for babies, like cream of wheat, as well as oatmeal, bananas, oranges, lemons, and many more items were still not available. We still had strict rationing but the electricity and gas weren't turned off anymore and curfew was eliminated. Oma had stopped locking the bread away, saying that we had a slight increase in our food stamps, but we still needed to ration our daily usage. We continued eating watery soups during the week. Oma still made her Karnickelbutter spread for my school and at home sandwiches, to help stretch the rationed marmalade. Only on weekends or special occasions would we have meat to eat.

Mutti and Oma talked of how the people living in East Germany were cut off more and more from the rest of the world. "The newspaper prints only what the regime allows us to know, and that is the glory of living the communist way where everyone is equal. Then, Oma said, "That's right! We are equal! Equally and together we go hungry, except for the top communists, the *Partei Bullen*."

Mutti added, "The radio, too, is controlled by the communists. They broadcast only what they deem necessary for us to hear."

As soon as I could, I had to ask Oma, "What are *Partei Bullen?*"

Surprised, Oma looked at me and instead of answering, asked, "Where did you hear that?"

"When you and Mutti were talking."

Oma shook her finger, "You're not supposed to listen when we talk about politics. You might slip and then we're in trouble. Don't ever repeat what you hear at home or use the expression in school, at your Pionier meetings or anywhere else."

"I know I can't, Oma, but who are they?"

Unsure, Oma looked at me, but she continued, "*Bullen,* (plural for bull) is a slang word used for the East German communist leaders and other Germans who are high in the Communist Party. They live in big houses and have all the food they want. They approve, support and believe in communism and Stalin and under his direction they rule East Germany. They're the ones who police us, so we do as we're told."

"They have food and we don't?"

Oma shrugged her shoulders, "That's the way communism works in Russia and now here. What Russia doesn't take out, then the *Partei Bullen* and their conspirators get what they want, they live like kings, while we have to scrape to survive. It all goes back to Hitler's big ideas in believing Germany was undefeatable, and now the Russians, their communism, and our Partei Bullen are suppressing us.

"So, those Germans believe in communism and Stalin?"

"Oh yes! They do! They're almost worse than the Russians. Even fanatics. Like Hitler and his Nazi's."

"How come you and Mutti know that?"

"It is common knowledge, only we're not suppose to know or talk about it. Don't repeat what you hear in our family," Oma warned me again.

"I won't, Oma," I promised. I knew talking negatively about the East German regime and its leaders, and most of all about Stalin, was not only forbidden but also dangerous.

Mutti, Oma, and many others who had a radio listened to *RIAS*, radio free Europe established in 1946, transmitted from West Berlin, the

American sector. *RIAS* broadcast the news of the free world and West Germany. They talked about Russia, telling the people in East Germany what the real truth was, discouraging everyone in East Germany from believing in communism and Stalin's regime. The sound low, their ears close to the radio, Mutti and Oma listened whenever they could to the six o'clock broadcast. Both instructed me, "Never mention to anyone our listening to the *RIAS* broadcast because the East German people are forbidden to listen. We'd be in big trouble if we were found out. Do you understand?"

I understood and I knew the danger. People had been caught, turned in by their neighbors, reported to the *Stasi*, a secret communist police agency operated by Germans. Everyone who listened to the *RIAS* broadcast kept the sound low and huddled near the radio. Some, like Mutti and Oma, even locked the door to be safe, to keep unexpected visitors out, to have a chance to turn off the radio or to change the station before answering a knock on the door. Mutti would say to me, "In or out." Usually I went out. I felt the less I knew of what was said from that broadcast, the better it was for me to keep us safe. Then, too, politics were so confusing. In school and at the Pioneers, we were told that all was good and well; that we were doing fine; that our leaders would lead us to prosperity and the good life. But, to achieve this goal, we needed to work hard and in solidarity. Only then would we fulfill our dreams, but they never told us when, only that it would take time. The more I thought about of what Mutti and Oma were saying and what we were told in school, the more confusing it got.

Later, when I saw Mutti or Oma looking out the window, I knew the broadcast was over. Sometimes after a broadcast I would hear Oma say, "It's almost impossible to hear anything at all anymore, only a word here and there. The high frequency signals East Germany sends out are so strong they almost block the broadcast."

"Yes," Mutti sighed. "The communists want to keep us in the dark. They want to control us and they'll do all they can, to do it. I wonder when it will end and they'll go home, all of them, even the occupiers in the West."

"The way I see it," Oma replied, "the war is over, Hitler is dead, so everyone can go home now, and the Russians can take the German communists and informers with them. But it won't be anytime soon. The Russians like it way too much in Germany. They never had it so good. Haven't we given up enough?"

I could tell Oma was sad, but her face showed strength, ready to throw the Russians and the Pole's out of our homeland and country. I had the feeling she missed her little house in the country and the now decayed apartment we could see when we looked across the Neisse River. Oma wanted to go home, back where she belonged and to the life she had lived.

But what had been her life and home was now in Polish territory, forbidden to the people who had lived there.

No matter how bad it was, our family, a fun loving family, seized any occasion to be together, to forget, and to enjoy the moment. That is what kept all of us going.

The teaching of communism continued in school as in the Pioneers. Continuously we were told to believe that our lives would improve by working hard together with the promise that Stalin, our friend and liberator, would show us the way, a promise emphasized with big posters of Stalin. On his birthday in December, every store window was decorated in red. Centered and framed with flower garlands, stood Stalin's picture among Russian flags with a hammer and sickle, the insignia of the Soviet Union, as we were told to refer to Russia. Also included in the decorations were the flags of the *Deutsche Democratic Republic* in short *DDR*, with its symbol of a hammer and compass, encircled by a wreath of wheat interwoven with a band of gold, red, and black, the colors of East Germany. Stalin's birthday meant always a big celebration and although it was winter and cold, we had to march with the flags of both countries flying high. The Pioneers and the *FDJ*, Free German Youth, carried their flags; some of the marchers held pictures of Stalin; others had small bouquets of flowers, waving them, smiling while they marched. People stopped and lined the streets or looked out their windows as we marched by singing. Children waved paper flags. At the conclusion of the march, we had to gather with the citizens of Goerlitz at the *Obermarkt,* in a public square. A podium covered in red cloth had been built with amplifiers all around it. A huge picture of Stalin draped in red covered the back wall. Chairs were placed on the podium where the Buergermeister and the dignitaries of Goerlitz were to sit. All around the podium and the public square flags were flying. A speaker, dressed in a suit and tie, greeted us, telling us how lucky we were to have Stalin and the Soviet Union as our friends, how we needed to work hard; how we needed to build up the *Deutsche Demokratische Republik*; how we needed to free the people in West Germany from the tyranny of capitalism. He closed his speech with, "Let's all of us work hard so that together we will and can accomplish our goals!" The dignitaries sitting on the podium clapped often. All of us standing and listening had to follow suit because no one knew who was watching the reaction of the people.

Communist slogans printed in big white letters on red banners hung in schools, restaurants, movie houses, and outside buildings. Again and again, we were told that Stalin and the people of the Soviet Union were our friends, who believed in us, and encouraged us to work so that we, too, could improve our lives. The Soviet Union and only the Soviet Union was the true friend of Germany.

In school we continued to learn everything about Russia, Stalin, and Lenin. Vladimir Lenin was a revolutionary and the forbearer of Joseph Stalin. We were taught that the people in West Germany were being misled, oppressed, and lied to by their conquerors. They had to endure the capitalism of the Americans who had divided Germany, who also had cut communications between East Germany and West Germany. The Americans didn't want anyone to know what they're doing to the Germans living in West Germany. But, we would always hear the truth from Stalin, our friend. He would never lie to us. He promised that someday, when East Germany was strong, action would be taken to free those poor lied-to people in West Germany, to release them from the tyranny of capitalism and to liberate them from the American occupation. We would send them and their collaborators, the English and French, back home. Then, we would unite Germany once more, making it the greatest country under the leadership of *Pieck* and *Ulbricht*, our East German Chancellors, and Stalin, our friend and advisor.

The Pioneers were not much different. Our group leader, a woman made sure we followed and respected her communist guidelines. She was also our choir leader and continued to teach us patriotic German songs and folksongs in Russian. It was important, she told us, to learn the traditions and customs of our Soviet friends, to love them, but to hate capitalism.

When I told Mutti and Oma what I was learning in school, how bad capitalism was, they shook their heads in disbelief at what they were hearing. Mutti said, "Don't tell us! You sound as if you're on your way to being a little communist."

Oma said, "That's all she hears and learns in school, so it's no wonder she is starting to believe all that false information." Turning to me, Oma asked, "Have you forgotten that we have not always lived like this? You remember before the war ended, when all of us lived in our homes and had food to eat?"

"I remember, Oma."

"Then I think you're old enough to understand and to see that we still have nothing. We can't go home because Russia gave our land away. It's been almost four years since the war ended and we still have no food to speak of. All that stuff you're being told in school is propaganda, so you children will believe how much better the future in East Germany will be when you grow up under the guidance of communism or, as you call it, our Soviet friends. They are trying to make Communists out of you children. We, all of us, are being used. We're being told to work hard to better ourselves, but, in fact, whatever we achieve goes to Russia and to the big communists that rule us."

"But why do people believe in communism?"

"Not all do, and the ones that do they were already communist, or they are what we call turn-coats, people who hang their coats in the wind and go wherever the wind blows them."

"That sure is a funny sounding expression, Oma."

"Yes it is, but that is what they're called because they change from one form of government to another without any scruples. They're the ones who turn in their own countrymen when they voice criticism of the current government. How do you think people get arrested for political reasons? The Russians don't know unless someone tells them, and those are the people who do that. Remember to be careful to whom you speak about politics. And do not tell anyone what is talked about here. It needs to stay right here and go no further. You understand, don't you?"

"I know, Oma." And that ended our conversation. I felt I was sitting in the middle. In school we were told how great everything was, and at home, how it was not. Thinking over what Oma had told me, I knew she was right. We had nothing, nothing at all. Everything was rationed. Even when I wanted a small cone of ice cream, I had to ask Oma for a stamp from our rations, and that meant Oma was a sugar stamp short for our monthly allowance. A small cone of ice cream was a rare treat, but it was not the sweet, creamy ice cream I remembered. This ice cream was frozen sugar water with color and flavor. The ice cream parlor was not always open either. It was closed when the owner ran out of supplies to make the ice cream.

Spring had come and passed, and, according to Oma's calendar, summer had started. The end of seventh grade was almost near and I would be fourteen in July. To complete eight grade, some of my classmate and I would fifteen because we had missed school because of fleeing. Because of those circumstances, the school didn't insist that we continue because normally children at fourteen have completed all eight grades. I asked Mutti, "Can I quit school?"

"Are you sure you want to do that?"

"Yes I am. I will be fifteen before I'm done with grade school, and I have another four years in the *Beruf-Schule*, a Trade School. I don't want to be one of the "old ones" in either school. Besides, many other children are stopping school. Can I stop, too, Mutti, please?"

Thus, at the end of July 1949, with written permission from Mutti and the agreement from the school, I was excused. Although Oma felt I should finish the eighth grade, Mutti said, "She'll be fine. Before you know it, she'll be married and no one will ask if she finished her eighth grade or not."

That same summer, the pastor came to Goerlitz to gather his belongings, taking them back to West Germany where he was living with his family. Then, our living room was almost empty. He took the china cabinet with all its contents, the chandelier, the overstuffed chairs, and all the oil paintings. I asked Mutti, "How can he do that?"

"He had permission from the East German government to cross the border to get his belongings, with the understanding that we allow him to take them from us."

"So you let him take them?"

"Yes I did, and he was grateful that we had taken such good care of his furniture, dishes and crystal. As a thank you, he left us six of the crystal wine goblets in different colors, the credenza, the dining table and chairs, the tea cart, some tablecloths, and three pictures, the holy picture showing the hill of Golgotha with the three crosses on top and the two pictures of the forest. He told me the photos of the forest used to be black and white, but his wife had colored them."

"Did you know that, Mutti?"

"No, but by looking close, you can see the fine strokes of each individual colored pencil. I always wondered who did that."

I went to where Mutti had hung them and I, too, could see the precise strokes of each colored pencil. "That must have been a lot of work, Mutti. I think that lady is an artist."

"The pastor didn't say. He was happy that I let him have what he wanted, so he gave us things, saying that his wife wanted us to have them too."

"I think that was nice of him."

"Yes, it pays to be nice and generous."

"Did he take the gramophone and the records, too?"

"Yes, he did. I told him he could take them. You haven't been playing with them anymore."

I hated to hear that because I had spent many hours listening, singing, and dancing around the gramophone. But it was not mine to keep and, as Mutti said, I had not been playing with it for some time.

Although I was out of grade school, going to the Beruf Schule I had to join the *FDJ*, and I continued in their choir. We had to participate in some functions, and I liked choir the most. Our songs were mainly patriotic with a few traditional German ones. Thanks to Oma, I knew all the old ones. I never learned how to read notes. Although we had it in school, the notes just never went into my head. But I had sharp ears and could pick up the notes of a song after listening just once. Oma thought it came from sitting for hours by the gramophone playing records, listening and learning the songs. My ballet classes came to an end, too, as I felt I was getting too big and knew I would never be a ballerina as much as I pretended to be one.

My friends started their apprenticeships, Jochen, I remember as a locksmith, but I don't recall what trade Siegfried was learning. Inge was in school and so was Regina, Jochen's sister. We would see each other on weekends, chat and just sit around. Oma and I stopped gleaning but our trips to the cemetery continued—every other Saturday. Thus, my childhood came to an end.

In spring of 1950, Mutti traded apartments with Onkel Heinz and Tante Hilde who had a baby girl, Heidi. After the baby's birth, Tante Hilde was hospitalized for six weeks with a gallbladder operation. Before the move my sister helped Onkel Heinz with the baby and Reiner, but soon it became my job because Christa had a job. I didn't mind. It gave me something to do, and I liked taking care of children. When Tante Hilde came home from the hospital, she needed a yard to recoup and for Reiner to play in, as well as Oma to help out. Thus, Mutti and Onkel Heinz traded apartments.

I was sad to leave Oma. She had been the main figure in my life, giving me love and care when I'd needed it most. Oma had been my teacher, my nurse and my keeper. I knew even then that I would never forget her. She would always be a memory close to my heart, a lady who cared so much for others, forgetting herself in the process. Next to Vati, Oma would be the person that I loved the most in my young life and that has been so.

Therefore, I dedicate this portion of the book to my loving, and caring Vati, who was, if only for a short time so much a part of my very young life, and to my dear and loving Oma, my grandmother. You have always been present as I walked through life.

My Parents
Engagement and Wedding 1930

Vati, 1939

Mutti, 1940

Goerlitz

Mutti, and Christa with Me
in the Buggy 1935

Me, Christa and Uschi
1938

Oma and Me
1937/38

Me, Uschi and Christa
1938

Vati's Visit with Mutti
in Goerlitz 1943

Liegnitz 1939

My Stepmother, Vati
and Me 1939

Uschi with Doll Rosewitha
amd Me with Fritz, my Teddy

My Buggy

First Day of School 1941

Me—1944

Back Home 1946

Mutti with her Daughters

Mutti, the Nurse

Oma in her blue Hat

Christa and Me 1948

Mending in the Backyard

Miscellaneous Pictures

My 1943 visit to Goerlitz
Christa, Uschi and Me

1952 Wedding
Mutti and my Stepfather

Little Claudia

Confirmation 1950

Carnival

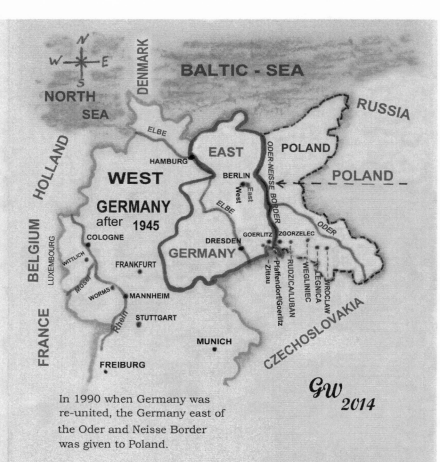

In 1990 when Germany was
re-united, the Germany east of
the Oder and Neisse Border
was given to Poland.

Book Two

My Teen Years and the Escape

The trading of apartments and moving was done before Tante Hilde was released from the hospital. Mutti, Martin Hentschke, and I were now living at our new residence—*Karl-Liebknecht-Strasse 42.* Christa stayed at the Langenstrasse and moved into Frau Hartman's former apartment, because her two children and she had moved away.

Our new residence was a four-story *Eck-Haus*, a corner apartment building that faced *Karl-Liebknecht Strasse* and *Leipziger Strasse* and consisted of seven apartments with a bakery on the bottom floor. Our apartment on the second floor was an *Eck-Wohnung*, a corner apartment directly on top the bakery. We had a dark kitchen, a living room with two windows and a large bedroom, with four windows, two of them facing *Leipziger Strasse.* We shared the water closet a half flight down in the stairwell with an elderly couple that lived in the apartment next to us.

Martin Hentschke, who was now working for the *Goerlitzer Polizei Revier*, the Police Department had become so entwined with our family over the last three years that he joined Mutti and me at our new location. I called him *Onkel Martin*, although he was not my real Onkel it was considered impolite and disrespectful to address a grown-up by their first name. When talking to friends and family, Mutti jokingly referred to him as "my co-tenant".

I liked Onkel Martin a lot. He was a nice, quiet man with a dry but quick sense of humor and we got along just fine, but I knew he never could replace Vati—no one could. We were a three-some, like a real family, only Mutti and Onkel Martin were not married. That didn't bother me—I liked having him move in with us. I didn't even question it. I was just happy where I was.

Although we only had one bedroom, it was big. Mutti partitioned it with two *Kleiderschraenke,* two clothes closets, setting them side-by-side, thus making a small bedroom for me behind them, with a curtain as a door. There was enough room for my bed, a nightstand, a small table and chair in front of one of the windows. It was a cozy little place, private, and it all belonged to me. Because we didn't have a big wardrobe, we shared the two closets. When we moved, Mutti had taken all the living room furniture, pictures, and the six colored crystal goblets the preacher had given her with us. I marveled at how quickly Mutti could make a strange place so welcoming and homey.

I missed Oma a lot, when we moved that spring of 1950. So often I'd make the twenty-minute walk and go to see her. Oma and I would sit in the backyard and visit, Tante Hilde joining us. Sometimes I played with Rainer or took Heidi, my new baby cousin, for a walk in her buggy—relieving Oma and Tante Hilde for a short time. Oma's and my relationship had developed a tear, though I still felt close to her. I knew her love for me had not stopped, but somehow the unseen ribbon that had tied us together had fallen apart. We had stopped going for walks, singing, talking, or just being together. Oma was too busy with Tante Hilde, who was trying to recover from her surgery, needing help with Rainer and the baby. Oma was so busy, there was not much time left for me—I was jealous.

Several times that summer, mostly on a Saturday when Onkel Heinz was home, Oma and I did go to the cemetery to take care of Vati's grave. After we were done weeding and planting flowers, Oma and I stood surveying the field where Vati was buried—it looked so uncared for, so sad and forlorn. Discouraged, Oma, said, "With the graves and walkways overgrown with weeds, we can hardly keep them off your father's grave. I don't know what we could do to stop that."

"Why aren't people taking care of their graves, like we do Vati's?"

"Well, there are no family members to care for these graves. Apparently these people died all alone with no one to mourn them and some are unknown—with no names. That's why these graves have no markers. Only your father has—and that's almost gone. Over time the weather has damaged the wood, and the paint is peeling off too, and we have no means to fix it."

Oma was right. I still remembered the rows and rows of caskets that had filled the church—no one had been there. No one followed the other three caskets when we'd buried Vati on that sad day. Only my stepmother and I had followed the hearse. "Does that mean the people lying here didn't have any relatives?"

"Oh, I'm sure they did—we all do. They probability have lost contact with their families because of the war. Maybe they got separated somehow, or got lost, sick, and died with no identification. Maybe their families were already dead, so they died all alone. No one will ever know what their circumstances were." While Oma was talking, I was thinking of Vati. I was comforted that he was not alone when he died, comforted, however sad, that my stepmother and I had been able to follow the hearse to his grave, glad that Oma and I now could bring him flowers. Oma stopped for a minute as if she were thinking, then continued. "Could be that their families might be looking for them, not knowing they died and are buried here." I listened to Oma and I thought, *that's what happened to Mutti when she was looking for Vati; she didn't know he had died.* Just then Oma interrupted my thoughts, saying, "I guess we're all looking, hoping, and praying to find a loved one, just as I keep praying, looking, and hoping to see my son Rudi again before I die."

Oma's words sent shivers through me and harshly, I interrupted, "Oma you're not going to die. Not right now."

"No, not right now, but someday, and my only wish is that before then I will see my son Rudi's safe return home." Oma gave me a nudge and turned to leave. "Let's go. I need to get back home, and we can't stand around here and stew about things we can't change—but can only hope for." Feeling it would be a long time before we came again, I bent down to Vati's grave and moved a little dirt, as if I wanted to rearrange something, but, in fact, I was giving Vati my silent good-bye, promising never to forget him. When I left, hanging onto Oma's arm, it felt as if Vati were walking beside me—going home with me.

That summer in 1950 Oma stopped gleaning, but would sometimes asked me to help her on her washdays. Then we made the trips to the Waeschemangel, the same one that had intimidated me, across the street from where we were living now. I didn't mind helping. I had nothing else important to do. It gave me a chance to spend time with Oma, as I used to. Because we had no wash facilities in our new apartment building, Oma took care of our wash too. But when winter came, Mutti and I, sometimes Onkel Martin, we carried our wash in the basket between us to the professional washhouse—picking it up washed, pressed and folded.

Our food was still rationed with nothing to spare. But with Mutti's strict management, a lot of plain soups and the use of all leftovers, we survived. Nothing had changed. People still stood in long lines in front of stores when shopping for food. Some grocers would only sell to their steady customers. When Mutti went shopping, I always went with her, not only to help carry things, but also to get to know the grocer, butcher, and the baker.

Because Mutti was working for the Russian doctor and I was at home doing nothing, she gave me chores to do, like washing dishes, making the beds, and doing general pick up and clean up. It amazed me that when

Mutti got home, she could tell what kind of a job I had done. The minute she walked in and looked around, she often said, "I see you cleaned the dance floor only!"

Puzzled, I asked, "What do you mean by that? How do you know that?"

"By just looking! I can tell you only mopped the middle of the floor. It shows where you stopped mopping. Dust is still in the corners and along the baseboards. If you want to help, then you need to clean the corners and baseboards on your hands and knees. I know you can do that well." I didn't mind Mutti telling me that. I was glad she didn't yell or glare at me, as my stepmother always had. I promised Mutti I would do a better job next time.

Eventually, armed with a list, the food stamp card, and money, I did the shopping with Mutti warning me, "You make sure and watch so they don't cut more stamps off than what is needed."

"Why would they do that?"

"It gives the merchant more stamps for extra supplies which they then can sell *out the back door* to their special customers, without stamps, but for more money. That is part of the black market."

"I have heard you and Oma talk about that. Isn't that illegal?"

"Of course it is. That's why it's called black market."

"Can you shop like that too, Mutti?"

"No, you have to know a merchant really well, like being related. If you're caught, people go to jail for it and with my luck . . ." Mutti trailed off, giving me the impression that her luck was not very good. "We'll just keep on shopping the right way."

The only rationed stamps we always ran short of were for bread because we liked to eat *Semmeln*, hard rolls for breakfast on Sundays with a soft-boiled egg and the good coffee that either Mutti or Onkel Martin got from somewhere. I think it was bought at the black market since it was not available in stores; but I never asked. With the good coffee, the hard rolls, the soft-boiled eggs and a very small amount of butter, our Sunday morning breakfast was a feast. While we ate, Mutti opened the window so we could hear the church bells ring from the *Luther-Kirche* a block away, calling for the *Sonntag Gottes Dienst*, Sunday Sermon. We never went to services. Mutti said she didn't need to go to church. She said. "To believe in God, I only need to listen to the heavenly sounds of the church bells and say a silent prayer." I followed her example.

I didn't mind doing the shopping, but I disliked going to our baker downstairs to buy our bread or the hard rolls. The elderly baker's wife, *Frau Jaeschke*, who waited on her customers behind her white, clean, shiny counter, was a rather plump but friendly lady, but I disliked her. Every time Mutti sent me downstairs shopping, she looked at me and crooned, "And what would you like today, *little one?*" I wanted to jump over her white, clean, shiny counter and tell her, "I'm not a 'little one'! I'm almost fifteen, a young adult and not 'a little' one anymore! I'm *Fraeulein Knebel* to you!" But I didn't do it. Instead I bought what Mutti had sent me to get and went back upstairs—fuming. "One of these days I'm going to tell her, "Stop calling me 'little one'! I'm *Fraeulein Knebel!* I'm a young adult and it's common courtesy that she should address me as *Fraeulein* and with *Sie* and not with the familiar *Du!* I'm a stranger to her! I want her to call me *Fraeulein Knebel!*"

Mutti listened to my spouting, finally interrupting me, "What are you talking about? Why are you so upset?"

"That baker-woman downstairs—she always calls me, 'little one'."

"Oh, that is what has you so upset? Well, you're not very tall and you do still look like a child, although you'll be turning fifteen soon. It's best not to make her mad, because she'll sell us bread when we're out of our bread ration. She'll note it in her book until we can pay her when we get the new set of grocery stamps for the month. We need to keep her on our side." I could tell to Mutti this was a minor thing. But to me, everywhere I went, I felt looked upon as a school child because I was small and puny. Even when I went to see a movie rated for those over fourteen, the owners who stood at the entrance to any of our five movie houses told me to go home and do my homework! Onkel Martin tried to console me by saying, "You just need to grow some more—and you will, just wait."

"Ja, but when is that going to happen?"

"It will happen; just have patience."

"Onkel Martin? Do you think I can tell that baker-lady downstairs not to call me little one anymore? Do you think Mutti would get mad at me if I did?"

"If she does, you know your mother. It would not be for very long. Maybe if you ask the baker-lady politely to stop calling you 'little one', but to call you 'Fraeulein Knebel' instead. It all depends on how you handle it."

I thought about that, and as much as I was carrying on about it, way down deep I was a coward, afraid to confront people. I knew it was disrespectful to correct grown-ups, but at fifteen, we were young adults so it was customary that strangers address us by our last name instead of our first. I wanted to be treated and respected as a young adult. I wanted to be called 'Fraeulein Knebel', but I didn't know how to handle the situation with the lady at the baker's shop.

One thing I was sure of. I didn't want to talk to her with customers in the store because I feared she would get mad and tell me off. I knew from my past how easy it is to tell a child off, and she saw me as a child. It would be so awkward if customers were to hear that and see me getting beet-red with embarrassment. I had to wait for the right moment and for my courage to be with me.

After a while when the time was right and I was the only customer, my heart pounding, my mouth dry with fear, I asked, "Please, Frau Jaeschke, would you not call me 'little one', anymore? Would you please call me 'Fraeulein Knebel' from now on?" She looked at me in amazement. I was waiting for her to tell me how disrespectful I was and that she would have to talk to my mother about that.

Instead, smiling, while handing me the bread, politely she said, "That will be fine." My knees weak I left the baker shop, went upstairs and sat down. I had jumped a hurdle I'd thought I could never jump.

Mutti asked, "What is the matter with you? You have a funny look on your face."

"I did it! I really did it!"

"Did what?"

In my relief I had forgotten that now I had to explain my action to Mutti who was looking at me, waiting for an answer. I knew Mutti was not like my stepmother—she didn't hit me or call me names—but occasionally she would get mad at me and I didn't like it. Leaning forward a bit, Mutti asked again, "What did you do?"

"Now, Mutti, don't get mad, but I asked Frau Jaeschke, very politely, not to call me 'little one' anymore, but to call me 'Fraeulein Knebel'."

Mutti shook her head, as if she couldn't believe what she was hearing. "You did what?"

"Just now, I asked Frau Jaeschke to call me Fraeulein Knebel."

"What was her answer?"

"She just said, 'That will be fine'".

"That's all she said?"

"Yes, that's all she said. And she was very friendly."

"Well I guess, you can say, 'You did it', but now we will see if she'll let us borrow when we run out of bread stamps again."

I looked at Onkel Martin sitting at the table listening, grinning as if he had heard a good joke, wanting to laugh.

Mutti turned to him, "I can see you agree with what Gisela has told Frau Jaeschke in the bakery."

"Well, yes, she is not really a 'little one' anymore, no matter what."

Resigned, Mutti looked at both of us, nodded her head, saying, "I can see right now, you two will stick together." I couldn't help but grin, and Onkel Martin gave me a wink, a twinkle in his eyes. I knew I had him in my corner for life.

Frau Jaeschke never mentioned the incident to Mutti. She greeted me with courtesy and I her. When the time came that we had to borrow bread against our next month's ration of stamps, she granted our request, always. We were not only her neighbor, but also her customer.

I wanted to be recognized as an adult so badly that I'd left school with out considering all the consequences. I hadn't realized I'd miss out on the religious study for confirmation, added at the eighth-grade levels an after-school function. It is divided according to individual students' beliefs, and taught by teachers from the Lutheran and Catholic faiths. After completion of religious study, and before the end of eighth-grade, came confirmation—a solemn festive occasion. Celebrated in the Lutheran and Catholic churches with organs playing hymns, singing, and bells ringing—signifying the coming of age—confirmation was a stepping-stone from childhood to adulthood.

We were Lutherans and I had been baptized in that faith. Oma and I had gone to church on Christmas Eve, believing in God and Jesus; and Oma had walked for her holy water on Easter, believing in its power. Still, we did not attend church at other times—except for weddings, baptisms, or funerals. However, I still wanted confirmation, that ritual to complete my childhood. I asked Mutti if I could join the non-religious group of young adults and participate in its *Jugendweihe*—a Youth Dedication that began in 1852 and developed in opposition to the Protestant and Catholic Churches confirmation. It was widely practiced in East Germany to inspire the young to love socialism. Mutti didn't like it at all, "It's all about communism. I don't know why you want to do that."

"Because," I told Mutti, "when I left school, I missed the religious classes and I would like a confirmation, too." Onkel Martin agreed with me, saying, "Just let her do it. She'll be fine."

Mutti gave in, I signed up, and for a short time I went to the required classes so I could participate in the Jugendweihe. I wasn't too interested in their teachings. It was just as Mutti had said, "All communism." No religion. I would have liked it to be in a church too, to bow my head to receive the blessing, and to feel the closure of my childhood, as well as the beginning of my adult life, my own stepping-stone. I wanted a confirmation.

We were a big group of young adults—the girls dressed in black, the boys, in suits and ties. Mutti allowed me my first permanent and had a dress made for me of my own choosing. It was black, with matching stockings and new shoes made of fake leather. The Dedication or Rite of Passage was held in one of the auditoriums of the Stadthalle, the Goerlitzer concert hall. Our auditorium was decorated with flowers and flags of Russia and East Germany. The only thing missing was Stalin's picture. We listened to the socialist speech, and instead of church bells and organ music, we had piano music, with the *FDJ-Choir*, dressed in blue, singing their patriotic songs. At the end of the program, we received a small diploma stating that we had participated in the Jugendweihe.

Mutti stayed home to prepare for my party afterward, but Oma and Onkel Martin went with me. When we got home, our family and a few of Mutti's friends had arrived—including Onkel Martin's two sisters. I was greeted with hugs and congratulations. We sat down to a beautifully set table to have coffee and cake, thanks to my two aunts and Oma who contributed food stamps needed so Mutti and Oma could bake the cakes. Later in the evening, Mutti served potato salad, heated Wuerst, like hot dogs, and beer, with lemonade for the younger generation and tea for the older. I received the traditional gifts—sets of cup/saucer/cake-plate, each set in a different pattern, lacey hankies, and books. None of my eight godparents who, customarily would have been present, were not. We didn't know their whereabouts. All in all, thanks to Mutti and Oma's baking, cooking, and shining up the apartment, it was a wonderful party. I was happy to have a confirmation, although not in church, but a confirmation I had wished for, the ending of my childhood and the beginning of my teen years

That July in 1950, when I turned fifteen, I applied and received the *Personal Ausweiss*, a personal identification with picture issued by the police department, which was the law. Now I had proof of age when I wanted to see a mature movie. I had entered the world of the grown-ups—another stepping-stone. It was time now for me to decide what kind of job I wanted to learn. To choose a profession as is expected of every youth leaving grade school. "Why don't you become a nurse?" Mutti suggested.

"Me, a nurse, for grown-ups? Like you are?" I shook my head. "I wouldn't mind being a baby-nurse, but a nurse like you?"

"What's wrong with being a nurse like me?"

"Well, I can't imagine wiping their . . . you know what I mean, but with babies I could."

"Oh that," Mutti laughed, "You get used to it after awhile." But just thinking about it gave me a tight stomach. No, nursing grown-ups was not for me.

I decided to go to the employment office in charge of placing youths fourteen and over in apprenticeship positions. "Guten Tag" I greeted the woman in charge sitting behind her desk. She asked me to be seated and inquired where my interests lay. I stammered, "I like to be a baby nurse, a florist, or a beautician."

She shook her head. "I'm sorry, but places for those apprenticeships are not readily available." Shuffling her papers, she found what she was looking for. "However, I do have openings in apprenticeships—with the usual requirements of a four-year training and schooling period—for carpenters, locksmiths, roofers, electricians, and blacksmiths. We're in great need of those professions and want to educate as many young people as possible."

"Aren't those professions for boys only?"

"Yes, indeed, they used to be." Leaning over her desk and looking at me she continued, "We have girls already working in male professions and liking it. We need educated, trained workers; we need our young generation to build for their future, to make our democratic and socialist country strong, just like our friends the Russians, who have men and women working in those professions, examples of what a country can do when men and women are equal, working side by side—to make their country strong and to protect it from enemies. Under the leadership of Stalin and our Soviet friends, we can and will do the same. I'll give you the paperwork. Fill it out at home, have your guardian sign it, and return it to me. Also, give some thought to what trade you'd like to learn." She handed me the forms, including the date for the entrance examination.

I got up, made a curtsy then said, "Auf Wiedersehen."

Done with me the lady just inclined her head. When I got home, I told Mutti where I'd been and found out.

"Why would you want to learn a man's job? That woman is a communist. They want to recruit as many girls as possible to do men's jobs. She's helping to make communists out of our younger generation, working to make East Germany into a second Russia, and doing a good job of it. We're not working to rebuild our country. We're working for them, our so-called friends, while Stalin allows us barely enough food to survive." Although Mutti worked for a lady Russian doctor, she had no use for Stalin's communism or the Russians. "Didn't she have any openings for a girl apprenticeship, like nursing?"

"No, Mutti. She said they were not readily available."

"Did you ask for baby nurse's training only?"

"Well, yes, but I also told her I'd like to be a beautician or florist. She had nothing like that, and I don't want to be a nurse."

"I keep hearing that from you. It's a very respectable profession and will always be in demand, better than a man's job."

"I know, Mutti, but it's not me. I can't do it!" She stopped. I think Mutti wanted one of her daughters to go into the nursing profession she loved so much.

I didn't want to be a nurse, not only because of what I'd have to do, but because I was afraid of not being good enough or smart enough. These fears stuck in my head, a voice from the past that followed me. I was unable to tell anyone of my fear, even Mutti. I was ashamed to feel afraid, but I wasn't able to shake that taunting voice of my stepmothers. I couldn't tell Mutti how that voice hunted me. It would hurt her feelings. She wouldn't understand, and trying to make me feel better, she'd laugh it off, saying, "Forget what that fat slob of a woman told you. You're not with her anymore."

Oh, how I wanted to forget, and at times I did. But whenever a situation arose that took courage, I'd hear my stepmother's voice. "Don't bother. You can't do it because you're stupid, ugly and no one likes or wants you." I wondered if I'd ever stop hearing her voice.

I filled out the forms; Mutti signed them; I returned them; I took the test with lots of other young adults, boys and girls alike. I had decided to become a carpenter, like Vati. I always had liked playing with wood, its smell, and smoothness when Vati had planed. Even the fumes from the paint he used, reminded me of Vati. I wanted to learn to work with wood, to stick the flat carpenter's pencil behind my ear, to feel and hear the fallen chips under my feet. I wanted to build furniture, just like Vati.

After a time Mutti was notified that I'd passed the test, but all the carpentry positions were filled. Locksmithing and other positions were available. Because locksmithing was my second choice, my name had been added to the list of my future employer. We filled out more forms. Before Mutti signed them, she asked, "Are you sure you want to be a locksmith? You do know when I sign this contract, you're committed, with no way out."

"Yes, I know I have to learn some trade, and that's all that's available!"

With Mutti's signature, I was now a signed and sealed locksmith apprentice. It was a four-year, binding commitment with no way out, except health problems or death.

I was notified by mail when and where I was to report to begin my apprenticeship. I was employed as a locksmith apprentice by the *Loren and Waggonbau of Goerlitz,* established in the 1850's, a company that built and manufactured railway cars for people and cargo.

September 1st 1950 was the beginning of my apprenticeship, when I approached the site, nervous and unsure, I saw groups of boys and girls standing in front of the oblong gray building where the locksmith and blacksmith apprentices were trained. The four story's building's many windows felt like eyes staring at me, daring me to come closer. Fear gripped me, as I heard the familiar cold voice from the past telling me, "You're not smart enough. You're ugly, and they won't like you." I stopped. I didn't want to go through the gate into the graveled, fenced-in yard. I wanted to run, turn back, when a voice startled me by asking, "Are you one of the new apprentices?" With a lump in my throat, I nodded. The gatekeeper, smiling and pointing as if he knew how scared I was, said, "You need to join the group over there."

Finding my voice and with a hint of a curtsy, I said, "*Danke schoen.*"

When I joined the group, I noticed they too looked solemn. Nobody said a word. We just stood and waited. At the exact time specified in the appointment letter, a man came to greet us, "*Guten Morgen!* I hope everyone is here. Let's get started." Motioning to us, he said, "Come with me."

We followed him to the third floor of the building, then through a double door into a large hall that had several rows of long gray wooden workbenches. The thick, wire-reinforced big windows that had intimated me didn't seem scary anymore. They were just windows, illuminating the white walled hall with bright sunshine. Again, we were greeted by a group of men dressed in dark work uniforms as if they had been waiting for us. "Gather around," said the man who had brought us upstairs, "and pay attention. I'm *Meister Keller* in charge of all the apprentices in this building, including you. These men are instructors. Each of them has a list with names. When your name is called, you'll answer, "*Hier!*" then stand with your instructor." With a few more words to the men and a nod in our direction, *Meister Keller* was gone. The instructors spread out as they called the names on their lists. When all was done, every instructor had eight apprentices, eight girls or eight boys.

Our instructor was a tall, slender, friendly, man who introduced himself with, "My name is *Hahn* and I'm your instructor." Of course, to us he was "*Herr Hahn*" because he was not only a stranger, but also our superior and instructor. When he spoke to us, he was informal, addressing us by our first names only. We girls agreed not to be formal with each other by using our last names and titles, as etiquette would have required, but to address each other by our first names.

Looking us over, he said, "First off, I will show you to your work stations and your work benches, so follow me." Like little ducks, we followed him along the wall opposite the windows to the far end of the hall. He stopped at the last two rows of workbenches. They sat back to back, with evenly space vices, four on each side, with two big drawers below them. "Now, pick your work stations."

I didn't want to be close to Herr Hahn, so I picked the first vice by the window, the farthest away from Herr Hahn, because the workbenches ran from the window into the room. Herr Hahn had a table and chair placed against the wall opposite the windows, with a walking space between his station and the end of our work benches, enabling him to watch us at all times.

When we stood in front of our vices, Herr Hahn, at the end of the workbenches, continued, "The station you picked will be your station unless I decide otherwise. For the first year of your apprenticeship, I'm your instructor. After that, you'll move to another instructor for your second year, and so on until you have finished the required four years of apprenticeship, either in being a locksmith or a blacksmith. Then, to call yourself a bona-fide locksmith or blacksmith, you'll have to pass a written test, as well as a finished product you've made."

Longingly I glanced out the window, thinking, *Four years, it seems such a long time to me and . . .*

Herr Hahn's strong voice overshadowed my thoughts, bringing me back to where I was supposed to be. "The top drawer below the vice belongs to you; the lower, to the person from the opposite shift." Handing each of us a key, he continued, "Because you're responsible for the tools in your drawer, you will lock it at the end of your shifts. Don't lose the key. Am I making myself clear?"

Meekly, some of us answered, "Yes."

We stood like marionettes in front of our vices, stiff and shy, afraid to crack a smile. Trying to break the ice, "I think we are a nice group of start-up apprentices, don't you agree?" Nobody said a word. Herr Hahn asked us to say our names once more, with him laughingly adding, "It will take a day or so before I'll remember your names correctly. Now, let's go and see the rest of the building and grounds, your home for the next four years." Again, Herr Hahn in the lead, we followed in duck order out of the hall, silently passing the other new recruits and work benches.

The bottom floor, occupied by the fourth-year locksmith and blacksmith apprentices, was equipped with anvils and fire holes. The floor above them, but below us, belonged to the second and third year apprentices. Next was our floor, for the youngest set, the newcomers, the dummies, the know-nothings, as were called by the older apprentices. Up a flight was the final floor, divided into schoolrooms, where we had to attend classes twice a week to further our education and to learn the concepts of locksmithing.

Back outside and adjacent to the big building was a smaller one that housed a nurse's station with separate locker rooms for girls and boys. There, we got a key to our lockers where we kept and changed into our work uniforms when we came to work. The lunchroom, equipped with long tables and chairs, had a kitchen where we could buy hot meals. "Here," Herr Hahn said, "We'll eat our lunches together, as a group." Back in the yard, he informed us that although we were separated from the main plant, we were still part of the complex. Herr Hahn also promised that at a later date he would take us on a tour through the main plant so we could see what would be expected of us.

Before we were excused, Herr Hahn handed each of us an ID card, "You need your ID card to get past the gate when you come to work, so always have it with you." We nodded our heads. Then, we received our work uniforms and caps to cover our hair. While handing out the uniforms, he told us, "Every Friday before you go home, you'll take your dirty uniform to the laundry room to exchange it for a clean one. Is that clear?" Once more our heads nodded in unison.

"For today you're excused. I will see you Monday morning at six o'clock sharp, dressed in your work clothes, standing in front of your vices, eyes clear and alert. The following week you will work the late shift from two o'clock to ten o'clock." Putting up his hand to stop us from leaving, he continued, "I'd like to add just one more thing before you go. This apprentice shop is run just like the real factory. Monday morning you'll receive your weekly time card to clock yourself in and out with. Our job is to train and school you to become real locksmiths. But for now, you're excused until Monday morning, bright and early."

We said, *"Auf Wiedersehen,"* and he replied with a smile as we passed him.

My stomach hurt as I walked home. It had butterflies. What had I let myself in for? Is this what I wanted? I was scared. In three days it would be Monday morning, but it was too late to turn back now. The contract was signed and sealed.

All too soon Monday morning arrived with Mutti's cheerful voice calling me, ending my carefree sleep, awakening me to reality. I lay there trying to wake up. *How come Mutti is always so cheerful in the morning? She is just like Oma; only Oma whistled the minute she was up.*

I hate to get up! Oma always said I woke up when the lights went on, calling me *eine Nachteule,* a night owl. Oma was right. I could stay up all night.

While I was getting ready, Mutti cooked our usual breakfast soup. I just looked at the bowl of steaming soup, as butterflies did flip-flops in my stomach. "You need to eat before you go to work," Mutti urged me.

"I feel as if I can't swallow. My stomach hurts and I'd like to go back to bed."

"Oh, you'll be fine. You're just nervous. It's always like that when starting something new. Once you get there, you'll make friends and forget about being nervous, you'll see. So chin up, and eat your soup. You'll be fine."

But I thought, *Mutti can talk; her job is not new, only mine!* Mutti handed me the *Aktentasche,* a briefcase containing my wallet, the uniform, a sandwich, and a thermos filled with sweetened coffee and milk. That coffee was now available in stores without food stamps, so Mutti and Oma stopped roasting wheat kernels.

I gave Mutti a peck on the cheek and I was on my way, with Mutti once more assuring me, "You'll be fine."

Onkel Martin, sitting at the table eating his soup, gave me a reassuring smile. "Good luck, head up, and have a nice first day, *Fraeulein Locksmith.*" I just nodded at him as I closed the door behind me.

Aktentasche in hand, butterflies fluttering, I walked twenty minutes to my destination. I was scared. I thought everyone who passed me on the sidewalk could see it. But no one even looked at me. They were in there own thoughts, walking swiftly past me. Some even bumped into me, then, with a hurried quick nod said, *"Oh, Entschuldigung, Fraeulein!"* Excuse me miss.

I wanted to go home, but I knew I couldn't do that; we'd signed a contract. I remembered Mutti asking me if that's the job I wanted. Now, I really didn't know. But the woman at the office had told me there were no other jobs available. I realized then that life was staring me in the face. I couldn't go to Oma to hold onto her. She'd tell me that this is life and to live is hard work, and that my childhood was over. I missed Vati. I longed to hear his voice telling me, "You'll be just fine, Spatz." I missed the caring way he had always looked at me, but I hadn't seen his eyes or heard his voice for so long, I couldn't recall them anymore. That saddened me. *If he were alive, would I be a locksmith? And what would my life be now? Would Mutti and he be remarried? Or would he be in jail, as my stepmother had threatened him so long ago? There were no answers to my thoughts and no Vati, not anymore. I had to do this alone.* I looked up. I was standing in front the factory building.

My butterflies fluttered again while my heart pounded. With my identification card held high so the gatekeeper could see it, I squeezed through the gate with the rest of the apprentices. They were shouting morning greetings and laughing, the boys slapping each other's backs, as if it was normal being there.

I went to the locker room to change into the work uniform. It too was filled with shouting and laughing—everyone seemed to know each other. I felt like an island surrounded by noisy waves. After changing I followed everyone across the graveled yard to the main building, then went up the staircase echoing with footsteps, talk and laughter to the third floor, through the double doors, and entered the big hall-like room with its workbenches.

When I got to the far end of the room, some girls were already there, but not our instructor. Silently we stood in front of our vices, shuffling our feet, measuring each other with sideways glances, afraid to smile. Although the room was warm, the atmosphere was like ice among us. At six o'clock sharp our instructor appeared with a bright smile on his face and greeted us, *"Einen schoenen guten Morgen!"* "A wonderful good morning." We mumbled a reply. His eyes scanning us, Herr Hahn said, "Well, let's do that again. I said, 'Einen schoenen guten Morgen!'"

A little louder and in unison, we returned his greeting, "Guten Morgen, Herr Hahn."

"That's better." He took off his jacket, hung it over the back of his chair, then hung the Aktentasche on a nail underneath the nearest workbench to his table. Not a gesture was wasted, as if he had been doing that for years. Straightening and arranging himself, he motioned for us to come closer, saying, "We don't want to disturb the other instructors and their teams.

Gather around so we can talk." When I looked, I saw that all instructors had their groups gathered around them, too.

Herr Hahn, now half leaning and half sitting on his table, said, "To begin with we're going to repeat our names so we know who is who." There was a small shuffling of feet from our section. Ignoring it, he continued, "Again, I'm Herr Hahn, and your name?" he pointed at the outermost girl of our half circle.

"Sigrid," she answered.

He continued to point, and we said our names one by one. "Erna, Margot, Gittel, Helga, Ilse, Gerda, Gisela."

"Good, in a day or two we'll get to know each other and work in harmony. But before you return to your workstations, at the front of the room there are stacks of wooden grids. Each one of you has to have one. They will help to elevate you above the vices." Looking at us, he added, "Some of you are not very tall." We were ready to tackle the job when he put up his hand. "One more thing, the grids are heavy, so help each other bring them to your benches." The grids were wide, oblong and the exact length of each work station. We hustled to get the job done, and it seemed like little ice had melted.

That done, Herr Hahn said, "now open the tool drawers, take out the tools, and tell me their names." There were files, oblong and round, from small to large, from lightweight to heavy; there also were hammers, pliers, big and small screwdrivers, and rulers that looked like L's and T's including a triangle. With the activity, we started to talk, even laugh—and the ice kept on melting.

Standing at the head of the row of our workbenches, Herr Hahn instructed us, "Do you see that small wooden box in the drawer?" We nodded. "Take it out and open it. There are ten metal pegs, with numbers from 0 to 9 protruding at the bottom. Take the little round aluminum disks from the drawer. Then, using the pegs, hammer the number of your factory pass on the disk. You will need those disks to check out additional tools. You'll get them at that small window next to the door." He pointed in that direction. Automatically we stretched our necks to see what he was talking about. At the far end of the room was a small window with figures moving behind it—mainly boys. We must have had grins on our faces. "I know what you're thinking. Let me tell you, all apprentices who are completing their last year of apprenticeship have to spend time loaning out tools, and when you get that far, you, too, will do that. Believe me, the boys behind that window want nothing to do with beginners." We glanced at one another with looks that said, "Let's just wait and see." More ice melted.

A loud tap on the bench got our attention. "Now start hammering your identification number on your disks—all of them." Immediately the hammering began. We smacked our thumbs; pegs were hitting the floor with a ding; disks were right behind them. What had looked like an easy job was not easy! It was as if disaster had struck. The little disks didn't hold still because they were not perfectly flat, and our benches had nicks and crevices that made the disks bounce all over. Watching us, Herr Hahn shook his head and laughed. "Take the metal plate from the drawer, lay the disk on it and with the hammer flatting out the disks. That was lesson number one. I promise there are many more to come." We glanced at each other. His remark leaving left a big question mark in the air. We continued smacking our fingertips trying to hit the peg while holding the small round disks on the metal plate. When we finally finished the job, all eight of us were shaking our hands, blowing on our fingertips as if we could shake and blow the pain and bruises away. Now we had something in common. The ice had had melted. Poor Herr Hahn . . .

By the time our shift was over, we had become familiar with each other. When changing from our work clothes in the locker room, we chatted like the older girls. My island had vanished. After going through the gate, we checked each other's walking home directions; two groups went in opposite directions. In our group, Margot was the first one to drop off because she lived at the outskirts of Goerlitz and rode the *Strassenbahn*, streetcar home, leaving Erna, Sigrid, and me. We talked about our new job adventure and, of course, about Herr Hahn. We agreed he was a nice, not too bad looking, quiet man, and we felt lucky to have him for our instructor. It also became clear to me that Erna and Sigrid knew each other from grade school, and were surprised to end up in the same group of locksmith apprentices. While walking, they chatted about people they both knew and met at dances they attended. It sounded like so much fun, and I wished I could go, too. Soon it was my turn to branch off, so I said, "*Auf Wiedersehen*," and Erna and Sigrid continued on their way. Erna lived near the *Postplatz*, the center of Goerlitz, but Sigrid had to walk further because she lived on the *Blumen Strasse*, near the Russian compound.

When I came into our apartment, Mutti was in the kitchen preparing our *Abendbrot*, the evening meal. "How was your day, Gisela?"

"It was fine."

Stopping what she was doing, Mutti looked at me, "Just fine? What about the girls in your group and your instructor? Did you get to meet some of the girls? Did you walk home with some? Tell me all about it."

"Yes, I walked with two girls, well actually three, Erna, Sigrid, and Margot. Margot lives in *Rauschwalde*, and rode the Strassenbahn home."

"What are the girls like?"

I felt Mutti was interrogating me, but I answered, "They're nice. I like them. Margot is my height with dark hair; Erna and Sigrid are a little shorter. Erna likes to laugh and has such natural rosy cheeks that Herr Hahn told her not to paint her cheeks when she comes to work. It was really funny because she told him she doesn't paint her cheeks; they're always red. When she rubbed her cheeks to show him that the red doesn't come off, they got even redder and Herr Hahn felt embarrassed. Erna's eyes sparkled then, it was really funny and we all laughed. I like her; I think she's fun to be with."

Mutti continued her questioning. "What about the other girl? What's her name? Sigrid?"

"Sigrid is really pretty. She has curly hair, big brown eyes and dimples when she laughs. And she wears the nicest clothes."

"Ja, they probably have a family member living in West Germany who sends clothes for her."

"It could be. I wish we had someone over there, too. But, Sigrid also told us that her mother is a seamstress and sews most of her clothes."

Mutti didn't pay much attention to my whining, but like an afterthought, she asked, "How old are the girls?"

"They're only a year older, I think, but I'd like to be friends with them both and Margot, too."

"You will. But remember they're a little older than you are and they probably go dancing and you know you can't. Not yet."

"But why can't I go dancing? I know how."

"I know you do, but you're not sixteen and you know the rule. No going to dances until then." Mutti returned to her task. The subject was closed and needed no further discussion. Yes, I knew the rule, and I wished for time to hurry, so I, too, could go to dances with the girls. "Will you set the table for us?" Mutti asked. "Onkel Martin is on the way home and I'm ready to serve up."

"What's to eat?"

"Scrambled eggs with fresh cut chives for flavor and color for the eye, as Oma says."

"Hmm, warm scrambled eggs on a slice of bread, like an open faced sandwich, my favorite. And to drink?"

"Hot *Kakao*."

"Hot *Kakao*? Where did you get it?" *Kakao* was not available in stores.

"Oh, I got lucky. I was able to buy it through the black market." I had learned over time the meaning of the term 'black market' but no one talked out loud about it, so I didn't ask Mutti any questions. She wouldn't have told me anyway. "When you get done setting the table, run across the street to the store and get a bottle of beer for Onkel Martin. You know what kind he likes." I knew he liked, *Landeskrone Bier*, brewed right in Goerlitz.

When finally we sat down to eat, I had to tell Onkel Martin about the whole day again. He asked, "And your theoretical classes, when are they?"

"School days are on Mondays and Tuesdays, starting next week."

"That'll keep you busy for the next four years," remarked Onkel Martin, and Mutti nodded in agreement.

Glancing out the window, Mutti said, "It's a beautiful fall evening. When we're done eating, let's go for a walk and visit Oma. You haven't been to see her for a while. We'll put the few plates and cups in the dishpan. I'll wash them first thing in the morning." Mutti was right. It had been awhile since I had gone to see Oma. Mutti and I cleared the table, stacked the dishes, and all three of us took off to visit Oma at our former home. When we got there, Oma and Tante Hilde, her baby girl Heidi on her lap, were sitting in the backyard. On an old partly rusted tricycle Rainer was riding around and around the circular walkway in the backyard, making noises like a racecar driver. Onkel Heinz brought out more chairs and we sat down to visit. After a while, Oma asked, "What made you decide to be a locksmith?" Without waiting for me to answer, she continued with dignity in her voice. "That's not a proper profession for a young girl, to be among all those men and to walk around dressed in men's pants! No, that's not proper!" Oma sounded so sincere it almost made me laugh.

But there was no stopping Oma from having her say. "We've become just like the women in Russia. I am telling you these kids will turn out to be communists. We're being changed into a second Russia!"

While Oma was coming up for air, I jumped in. "That's all there is, Oma. There are lots of girls learning male professions. That's the way it is now."

But Oma was unstoppable. "When I was a young girl, that was unheard of!" Oma leaned back, but she was not done yet. "Girls wearing long pants! I don't know what's happening to this world. It's turned upside down." Oma shook her head, motioning with her hand as if she wanted to chase that upside-down world away. I wondered if Oma was right. Maybe the world had been turned upside down.

Soon we said our good-byes. I hugged Oma and, as always, felt sad to leave her behind. I wanted to believe that she felt the same way, although she never said so. I think that over the years Oma had learned to control her feelings, to be a strong woman, to tackle life, while raising her children. But when I looked into her blue eyes, I could see she still loved me, and that made me feel warm inside. Oma walked us to the front door. Just before we turned the corner, I looked back. Oma was still standing there. I waved at her and shouted, "Auf Wiedersehen, Oma!" She, too, waved and then disappeared into the house.

Going to work became a daily chore. Sometimes along the way I'd meet Erna and Sigrid and, while walking, they chatted, mainly about the latest dance they'd gone to and how much fun they'd had. Erna said, "Why don't you come with us? I know you'd like it."

"I know I would! I love to dance, but Mutti is not going to allow it until I'm sixteen and that's not until next July."

"That's a while away; it's only October now," Sigrid remarked.

"I know," I agreed. "I wish time would hurry."

"Maybe after Christmas, when your birthday is a little closer, maybe we'll talk to your mother. Maybe she'll allow you to go with us."

"I'm not sure. Mutti is pretty firm when it comes to that subject." That ended our conversation because we arrived at the factory.

That morning Herr Hahn handed each of us a raw, un-worked thick iron metal plate, about six or seven inches long, four inches wide, and two inches thick. It was covered with lumps, bumps, and black spots as if it had the pox. The sides weren't any better. In fact, the whole thing was not a precise, oblong piece. The sides and corners were uneven, too. We turned it over and under, wondering what to do with it until Herr Hahn drew our attention to him. "Your first job will be to make an iron hinge. This piece I gave you will be half of a hinge. When you're finished with this part, you'll make the second. By the time your first year of apprenticeship has passed, you'll have made a complete hinge." Then, as if he knew what we were thinking, he said, "Yes, under your hands and my teaching, this piece will be the beginning of a hinge."

We glanced at each other, thinking, "Make a hinge, out of that? Was he kidding? How could we transform this deformed piece of metal into a hinge?"

Herr Hahn continued, "I have an example to show you." He turned, and from his table behind him he produced one half of a finished hinge. We gathered around to examine it. It was part of a hinge, shiny and perfectly smooth. Herr Hahn had a sliding measuring device in the shape of a hammer, or 'T', only it was flat and made of stainless steel. What was usually the handle of a hammer was a ruler. Part of the hammerhead was split crossways, allowing the lower part to slide up and down the ruler to measure width or length. With this tool he showed us that the metal piece was a perfect four by six inches, and one and a half inches thick. It had five evenly spaced sunken drill holes for screws, one near each corner with a fifth in the middle. On one side of the piece were two evenly spaced and drilled out protruding wings.

Herr Hahn went on, "After completion of both pieces, you will position a pin through those already bored wings connecting the two halves together, thus making a complete hinge. It is my job to teach and yours to learn. You will see that by filing and precisely measuring your piece, it will eventually look just like the one I have. You'll start to work on one side, file it smooth, and take out the black marks. You glide the file with even, smooth strokes over the metal, leaving no dents or grooves. Because of the filing, when you're finished, your piece will measure a half-inch less in width." As Herr Hahn was talking, he took Erna's metal piece and put it in the vice. Then he picked up the biggest and heaviest file and showed us how to hold it and how to file with even smooth strokes. We stood and watched him with blank faces, unsure how to do what he was telling us.

Smiling while looking at us, he clapped his hands and said, "Let's start working and create a smooth and even piece, just like the one I showed you. I'll come to check your work to see how it is coming along. Begin to file the flat side first where the wings are to your left. After you finished one side, you'll do the other side. You'll work the edges last. Eventually you'll have a perfect rectangle. Then, the final touch is to bore the holes, but it will be a long time before you get to do that." All of it sounded so complicated, we didn't show any enthusiasm. Looking at us with an encouraging smile, he clapped his hands, "To your stations, put the iron in the vice and start filing, by using the big, heavy file first. Always position the file straight and flat on the metal. If you don't, you'll have rounded edges. I'll be checking on each of you and your progress."

So the filing began with howling and squeaking. Some of us, including me, had to retrieve the plate from the floor where it had hit with a loud clang, because we hadn't restrained it tightly enough in the vice. Pretty soon our arms cramped up and our shoulders started to ache as we leaned heavily into our filing job. We realized the lumps were not easy to file off. They were obstinate and the black marks were deeply imbedded. Herr Hahn walked around checking, straightening our backs, relaxing our shoulders, reminding us, "Keep the file flat on the piece; engage your body with the filing motion; apply an even amount of pressure on the file as you move it back and forth." It was a hard and tedious job, and at day's end, we had made no big improvement at all. Before our shift ended, Herr Hahn told us to wrap the piece in an oilcloth to keep it from rusting.

Every day we filed and filed, and our arms and shoulders got stronger and stronger, while our legs got used to standing all day. Herr Hahn walked among us; he'd stop, check, and explain. He'd take the ruler, set it on edge and slowly glide it over the filed surface, holding it up against the light to show if our filing was smooth, with no dents or valleys. Or with the sliding device, he'd test the width of our filing. He showed us how to check our own work with the ruler. He also taught us how to use the L-shaped ruler when we filed the sides and corners. The ruler had to fit exactly over the corner and down each of the sides. It took a long time to get that piece filed down to the specific measurements. Although we had an instructor, every step of our work had to be approved by Meister Keller in charge of all the apprentices, before we were allowed to continue on.

On Mondays and Tuesdays we were in school all day on the upper floor, learning the theoretical part of being a locksmith. We had lots of math because it was used daily on the job. We had history, mainly of Russia, as well as a continuous teaching of good communism compared to bad capitalism. We were taught that the people living in West Germany were being oppressed by capitalism. That we, the people of East Germany, needed to work hard so we could free them of their capitalistic oppressors. Continuously we were taught how great it was to have Russia at our side, Stalin as our friend showing us our way, treating us as equals, and how great this country would be after we accomplished our goals. Only the teachers never taught us just when our goals going to be accomplished. We also had to attend FDJ meetings for which we had to buy the required blue blouse, black skirt, and red scarf.

When I asked Mutti for money to buy the required items, she'd get upset. The communist color was red, and Mutti saw red, too, only not "Their red!" So, I decided not to mention Russia or politics to Mutti.

Although we were apprentices, we had total medical coverage, called Socialized Medicine and received a small pay, which increased according with the number of years we had completed. We were paid cash in small brown envelopes with our names on them. On payday, which was twice a month, Herr Hahn collected our pay envelopes at the office and handed them to us at the end of our shift. It was enough for pocket money. But part of my earnings I had to contribute to our household expenses. It was common practice that sons or daughters, living at home and working had to contribute to the household. I didn't have to pay very much, but as Mutti said, "It's part of being responsible." But when I ran out of money in-between paydays, I borrowed from Mutti and seldom re-paid her. Mutti didn't mind, it was as if she were safekeeping it for me. She always said, "We have money, and nothing to spend it on.

Mutti was right: our daily survival hadn't changed much. From time to time we received increases in food stamps, but not enough to make a big difference. We still only were allowed the bare necessities. And since I had turned fourteen, the special children's ration that Mutti had once gotten for me was gone. Somehow we got by.

But people did become lethargic. They were embittered, disillusioned. It was 1950; five years after the war, and the ruins still lay where they had fallen. Everywhere the city was in need of repairs, but because there were no allowances for material, nothing was done. Eventually the whole city had a gray look of hopelessness and despair, just like the people. There were whispers, like a murmur, that some of the mail from West Germany was held back—even destroyed. Packages coming from West Germany didn't arrive. The murmur continued that the German Commies, as they were called, confiscated the packages for their own use. It also was murmured that East Germany with the support of the Commies wanted to cut off all communication with the West; that letters written from East Germany never arrived in West Germany or the other way around. It was like a fist was squeezing, tighter and tighter, and because there were spies everywhere, it was impossible for the people to fight back.

That didn't make any difference to us, because we had no relatives who lived in West Germany. All of our immediate family was living right in Goerlitz, except for some of Oma's siblings who lived in Erfurt and that, too, was in East Germany. Like many others, we lived according to what we had, which wasn't much. People had resigned themselves to the fact that there wasn't anything they could do to change that. Germany had lost WW II, and Hitler, the cause of our problems, had killed himself. Now, Stalin's communist Russia used the people of East Germany as their workhorse.

All the goods produced by the people of East Germany most of them were not seen in our stores. People walked around in clothes that showed wear and tear. They used two coats or dresses to make one, or they made one smaller for a child. Nothing went to waste. Done by a seamstress, Mutti had a winter jacket made out of a gray blanket and it didn't look bad at all. Whatever people found or had, they made into something either to use or to wear. It was as if they were saying to Stalin, "We have lost the war, and you're the conqueror, but we Germans have pride and refuse to act like uneducated people, no matter how hard you try to suppress us."

Once in a while Oma would talk about the things we once had, how our past was filled with sad memories, pain, and losses, then, Mutti would say, "Let's forget about it. It's gone, and all the talking is not bringing it back to us." Mutti was the one with the up-beat outlook on life. She took everything in stride, just like the younger generation. So we managed to cope with those memories, to leave them behind, but for Oma they never vanished. And just like Mutti, we learned to live in the now, the present.

At work we got used to each other, and soon we became a mischievous group. We had to do the work assigned to us. Herr Hahn made sure of that. But some times we played tricks and Herr Hahn he never got mad at us when we played pranks on him. We noticed that when Herr Hahn walked off with the newspaper under his arm, he would be gone for a while. After he was out of the hall, the filing stopped and we visited, hanging over our benches so we didn't have to shout to each other. Erna, Helga and I could see the door in front, so it was our job to watch for Herr Hahn's return. We started to time him and figured out that he was gone from twenty to thirty minutes. But sometimes he was back faster than what we'd thought, so our lookout was important.

One of the first things we did was to attack the leather Aktentasche he carried his lunch in. Well used, it showed its age. Erna suggested hanging it in the way back underneath the workbench, but Herr Hahn found it in no time, spoiling our fun. He only smiled when he found it and carried on without saying a word. It seemed we were not the first ones to have played that trick on him. We decided more drastic measures were necessary. At our next opportunity we put our heads together, and everyone had ideas. "Let's nail the Aktentasche to the bench where Herr Hahn hangs it every morning. He'll never suspect a thing," I suggested.

"Nail it on the bench? How are you going to do that?"

"That's easy; we'll leave it hanging where it is. Then, we'll open the flap and nail it from the inside to the bench and close it again. When lunch time comes and he reaches for it, it will stay hooked." Everyone agreed.

The next day, we could hardly wait for him to take his newspaper walk, and as soon as he was gone, our work began. With laughter, but not so loud that we drew attention from the other instructors, Erna and I took a hammer and a nail, and crawled under the bench. The rest of the girls were the lookouts. Erna's job was to hold the Aktentasche straight on its hook while I nailed it from the inside to the bench with one small nail. When we closed the flap, the Aktentasche looked undisturbed, like always. Needless to say, there was lots of giggling going on. And being crouched down laughing with Erna in the excitement, I smacked hers as well as my fingers.

The job was done, and when Herr Hahn returned, we were busy filing, concentrating on not laughing as we exchanged sideways glances. We were filled with suspense, wondering how Herr Hahn would react to our new mischief. He watched us as he stood at the end of our row of benches with squinted eyes and a puzzled look on his face. Why were we so busy filing, never looking up at him when he came back? The suspense was almost unbearable for us. We were close to breaking out with laughter when we were saved by the bell that rung for lunch.

Rather slowly we gathered our lunch bags, all eyes on Herr Hahn. He became more suspicious. Cautiously he reached to grab the Aktentasche and came up empty handed. It was still hanging on the hook, not coming loose.

We watched him as he tried again. We burst into laughter. Herr Hahn, realizing we had played a trick on him and were laughing about it, laughed too. "That is a new trick and if all of you do your work with that kind of enthusiasm, you will make it to the top of the classes before the year is over. Now, if you would release the Aktentasche, we'll have lunch." Erna and I rescued the Aktentasche, and our group went to the lunchroom, laughing about our successful prank.

But that was not the end of our practical jokes. Often, but not daily, we continued our mischief. We put steel shavings from the bore machine in his thermos filled with coffee he'd brought from home. All eyes were on Herr Hahn when he opened his thermos to pour coffee in his cup and steel shavings mixed with coffee came out. He looked at us with a twinkle in his eyes, smiling, shaking his head in disbelief at how a group of such nice girls could think of such naughty things to do. But before we messed up his coffee, we made sure we had money to buy fresh coffee for him in the lunchroom. Other times we took safety pins and pinned the sleeve lining of his jacket together, so when he tried to put it on, he got his arm stuck in the sleeve. Once we glued his newspaper together in places, and then folded it so that it didn't show until he opened it. The suspense was almost unbearable and we could hardly wait for him to put it under his arm, hoping that he wouldn't unfold it until he got to his destination. Laughing at another joke well done, we watched for his return. When he came back, he calmly put the folded newspaper back on his table, as if all was normal, only it wasn't, because all eyes, again, were on him and we couldn't stop from laughing. From then on, he was not so careless with his paper. He never got mad at us. He'd just smile or laugh right along with us. But when he ignored our pranks, it was a sign for us not to do that again, and we didn't. He truly was a nice man with lots of patience for the mischief we played on him.

Fall passed and winter returned with lots of snow by Christmas. Everyone in the family had saved the necessary ingredients so Oma could do the baking. It was as if Oma had inherited that job, only I wasn't there to help or to beg for five raisins because now I was working. While Oma was busy baking the Stollen at the Langenstrasse, Mutti, Onkel Martin, and Onkel Heinz were making preparations to brew their own liquor for the holidays at Karl Liebknecht Strasse—our apartment. Mutti had already collected and cleaned the bottles to hold the liquor. Then, late one evening when it was dark, Onkel Heinz came with his share of potatoes and a big glass crock used for the fermenting. "Where did you get the crock?" Mutti asked.

Onkel Heinz said, "Oh, you know. I have my ways."

"I'm always surprised you can find things like that. I hope no one is wondering why you wanted a crock."

Onkel Heinz just said, "Don't worry, Lenchen; all is fine."

I, too, wondered where he got that big crock. It was almost table height, and a crock like that was not available in stores.

Mutti, Onkel Martin, and Onkel Heinz filled the crock with cleaned, unpeeled cut up potatoes and sprinkled yeast between the layers. When the crock was full of potatoes, they added sugar water and, like a crown, set a glass coil on top of the crock. Then all three carried the full crock into the living room. Because there was a step down from the kitchen, they moved slowly, their backs bent, saying to each other, "Careful, watch out, don't trip!" Finally, red-faced from the strain, they sat the crock near the Kachelofen for warmth.

Days earlier, Mutti had sent me to bakery shops away from our neighborhood to buy yeast. Mutti had already bought yeast for Oma's baking at our bakery, so she was afraid she would arouse suspicion if she came for more yeast, because yeast was still in short supply. Most bakeries I went to liked to sell only to regular customers, if they did sell yeast, and then they only sold small amounts, so I had to go to several bakeries because some told me they had sold out. Eventually, though, I got the needed yeast.

While the fermenting was taking place, our apartment smelled of yeast, like a brewery. When there was a knock at the door, Mutti opened the door carefully, wanting no surprises. But after some time the fermenting was done, and the cooking started, which took all night. The fermented potatoes were cooked in a pressure cooker, with a spiral copper tube attached to the lid. That spiral tube went through a bath of cold water into our dishpan. The end of the spiral stuck up over the rim of the dishpan, and a container was placed under the spout to catch the drips. When it started to drip, the first several drips were tested away from the cooker and the spiral. The liquid was lit on a spoon, and when it flamed up in a blue-violet glow, it was perfect. Mutti, Onkel Martin, and Onkel Heinz cheered quietly over their success. They sat in our candlelit kitchen and talked in whispers as they watched the kettle cook on the stove and the spiral drip.

Although Tante Elfriede and Onkel Richard contributed their share of potatoes and sugar, Onkel Richard never participated in the brewing. Mutti jokingly called him a *Feigling,* a scaredy-cat or chicken, which didn't bother him. He only smiled at Mutti. Well, I guess he had his reasons. It wasn't just that it was illegal—Onkel Martin was an officer at the Goerlitzer Police Department and sworn to uphold the law. But even that didn't stop their brewing of pure alcohol.

With additional purchases from the black market, Mutti turned the raw alcohol into tasty liquors, like *Eier-Liquor, Kaffee-Liquor,* and *Schokoladen-Liquor* (egg-café-coco). Because there were no refrigerators to keep the bottled liquor cool, the bottles were placed between the double set of windows in our bedroom along with other items needing to be kept cold. It was a common practice in the winter to use the double set of windows for refrigeration. Therefore, anyone walking on the street below us could see that Mutti had brewed liquor. I think Mutti, Onkel Martin, and Onkel Heinz were not the only ones who did brewing for the holidays. Oh, yes, the crock disappeared just as mysteriously as it had appeared with Onkel Heinz.

On Christmas Eve morning Mutti and I decorated our Christmas tree. As a final touch we added the candles that were a special Christmas allotment for every household. And, as always, Oma and I went to church. Mutti had saved stamps from the monthly meat ration for the traditional Christmas Eve dinner. When Oma and I came from church, Mutti and Christa had prepared bratwurst, sauerkraut, and mashed potatoes. Afterward, we did the dishes and exchanged small gifts. It was a clear, crisp winter night when I walked Oma home. The stars twinkled like the lights on the Christmas tree. In the distance bells were ringing from the Catholic Church, calling the midnight mass. Their ringing wove through the winter air with a sound I never tired of hearing. It filled my heart with loving thoughts of Vati and hope that the coming year would be good for all of us.

The following day, the first Christmas holiday, and after our noon dinner, the family, as usual, gathered at our place for coffee and the cake Oma had baked. Then, later in the evening, with their pooled food allotment, Mutti, Tante Elfriede, and Tante Hilde served sandwiches with potato salad. The grown-ups drank beer and tested their brew, smacking their lips, nodding at Mutti for a job well done.

Before we knew it, the celebration for New Year's Eve had come. Our apartment was humming once more, ready for the New Year's Eve celebration. Thanks to Mutti, the New Year's party with the usual paper decorations, the shared food, the homemade liquor—which Onkel Richard drank—all of it was a success. Mutti, as always, joined by Onkel Heinz entertained with laughter and humor. Then, at midnight, when the church bells were ringing in the New Year of 1951, we parted shouting, "Happy New Year!"

After the holidays, our lives continued like a waterfall, never stopping, regardless of happiness or sorrow. Although we had started a new year, 1951, there were no changes in our daily lives. People walked around sullen faced. They stood in line at grocery stores, sometimes before the store opened its doors. They stood in the freezing cold with their faces covered up to their eyes, moving from one foot to the other to keep warm, just so they could be the first ones in the store before the grocer ran out of merchandise.

Living in a corner apartment building at a cross street, we didn't have far to go to shop, and we could see the people standing in line. We had five stores nearby—two grocers, two bakeries, and one butcher shop. The grocers and bakers were corner stores. The butcher shop was a little ways down the street. All stores were small, and from behind their counters, the owners waited on the customers. Mutti hated to stand in line, so sometimes, when I was home from work, she'd send me and I didn't mind because I had done that for Oma too. But no matter how bad things were and how much the grown-ups grumbled, we, the younger generation, took it in stride. We weren't the ones who had to fix meals, to make the food stamps last through out the month, or to make do with what was available in stores. We were the ones laughing and enjoying life as much as possible. We didn't like the regime and didn't remember the past as well as the older generation did. Yes, we remembered the war—the bombs, the fleeing, and the hardships involved. All of us had horror stories to tell, but we didn't talk much about the bad times.

Because of the war, many of us who had lost our fathers were labeled *Halbweisen*, meaning half orphans. Others who had lost both parents were marked as *Weisen*, orphans. When I had to fill out legal papers, we had to declare ourselves as such, and it felt like a stigma. Those were our wounds, and almost six years after the war, we slowly began to heal, leaving us all with scars. The rushing waterfall was healing our wounds, washing away our hurt and pain. Its swift tumble was telling us to move on with our lives—and move on, we did.

At home, Mutti, Onkel Martin, and I lived as a happy threesome. I disliked admitting how much I enjoyed having Onkel Martin living with us. He and I got along great. Mutti claimed that we stuck together like glue. It was easy as Onkel Martin left my restrictions and disciplining to Mutti. He was like a fatherly friend to me. When Mutti got mad at us, she'd start to stutter. That's when we never said a word or made a peep. We knew it was best to let Mutti have her say. After a while, Mutti would realize she was doing all the talking. Then, she'd stop and look at us, laughing, saying, "All right, you two, I can see I'm losing the battle again."

Other times Onkel Martin would take me by my upper arms and squeeze them, saying, "Let me feel your muscles to see if they have grown some due to the filing you're doing now." Then he'd roll up his sleeve and we'd compare muscles. Laughing, we'd end up in a mock fistfight or wrestling, so we'd push the dinner table to one side to have room. Watching us, shaking her finger, Mutti would say, "What am I going to do with the two of you? And you, Martin, are just as bad, in provoking a wrestling match with Gisela." He'd just grin at Mutti. Needless to say, I lost most of the time. But I had learned when to dodge and when to punch, and I got him with a few punches of my own, too. When Mutti got too close, we turned on her. She never lasted very long because she'd laugh so hard she was unable to fight back and had to beg us to leave her alone.

Yes, I liked Onkel Martin a lot, but I also knew he could never replace Vati. Sometimes when I was alone and I thought about Vati, I felt guilty for liking Onkel Martin. I felt like a traitor, a defector, and my guilt overwhelmed me. But I was sure Vati wouldn't want me to be sad, that he wanted me to be happy, to love him and never to forget him—and that I promised with all my heart.

And then something happened, something I've never forgotten.

I was at home doing nothing when Mutti asked me to take the mending to Oma. I didn't mind because I hadn't seen Oma for a while, and because it was a weekend I had lots of time. Mutti packed the mending in a cloth bag and handed it to me, saying, "Oma knows we have mending for her. Be sure to tell her I'm not in a hurry for it."

"I will." A kiss on Mutti's cheek, a good-bye nod to Onkel Martin, and I was out the door. It was a warm, sunny early spring day so I took my time walking, mostly because I was engrossed in my thoughts about Oma, how she did the mending for her family, either by hand or machine. I'd never seen Tante Elfriede bring her mending to Oma, but Mutti did because she was not a mender, maybe a button or two, but the rest went to Oma.

Wherever the need arose, Oma was there. Like when I'd returned to my family, Oma came to take care for me. Later, Oma guarded, loved, and cared for me when I was sick. She was my guide, my mentor, and I missed not having her live with us. But Onkel Heinz, Tante Hilde, and the children needed her now. Oma, uncomplaining, was always there, as though it was her mission in life to care for her family.

Deep in thought, before I knew it, I was walking underneath the arches of the *Reichenbacher Turm*. Then I turned left, entered the *Breitestrasse*, and with another right I was at my destination—*Langenstrasse*.

First, I went upstairs, but Tante Hilde told me that Oma was in the backyard doing her mending and watching Rainer. When I walked into the backyard, I saw Oma sitting in her favorite old wicker chair in the shade of the gnarled cherry tree while Rainer was running around, playing. On a bench in front of her sat the mending basket. "Guten Tag, Oma. I brought the mending and Mutti said not to hurry with it." I bent down to give her a kiss on the cheek.

"Just lay the bag on the bench. I'll look at the mending later." Looking up at me with a smile, she said, "Come sit with me. It's nice to see you. It's been a while."

"I know, Oma, but with working I just don't have much time."

"That's the way it is. Children grow up, get busy, and have little time left for others."

Then, Tante Hilde with Heidi in the baby buggy joined us. We sat and visited. Oma and Tante Hilde asked me how the locksmithing was going, and I told them it was all right. "You don't seem too excited about it," Tante Hilde remarked.

"No, not really."

"What's the problem?" Oma wanted to know.

"It's not for me. It's heavy work. It's more of a guy's job. But I'm in it now."

Trying to encourage me, Oma said, "You'll feel better once you're done being an apprentice; then you'll work in the main factory with the others."

"Yeah, maybe." I stayed a little while longer; then, I left for home. Oma got her customary kiss on the cheek and Tante Hilde a handshake.

I decided to take a different route home. I walked across the *Obermarkt*, along the *Stein Strasse*, past the *Frauen Turm*, and the HO department store. I crossed the *Postplatz* in the direction of the *Berliner Strasse*. Just as I entered the Berliner Strasse, a man came toward me—facing me. His black corduroy pants and cap were dusty looking, and his sleeves were rolled up, like he'd just stopped working. Because he was limping, he supported himself with a cane. His blue eyes caught my attention because he was looking at me. They seemed familiar, sending shockwaves through me. He nodded his head and smiled, like he was glad to see me. My mind went blank, and in a haze, I stood staring—confused. People bumped into me, but I didn't feel it. Instead, I wanted to shout, "Vati, Vati!" But not a sound escaped my lips. I just stared, not able to comprehend what I thought I saw. A feeling of weightlessness streamed through my body, filling me with unmatched happiness. A dark cloud was lifting, and I, too, smiled. I wanted to run to that man who was smiling back at me. I wanted to say, "Vati, Vati, you're alive!" But then I shook my head. I stopped smiling as I told myself, "It can't be! Vati is dead! I saw him in the casket! I stood at his grave!" And that dark cloud of sorrow and sadness returned. But who was that man who had passed me, whose blue eyes had smiled at me? And when I looked back, the man was gone.

I turned and ran to the corner, but there was no man with a cane walking. I ran to the corner of the *Jacob Strasse*. I didn't see him. I looked across the Postplatz, but he wasn't there either. Like a flash before my eyes, he had come and gone—disappeared. I leaned against a house wall, my mind reeling and my body shaking. What had happened? I knew in my heart I had seen Vati. But how? How was that possible? I had to hurry home and tell Mutti. But then I thought, *No, Mutti might not understand; she'd humor me, tell me I had seen a ghost.* But it wasn't a ghost; it was Vati! Then I thought, "Oma, I have to go back and tell Oma, she'll understand." And I ran all the way to tell her.

Oma was still sitting in the backyard. She had stopped mending and sat enjoying the sunshine. Tante Hilde and the children had gone upstairs, so Oma and I were alone. "Did you forget something?" Oma asked when she saw me.

Out of breath, I said, "Oma," as I sat close to her so no one could hear, "Oma, I have to tell you something, but don't laugh when you hear what just happened to me."

Shaking her head, Oma said, "I won't laugh." And looking at me she asked, "Have you been running? You look flushed."

"Yes, I have, but Oma listen . . ." And I told her what I had seen. "And, Oma," I finished, "it was a short minute. He was so real, his dusty woodworking clothes, his cap, the rolled up sleeves, his cane, the limp, the pipe, and the way he smiled at me, his blue eyes shining—just like Vati . . ."

"Calm down," Oma said as she took my hand. "It might be so. You might have seen your father."

"But, Oma, he is . . ."

"Yes, he is dead. But, think. Your father, was he able to say good-bye to you before he died?"

"No! When they came to take Vati to the hospital, she, you know, my stepmother, pulled me away. She was going to spank me because instead of going to school I'd stayed home to take care of Vati while she had gone to see her parents. And then he died during the night in the hospital, without saying good-bye." Tears started to well up as I recalled that dreadful day almost six years ago.

Oma looked at the ground as if she was thinking, then said, "Sometimes," she stopped and took a deep breath, "sometimes, the souls of the dead come back to us, waiting for the right moment—like your father, today."

"Why, Oma?"

"They can't rest because of things they have left unfinished on this earth. I believe because your father wasn't able to say good-bye, he came to say good-bye to you, today. He wanted to see you once more, to see that you're all right and happy, to let you know that he loves you." Oma stopped for a minute and then continued, "Also, he died before he was able to get you back where you belonged—with us. So, you see, it's not that astounding. I believe that your father was given a second chance to say good-bye to you. And now, after seeing you, now he will rest in peace—at last."

Wiping my tears, I said, "I wish it could have been Vati. I wish he had come back to life again."

But now Oma smiled. "That is a wish that will not come true."

Silently we sat for a moment. Then, I gave Oma a hug and a kiss and went home. Oma had eased my mind. I knew she'd have an explanation of what I had experienced. Oma was old, a wise old Oma. *I thought about what she's said, maybe Vati had come to see me, to say good-bye, to tell me he had not forsaken me; to let me know he'd always be wherever I am.* I clung to that. As I walked home on that sunny afternoon, I felt happy because I knew I had Vati and that dark cloud seemed not so dark anymore. Then, I told myself that Vati wouldn't mind and that it was all right for me to like Onkel Martin.

When I got home, Mutti said, "You were a long time at Oma's."

"Yes, we visited and the time passed fast." I never told Mutti what happened that day or anyone else—it was Oma's and my secret.

Every day I thought about my recent experience and every day, I went to work, except for the two days of each week we had to attend class. There we continued playing tricks on Herr Hahn, every now and then, so one day rolled into the next. Erna, Sigrid, and Margot became my friends, and many times when they went out dancing, they'd ask me to join them. But my sad answer was always the same, "I can't. Mutti won't allow it until I'm sixteen."

"Have you asked her yet?"

"No, I don't have to. I know what she'll say. Mutti is pretty firm on that subject."

"You're already fifteen and a half," Margot argued.

"That's right. So why don't you ask if you can go with us, and, if it helps, tell your mother I'll watch out for you and I will bring you home again," Erna suggested. I wanted to go, but I knew what Mutti's answer would be. Erna and Margot kept on encouraging me to ask Mutti. "Today is Monday. You have a whole week to convince your mother to let you go with us."

"You want to go, don't you?" Margot asked me.

"Yes, I do, but . . ."

"Then ask, and don't be a scaredy cat!" Erna piped up. Looking at them, I thought they could talk—they were sixteen. But I? *Maybe I was afraid to ask because I already knew what Mutti's answer would be and I shied away from situations like that.* It was different living with Mutti. When I had returned to my family in 1946, I spent my first four years in Oma's care because Mutti was working on the train and was seldom home. Oma was what an Oma should be—loving, cuddly, and fun, even though she had strict house rules. Now that I was living with Mutti, she had to take over the role of disciplinarian. Not that Mutti restrained me. No, but it was a different life with Mutti. And it wasn't that I didn't love or respect her, or Mutti didn't love me—it was just different. On the other hand, maybe Mutti, too, had to learn to live with me, to be a mother to me, something, which for many years had been forbidden to her. I felt guilty about my feelings because after Vati had died, Mutti came and took me back, rescuing me from the sad and terrible life that my stepmother had planned for me. Because of what Mutti had done for me, I felt guilty. Mutti was just different from Oma; she was like a friend with rules and restrictions.

When we left work, Erna once more reminded me, "Don't forget to ask!" I nodded my head, unsure what to do. "I'll ask you in the morning. Don't forget," Erna shouted as we parted.

"What was that all about?" Mutti asked me when I came upstairs. When Mutti was home from work, she always looked out the window with a pillow propped on the windowsill to rest her arms on while she was watching for Onkel Martin or me to come walking up the street. Also, conversation and sounds traveled up from the street to our second floor open windows.

"What?" I asked in surprise.

"Erna said something like, "Don't forget to ask." Mutti, with her back to the window, was looking at me, waiting for my answer. But I didn't know what to say or do. I didn't have time to get my words in order or to wait for the right time to ask, so there I was, my throat suddenly dry, while Mutti waited for me to answer her. I stammered, "They . . . ahh . . . I mean Erna and Margot . . . ahh . . . you know from work . . . ahh . . . they keep asking me if I could go to the dance with them." It was out, and I was relieved.

Slowly I raised my eyes, afraid that I might see that hateful face of my stepmother with her fierce, ice-cold eyes. *Why did I always see her mean face from the past? When was it going to stop intimidating me?* But when I looked up, her face wasn't there. Mutti was looking at me, with her head tilted sideways, the sun highlighting her shiny black hair like a halo. Then, Mutti moved, and the halo disappeared. In a low, calm voice Mutti spoke, "So the girls invited you to go to the dance with them?" I just nodded, still standing where I had come in. "You know the rule, don't you?"

"Yes, I know." Getting a little braver I added, "But Mutti . . . ahh, maybe I could . . . ahh, just once, please?"

"I don't know. I have to think about that. You're not sixteen!" That was the big exclamation mark that hung over my head! But, my spirit soared because Mutti's remark, "I have to think about it," was a lot more than I had expected. There was hope, and I didn't push any further. This was Monday and the dances were not until Saturday, so there was time.

When I told the girls the next day, they agreed to let it rest and not to push it. Erna again told me she'd come to see Mutti, if that was what it took for me to go with them. Every day I wanted to ask Mutti if she had made a decision yet, but I kept quiet. Then Thursday came and Mutti still had not said a word. We were having our evening meal, and I pulled all my courage together and blurted, "Mutti, can I go?"

"Go where?" Onkel Martin threw that question in the air before Mutti was able to give me an answer. Oh, I thought, please be still, Onkel Martin; don't make Mutti change her mind . . . please. But he continued, "So where do you want to go?"

I looked at Mutti for help, but she waited for me to answer him. "I'd like to go dancing with my girlfriends this Saturday."

"So? . . . And? . . ." he leaned forward as he questioned me.

I had to answer, "I asked Mutti, but she has not given me permission yet."

"And why not?"

"Because Mutti said I'm not sixteen yet." What was he doing? If Mutti was going to let me go, his line of questioning would be the end of it. But things took a different turn. Onkel Martin asked Mutti, "Have you come to a decision, Lenchen?"

"I'm not sure. I think she is too young to be out dancing." My boat was sinking. Then, I realized Onkel Martin wasn't saying that he was against my adventure. I grabbed my opportunity and looked at him with pleading eyes.

Onkel Martin looked across the table to Mutti. "Why don't you allow Gisela to go? Most dances start at five in the evening and end at two in the morning, but her curfew should be ten o'clock." I was thinking *I could be at the dance until nine thirty and be home by ten.* I wanted to shout, "Oh, Onkel Martin, you're the best." But I had to wait for Mutti's final answer, and I didn't want to look too happy or too anxious, so I kept on eating.

"Well," Mutti laid down her silverware and took a deep breath, while I was holding mine. "I guess you're lucky, Gisela, to have Onkel Martin on your side. I hadn't made up my mind, but I agree. I will let you go, but," Mutti raised her finger and shook it at me, "do not expect to go every Saturday. Do you understand that?"

"Yes, Mutti," I replied happily. "But does that mean I can really go?"

"Yes, but I want to meet Erna before you go so I can have a talk with her. And if she doesn't come and talk to me, the dance for you is canceled."

"Yes, Mutti, I'll tell her. You'll like her. She is really nice." I was so happy I jumped up and gave Mutti a kiss and Onkel Martin a big hug. I could hardly wait to tell the girls Friday morning that I could go.

Erna, as promised, said, "I'll come up to talk to your mother Saturday afternoon at four o'clock when I pick you up." I was so excited to go dancing that I could hardly wait for Saturday to arrive.

Finally it was Saturday morning, and I could hardly eat breakfast I was so excited. Looking up from his, Onkel Martin smiled, "Slow down. Erna is not going to be here until four o'clock."

"I can't help it, Onkel Martin. I've never been to a dance, and I'm excited and scared at the same time."

With a grin and a glint in his eyes, he said, "Well, maybe after we've eaten breakfast, we need to wrestle so you get your mind off the dance for a little while."

"You are funny, Onkel Martin. I don't have time to wrestle. I have a hair appointment at her *Friseur,* the beauty shop this morning."

When I got home, after my hair was done, I checked which of the two dressed I should wear for the dance. There was the black dress from the Jugendweihe, but black wasn't for dancing. That left the green dress I hated, an unpleasant reminder of my sister, and her girlfriend Rosel. Holding the dress, I remembered that day as if it had been yesterday.

We were still living at the Langenstrasse with Oma, the latest fashions were three-quarter-length dresses, flared skirts, high collars, wide belts, with sleeves, like on a preacher's robe. My sister had a dress like that of grayish blue material. Almost fifteen and out of school, I wanted a fashionable dress for Christmas. But first I had to convince Mutti I was old enough to have such a dress. Mutti agreed, but not Oma, "That's not for you. You're not old enough to wear a fashionable dress like that. It's for girls your sister's age."

"But, Oma, I'm out of school, almost fifteen, and I'd like to have a three-quarter-length dress instead of the baby dresses I have."

Oma shook her head, "You're only fourteen right now and your dresses are not baby dresses. Be glad you have dresses to wear. Why do you need a dress like that? Are you going out dancing like your sister?"

Everything revolves around my sister, I thought. "No I'm not, but Mutti said I could have a new dress like that for Christmas."

"I know what your mother said, but I think you need to wait for a dress like that until you're a little older." Looking over the top of her glasses, Oma frowned slightly at me. I loved Oma, but I wished she would stay out of this and let Mutti make the decision.

As soon as Mutti came home and Oma was in her room upstairs, I approached her. "Oma does not want me to have a three-quarter-length dress."

"Why not?"

"Oma thinks I'm not old enough to wear a fashionable dress, but I told her I am." I was near tears. "Why is Oma so against my wanting a new dress, Mutti?"

"Oma is not against your wanting a new dress. She thinks it's inappropriate at your age to wear the latest fashion. I will speak with Oma. You'll have a new dress for Christmas, but it might not be exactly what you want. Oma is right. You're not going to dances like your sister and won't be for a while." *Uhh . . .* I thought, as I gritted my teeth. *There it is again, my sister, always my sister!* I said nothing. I didn't want Mutti to get upset or there might be no dress at all. "Why do you have to talk to Oma about it?"

"Because we live with Oma, and, when I'm not here, she takes care of you and the household. I don't want to ignore or overrule her. It may sound funny to you, but Oma loves you and wants to do what she believes is right for you."

"What's right for me is that dress, Mutti! I hope you can convince Oma to change her mind."

Mutti did get Oma to agree to a new dress, and the hunt for material began. Goerlitz had a four-story department store, called *Karstadt*, a familiar department store all over Germany. The Goerlitzer Karstadt had been closed since the end of WW II. Then, in 1948 a *Handels-Organisation*, H.O. or Trading Organization had been established with stores all across East Germany, including Goerlitz. In Goerlitz they removed the name Karstadt, replacing it with, big white H.O. letters. There, if people could afford the prices, without food stamps, they could buy clothing and some goods not available in privately owned stores. The H.O. still didn't have items like bananas, oranges, and chocolates. If, by chance, they had the real coffee or cocoa, people stormed the store but sales were restricted—a half pound each of coffee and cocoa per costumer. And that's where we had to shop for the material.

Several days later, my sister said, "if you'll meet me at the entrance of the H.O. store about one o'clock, I'll help you pick out the material." But when I met my sister, her friend Rosel whom I still couldn't stand was with her. Whenever they were together, my sister was twice as mean and Rosel would have a spiteful grin on her face. Here they came, laughing and talking, barely acknowledging my presence. Like a stranger or subordinate, I followed them.

I had never been inside the store, but it was easy to see the interior had once been modern and lavish. The wide staircase with its elaborately designed banisters still showed remnants of gold underneath the dust and grime was blocked off. The domed ceiling made of colored leaded glass was partly broken and crudely roofed over. The chandelier once shiny and bright, hung dull from the center of the ceiling, with barely enough light for the shoppers.

I trailed Christa and Rosel to the material counter where people were waiting to buy material. My sister and Rosel made their way to the counter past the people. I couldn't catch up with Christa, so I gave up trying. I waited opposite the counter for Christa to make the purchase, hoping she'd pick nice material.

When they reappeared with grins on their faces, Christa tossed a brown package at me. "Here is your material. Go home and give it to Oma." Laughing, they disappeared in the crowd.

I hurried home to see what Christa had picked out. I knew my sister had good taste. When I unwrapped the package, I stood there, horrified! It was ugly! It was a bright yellowish green with brown stripes that made squares, like a large plaid. Christa had picked out brown material to offset the dress. "Oma," I cried, "That's the ugliest ever! I hate it!"

"Na, na," Oma soothed, "It's not that bad. Maybe there were no other materials available?"

"Oh, yes there were! I saw them, only I couldn't get near the counter. People were so pushy. Christa never asked me. She didn't even look for me! Rosel and she were too busy laughing and talking. She knew this dress is special to me. Now I know why they laughed when Christa tossed me the package. They did this on purpose so I'll look ugly! I hate both of them! I don't want a dress anymore. They can have that ugly material!" Tears of loathing ran down my cheeks. How could my sister do that?

But Oma, her hand stroking the material said, "It's not that bad. After it's sewn, it'll look much better. You'll see."

I just looked at Oma, not believing her. Again, I wondered why everyone agreed with my sister, never with me.

Although Oma sewed, she and I went to a seamstress. From a magazine, I picked a pattern, a three-quarter-length, flared skirt dress, with a small v-cut in front, a stand-up collar, a belt, and sleeves like those of a preacher's robe. Oma watched as I picked out the pattern, but said, "No, no, that's not a dress for you!"

"Why not, Oma?"

"Because a v-front is not for a young girl like you and the sleeves aren't either." The whole thing began to be a big disappointment for me. I loved Oma, but she was old fashioned. The dress became a mish-mash of fashion. When we went for my first fitting, it wasn't three-quarter-length, but just below the knee, befitting a young girl, Oma explained. The dress flared, but the sleeves were not flared. According to Oma, they too were inappropriate, so they were gathered in a cuff, then, closed with little brown buttons at my wrists. The v-neck had disappeared; instead the dress had a button closure from the belt up to my throat. Then, Oma told the seamstress to make a brown bow to cover the button closure. The only part that resembled the original pattern was the high collar and the wide brown belt.

When my sister saw me in the dress for the first time, she burst out laughing. Mutti and Oma told her to stop laughing, but she continued laughing, looking at me, saying, "You look like a green frog with brown stripes. I can't wait to tell Rosel," and still laughing, out the door she went.

Although I was unhappy with the dress, I never talked to Mutti because complaining about my sister was useless. I decided it was better than no dress at all, but I promised myself that my sister would never shop for me again. I realized once more that the sister I had hoped and longed for was never going to be. Much later, I learned that Mutti had given Christa enough money to buy nice material, but by buying the cheap material, Christa had saved money for Rosel and her to spend.

I was still standing in front of the open Kleiderschrank, holding the dress, memories floating in my head, when Mutti came into the bedroom. "What are you doing? You look far away."

"I wanted to see what dress I should wear, but I have no choices. I have to wear the ugly green one."

Looking at me and at the dress Mutti, said, "It's not that bad. With your hair all done, you'll look fine. It's your first dance, and in time you'll have other dresses—you'll see." I knew better. It was ugly and no hair-do, however good, could change that.

I sighed. "It has to do. But Christa will never shop for me again nor will she have any say in what I should wear! Oma will not either—I will choose and dress the way I want to look!"

"Na, na, don't get sassy with me. Remember, I was not there when that dress was made. You wanted a dress and you got one! And Oma did what she thought was right. If you want to go to the dance, then that is what you'll have to wear."

Feeling bad for the way I spoke to Mutti, I said, "I know, Mutti, but I will never forget nor forgive Christa for choosing such ugly material, and . . ."

Mutti made an outward gesture with her hand. "It's time for you to forget and to get ready—that is if you're still going."

Resigned, I closed the doors of the Kleiderschrank, took the dress, and went to my bed behind the partition Mutti had made in the bedroom. Then, panic struck me, "Mutti! Mutti!"

"What's the matter now?"

"I haven't any stockings to wear! What do I do now?"

Mutti shook her head, "You have more problems. I wonder if you'll make it to the dance today." Mutti went to her nightstand, handed me her stockings and said, "I'll loan you my stockings. Try not put a run in them. Those are the only good ones I have left."

"Oh, thank you, Mutti! I'll be very careful—I promise."

I was ready and waiting long before Erna arrived. Mutti was right— when I was dressed, my hair done by professionals, Mutti's stockings, and my brown fake leather shoes, I was color coordinated and felt a little better. But when I looked in the mirror, I noticed my fair face was blah looking. So I rubbed my lips with my teeth to add color, but that lasted for just a short moment. Still looking in the mirror, I asked Mutti. "Can I use your lipstick?"

"No, lipstick! That's for grown-ups! You're too young for that. Wearing lipstick at your age gives the wrong impression."

"What wrong impression?"

"Street girls wear lipstick but for you, not until you're sixteen. It doesn't look right." I wanted to ask, "What street girls?" But I didn't want to push it any further.

Waiting for Erna, I paced around the table, to the window; back around the table, and to the window again. Onkel Martin was sitting at the table doing his crossword puzzle. Without looking up, he asked, "Is the front door open? I feel a draft passing me every so often."

I stopped pacing, "No it's not open. Why do you ask?"

"Well, it's awful drafty in here."

Then, I realized that I was the draft he was talking about. "Onkel Martin, you're too funny."

"Relax. She'll be here soon."

"I can't. I'm too nervous." About that time our doorbell rang, and Mutti answered the door. I recognized Erna's voice.

Then, I heard Mutti say, "Come in, Fraeulein Erna."

Erna shook hands with Onkel Martin and smiling, said, "Guten Tag, Herr Hentschke." After that she and I shook hands.

Mutti offered Erna a chair. Then, she too sat down. Onkel Martin laid down his pencil and folded the newspaper because it's impolite to ignore company. I leaned against the credenza, waiting for Mutti to question Erna.

Erna, looking a little uncomfortable but smiling, waited for Mutti to speak, "This is Gisela's first time to a dance, and I'd like it if you would stay close to her." Erna nodded and Mutti continued. "Also, I want her home by ten o'clock." Then, looking at me, Mutti said, "You have to take the streetcar home no later then 9:30.

"Don't worry, Frau Knebel. Margot and Sigrid are coming too, and we'll make sure that Gisela gets home on time," Erna assured Mutti.

Satisfied to have made Erna's acquaintance, Mutti said, "You girls have a good time, and enjoy your evening." Turning to me, she repeated, "Make sure you're home on time."

Before I could reply, Erna said, "She will." With a smile, Erna said, "Auf Wiedersehn" to Mutti. Onkel Martin stood up and with a slight gentlemanly bow, shook Erna's hand. Then, out the door we went, down the stairwell, and out the front door of the apartment building, laughing, glad to be turned loose.

When we got outside, there was a shout from above. "Have fun!"

Mutti and Onkel Martin were looking out the window, waving at us.

"We will!" Erna and I hollered, waving back while walking up the street.

"See, that wasn't bad. Your mother and your Onkel are very nice."

"He's not a real Onkel, but my mother's friend, and he lives with us."

"I know. You already told me that. I'm so glad my father returned from the war, but he is sick most of the time."

"What's wrong with your father?"

"I don't know. It's something from the war. He never talks about it around us kids. But your Onkel is very nice. Did you see the way he bowed when I shook his hand? He's a real gentleman." I think Erna was smitten with Onkel Martin.

"Yes, he is a gentleman and he's fun to be with. I like him a lot."

For just pennies, Erna and I took the streetcar, a thirty-minutes ride to Rauschwalde, a suburb of Goerlitz. I noticed that Erna was wearing lipstick, reminding me of my conversation with Mutti. Not wanting the passengers or the conductor lady on the streetcar to hear me, I whispered, "Mutti wouldn't let me wear lipstick. She said I was too young—not sixteen. But my face is so blah, I wish I could."

"My parents don't like it too much either, but if you want, you can use my lipstick, but be sure to take it off before you go home."

"I'll do that." We got off at the *Endstation*, the final stop and turn around of the streetcar, the *Gasthaus,* a restaurant, our destination, across from it. Its lit up sign said, *Flora*. This place had a dance hall in addition to the Gasthaus for Saturday and Sunday dances.

When Erna and I got off the streetcar, Margot and Sigrid were already waiting us. After we greeted each other, we entered the Gasthaus, filled with blue cigarette smoke and loudly said, "Guten Tag!" Some of the other guests at the tables covered with white table clothes, stopped their conversation and returned our greeting with a smile.

We walked to a wide open door where a woman sat behind a small table, covered with a white cloth. In front of her was a square metal box—a till for the entrance fee for the dance. We paid, she gave us our tickets, and we continued into the dance hall.

What a dance hall! Its centered parquet dance floor reflected multi-colored lights of from all angles. Under a high, arched natural wood ceiling, directly above the dance floor, lit in diffused multi-colors, hung a twelve-foot high chandelier, a huge grape cluster made of milky glass globes. Evenly spaced along the walls were repeats of single milky glass globes, the same size as the ones on the chandelier. They too were lit, reflecting in the mirrors behind them. Rows of chairs and tables covered with white tablecloths were grouped around the dance floor, and underneath the lit globes along the walls and mirrors.

I stood staring. What a dance hall! And the chandelier! Across the dance floor, I saw the stage with its deep blue velvet curtains showing in glittering letters the bandleader's name *Martin Viertel.* A grand piano stood to one side and the musician's stands too had glittering *MV*'s on light blue backgrounds. Towering over the band were the drummer's cymbals. The musicians, dressed in black slacks, white shirts, ties, and light blue jackets, were tuning their instruments with squeaks and squeals while the piano player played the keynote. The slender bandleader in his blue suit leaned forward as he talked to his men.

I stood planted. I couldn't take it all in, especially the chandelier. "Are you going in or are you just looking while blocking the door?" Erna asked

"I've never seen a chandelier shaped like a grape!"

The girls nudged me. "You're stopping us and others from going through." My eyes on the chandelier, I followed them to a table near the dance floor.

"How long are you going to stare? Take a chair, and have a seat!"

Shaking my head I said, "I can't believe that chandelier!"

"Yes, believe it! And it changes colors."

"It changes colors?"

"Yes, from what you see now to a steady dark red or blue for slow dances, like tangos and English waltzes. Then, you want to dance with a super dancer, gliding all over the dance floor while he is holding you close." I could tell Sigrid was really into dancing because her eyes sparkled with excitement and her body swayed as she talked.

But I shook my head. "I don't think I'd like being held close."

"Hah, just wait! That's what you say now, but we know better!" They laughed and nodded at each other, but I was not so sure.

While the girls were busy talking, checking who was here, concentrating on the boys, the musicians left the stage, the tuned instruments next to their chairs. I noticed young men in suits and ties sitting at tables, talking and laughing. Groups of girls were talking, laughing—behaving like young ladies. There were couples and even a few older people. But most were young adults. Steadily, people came, to dance at the Flora Restaurant.

Looking and watching, I realized no other girl wore a dress of ugly green and brown big plaid material. I wanted to hide! I had been so excited and anxious to go, but now I wanted to hide. The girls wore either skirts and blouses or dresses, even three-quarter-length, but made of more eye-pleasing colors than my dress. Sitting next to the dance floor, I realized that everyone could see my glaring green frog dress. I asked Erna to trade places with me. "Why do you want to trade places? I thought you might like sitting next to the dance floor."

"I do, but everyone can see my ugly dress."

"Your dress is not so ugly that you have to hide," Erna reassured me, with Sigrid and Margot agreeing.

"My dress is ugly! No girl here wears a dress as ugly as mine."

Erna got up and we exchanged seats. Although I didn't feel any better about my dress, at least I was not sitting beside the dance floor. As the dance hall filled with people, my dress and I drowned in their talk and laughter. Soon the band reappeared and played an opening short tune. Then, the bandleader introduced himself and his band, wishing the guests a happy and enjoyable evening. Everyone applauded and my first dance evening began. Turning to his band, the bandleader raised his arms, moved them downward, and the band began to play, the horns, violins, clarinets, and saxophones filling the air to the drummers beat. The dance hall came to life. Young men approached tables where girls were seated. They bowed to the girl of their choice, asking her, "*Darf ich bitten?*" May I, please? The girl got up, the young man moving her chair back, escorting her to the dance floor. Facing her, he bowed, and she inclined her head. Then, his arm around her waist, they were off—dancing.

Young men arrived at our table and with bows, asked Erna, then Sigrid, then, Margot for a dance. The dance floor was filled with whirling couples as dresses flared. But here I was, alone, activity all around me. I didn't know were to look. I wanted to hide, but I was glued to the chair. *Maybe it was a mistake to come. Maybe I wasn't ready. Maybe my dress was too ugly.* My mind, like the dancers, was whirling. Slowly, without moving my head, I let my eyes roam. I was not the only one who sat alone. Others weren't dancing. I relaxed. I took a sip of my beer. Clasping the handle of my beer glass, I told myself, "Sit up straight and act natural." After the customary three sets of dances, which seemed forever, the girls, returned to our table. The boys bowed, said, "*Danke schoen.*" The girls slightly nodded, and said, "Bitte schoen." Our table was complete, and I was glad.

"You didn't dance?"

"No. I wasn't asked."

"You'll be asked to dance. Don't give up."

"I know!" Margot quipped. "The next dance, you and I will dance, just to show you can. But if the lights dim, then it's a slow one and I want to dance with a man."

I was lucky the lights didn't dim. Margot touched my sleeve and said, "Let's go, before I'm asked to dance." Margot took the lead and away we went all around the dance floor. She was a good dancer and knew how to lead. It was also nothing unusual to see girls dance together. I had fun, and all too soon we were back at the table just as Erna and Sigrid, escorted, returned from the dance floor.

"That was fun, Margot, thank you."

The multicolored chandelier, the globes along the wall, and the stage changed color, to semi red darkness. An "ah" floated into the air. The band picked up their violins as the drummer slowly worked his drums. Young men hurried to their favorite dance partners, and in no time Erna, Sigrid, and Margot were on the dance floor. I was resigned to sit and watch, when someone bowed and asked, "*Darf ich bitten?*"

Surprised, I looked up. He was a blond, nice looking young man dressed in a suit and tie. Trying to look collected while embarrassment attacked me, I nodded my head and got up. When we got to the dance floor, he bowed and, again, I nodded. He was barely my height, and I could feel he was just as nervous as I. Before we did the first step, he stepped on my foot. Beet red, he apologized, "*Entschuldigung, Fraeulein.*" I nodded my head not wanting to look at him. Embarrassed and confused, I seemed to have forgotten how to dance. I could feel my face turning red. We stumbled around the dance floor, excusing ourselves every time we tripped over each other.

Then, without warning, he dipped me, nearly ending in disaster. He didn't have a tight hold on me, so I almost landed on the floor. His apologies were never-ending, "This is my first time to a dance. My friends invited me. Have you been here before?"

"It's my first time too. My girlfriends invited me." We laughed and relaxed. We stopped tripping over one another and he didn't try to dip me again. By the time the chandelier returned to multi-colors, the tangos were over, and we had managed to dance in unison. My dance partner escorted me to the table and before bowing, he asked, "May I come for a second dance?" I accepted. The evening was fun. I even forgot my ugly dress as my partner and I relaxed and spun around the dance floor.

But something else happened at my first dance evening. The band, after playing for an hour was taking a ten-minute break when Erna asked me, "lets go to the restaurant portion of the Gasthaus.

"What do you want there?"

"I just want to see who's at the bar." So, I went with her. Among others sitting at the bar having a drink were two young men. They saw Erna and called to her. Turning to me, she said, "Come on, and let's see what they want." I hesitated.

"Come on, they're friends of mine. I know both of them. They're nice." So, I followed.

They shook hands and when the introductions came to me, leaning forward, they asked Erna, "Who is that Fraeulein with you?"

"My friend and work buddy, Fraeulein Gisela Knebel. It's her first time here. We both work in the same apprenticeship—you know, locksmithing?" Silently, I wished that Erna had not told them that this was my first time out or that I too was locksmithing. I heard their names, but they went right over my head—I was so nervous.

The one fellow still holding my hand asked us, "Can we invite you to a liqueur?" I pulled my hand away, wanting to decline the invitation.

But Erna said, "Sure, thanks, we'll accept." When I was asked what kind of a liqueur I'd like, I had to think fast. I didn't want to look immature. So I said in a sure cool voice, "An apricot brandy, please!" After the brandy was served in small-stemmed glasses, we toasted each other by lifting our glasses. Erna and I took a sip, because it's not lady-like to drink it in one swallow.

Erna and the young men talked while I stood there like a green and brown statue, but I had time to look them over. I had to admit both were clean, nice looking men in suits and ties, older than I. They spoke and laughed with Erna in a respectful tone. Turning to me, one of the young men put his arm around my waist, pulling me nearer to him, saying, "I'm sorry we left you out of our conversation, Fraeulein."

I stiffened. I didn't like him pulling me close. He didn't know me and I didn't know him. So I told him, "Excuse me! Please, remove your arm from my waist." *Had I really said that?* I felt the heat creeping into my face. I wanted to sink into the floor.

His brown eyes flirting, he released me. "You have pride! I admire that in a girl!"

That did it! My heart pounding, my head spinning—I fell head over heels. It came without warning, like an arrow from nowhere. My face burned and I wanted to get away. Embarrassed, because I knew he could see it too, I thanked him for the liqueur and started to walk away when he inquired, "Fraeulein Gisela, may I have the next dance?" All I could do was nod.

I left Erna standing there, puzzled. When Erna retuned to our table, she asked, "What was that all about?" But I just shook my head, not wanting to talk about it.

The band started up, and after several dances the chandelier, again, darkened to a red as the band began to play a set of English waltzes. Out of the corner of my eye I saw him approaching our table, asking for the dance I had agreed to. With pounding heart, afraid to look at him, I went with him to the dance floor. He was a head taller than I, and a great dancer. I danced as in a dream—floating, never feeling my feet touching the dance floor. Now I know what Sigrid meant by gliding in semi-darkness under the chandelier in the arms of a fabulous dancer. Just before the dance ended, he looked at me and said, "You are a wonderful dancer. Have you been dancing for long time?" Unable to speak, I just shook my head. Back at the table, he bowed to thank me for the dance, but I could scarcely look at him. When he was gone, I asked Erna, "What is his name?"

"Wolfgang, but, don't get hooked. He has a girlfriend."

Too late, it's done. I thought.

All too soon I had to meet the streetcar. Erna wanted to go home with me, but I told her, "I know my way home. Stay with the girls and have fun."

"But I promised I'd bring you home."

"I know my way!" The streetcar was ready to leave and I called to Erna, "Thanks for taking me. I had fun and *Gute Nacht.* I'll see you Monday at work." Erna waved and I was on my way with my head in the clouds as the streetcar rattled down the street. I heard his voice telling me that I had pride and he liked that. I was still dancing, hearing his compliment that I was a wonderful dancer. But I knew we'd never date. He had an air of superiority and arrogance about him, and I knew that a girl locksmith was not up to his standards. It was only one dance, but a dance so wonderful, so filled with enchantment and fascination, that when I got home I was still dancing, floating to the English waltzes in his arms.

Mutti and Onkel Martin were still up and wanted to know if I had had fun. Wanting to keep my memory alive, I said, "Yes it was lots of fun." Then, I excused myself and readied for bed. In my sleep I was dancing under the chandelier in semi red darkness with the man of my dreams. The dance and he lingered in my mind for a long time. It was months before I saw him again, and, then, he remembered me only faintly.

When I came to work on Monday morning, and walked across the gravel yard, with my head still in the clouds, I noticed that someone was smiling at me. Looking a little closer, I recognized my blonde dance partner from Saturday night. I felt awkward to be seen in work clothes—not that my dress had looked any better. Embarrassed, I ignored his smile and quickly walked past him. He didn't interest me; and I wasn't dating because Mutti didn't allow it—"not until you're sixteen." Still, working in the same place, our paths crossed often; he'd smile, I looked away, and we never spoke. Besides, my thoughts were elsewhere, somewhere no one else knew of. When I met up with Erna and the girls, with a glee in their eyes, they said, "Guess who we saw this morning walking into our building, stopping at the second floor?"

"Yes, I know. I saw him, too."

"Did he talk to you?"

"No, I ignored him. I don't want to talk to him."

"Why not? He's cute," the girls said as they huddled around me.

"I just don't want to." I didn't want the girls to know I was too shy to speak to him. Then, Erna came to my rescue. "Gisela can't date. Her mother won't allow it."

"Erna is right. I can't date." That ended our conversation as Herr Hahn greeted us with his customary "Guten Morgen." Automatically we took out the everlasting piece of iron, the future hinge, squeezed it in the vice and continued our filing. Herr Hahn walked among us, and with his L-shaped tool he checked our progress. "You're too high here, too low there, your piece is not smooth on top, and the edges need to be precise, not round. Don't wobble while you're filing. Hold the file straight, and file with even strokes. The piece has to be even and smooth all over, the edges sharp and precise. Also, don't forget the required measurements." So for several months we filed and filed, until finally, with the required precise measurements and smoothness, the first phase of our half hinge passed inspection.

Now, it was time for us to learn how to operate the boring machine so we could bore holes into our piece. The boring machine, big and oppressive, squatted like a monster in the middle of our hall and was used by all the apprentices on our floor. Herr Hahn showed us how the machine worked. To prevent accidents, he taught us to be aware and use caution when using the boring machine. He told us in a strict firm voice, "When operating this machine, pull your cap over your forehead so no hair is sticking out because the boring machine will grasp your hair and pull your scalp off before anyone is able to turn the machine off." We were horror-struck. Seeing our fear, Herr Hahn said, "Don't be scared. If you do what I tell you, you'll be fine. Remember, you're in command. But," he raised his finger at us, "you must use caution and never hurry. That's when accidents and mistakes are made. Keep your hair under your cap, and your fingers away from the borer. I'll be standing by until all of you have learned to use it safely. After that, you're on your own." Herr Hahn gave each of us thick metal plates for practicing with the boring machine. We learned how to change drill bits from small to large sizes. So that we didn't hold the plate with our fingers, Herr Hahn showed us how to use the built-in vise on the boring machine. He taught us how much pressure to apply while the borer was in motion, teaching us how to make sink holes for screws—and more.

While I was busy with work and learning what I was not too enthusiastic about, spring of 1951 arrived. That June a month and a half before my sixteenth birthday, I got sick and landed in a small clinic for women. My monthly cycle had started for the first time, and when I told Mutti, she said, "Well, it's about time. You're old enough." But, it wouldn't stop; it was an on and off again situation. Being a nurse, Mutti was not too concerned about it, following her motto of, "What comes by itself; will go by itself." But it didn't. I confided in Erna, and she urged me to see a doctor, "a *Frauen Arzt,* an Gynecologist. I'll ask my mother to give you the name of one."

Without asking Mutti, I went to see the doctor. He was a friendly, elderly gray haired man. He wore a white linen coat that showed his white shirt and tie, and he treated me like a little girl. After asking what my problem was, he examined me. I was embarrassed because I was not expecting it and knew nothing of a female examination. When he was through, he told me to get dressed and come to his office, the adjacent room. Nervous and shy, I entered his all-white office. He was sitting behind a big impressive desk that matched his stature. He said, "Sit down, Fraeulein Knebel." Then, he rested his arms on the desk, looked straight at me and asked, "Who is your mother?" When I told him, he exclaimed, "Oh, I know your mother, Schwester Helene. Does she know you came to see me?"

Every doctor in Goerlitz knows Mutti. But I told him, "No, I didn't have a chance to tell her. She is busy working." Red-faced, I felt ashamed, like a little girl that hasn't told her mother what she is doing.

Leaning back in his chair, the doctor said, "You go home, and tomorrow you come back with your mother, ready to be hospitalized in my clinic."

"Hospitalized? For what?"

In a fatherly tone he said, "It's nothing for you to worry about. I will discuss it with your mother. We have to get you well again." He started to write, then handed me a page with his name printed on top in bold letters. "This will excuse you from work because you will stop working immediately."

I was speechless. What was he talking about? I wasn't sick! All I wanted and needed was for my monthly to be a monthly and not a daily! And again, I sat feeling like a little girl who'd done something wrong.

He got up and, coming around his desk, he reached out his hand and said, "Auf Wiedersehen!" We shook hands. I sort of curtsied, and with a reassuring smile he said, "Don't worry; we'll get you well again." I wasn't really worried because I didn't feel sick. I was more worried about what Mutti would say when she found out I had seen a doctor without telling her.

First, I went to work and notified the office with the doctor's orders. After that I went to tell Herr Hahn and the girls that I wouldn't be coming to work for a while, asking the girls to visit me at the clinic. At home, Mutti wasn't mad at all. She said, "Yes, I know the doctor, and I think it was a good idea for you to get checked out." I was surprised and relieved.

When Onkel Martin heard that I would be gone for a while, he said grinning, "Now I have to wrestle with your mother." Mutti only smiled.

The next day, toting my essentials in a cloth bag, I went with Mutti to see the doctor. First, they talked about surgery, but his associate, also a doctor, she didn't think that was the thing to do, saying that I was too young. I had no idea what she meant and I didn't ask—glad I didn't have to have surgery. Finally, they agreed to put me on a daily regimen of four shots instead of surgery. Mutti signed papers, and I was lodged in a five-bed room with four ladies.

The ladies were very nice and nicknamed me Dolly because I was so small, they said. They also used the familiar "Du" when they spoke to me, and I didn't mind. They were careful not to have conversations that they thought were inappropriate for my ears. Every morning before breakfast, the nurse would come into the room carrying a tray with four syringes. She'd stop at my bed, smiling, and in a melodious tone she'd say, "Just for you!" Three of the shots went into the fleshy part of my hip, rotating daily between the right and the left side. The fourth shot was given in my arm. Because the serum was kind of thick, the syringe and the needle were big. It hurt when she poked it through my skin. The serum also had to be given slowly into my bloodstream, and I was to tell the nurse when I could feel heat under my tongue. Then she'd stop injecting and, instead, drew blood into the syringe, thinning out the serum. It was a funny feeling. I felt the heat in my feet first. Then, it traveled upward until I felt it in my mouth. This regimen went on for three weeks.

It wasn't that bad in the clinic, but I had quite a scare so that I wanted to go home. For the first week I shared a room with the ladies. Then, without explanation, I was moved upstairs to a twelve-bed room where the first night was frightening to me. There had been an emergency surgery, and because there were no beds available elsewhere, they rolled an additional bed in and set it crossways at the foot of my bed, blocking me in. In the middle of the night when the woman who had had surgery was brought in, still in her ether delirium, she kicked and screamed profanities while fighting off the nurses and the doctor. I was afraid she'd jump right into my bed. I was so frightened that I hid under my covers, shaking and sweating, with my legs pulled up. When morning came, I was still afraid and refused to have my shots. I wanted to go home.

Mutti was notified and on her way they told me. The woman still in front of my bed had settled down and was sleeping. By the time Mutti arrived, I was dressed and ready to leave, but Mutti said, "I can't take you home. You're not done with the procedure."

"I don't care, just take me home. I don't like being here in this room with all these women." I begged, but Mutti just shook her head no.

The doctor came, and Mutti and she had a heated discussion. Upset, Mutti told the doctor, "The patient should have been left in the recovery room if there was no room in here. To bring her in and place her in front of my daughter's bed was not good. If you had to, then she should've been put near your mature patients and not in front of a young inexperienced girl, scaring her." I was so proud of Mutti. Being a nurse, she spoke with confidence and knowledge.

They apologized to Mutti and me, and while Mutti was standing by, I got my shots. Then, they moved me to a glassed-in veranda with three unoccupied beds. The outside was overgrown with vines like a curtain made by nature. The veranda was at the back of the house, and when I looked out the window, I saw a small garden below with a water fountain, flowers, trees and benches for the patients and their visitors to sit. But when I needed to leave the veranda, I had to walk through the twelve-bed room. I didn't like that very much, and I kept my eyes on the floor. Before Mutti left, she made sure I was all right. Relieved, I told her, "Yes, I like it out here; it's like sleeping under the stars."

Later during the day the doctor came and she, too, asked, "How are you doing out here?"

"I like it. With the window wide open, it's like sleeping outside." The following day two girls, older than me, were moved on the veranda. I never asked about their problems, and like me, they weren't in pains and so we had lots of fun.

Oma and Uschi came ever so often for a visit and the girls almost every day. They brought rhododendron they had stolen from the city park, which made Oma frown. When the girls came, we'd laugh and talk, because we were the only ones on the veranda. They told me of dances they had gone to at the Stadthallen-Garten, dancing under the stars. "We can't wait for you to get out of here so you can go with us."

"I can't go."

"And why can't you?" Erna wanted to know.

"Because I don't have a dress. That's why I can't."

"No problem," Sigrid intervened. "My mother sews. She'll sew a dress for you, I'm sure."

"I have to have money first."

"You'll get paid from work, and we'll help you pick out material," Margot suggested. It seemed they had it all figured out for me.

"Yeah, and my mother has all kinds of magazines with patterns that our family sends to her from the West."

"Do you think she'll make me a dress the way I like it?"

"No problem."

The regimen of four daily shots continued almost to the day I was released from the clinic, and they did what they were meant to do, but my hips were sore and my arms were a purplish blue. I thought they'd never be normal again. After being home for a week I developed a rash, luckily on my backside where no one could see it, but forcing me to sit down carefully. To make matters worse, Onkel Martin promptly nicknamed me "Blister Butt".

On my discharge day, Mutti came to the clinic to sign my release and for us to see the doctor. Again, I sat in his office, Mutti in her nurse's uniform, beside me, the doctor behind his desk. He opening a folder and said, "Schwester Helene, we need to talk about Gisela's situation."

"Is there something else wrong with my daughter?"

"No, there isn't. She will be fine, but I recommend that she does not continue in her present profession. She is not strong enough to do heavy work, and locksmithing is heavy work. It could lead to future problems, so I recommend she discontinue her apprenticeship."

"But we've signed a four-year contract."

"That can be broken. I'll write a memo requesting a release of contract for health reasons." Looking at me, he said, "You need to grow, and you will because the shots in your arms were a multi-vitamin and iron you needed to help you develop physically." Then, he spoke to Mutti, "I need to see Gisela after her first monthly or sooner if problems occur. By then, I'll have the memo ready requesting her release, but for now she is on sick leave." The doctor closed the folder and got up, then, he shook hands with Mutti and me. I did a slight curtsy, while reminding myself to stop curtsying—I wasn't a child anymore.

Walking home, Mutti asked, "Do you want to be released from the contract?"

I shrugged my shoulders, "Oh, I don't mind. Locksmithing isn't really for me, but I will miss the girls." Mutti seemed satisfied with my answer. We didn't talk about it anymore, and I was glad. I didn't care for locksmithing or school. I really didn't know what I wanted to do. I felt like a leaf hung loose on a small branch, turning this way and that way with each breeze, not falling off to settle someplace. I knew, too, that I had to find a new job. But, until I was released by the doctor and from the contract, my apprentice pay continued.

Saturday morning, my second day at home, when Mutti was out shopping for our weekend groceries, the doorbell rang. Thinking it was Mutti; I opened the door still in my housecoat. Werner, my second cousin, was at the door, dressed in a suit and tie. Surprised to see him and embarrassed, I said, "What are you doing here?"

"Can I come in first?"

I motioned for him to come in. "Mutti is not home, but she should be home soon." We shook hands as is customary, and I offered him a chair to sit.

"Actually, I didn't come to see Lenchen. I came to see you."

"Me? What for?"

"I want you to go to my brother's wedding with me."

"No, I don't. Uschi is going with you."

He shook his head, "No, I want you to go with me."

I knew Werner's brother Jorg was getting married this weekend because Oma was in charge of the cooking.

"I was told that Uschi is your escort at the wedding. Besides, I can't go with you. I'm just home from the clinic. My hair is a disaster, and I don't have a dress." *The frog-dress is out,* I thought.

"No excuses; I want you to go to my brother's wedding with me."

"Why can't you take Uschi?

"She isn't as much fun as you are, so you have to go with me." He was right—Uschi was always more prim and proper. Because I liked to laugh and have fun, I was often told, "You're just like your mother!" Just then Mutti returned from shopping, and behind her was Tante Klara, Werner's mother, also dressed for the wedding.

"Gisela doesn't want to go with me," Werner told them.

"That's not what I said! I'm sure Uschi is expecting to go. And Tante Elfriede will be mad when she hears I'm at the wedding instead of Uschi. And besides my hair, I don't have a dress to wear." I was hoping my excuses would convince Werner to take Uschi. Mutti and Tante Klara looked at each other, trying to think of something to convince me to accept the invitation.

Then, Mutti said, "If Werner wants you to go with him, then go. You can wear my new dress and my high-heeled shoes. Don't worry about Tante Elfriede. I'll take care of that."

Tante Klara, nodded, "That's right, and the bride's hairdresser can do your hair, too. Just wash your hair before you come, it'll be less work for her."

"But there isn't time for all that!"

"Yes, there is." Tante Klara answered. "Right now the bride and groom are at the justice of the peace for the civil service. The church wedding is not until 1:00 o'clock this afternoon; you have plenty of time to get ready. Werner wants you to be his escort, and I'm asking you to accept."

I didn't know what to answer, so Mutti made the decision and told Tante Klara, "Give me an hour to get Gisela ready." *I guess I'm going.*

"Yes!" Werner said, beaming, "I'll be back in an hour to pick you up," I waved him off as Mutti closed the door.

Unsure and nervous, but with Mutti's urging I got ready. Mutti's dress, although fashionable, was both a bit too mature, and too big around my waist, but belted, it worked well.

One hour later, Werner was at the door with a small bouquet of beautifully arranged carnations, which I later, like the other ladies in the wedding party, carried to the church service. When we got to the bride's house the hairdresser did my hair. Now, I felt presentable.

Oma was surprised to see me, "Isn't Uschi going to church with Werner?" But Tante Klara told her that Werner had asked for me instead. Oma said nothing, and returned to supervising her kitchen help.

I knew Oma was thinking of Tante Elfriede and how mad she'd be when she saw me stepping from the horse drawn coach in front of the church. I was nervous, too, almost afraid of that moment. I liked my cousin Uschi and I didn't want her mad at me over this. Because the wedding was small, Mutti and Tante Elfriede as cousins were not included, only close relatives. I was invited only because the brother of the groom needed a female escort.

I knew I would see Tante Elfriede and Uschi at the church because anyone could join the wedding ceremony. I was not looking forward to that.

The groom's parents had hired four shiny black carriages drawn by black horses with white and blue plumage on their heads to take the wedding party to the church. The two coachmen, for each coach wore light blue uniforms with white braids across their chests, white gloves and top hats. The creamy white bridal carriage was drawn by four white horses. The carriage upholstery was light blue with frilly white curtains on its beveled windows. Those horses, too, wore plumage of white and blue, matching the coachmen's dress uniforms. Every little girl dreamed that on her wedding day she'd ride in a carriage like that to church.

It's the custom for the groom to pick up his bride with that white carriage and to bring her the bridal bouquet—this one was of yellow roses. But before Jorg came to pick up his bride, we, her wedding party, left in the other coaches. When we got to the church, we lined the aisle, the men on one side, the woman on the other, facing each other, waiting for the bride and groom. As the bells rang and the organ filled the church with its hymns, the carriage with Jorg and his bride drew up. Holding their flower baskets, two little girls in frilly white dresses were lifted by a coachman from the carriage. Then, the bride in her snow-white gown descended from the carriage with the help of her groom. Her long white veil flowed from atop her head where she wore a crown of small green leaves interspersed with tiny white flowers, of *Myrte,* the symbol of purity. Smiling, she took Jorg's arm; and while the organ played, the flower girls scattered their flowers in front of the bride and groom walking down the aisle to the altar where two ornate chairs awaited them.

As the bride and groom walked past us, we followed arm in arm with our partners to the designated pews near the altar. After we were seated, everyone else, distant relatives and friends who had stood outside the church watching and wanting to observe the ceremony, were allowed to enter, sitting behind the wedding party. The bells stopped; the organ was silenced. Then, with a rumble that echoed through the church, the church elder closed the big heavy wooden doors. The pastor, in his robe, stood in front of the altar, facing the bride and groom in there ornate chairs, they waited for the pastor to join them together as one.

Sitting next to Werner, trying to listen to the pastor, my mind wandered. I had spotted Tante Elfriede and Uschi when I arrived. I could feel their presence behind me now. Tante Elfriede didn't look at me, but Uschi smiled and waived as I'd stepped with the coachman's help from the carriage. Uschi wasn't angry; I'd relaxed and enjoyed the ceremony.

Finally the organ thundered a hallelujah, the bells from the church tower rung. The smiling bride and groom, got into their carriage, then, we got into our carriages. With the bridal carriage in the lead, we made our way along city streets to her parent's apartment. People stopped and smiled; some waved just like in a movie. Shiny-eyed little girls watched as the bride, sitting next to her groom in her white carriage rolled past them.

While we had been in church, Oma had set the table for dinner. Delicate twigs with white star-like flowers and tiny green leaves clipped from the *Myrte* plant graced the table. Glowing candles filled the room with warmth and serenity for this festive occasion. The wedding party of about twenty people gathered at the table marked with place cards. Speeches were given, and toasts were made to the newly married couple with laughter and enthusiasm. Then Oma, wearing a black dress, covered with a clean white starched and ironed apron, supervised the serving of dinner. Oma had prepared a bouillon soup with sprigs of carrots, onion, and parsley. For the main dinner Oma served sliced roast beef and gravy, potato dumplings, with sweet and sour red cabbage. The drink was mainly beer, while the bride and groom had a glass of Champagne. It was not a fancy wedding dinner, but fancy for us. Because of food rationing, parents and families on both sides contribute to the food needed either with saved food stamps, black market or at the H.O.

Everyone complimented Oma on how good it tasted and what a good cook, chef and organizer she was. But then, Oma was known for her cooking skills. I remember her telling me that for a long time, almost for all her life, she had cooked for large events, sometimes to supplement her income. I felt especially proud to be her granddaughter.

After dinner, coffee and cake, conversation floated around the table, and Oma, without her apron, joined in. But Werner and I got bored and decided to move out to the balcony with a table and chairs as well flower boxes with blooming geraniums making it a cozy place to sit. It was a warm evening, and Werner and I were having a beer. Soon an older man, an Onkel of the bride, came out on the balcony—also carrying a beer, asking, "May I join you two?" Werner pulled out a chair, inviting him to sit with us. He was a jovial man with a kind face, and soon the balcony filled with laughter. Because of our laughter, two more men joined us. Werner and I enjoyed our beer, laughing and listening to jokes told around the table. Because I was a young girl among grown men, the jokes were mild, but funny.

But while sitting on the balcony, I almost broke one of my teeth. It was ill mannered to drink from a bottle instead a glass when sitting at the table with company. Forgetting our manners, Werner and I were drinking our beer from the bottle. I was listening to a joke, my head tilted back to take a sip from my beer bottle, when I suddenly wanted to laugh. With the bottle still on my mouth, I bent forward, hitting the edge of the table and jarring the bottle against my front teeth. I heard a crack. I ran for the mirror, fearful I'd broken off a tooth. When I returned, the men had gone back inside to join the conversation there. Werner asked, "How is your tooth?"

"I was lucky. I broke only a very small corner off from one of my front teeth, and I don't need to see a dentist." I was so glad I hadn't ruined my teeth that after the incident for many years I didn't drink from a bottle again.

It was getting late, so Werner and I decided to say our "*Gute Nachts*" or good night, and, with the moon watching, Werner walked me home. Slightly woozy, we laughed, sang, and sometimes danced along the sidewalk, happy to be alive. I liked Werner; he was fun to be with. Had he not been my second cousin, I could have liked him a whole lot more. So we became good friends. Also, a certain young man was still dancing in my head.

S ince I was not working, I had house duties, mainly to tidy up by making beds, dusting, and washing dishes by hand because there were no dishwashers. On weekends, Mutti took over. Friday's housework was more thorough because the apartment had to be clean for the weekend. The floor had to be washed from corner to corner, not what Mutti called "the dance floor only". I was like any other teen, not too fond of doing housework, but as Mutti said, "It has to be done and you're living here, too." Before washing the floor, I had to sweep. I'd turn on the radio, rather loud; then, I'd opened the windows. Then, since there were no vacuums, with broom in hand I'd waltz across the floor, sweeping and singing from the bedroom to the living room and kitchen. I liked listening to the West German station because they had the latest hits. It wasn't strictly forbidden to listen to the music from the West, but when the news came on, then East Germany scrambled the radio waves, making it almost impossible to understand. It was wise either to turn the radio off or to turn it to an East German sender.

I was not allowed to cook, and I was glad. Mutti said, "Due to our food shortage, we can't afford for you to practice cooking or baking." So I watched while I helped sometimes with peeling potatoes or cleaning vegetables. Mutti knew how to make dinners from almost nothing, how to make gravies using sautéed onions or liverwurst she had purchased with stamps from the butcher. Mutti even made gravy with mustard then added hard-boiled eggs—one for each of us to the mustard gravy. Those gravies we used over mashed potatoes, rice, or noodles. I learned to make them, too. Because we could have meat on Sundays only, Mutti cooked to be sure the meat was well prepared. Besides, for Onkel Martin it wasn't Sunday if Mutti didn't make *Sauerbraten* with potato dumplings and sweet and sour red cabbage. It was my job to take the beer pitcher and money to the Gasthaus on the corner of our block to buy the beer for our Sunday dinner.

Although Onkel Martin liked sauerbraten, I liked something that was almost vampire like. The butcher catty-corner from us butchered once a month. He told his customers when he was butchering. Mutti, like all of his customers, brought pitchers and containers with their names on them to his shop. When he butchered, he'd catch the blood, dividing it among the containers furnished by his customers, charging them a couple of *Pfennings*, pennies for it.

Once the blood was home, Mutti soaked two-day-old hard rolls in water. While the rolls soaked, with tears running down her cheeks, Mutti chopped up a big onion. Then she took the softened rolls, squeezed out the excess water, and mixed them into the blood, after that she added the chopped onion, marjoram, salt and pepper. Next, she put the mixture in the frying pan where small pieces of bacon were browning; stirring it until it turned solid, like scrambled eggs. We ate it as a spread on open slices of bread. It tasted almost like sausage from the butcher, only not smoked. But before Mutti cooked it, I already was waiting for her to finish mixing. I had to have a small amount in a tiny bowl because I liked to eat it raw. Mutti just shook her head, not believing what she saw. "How can you eat that raw?"

"I don't know. It just tastes good to me."

Mutti, puzzled but resigned, only said, "Well, maybe there is something in the blood that your body craves and needs. It might be the iron."

Onkel Martin asked me to open my mouth, which I did. He looked all around. Then, rather seriously, he said, "You can close your my mouth again."

Dumbfounded, I asked, "What were you looking for?"

With his usual grin, he said, "I just wanted to see if you have grown fangs yet." Then, he laughed because he got me again. I never got sick from eating the raw blood, but every body in our family teased me about eating the raw prepared blood, and in time I eventually stopped my vampire habit.

Several months later, the butcher shop, after being closed for the weekend, Sunday and Monday, didn't reopen on Tuesday. There was no sign in the window and people were puzzled when they came to shop. But when he didn't open after several days, then quiet speculation started that maybe he had done or said something against the East German regime and its communism and his family and he had been arrested. Others thought his family and he made an overnight escape to West Germany. Mutti said, "If the butcher with his family escaped, then lets hope they made it unharmed." Everyone knew what happened to people who were caught trying to escape to the West. If they were not shot first, then they were sent, no questions asked, to Siberia, never to be seen again. There were whispers of people who had tried to escape, some lucky, some not, or so presumed, because the family never heard from them. Those of us who lived in the East we'd learned to be cautious to whom we spoke. It wasn't safe to express any political opinions. Mutti, Onkel Martin, or the family seldom talked about politics outside our apartments, and, if they did only in subdued voices.

Most days, and on her way home from work, Erna would stop to see how I was doing, and, of course, I was doing fine. I had no pain, and it seemed odd not to go to work, but I didn't miss it. I did miss the girls and they, me.

Talking with Erna, I asked, "Are you, Margot, and Sigrid still going with me to buy the material for the dress?"

"Yes, we told you we would."

"But I need to ask Sigrid to make sure that her mother will sew this dress for me."

"I'll check with Sigrid when I see her at work tomorrow."

"I have the money and can go anytime. I already told Mutti. It's fine with her."

"I'll stop by after work tomorrow and let you know when we'll go."

We met the following Saturday at the HO store, but only Sigrid and Erna were there. "Where is Margot?" I asked.

"She couldn't come. She had to help her mother."

"Oh, I was looking forward to seeing her." Turning to Sigrid, I asked "Are you sure your mother wants to sew this dress for me?"

"Yes, she sews for our living and wants you to bring the material. So let's go." As we walked in the store, I thought how different this was from when I was here with Christa and her friend Rosel. Now I was with friends, talking and laughing, not walking behind or being ignored. I was excited. I had money in my purse when we went inside the HO store.

Although it had been two years since I had been inside the HO, it still was dingy and dark with little material on the shelf. The sales lady didn't know when there would be more material. "And when it comes, we sell out fast," she told us. I considered myself lucky to find a lightweight, nice looking summer material. It was white with tiny flowers printed all over. I was satisfied, happy, because for the first time I had made a decision all on my own.

With the material wrapped in brown paper, we walked to see Sigrid's mother. After shaking hands, we sat around the table and pored over magazines, Erna and Sigrid exclaiming. "Look, Gisela, that's a nice dress! Look here! What about this one? Oh, I like that one!"

I didn't know where to look first! Sigrid's mother, a stout but kind woman interrupted, "Slow down, girls." Taking the magazine, she said, "Let me see what you're looking at. Yes, that is a very attractive dress. It would look nice on you." It was a sleeveless dress, with a flared skirt, and a short-sleeved jacket that stopped at the waist.

"To give it a personal touch," Sigrid's mother continued, "let's add blue piping around the little jacket and around the top of the dress. You check at the HO store to see if they have blue lightweight material. I'll need just a very small strip, about a quarter meter. What do you think?"

"Oh, I like it! I'll check tomorrow, and I'll bring it to you right away," I replied, overjoyed.

"You can bring it when you come for the first fitting, a week from today. The piping is one of the last things I will do."

When I got home, I told Mutti about the dress I was having sewed.

"I'm glad you found what you wanted, and I'm eager to see what it will look like. I hope the HO will have what you need because they never have many choices on hand."

"I know. They didn't have much material to choose from when I was there. I was lucky they had something I liked." But when I went for the blue material, they didn't have any blue at all. Then I went to Oma's to see if she had some blue material in her scrap basket. She didn't. Excited, but without the material, I went for my first fitting. "The HO didn't have any blue material," I told Sigrid's mother.

"Don't worry. I found some blue material in my scraps. I have to sew it together to make a strip, but it will be fine when I get done with it. I thought they probably wouldn't have it. It's always the same. We're never able to buy the simplest things." Her voice sounded sad, but matter-of-fact, like all grown-ups when they talked about things that were not available in stores.

While I had the dress on, she pinned here and there. Then with a satisfied smile and a critical look, she stepped back, her eyes were going over me, "I think, the dress will look really nice on you."

And it did. I was proud of my first dress, a dress of my own choosing. When my sister saw it, she looked down her nose at it. "It's a baby dress." But I knew it was not a baby dress. I also knew that all Christa wanted was to dampen my spirits, but I wouldn't let her. I had matured a little, and most of the time I wouldn't let Christa get the best of me. Also, I didn't see her often because she still lived at the Langenstrasse and I was glad.

However, when she came to see Mutti, to borrow money that she very seldom repaid, I tried to stay out of her way because I knew we'd end up fighting. She'd say to Mutti, like, "Why do you let her do that?" Or "She shouldn't be allowed to do that."

Then, the fight was on and I'd tell her, "That's none of your business. I don't stick my nose in your business so don't stick yours in mine and, furthermore, you're not my mother!" My sister always had to have the last word, sniggering as she went out the door. But I never backed off. Mutti would get upset with me because I stood my ground, and that hurt my feelings. At those times I felt like an intruder, an unwelcome newcomer and I never told Mutti about my feelings, or even Oma. Sometimes, not very often, Mutti would ask Christa to leave. Onkel Martin didn't like listening to our fighting because sometimes Christa was downright nasty. Then, he'd give me a look that said, "Don't take that from her." I wanted to believe he wasn't that fond of my sister. He never wrestled or kidded her like he did with me—he was in my corner and that made me feel good!

It's July and my sixteenth birthday had arrived. I was still sleeping when I felt a gentle tapping on my shoulder and heard a cheery voice saying, *"Wir gratulieren Dir zu Deinem sechzehnten Gebrutstag"* Congratulation to your sixteenth birthday. Through barely opened eyes, I saw Mutti, bent over me, her hand on my shoulder while Onkel Martin in his police uniform stood at the foot of my bed holding a bouquet of flowers, beaming. Mutti dressed in her nurse's uniform and always chipper in the morning, pleaded, "Come, and get up. The breakfast table is ready and waiting for you. Come on get up. We want to have breakfast with you before going to work." Onkel Martin tugged on my foot sticking out from my bed cover.

Stretching, I rolled out of bed, and, half asleep, made my way to the breakfast table. Mutti had brewed the good coffee. While she poured, I opened my eyes. It was Wednesday, but the table was set for a Sunday breakfast with fresh rolls from the bakery, butter, marmalade, and a hard-boiled egg for each of us. Next to my place setting glowed the customary birthday candle, the *light of life,* a symbol, and a belief that with every newborn a new light—his light—begins to shine. It guides and illuminates our paths and when we leave this world, the light fades away again.

While we ate breakfast, Mutti said, "We'll celebrate your birthday Sunday afternoon." Birthdays were mostly celebrated with family members, and since I was a young adult, the afternoon coffee was appropriate. That Sunday the table was set; the birthday candle flickered, and on a big round cake platter was the cake Oma had baked, my favorite, Streuselkuchen. All was ready, and I, the person of honor, wearing my new dress, waited for the guests to arrive.

Tante Elfriede came with Onkel Richard and Uschi. Then, Oma came with Onkel Heinz, Tante Hilde, Rainer, and Heidi. Because flowers were customary gifts, everyone came with beautiful bouquets, arranged in flower shops. Lingering with their sweet scent above us were my favorite flowers, sweet peas, a bouquet Uschi gave me every year for my birthday. Mutti was busy putting the bouquets in vases and placing them throughout the living room so that it looked like a florist shop. There were small gifts, three handkerchiefs in a gift box, a book, boxed stationary with matching envelopes, perlon stockings, but flowers were always my favorites. Even Christa came with a bouquet, which she stuck in my face with a sheepish grin, hiding her embarrassment.

Except for my sister, everyone shook my hand, congratulating me on my sixteenth birthday, wishing me health and happiness. While pouring the good coffee, Mutti asked everyone to gather around the table and be seated. Onkel Martin stood behind his chair waiting for everyone to sit down. It's impolite for the man of the house to sit down before the guests are seated. Soon after we had coffee and cake, my sister left, saying Rosel and she were going dancing.

Sitting at the table, I watched the candle as its reddish-yellow flame flickered and thought, *the much waited and looked forward to sixteenth birthday has arrived, been celebrated, and is almost gone.* But I was content and happy. While I blew out the candle, I thought of Vati and how I missed him at these special times. With everyone deep in conversation, Uschi and I took a walk in the late afternoon sunshine with Rainer and Heidi in here stroller. When we returned, the family was ready to leave. Shaking hands, I thanked everyone for the flowers and gifts, but gave Oma a hug and a kiss on the cheek. My birthday was over, leaving Mutti and me to clean up the table, wash the dishes, and prepare our evening meal.

A couple days after my birthday, Erna came by. "So, you're sixteen now. My best wishes afterward."

"Thank you." Beaming at her I said, "Yes, isn't it great? I, too, can go dancing now."

"That's why I'm here. The girls and I were planning to go dancing in the *Stadthallen Garten* this Saturday. We want you to come with us."

"I'd like that, but I still need to ask Mutti first."

"I'll stop by tomorrow on my way home. Auf Wiedersehn."

"Ja, until tomorrow! And auf Wiedersehn!"

As soon as Mutti came home, I told her, "Erna was here this afternoon she asked if I could go with her, Margot, and Sigrid to the dance in the Stadthallen Garten Saturday evening, but I told her I needed to ask you first if I can go."

Mutti looked at me, "Of course, you can go. You're sixteen."

I was sixteen! I was free! Mutti had just set me free. It felt odd. *Have I just added another stepping-stone?* Mutti interrupted my thoughts. "You have to be home before midnight. Let's say eleven."

"Yes, I'll be home on time." Well, I was almost free.

Erna stopped by the next day and was glad to hear that I could go. "Now, this is the way we'll do it. The dance doesn't start until five o'clock. Margot is coming on the streetcar about four o'clock. You and I will meet her when she gets off the streetcar at the Postplatz. Then, on the way to the Stadthalle, we'll pick up Sigrid. Agreed?"

"Agreed. Only I have to be home by eleven," I told Erna.

"Margot has to be home by midnight. She has strict parents."

"But she's a year older than I am."

"Yes, she is, but her curfew is always midnight. Sigrid's mother is more lenient. But then it's just her and her mother because her father was killed in the war."

"Yes, I know; she told me. So many of us lost our fathers in the war. Sigrid's mother is nice. I like her and the dress she sewed for me." Trying to shake off the unhappy thoughts, I said, "I'm so excited. My first evening of dancing under the stars."

"Let's hope it doesn't rain."

"It can't rain. I want to know what it's like to dance under the stars." I pictured myself dancing to the sound of the band in the warm flowery air.

"Well, if it does, then the dance is inside the Stadthalle." Looking at the clock she said, "I've got to hurry; my mother is waiting for me. I'll see you Saturday."

"Yes, Saturday. I'll be there!"

All week long I had one thought: dancing, dancing, and dancing!

I was sixteen and allowed to go out! While playing the radio, I whirled and two stepped around the apartment, sweeping and dusting. Onkel Martin claimed I was a wild broom turned loose, whereas Mutti hoped my cleaning spirit would stay. But like any teen, the cleaning spirit fizzled out because dreamy thoughts were dancing in my head. *Would I see him again? Would he be at the dance? Would he ask me for a dance?* When I closed my eyes, I felt his arm around me, guiding me over the dance floor, as I melted into the rhythm of the dance and him. I was filled with anxiety for Saturday to come, hoping it wouldn't rain and that I would see him again.

When I woke up Saturday morning, the sun was shining and the sky was blue. Because I had an appointment at Mutti's beauty shop, I jumped out of bed and ate a hurried breakfast. Mutti and Onkel Martin looked at each other. "What's your hurry? We've never seen you get out of bed so quick."

"Well, I have an appointment for my hair, and then I have to get ready for tonight."

"Slow down. You have lots of time," Mutti told me.

Onkel Martin teased, "Maybe our Fraeulein has a date that we don't know of."

"No, I don't!" I replied way too fast, as my face turned red, like being caught in a fib, but I thought, *I don't have a date—only hope.*

Under a clear blue sky, I walked to the beauty shop. Women and teens had their hair done in beauty shops because washing hair at home and using rollers was not done. Only children and older people like Oma washed their hair at home and let it air dry.

Shortly before four o'clock, in my new dress, my hair done, I walked to the Postplatz to meet Margot and Erna.

Whenever I went in the direction of the Postplatz, I had to walk down Berliner Strasse, passing the place where I thought I had seen Vati. For the longest time, I watched and hoped that I would see that man again, but I never did.

Because Erna lived just around the corner from the Postplatz, she was already waiting. Soon the streetcar came and Margot got off. After our customary greetings, we were on our way to pick up Sigrid and then to the Stadthalle and the garden.

That evening, laughing and talking, Erna, Sigrid, Margot and I made our way to the Stadthalle. It was a beautiful warm summer evening as a gentle breeze carried the scent of roses from the flowerbeds along the walkways in the park. The closer we got, the more eager I was. The Stadthallen Garten had palm trees; two tiled dance floors, tables covered with tablecloths, and placed here and there, sun umbrellas with strings of colored lights all around. We paid our entrance fee and found a table near one of the dance floors. Seated, I slowly looked around, my heart throbbing. Was he here? I didn't see him; there were too many people. Then, the band, sitting on a roofed over-stage started to play. Margot and I went to the dance floor and so did Erna and Sigrid. Most of the time girls danced the opening dance, as if to say, "Here we are, so come and get us."

As the evening progressed, I danced, but it wasn't like the first time I had gone out with the girls. I was a little surer of myself because I didn't look like a frog anymore. As I danced, I watched over the shoulders of my partners for that one particular person. I almost lost a beat when I saw him dancing past my partner and me while my heart was doing double duty. *Will he ask me for a dance? Will he remember me?* I looked at him when he came close to us again, but there was no recognition, not even a glance as he danced past us. I just knew he would never ask me for a dance. Or would he? When I came back to our table, to get Erna's attention I touched her arm and whispered, "He is here."

"Who?"

"You know, Wolfgang."

"Ja, I saw him on the dance floor."

"Is he alone?"

Erna looking around said, "Yes, I think so. Are you hung up on him? Better forget it; I told you he has a steady girl."

"Then, why is he here alone?"

"I've seen him alone before, but forget it. I mean it." Before I could answer, the band started to play. Erna and the girls were already dancing, and I sat alone at our table. Then I heard someone coming up, asking, "May I have this dance?" Looking, while getting up to see who was asking me for a dance, I nearly lost my composure. He was here, asking me for a dance! My face felt hot, my heart was racing, so much so that I thought he could see my infatuation. While we walked to the dance floor, I told myself, "Be calm, relax, he doesn't remember you." But I had all I could do to control my emotions. With a slight bow, he placed his arm around my waist, then, I placed my hand in his, while my other hand rested near his shoulder. I was floating in his arms, my feet never touching the dance floor. We danced in perfect harmony. I felt as if I belonged in his arms and I didn't want that dance, ever, to end—but it did.

"You're a wonderful dancer," he started the conversation.

Taking hold of myself, realizing he really didn't remember me, I smiled coquettishly and said, "Thank you." Then holding me at a slight angle, looking at me rather puzzled, he said, "Somehow you look familiar to me, like I've seen you before. Have we met?"

It reminded me of a cat and mouse game. I remembered him, but he didn't remember me. So I flirted even more, "Well, maybe we have."

"Then why don't I remember you?" Somewhat more assured he said, "I know I have met you! But I'm not sure if you're the girl I'm thinking of." Rather carefully he asked, "Were you the girl I met awhile back at the Flora with Erna?"

I looked at him, "Yes, the very same." While my mind shouted, "He did remember you!" and at that moment, I was the happiest girl on the dance floor.

Surprised, he looked at me, his eyes showing admiration, "I would have never recognized you. You have changed. You look so different from when I saw you at the Flora. You have become very attractive." And I was thinking, "That's because the frog has shed its green color." Embarrassed, but flattered to hear him say I had become attractive, I cast my eyes downward while I thanked him for the compliment. When he escorted me to the table, he thanked me for the dance, and then greeted Erna. When he was gone, Erna just looked at me and shook her head.

"What? I'm only dancing with him," I said, shrugging my shoulders, but my evening was made. We danced several times that evening and by the time I went home, my head was spinning again. I knew for sure that I had fallen head over heels. I also knew it was one-sided, and nothing ever would come of it but that didn't stop my heart from racing every time I saw him. Many times I would see him with his girl when I was out dancing. He'd always ask me for a dance or two, making polite conversation while dancing. I made myself believe that he must care some, or why would he dance with me whenever he saw me? So I carried this secret, my first love, for a long time. Still, that secret didn't stop me from having fun, going dancing, or meeting new friends along the way.

While I was still under doctor's care, the locksmith contract was terminated, but I was not excused from the *FDJ, Freie Deutsche Jugend,* the Free German Youth. Instead, I was assigned to a different troop, of members with no special trades or training. The FDJ, a socialist's organization, required all youth, aged fourteen and up to be a member and attend regular meetings. I never liked joining new groups, because I didn't do well meeting new people. At the first meeting I attended the group leader, informed me I was expected to travel to East Berlin with the troop.

"Travel to East Berlin? What for?"

"To sing and march in the parade at the *Weltfestspiele der Jugend,* a World Youth Festival."

My face burned with embarrassment, because everyone was watching me as she was talking.

"Apparently you are not informed, so let me clarify this for you." I wanted to slide off the chair, or sink in a hole, but instead, I had to sit and listen to her speech.

"The *Weltbund der Demokratischen Jugend,* a World Federation of Democratic Youth was organized and established in November 1945 in London, England. Its first meeting was in 1947 in Prague, Czechoslovakia. In 1949 its meeting was held in Budapest Hungary; in August of this year, 1951, East Berlin is hosting the meeting. To cover your travel expenses, you need to bring money to our next meeting. Don't forget!"

Mutti wasn't happy when I told her about the travel expenses. It wasn't the money but where it was going. "You just joined the group and paid your monthly dues, so why pay travel expenses? Ask your leader what she does with the money she is collecting."

"I don't want to ask her." Confronting people wasn't something I liked to do and having to ask our group leader, "Why?" wasn't easy for me, for all she had to do was glare at me and I would shrink away. Then, I know I'd hear my stepmother's voice, "You're too dumb. Don't even try it." And I wouldn't.

Next Mutti suggested, "Tell her you can't go. Tell her you're sick."

"I already tried that, and she said, "You don't look sick. We will go as a whole group. We will show solidarity. We will show the world that we are strong, that we believe in socialism, that we trust our friends and leaders, that in unison and with hard work, we'll build a better future. Our future," I mimicked the leader's clenched raised fists and stern face.

Mutti shook her head. "Do you and the rest of your group believe all that?" Getting louder, she continued, "Your leader is a communist and a socialist. She is a hammer and sickle red flag waver who is filling your heads with lies and false hope." Listening to Mutti, I knew it was best not to mention communist functions to her, but sometimes I had to.

Onkel Martin intervened, saying, "Not so loud, Lenchen, someone could hear you. Don't get yourself all upset over it. You know Gisela has to participate in the East Berlin Youth-Festival."

Mutti closed the window and turning to Onkel Martin, said, "Yes, I know, but it makes me mad. We hardly have enough food. Then, they dominate us. Fill our youth's heads with their Russian ideals and communism, as if the Germans were a bunch of stupid, uneducated people who don't know anything. All the red flag hammer and sickle wavers can go to Russia, but I bet the Russians don't want them either. They just use them to make communist's out of our youth." Mutti was so upset she started to stutter.

Onkel Martin said, "Lenchen, there is nothing we or anyone else can do. This is where we live and this is the way it is. Getting mad over it will not change anything. If some commie hears the way you talk, we may end up in jail or worse." Wiping her forehead with her hanky, Mutti nodded in agreement.

I could have told the leader we didn't have the money for me to go, but I didn't. Secretly, I was thinking of crossing over to the *other side*—West Berlin. I wanted to see what the West was really like and if they really had all the food every one was whispering about. I couldn't tell Mutti or Onkel Martin because they'd tell me it would be too risky and dangerous and might cause trouble for all of us.

Silently Mutti handed me the money for the trip, adding, "And don't let her ask for more. If she does, she can pay for it or you stay home."

I hastily took the money and gave her a peck on the cheek. "Thanks Mutti." And out the door I went before Mutti could say another word.

Soon after, I packed a small suitcase. Nervous but curious, I said good-bye to Mutti and Onkel Martin, both reminding me to be careful. "Berlin is a big city. Don't do anything foolish, like crossing the border!"

"I'll be fine. Don't worry." With suitcase in one hand, a brown paper bag containing my sandwiches for the train trip in my purse, I was ready to explore Berlin.

Because several FDJ groups were traveling from Goerlitz, all members and leaders met in the vestibule of the deserted train station. Then, in groups, we walked into the tunnel and up the stairs to the platform where the empty train was waiting. The platforms—five of them—were empty and looked forlorn. There were no uniformed stationmasters. No hissing and rumbling trains. No happy travelers shouting and waving. There was no activity—none. This was the end of the line. Trains couldn't travel further east because in 1945 after WW II ended, Goerlitz became a divided border city.

Beyond the platforms, I saw railroad cars, rusted and forgotten, sitting on tracks with weed and grass growing around them. The switch master's red brick tower was deserted, its windows broken, hanging from their hinges on the outside of the tower. The red bricks scarred with bullet holes brought back the memory of shooting planes.

Our voices echoed from the arched glass ceiling, supported by black iron rafters and pillars that spanned the five platforms. Many of its glass panes were shattered, in jagged sections ready to drop—sad reminders of the war and of what a grand train station it once had been.

How different this trip is, I thought. *The last time I rode the train was after I had visited my family in Goerlitz. How happy I had been visiting Oma, Mutti and Christa. How sad I was when I returned to my stepmother, who was waiting for me at the train station in Kohlfurt.* But leaving Goerlitz this time, there is no stepmother I had to return to—only a trip to Berlin.

A lot had happened since then. All our lives had changed dramatically. But we were young, the war was behind us, so we sang and laughed as the train rolled on. I glanced out the window as we traveled. Some farms lay in ruins, deserted, while others were only partially damaged or not at all. People lived and worked the land, only to have their crops confiscated by the East German Government, leaving the farmers just enough food to survive. Still, they had more food then what was allocated for the people in the cities. The factories, that hadn't been destroyed, were working, but few of their products were in any East German stores. Although the war had ended six years ago, in every town we passed destruction and devastation were still visible. Houses lay in rubble, roofs hanging precarious, ready to collapse, leaving nothing then a deserted shell with no sign of reconstruction.

What should have been a three-hour trip to Berlin, took eight hours because of stops along the way, either to pick up additional troops or by moving our train on to a sidetrack so other trains could pass. Ones in Berlin we changed to busses, which took us to our assigned quarters for the four-day stay, in the attic of an apartment building where layers of straw covered the floor. We received two blankets each: one to lay over the straw, one to cover up with. We piled bunches of straw underneath the blanket to make a pillow. Every day we were handed our ration of bread, a ring of smoked hard salami, and milk. What I couldn't eat, I tucked away in my suitcase to take home; in time, my clothes and I smelled like walking salami. I don't remember where we washed or ate a hot meal, only sleeping in that hot attic. We were left to our own devices, for our leader only showed up to pass out rations or to gather us to march in the parade. I managed to avoid participating in the parade all but one time; because our leader was so disorganized she didn't even know when some of us were missing. She never asked me where I'd been or why I was missing. I would have had a simple answer, "I got lost."

Then, one evening one of the girls who slept next to me whispered, "Have you been to the *other side* yet?"

"No," I whispered back.

"I have. It's easy. Just take the *U-Bahn*, the underground subway, and don't wear the FDJ uniform. If you do, you stick out." Ending with, "and I never told you anything. You know what I mean?"

"Don't worry. I understand." We didn't talk again.

Because I wasn't well acquainted with the girls in my group, it was easy for me to leave, to explore the other side. The day after the parade, right after receiving our rations I took off, my heart pounding with anxiety. I didn't ride the *U-Bahn*. I wanted to save my money and I wasn't afraid of getting lost. I had also overheard other girl's whisper that we were not far from the street or border dividing East Berlin from West Berlin, and marked by warning signs. I decided to walk in the general direction of the West Sector by taking several side streets where apartment buildings three and four stories high had been reduced to piles of rubble. Jagged house walls stretched into the air, some with partial floors still attached. I saw what had been a bathroom, the fixtures still in the wall, the tub standing at the edge where the floor hadn't totally broken away. I could see the wallpaper the occupants had in their rooms. There was even broken furniture on some floors, bleached and warped from the elements. Some of the ruins looked like roofless dollhouses, their fronts crudely torn away, with holes where windows had been, exposing sloping hanging floors and partial staircases. In some ruins the rubble had been piled to one side, revealing a gaping black hole that led to a basement. I asked myself, *were they found alive?* I felt a deep sorrow for the people and their children who had lived in those apartment houses, for the ones who'd been killed in basements or on their way to the basement because the planes were coming fast and furious. I, too, had sat in the basement, in Kohlfurt and in Zittau, but it did not compare to what these people and their children endured. Looking at the ruins, thinking of the people who'd lived here, I thought, *How horrified they must have been to hear the deep droning of the low oncoming planes loaded with bombs, knowing what will happen as the planes came closer and closer, dropping their bombs. The horrific explosions, the vibrations, the tremors shaking the apartment houses as the bombs where hitting the ground. How mothers must have tried to comfort their children while listening to the whistling of the falling bombs. They must have sat fearful and powerless, afraid of being hit and killed while sitting in a basement.*

Looking at the ruins, I could see their fears had come true. These ruins were like hallowed ground to me. They were ghostlike, eerie to look at. I couldn't understand the enormity of what had taken place here and elsewhere. I never had had to endure such horrific bombing attacks, but I had felt the vibrations if only from a distance, heard the sounds and seen the fiery red and yellow explosions while I was lying in a ditch watching the bombing of Zittau. Feeling the fear that hovered like a ghost over the rubble, I was thankful to Vati for keeping me alive and away from such gruesome attacks. I walked on, sad, but glad to be alive.

Shortly, I came to the street that was the border between East and West Berlin. Just as I heard the girls tell, there were big white wooden signs, with black lettering, warning pedestrians they were leaving East Berlin. I stopped at the corner and looked carefully up and down the street. I almost stopped breathing when I saw a Russian and a German MP with rifles, patrolling the dividing street. They were stopped and had their backs to me, so they didn't see me. In fear the might come walking up the street, discovering me, asking me what I was doing here, I dove into the nearest cover I could find. It was an entrance to what used to be an apartment building but now was only an arch without a house door. The rest was in ruin. There I waited. After what seemed a lifetime of waiting, slowly, I made my way to the corner again and when I peeked I saw them walking further down the street. Now was my chance. My heart in my throat, I hurried across the street to West Berlin. Then, I ran down the street to the next corner, looking back to see if I had drawn anyone's attention. I hadn't.

Feeling safe, I slowed to catch my breath and to calm myself. Knees shaking, my heart aflutter, I leaned against a pole that once had been a gas lantern. All I could think was, *I made it!* I actually made it to the *other side*—West Berlin. Mutti had warned me not to go, because of the danger of getting caught by the Russian and German MP. But here I was! People were walking, passing me, but I felt like a trespasser, a foreigner in a land forbidden to me by my government. Leaning against the pole I looked around. No one was paying attention to me, not even a glance. No one seemed to care about an East German girl who had just sneaked across the border. *Maybe they don't mind.* I thought. Shaking off my fears, my spirits high, I walked down the street lined with new looking three and four story apartment buildings, some with stores. I was ready to explore, but not ready for what I would see.

The first store I came too made my eyes pop. It was a small grocery store, it's awning stretched out for protection from the sun. In front of its big window was a stand holding several small wooden crates, each displaying different fruits and vegetables. Oranges were nestled in long wood shavings, red apples were snuggled in frilly paper cups, and bananas lay neatly row by row like small humpback whales in crates lined with green paper. Last were the crates of tomatoes, carrots, lettuce, and vegetables I had never seen before. I stood rooted. People walked around me and shopped, as I gazed at the abundance of food.

I raised my eyes to the big store window. I could not believe what I saw behind the glass: On different levels, covered with a beige cloth that fell in big folds, were boxes of chocolates with big colorful bows. Sitting in fake green grass were big and small chocolate ladybugs, covered in red foil with black polka dots. Chocolate bars of all sizes were stacked in pyramids in-between the cloth's folds. Glass jars of candies sat on lower mounds. They too, had, big bows on top. And close to the window sat tiny baskets filled with colorful fruits and vegetables made from *Marzipan.* Tilted on the tallest mound, their lids slightly open, were beautiful decorated canisters filled with cookies and chocolates—ready for gift giving. Colors exploded in my head. I soaked up the warm scent of fresh fruit. From the open store door, the sweet smell of chocolate laced with the aroma of coffee tickled my nose like an unseen veil.

I had reached *Schlaraffenland,* the land of plenty. Now I knew what the whispering was about. It was true. The people living in West Berlin and West Germany had food and lots of it. Standing there staring, my eyes wandered back to the humpback bananas. It had been so long since I had eaten a banana that I only faintly remembered the taste. I wanted to buy a banana, but I couldn't recall how to peel it—properly.

"Na, kleines Fraeulein kann ich Ihnen helfen?" "Na, little lady can I help you?" Startled, I turned my head to see who was talking to me. A middle-aged man with sparkling eyes and a smile was standing next to me.

"*Nein Danke!*" I uttered.

But he was not discouraged. "You're from the East, aren't you? You're here for the competition!" His eyes looked me over as he spoke. Not knowing how to answer, afraid to tell him that he had guessed right, not wanting to be rude, I said the first thing that came into my mind. "I'd like to buy a banana."

"A banana!" Walking over to the box of bananas, he broke one off, leaving a hole in the humpbacks line-up, and handed it to me. "Here you are!" I handed him the money, but he stepped back with his hands up. "No, I don't want your money. East German money has no value here."

Embarrassed, I curtsied and said, "*Danke schoen!*" Hoping he'd go back inside his store.

He didn't. Instead he called to his wife. "Look who we have here, *ein kleines Fraeulein* from East Germany." I stood shy and speechless. I wanted to eat my banana, slowly turning it, not wanting anyone to know how unsure I was about which of the two ends was the appropriate one to break a banana open.

His wife came out of the store. "Oh, how nice." She clapped her hands in delight. Coming closer she asked, "What's your name? And where is your home? Is this the first time you're in West Berlin? Come into the store with me. I have something for you." Not waiting for an answer, she took my arm and led me into the store, where she walked behind her counter. The store was packed with dry goods, almost to the ceiling. Every shelf was neat and clean and, oh, there was more chocolate! Behind the counter, off to one side, sat a gleaming copper grinder, filling the air with the scent of freshly ground coffee. Good smells were everywhere, bringing back long ago, and almost forgotten memories. I wished Mutti and Oma could be here to see all the food and to smell the good coffee.

The woman kept talking as she busied herself behind the counter. Then, the man said, "Mother, let the girl eat her banana. She's been holding it for a while." Bashful and embarrassed, I looked at my banana, thinking, *I don't know where to start.*

"You look a little puzzled," the man said. Then he smiled, as if he had just realized why I was not eating the banana. "Here, let me help you. You haven't seen a banana for a long time. Right?" I just nodded, not able to speak. This was more than I had expected. He peeled the banana half way, handing it back to me with the peels hanging limp like broken propellers. Again I curtsied, forgetting that I had decided not to curtsy anymore. *But these people were so nice and kind, how could I not?*

When I had eaten my banana, which tasted just as I had faintly remembered, the lady handed me two big *Schokoladen-Tafeln,* chocolate bars. "Here," she said, "take them home with you and share them with your family. We know that all of you poor people *da drueben,* over there," tilting her head in the general direction of East Germany, "have hardly any food. You're being starved to death by the Russians, and the sad part is, no one is doing anything about it."

She reminded me of Mutti, and I didn't know how to answer her. So I smiled at her, curtsied and said, *"Danke Schoen,"* while I put the chocolate bars in my purse.

In the meantime, a lady about the same age as the owners came in. It seemed that the owners and the lady were well acquainted because "Mother," as her husband called her, told the lady I was from the East, from Goerlitz, and here for the Youth Rally in East Berlin. That put the lady in action. Facing me she asked, "Are you hungry? When have you eaten last? You come home with me and I'll feed you some good food. Food that you don't have over there." Without an answer from me, she started to shop. "Do you drink coffee or do you want *Kakao*, hot chocolate?"

"I can't go home with you. I have to go back again," I finally stuttered.

"Yes, I know you have to be back before nightfall, but first you go home with me." Putting her hand on my shoulder, facing me, she explained. "The people of West Berlin have been asked when we meet a youngster from East Germany participating in the Youth Rally to feed them, so you'll be my guest."

"Yes," Mother from behind the counter added, "that's right. That's what we were asked to do. You can go with her. She's a long time friend and customer of ours. You have no need to be afraid." Then, back she went to the business at hand. The woman, too, returned to her shopping. For her the matter was settled. I was still hesitant, but seeing all that food, I felt my stomach wake up, making little growling noises.

Mother and the woman were busy. The woman gave orders about what she wanted, and Mother went back and forth weighing different cheeses, wrapping each in white paper that she ripped with a "s-s-s-ssid" from the big paper roll attached to a holder. The final purchase was coffee that Mother ground with the gleaming copper grinder, then put in a see-through little bag, set on the scale, and finally closed with a narrow brown ribbon. The shopping was done and the lady paid. Several small white packages lay on the counter, one for each of the different freshly sliced cheeses. Butter, coffee, chocolate powder, oranges, banana and more chocolates lay beside them.

Placing some of the packages in a shopping net she pulled from her big handbag, the lady then handed it to me, and said, "Here, you can help me carry this. On the way home, we'll stop at the butcher's and the baker's, just down the street from here." Although I wanted to eat the food she had bought, I still was unsure. I didn't have the courage to tell her that I should go back over the border instead of going home with her.

Mother came from behind the counter to shake my hand, wishing me luck for a safe crossing to the other side. She said, "Before you go back, enjoy your afternoon with our friend and, most of all, enjoy the food. And don't worry. She's a very nice person." The man, placing his hand in a fatherly manner on my shoulder agreed with Mother. It seemed that my fate was sealed. All I could do was to say, *Danke Schoen,* and to curtsy once more.

With a wave and one last look, the lady and I said, *"Auf Wiedersehn,"* and left the little shop leaving Mother and her husband behind. Our next stop was the butcher's, a few steps from the little grocery store. There, the lady told the butcher and his wife that I was from Goerlitz, and here for the Youth Rally in East Berlin. "I met her at the grocer's, her name is Gisela and she is my guest this afternoon."

When the butcher, his tummy round beneath his white apron, heard I was from Goerlitz, he said, "I know Goerlitz. During the war, before I was sent to Russia, I was stationed in Goerlitz, but I heard that the garrison is on the Polish side now. I remember Goerlitz as a beautiful city, with very interesting architecture, and word in the garrison was that Goerlitz had the best-looking girls anywhere around." With a wink at his wife, he continued, "and they were right." After a statement like that the joking reply always is, *"It's that good water from the Neisse River!"* Embarrassed, I just nodded my head lightly. The butcher shook my hand and wished me a safe border crossing, then told his wife to wrap up an extra sausage. Again, I curtsied with a, *"Danke Schoen."* The lady said *"Auf Wiedersehn"* and we left the butcher's shop to walk across the street to the baker's.

At the baker's, we weren't greeted only by the owner from behind the counter, but by the suiting aroma of sweet pastries and fresh baked breads. I wanted to immerse myself in those sweet smells. My eyes roamed over loaves of white and dark bread neatly stacked on clean shelves along the wall behind the counter. Big wicker baskets were filled with crispy breakfast rolls—with or without poppy seeds—and an array of cakes and tortes set on the counter behind a low glass panel. All I saw was food, food, and more food. Every store I had been in was filled with food. No one was using food stamps. Here it was money only. It felt as if I was in a different country, only we spoke the same language.

And just as the butcher's when the lady said I was from Goerlitz and here for the Youth-Rally in East Berlin, the baker-lady added an extra sweet roll for me and said, "I'd like to give you a loaf of bread to take home. We know you have no food over there." Again she gave a backward nod towards the east as she continued, "Hitler's war cut our homeland in two, and now we have to stand by and watch, unable to help our countrymen and families who have to live under Stalin with barely enough food to survive." I didn't know what to say, but I realized the people in the West didn't like the Russians. Still, I didn't voice my opinion because in East Germany we weren't allowed to criticize the government. So I listened as she leaned over the counter towards me and continued, "I understand your silence. You're trained to fear the Soviets, but believe me, those commies don't go hungry like the rest of you."

"We'd better be on our way," my hostess intervened. "You must be hungry. It's just a little further down street." With a polite, *"Danke Schoen,"* a curtsy from me, and, *"Auf Wiedersehn,"* we left the bakery shop.

The lady lived on the second floor in an apartment building. Her apartment was small, clean and inviting. She pulled out a chair, asking me to sit while she brought plates, cups, saucers, silverware, and napkins to the table. Then, came a platter with the lunchmeats and cheeses, a butter dish, a small glass jar of mustard and the basket with heated hard rolls. A platter of different cream cakes from the bakery finished the setting. All the while she talked. "Would you like coffee or *Kakao?*" Talking to herself she said, "Oh, I'll just make both. Then, you can have what you like best."

While she was busy going between the kitchen and the living room I had a chance to observe her. She never told me her name and it was impolite for me to ask. She was not very tall, not too slender, with graying hair, caring eyes, and a kind voice, maybe a little older than Mutti. When finally she joined me at the table, she said, "Now, you eat what you want and as much as you want and take your time. My son will be home soon. He'll take you safely back over the border via the underground subway. Do you know the address where you're staying?" I only nodded because my mouth was full of food.

Seating herself, she said, "I've been doing all the talking. Now it's your turn."

I quickly swallowed, then said, "You have so much food! Stores are filled with food of all kinds! You have real coffee! Chocolate! And all kinds of fruits and no food stamps!"

"Yes, we have plenty now. Food stamps were discontinued in 1950 but, even than, we still had more then what you have in the *Ost-Zone,* the East-Zone. But there was a time when the people in West Berlin didn't have any food—even the Allied troops were affected by it."

Surprised, I looked at her. "Yes, it's true." Leaning back and taking a sip of coffee, she continued, "It started in April of 1948 when Stalin and the Western Allies got into differences. The Western Allies—Great Britain,

France, and the U.S.—wanted to reunite and rebuild Germany. Stalin didn't agree. Because of these differences, Stalin tried to get the Western Allies out of West Berlin, to claim the whole of Berlin for his eastern block.

Because West Berlin is an island sitting in the middle of East Germany, Stalin planned to cut West Berlin off from all food and fuel supplies. He ordered that all trains coming from the western Zone, traveling through the Russian occupied block, carrying food and fuel to West Berlin, be stopped and, under Soviet armed guard, returned to West Germany. He also closed all land and waterways. We were cut off. No more food supplies got to West Berlin. It was a difficult time and we feared we would be taken over by the Soviets."

Taking another swallow from her coffee, she continued, "That's when the U.S. started the Airlift. At the beginning it was slow until they got organized. Planes from the western sector came flying in all day long until late at night. It was a continuous droning of planes overhead, not with bombs but with food. The people living here helped unload the planes. Neither the Russians scare tactics of shooting at them nor bad weather stopped the planes. Although food and fuel were strictly rationed, we were glad for whatever we got, but mostly happy that the Allies didn't give in to Stalin's demand. Operation Airlift was a success, but, sadly, American and British airmen lost their lives."

"How is that?" I wanted to know

"The Airlift continued over the winter with bad weather contributing to plane crashes."

Mesmerized by her story because I had never heard of the Airlift, I asked, "Do you still have the Airlift?"

"No it's over. It lasted a year before Stalin finally gave up in 1949, realizing that he wasn't going to win. Since then, we have started to rebuild our West Berlin."

"You're lucky you don't have to live under the Russians. They don't help us. We still have ruins and rubble in East Germany.

"We know they don't help. They take everything out to Russia, leaving you people with the bare minimum. I see the sadness in people's eyes, the empty stores, and the lines for food. I see it all when I visit my family in the east sector when smuggling small amounts of foods to them."

"Can I ask you something?"

"Sure you can."

"Were you here in Berlin during the bombing and air raids?"

"At the beginning the children and I were, but then we left. We fled to the country and lived with a farmer's family where I worked for our stay. If we hadn't, we wouldn't be alive today, because Berlin had over three hundred air raids."

"Three hundred?"

"Yes, over three hundred."

"But where was your husband?" I was thinking that he must have been with her and the children, like Vati was with me, but when a shadow went over her face, I felt bad for having asked her.

"My husband is still missing somewhere in Russia."

"Oh I am sorry. I lost my father right after the war, and Oma has a son who is still missing in Russia too."

"Yes, we all lost loved ones. But let's not talk about sad things anymore. I want you to eat."

Holding my stomach, I said, "Thank you, but I can't eat anymore. Everything tasted so good. I will remember you and this for a long time."

"I wish you could take some home with you, to Goerlitz."

"Thank you, but I can't. It'll get me in trouble."

"Before you return home to Goerlitz, you need to have a walk along *"Kurfuersten-Damm"*, our famous fashionable boulevard. I'm sure you've heard of it."

"Yes, I have heard of it." Looking at the clock, realizing it was getting late, I said, "I have to get back over the border before I'll be missed. Thank you so much for having me."

While we had been talking, her son, attractive and a bit older than I, had arrived. His mother told him to take me back over the border. The lady wished me a safe crossing and, shaking my hand, she put something in it explaining, "It's just a little contribution towards your stroll on the *Kurfuersten-Damm*. Maybe you'll find something nice." I didn't want to take the money because it embarrassed me. No one had ever given me money, but she insisted. Turning to her son, she told him to point out which subway I needed to take to get to the *Kurfuersten-Damm*, or *Ku'damm* for short, the following day. One more curtsy with many thank you's, I left with her son. While riding the subway, he showed me on a map above the window which direction I had to take to the Ku'damm. After we got off, he walked me close to the street where I stayed. I was glad he saved me from walking in the late evening hours along the ruins or meeting a guard patrol. When we shook hands and said "Auf Wiedersehn," I thanked him for bringing me safely over the border, but this time I didn't curtsy.

The following morning, after receiving our ration I was on my way to explore Berlin's famous boulevard, the *Kurfuestendamm,* Germany's fashionably boulevard, dating back to 1885. Since the split of Germany, the *Ku'damm* had seldom been mentioned in East Germany. According to our communist teaching, the capitalists of the western world dominate West Berlin and West Germany and capitalism is bad. Bad or not, my mind was made up to explore capitalism and the *Ku'damm*.

While on my way to the U-Bahn, I was thinking about the conversation the lady's son and I had when he walked me to my quarters the previous night.

"I overheard my mother suggesting you should visit the *Ku'damm* before you go home. Are you going to?"

"Yes, I'm anxious to see what it's all about."

"You'll like it. There's a lot to see, but be careful. Don't talk to strangers, most of all not men. You could end up in places you don't want to be."

"What do you mean by places I don't want to be?"

He stopped walking, and said, "Let's just say it's not Goerlitz but Berlin, a big city with lots of happenings. West Berlin is a free city where anything goes." Stepping a little closer and looking down at me, he asked, "Do you understand what I'm trying to tell you?"

I didn't want him to think that I was an inexperienced girl from Goerlitz. "Why would I want to talk to strangers? They don't scare me. Besides, I have no intention of speaking to strangers."

Unimpressed, he shrugged his shoulders, "I'm just saying, don't talk to strange men no matter how gentlemen-like they seem! You're a good-looking young girl with innocence written all over you." I blushed both at the compliment and at what he was trying to tell me.

Thinking back on how embarrassing and amusing our conversation had been, I must have had a smile on my face, because as people passed me, some smiled back. Lowering my head and looking serious, I walked down the stairs to the U-Bahn station in the east sector to purchase a round trip ticket to the *Ku'damm* with my East German money. I was nervous because I didn't know if I would be asked what I wanted on the *Ku'damm*. But the uniformed man behind the window who took my money never said a word, other than the usual *"Guten Tag."* He gave me the ticket, and with a friendly *"Danke Schoen"* from me, I left the window, thinking it must not be unusual for people to ride the U-Bahn to the west sector of Berlin.

At the platform where I waited to catch the U-Bahn the odor of diesel surrounded me, the smell of big city life. Trains came rushing out of dark tunnels in both directions, then stopped. Doors opened and closed; people poured in and out as the trains disappeared in those black tunnels again, leaving a tail of diesel odor behind. I stood and took in the noise, the rush of air from the fast moving trains that passed me pulling me into the life of the city. I liked it. After a few stops it was my turn to get off the *U-Bahn*. Excited, I walked up the steps to set my feet on Berlin's famous boulevard.

I stopped and looked around as people passed me. The Ku'damm is a broad and specious street, divided by a wide grassy center strip with trees and benches and traffic on both sides, like one-way streets. No ruins were left, only clean open spaces. Rebuilding was everywhere. The only ruin left standing, pointing to heaven like a half-broken finger, was the bell tower of the *Kaiser-Wilhelm Gedaechtniskirche*, a church built in the 1890's.

Young girls wearing high heels, fashionable dresses, carrying small leather handbags, walking, laughing, and talking to their friends, gave me awkward passing glances. I knew they knew by my dress and shoes that I was from the Russian sector. I stood staring, feeling out of place, envious of their clothing. Maybe the lady's son's advice was not necessary. I could see I was not dressed to arouse any interest—only sideways glances. Ignoring the glances, I walked along the boulevard. There was so much to see. I stopped at shoe-store-windows, my eyes aglow over the colors and stiles of lady's shoes made with real leather and suede, as if they competed with each other. Fancy dress shops with window mannequins wearing colorful dresses, shoes and handbags to match, posed as if to say, "See, we get to wear these beautiful dresses and you don't." Jewelry stores, displayed expensive rings, necklaces, and watches. I saw Flower shops nestled next to expensive china and crystal stores. At sidewalk cafés, people sat at marble tables under colorful umbrellas, having coffee, eating cake, sipping cognac or drinking beer, talking, laughing, and enjoying life. I stood and gaped at all those beautiful things, so different from what we had in East Germany. I asked myself *"How come these people live in such abundance and we don't? Aren't we all Germans? Is this what the communists call capitalism? I wouldn't mind being part of it—living in it."*

Seeing the prices, I knew I couldn't afford much even with the money from the lady, but I didn't give up hope. I had to find something to take home. My mind and eyes were focused on shoes, pretty ones, not available in East Germany. Watching and checking, I discovered a rack outside a shoe store filled with shoes and a sign that said "Summer Sale". Like other pedestrians, I, too, looked through the shoes, my eyes zeroing in on a pair of open-toed, white leather sandals with a two-inch wedge heel. The top of the sandal was made of an intricate lace pattern while the back extended above the ankle with a small buckle closure around the ankle. I had to have those shoes! When I looked at the sale price, I realized I was a couple of West Marks short, but I had East German money. Shoes in one hand, courage in the other, I entered the shoe store, where an elderly man in a suit and tie approached me. "Can I help you?"

"Ja, uhmm . . . I would like to buy these shoes, and I'd need to . . . ."

"That is a very nice sandal. Please, be seated, while I get the second one for you." And off he went, returning shortly with a box containing the other sandal. From underneath my chair he pulled out a low stool, like a footstool for him to sit on. Then, he removed my fake leather East German shoes and replaced them with the leather sandals, telling me that I had good taste, how nice the sandals looked on my feet, and how much I would enjoy wearing them.

I, red faced with embarrassment, not wanting to tell him that the sandals slightly pinched, not to mention my money situation, just sat, staring at my feet, realizing that I should never have come in or even let him put those sandals on my feet since I didn't have enough money in my pocket to pay for them. The man waited patiently for me to make a decision, then finally asked, "Don't you like the sandals?"

I knew I had to do something and in a low voice so no one would hear I said, "Oh . . . I like the sandals very much, but I don't have enough West Marks. Can I pay the rest in East German money?"

Smiling as if he already knew what my problem was he said, "Tell you what. I don't want your money. It has no value and causes more trouble than it's worth. You give me what you have in West Marks, and the rest is a gift from me to you." I was overjoyed! I had bought a pair of shoes in the West from the capitalists.

I gave the man what West Marks I had. He handed me the sandals without the box and said, "Stuff them in your purse because if you happen to run into the East German border patrol in the U-Bahn, and they see you're coming from the West Sector with a package, they will want to know what you have and possibly take them from you."

"There are guards on the subway?"

"Yes, but you can't tell because they're in civilian clothing watching people coming from the West Sector carrying packages over to East Berlin."

We shook hands, the man wishing me a safe crossing. My old shoes back on my feet, the new ones stuffed in my purse and an ever so slight curtsy, I said *"Auf Wiedersehn und Danke Schoen."*

While riding the U-Bahn back to East Berlin, I scrutinized every man, wondering if he were an East German border guard. After several stops, I got off the subway, relieved to have had no mishaps. When I arrived at the quarters, the girl who slept next to me told me in a low tone, "You just missed our troop leader. She asked if we knew where you and some of the others were, but we told her we didn't know. We'll be leaving tomorrow morning at 6:00 a.m. She asked us to pass it along because she isn't coming back tonight." With a conspiratorial look, she added, "I'd just gotten back myself when she came to check on us."

"Thanks for letting me know." I felt bad for being short with her, but I knew when we got home, I would never see her again, so I wasn't too quick to start new friendships.

Not to be too obvious, I took my new shoes from my purse and put them in the suitcase next to the brown paper wrapped salami. Then I put my head on the straw pillow and went to sleep.

The next morning we were up at five. We cleaned our area, except for the straw, and were downstairs by six. While waiting for the bus, we received rolls and jam with coffee—not the good coffee like the lady had, but the kind Oma made from roasted wheat.

Soon we were on the train bound for home. The trip took all day as we moved at a slow pace because of stops and waits, and for groups to get off. We were tired and glad when the train pulled in at the end of the track because the Goerlitzer groups were the last ones to get off. I was glad to be home again and then not, because I had seen what living in the *West* was like and wished we, too, had food and were free of communism and the Russians.

When I got home and had hugged Mutti and Onkel Martin, I was anxious to unpack the salami, the chocolate bars, and my capitalist purchase. Mutti was glad about the salami, but the chocolate bars and my shoes made her forehead wrinkle. "I thought I asked you not to go over to West Berlin?"

Onkel Martin, laughing, said, "Lenchen, you didn't think that the kids wouldn't sneak over to West Berlin, when they're so close!"

Glad Onkel Martin made light of Mutti's question, I said, "I know you asked me not to, but Mutti, I wasn't the only one. I think almost everyone sneaked over to West Berlin—only we didn't tell each other."

"Just because they do, that's no reason for you to do the same. Didn't the leader miss any of you?"

"No, she didn't stay with us or even pay much attention to us."

"What about the marching? Isn't that why you kids went?"

"Our troop marched once and then only for a very short time. The whole thing was so disorganized. I don't know why we went, but I'm glad we did because I was able to see West Berlin."

Sitting down at the table, I told Mutti and Onkel Martin about the invitation from the lady. "You went to some strange woman's house?" Mutti asked horrified.

"She was a nice lady, a bit older than you." Mutti shook her head. "That was risky. A good thing I didn't know."

"At the beginning I wasn't sure either but the food won out. The lady was very nice, and so was her son who walked me back to my quarters. The lady told me about the food and fuel shortage and how the western allies flew supplies into West Berlin from West Germany, because the Russians stopped their supply trains. She called it an airlift. Have you heard of it?" Mutti and Onkel Martin nodded their heads. "We've heard. Our media told us that Stalin was trying to protect the people in West Berlin from the western allies and their corrupt ways."

Onkel Martin added, "Controlled by Stalin, our government invited the people from West Berlin to shop with their food stamps in the East Sector. It didn't work. They didn't shop in East Berlin because they didn't want communism. But we were not told any of that. Only through whispers did we hear about the Airlift and Stalin's real reason—he wanted the allies out of West Berlin. Then, the allies would have no reason to cross through the Russian occupied territory of East Germany. But his plan failed. The West is once more crossing through East Germany to bring supplies to West Berlin." Listening to Onkel Martin, he sounded happy that Stalin didn't win.

"How come I never knew?"

"That's because you're too busy with your own life and dancing, and, as Onkel Martin explained, it was all in whispers." Mutti said while she handed me an opened envelope. "A letter came from the LO-WA, your locksmith apprenticeship, your health coverage has run out, which means no more monthly benefits. You are unemployed now and could apply for unemployment benefits or better yet, find a new job, and soon."

Like a balloon losing air, I exhaled, "Yes, I know. I just don't know what kind of a job I want."

"Go to the unemployment office; they'll find something for you," Onkel Martin encouraged me.

Trying to change the subject, I asked Mutti, "So how do you like my capitalist shoes?"

"Why do you call them capitalist shoes?"

"Simple, I bought them from the capitalist sector," I happily replied.

"They're very pretty and nice for when you go out dancing. Don't wear them when you apply for a job. The person at the employment office or your future employer, if they're strong communists, could see you've been in the West and you could miss a job opportunity." For Mutti the subject was closed. Picking up the chocolate bars, she said, "Tomorrow on your way to the unemployment office, take one to Oma." Tired, I nodded my head and said, "Gute Nacht" and went to bed—not ready to face job-hunting.

The next morning, Mutti roused me from sleep. I made my way to the kitchen where Mutti had warm water, my toothbrush and a towel waiting for me. After breakfast, Mutti and Onkel Martin went to work, but not before I was told my duties: stopping at Oma's, but most of all, looking for a job. "Don't wear the shoes!" Mutti once more warned me.

After doing the breakfast dishes, the beds, and general pick-up, I went to see Oma. I told her about my trip and handed her the chocolate bar. At first she didn't want to take it, but then she changed her mind, saying, "I'll share it with little Rainer." I knew then Oma wasn't going to eat any of it.

Sitting upstairs in Oma's room, looking unhappy, I heard Oma ask, "What's wrong? You look as if the cat has eaten your breakfast this morning."

"Mutti told me I have to look for a job."

"Oh, that's not an unreasonable request. We all have to work. And when you're done working and retired, well, then you're old like me."

"Oma, you're not old."

"That's what you say, but I am, and that's the way it is. Don't go around sulking. You just make yourself unhappy. We've had and still have enough unhappiness to last us for the rest of our lives. You're young and free. Have fun and enjoy life while you can. The seriousness of life will catch up with you soon enough." Looking at me, she said, "Some day you'll remember my words."

"But I don't know what kind of work I should be looking for."

"You'll find something. We're the working class with no special education, with no opportunity or choice to be anything else because of how we have to live and survive. I always thought you should have finished the eighth grade. It's not good to drop out early just because you were fourteen, but you convinced your mother and she agreed. Maybe you could've gotten a better apprenticeship than the one you had. Now you're sixteen, too late to start a new apprenticeship. I'm sure, you'll find a job."

"I hate to start new jobs and meet new people."

"You'll be fine. It'll work out. You'll see. I remember my first real job, in a mental hospital. Talk about scared, I was only sixteen."

"You worked in a nuthouse?"

Oma shrugged her shoulders. "I wouldn't call it that. It was a hospital for mentally ill people. It was a sad place, but some patients were rather entertaining because of the crazy things they did."

"Then you were a nurse like Mutti."

"No, just a worker doing the dirty work, mainly cleaning up after the patients and doing jobs the nurses didn't do, like bedpans and so forth."

"Yogh," I said, crinkling up my face, picturing myself carrying stinky bedpans, my stomach revolting, "That I'm not going to do. Mutti tried to get me interested in nursing. Not me! Never!"

"It's not for every one," Oma agreed.

"I'd better go, Oma. I'll let you know if I find a job and what kind."

"Yes I, too, have to go downstairs to help Tante Hilde with the children, and you can say "Guten Tag" to her before you leave?"

I walked over to where Oma was sitting and gave her a hug and a peck on her wrinkled cheek. Then, we both went downstairs to our former apartment where Tante Hilde and Onkel Heinz were living now. I stayed for just a minute. Then I was gone—job hunting.

I found a job that same day. The unemployment office sent me to a small factory that produced handmade lampshades. After the interview, the tall, young, handsome manager dressed in suit and tie, told me to report for work the following Monday. Then, I filled out the necessary papers and he signed them. I was hired. I returned to the unemployment office to verify my hire, canceling my unemployment pay.

When I got home, Mutti was preparing our evening meal. "Did you look for a job?"

"Yes. I'll start work on Monday morning at a lampshade-factory on the *Luisen-Strasse.*"

"That's just a couple of minutes from where we live! How did you get that job so fast?"

Mutti seemed glad, but I shrugged my shoulders. "I guess I was at the unemployment office just at the right time. The factory manager told me they already have two other girls my age working there, but the majority of workers are older women."

Getting plates and silverware, Mutti turned to me. "Here, you can set the table. We're ready to eat."

Watching me setting the table, Onkel Martin said, "See, I told you you'd find something."

"Yes," I grumbled while I sat down to eat. "I'm nervous. I know my stomach will be flip-flopping again. I wish the first day was behind me."

Mutti and Onkel Martin chorused, "You'll be fine. The first day is difficult for everyone."

I thought, *"Yeah, I've heard that before!"*

Monday morning came. My stomach flip-flopping, I walked to my new job. When I checked in at the office, the manager said, "I am not able to walk you through our factory, but your supervisor will. Let's go up to the second floor so you can meet her and your co-workers."

Dry mouthed, I followed. We entered a big room where women sat at long tables quietly talking while working. In a low voice the manager said, "May I have your attention, please?" The busy hum stopped. I felt as if a thousand eyes were looking at me. "This is *Fraeulein Knebel*, our new employee." Some heads nodded an unspoken "Hello." Then, the supervisor, a middle-aged woman, approached, and the manager told her to walk me through the building.

It was a small factory with the office on the bottom floor. In the workroom on the second floor, is where the women sat facing each other at six extra long tables, hand sewing material or precut panels onto pre-formed lampshade frames. Across the hall was the painting room with a large noisy fan for ventilation. Three painters with spray guns filled with green, red, blue, brown, yellow and black paint sprayed flower patterns on the panels of the finished lampshades. To give some of the lampshades an antique look, the painters used a color mixture of light and dark browns. Then, all lampshades were sprayed with a clear topcoat.

After drying in the adjacent dry-room, they were packed in crush proof containers, stored in the stockroom, to wait for shipment. On the third floor was the women's lunchroom and a supply and storage room. After meeting everyone, I realized the three painters and the manager were the only male employees.

Back in the workroom, the supervisor pointed to one of the ladies. "I want you to sit next to her and watch so you learn the work we do here. Tomorrow I'll have you sit with someone else."

For the next several days I sat, watched, and listened. The lampshades were of different sizes, from nightstand lampshades, to floor lampshades, and ceiling lampshades. The materials used varied, from plastic to strong cardboard to a cream-colored silk-like material. Whoever I sat next to explained and showed me what their particular job entailed. I barely lifted my head. Everyone was so serious, not like the locksmith girls, always joking and laughing. Just as the manager had said, there were two girls my age, and sometimes when I glanced up, they smiled.

Every day when I got home, Mutti asked, "How was your day? Did you talk to the girls yet?"

"No, I haven't. The supervisor isn't having me sit with the girls."

Mutti nodded her head, as if to agree with the supervisor. "She knows you girls would be talking and not working. What are their names?"

"Renate and Brigitte. I think they're friends and I don't want to get between them."

"You'll be friends in time. You still have Erna, Margot, and Sigrid."

"Yes, I do, but because of our different jobs, I seldom see them."

Finally, I did get to know Renate and Brigitte. One day they asked if I wanted to join their lunch break, and I did. While eating our lunch, questions went back and forth: "Where do you live? Do you go dancing?" Dancing was on everyone's mind! I learned that Renate lived around the corner from me and walked past our apartment building every day to work. "I'll stop and we'll walk together," she offered. Brigitte didn't walk with us because she lived on the outskirts of Goerlitz, near the Landeskrone and rode the streetcar to work. I liked them both and sometimes it felt as if I were bouncing between them. As we got to know each other, the three of us livened the workroom with laughter. Smiling the older women claimed that peace and quiet had left the workroom.

Renate, Brigitte, and I were like stair-steps. Renate was tall and slender with long natural platinum blonde hair that she cherished as a queen would her crown. She was funny at times but mostly serious. Brigitte with dark hair, energetic and attractive, was the shortest and always ready to laugh. I was in the middle, dark blonde, blue eyed, ready to laugh, and complimented on having the best looking legs. Brigitte and I liked fun and laughter, but Renate, kept a lid on us. Mutti wasn't too fond of Renate. "I don't know about her. She is nice, but I like Brigitte." I knew Mutti would like Brigitte. She was open, easy to get to know, and, like Mutti, enjoyed laughing and joking.

But there was a kink in our fun—school. By law, all young adults between fourteen and eighteen with no specific trade or apprenticeship had to attend twice weekly the *Berufs Schule,* like a High School. There we had the basic subjects: reading, writing, math, history, geography, and, most of all communist teachings. Thus, with no loss in pay, we attended school, but Renate and Brigitte had different school days than I. School was a bore to me. Most of the time I'd leave after our homeroom teacher, a little old lady, checked me present. I didn't do much of the homework, and Mutti never asked, so I slid through with an average grade.

I knew nothing important was in my future, except marriage. I knew it was essential to know how to clean, cook, and mend, as well as how to raise children. For me such teaching was split between Oma and Mutti, only I wasn't allowed to cook or bake. Mutti said, "We can't afford to waste food."

Food rationing continued, as well as the daily long lines of people waiting in front of stores. It was part of living and surviving, a familiar site throughout the city. We had to accept not having the abundance of food enjoyed by those in West Germany and also knew there wasn't anything we could do about it. We were glad when we received a small increase in our monthly food allowance. These always came with big announcements on the radio and in the newspapers so the entire world could hear how our friends, the Soviet's, were helping us to regain our independence; how, with continued support and leadership from them and our unceasing hard work, step-by-step they were advancing us toward success and freedom.

To that, Mutti sneered, "What? The Russians helping us regain our independence and freedom? Never! It will take another war to throw them out! They'll never give us our life and country back." Many others felt the same way but didn't voice their opinion in public. Neither did Mutti. So nothing changed. Pictures of communist leaders—usually Stalin's or Lenin's decorated the empty store windows. Red banners with communist slogans hung in schools, as well as outside and inside office buildings, restaurants, and movie houses, always reminding us of our pledge to work hard. I often wondered who signed or supported that pledge. Then, I thought of West Berlin, where I hadn't seen any banners or pictures of capitalists—only food. I wished we had capitalism. Then, we'd send the Russians back home, but I knew those were stupid thoughts.

At this point, life for us young people was mainly fun. Renate, Brigitte and I, knowing we couldn't change politics or the way we had too live never talked about those things. We didn't go to *FDJ* meetings, but had our monthly dues automatically deducted from our work pay. We were busy with movies, walks, and dances every weekend, perhaps a new dress twice a year, one for the *Pfingstfest*, a holiday in June and one for Christmas, an absolute must for attending holiday dances.

Before we knew it, we were shrouded in snow. Christmas was on its way, signifying the end of 1951 and the beginning of 1952. On Christmas Eve, the church bells ringing, Oma and I walked to church, at the *Luther Kirche* down the street from where we lived. Then, after dinner and gift giving—with Mutti receiving a new-antiqued lampshade for the dining room ceiling fixture—I walked Oma home proudly wearing my new coat. It was a cold clear night. The snow sparkled and crunched under our feet as we strolled to the Langenstrasse. "What are you thinking? You're so quiet," Oma asked.

"I was thinking that the crystal clear night doesn't have the magic it once had when we walked on nights like these."

"You're growing into a young adult. Soon you'll be seventeen and the magic of childhood is being left behind, a happy memory."

"*Ja*, but some of my childhood memories weren't happy ones."

"Yes, I know, but think of the happy memories, not the sad ones. You don't want to go through life unhappy. There are many hurdles to jump over, good and bad, before you get as old as I am. So, stay positive. Enjoy your teens. Life will grab you before you know it."

"I can't help but think of Vati and how it would be if he were alive."

"Nobody knows what it would be like if your father were here with us now. You should not ever forget him, but think happy thoughts of him."

Snuggling closer to Oma, her arm in mine, I felt her warmth, and, although she never said it, I knew she loved me. This crystal clear night was Oma-magic.

On Christmas Day the family gathered for the usual good coffee and cake, with evening sandwiches and potato salad, home brewed liqueur, and bought beer. Onkel Martin, excited and somewhat embarrassed, announced their wedding plans. After all the congratulations and a hardy *"Prost"* to the bride and groom, I went dancing. I didn't have to walk Oma home because she'd come with Onkel Heinz, Tante Hilde, and the children. On the second Christmas holiday, Mutti and Onkel Martin had friends in, including his two sisters. Again, congratulations floated all around the living room. Then, I went to the movies with Renate and Brigitte.

Goerlitz had three big movie theaters, but we went to a small, cozy one, decorated in red velvet with indirect lighting and cushy red velvet seats. We'd bought our tickets several days ahead because when any of the theaters showed a film from West Germany, they sold out fast. The lights in the theater were low. We were sitting in the center of the middle row waiting for the movie to start when I told the girls about the perfume I had gotten from my sister for Christmas. "It stinks." I whispered.

"Let us smell it," I took the little bottle from my purse and unscrewed the cap for the smelling test. I held the perfume bottle in my hand as Renate smelled, making a funny face. "You're right. It stinks."

"I want to smell it, too." I stretched across Renate for Brigitte to smell it when Renate smacked my arm from underneath. My perfume escaped—airborne, like a small shower. It missed us, but seated directly before us was a bald headed man, who startled, looked up to the ceiling. We knew he was wondering, "Is the ceiling leaking?" With a second glance upward, he wiped his baldhead twice, each time smelling his hand. We almost rolled out of our seats as we tried to suppress our laughter, watching him try to figure out where that smell had come from.

He never turned around. That was good because we would never have been able to keep from laughing out loud. All through the movie we hid behind our scarves and coat collars so our giggles wouldn't escape. Before the lights came on, we hurried outside, and exploded with laughter. When I checked the perfume bottle, it was almost empty. Brigitte, between laughs, took the perfume bottle and sprinkled the rest on the sidewalk. Then, handing me the empty bottle, she said, "You didn't like it anyway."

Renate was still laughing. "I bet the baldhead is still wondering where that stinky smell came from." And once more the three of us burst out in laughter as we walked arm in arm down the Berliner Street.

Yes, for us, life was mainly laughter.

Not long after this Mutti asked, "Were you at the theater with Renate and Brigitte recently?"

"Yes, the second Christmas holiday, when you and Onkel Martin had company. Why?"

"Your sister's friends saw the girls and you outside the theater breaking up with laughter, sprinkling something on the sidewalk."

"What business is it of her friends what we do? We were just having fun."

"What were you girls sprinkling on the sidewalk?"

I said as nonchalantly as possible, "I don't know what they're talking about." Then, I snapped, "Are her friends spying on me?"

"Don't get cross! They meant no harm. It's your sister who is taking it so seriously."

"So now we can't laugh? We have to be careful because of her friends?"

"No, you don't."

"Then tell her to stop spying!"

Mutti walked away from me with a sigh. I knew she was thinking: *Why can't those two get along?*

And I was thinking. *It's always the same. My sister! My sister!*

The very next day Christa was at our apartment, so she started in. "Your behavior is unacceptable. I'm ashamed to be your sister, you're . . ."

"Then, don't be my sister! Tell your friends what my friends and I do is none of their business! And further more, who appointed you as my guard?"

She started to lunge at me, but Mutti stepped between us, "Stop your fighting. Now! The neighbors will hear and I'll be ashamed to meet them on the staircase." My sister just glared at me.

Furious, and near tears, I grabbed my purse and coat and headed out the door, hissing at my sister, "You and your spying friends can kiss my you know what!" I forced myself not to slam the door because Mutti hated slamming doors. When I returned home my sister was gone. Mutti told me that my sister's friends weren't spying, but had told her, "Every time we see your little sister, she's always laughing with her friends."

And so, the Christmas season of 1951 ended. The New Year of 1952 was approaching fast. Mutti had decorated the living room with garlands and paper snakes for her usual New Year's Eve celebration with family and friends. The girls and I celebrated the arrival of 1952 with dancing at the Flora until three in the morning.

One of our escapades in early 1952 was going once a month, on a Saturday afternoon after payday, to the *Hotel Dresdner Hof.* Across the street from the Bahnhof, this hotel had been one of the leading hotels in Goerlitz. Untouched by bombs, it stood several stories tall, trying to overcome the after effects of the war.

Dressed up, our hair done at the hairdressers, a small pack of cigarettes for the three of us in one purse, we entered the *Dresdner Hof* through the big glass doors—young ladies. We walked up four steps on the wide marble stairs, where a waiter in a black suit and tie greeted us with a bow. We nodded our heads; then, he escorted us to the dining room, where white lace curtains covered the tall windows. The tables, too, were clad in white linen, with crystal ashtrays and small bud vases. Palm trees in decorative containers stood throughout the dining room.

With only a few guests because few travelers now came to Goerlitz, the dining room had a muted atmosphere with conversations in low tones. The waiter, a starched white and precisely folded napkin over his left arm, showed us to our table. He ceremoniously pulled out the chairs, and, bowing slightly, invited us to be seated, asking what our wishes were. We each ordered a beer. With a *"Bitte Sehr,"* my pleasure, he was gone, returning with a tray that held three glasses of beer topped with a thick layer of foam like whipping cream. With a flourish he placed the beers in front of us, saying, *"Zum Wohlsein!"* to your health" and like a shadow, he was gone.

We lifted our tulip shaped, gold rimmed beer glasses to toast each other in a silent *"Zum Wohl,"* took a swallow, set our glasses down, then lit our cigarettes—trying not to cough with the first puff. Soon, the waiter came to check if we wanted anything else.

We ordered bouillon soup that required no stamps, only money. Served in fancy soup cups with matching saucers, the bouillon soup had sprinkles of parsley on top and, on the bottom, a freshly cracked raw egg—looking up at us through the green parsley like a yellow bubble. When we stirred the very hot bouillon, the egg bubble turned into white and yellow flakes. We also were served a warm roll, but no butter. Daintily we ate our thin soup. When the waiter took our dishes away, we ordered a liqueur. After the waiter set the tiny delicate stemmed glasses before us, with a *"Zum Wohl"*, we sat in quiet conversation, cigarette in hand, blowing smoke—ladies of the world.

Three months into 1952, my sister surprised the family with an announcement: she was expecting a baby in September. We knew she had a steady boyfriend, Werner, but her pregnancy was a surprise. The family liked him a lot. I thought him handsome. He had wavy, reddish blonde hair, was tall and slender, reserved with a smile that showed his perfect white teeth. When Christa and Werner visited, I joked and laughed with him, but after they were gone, Mutti said, "You'd better stop your teasing and laughing with Werner. Your sister doesn't like it." I just shrugged my shoulders.

"When is Christa getting married?" I asked Mutti.

"I don't know. She hasn't mentioned it and I'm not asking."

After that, I didn't ask again because it really didn't mater to me.

And so, our family was not only having a tiny addition, but a grown-up one as well. Onkel Martin, who was fast becoming my favorite person, and Mutti had set their wedding date for October 1, 1952. I was excited that Mutti and Onkel Martin were getting married. He was funny—but quiet, so Mutti's liking parties, friends, and laughter balanced the scale. Plans were made for my sister to have the baby at our apartment. Because the wedding date had been set before anybody knew about Christa's pregnancy or due date, Mutti and everyone else wondered what would come first, the wedding, the baby or both at the same day? The only person not too concerned was Onkel Martin, stating with his usual grin, "I believe I am the first groom whose bride is a thirty-nine year old grandmother."

If Renate's, Brigitte's or my lives weren't entwined with family happenings, they revolved around going to work and dances on weekends. Every Saturday mornings, and because our apartments had water closets only, Renate and I took our showers for a small fee at our local *Schwimmbad,* a swimming pool house with individually bath facilities. Then, we went to the beauty shop to get our hair done, and, because we had to sit and wait our turn, it was often early afternoon by the time Renate and I parted to go home. Most of the time Mutti had dinner from the noon meal waiting in the oven for me. Although it was dried around the edges, I ate it hungrily. Then, it was time to freshen up my dress for to the dance. When Mutti and Onkel Martin weren't home, I'd iron out the wrinkles in my dress while listening to the radio, singing, and swinging my hips in anticipation of the evening. When they were home, Onkel Martin would do his crossword puzzle with a beer beside him. Mutti, cigarette in hand, blowing blue clouds into our living room, would watch me, and with a smirk asked, "Should I make you a sandwich?"

"A sandwich, what for?"

"You might get hungry with all that dancing late into the night." Onkel Martin, not looking up from his newspaper puzzle, added, "Maybe with some smelly cheese, like Limburger?"

Realizing they were teasing, I replied, "You're both too funny!"

Or Mutti would say to us girls, "You're the first ones to arrive and the last ones to depart!" Well, I guess Mutti was right! But we were not the only early ones at the *Flora;* everyone wanted a table along the dance floor. However, staying late was a different matter. We were allowed to buy alcoholic beverages, but an eleven pm curfew existed for any youth under eighteen—and that included the three of us—unless accompanied by an adult. At ten-forty-five p.m. the band's drummer did a short solo. The bandleader then announced that all guests under eighteen were to depart while the band played a few soft notes from *"Auf Wiedersehn".*

But who wanted to leave? Not us. So we ignored the curfew announcement. We knew there could be a police patrol, a *"Razzia"* anytime after eleven pm and the ending of the dance evening. If a youth was written up three times, the parents were notified and had to pay a small fine. When some times the police did arrive the band stopped playing, lights went bright. One police officer stayed at the door while the other walked along the dance floor and in-between the tables, checking ID's sporadically. We were lucky because the three of us never got caught. A notification to Renate's parents would not have been good, because she had a very strict father.

At one o'clock in the morning the band played the final song, always the same, *"Auf Wiedersehn, Auf Wiedersehn . . ."* with a second one added, *"Die kleine Stadt will schlafen gehn,"* the little city wants to go to sleep. Girls' hearts, including mine, were thumping in hopes that a certain young man would ask for the final dance, and while dancing ask for permission to escort her home. Since the last streetcar had left, the couples walked arm in arm, with the young man carrying her purse, like a cavalier should. Sometimes we'd walk in groups, our laughter and talk echoing from the house walls in the quiet of the night. The lit gas lanterns stationed along the side-walks were turned off by the young men who turned into mischievous boys, dressed in suits and ties, kicking the posts, claiming, they made less work for the night watchmen, who walked with poles early in the morning all over the city, extinguishing gas lanterns. On some streets, the lanterns were already off. That's when we knew we weren't the first group to walk down that street.

Gradually, winter turned into spring, and there was another surprise. Without warning, Renate quit the lampshade factory and went to work at another factory. The three of us still saw each other and did things together, but now it was mainly Brigitte and I. Also, Margot and Sigrid had steady boyfriends and Erna, too, was expecting and busy with wedding plans, so I saw them very seldom.

Brigitte and I didn't have steady boyfriends. We liked being solo, going dancing, meeting friends, but most of all not interested in becoming a mother any time soon. Since there was no Renate to restrain us, we had fun. With a letter from work I was able to change my school days to the same two days as Brigitte's, with both of us skipping right after roll call. We went to early movies, roamed the city, or went to the apartment, with Mutti exclaiming, "Did you girls skip school again!"

Also, Brigitte didn't care for the *Flora* where we had been dancing, proclaiming, "That's for beginners, not for us mature women!" So we changed to the *Konzert Haus,* just around the corner from where I lived.

Mutti told me that at the beginning of WWII, dances sporadically had been forbidden by the Hitler regime, with dancing prohibited altogether in 1943. For a time after WWII dancing hadn't been popular, partly because surviving had been critical and the men either had been killed, lost in the war or were broken in mind and body. By 1947, bands slowly re-established themselves in Goerlitz, and, in spite of despair, a spirit of optimism emerged and dance places reopened.

Brigitte and I, as well as Mutti loved to dance. Onkel Martin had never been a dancer. Mutti tried to teach him, but gave up and said, "It's no use; he has two left feet." Onkel Martin, happy to be released, grinned.

Every Saturday and Sunday evening, Brigitte and I danced at the *Konzert Haus.* Sometimes Mutti joined us for an hour or two. My friends envied me my petite and full-of-life mother. Because Mutti was a good dancer, they liked dancing with her. "You have the best mother," they'd tell me with envy. I agreed, thankful she had rescued me from my stepmother and a life of misery.

Mutti was fun at all times, so my friends would often stop by to visit. We'd sit around the table, enjoying a glass of beer, Mutti smoking her cigarette, talking and laughing as if she were one of us. Sometimes Mutti would cook a big pot of noodle soup made with substitute bouillon cubes that she'd set on the table, ladling out a bowl of soup for everyone. Although it was a cheap meal but with laughter and talking, we ate the watery noodle soup as if we'd never eaten anything so good before.

Brigitte, living on the outskirts of Goerlitz, would often stay overnight with us on weekends. Then, after the dance, to not wake up Mutti or Onkel Martin, we crept behind the partition Mutti had made for me and huddled liked sardines in my narrow bed. If one of us needed to turn, then, on command, we both turned. The next morning, Mutti, sitting on the edge of my bed woke us up, not for Sunday morning breakfast, no—it was already mid-morning—Mutti only wanted to know if we had had fun at the dance, whom we'd danced with or if we had any new *victories* to report. We mumbled, but Mutti didn't give up until we were awake. Most of all, she wanted to know if Brigitte had fallen in *love* again, which she did quite often. Brigitte fell in love, as fast as she fell out, but there was a procedure in falling out of her *love* that only Mutti could fix according to Brigitte. Often Brigitte would fall in *love* with a guy she had only seen from a distance or had danced with, unaware that he was Brigitte's *love object,* didn't pay any attention to her. My trying to talk her out of her infatuations didn't do any good.

As Brigitte got to know Mutti, then, the two had teary heart-to-heart talks over Brigitte's many lost *loves,* talks eased with liquor. That's when Mutti would suggest, "Why don't you get a bottle of liqueur, then, you and I will talk about it." So, Brigitte, feeling sad and unhappy, would walk across the street to the grocer's to buy the liqueur, while Mutti got one of Onkel Martin's big hanky and two liquor glasses. They would sit, and, with a *prost,* have a shot ever now and then, drowning Brigitte's sorrow. Mutti, smoking a cigarette with Brigitte trying too—coughing and choking—listened as Brigitte, between laughs and tears poured her heart out about her lost *love,* while soaking Onkel Martin's hanky. If I tried to rescue her, then, Brigitte, shaking her finger at me would tell me, "You stay out! Your mother and I are having a serious conversation."

I gave up. It was a ritual. I felt that Brigitte had a special bond with Mutti that she didn't have with her mother. If Brigitte weren't falling in or out of *love,* Mutti would ask, "Are you all right? Are you having a dry spell?"

Brigitte would reply, "Don't worry, Frau Hentschke. I'll see what I can do." And sure enough, Brigitte managed to fall in and out of *love* time after time.

After their talks Brigitte sighed, "I always feel so much better after I have a heart-to-heart talk with your mother."

Laughingly I replied, "Yes, I can see that. It's you, Mutti, and the bottle."

After many years I visited Brigitte in Germany. She said then, "I still remember the broken-heart crying sessions I had with your mother and how sympathetic she was. She was so much fun!"

Later, after Germany's unification in 1990, after being gone for thirty-eight years, I went home to Goerlitz. When I met old friends, the first thing they said was, "Do you know what we remember most from our youth? Your mother! Dancing with her at the Konzert Haus, sitting around the table and eating that watery noodle soup! Those were fun times!"

To that I only smiled and nodded, thinking, "Yes, that was my mother, remembered by my friends for a lifetime."

Winter gave into the spring of 1952, seven long years after the end of the war, seven years of silently enduring Soviet oppression. Food rationing was still at the bare minimum, including coal for heating and cooking. Fruit, like bananas and oranges was nonexistent. Specialties items for cooking, like spices, oatmeal, cream of wheat, chocolate, cocoa and coffee, and many more items were still not in any store. We could buy a chocolate substitute, but it didn't taste or look anything like chocolate. Mutti said, "They must think we don't know what real chocolate tastes or looks like."

People, solemn faced, still stood in lines at the butchers and grocer's, grumbling, "It's been seven years since the war ended and our lives still have not improved." Over and over we were told not to look to the *West* because those people were influenced by capitalism and capitalism was bad. But here the people in the *East*, here, everyone was equal. Here, with the help of our friend Stalin, we would prosper by working to better our lives.

Making sure no communists were near, people responded, "We need Stalin to show us how to better our life? How to prosper? All we need is for Stalin to stop converting our youth to communism, and take his Military and go back to where *he* and *they* had come from." Others whispered the often-heard phrase, "It'll take another war to get the Russians out of our land and lives." Everyone longed to be freed of the Russians, to better our living conditions, but everyone knew it would not be soon—if ever.

Just as at the Langenstrasse, behind closed windows and locked doors, Mutti, Onkel Martin, and Oma, when she was there, still listened to Radio Free Europe, the West Berlin broadcast. But, it had gotten more and more difficult to hear, because it was overplayed with the Russian or East German national anthem. Sitting crowded near the radio, straining to hear, they sometimes wouldn't hear me unlock the door and come in. Then, looking up startled, they sighed, "Oh, it's you!"

So, nothing had changed, except Brigitte started to cough. She and I continued working at the lampshade factory, ignoring Brigitte's coughing, looking forward to each weekend so we could go dancing, our favorite one and only entertainment.

In time, Brigitte's coughing worsened. Sometimes she could hardly stop. Then, laughing, Renate and I took her arms and held them above her head as mothers do to keep their babies from choking. Only Brigitte was laughing too, which made her coughing and choking even worse. Finally, she went to see a doctor. He sent her to an out-of-town sanatorium for treatments and a change of air.

We were shocked when Brigitte told us and felt bad about having made fun when she was coughing and choking. But, confident as ever, she said, "I'll be all right. I'll see you when I get back. In the meantime, I get a nice vacation." Renate and I hugged her good-bye. Then, Brigitte was gone, leaving an empty spot in our threesome.

With Brigitte gone, I didn't enjoy working at the lampshade factory anymore, because I was the only young person left.

Renate urged me, "Quit that job and come to work where I'm working. They're always hiring. Then, we can walk to work together!"

When I told Mutti I was thinking of changing jobs, she said, "Whatever you do, just make sure, before you quit one job, you have another." I put in my application where Renate was working, a factory that manufactured electric condensers, and I was hired. After completing the two-week notification period at the lampshade factory, in September of 1952, I started working at the *VEB Kondensatorenwerk Gera/Zweigstelle Goerlitz.*

That first morning, at six thirty sharp Renate rang our downstairs doorbell, letting me know she was ready and waiting for us to go to work. "Guten Morgan," I said when I came downstairs. "I'm so nervous this morning, I could hardly eat breakfast."

Walking, arm in arm, Renate said, "Don't be! Everyone is really nice and it's not a difficult job." But my stomach stayed in knots as we neared the big three-story, red brick building, built in the early 1900's near the bank of the Neisse River.

There, I had to fill out additional forms for taxes and deductions like health insurance, church taxes, and dues for the FDJ organization. Then, I was handed the punch card for clocking in and out of work. After the paperwork was done, my supervisor, *Herr Brand,* a middle-aged man wearing a blue linen overcoat, was called over the intercom system to come to the office. Overcoat flapping behind him, he motioned me to follow him, and while climbing the stairs to the second floor, he informed me of the alternately biweekly morning and evening shifts.

The room we entered where the condensers were made was large, like a hall with windows on each side. Its center walkway split it into two sections, both with rows of long tables. Each table held three cast iron winding machines, spaced five feet apart, with power meters the size of small radios sitting next to them. The room was abuzz with voices, and at almost every machine operators sat rolling condensers.

At Herr Brand's loud, "Guten Morgen," the workers stopped and turned around. "We have a new employee. Fraeulein Knebel is joining us." Renate beamed. Others nodded, and turned back to their jobs. Motioning to me, he walked between tables and stopped by a woman sitting in front of her machine, waiting. After the introduction he said, "Fraeulein Knebel, for today and tomorrow, you will watch *Frau Richter* and learn how to roll condensers. Then, under her supervision you'll practice on the machine next to hers." Herr Brand, pulling the chair from that machine near, said, "Have a seat and watch. Frau Richter is our instructor and trains all new employees." With a pat on her shoulder, he walked away.

Frau Richter, much older than I, smiled, then explained, "An electric condenser is made in five layers: two layers of foil and three of a thin, clear, plastic-like material in different sizes and widths, depending on the size of the condenser. Also, the foils are always narrower than the plastic strips, so that when the condenser is baked, the plastic strip seals around the foil."

As she talked, she slipped five rolls, three plastic and two foils, that looked like wrapping tape—each six inches in diameter—onto five separate dowels on the machine. First, she threaded the plastic strips over three separate wooden dowels. Then, she threaded the two narrower foil strips over two metal dowels, with the foil strips running between the plastic strips. Next, she gathered all five strips, pulled them downward and attached them to a spindle.

Then, with her right hand, she slowly turned the spindle with the attached small crank, making sure all five layers were straight, flush and winding. "Now, do you see the power meter on the left of the machine? That meter is connected to the two metal dowels and measures the length of foil needed for the condenser's specified voltage storage." Slowly, she cranked and rolled, watching the meter and the rolls, insuring that all five strips stayed in line so the condenser was rolled evenly and tightly.

When the power meter needle reached the first red mark—set to the size of the condenser—she laid two short, flat, thin metal strips on top of each foil, on the right and left side of the condenser. Then, she cranked again as she watched the power meters needle advance to the center of the red field. She stopped and again placed metal strips on top of each foil. Pointing at those strips sticking out on each side of the condenser, she explained. "They're needed for measuring the voltage after the baking process."

She continued to wind until the needle reached the end of the red field. There, she stopped. "Now we have rolled the required foliage into the condenser." I watched her cut both foils from the main rolls with a small scissor, explaining, "It's important to cut the foil at this precise point, so it will measure correctly. After that and to seal the foil in tightly, we do two more turns with the three plastic strips, then, cut away two of them. Several more turns with the last strip, then we cut it off and seal it with the electric gun."

When she was done, she removed the small crank and gently pulled the finished condenser from the spindle and handed it to me.

"That's how we make condensers. This size, not no bigger than your thumb, is one of the smaller ones, but we also make much larger ones. The small ones are quick to make, but the larger ones take time. Whatever size you make, remember that the foil is the important factor. If you roll incorrectly, the condenser will measure incorrectly, therefore, pay close attention to the power meter. Also, you need to roll straight and tight, so watch the tensions of your rolls." She took the condenser from me and placed it in the finished tray. "When the order is filled, then the tray of condensers, including the work order with your name, is taken to another department where they're baked at a high temperature. Then, using the metal strips I inserted earlier, each condenser is attached to a very precise power meter and measured for its voltage storage or capacity—specified on each work order. There is a very small leeway, but it's best to have your work be precisely in line with the correct measurements—if you want to keep your job."

Having said that, she went back to work. I watched as she efficiently produced one condenser after another, talking very little. I couldn't resist asking, "How long have you been doing this?"

"Going on three years. I like my job. It's easy work."

"I hope I'll get as good as you are."

"You will. Just give it time." When her order was filled, I walked with her to another section of the room where the bake ovens were. There I was shown the baking process and the measuring of the condensers.

After two days of instruction, I began working on the machine next to Frau Richter. Then after my two-week training, I was moved to another machine, expected to fulfill my hourly quota. There was no dallying on the job. Depending on the sizes of the condensers, different per hour quotas had to be filled. If the quota was easily reached, it was increased.

I never tried to be as swift as Frau Richter. Neither did many other workers. Her swiftness upped the norm some, but we made sure to stay just below hers, so that when averages were taken for the individual sized condensers, the norms barely increased. The factory, managed by believers in communism, encouraged us to produce, saying, "We need condensers to rebuild our country." We knew what was behind their explanations. We knew the condensers were not for our country, and we also knew not to voice our opinions.

I liked the work, mostly the late shift. I didn't have to get up early and the bosses were at home. We had a shift leader on the evening shift, a woman who was the mother of two sons who were boxers. She was a pleasant lady and not a communist. While working the evening shift, we sang songs, from folk songs to the latest hits. But we were forbidden to sing Hitler's marching songs or songs about the folklore of the part of Germany now in the hands of Poles. Because the factory was part of the government and managed by communists, we younger workers were required to attend FDJ meetings, but Renate and I would attend only every other meeting. It was important to keep our attendance records up to date, to show patriotism and to secure our jobs.

With Brigitte gone, Renate and I were chumming around. She was fun but not like Brigitte. Renate didn't stay overnight, and didn't fall in or out of love the way Brigitte had. I missed Brigitte and the fun we'd had, but Mutti missed her even more because she'd lost her drinking partner.

We had not heard from Brigitte, but when we saw her sister she told us that Brigitte was still in the out-of-town sanatorium, and doing well. We asked her to tell Brigitte that we're waiting for her to come home.

Renate and I didn't do anything important except go to work, to a movie or dancing at the Konzert Haus on weekends. Out of five movie houses, three of them had been closed permanently at the beginning of 1952. Films made in East Germany were made in black and white and always had a communist theme in the background and not worth seeing. But once in a while a color film made in West Germany would be showing. Then, people stood in long lines for tickets. Those films were never political, but love stories. The stars wore beautiful clothes and portrayed a normal, happy life, something we could only wish for. Some stories had sad endings, then, Renate and I left the movie house with red-rimmed eyes.

One day, while walking home from work, Renate said, "This Saturday, let's not go dancing; but go to the boxing tournament at the Stadthalle."

"You want to see a boxing tournament? Why? I don't like boxing and don't like to watch guys smash each other's noses and faces until they're bloody! You have to go without me because I don't like violence!"

But she didn't give in. "Oh, come on. It's not violent. It's a sport! You'll like it! Its fun!"

"No, I'm not going! Since when are you interested in boxing?"

"I went with my sister once and I liked it. This weekend is a big boxing tournament, and I'd like to go. It's something different from always dancing.

Just for once," she begged, "go with me, please?" I agreed to go only once, but my heart wasn't in it. Even Mutti and Onkel Martin were surprised when I told them where I was going.

It was a two-day tournament with boxers from all over East Germany. Goerlitz had a boxing club that participated in the tournament, including the two sons of our shift leader. Both were in their twenties, the older a heavyweight, and the younger, a lightweight. The boxing tournament was held in the auditorium of the Stadthalle where all special events took place. The main floor had to be re-arranged so the ring sat in the center with seating around it. Renate and I had balcony seats right over the ring. At the beginning of the fights, I felt uncomfortable and uneasy and looked away. I didn't like the mushy, squishy sounds when they hit each other in the face reminding me of the butcher smacking a piece of meat with his cleaver to flatten it for a Schnitzel. But Renate kept poking me with her elbow. "Look, you're missing the action!" So I swallowed my apprehension and watched. To my surprise, the villain in me appeared and soon I, too, cheered along with the fans. When it was time for the two sons of our co-worker to box their opponents, I was swept away on a wave of excitement and cheered and yelled. That was the beginning of my interest in boxing and we went to every tournament. Then, with a grin, Renate said, "See, I knew you would like it!"

Yes, I liked it, so that at times I was so engrossed in what was happening in the ring, I'd box Renate. Rubbing her arm she warned me, "At the next boxing event I'll surprise you and sit on your other side." She did just that, excited, I forgot Renate wasn't on my left and promptly boxed the man who sat where she'd always sat. Red faced, I apologized, while Renate burst into laughter. "I had warned you!" To save Renate's arm, I curbed my enthusiastic boxing movements.

July arrived, and with that my seventeenth birthday. Mutti asked, "What would you like to do for your birthday?"

"I don't know."

"Let me make a suggestion. Your birthday is on Friday. So, on Saturday, we'll invite the family, Oma, Tante Hilde, Tante Elfriede, your cousin Uschi, and Renate for coffee and cake. I'll make some sandwiches for the evening meal and after eating you three girls can go dancing at the Konzert Haus."

"That's a good suggestion, Mutti."

"I know it's a small celebration, but we need to save on food stamps because soon we have a baby coming and a wedding with a dinner afterward."

"I understand, Mutti, but next year we'll celebrate my eighteenth birthday because I'll be a grown-up. Then I can stay at the dance legally all night and no one can stop me."

"Na, na, don't get carried away. You are still living under my roof and no matter how old you are, there are still house rules."

"I know about your house rules, Mutti. They're easy. I'm talking about the police, appearing after the eleven o'clock curfew to check for those under eighteen. Next year they can check all they want because I'll be eighteen."

"So far you've been able to avoid getting caught. Let's hope your luck holds out for another year."

"Me, too. It's always scary when the police show up. But I'll never forget when Brigitte and I were at the Konzert Haus and they came to do their eleven p.m. raid. Brigitte and I hid on stage behind the curtain in a wooden breast high gym box. Two of the band players helped us get inside it, saying, "they'll never find you here." Soon, the bandleader announced, "Ladies choice!" The band played three tangos, while we were stuck in the box. Brigitte almost cried. Here she was, trapped, while the young man she was flirting with was more than likely asked by another girl to dance the tangos. When we finally were freed from the box, Brigitte vowed never to hide there again, but instead, she'd take her chances with the police."

"Why didn't they let you out before the ladies choice?" Mutti asked.

"They couldn't because just as the police were leaving, the band leader announced ladies choice. So they had to play and we had to wait for them to finish. We tried to lift the top off, but it was too heavy."

"What happened to the young man?"

"Nothing. Brigitte danced with him the rest of the evening. But she never went near that box again."

Mutti laughed. "Yes, that sounds like Brigitte."

The day before my seventeenth birthday Oma had baked my favorite, *Streussel Kuchen*. Then, on the day of my birthday party, Oma arrived with Tante Hilde; Tante Elfriede came with Uschi, and lastly Renate. Uschi brought my favorite flowers, a bouquet of sweet peas. I loved their sweet scent and asked Mutti to set the small vase in the center of the table. There was no big gift giving—maybe a gift box of three handkerchiefs, a book, or a pair of *Perlonstruempfe*, a nylon like stockings, precious because they were expensive and not always available. Later on, Renate, Uschi, and I went dancing, although Uschi, just three months from her seventeenth birthday, was allowed to stay at the Konzert Haus for only two hours while Tante Elfriede visited with Mutti, Oma, and Tante Hilde. It was a nice birthday celebration, but I was looking forward to 1953, my eighteenth one.

September had arrived, and plans were made not only for Mutti's and Onkel Martin's wedding on October 1,1952, but for the arrival of my sister's baby due anytime. The wedding was to be small, with only family and close friends. I liked the thought of their being married and so did everyone else in our family. Onkel Martin was a likable, quiet person and a good match for my lively mother.

On September 26,1952, shortly before the wedding, my niece Claudia Martina was born. Mutti had made arrangements for a midwife, because my sister had the baby at our apartment. The midwife was the same one who had delivered me—seventeen years ago. On Mutti and Onkel Martin's wedding day, my sister was still recuperating with the baby basinet beside her in our bedroom.

It felt as if a whirlwind had hit our small apartment and me. Everyone was busy. Every morning Oma came to help care for my sister and little Claudia who had a pretty strong voice. My sister was, as always, her grumpy self and nobody could do anything right, so I stayed away from her. Only little Claudia—sweet, pink, and pretty—took my heart in her little hands.

While I held her, I couldn't help but think of Vati and of what he would say could he see his first grandchild. Seven years had gone by since his passing. Seven years, and I felt guilty for not remembering his face clearly anymore, for not thinking of him as often as I had before, for not going to the cemetery as Oma and I had done, and for attaching myself more and more to Onkel Martin, feeling as if he were my father. All these thoughts were buzzing in my head, and I consoled myself that Vati knew that he was and always would be in my heart.

On the evening before the wedding, porcelain was crashing outside our door. The wedding-eve was in full swing. Oma was busy setting trays of sandwiches, potato salad, and the hot Wurst on the extended table in the living room. Mutti and Onkel Martin were setting out beer, Schnapps, and liquor glasses as the crashing and laughter outside our apartment door got louder and louder. It was *Polterabend* an old long-standing tradition. It's a party for the bride and groom at the bride's home on the eve of their wedding day. Friends of the groom throw *only* porcelain—collected from anywhere— at the bride's front door. Broken porcelain symbolizes, good fortune, luck and happiness, for the soon-to-be-married couple. Since we lived on the second floor, Onkel Martin's friends threw the porcelain near our apartment door on the stairwells stone steps. When the crashing stopped, Onkel Martin, broom in hand, wearing an apron—as is customary—and Mutti, carrying a tray of *Schnapps-filled* shot glasses, stepped-out in the stairwell to greet his friends. Standing, surrounded by broken porcelain they drank a toast to the bride and groom. Then, Mutti and Oma invited everyone in, while the groom, as is his duty, cleared the good luck debris into a previously obtained barrel to be taken away later. When Onkel Martin joined the party, the well wishing, drinking, and eating was in full swing. It was a noisy evening, and, although we lived in an apartment building, no one complained.

Mutti, Onkel Martin, and their witnesses were due the next day at one thirty pm, at the Justice of the Peace in the *Rathaus, Am Untermarkt*. Mutti was dressed in a black suit, white blouse and carried a bouquet of yellow feather chrysanthemums intertwined with green asparagus fern. Onkel Martin wore a black suit, white shirt, and black bow tie. The bride and groom looked so handsome when the horse drawn carriage arrived to pick up the small wedding party. Mutti had asked her best friend Annie to be her witness, and Onkel Martin had asked a long time friend to be his witness.

I didn't mind that I couldn't attend the wedding ceremony. I knew Oma needed my help in the kitchen, and little Claudia had her own demands and seemed not to care what was going on around her. To ready for the return of the wedding party, I set the table for dinner with candles and sprigs of flowers. The previous day Oma had prepared the *Rouladen*, beef rolls, and the *Blaukraut* a sweet and sour red cabbage. While the Rouladen were simmering in their own brown juicy gravy, and the Blaukraut was re-heating, filling the kitchen with their tantalizing aroma, Oma was preparing the dough for the *Kartoffelkloesse*, the potato dumplings.

Soon, all other guests arrived to wait for the bridal parties return. Later, after Oma's much praised dinner, coffee and cake were served and, to toast the newlyweds, cognac and liqueur. It wasn't a big and elaborate dinner, but everyone felt it was a dinner made for royalty. The wedding celebration was a success, and the partying went on until the early morning hours. Since it was Saturday, I excused myself and went dancing with Renate and Uschi at the Konzert Haus.

After all these events, a birth and a wedding, life went back to as normal as possible, only now we had two new member's added to our daily lives: a husband and grandchild for my mother; a stepfather and niece, little baby Claudia for me. Before Christa gave birth, it was decided that Mutti would quit her job to care for the baby. Thus, when Christa was well, she went back to her place at the Langenstrasse, giving Claudia into Mutti's care.

Three months later, at our second Christmas holiday, Claudia was baptized in the Lutheran faith in the *Luther Kirche am Luther Platz*, just down the street from where we lived. Afterward, Mutti had a baptismal party for our whole family, supported by Christa and Werner, Claudia's parents.

Then, with Mutti's usual New Year's Eve party, 1952 came to an end while Renate and I danced at the Konzert Haus into 1953.

At the stroke of midnight the cold, crisp air was filled with the ringing of church bells, floating above snow-covered rooftops that glistened in the moonlight, echoing along every street and alley. All over Goerlitz, every church was ringing its bells welcoming the new year of 1953.

With a fanfare the dance band at the Konzert Haus stopped playing and a chorus of voices, including Renate's and mine shouted a *"Prost Neues Jahr!"* Throwing paper snakes and confetti, blowing paper horns, everybody went outside into the fresh night air, their *"Prost Neues Jahr!"* mixing with the sounds church bells.

People leaning out the windows listen to the bells, joining in shouting of *"Prost Neues Jahr!"* My family too was at the window, shouting, and blowing paper horns. So as not to sink into the snow, I carefully made my way across the street and up to our apartment where Mutti and Onkel Martin were having their usual New Year's Eve party with friends and family. Mutti, Onkel Martin, and Oma got a kiss on the cheek from me and everyone else, as is the custom, received a handshake, and a smile with a wish for a Happy and Healthy New Year. Then, I hurried back to the Konzert Haus; where Renate was waiting, there we danced until three in the morning.

That New Year 1953, it would bring a change to our families, and, most of all, to my future. But while shouting "Prost Neues Jahr!" dancing and partying, it never crossed my mind that it would be the last time I'd hear the church bells ring in my beloved Goerlitz. That I would never dance or party, ever, at home again. That this is the year I would say good-bye once more to my home, leaving friendships, and people I love, eventually to make my home halfway around the world.

January began like any other month, but after baby Claudia's baptism, I noticed that Mutti, Christa, Werner, and Onkel Martin were talking in hushed voices. I paid little attention because anything concerning my sister I didn't care to know. But, soon after the New Year I noticed that I hadn't seen my sister or Werner at the apartment. It seemed odd they hadn't come to take baby Claudia for her outing in her buggy as they did every weekend with Mutti cooking a meal for all of us. It was even stranger yet when Mutti, holding the baby, asked me at our Sunday morning breakfast table, "What are you doing this afternoon?"

"Not much, it's a nice January sunny day. Maybe Renate and I will go for a walk."

"Would you mind taking Claudia with you in the buggy, just for a short while, maybe an hour or so? The fresh air will be good for her." I'd taken Claudia for outings in her buggy before, so why was Mutti asking me so hesitantly? This was Christa and Werner's Sunday. Puzzled, I asked, "Why? Aren't Christa and Werner coming?"

"No, they're not coming. They're gone."

"Gone? Gone where?"

"Gone."

"Mutti, don't be so secretive. Gone where?"

"Christa and Werner have fled to West Germany."

"They have what? They fled to West Germany?"

"Keep your voice down," Mutti warned me. "Do you want the neighbors to hear you?"

Trying to lower my voice as my thoughts raced, I looked at Mutti, then at Onkel Martin, "When? How? Why wasn't I told?"

"It had nothing to do with you. You know the risks to flee to West Germany, and the less people know, the better it is."

Still not believing what I'd heard, I asked, "When did they leave?"

"A couple days ago on the three thirty a.m. train to East Berlin. I'm worried. I hope they made it over the border to West Berlin. Christa promised as soon as she could she'd send a picture post-card signed with the name *Alma* to let us know they had safely crossed the border."

I sat, shaking my head in disbelief. "I know Christa and I weren't the best of sisters, but she could have said good-bye. And Oma? Does she know?"

"Yes, Christa said good-bye only to Oma. You know she doesn't like emotional situations or good-byes."

It took me a while to get used to the idea that my sister had left. I felt sad, even though we fought a lot. She was my sister after all. But why had she left her baby? So I asked, "What about Claudia? How come Christa didn't take the baby? Why is she escaping now and not before she had a baby?"

"Things don't always go as we plan and Claudia was a surprise to all of us," Mutti replied. "To take a baby through a camp in West Berlin would be too difficult. When they're married and settled in West Germany, I'll take Claudia over to them. Until then, she'll stay with us."

And that's the way it was. I didn't ask any more questions. I liked having Claudia with us. Whenever Mutti had something to do, I'd take Claudia for her afternoon outing. I loved pushing her in the buggy. When people asked if she was my baby, I hated to say, "No, it's my sisters baby." Sometimes they'd ask about Christa and Werner's whereabouts, but I told them I didn't know, and, in time, they stopped asking because they suspected where Claudia's parents might have gone.

About two weeks after they left, to everyone's relief, a picture postcard came that said, "Having a wonderful visit. Best wishes, Alma." Then, after eight weeks of waiting and hoping, news arrived. Mutti cried with relief, wiping her tears as she read the letter. My sister wrote that after six weeks of encampment in West Berlin, they were flown to Worms, a city in West Germany, from there by train they were sent to a town called Wittlich; near the Mosel River. She wrote of their marriage in Wittlich. They were renting a room with kitchen privileges from a very nice family with six children. When they first arrived in West Berlin, and, because they weren't married, they had to live in separate camps. Christa was in a camp for women and Werner in a camp for men. Listening to Mutti reading the letter, I was glad they had made it to West Germany and married, but I still didn't understand how my sister could have left her baby behind.

Even though we had a small member added to our household, my carefree living didn't change. I went to work and helped whenever I was needed. I still was not allowed to cook because Mutti said, "We don't have the groceries for you to practice cooking." I was free to do as I wanted, but *within reason* as Mutti put it. Because I hadn't seen or heard from Brigitte since she left, almost every day Mutti would ask me, "Have you seen Brigitte yet?"

"No I haven't, but I think she should be home by now."

"Why don't you go and see her?"

I shook my head, "I've never met her family except her sister and Brigitte told me that her parents don't like it when friends come up to their apartment. I'll just wait." Sure of our friendship, I added, "She'll come when she is home again," but Brigitte never came. Then, one day when I was taking Claudia for her outing in the buggy, I saw Brigitte walking arm in arm with a girl I didn't know. They were busy talking and laughing, strolling leisurely down the Berliner Strasse, our main street.

Glad to see her, I called out, "Brigitte! When did you get back?" Brigitte was aloof. Her cool look made it clear she didn't want to be bothered. Looking at her with her new friend, I realized Brigitte had built a new relationship while she had been away to recover from her illness.

When I saw her alone another time, I asked her why she hadn't come to see Mutti or me. Shrugging her shoulders, she said, "Since you and Renate work together you've become close friends. She is all right, but I really never cared for her."

I was surprised to hear Brigitte say that and when I got home, I told Mutti about it. She said, "I'm sorry to hear that. I always thought you two were good friends because of all the times Brigitte had spent with us."

Nodding my head I said, "Yes, I'm sorry too. We had lots of fun together and I will miss her, but I can't suddenly drop Renate because Brigitte doesn't care for her anymore."

The three of us would meet once in a while, but I could feel the strain between Renate and Brigitte. I was caught in the middle and didn't want to lose either one of them. In time, we saw less and less of Brigitte because her new circle of friends kept her busy.

Renate and I continued to have fun. We especially anticipated the *Fasching*, the carnival starting in January, ending in February on the eve of Ash Wednesday. In Fasching, every Saturday evening all dance places had *Maskenballs*, masquerade balls. Renate and I were busy deciding what kind of costume to wear and what to make it with. Our costumes had to be simple and homemade. Whenever going to a dance, it was important to wear a costume, however plain, and a facemask. Unlike groceries, facemasks at carnival time were readily available, full faced or half faced, sold in paper and writing supply stores. All were plain, made of thin cardboard with a matte finish on the outside. The mask was worn before entering the dance hall so everyone would have to guess, including Renate and me, just who our dance partners were. Then, at midnight to the band's fanfare, the masks fell and we discovered the identity of our different dancing partners. Laughing, we'd say to friends or acquaintances, "I guessed it was you!" Often I was told, "I knew it was you!"

"And just how did you know?"

"It's your smile, your blue eyes, your laughing and talking. That's what gives you away every time." I had tried not to talk, laugh or smile, but dance partners said funny things to figure out their partners identity, so I'd laugh and talk, giving myself away. Renate on the other hand, kept quiet, but her long blond hair, slenderness, and height gave her away. I was even told that being seen with that slender blond gave me away, but it didn't matter. We had fun and that was the important part.

I didn't want to dress as I had the previous year as a *Reiterin*, a lady horseback rider, which didn't fit me because I was afraid of horses. In pictures, lady riders wore long dressy skirts and hats with veils flowing down their backs, but I didn't have the material. Besides, I thought a short black skirt would make the costume look frisky. It was easy to put together, with matching black vest, a white blouse of Mutti's and black boots I borrowed from Tante Hilde. Instead of the traditional riding hat and the long veil, I put a white bow in my hair and wore a black mask. Oma sewed the skirt and vest, but she thought my skirt was too short, "It's inappropriate for a young girl to walk in public in a skirt above her knees, and, walking bare legged in the winter could give you a deathly cold."

"But, Oma, I won't catch a cold. I'm going to the Konzert Haus around the corner from us. And I can't wear stockings, because the garters would show beneath my short skirt."

"That's why the skirt should be at least below your knees."

I could see that pleading my case with Oma wasn't getting me anywhere, but Mutti came to my rescue, saying, "Let her have a few hours of fun. That's all we have anymore. She is young and won't be the only one at the dance in a short skirt and bare legs." With a sigh, Oma gave up and made my costume of bits and pieces when I was just shy of seventeen, that Fasching of 1952.

But this year, I didn't want to wear the same costume, so I chose a Hungarian peasant girl's traditional costume that I'd seen in the magazines at carnival time. The traditional Hungarian costumes were elaborate with embroidered white blouses, bright red gathered skirts, lace trimmed petticoats and red leather boots. On their heads the girls wore a wreath made of flowers or a diadem with streaming ribbons. I had to improvise because I didn't have the beautiful material the magazine showed.

I was able to purchase a couple yards of red material and black ribbon. Again, I went to Oma who made me a slightly gathered short skirt with the black ribbon sewn around the hem. Oma didn't say anything this time about the length or my bare legs. When she handed me the skirt, I gave her a hug and a kiss on the cheek. She just said, "Oh, go on and have a nice time." I made a diadem from cardboard, covered it with leftover skirt material, and glued a strip of gold paper along the top edge of the diadem. From the scraps of the gold paper I glued tiny dots all over the diadem to make it shimmer. To finish the look, I added colored streaming ribbons. Because I had no red boots, Tante Hilde's black ones had to do, as did her Hungarian embroidered blouse. I still had the black vest from the previous year, so I only had to buy the red mask.

I never got a prize for my costume, but that didn't matter. Renate and I had the best time dancing every weekend in our costumes until the eve of Ash Wednesday. Then, all the dance places were closed until Easter. It was fasting time.

My sister's leaving was not the only change in the early months of 1953, but it lingered in the air like a foreboding. More and more private stores were open one day and closed the next. There was no note posted on the door, no explanation—just closed, just like our butcher across the street had done. Mutti, surprised too see the butcher's store stay closed on Tuesday morning—Mondays are always closed days—said, "It's odd, on Saturday when I was in the store, I talked to his wife and she behaved as always and today they're still closed. I wonder what's behind it."

Then, the whispering started. Everyone in the neighborhood was guessing what could have happened to the butcher. "Did he or his wife speak against the communist regime and got arrested? Or have they fled to West Germany in the middle of the night? Every night their apartment is dark with no movement at all!" Others said, "If they fled, let's hope they made it." But no one ever knew what happened to our butcher.

In early March, rumors were going around that Stalin was in bad health. Just exactly what ailed him, no one knew. It was whispered that he was on his deathbed and could die most anytime. There were even hopeful whispers, should he die, would we Germans be freed from communism?

With no dancing until Easter, because of fasting, the movie houses weren't close. So Renate and I had a Saturday evening movie date and said, "Stalin had better not die this weekend and ruin our dates. He can die Monday." But he didn't listen to us and died Thursday, March 5, 1953. The next morning when we walked to work, the Russian hammer and sickle flags and the East German flags were flying half-mast with Stalin's picture draped in black in every store window. German communists displayed Stalin's picture draped in black on their windowsills. Renate and I just looked at each other. "Now what? Why couldn't he wait till Monday? There won't be a movie house open anywhere." We were right. No movies. Gasthauses were allowed to stay open, but only for food and drink. The radio played nothing but *Trauermusik*, mourning music all day long every day for four weeks. All fun places and entertainments were closed and canceled.

Renate and I met our dates and went to the Gasthaus for a while, but when we laughed out loud, we got frowns from other patrons. It was the longest most boring four weeks for us. Even Mutti grumbled quietly because it wasn't safe to say, "I am getting tired of that whiny music day after day. He is not our leader! Let the Russians cry over him!" Finally the mourning period ended. We had survived!

The older generation said with a sad undertone, "It doesn't look like with Stalin's death, Russia will give us our freedom and Germany back."

June 17th a Wednesday morning, started like any other morning. When I awoke, the sun's rays tickled my face, a promise of a warm, feel-good summer day. Drifting in from the open window I smelled the fresh morning air as I ate my breakfast, a jelly sandwich and coffee. Soon I heard Renate calling from downstairs, "Gisela, are you ready?"

I leaned out the window and waved to her. "I'll be right down." Arm in arm, we walked to work while we chatted. We started our shift getting the machines ready for the rolling of condensers while talking with our co-workers. At ten o'clock, our half hour break, Renate said, "Let's play table tennis in the day room downstairs."

"I don't feel like playing table tennis this morning. You always beat me." Renate, taller than I, had better control of the ping-pong ball.

She smiled, answered, "No, I don't always beat you. Sometimes you win." I gave in because Renate was the domineering one in our friendship. To get to the hall where the tennis table was set up, we had to cross the factory courtyard. When we entered the courtyard, the high, heavy, ornate cast iron gate, normally open during working hours, was closed and guarded by our bosses. Outside the gate was a large group of men in work clothes, their faces smudged, their clothes and hands grubby and greasy, as if they'd just walked off their jobs. Some held the big heavy sledgehammers used by blacksmiths; others carried shovels or smaller sledgehammers. Yelling, "Open up this gate! Now! Or we'll smash it in!"

"Go back to your jobs!" Our bosses told the mob, while backing away from the gate in fear of getting injured.

"If you don't open the gate, we will!" Others, their fists raised, yelled, "Break it down!" The heavy, black sledgehammers crashed against the gate, their screeching noises echoing in the wide, high archway.

Renate and I stood rooted to the ground. We looked at each other. "What's going on? What are they doing here?" Looking closer, we saw that two of the men in front, carrying the biggest sledgehammers, were the boxer brothers, the sons of our co-worker—blacksmiths by trade. Renate and I knew them both from boxing and from dancing with them. We stood like statues as the gate broke open and the mob rushed in. "What's going on? Why are you here?" we asked the brothers.

"You don't know? There's an uprising all over our city and East Germany. We're throwing the Russians out of our land. No one is working today, so just leave." Renate and I grabbed our purses and left. Just as we had been told, the streets were filled with enthusiastic people, their faces aglow with joy and happiness. Men, women, young and the old, were carrying all sort of weapons—hammers, shovels, strong sticks, even rakes—but no guns, because no one had a gun.

When we got near the center of the city, somewhere in the rioting crowd, I lost Renate. I knew it was useless to try to find her. I went on alone, fed by the energy of the rioters. As people passed me, I could feel their force and heard their shouts. "Now *they* will come and help us! Now *they* will free us from the Russians!" Others shouted, "Let's send the Russians home!" Everyone was high with excitement. Confident we'd be freed from the Russian occupation, from communism and its iron fist.

I kept on walking, not believing what I saw. The crowed didn't destroy stores or properties. They only ripped the Russian and East German flags off buildings and tore the communist banners to shreds. Then, I came to the *Postplatz*, where the big red brick post office sat, and across from it, the red brick three-story jail and courthouse. To one side of the jail, was a wide, high sturdy wooden gate. A crowd of people had gathered there.

I forced my way through the rioters to see what they were doing. The group of men who'd been at the factory, including the boxers, worked with their sledgehammers to break the jailhouse gate open. As the gate broke, the guards inside ran to hide. The men caught some and beat them up. I didn't want to watch, so I followed the other men as they stormed through the jailhouse, breaking cell locks with their sledgehammers, leaving holes in the bricks where the locks had been. They knocked cast iron bar doors off their hinges, leaving them on the floor where they had fallen. People in cells screamed, their hands stretched through the iron bars, to seize their opportunity to be free, to run. Most were political prisoners and held too be sent to Siberian work camps. A woman, Mutti's age, her cell door open, sat on her wooden coat and cried, lost, not knowing what to do because she was not from Goerlitz. I wanted to take her home but knew that would cause trouble for our family.

I followed the rioters into the office, watching as they pulled out file drawers, dumping them onto the floor or throwing them out the window. A uniformed office lady, her eyes big, sat tied to her chair with a gag over her mouth. One man leaned over close to her face, muttering, "You're lucky we're not beating you up." Watching, I realized the thick dusty air was filled with hate for those Germans who'd guarded their own people for the communists.

I don't know how long I was in the jailhouse, but when I wandered out, it was late afternoon. Shreds of red cloth from flags and banners covered the streets. Smashed glass from broken picture frames, torn pictures of Russian's new leader Khrushchev, and Stalin who'd died, littered the sidewalks as well as those of Ulbricht and Pieck, the communist leaders of East Germany. Strewn all over the streets were ripped documents, blackened from people walking on them. The streets reminded me of the war bombings; only this one was with paper and cloth. Although they carried only meager weapons, people in the streets were confident help would come from the western allies, to free us from Russia's tyranny.

Then, *they* came! Not the liberators, but the Russians, driving halftracks, a half truck/tank, with guns pointed at us. *They* came clattering down Berliner Strasse, our main street with rackets that vibrated and bounced of buildings. *They* clattered down the street, spread out like a wedge, they drove, never stopping, herding people like cattle forcing everyone to run. People escaped into side streets or pressed into entrances to save themselves from being run down as the Russians drove their halftracks as close to the house walls as they could. I, with others crammed into the archway entrance of a store, their faces now hopeless and fearful. Pressed so tightly, we almost couldn't breathe, no one complained. Loudspeakers blared in German ordering us off the streets by nine p.m. Windows had to be closed. Violators would be shot. As soon as at the halftracks had passed, people hurried home. This was the end of the East German people's fight for freedom, to be freed from Russia's communism. We were defeated and martial curfew was enforced once more.

It was getting late and I knew I was in trouble. All day I had not thought about Mutti being worried because she didn't know where I was. I ran, only to meet another Russian halftrack, guns pointed, coming down my street. It wasn't nine o'clock yet, but, scared, I dashed behind the door of an apartment house and waited for them to pass. When I came upstairs to our apartment, Mutti's red, angry face greeted me. "Where have you been all day? Do you have any idea how worried I've been? Do you know I've been looking for you all afternoon? I even went to Oma's, but no one had seen you." I'd never seen Mutti this angry. I just stood and said nothing because

I had no excuse. "I was afraid you'd been arrested. Someone said they'd seen you in the jailhouse. Were you there?"

I just nodded me head. Mutti started to stutter, a sign she was stressed, then cried. "You had no business going inside the jail house!" With a stern look at me, Onkel Martin got up and put his arm around Mutti, guiding her to a chair. "She is home now and you need to relax."

Still standing near the door, I said, "I'm sorry, Mutti. I should have come home when the riot started, but there was so much going on I forgot all about it."

After a while, as I told them what I had seen Mutti settled down. "But to go into the jailhouse? What were you thinking? The Russians and German guards could have taken the jailhouse back, closed the front gate, and you would have been inside with me not knowing what had happened to you! I just hope, no one we know, saw you?"

"No, I don't think so." I wasn't going to tell Mutti that the two boxers with their sledgehammers had seen me. When I went to bed, I thought about the day's events. The thought of getting caught inside the jail never crossed my mind because among the people was such a strong feeling, believing their rioting would lead us to a better life, to liberate us, and to force the Russians out of our land. But hearing Mutti's worried words, I now realize how careless and thoughtless I had been to go into the jailhouse.

When I awoke the next morning, yesterday's events came back, Mutti's words echoing, "I hope, no one we know, saw you!"

Now I realized my actions could have horrible consequences. The morning sunshine, a promise for another summer day, didn't lessen my fears. Quietly, I ate my breakfast, a jelly sandwich and a cup of wheat coffee. "You're so quiet. What's wrong? Are you sick?" Mutti asked, holding little Claudia in her lap and feeding her breakfast.

I shook my head, "I'm just tired."

"Didn't you sleep last night?"

"Yes, I did, but I'm still tired." I didn't want Mutti to know I was worried that someone might have seen me inside the jailhouse. I'd not thought the Russians could come and barricade the broken entrance, just as they had come with their halftracks on the streets. They wouldn't have believed or cared that I was just watching, wanting to see inside a jail. I would've been caught along with the rioters, able to see the inside of a jailhouse for a long time, or, worse, spend the rest of my life in a Siberian work camp. The only ones who knew me were the boxer brothers. Maybe they'd been so busy smashing cell doors, they hadn't realized I was there. I also didn't know the uniformed matron tied up in her chair. Mutti was right! I'd no business inside the jail.

When I heard Renate call from downstairs, I grabbed my sweater and purse. With a peck on Mutti's cheek and another on baby Claudia's head, she waving good-bye with her little hand—I went downstairs. As soon as I stepped out of the house, Renate asked, "Where did you go yesterday? I couldn't find you in the crowd of rioters."

"I looked for you and when I couldn't find you, I just walked around and watched." I didn't want to tell Renate where I'd been. She'd tell me the same thing Mutti had and I didn't want to hear it again. I felt embarrassed and stupid. I didn't trust Renate nearly as much as I had trusted Brigitte, a feeling I couldn't explain. Maybe it was because Mutti always said Renate was different, and the way things were politically, no one could trust anybody. But Brigitte, I knew, would have looked me straight in the eye and given me a lecture, but it would have been different, more caring, more from a kindred spirit.

"When I couldn't find you," Renate interrupted my thoughts, "I went home."

"Yes, I did too."

When we crossed the Berliner Strasse, I saw not a fragment of debris left on the street. It looked just as always, clean. Only pictures, flags, and banners with their communist slogans were missing. We walked on over the Postplatz, past the marble water fountain where once in the center on a pedestal, a tall bronze figure had stood, holding a large flat oyster shell above her head from which a gentle waterfall had fallen. During WW II she'd been taken down and the bronze melted. Ever since then, the fountain had been turned off. Passing the fountain, I glanced over my shoulder at the jailhouse and noticed its big wooden gate was upright again with a halftrack parked in front of it. Russians, shouldering rifles and uniformed Germans strapped with pistols, stood guard. When I saw that, I realized how easy it really could have been for them to close that gate with me inside. A shudder ran down my back. I took a deep breath of relief, and Renate asked, "Are you all right?"

"Yes, I'm fine."

At work, the factory, too, showed no signs of looting. Nothing was broken, and the machines sat as always waiting for the operators. I was curious to know what the rioters had wanted here, but no one spoke of the uprising. It was as if it had never happened.

Then, I saw the mother of the boxers. Her eyes were red, her face drawn, and my heart skipped a beat. I knew why she looked so sad. Her sons had been arrested. A wave of fear went through me. I wanted to ask her about her sons, but now, I was afraid. Someone might connect me with them. A short whistle told us it was time for work to begin. Silently, heads down, we tended to our jobs while our bosses, even the manager of the factory whom we knew to be a communist, walked back and forth among us—row after row. Without raising our heads, we glanced at one another with a silent question, "Why are we being watched?"

Every time one of them walked behind me, my heart did double beats. I practically froze, expecting a tap on my shoulder and a low voice saying, "Fraeulein Knebel, come to the office with me." At the end of our shift I was glad that I could escape our bosses roaming eyes.

As soon as we were outside the factory and on our way home, Renate asked, "Did you hear what happened to Manfred and Rudi, the boxers?"

"No, I didn't, but I noticed their mother. Her eyes were red and swollen, like if she had cried. Did you talk to her?"

"Yes, I did. She told me her sons were on the run. They and others knew when the Russians took control of Goerlitz again, they'd be arrested."

"I bet they're trying to escape to West Germany."

"Yes, they are. Their mother told me, they planned to walk at night and hide out by day in the woods, hoping to cross the border into West Germany, undiscovered."

Remembering our hardships when we were fleeing, I said, "I hope they make it."

"Yes, I do too. They were so out in front of the rioters, almost like leaders, supporting the uprising. If they're caught sneaking across the border, Russian border guards will shoot them. Or worse yet, they'll be interrogated and sent to a Siberian work camp." Siberian work camp, the very sound of that name made people afraid. Everyone knew that to be sent to Siberia was a death sentence because no one returned from there.

I hated to hear that her sons had to run, to leave their mother; hated to think of the hardship and sorrow she would have to endure not knowing if her sons were alive or dead.

The curfew, now eleven o'clock in the evening, lasted for one week. Enforcing the nightly curfew, the Russians halftracks continued to clatter over dark, empty streets, the roar of their thread chains bouncing off house walls—a flashback to 1945. Once again we felt the Russians iron fist, demanding total surrender. The communist controlled radio and newspaper wanted us to believe the uprising was the work of western capitalism who'd planned to destroy our trust and friendship with Russia, our leaders to a greater future. We were told be to be thankful our Russian friends had taken swift action to re-establish order in our land.

After a week the curfew was lifted. Restaurants and movie houses opened their doors again. People had resigned themselves to never being free from Russia's tyranny. Everyone tried to over come the disappointment at not getting the help from the *West* they'd desperately hoped for, realizing anew we were isolated, prisoners in our own land, left to the Russians to do with as they pleased.

Lingering in the air was a dark unseen shroud, pressing down. People walked around grim faced. Spies seemed to be everywhere, listening. Communist propaganda banners were up again on house walls, in restaurants, movie houses, factories and schools. They spoke of solidarity and of the great opportunities awaiting us, to be achieved only by working hard, united with our Russian friends. They assured us of the freedom we have with Khrushchev, their new leader after Stalin's death. People still whispered, but Mutti would say it out loud, "Nothing has changed. We're sold out to the Russians, and the *West* isn't giving us a second thought."

Onkel Martin, eyebrows raised, said, "Now, Lenchen, be careful what you're saying, to whom you're talking. You know spies are everywhere."

"Yes, I know, but I know and you know it's true. We've been forgotten, sold out to the Russians by the allies in the West."

Life resumed as normal as possible, but with one difference; rumors started, quietly. The uprising had begun the day before in East Berlin, about175 miles northwest of us. It had taken twenty-four hours for the news of the uprising to reach Goerlitz. The communist controlled media had been silent, so news only passed by word of mouth. By the time the Russians had squashed the uprising in East Berlin and other cities in East Germany, we had barely started in Goerlitz. The Russians in Goerlitz hadn't thought the uprising would reach us, the most eastern city in East Germany. Taken by surprise, they hadn't crushed our rioting until late in the afternoon.

Stories flew like unwritten underground letters. A two-story villa and former home of a doctor sat secluded, hidden by high bushes on a big corner lot bordering the Russian compound. This villa, its garden overgrown with weeds and shrubs, its ornate wrought iron fence now rusted, its shutters closed, looked unused. Daily, people had walked past it, believing it deserted. In the summer, when we went to the dances in the Stadthallen Garten and talked and laughed on the way, we girls never thought something had been going on inside that villa. Apparently, it had not been deserted.

Another group of rioters had stormed that two-story villa and found, so the rumor went, a basement filled waist high with water, with poles standing throughout, where political prisoners were chained to. They had been released, where to unknown, and the poles had been destroyed. The upstairs rooms had held files of political prisoners and suspects, unopened mail, letters from West Germany confiscated by the communists. All those had been thrown out the windows. People standing on the street and in the overgrown garden had scooped them all up. At a later time, the letters secretly were given to the people to whom they were addressed. It was also rumored, the villa, used by the Russian and German communists to interrogate German political prisoners, continued its gruesome activity after the riots. But no one could stop them without ending up in that with water-filled basement.

That was the only political uprising ever tried in East Germany. Resigned, people grumbled, "It was lost before it started."

For a while, when the grown-ups in my family were together, their conversation centered on the sad ending of the uprising and additional rumors they'd heard. Finally, with a sigh and a shrug they joined in saying, "It was lost before it started!"

People went back to their daily lives. Renate and I too, picked up where we had left off: going to work and dancing, but we noticed at the dances some young men were missing. We knew they either had escaped to West Germany or had been arrested for participating in the uprising. For a short while I worried the police would come for me too because I had been in the jailhouse, but they didn't, so, finally I put it out of my mind.

But the reins had been tightened. Although open, the movie houses didn't show movies from West Germany. They were banned. Eventually, more movie houses closed, perhaps because of low attendance or because the owner had fled to the West Germany. No one really knew the reason or what had happen.

Then, the Flora, the dance place where I'd gone with Erna, Margot, and Sigrid, closed its doors. It made me sad. There I'd experienced my first crush, my fascination with an unanswered love. I'd seen him last at the Konzert Haus. He was just as handsome as ever in his suit and tie, his dark hair combed to perfection. Within an air of confidence, he'd approached our table to ask me for the next dance. My heart pounding, I accepted. Then, with his arm around me, I'd danced with my feet barely touching the parquet. While dancing, looking down at me, he'd asked politely, "How are you? It's nice to see you again."

Trying to ignore my pounding heart, I'd answered just as politely, "Thank you. I'm fine." After the dance, he'd escorted me to my table where, with a bow, he'd thanked me for the dance and I'd nodded my head in return. I hadn't known it was the last time I would ever see or dance with him.

With the riot behind us but not out of our minds, on sunny Sundays when blue spanned the sky, people walked about, along the main street, the Berliner Strasse, in the city park; or visited with friends and relatives. On those Sundays Mutti and Onkel Martin sometimes walked to Onkel Kurt, Oma's brother, and Klara, his wife. At times Oma, Tante Elfriede, Onkel Richard, Uschi, and I, would walk together, me pushing my favorite niece in her buggy. Claudia, ten months old now and sitting up, babbled while playing with her fingers or chewed on a baby toy Mutti had tied to the buggy. Pushing her, I'd talk to Claudia and her giggle would make us laugh. Our walk took about an hour because they lived near the foot of the Landeskrone, where they owned a small house. I always enjoyed seeing Onkel Kurt, Tante Klara, and Werner, my partner at his brother's wedding.

I liked their yard planted with flowers, vegetables and fruit trees, as well as Tante Klara's two goats; who followed her like puppies. But Tante Klara, whenever she saw me, asked the same question over and over, "It's been almost a year since your mother married Martin. When are you going to call him Vati instead of Onkel Martin?" To make matters worse she'd add, "You call him Vati and I'll reward you with a dozen eggs." A dozen eggs! Like an offering of gold! I looked at Onkel Martin, but he never showed any response at all. I think he knew I was embarrassed because everyone was looking at me. My eyes downcast, I shook my head no, just a little.

Vati! I knew that I would never be able to call another man Vati no matter how nice he was to me and how much I liked him. I knew that name would never cross my lips. It would be stuck in my throat. Although Mutti had never asked me to do so, I had thought about calling Onkel Martin, Vati, but I just couldn't do it. It was a fine line I couldn't cross, no matter how fond I was of Onkel Martin. I had had a Vati. The last time I'd said the name out loud was the day Vati was taken to the hospital, when he promised me, that he would return, but he didn't. For me, the title Vati was for one person alone, and although Vati was not living anymore, he was still living within me.

I never collected Tante Klara's dozen eggs, but it's surprising how unexpectedly and in a short time, the circumstances of an unforeseen situation would force me to change my child-like values and strong beliefs.

July arrived and with that my so awaited for eighteenth birthday which fell on a Saturday. "You can invite your friends for afternoon coffee and cake," Mutti told me. "And for the evening, I'll make Kartoffelsalat und Wurst."

"Thanks, Mutti. That sounds good to me."

"You can't invite no more than six, including you because that's all the room and chairs we have."

"I already know who I want to invite."

"And who is that?"

"Well, Renate and her friend, Uschi, Werner, and Karl-Heinz. That makes six, including me, three guys and three girls. I'll seat Uschi with Werner, Renate with her friend, and Karl-Heinz with me."

Mutti, nodded in agreement, "I'm glad you're inviting your cousins, Uschi and Werner. And Karl-Heinz has been a friend of yours for some time."

"Ja, he is a good friend. I like Karl-Heinz. He is always good for a laugh and a great dancer." Mutti agreed, because she had danced with him too.

Saturday morning Renate and I walked to the local bathhouse, then to the beauty shop to get our hair done. When I got home, Mutti had already set a pretty coffee table with a gleaming white tablecloth. In the center of the table strewn with colorful confetti and paper snakes, was the *Apfel-Streussel-Torte,* the apple streusel torte Mutti had baked. In front of my place setting was the customary, white birthday candle. Although this candle had served at other celebrations in our household, because candles were not readily available, it was still special to me. Mutti had decorated my eighteenth birthday table with care and love, looking pretty and inviting.

My nose in the air, I smelled the aroma of real coffee and asked, "Mutti, are you making real coffee for us?"

"It's your birthday!" Mutti almost always managed to come up with real coffee for special occasions and I didn't ask. "It's better," Mutti always said, "if you don't know everything." I just gave her a thank you peck on the cheek.

My guests due to arrive between three-thirty and four p.m. were punctual as always. Everyone brought me beautiful arranged bouquets from a florist shop. Mutti got vases and set them around our small living room. But Karl-Heinz was the life of the party. When the doorbell rang and I opened the door, all I saw was a huge bouquet hiding a face. Then, a voice spoke through the flowers, "*Lass Blumen sprechen!*" Let flowers speak. He then recited a funny poem he had written for my birthday. Everyone came to the door, so he had to do it all over again, amid loud laughter.

Mutti placed the white porcelain *Kaffeekanne* that matched the dishes on the table and told me, "I'll leave you to take care of your guests. I'll go and visit with Annie for a while." Mutti's longtime friend Annie lived in the apartment building across the street from us. I think her living across from us was one reason Mutti had been anxious to trade apartments with Onkel Heinz and Tante Hilde.

Before Mutti went out the door she stopped, and looking at us, said, "*Einen Guten Appetiet wuensch ich Euch*" Good appetite!

We chorused, "Thank you, we will!" While having coffee and Kuchen, we told funny stories, and laughter flew back and forth over the table.

Before we knew it, Mutti was back. So Mutti could join us, I pulled the wicker armchair from in front of the window over to the table. Leaning back in her chair, blue smoke rising in waves from her cigarette, she asked, "So, what are your plans for the evening?"

"I'm not sure. We've been talking about going dancing at the Konzert Haus. It's Saturday evening and the band is playing." My guests nodded in agreement.

"That's a marvelous idea. The potato salad is made. All I need to do is heat the Wurst. Since the Konzert Haus is just around the corner, I'll bring the food over there."

"You can't do that Mutti!"

"Why not? Isn't it your birthday?"

"Mutti, please don't! That will be so embarrassing!"

"Why not? What is so embarrassing?" My guests chimed in.

"It's just embarrassing! That's why!" The debate was on. I was overruled. Everyone agreed that it was a great idea. Mutti beamed, her eyes, shining. She loved adventure.

Renate, Uschi, and I, helped Mutti clear the table. While we stacked the dishes near the kitchen sink, Mutti told us, "I'll do them later. The cake we'll leave on the table, for Martin after his dinner." By the time we had finished clearing the table, Onkel Martin returned from visiting his sisters. He sat with us until it was time to leave for the Konzert Haus. Renate, Uschi and I did a quick check in the mirror, applied lipstick, then, checked our hair and our outfits. Pleased, we motioned to our escorts that we were ready to leave. Laughing, we left with Mutti holding the door, saying, "I'll be over in a little while with the Kartoffelsalat and the Wurst!"

"Yes!" everyone shouted as we walked down the stairs. I still wasn't happy, but when Mutti made up her mind to do something she considered fun, that was that. So I consoled myself that as long as everyone else thought it was fun, then so be it. At the Konzert Haus, we decided to take a table close to the dance floor and the band. To toast my birthday, we ordered cognac and beer. When our drinks arrived, the waitress sat a glass of beer in front of each of us, but the small tray that held the six filled with cognac shot glasses, she placed in the center of our table. While the waitress served our drinks, the band did a fanfare with a drum roll joined by the trumpets with a "tat-taaa." I wanted to slide underneath the table. All eyes were on us, to see what would happen next. They didn't have long to wait. Reaching for a cognac, Karl-Heinz stood up, and gave a short funny toast. We laughed. Then, red-faced, with my cognac in hand, I stood up to thank Karl-Heinz. Standing up, holding our cognacs, all of us even the band held up our drinks in a birthday saluted and said, *"Prost."* It's customary to buy the band and the bandleader a round of cognac when asked to perform a toast. As I was toasted even some of the neighboring tables lifted their drinks in a birthday salute.

The band began to play a *Wiener Waltzer*. Karl-Heinz, with a swooping bow asked, "May I have the honor of this dance?" Matching his gesture, I curtsied ceremoniously. We danced a short birthday solo. Then, everyone joined in. While we were dancing, "Happy Birthday" wishes came from all directions—from people I didn't even know. I felt like a queen, the center of attention.

As the evening progressed, I nervously watched the entrance to the dance hall. I knew at any minute Mutti was going to appear. The door opened with a swoosh and there was my mother with Tante Elfriede in tow, carrying two shopping bags, the kind used at the weekly farmers market. The band wasn't playing at that moment, and Mutti walked straight across the dance floor to our table with Tante Elfriede following. My birthday guests cheered as Mutti approached us. The patrons of the Konzert Haus watched. I wanted to hide my red face, to be invisible. Tante Elfriede, also embarrassed, helped Mutti set the shopping bags on two chairs. Then, as if from a magic carpetbag, Mutti pulled out a big bowl of potato salad.

From her second bag appeared a lidded big pot that held the Wurst, still swimming in hot water. Then Mutti produced spoons, and, with a loud clank, strewed them over our table. The napkins followed and several small jars of substitute mustard. Mutti was the center of attention, everyone watching to see what would come next from her magic bags.

As I watched my mother plunk those big containers on our table, I didn't feel like a queen anymore. My imaginary crown had been tarnished and was now slowly sliding off. Looking for plates for the potato salad, I asked Mutti, "How are we supposed to eat the potato salad and the Wurst? We have no plates."

Mutti shrugged, "Everyone has a spoon, just pass the potato salad bowl around the table and hold the Wurst in your hands!"

"Yes, what's wrong with that?" Laughter followed Mutti's suggestion as my guests reminded me. "You know the famous saying? *Wer keinen Loeffel hat, isst mit den Fingern!*" If you don't have a spoon, then you eat with your fingers. For the second time, I told myself to let it be. If my friends didn't care, then neither should I. So I decided to enjoy my eighteenth birthday party. The boys ordered beer in a tall glass boot and the party was on! When the waitress returned, she placed the beer-filled glass boot on the table with a *Prost*. With another *Prost*, Werner lifted the glass boot, and, standing on his chair, drank from the boot as we applauded with the bands, "tattaaa!" Then, the boot was passed around our table with the boys, dressed in suite and tie, standing on their chairs—as is the custom. The custom also decrees that when the beer was near to the foot of the boot, the trick was not to have it make a bubble—avoiding it by slowly turning the boot while drinking. The person caught with a bubble had to buy the next boot. Girls not standing on chairs when drinking from the boot, stopped when the beer got low because the bursting bubble sprayed beer in the drinkers face. But it was a challenge among the boys not to have it bubble, creating yet another reason to cheer the winner. Drinking out of the glass boot was done only on special occasions, it was fun to watch and do.

Eventually Mutti gathered up the empty bowl, the silverware and the pot with the now cold water. She took it all home. Then, she returned to join the party. Now, Mutti was dancing on the dance floor instead of walking across it as she had done earlier. Again, I was told what a wonderful and great mother I had and how much fun she was. Tante Elfriede, Mutti's sister, was more serious. She wouldn't dance and took Uschi home before the party ended.

My birthday celebration came to an end as the band played the closing song *"Auf Wiedersehn."* Everyone said it was a wonderful, fun-filled celebration.

On Monday when Renate and I came to work, a woman co-worker asked if we had been celebrating my birthday Saturday evening at the Konzert Haus. Perplexed, Renate and I said, "Yes, why?"

"A family member of mine was there and spoke of a fun birthday celebration. I figured it had to be Gisela's party."

Renate and I smiled. "Yes, it was fun!"

Repeatedly I was told how everyone had enjoyed Mutti and her unique way of serving at my eighteenth birthday party. None of us thought that this was the last time we'd be celebrating together, but it was.

Although I had not been too happy with Mutti's way of serving our food, I now have to admit it was different. Hadn't I wished for a loving, fun mother when I'd lived with my stepmother? Yes, I had! I had the best fun loving mother and friend ever. Thanks to Mutti it was a party filled with fun and laughter, a party and a mother remembered for a lifetime.

Over the months since Christa and Werner's leaving, Mutti got mail pretty regularly, but the news wasn't good, so Mutti worried. The small town they had been sent to near the Mosel River, was mainly Catholic, with no factories near because that region was one of wine growers and their wine cellars. Being a refugee from East Germany and a Protestant, Werner had had part time jobs only. Christa also wrote that they we're still renting from the same family but needed to find a new place of their own soon because a new baby was due in December. My sister's pregnancy stunned Mutti who soon was beside herself. However, I didn't worry because Christa and I had never been close.

Marriage, children, and sex weren't on my agenda. Yeah, I had boyfriends, we kissed, but when it got serious, I shied away. I liked being free to enjoy my life without commitments. Some girls became pregnant and married, but they didn't look too happy. Then, there were those girls who passed favors out freely and I didn't want be known for that either. My present boyfriend Kurt, a student at the college of agriculture, a super dancer, sometimes wouldn't show up for our date. Then, days later a girl I knew stopped me, "I saw Kurt out dancing with another girl the other evening."

"Thanks for telling me," and I started to walk away.

"Aren't you mad at him? Aren't you breaking it off with him?"

I stopped and tilted my head to one side as if thinking about it. "No, I don't think so." I left her standing with her mouth open.

After I told Renate about my encounter and we finished laughing about it, she said, "You know, she is hoping you'll break up with Kurt so she can go after him. I don't blame her. He is good looking, a super dancer, so you're the envy of the girls because he only dances with you. Well, some times, he'll dance with me just to be polite."

The next time we met, I asked Kurt about it. He freely admitted being with another girl. "A man has to take care of its needs!" I knew what he meant and I never asked again and whenever he didn't show, well I knew. He'd talk about those girls, telling me never to be like them. He put his arm around my shoulder, and with a smirk, say, "Of course there isn't any danger you'll ever be like those girls!"

"You're right! I wont! I have lots of freedom because Mutti trusts me and I don't want to lose that trust."

I liked blond, slim, blue-eyed Kurt. I loved to dance with him while other girls watched in envy but I wasn't in love with him. Was it because someone else still was dancing in my head? He had a longtime girlfriend, and she fit him. Both had the same air of superiority, something I could not compete with. Still, it made my heart throb whenever I thought about him.

Then, there was my buddy and friend Karl-Heinz, always a gentleman when we saw each other. Mutti would tell me, "He really likes you and I wouldn't be surprised if he isn't in love with you. Hasn't he taken you to meet his parents? And didn't you tell me how friendly and outgoing they were, making you feel welcome?"

"Yes, he did, and yes, he has nice parents and yes, I liked them too, but he is just a friend. We haven't even kissed and I don't want him to kiss me."

"Why? He is a good-looking, reliable young man, with a good job at the Siemense Company. What's the problem?"

"Have you ever taken a good look at his teeth, Mutti?"

"What's wrong with his teeth?"

"They are straight and clean, but they have little tiny black speckles all over them."

"Oh that," Mutti said. "Those speckles could be from an insufficiency of vitamins because we haven't had decent food for years or its genetic."

"Whatever it is, I just don't want to be kissed unless they guy has nice, clean teeth."

"How long have you known Karl-Heinz?"

"Almost two years."

"And you've never kissed?" Mutti shook her head in disbelief.

"No, and I've never encouraged him either. I know it sounds stupid but that's the way I feel. Besides, Karl-Heinz has kind of an on and off girlfriend. She was at his birthday party, celebrated with family and friends at home. I was invited too along with Manfred, his long time friend. I could like Manfred. He is tall with dark hair and good looking, but he is not interested in me. I'm not sure, I think he likes another girl."

"Does he have nice teeth?" Mutti wanted to know.

"Yes, he does. Mutti, you've met Manfred. He was with Karl-Heinz and me when we stole the lilac for you on *Muttertag*, Mother's Day. Remember?"

Mutti nodded her head. "Oh yes, I remember when the three of you came singing up the street at five in the morning."

Listening to our conversation, Onkel Martin winked at Mutti, then said, "It would seem that if Gisela doesn't find someone with perfect teeth, she won't be leaving us anytime soon."

Smiling, I walked over to where Onkel Martin was sitting, laid my arm on his shoulder, leaned forward and I said, "You're right. I like nice teeth and until then I'll just grow old with you and Mutti."

"What a three some we're going to be!" Onkel Martin exclaimed. After that my obsession with perfect teeth was the joke in our family, because whenever I met some one new, I was always asked, "And his teeth?"

Onkel Martin became a special person in our daily life. Shortly after they were married, he quit the border patrol job, saying he didn't like pointing his rifle at smugglers who were trying to survive to make a living. Also the border watch was becoming more tightly enforced as young communist believers were hired, spying on their own patrol guard, turning them in for looking the other way or taking bribe. So he quit before he got in trouble.

His new job was at the steel factory in Goerlitz, but a shortly after the factory closed, and the workers were sent to a steel factory in Riesa, not too far from Goerlitz. He'd come home by train on Friday evening, then returned to work on Monday morning. Often Mutti would take train, Claudia, buggy and all, to spend a week in Riesa with Onkel Martin at a couple's home, where he was a boarder. I didn't mind Mutti's leaving when I was on the late shift, but when I had the morning shift it was different. Then, to get me up in time Renate got permission from her parents to keep me company. We took Mutti's big stainless steel dishpan, and set it on the floor next to the bed. Then, we put spoons and forks in the dishpan along with the big hammer alarm clock, hoping the rattling of the silverware and the jumping of the alarm clock would wake us up. That didn't work too well, because sometimes neither Renate nor I would hear the alarm clock or go back to sleep. After that, Mutti would leave only when I was on the late shift.

In September Mutti had a party with our family for Claudia's first birthday. It was a quiet party because Mutti was talking of taking Claudia to Christa and Werner in West Germany. Mutti had to request permission from the East German government, specifying the reason, the date of her departure and her return in order to cross the border to West Germany. The regime used permission as tools to control and to discourage East German citizen's from traveling to the West. West Germany had no such requirements.

After Mutti and Onkel Martin's first wedding anniversary, October first, Mutti started to pack, so when the permission arrived, she was ready. But our real plan went beyond Mutti's packing, because once she was in the West, we had all decided she should stay. "We'll never be free of the Russian's dictatorship and the shortage of food. There is nothing but a depressing future for us here." Because Onkel Martin and I had no valid reason for leaving and couldn't apply for permission, we would have to follow by escaping to West Berlin.

The day Mutti left with Claudia, I was sad. Claudia had become so important to me that I hated to see the train pull out with Mutti holding her at the window, both of her little hands waving, smiling happily, because she was going *atta-atta*, by-by, with her Oma.

With Mutti gone and Onkel Martin working out of town, I had the apartment to myself, but I was busy with work and sorting out our household. I had a list of things Mutti wanted me to mail to my sister's address: sheets, towels, a tablecloth or two and small sentimental items. We didn't have much, but we would need some things, like our clothes when we got to Mutti's. I couldn't take the risk of mailing packages to West Germany myself because mailing packages of personal belongings to the West would arouse suspicion, with Mutti there. If one of the packages were opened, its contents would be a tip-off of a possible escape. My sister's escape and with Mutti being in the West, it would make us even look guiltier. Then we'd be watched. Tante Elfriede and Oma picked up the items and mailed them. They came separately to fill a shopping bag that they took to Tante Elfriede's. There they made small packages and Oma and Tante Elfriede took turns mailing them, because we had only one post office, the packages were mailed at different intervals—one at a time. It was a slow and dangerous process, because if too many were mailed to the same address a postal worker, a possible communist informer, could get suspicious. Then the package would be opened before it left Goerlitz. It was dangerous for anyone to assist people to escape, because if found out, they too risked being arrested.

Because Mutti had taken our only two suitcases, Tante Elfriede and Oma, separately bought two small ones for us. Then, Onkel Martin also at separate times brought them home when it was dark. Made of brown heavy cardboard, they were the size of a weekender. Anything bigger would arouse suspicion on the train to Berlin. Onkel Martin and I decided that when we were on the train, we wouldn't show we knew each other. Because he had a different name, the patrol checking ID's wouldn't think we belonged together. Also, should either one of us be asked why we were coming to Berlin and how long we were staying, Onkel Martin would say, "Just for the weekend, to see the Stalin Allee." The Stalin Allee was a newly built wide street, the pride of the communist regime, trying to rival the Kurfuersten Damm in West Berlin. Should I be asked, I would use Vati's brother in East Berlin for my alibi, although I had seen him only once, a long time ago. All this we thought through carefully and calmly in our living room, but that's not how it worked in reality.

In the meantime my daily routine had to continue. I went to work with Renate, to dances or on walks. I told no one of our escape. Not Renate, Brigitte or even Karl-Heinz, my closest friend. That was not easy. Leaving my home, my friends, most of all Oma, unsure if I'd ever see them again because I could never return as long as Russia occupied East Germany. I cried sometimes. But, other times I was anxious to go. Yet, others times I was frightened, scared of the unknown. Would we get to West Berlin or be caught? What would life be like in West Germany? Those questions surrounded me day and night like a thick fog I couldn't penetrate.

Then, one day when I was getting ready for work, the doorbell rang. When I opened the door, our landlord was standing there. He used to be the owner of the apartment building, but the building had been confiscated by the regime, making him the manager. "*Guten Tag, Fraeulein Knebel,*" he said, shaking my hand, leaning forward, trying to peek inside our apartment.

"Why are you here *Herr Brandt*? You know my mother isn't home yet."

Still shaking my hand, he asked, "May I come in?"

Before I could react, he stepped forward and with his other hand pushed the door further open, then walked straight into the living room where his beady eyes roamed. I knew why he had come. He was snooping, a form of communist spying. Overtaken by his boldness, I watched as he scrutinized our living room, waiting for him to speak. Looking at me, his eyes squinting, he questioned me. "When is your *Frau Mutter* coming home? I don't see any of the pretty things she always has sitting around?"

My inner self shook at the audacity of this man, but I was ready for him and answered as calmly as possible, without being rude. "*Herr Brandt*, my mother will be home soon, and I'm cleaning before she returns."

Not satisfied with my answer, his eyes still roaming, with a sly grin about his mouth, he asked, "You took the pictures off the wall? To clean? And the doilies?"

"Yes, I did! I'll have it all back up when I'm done cleaning. I'm working and can only clean when I'm home." Trying to keep my composure, I edged towards the door.

He didn't move, instead asking, "Where is *Herr Hentschke*?"

Shrugging my shoulders, I said, "He is working. He'll be home this weekend."

He gave a slight nod, but I could see by the look in his eyes he was skeptical about what I had told him or what he saw. I wanted him out of the apartment before he found more things missing or had more questions. As politely as I could, opening the door, I said, "*Herr Brandt*, I have to go to work. I'll tell my mother you came to see her." With another glance around the living room, he left. After I closed the door, knees shaking, I muttered, "Nosy old communist! It's none of your business when or if Mutti ever comes home."

Thinking of what just happened, I realized we'd need to be even more cautious taking things from the apartment, because he lived next door in his other former apartment building. Tante Elfriede and Oma also thought that his visit was suspicious, because Mutti wasn't home yet. We stopped taking things from the apartment. Most already was out, except for the furnishings we had to leave behind.

About a week before our planed escape, set for the beginning of November, Onkel Martin came home on a phony sick leave. I continued to work until the end of October and then took vacation, so I could finish cleaning before Mutti's return—so I told everyone. My two pays and Onkel Martin's pay would give us a little cash after the exchange for West German money. Everything was planned down to the day—except for me.

Sometimes on Fridays when Renate and I had completed our late shift for the week, sometimes on the way home, we'd stop at dance places just for a look. Since the uprising little was happening and this evening, my last working day, wasn't any different. Our final stop was the *Rheingold*. We had just walked in when the police came to check for under age patrons. I, eighteen and sure of myself, watched as the police made their way from table to table. Renate and I were standing in the walkway when I said, "There are more policemen here than dancers. Looks as if they haven't much to do since the uprising because no one is out dancing." About that time a voice in front of me said, "*Genossin*, the informal name for a communist comrade, could I see your ID please."

Insulted, I replied, "I'm not your *Genossin*!" Renate elbowed my ribs, but I paid no attention. "Furthermore, you will address me as Fraeulein Knebel!" He took my ID, gripped my arm and walked me towards the door, with my telling him, "Let go off me!"

"No, I'm not! I'm taking you to the station!" Suddenly I didn't feel so bold, but I wouldn't let him know it. Outside he told me to get in the car, a jeep like patrol car. Onlookers stopped and stared. Soon, the other policemen came. As we drove off, I saw Renate, her purse slung over her shoulder, a lost look on her face.

At the station, only three blocks away, he took me upstairs to a foyer like room with chairs along the wall. "Have a seat!" I sat down as he went to one of the rooms that branched off the foyer. As I sat, around me was stillness as if the building had been dipped in silence. I could hear conversation on the other side of the door.

"I have brought a girl, eighteen, who didn't like being called *Genossin*. She also stated loudly that there were more of us in the Rheingold than dancers. To teach her a lesson, I brought her in. What do you think? Do you want to talk to her?"

A rather bored voice answered, "Yes, let's have a look at her. There isn't much else going on tonight." That made me mad! The nerve of that little pipsqueak to haul me in, just for fun! *Calm yourself,* my inner voice told me. *Don't make waves. Remember the plan. Don't cause trouble for yourself and Onkel Martin.* I looked at my watch. It was one thirty in the morning. I knew Onkel Martin would be worrying, wondering what had happened to me. *What will he say when I get home, if I get home?*

"Fraeulein Knebel, come in, please," the little pipsqueak said, holding the door open.

My head high, I swooshed past him. Inside the small room sat another policeman behind a desk with a chair in front where I was to sit.

"So," he said, his voice low while he leaned back in his wooden armchair, "You have never seen so many policemen all in one place?"

I shrugged my shoulders, because my inner voice said, *Keep calm and keep your mouth shut.*

Checking me over, he said, "I can arrange a whole platoon for you to parade your pretty face by."

That did it! I sat straight up. "I don't need you to tell me I'm pretty." My inner voice was shouting, *Keep you mouth shut!* But it was too late.

Seeing that he hadn't scared me, he leaned forward, his eyes so cold I shrank back in my chair. "Let me advice you!" His eyes locked onto mine. "In the future, don't remark when you see us doing our job. Is that understood?" I nodded. Then, he handed me my ID, turned to the little pipsqueak and said, "Show Fraeulein Knebel out and come back up."

"Yes, Sir." the pipsqueak replied, standing at attention.

Downstairs, before we reached the main door, he asked, "Fraeulein Knebel, I'd like to see you again. Could I have a date with you?"

The nerve of that pipsqueak to ask me for a date! My composer back and with eyes fluttering, I said, "That would be nice."

"When can we meet?"

"How about next Friday?" Thinking, if all goes well by next Friday I'll be long gone.

"Where?"

"Near the fountain at the Postplatz," I smiled.

"I'll be there!"

Again I thought, but I wont, you little pipsqueak!

When I thought I was rid of him, he called, "Fraeulein Knebel, Fraeulein Knebel, what time are we going to meet?"

Over my shoulder, without stopping, I shouted, "Eight p.m.!" I briskly walked around the corner. There, leaning on a house wall, my mouth dry, my knees shaky, my stomach churning, I realized the self-assured, sassy girl was gone. She had disappeared, leaving me leaning against a house wall at two thirty in the morning. *What have I done? How will I tell Onkel Martin about my arrest?* Although no fingerprints were taken, no papers filled out—I was arrested. *Oma! What will she say when she hears? How can I have been so careless? And Renate, tried to stop me! But I paid no attention.* Leaning against that house wall, I knew I had to go home, to face Onkel Martin. *How will he react when I tell him? He's never been mad at me.*

Slowly I made my way home, only a few blocks from the station. I had to face Onkel Martin. There was no way around it. Carefully, hoping not to wake him, I unlocked the door. When I walked into the living room, Onkel Martin, smoking, sat at the table fully dressed, his face white, his eyes, accusing, almost saying, "Where have you been?" I couldn't bring myself to tell him right away. I took my empty lunch bag into the kitchen, put my purse in the cabinet underneath the mirror, hung up my coat on the hooks next to the mirror. Stone-faced, Onkel Martin watched. Finally, taking a deep breath, he penetrated the icy silence. "Are you going to tell me where you've been until two thirty in the morning? Your shift ended at eleven o'clock!"

Taken aback by his straightforward question, I thought of acting surprised that it was two thirty in the morning, but I had to tell. I sat down across from him, "Onkel Martin, you're going to be real mad when I tell you what happened to me."

"Let me be the judge of that."

Unable to look at him, I blurted, "I was arrested!"

"What?" Onkel Martin sat straight up in his chair, shaking his head. "How did you manage that?" I told him the whole story. Then, he shook his head. "You're right I should be furious with you, but that wouldn't change anything. It wasn't smart to talk to a policeman like that. What you've done could put us in real danger."

"I know Onkel Martin. I should have not spoken that way, but the policeman made me mad. I'm not a communist, and I don't like for anyone to speak to me as if I were."

"Did they write your name and address down? Did you have to sign anything?"

I shook my head, no. "They know my name, and the officer who spoke to me never wrote anything down."

"The name is enough. If they decide to investigate, we'll be in trouble. So let's hope the officer in charge never wrote up a report, considering you their entertainment for the night."

"Onkel Martin," I whispered, "I'm glad you're not too mad at me."

He leaned back and lit another cigarette. "I should be," he rubbed his brow, "But we have more trouble. Your episode with the police might make it worse."

"What do you mean, more trouble?"

Blowing out a blue cloud of smoke, he answered, "I think we're being watched."

"Watched? When?"

"The last several evenings I've noticed a man standing opposite our apartment building, watching."

"Watching us?" Cold fear crept into my heart.

"I don't know, but it's a man in a black leather coat, like the one I had on the border patrol. I'm almost sure he's watching us because he posts himself across from us at the opposite corner where he can see and observe. But I've been watching him too. He comes and goes. One time he is here, then, he is gone, only to show up again. I think he has a replacement watching from a different angle, but I haven't been able to see from where."

"Do you think our landlord turned us in after he was here last week snooping and asking for Mutti? He didn't quite believe what I told him and he is a communist."

"It could've been him," Onkel Martin agreed, squashing his cigarette in the ashtray.

Fright showered down my spine. My face must have shown fear because Onkel Martin said, "If he is watching us, we don't want to look suspicious. Let's just keep going as we have. Most of all, let's be calm. Don't take the sheers or the drapes down, to take to Elfriede. They need to be left hanging at the window. If we take them down the landlord will snoop around again and we don't need that." I nodded. "We'll pull the drapes closed at dusk, turn off the lights about the same time as we have in the past so that everything looks as usual—no changes." For once I didn't know what to say. I had a knot in my throat the size of a dumpling. So far the plan had been talk only, but now it was serious, a reality. I was scared. I thought about those people I had seen in the jailhouse, the villa with the poles in the water. In my imagination I saw . . . .

"Are you listening to me?"

I jerked my head up, cleared my throat. "Yes, Onkel Martin I'm listening. But why are you still dressed? Haven't you been to bed?"

"Yes I was, but I worried and couldn't sleep. Then, when it was two and you still hadn't come home, I got dressed. I feel responsible for you since your mother is not here. I was going to look for you, as soon it got a little lighter, although I wouldn't have known where. But I'm glad you're home."

I wanted to say, *you don't have to worry about me. I'm an adult now.* Thinking of what I'd done, I just walked over to Onkel Martin and gave him a peck on the cheek. He smiled. I was glad he wasn't mad at me. He was a father to me even though I couldn't call him Vati.

I began to yawn. The night was almost over, "I'm going to bed. Tomorrow is . . . no today is Saturday and Renate and I, we're going dancing."

Onkel Martin grabbed a blanket and nodded. "I'll take a little snooze on the couch and wake you at midmorning. But first I'd better have a slice of bread with jam and coffee."

"Oh, me too," I called out. We ate, and left the dishes sitting. I was asleep when my head hit the pillow.

Onkel Martin never told Oma or the family about my arrest, and I was so glad. When Renate came, she said, "I was so worried about you I hardly could fall asleep. I'm glad you're here but don't make any more remarks like that again." I wanted to tell her she needn't worry because I'd be gone soon, but I didn't. Instead, we went to the dance, talked and laughed like nothing was going to happen. After the dance, we cheerfully said goodbye with a "see you next Saturday"—while my stomach was twisting.

For the next several days we did as Onkel Martin had suggested. The sheers continued to hung on the windows, the drapes were pulled closed at dusk, and the lights went out at about ten thirty. With fast beating hearts, we then watched the man in the leather coat through a very small gap in the drapes and noticed that about an hour or so after we turned off the lights, he left. All this time, while we watched him, we sat in the dark and talked in whispers only.

Our last day at home, a Wednesday in early November had arrived and because I didn't have to go to work, none of my friends would know I was gone, not until Saturday morning when Renate and I had planed our usual trip to the bath house and beauty shop. Then, she and every one else would find out I was gone. Escaped to West Berlin!

That last day, I walked to see Oma, to say good-bye. My feet felt like lead and my heart cried. My sorrow felt like when Vati had died. I was hugging Oma, crying, I didn't want to leave her. I had never seen Oma cry, but I saw tears in her eyes that she tried to control. I had to say good-bye to that loving, caring person who'd nursed me through my illnesses, taught me how to be happy again, a person I loved dearly—my Oma. *Would I ever see her again?* Deep down we both knew it was not likely. My escaping would close the door for a long and unforeseeable future.

I didn't want to leave Oma. She'd been my mentor, dried my tears, nursed me when I'd been ill, but, most of all, loved me unconditionally. Here I was, eighteen, crying, walking with my head down, handkerchief in hand, every step carrying me further away from Oma. *Why do I have to leave people I love? Has the war torn our lives totally apart? Yes, I'm leaving hopefully for a better life. With food, freedom from communism and its iron fist. But I have to give up Oma. It's like being re-united with my family but only after Vati had died. Or when Vati had taking me away from Oma. Every time my life has changed, I have to say good-bye with tears and heavy heart.* I heard, "Entschuldigung!" As someone almost knocked me off balance, bringing me back to reality. I knew then that I had to close the door on another chapter of my life, but the door didn't want to close—it stayed open just enough for me to glance back.

When I got home, Onkel Martin was packing his small suitcase with underwear, socks, shoes, pants, a jacket, two shirts, a tie and his toiletries. Seeing my swollen eyes, he gave me a hug that said more than words. I got my suitcase and started packing too. We didn't have much to pack. Most of it had been sent to my sister's. I packed underwear, a dress, but not the ugly green one, a skirt, stockings, a pair of shoes, and toiletries. We packed as if for a weekend trip, but planned to wear and extra layer clothing under our coats. We packed loosely so when we took our extra clothing off, it would fit in the suitcases. I packed no keepsakes because they would arouse suspicion if I were told to open my suitcase by the Russian and East German patrol before entering East Berlin.

Packing my clothes had taken my mind off Oma. When I was done, I looked around the bedroom. Our suitcases were ready to be closed, our extra wear ready to be put on. The bedroom was clean. The beds made. Everything looked normal, but it wasn't. Panic about the unknown took hold of me. Would we make it safely to East Berlin and across the border into West Berlin? I felt as if I were on a wave riding up and down, not knowing if it would drown Onkel Martin and me or carry us to the other shore. I went behind the partition and sat on my bed, tracing the flower pattern on the bedcover with my finger, thinking, *who will sleep in my bed?* Nothing was left in my small corner. The keepsakes I'd collected and gifts I'd received were stored in the attic at Oma's. *Will I ever see them again? No! As long as Russia controls East Germany, I can't return. In time some one else will have my things just like the toys I had to leave behind when we fled from Liegnitz. Now I'm losing everything again because, once again, I'm fleeing with only a small suitcase.*

With a sigh I stood up and went to the living room where Onkel Martin was coming in from the kitchen. A smoking cigarette between two of his fingers, a bottle of beer with an empty glass in the other hand, he sat down at his usual place at the table. "Come have a glass of beer with me," he said.

"No thanks, my stomach is too upset." I was astonished at how calm he was. "Aren't you worried?" Sitting across from him at Mutti's place, I watched Onkel Martin slowly pouring the beer that foamed high above the rim of his glass.

"Yes, I'm worried and scared too, but sitting and wringing my hands will only make it worse." He took a couple of swallows of his beer, wiped the foam off his lips and asked, "Have you peeked through the sheers lately?"

I went to the window, and, without moving the sheers, I saw him standing across from our corner in his leather coat, wearing a narrow brimmed gray hat. His collar was turned up, his hands tucked in his coat pockets. Because of the wintry icy breeze, he stepped from one foot to the other. "He is cold." I said. "Why doesn't he go home?"

"I wish he would."

"What if he's still here when we leave for the train?"

"That's not until three thirty in the morning. I hope after we turn the lights off, he'll go home as he's done in the past."

"But if he hasn't. Then we can't leave."

"Let's just wait." Was his calm and collect answer.

I turned from the window and looked at Onkel Martin, sipping his beer and smoking his cigarette, "Did Tante Elfriede give you the train tickets when we were there yesterday to say good-bye?"

"Yes, I have them in my wallet." He put his arms behind his head, stretched and said, "I'm glad she offered to get the tickets for us. If they're really watching us, getting the tickets would only confirm their suspicion."

"Do you think maybe they're not watching us?"

"I'm pretty sure they are. There are too many reasons for them not to: first Christa escapes, now your mother is past due to be home, you've been arrest, maybe they now know you were in the jailhouse at the uprising; also your participation in the Free German Youth, the FDJ isn't good either."

"That makes you the innocent by-stander, Onkel Martin."

"Not anymore. I'm just as guilty for participating."

"You know, when I stopped to say good-by to Onkel Heinz and Tante Hilde after I saw Oma, they said we shouldn't leave, but Mutti should come home."

"That doesn't surprise me. Your mother and her brother always argued over politics because both Heinz and Hilde are starting to believe in communism."

I nodded my head. "Yes, Mutti liked arguing with Onkel Heinz over politics. But did you see Tante Elfriede? She had tears in her eyes when we said good-bye and Uschi too but Onkel Richard didn't say anything."

Leaning forward again, Onkel Martin answered. "Elfriede is soft hearted and concerned. Oma and she will worry until they know we're safe. Richard, I'm sure, doesn't like Elfriede and Oma's involvement in our escape, and I don't blame him. It's dangerous!"

Biting my fingernail, I said, "It's our last day at home and I'm scared"

"Just keep calm. If we get upset, then we'll make mistakes. I hope they're not watching the train's departure to Berlin. When we get to the Bahnhof, we'll go straight to the controller. After he validates our tickets, we'll go quickly up the stairs and into the waiting train. I think the less we're seen, the better."

"What about the patrol, boarding the train just before entering East Berlin to inspect the passengers?"

"You know the plan, so let's not borrow trouble." Holding the empty beer bottle with the label that said, *Landskron Pilsner* from the *Goerlitzer Brauerei*, Onkel Martin announced, "I'm hungry. Are you?"

I went to the kitchen where I got the elbow macaroni, the last of our food supply. With that and a couple of imitation beef cubes, I made noodle soup. It was hot and filled our nervous stomachs. Although Onkel Martin claimed to be hungry, he didn't eat much and neither did I. Every so often Onkel Martin would crane his neck to see the other side of the street. "Doesn't he ever go home to eat?"

After we ate, I washed and dried the two bowls, two spoons and the pot, then left them sitting on the kitchen table and went back to the living room. The lights were on and the drapes closed. It was seven in the evening. The leather coat was still standing guard. Or was it a different one? *If they're watching us, why haven't they come for us? In several more hours we have to leave for the train. Were they waiting for us to make the move, to catch us in action?*

As I sat, hands in my lap, head down I felt like a prisoner. I had to do something. Not knowing when I'd be able to wash myself again, I went to the kitchen, set the big stainless steel washbasin filled with water on the gas burner, told Onkel Martin who was doing his crossword puzzle, "I'm going to wash myself." That meant for him to stay in the living room until I was done. Our kitchen doubled as a bathroom and we shared the water closet in the stairwell with our neighbor on the same floor.

When I came back in the living room dressed and clean, Onkel Martin said, "I'd better do that too, but it'll be later, after my crossword puzzle is done. Why don't you lie down on the sofa? Maybe you can sleep some?"

"I can't sleep." But I must have slept some, because the doorbell penetrated the silence with loud rings.

I jumped off the sofa, my head in a haze. I saw Onkel Martin's ashen face. My heart was jumping, choking me—it was nine. Onkel Martin went to the darkened bedroom to look downstairs, and when he came back, his eyes showed fear. In a shaky voice he said, "I can't see him!"

The doorbell rang again, more forcefully, and I went to the door. With clammy hands I opened the door. I felt the panic drop as I exhaled with relief, leaving me weak, barely able to say, "Karl-Heinz? What are you doing here?"

"Can I come in?"

I opened the door further. He came in and shook hands with Onkel Martin, whose color had returned. He offered Karl-Heinz a chair. Without any preamble, looking at me and then at Onkel Martin, he said, "You're escaping tonight. Am I right?"

Surprised, still reeling from fright, I didn't know what to say. I looked at Onkel Martin. "Yes, we're leaving tonight, but how did you know?"

"I didn't. I was in bed but I couldn't sleep because I had the feeling since Frau Hentschke is in the West you'd be taking off too. So I dressed again. I had to find out. I wanted to see you before you're gone."

Unsure how to answer Karl-Heinz, I heard Onkel Martin asked him, "Did you see a man standing on the opposite corner from us?"

"I wasn't paying attention. Why?" We told him about being watched and about my stupid arrest. He shook his head with a look that said, "That's just like you." We discussed life under the communist regime, a life with no future.

"Yes," Karl-Heinz said while he put his coat on, "If it weren't for my parents, I'd go with you right now, but I'm the only child and I won't leave them." He shook hands with Onkel Martin wishing us good luck and a safe arrival in West Berlin and eventually West Germany. While Karl-Heinz was saying good-bye, I went in the kitchen to get the key for the downstairs house door, locked every night at ten. Downstairs, before he went out, Karl-Heinz took me in his arms and kissed me tenderly. Then, he walked away, leaving me standing—breathless.

What was that all about? Mystified, I watched Karl-Heinz walk away, his head down, the collar of his winter jacket pulled up, bracing himself against the cold wind. Never looking back, he walked up the street, crossed to the other side, and disappeared around the corner. Locking the house door I thought, W*as Mutti right? Does he really care for me, not just as a friend? That kiss wasn't only a good-bye kiss, but a tender kiss of love.*

When I came into our apartment, Onkel Martin was placing the big stainless steel washbasin filled with water on the gas burner. "That was a surprise to see Karl-Heinz this evening."

"Yes, he surprised me too."

"For him to get out of bed, get dressed, and walk in that cold wind so he could see you means he must like you a lot."

"I think Mutti was right. She always said he liked me more than as a friend, but I never looked at Karl-Heinz that way. It's too late now. Soon we'll be on the train to Berlin. Are you glad we're escaping to West Germany?"

Onkel Martin shrugged his shoulders. "It's too late to change our minds. Besides wherever your mother is, that's where I'll be."

"Ja, I know, but would you have wanted to go if it weren't for Mutti?"

Checking the temperature of the water, he said, "Well, if it weren't for your mother, I'd stay home. Goerlitz used to be a rich and prominent city, but the war and the Russian occupation have changed all that. I would never be a communist, but I wouldn't leave either. I've lived here all of my life. I will miss it." He took the washbasin off the burner, set it on the kitchen chair, hung a towel on the back of the chair, and dropped the washcloth in the water with the soap dish alongside the washbasin. From the kitchen shelf, he got the ceramic candleholder with the candle, and after he lit the candle he set it on the floor and turned off the kitchen light. Watching Onkel Martin I wondered, *what is he doing?*

When he said, "It's way past ten, and we need to turn off the lights. Did you see the leather coat when you were downstairs with Karl-Heinz?"

"No, I was too stunned by Karl-Heinz kissing me good-bye. I didn't look."

"You allowed Karl-Heinz to kiss you with his imperfect teeth?" He smiled.

"Yeah, I know. He caught me by surprise." Changing the subject I asked, "Why do you have the candle sitting on the kitchen floor and not on the table, Onkel Martin?"

"We can't have even a glimmer of light showing through the curtain, if the leather coat is watching. With all the lights off, I need to see what I'm doing. Now, please leave the kitchen so I too can wash up. Better yet lie down and try to get some sleep. When I get done, I'll stretch out on the bed. Open the bedroom door so it warms up a little from the warmth of the living room."

Before I lay down on the sofa, I peeked through a small slit in the middle of the curtain to check on the leather coat. Relieved, I half whispered, "Onkel Martin?"

"Yes?"

"The leather coat is not here. Maybe it got too cold for him."

"Let's hope so." Without undressing, I lay down and covered myself with the sofa blanket. Unable to sleep, the minutes ticking away, I waited for the time for us to leave. My mind was already traveling on the train. *What if we get caught on the train? Will Mutti know? Will she ever know? What if one of us is arrested on the train, while we've pretend to be strangers?* All those *ifs* made my stomach ache, so that I wanted to throw up, but I knew I couldn't.

Coming from the kitchen, Onkel Martin stopped in front of the sofa, bent down, and said, "It's midnight and in three hours we have to go, so try to get some sleep."

"I can't sleep, Onkel Martin. I'm so scared my stomach hurts."

"I know. I am nervous too, but we have to stay calm. Once we arrive in East Berlin, we can breathe easy again. I'm even thinking of going to the Stalin Allee to see what's it all about."

"To the Stalin Allee?" Surprised, I sat straight up. "The Stalin Allee in East Berlin? Shouldn't we go straight to West Berlin?"

Looming like a dark silhouette, Onkel Martin said, "I think it would be safe for us to do that because should they realize this morning that we have escaped and we're off the train by then, they wouldn't know where to look for us. Berlin is a big city."

"I don't know, Onkel Martin. It sounds risky."

"Well, let's just wait and see. First, we have to get to the Bahnhof, unnoticed. Then, we need to arrive undiscovered in East Berlin. So try to sleep some."

That was the last I heard until I felt a light tapping on my shoulder, and someone calling softly, "Gisela, Gisela, its time to get up." Startled, I saw Onkel Martin bent over me in the dark living room, "I've made coffee and a slice of bread with jelly, so get up and eat something."

My stomach began to churn as I put on my shoes. The hour was near. "I can't eat, my stomach . . . ."

"Yes, you have to eat something." We ate in silence, the lit candle sitting on the kitchen floor. I watched Onkel Martin's gray face in the flicker of the candlelight. He was just as worried as I, only he didn't want me to know it. I never thought that eating a slice of bread with coffee could be so difficult. The bread kept rolling around my mouth until it finally found its way to my stomach. My upset stomach wasn't ready for food at this early hour, but Onkel Martin made sure I ate. After we were through, we washed the few dishes and Onkel Martin dried. When the dishes were back in cupboard, I got the liver-wurst sandwiches Tante Elfriede had made, gave one to Onkel Martin for him to put in the Aktentasche, along with a bottle of beer. My sandwich and a bottle of lemonade went in my purse. Then, still in the dark, we went to the bedroom to close our suitcases. Silently we put on our extra clothes and coats. With our suitcases, we walked carefully so the floorboards wouldn't squeak, through the dark living room into the kitchen. When Onkel Martin blew out the candle, it felt as if our dark apartment crackled; ready to explode with any sudden noise. In that ghostly darkness, Onkel Martin removed the ring of our apartment keys from the hook. My senses high, I could hear him softly turning the knob to open the door for us to tiptoe into the stairwell, pulling the door closed with a soft click, locking it soundlessly. Without turning the lights on in the stairwell, we crept downstairs.

When we reached the house door, my mouth felt dry, my heart pounded so my body almost vibrated. We looked through the inlaid clear glass panel of the house door to see if the leather coat was standing across the street. No leather coat. Turning the key slowly and smoothly, Onkel Martin unlocked the house door and went outside, leaving his suitcase and me inside the door. When he came back, he only said, "Let's go!" My purse slung over my shoulder and both suitcases in my hands, I slipped out, while Onkel Martin just as quietly locked the house door behind us. Then, taking his suitcase, without a backward glance, we briskly walked away, up the street and around the corner to the Bahnhof.

Although it was only a fifteen-minute walk to the Bahnhof, because of my extra clothes walking was difficult. I felt like a mummy, as the icy air attacked my face. Shortly before the Bahnhof, Onkel Martin gave me my train ticket, made of brown cardboard, the size of a movie ticket, imprinted with bold letters, *Hauptbahnhof East Berlin*.

When we entered the big high Bahnhof Halle, we walked without looking right or left to the ticket controller. Our tickets validated, punched with holes, we walked up the wide stairs and boarded the waiting train. In the train, Onkel Martin and I took deep breaths of relief. We took a window seat opposite the platform, "just in case" so Onkel Martin said, "some one should see us." Sitting across from Onkel Martin, I looked out the window. *Will I ever see Goerlitz again, Oma, my family, and friends? And Vati, this was a final good-bye to him too.* Tears began to flood my eyes. I knew this was a good-bye for a long time to a home I had returned too only seven years ago.

I heard the stationmaster blow his whistle, and slowly the train began to move out. I couldn't help it. My tears just ran down my face. Even though our lives were depressed and hopeless, I was leaving my home for an uncertain future. Onkel Martin reached over, handing me his handkerchief, with a look that said, "You will be fine." I wiped my tears and said, good-bye to my home with a promise that someday I would return.

Leaning back, trying to relax, I watched as the train rolled through the almost flat countryside, past the Landeskrone with the castle on top, landmark and pride of Goerlitz's citizens, surrounded by farmlands, pastures, and houses, still showing the scars of war. Watching as Goerlitz vanished, I realized we had cleared our first hurdle, but we were not safe yet.

For the next four hours, the train stopped along its route of seventeen towns like, *Kodersdorf, Weisswasser, Cottbus, Kunersdorf, Luebben, and Koenigs-Wusterhausen*, the last stop before East Berlin's Hauptbahnhof.

Koenigs-Wusterhausen was our next crucial hurdle. The closer we got, the more I worried. In Koenigs-Wusterhausen all trains to Berlin were held up, not permitted to continue until all passengers had been checked. It didn't matter that we were East German citizens traveling to East Berlin. Because West Berlin was so close and people were using the train to escape—as some had been caught—trains to Berlin were watched by the communist regime, searched by German police and a Russian guard. Questions tumbled in my head, as we got closer to Koenigs-Wusterhausen. *Has our escape been discovered?* Did *the leather coat become suspicious when he saw our drapes still closed? Have they broken into the apartment and found us gone? Has the patrol in Koenigs-Wusterhausen been notified to look for us, arrest us?* Despite how scared and nervous I was, the train began to slow down, and as if in protest, the wheels squealed until the train stopped. I sat across from Onkel Martin, my heart pounding. He pretended to ignore me as he had ever since we'd left Goerlitz. Looking out the window, I saw both a Russian and German guard, rifles over their shoulders, walking along the train. A picture flashed into my mind from the war, when I had seen German soldiers with rifles and dogs walking along the train, herding people as they climbed into cattle cars. I glanced at Onkel Martin. He shook his head lightly with a look that said, "Keep calm."

Then I heard an authoritative voice, "*Ausweis bitte!*" ID, please. Acting as normal as possible, I sat and watched the guards out the window watching for escapees jumping off the train, running. With a sinking feeling our escape had been discovered, I heard "Ausweis bitte!" as they came closer us.

They stopped at our compartment, the Russian carrying a rifle, the German policeman with a pistol attached to his belt. "Ausweis, bitte!" The policeman checked the identification of the person next to Onkel Martin. Then, Onkel Martin handed his identification to the German officer. My heart racing, my throat dry, I tried to read his expression, as he checked Onkel Martin's Ausweis, but it was set in stone. "How long are you staying in Berlin?"

"Just over the weekend," Onkel Martin politely answered.

"Well, enjoy your stay." He returned Onkel Martin's Ausweis. With a "Danke Schoen" the officer next handed the Ausweis back to the woman beside me. Then, he faced me. "Fraeulein? Ausweis, bitte." His arm stretched forward. I handed him the Ausweis. Eyes fixed on me he studied it. My face turned red embarrassed, my heart racing in terror. He kept looking at me with eyes revealing nothing. "How long will you be staying in Berlin?"

"Just for a few days," I answered with a dry mouth.

"And where are you staying?"

"At my Onkel's."

"Aha, and what's your Onkel's address?" Pulling out his notepad, he made note of my Onkel's address in East Berlin. Seeing what he was doing, not knowing why, panic raced through my body. *Are they going to check with my Onkel, before the train reaches East Berlins Hauptbahnhof?* I broke into a cold sweat. I glanced at Onkel Martin and his eyes told me, "Keep calm!"

"And do you have a suitcase?"

"Up in the luggage rack," I replied.

"Take it down and open it!" Shaking, but outwardly controlled, I got the suitcase, set it on my seat, and opened it. Followed by the Russian who had been watching, the policeman motioned for me to step aside. Then, he started to search through my clothes.

Why is he doing this? Does he know? Is he playing a game? My panic was turning to a silent loathing. I wanted to slap those hands rummaging through my belongings, as the Russian watched over the officer's shoulder. But I stood, my mouth clamped tight, my hands in fists tucked in my coat pockets with Onkel Martin's eyes fastened on me. Then, with a cool "Danke schoen, enjoy Berlin," they walked to the next compartment.

I straightened up my suitcase, closed it, ready to return it to the luggage rack, when a voice behind me said, "Can I assist you, Fraeulein?" When I stepped aside I saw Onkel Martin's beaming face. He placed my suitcase back on the rack.

"Danke schoen," I said, trying not to laugh out loud because Onkel Martin's formal approach was just too funny. Soon I heard the stationmaster's whistle and the train began to roll out of Koenigs-Wusterhausen, destination East Berlin Hauptbahnhof. We've made it! I wanted to shout. They hadn't discovered our escape in Goerlitz by the time the train stopped in Koenigs-Wusterhausen. Onkel Martin, leaning back, relaxing, grinned. But his eyes warned, "Keep calm. Remember we're still inside the train and not in Berlin yet, so keep calm." I was so anxious for the train to get to Berlin that I wanted to run ahead of it. At seven thirty a.m. we arrived in East Berlin's Hauptbahnhof. We had cleared our second hurdle.

Still in the Bahnhof, we went to the restrooms to get rid of our extra clothing, and, when I came out, my clothes packed, Onkel Martin was waiting for me. "Do you want to see the Stalin Allee?"

"Should we do that, with our suitcases?"

Motioning, he said, "I see lockers to rent over there."

I was so excited I hardly kept my voice down when I asked, "Aren't you glad we escaped undiscovered, so far?"

"Not so loud! "Do you want to be heard?" Automatically I looked around but there was so much noise from trains rushing, people talking and walking around us, nobody had heard us.

Our suitcases in the locker, the key in Onkel Martin's pocket, we were off to see the Stalin Allee, a short ride with the S-Bahn. The Stalin Allee wasn't much to look at. At the beginning of the wide street on a pedestal stood Stalin's oversized figure. Planted in the center strip that divided the street were young trees, their bare branches stretched into the crisp wintry air. Three story apartment houses on both sides were unadorned, looking like boxes with windows. Below the apartments were stores filled with merchandise not available anywhere else in East Germany. The Stalin Allee was competing with West Berlin's Kurfuersten Damm, but it was no match.

As we walked along, Onkel Martin discovered an ice cream parlor. "I know it's cold and early, but how about an ice cream cone?"

"Yes, that sounds good!" I agreed. Inside the store people were standing in line. "What flavor do you want?" He asked.

Before I was able to answer, an old lady standing next to me, whispered, "You have a nice *Geldonkel,* a sugar-daddy, so order up!"

"Geldonkel? He is not my Geldonkel. He *is* my Onkel," I told her.

With a gleam in her eye and a toothless smirk, she said, "Ja, ja, that's what all the young girls say."

When Onkel Martin handed me the cone filled with half vanilla and chocolate, we went outside. There, I burst out laughing.

"What's so funny?" I told him what the old lady had said. Then, we both laughed. "If she only knew how poor the Geldonkel is!" However, it got me thinking. *How many other people will think I'm a young woman, escaping with an older man—an Onkel?*

Then, I did the only thing I could do. I stopped licking my ice cream. "Do you mind, Onkel Martin, if I call you Vati? You're my stepfather, and I should stop calling you Onkel." Looking at him while standing on the Stalin's Allee, I asked again, "Do you mind?"

His nose red from the cold, his collar turned up, his scarf almost up to his chin, his hat tilted forward, he grinned. "I'd like that because you're like a daughter to me."

Then, hitting my forehead with my hand, I said, "Now we have to go back home!"

"Back home, why?"

"Tante Klara, she owes me a dozen eggs! She promised that when I called you Vati, she'd give me a dozen eggs."

Laughing he said, "I remember, but you'd better forget about it. We're not going back! Better eat your ice cream before your fingers freeze."

Side by side, licking our cones, our hands cold, we took to the subway back to collected our suitcases. Our third and final hurdle was near.

When Berlin had been divided into east and west, the subways had come under the jurisdiction of East Germany. Because of that, East Germany had the power to arrest people inside the subways even when traveling in the west sector of Berlin and held until the subways returned to the eastern sector of Berlin, so I was on edge. Taking the S Bahn to West Berlin, we sat near the door trying to look inconspicuous. To hide our small suitcases behind our coats, we opened them so they touched the floor. Then, at the first subway stop in West Berlin, we grabbed our suitcases and got off. Once on the platform, we were safe from East German control. I watched as the subway disappeared in the distance like a snake, wondering. *What's ahead of me? What's my future?* Standing on West Berlin's subway platform, happy to be free and safe, with a guarding angel by our side, I hugged Onkel Martin. I mean Vati.

Faith had given me a reason to change my mind without guilt, but it took a little while for me to say Vati again. At first I tried not to address Onkel Martin at all, but soon I liked calling him Vati. It was so much easier and I told myself that my Vati would understand and know that he would always be where I was, in my heart.

Not knowing what to do next, we looked around and saw a man wearing a blue uniform, waiting for the subway. His hands were tucked in his pant pockets, pushing his uniform jacket up into a big wrinkle around his waist. But what drew my attention to him was his mouth. It was moving as if he were eating or talking to someone. But he wasn't talking to anyone. What's he doing? "Onkel Martin, eh, ah, I mean, Vati, you see that man over there? His mouth is moving non-stop as if he's eating, but he's not putting any food in his mouth. What's he doing?"

"What man?"

Tilting my head, I said, "Over there! Do you see him, in the blue uniform?"

"Yeah, I see him. I don't know what he's doing. I read in a book once that there is a rubber like substance you can chew. Maybe that's what he's doing. He looks like a cow chewing the cud." We laughed.

"Chewing on rubber? That sounds awful." I couldn't take my eyes off him. How inappropriate for a man to have his hands in his pant pockets when wearing a suit or uniform. "I don't think he's German. Do you know what he is, Vati?"

"Well, I'm not sure, but he could be an *Amerikaner.*"

"An Amerikaner? That's what they look like?"

"What did you think they should look like?" Vati smiled.

"Well, I don't know, but in school they taught us how bad the Amerikaner were, but he looks just like us!" Laughing now, my stepfather took me by the arm and said, "Come on; let's go before you stare the poor man down. We have to find the office for refugees to sign in. I heard that every subway station in West Berlin has a place like that." But like a little kid having discovered something new, I kept looking back at the Amerikaner, his hands in his pockets, still chewing rubber.

"Watch where you're going!" Vati warned as I bumped into another one of those blue uniforms, but that one said, "Pardon me, miss!" as he rushed by me.

I looked at Vati. "What did he say?"

"I think he said, "Entschuldigung, Fraeulein.""

Not used to seeing foreigners, because the Russians stationed in Goerlitz were never on the street, I asked, "What are the *Auslaender*, the foreigners, doing here?"

"Well, we're in West Berlin, so probably we'll see more of them. Look, I see a sign over there that says, 'Refugees Here.' Seeing the word refugee, I realized I was a refugee again. I didn't like it. The war had been over for eight years and so had the fleeing, but, now, I was an East German refugee.

We knocked on the door and a female voice answered, *"Herein!"* After the customary greeting of "Guten Tag," we told the lady we were here to ask for asylum. "Have a seat," she said and began to ask questions, like where we came from, but when it came to our names, she stopped and looked up, "You're not father and daughter?"

"No," Vati explained, "Gisela is my stepdaughter. My wife is already in Wittlich, West Germany, and we're here to follow."

She looked at us as if she had heard that story before. "You have to stay in separate camps because you're not considered a family." Looking at her notes, she continued, "Herr Hentschke will be in a camp for men, and Fraeulein Knebel will stay in Marienfelde, a girl's camp." We nodded, because there was nothing else to say. Using a softer tone, she looked at me. "However, I'll place your stepfather in a camp that's in walking distance from yours." After making several calls, she gave us tickets for the bus, telling us the bus number we needed to take, adding, "While you're in West Berlin, do not take the subway!" Again we nodded, and I realized we were not in control anymore. She got up from behind her desk, shook Vati's hand, then mine, and wished us good luck.

With a "Danke Schoen," we left her office and walked to the terminal outside the subway station where busses and streetcars were coming and going. Everybody knew where they were going, except us. Waiting for our bus, Vati said, "I'll take you to your camp first. Then, I'll walk to my camp."

"But you don't know the way."

"The woman gave me the address, so I'll ask." The bus came and several stops later we were at Camp Marienfelde.

"Oh my," I groaned when I got off the bus. I had been in a camp with Oma and Christa when I'd first come back to my family, when I'd been eleven. But this felt different because I didn't have Oma to protect me. The camp looked like a jail! Like the camp in Goerlitz, it had individual barracks with a high chain length fence topped with barbed wire around them. The entrance had a wide gate for motor vehicles and a smaller one for pedestrians with a booth where a plainly dressed man stood guard. My shoulders slumped. My courage collapsed. I mumbled, "I'll never survive this! I wanna go home!"

"We can't! It won't be as bad as you think. I'm sure we'll see each other every day because of legal things we have to attend to before we're allowed into West Germany. And tomorrow being a Saturday, I'll be here at the gate about ten a.m."

I nodded as Vati led the way to the gate, where the man asked for my name. He checked his notepad and said, "Ah, yes, Fraeulein Knebel, come on in. Our camp director, Frau Ziegler, is expecting you." Then, turning to Vati, he commanded, "You can't come in; this is a girl's camp."

"I know. I'm just dropping my daughter off. Then, I'm walking to my camp. I have the address right here. Maybe you can tell me the best way to get there." I observed the man's expression when Vati said, *my daughter*. His expression said, "Ja, right, your daughter." And I thought *this is getting to be a very interesting situation*.

I gave Vati a peck on the cheek and as he walked away, he said, "I'll see you tomorrow." Another wave and he was gone. I went to see Frau Ziegler, the camp director.

"First building to your right," the gatekeeper told me.

"Thank you."

Nervous and alone, my heart beating fast, I entered the wooden building. Inside were several doors with plaques. When I knocked on the door labeled "Director," a voice answered, "Herein!"

"Guten Tag," I said to the lady sitting behind the desk, looking at me. With a friendly smile, she asked, "Are you Fraeulein Knebel?"

"Yes, I am."

"Please be seated." She pointed to the chair in front of her desk. Sitting down and looking at her I thought, *she has a kind face.*

"So, you're from Goerlitz. I was in Goerlitz once. It's a nice city"

"Yes, I was born there, but because of the Oder-Neisse-Border, part of Goerlitz is in Polish territory now."

"I know. That's so sad." Taking a lighter tone she said, "But now to you." Again, I thought. Yes, *she has a motherly way about her.*

After she asked me questions—date of birth, my mother's name and so on—she closed the brown folder, "Now we'll talk about house rules, and I hope you'll abide by them. These rules are not made to keep you in, but to protect you while you temporarily live here." Taking her glasses off, she looked straight at me without blinking. "No dating! No getting into cars! I repeat. No dating and do not get into a car! Do you understand?" My last bit of confidence left me. I shrank back in my chair, feeling it was bigger than I, thinking, *I'm in jail with a motherly warden!* I listened to her. "Dating is dangerous. More girls have disappeared from camp because they ignored our rules. East Germany has agents lurking about with fancy Mercedes. They promise to show you West Berlin's night life, but once you're in their car, they'll take you back to East Germany and there is nothing we can do." Leaning forward she asked, "Do you understand why I'm telling you this?"

She had my attention. "Yes, I understand. I won't date."

"Good. Now the other rules: curfew is at nine, lights out at ten. Breakfast between seven and nine, lunch from eleven to one. You'll receive two

Deutsche Mark per day for lunch money when you have to be at consulates or other places. Dinner hours are from five to seven. Your bed area has to be kept clean at all times and your bed made before you leave for the day. If you have a key for your suitcase, lock it; we're not responsible for lost items. Monday morning, you stop at my office and I'll get your process started. But for now, I'll take you to your quarters. Also, the kitchen will open shortly, so get something to eat. Except for Saturday and Sunday, I'm here every day from eight in the morning until five in the afternoon. Do you have any questions?" I shook my head. I was exhausted, tired, and hungry.

She got up and came around the desk, and unlike her forceful voice, she looked kindly, a short, rather stocky lady, reminding me of Oma, only younger. With the key she had taken from her desk, she unlocked a closet, handing me two blankets and a pillow. "This is your bedding. When you leave, please return them to the office."

Blankets clamped under one arm, the pillow under the other, my purse slung over my shoulder, I picked up my suitcase and followed her through the courtyard to another building with the number five in big black letters next to the door. Inside the hallway were several doors. Without knocking she opened the second door to the right. Quickly I surveyed the room furnished with eight crudely made bunk beds, set by four's on opposite walls so that the foot ends were toward the middle of the room, with narrow walkways between them. In the center was a small, well-used wooden table with eight chairs. "Hello, ladies, I'm bringing you a new roommate." The room turned silent, all eyes on me. "This is Fraeulein Gisela Knebel, and she comes from Goerlitz." Frau Ziegler turned to me. "Well, I see there are three empty bunks, so pick the one you want. You ladies get acquainted and help each other." Out the door she went.

Walking across the room, feeling eyes were following me, I took the upper bunk by the window. The bunks had low sides and a straw filled sack as a mattress. I spread one blanket over the straw sack; the other I left folded and put it over my suitcase at the foot of my bunk with the pillow at the other end. Then, I sat, my feet dangling, my chin propped in my hands. I almost cried. *I wanna go home!* But a voice within said, *You can't go home; you're a refugee now.* I felt as if once more refugee were written on my forehead.

An older girl, lying in her bunk next to mine, propped herself on her elbow and said in a kind voice, "You're homesick. It happens to just about all of us. But it's not that bad. You won't be here long because they're fast in moving us out of West Berlin and into West Germany. The most you'll be here is about two weeks. I'll be leaving within the next day or so." I tried to smile.

At five o'clock, the girl and I went to another building for dinner. There was no kitchen, only a mess hall room with tables and long benches. I was given silverware and two metal containers—one for soup, the other for coffee—to keep while I was there. The food was mainly soups, delivered in big stainless steel containers. We also had bread, butter, different lunchmeats, fruit and an occasional chocolate bar. Breakfast was bread, butter, lunchmeat and real coffee, not the wheat kind we drank in East Germany. When we got back, I fell into my bunk. It had been a long, stressful day. Straw mattress or not, I slept soundly until morning.

I got to know the girls, but not well because within a short time and with smiles on their faces, they said, "Good bye." But the prediction of only being here for two weeks didn't come true.

When I awoke the next morning, I had to think where I was. From my upper bunk, propped on my elbow, I watched the girls going in and out of our small dimly lit room, abuzz with chatter and laughter, a transistor radio playing the latest dance music. When I looked at my watch, I saw it was seven thirty, not totally daylight yet. Watching the girls, I wondered where they were going so early on a Saturday morning?

From a bunk in the far corner opposite my bunk came a, "Quiet! How can anyone sleep with that racket going on? I want to sleep!" For a moment there was silence. Then, the girls looked at each other, shrugged their shoulders and snickered as if they'd heard that protest before. The chatter and laughter resumed.

I lay back down and stared at the ceiling, only two feet from my face. The straw from the mattress was scratching me. I hadn't felt it last night but now I did. My mind started to wander. I missed my home, my bed with a real mattress that Mutti had bought for me. Hearing the latest hits from the transistor radio stirred up memories of dancing at the Konzert-Haus and the Stadthallen-Garten. A voice within me said, "*Do you really want to be here?*" *Granted life is miserable in East Germany, and here there are food and freedom, but is life really going to be better in West Germany?* Then, my other voice said, "*You're just scared. Get up, shower, get dressed, eat some breakfast, and meet Vati outside the gate.*" I climbed out of my bunk and asked one of the girls where the bathroom with the showers was.

The oblong bathroom had one wall of sinks with mirrors above. The opposite wall had five shower stalls with no doors. A row of plain wooden benches sat in the center. Although we were all girls, to undress in front of strangers embarrassed me. I looked around, but none of the girls were paying any attention to me, so I quickly took my shower and dressed. Then,

I had a breakfast of bread, butter, lunchmeat, jelly, and barely warm coffee. I was hungry, and, no matter the circumstances, I could always eat.

I washed my metal dishes, made my straw bed by smoothing out the blanket over the straw sack and folded the upper blanket. Before placing the metal dishes and the blanket on the suitcase, I unlocked it, got my purse, relocked it, placed the dishes on top of the suitcase, and covered it all with the blanket. We had a coat closet in the room, but I used my coat both as an additional cover during the night and as a way to keep my only coat secure. It was now ten, with my coat on, my purse slung over my shoulder, I went to meet Vati at the gate.

There, a different and younger guard greeted me. "Guten Morgen!"

"Guten Morgen." I replied, walking past him, waving at my stepfather already waiting outside the gate.

"Just a moment, Fraeulein!" The gatekeeper called, motioning me to come back. "You need to sign out!"

"Sign out? Why?"

"So we know you have left the premises and when you come back, you sign in." Standing, a figure of authority, tablet in hand, pencil poised, he asked, "Your name, please?" I gave him my name. "Oh ja, here it is. You're Fraeulein Knebel. Now you're signed out. Have a nice day, and we'll see you when you return." Then, with a glance at Vati he added with a funny grin, "Be careful, and don't forget curfew is at nine!" "*You mean jail time, warden,*" I wanted to reply but thought the better of it. I had to stay here, like it or not.

I greeted Vati with a peck on his cheek and a cheerful "Guten Morgen". Then we walked arm in arm down the street.

"How was your night?" Vati asked. I told him about my room, the girls, no shower doors, the rules we had to follow, how I missed my bed and everything else.

"It will take a while for us to get used to our new surroundings, to live with strangers with no private space or time, but we'll get through this."

Trying to snuggle a little closer to my stepfather, not wanting to talk about camp anymore, I said, "It's cold this morning."

"Yes, it's a little nippy, but if we walk briskly, it'll warm us up."

"Where are we going?"

"To my camp, so you know how to get there. It's not far, only about a thirty-minute walk from your camp. So we won't miss each other, we'll walk the same streets every time." We walked up the street I lived on, around the corner and down another street, where we crossed over, and around the corner again until finally we came to a round, red brick building, with a slightly peaked roof flanked by restored apartment buildings on both sides of the street. Vati stopped across the street, "That's where I'm living."

"You live in a round building with no windows?"

"It was a bunker during the war."

"A bunker? In the middle of these apartment buildings?"

"Yes, a bunker. It was built for the neighborhood to seek shelter when Berlin had their air raids. A worker in the bunker told me that the walls and the roof were thick and steel reinforced to withstand a bomb."

I stood there, looking, imagining people running into the bunker as sirens howled and bombs exploded. The red brick walls were scarred with big bullet holes from low flying fighter planes with machine guns. It brought back memories of the attack I'd experienced in 1945 in Zittau just before the end of war when I was nine. My stepmother had sent me to the butcher's when the sirens howled and enemy planes flew low, shooting along the streets. A woman had pulled me inside an apartment building. I remembered how scared I'd been sitting in the cellar.

"Come on," my stepfather's voice interrupted my memories. "I'll show you inside. Then, when you come, you can wait for me in the entrance hall."

"I'm allowed inside?"

"Yes, you are. So come on." We crossed the street to the entrance where a man sat behind a window. There we stopped. Vati gave his name and told him that I was his stepdaughter that he wanted to show me the lobby where I could wait when I came to meet him.

With a friendly nod, the man asked for my name and wrote it next to Vati's. Then, he explained to me, "When you come to meet your stepfather, all you do is give your name and his, and you'll be allowed to wait in the lobby. But in the lobby only!" I nodded. I thought it rather odd that he'd never blinked an eye when Vati told him I was his stepdaughter.

The lobby was a big room, painted white with several rows of wooden benches. A big bulletin board hung on the wall with notes attached, giving names of people still missing from the war, asking anyone if they knew of their whereabouts. Off the lobby to one side were a hallway and steps that lead below ground, but they were roped off. "So," Vati said, "now you know where I'm staying. If we miss each other while walking between our camps, you stay here. I'll come back here to check for you."

I nodded, my eyes scanning the room, "Where is that hallway leading too, Vati?"

"To several big rooms with bunk beds, and bathrooms with showers. This is a big place!" Vati sounded just as amazed as I.

When we were back outside, I was still thinking how easy it was to be in Vati's bunker, so I said, "Your camp is not like mine. That guard didn't act funny at all when you told him who I was."

"It's a men's camp and we're not watched that closely. But have rules just like you and we do have to sign in and out."

Being around my stepfather was relaxing. I was more at ease, so everything didn't look as bad as it had earlier. We walked and checked out our surroundings. We took a bus to downtown West Berlin, walked around, and exchanged our East German money. Vati bought a pack of cigarettes and a chocolate bar for me. When we got hungry, we stopped at a *Bratwurst* booth and bought a Bratwurst on a bun with mustard and a beer to drink. We felt like royalty as we wiped the juice off our lips. Later in the afternoon, to save money, we walked back to camp, almost two hours.

On Sunday, to save money, Vati came after lunch. Along the way, we bought a picture postcard for Mutti to let her know we'd safely crossed the border and dropped it in the mailbox with both of our mailing addresses. And so our first two days in West Berlin ended.

I hated signing in and out like a prisoner, hated the questioning look from the gatekeeper when I met Vati and when he dropped me off. Even the girls looked at me with question marks in their eyes.

When I returned Sunday before the dinner hour, one of the girls approached me. "You have a boyfriend. Don't you know we're not to date, not even for a walk?"

"I know we can't have a boyfriend, and I don't have one."

"Then, who is the man you've been going with yesterday and today?"

"That's my stepfather!" She didn't believe me, so I explained our circumstances, but that fell on deaf ears.

This was a different world I had to live in for a short while, a world filled with strangers, uncomfortable, impersonal, cold world. The camp had makeshift surroundings and felt unclean even though the buildings and rooms were scrubbed with disinfectant every day, it's smell accosting me. I had to lay my feelings aside by telling myself this was not for ever. Still, it felt as if I were hanging on a limb, swinging in the breeze with no ground below me. I hated returning to camp after Vati and I had been out walking.

Monday morning arrived and so did my appointment with the Camp Director, Frau Ziegler. I hurried through breakfast, straightened my bed, and at nine o'clock sharp, when I knocked on her door, I heard Frau Ziegler's cheerful "Herein." I entered her office.

"Guten Morgen!" I said, my voice not as cheerful as hers. I had had a restless night, my heartstrings pulling me home. I missed Oma, my friends, and my comfy bed that I didn't own anymore because the nosey landlord and the police had probably broken into our apartment.

"Have a seat, Fraeulein Knebel." Instantly, her invitation to sit brought me back to where I was, the barracks. Sitting behind her desk, Frau Ziegler inquired, "How was your weekend?"

"It was fine." My flat tone seemed to make no impression on her. *Maybe she was used to girls being unhappy when first they came here.* "Well, then let's get started. I have here," she said, "the outline of a *Laufzettel fuer das Notaufnameverfahren, an* Application for Emergency Entrance Permission. We call it the walking paper, because you'll be going, by bus and on foot from agency to agency listed on this form. Every East German refugee who asks for asylum in West Berlin is required to see those agencies before permission to enter West Germany is granted." Laying the printed form with its outline down, she looked at me. "First stop is the *Gesundheitsamt,* the Health Department, for a medical evaluation. That's to make sure refugees don't bring contagious diseases into West Germany."

Offended, I said, "I'm not sick."

"After the Health Department, then to the *Polizei Amt,* the Police Department. They'll search in East Germany to see if there is a warrant out for a non-political arrest to make sure refugees asking for asylum haven't killed or needed to be jailed for other than political reasons."

Facing Frau Ziegler, sitting in front of her desk in a well used wooden straight back chair, my hands resting in my lap, I said, "No, I didn't kill over there or have to be jailed."

Again, she ignored me and continued her rehearsed speech, "You work your way down this list, and eventually you'll meet with the *Jugend-Amt,* the Juvenile Board. They will examine all the findings and determine your eligibility to transfer to West Germany. After your application of asylum has been approved by the West German government, then you'll meet with our Allies."

"Meet with who?"

"Our Allies, the Americans, English, and the French at their consulates." Her tone was matter of fact.

"Why?"

"We are not a free country, so to speak, and whatever we do has to be approved by our Allies. Also, they're very interested in the refugees coming from a communist controlled country."

"But I don't speak English or French."

"They have German-speaking people there. The application will take about two weeks or more, depending on what the findings are. There are no appointments for these agencies, so you need to be there as early as you can. On your arrival, give them your name; then, wait."

Taking a sip of coffee from her white coffee cup with matching saucer, she leaned back for a moment. "Your first order on this form is the Gesundheitsamt, the Health Department." Getting up from behind her desk, she handed me what she called the walking papers. "Fill in your name and date of birth. As proof of residency the address, *Mariendorf, Ring-Ecke Gersdorferstr. 73-79 Askania Lager, West Berlin,* is stamped on the head of the application. Frau Ziegler handed me a pen, and I wrote my name and date of birth on the line above the address. Then, I saw, written in by Frau Ziegler and above my name, the registration number for my application. Seeing that number, I thought, *I'm not only a refugee but also a number.* Again, my homesickness felt worse than the miserable life I had left behind.

I handed the application back to Frau Ziegler who said, "I'm almost done with instructions. Because we're in a suburb of West Berlin, to get to these agencies, you have to ride the bus. Every morning, my secretary will hand you a bus ticket with directions and lunch money. Then, when you leave, the agency will give you the return ticket. Dinner is in camp." Standing across from me, looking at me, her voice firm, she said, "One last reminder, do not take any other transportation and that includes the subways. Take only the bus routes given to you. You understand?"

"Yes, I understand."

Then, handing me the walking papers in a milder tone, Frau Ziegler said, "Good luck, and if you have any questions, talk to my secretary. She will inform me."

I shook her hand and almost curtsied as I replied, "Danke Schoen." Frau Ziegler nodded to her secretary, a young woman who sat at a desk behind hers, a sign that she was ready for the next girl waiting outside her door. As I walked out of the office, a new girl walked in. That's when realized I had joined the brigade of walking refugees. So began my daily duties for the next several weeks.

Excused by Frau Ziegler, I hurried to meet Vati, to see what his schedule was. Luckily, he was still at the bunker. He had the same walking papers as I, with the same places, so we went together, and I was glad because we had to ride the bus all over West Berlin.

By the time we got to our first stop, the Health Department, they gave us a return ticket, telling us to come back the following day. So the next morning I got up at six o'clock, had my ticket and lunch money by eight o'clock, then met Vati halfway, and took the bus to our destination. At the Health Department, we gave our names. Then, we sat, waiting. When finally I was called for my examination, I had to undress and was given no gown or cover. My head was inspected for lice, my body scrutinized for fleas. Then I was x-rayed, poked with needles, and told, "Take a deep breath, now out, then in again, and out again." After that I was questioned about my past activities, including my sex life. The last was embarrassing.

When Vati and I were on our way to camp, we talked about the examination. Indignant, I told him, "And then, the doctor, about your age, asked me if I had a sex life! Do you know how embarrassed I was? Why do they have to know all that?" Disgusted, I shook my head.

"I understand how you feel. I was asked the same questions. It's part of the requirement and their job to make sure refugees don't bring venereal diseases into West Germany."

"Well, maybe it's their job, but I didn't like being prodded or questioned about my earlier life."

"Just think of it this way. It's like entering a foreign country. East German refugees want to enter West Germany. Although we're all Germans, we're two countries now."

"I hate that whole refugee business. I wish I was home again!" I was about to cry.

Putting his arm around me, he said, "Just be patient and keep your chin up. I don't like it either, but we're here now. Together, we'll get through this." His arm around my shoulder, me leaning into Vati, we walked up to the gate where the gatekeeper gave me a look that said, "You're not to have a boyfriend." Ignoring him, I gave my stepfather a kiss on his cheek. With a, "See you tomorrow," I walked up to the gatekeeper, signed in, and, smiling to myself, went to my home away from home, thinking, At least that is entertaining.

I ate the usual soup and sandwich. Then, I showered, because it was almost impossible in the morning with everyone wanting to shower at once. After brushing my teeth, I curled up in my straw-bed, adding my coat for safekeeping and warmth. Exhausted, I fell asleep.

The daily routine of meeting with agencies was a job. Get up at six. Clean and dress. Eat breakfast. Pick up the bus ticket and lunch money, and join the marching brigade to the next agency on the walking paper. Depending who left their camp first, Vati and I met along the way, on our specific street route.

When I stepped out from the barracks, a piercing, cold wind attacked me. Although I was bundled up with a sweater beneath my coat, a scarf around my neck and head, my mouth hidden behind my upturned coat collar, and my gloved hands in my coat pockets, the icy November wind let me know my East German coat was no match for him.

By the time I met Vati I was shivering. Because girls didn't wear long pants in the 1950's, my stocking legs felt like ice sticks. "Brrrrr!" I said, "It's so cold, even my breath is making small white clouds."

Vati his coat collar turned up, his hat low over his fore head, said, "Yes, we're having a cold spell right now. Get close to me so we can keep each other warm." Arm in arm we walked to our bus station, then to the next agency on our walking paper, the *Polizei Revier*, or police station.

There we filled out forms with date of birth, past and present addresses, arrest records and more. We were fingerprinted and had our pictures taken front and side views. I felt like a prisoner. The official who took my fingerprints was curt, making me feel low, not worth bothering with. "I hate going to all those agencies. Some are not very nice!"

"I suppose they're tired of the influx of people coming from East Germany day after day." Vati countered.

"That might be, but they could be a little friendlier. They need to live in East Germany for a while. That'd change their minds."

Vati smiled. "That will never happen."

I also hated having to explain our relationship when we asked to process our paperwork together. Because our last names were different, we had to explain that he, Martin Hentschke, was my stepfather and that my mother, his wife, was already in West Germany. The receptionists listened with cynical grins. That behavior infuriated me. "I wish they'd stop their stupid grins. Can't they see you're old enough to be my father?"

My stepfather shrugged his shoulders. "Don't let it bother you. Maybe they have seen cases where older, married men have tried to flee with young girls to West Germany."

"Do you really think so?"

"Well, it could be."

One day, when we got back from one of the agencies in the early afternoon, Vati dropped me off at my camp. With a peck on his cheek and a, "See you tomorrow," I walked up the gate to sign in. The young gatekeeper sneered. "Fraeulein Knebel, Frau Ziegler wants to see you right away."

"Me, why?"

Grinning, and glancing at Vati, he said, "You'll find out! I tried to warn you."

Warned me of what? I turned to Vati who'd heard what I'd been told. Shrugging my shoulders, I said, "I don't know what it's about, but I'll tell you tomorrow." Then I went to see Frau Ziegler. After knocking, and waiting for her "Herein," I walked in. "Guten Tag, Frau Ziegler."

"Oh, Fraeulein Knebel, please sit down. We need to talk."

"Talk?"

"Yes, talk."

Sitting in her high backed chair, her left arm resting on the armrest, her right elbow on the other armrest, her hand under her chin, Frau Ziegler's sharp eyes roamed over my face.

Talk about what? I felt my face turned red and I looked down. *Why is she looking at me like that?*

Frau Ziegler cleared her throat, leaned forward, with her lower arms now resting on her desk, her hands folded, said, "Fraeulein Knebel, did I not tell you the rules when you came? Did I not repeat our rules so you understood them? Yet you have chosen to ignore them, and I must say I'm disappointed in you because I had thought you to be a nice, decent young girl." Her watchful eyes still on my face, she asked, "Why haven't you respected our rules?"

"I don't know what you're talking about, Frau Ziegler." I stammered, feeling guilty, for what, I didn't know.

"Your boyfriend!" Leaning further over her desk, her voice rising, she said, "You have a boyfriend! You know it's forbidden to have a boyfriend while going through processing!"

So, that's what it is! Relieved, I wanted to laugh, but I knew not to. "Frau Ziegler, I don't have a boyfriend. That's" . . .

"Fraeulein Knebel," she interrupted me, "I know you have a boyfriend. It's the gatekeeper's job to inform me of such matters, and he reported that every day a gentleman escorts you too and from our camp. You kiss him and tell him, 'See you tomorrow.' Is that not so?"

"Yes, but he is not my boyfriend. He's my stepfather, and I do not kiss him. I only give him a peck on his cheek." And there it was: Frau Ziegler had the same unbelieving look I had seen so many times. Then, I told her our story, beginning with Mutti's taking baby Claudia to my sister, her mother.

Still skeptical Frau Ziegler said, "It's not that I don't want to believe you. It's my job to protect you girls as much as I can. We've just lost another girl. I don't know what happened to her. What's your stepfather's name?"

"Hentschke, well, Martin Hentschke," I corrected myself.

In a much friendlier tone she said, "I'd like to meet your stepfather the next time he is here. And you say you have letters from your mother and Herr Hentschke too. I'd like to see them. Can you bring them to me?"

"Yes, I can, and I will introduce my stepfather to you." Trying to be funny, I added with a smile, "He is too old anyway."

Ignoring my remark, Frau Ziegler walked around her desk. "I'm glad you didn't disobey our rules." We shook hands and said, "Auf Wiedersehn."

After eating and showering, I lay in my straw bunk. The room, as always, was filled with talk and laughter. I looked at the empty bunk a foot away from me. I missed the girl who'd slept there; she was the only one I had talked with. I'd enjoyed listening to her adventures with her boyfriend. When she'd come back in the evening, she'd tell me how much fun she'd had, and the places her boyfriend had taken her in his Mercedes. Then, quietly and partly hidden under her blanket, she'd show me the jewelry and clothes he'd bought her. Seeing the gifts, I asked, "Aren't you afraid he'll take you back over the border to East Berlin and you'll be unable to come back?"

But she'd shaken her head, her bobbed black hair swooshing around her head. "No, my boyfriend loves me and he wouldn't do that."

But for three days there'd been no sign of her. Lying in my bunk, I wondered. *Did he take her back to East Berlin? Or did he really love her and now they're living somewhere in West Berlin or West Germany, happily ever after? Frau Ziegler is right, dating, is way too dangerous.* Hoping the girl was well and happy. I closed my eyes and went to sleep.

The following morning when Vati came to pick me up, I had him meet Frau Ziegler. Reassured that he was not my boyfriend, Frau Ziegler shook his hand. "Herr Hentschke, I'm glad to have met you. Please feel free to come in and wait in the day room when you pick up your stepdaughter. It's too cold to be standing outside." Frau Ziegler notified the gatekeepers that Vati was allowed to enter whenever he came between the hours of eight a.m. and six p.m. Having a man in the day room, a stepfather of a fellow inmate, was quite a change from the regular routine of the camp. The girls liked Vati and I became a novelty because no one else had a father or family members going through processing with them. On weekends, waiting for me in the day room, Vati was entertained by the girls and I could tell he enjoyed that.

Almost done with our walking papers for the West German authorities, we both got a clean bill of health, and I was cleared after the police's investigation. But Vati's police clearance hadn't come back. "I wonder what's holding it up?" I asked.

"I think it's because I was a border patrol trooper for the East German government."

"I hope we have no problem getting permission for West Germany."

Vati shook his head and in his usual quiet manner said, "I haven't done anything against the law. I didn't shoot anyone or turn anyone in for smuggling. Grown-ups just have a longer history. Besides, the authorities have a lot to check because so many people are asking for asylum."

Soon after our conversation with Frau Ziegler, Vati was told that his police record was clear. We were so happy. The only thing left was to wait for a final oral examination conducted by a board of the West German administration. This board will judge our request for political asylum and permanent residency in West Germany.

While we waited for those appointments, next on our walking papers were the French, English, and American embassies. Although cold, the weather was bearable, the sun peeking out from behind the clouds as Vati and I walked to the French consulate. As we came into the building, uniformed French speaking people kept crossing my path. *Was I in a foreign country?* After I stated my business to a German-speaking lady behind the visitor's desk, she ushered me into a room where a young uniformed Frenchmen was sitting behind a desk. He hardly looked up at my "Guten Tag!" Wordlessly, he reached for the form in my hand. He signed it, handing it back to me without a glance. I took the form and, rather noisily, I closed the door behind me. *Stupid Frenchmen!* When I complained to Vati, he said, "Don't let it bother you. The Germans and the French haven't been the best of friends for a long, long time."

"I wonder what will happen when we go to the English? I'd better brace myself."

But to my surprise the older Englishman, a Captain, was cool but polite. He invited me to sit and, with a smile, offered me something in a narrow tiny wrapped in silver package. "Gum?" Not knowing what to do with it, I shook my head, no. Then, he opened the drawer of his desk and pulled out a pack of cigarettes. "Smoke?" he said, reaching over his desk with the pack in his hand.

I nodded, "yes". After I tried to extract a cigarette from the half empty pack, he handed me the package. Red-faced, I put it in my purse, saying "Danke Schoen."

He signed my form, shook my hand, and said, "Good bye!"

Vati was waiting for me. When we were some distance away, I said, "Well, that wasn't too bad and I have something for you." I handed him the cigarettes.

Vati laughed and showed me a pack of cigarettes of the same brand, "I got one too!" Because we didn't have much money, Vati watched his smoking, so free smokes pleased him.

The next day we went to our last stop, the American consulate. Although my experience with the English hadn't been bad, I didn't look forward to meeting the Americans, because I remembered the East German communist teachings, saying Americans were bad. Walking with Vati, I remembered the song, "Go home, Ammy, Ammy go home . . ." a hate song we'd been taught in school. I remembered the bombs, the destruction done to my country. I disliked the Americans! *But you didn't mind the English? Well, it's because I never heard much about them, and the English man was friendly not rude like the French. The Russians? They're on the top of my hate list. I wish all of them would go home so I could go home too.*

"You're so quiet. What are you thinking?"

"I'm thinking about the Americans. I hope they won't be as rude as the French."

"You're worrying too much. You'll be just fine." *Vati and his calm manner, does he ever worry or get mad?*

The American consulate looked like a new building with big windows and swinging glass doors. As in the other consulates, uniformed men and woman were going about, talking in a strange language. Again, a German speaking uniformed lady behind a desk in the lobby asked me about my business, then escorted me to a room with several upholstered chairs where I was to wait. While I sat there, I listened to the strange language. My heart started to thump, and I twisted my fingers. *I don't want to be here!* A door opened, and an a man with gold bars on his shoulders and small colored ribbons pinned to his blue uniform came to where I sat. In perfect German, he said, "Are you Fraeulein Knebel?"

I nodded. "Yes."

"Please come into my office." With a sweeping gesture of his hand he invited me to go ahead of him. Once inside, I saw a flag of red and white stripes with a blue field filled with white stars standing upright near a corner of the brightly lit room. He pointed at the chair in front of his desk. "Please sit down." Then the tall middle-aged American man walked around his desk, and, just like the Englishman, offered me gum. *Why is everyone offering me gum?* Unable to form words, I shook my head. With a broad smile that showed a perfect set of white teeth, he asked, "Do you smoke?"

"No, I don't smoke, but my father does!" I popped off.

Amused, he said, "So you do talk. Here is pack of cigarettes for your father and a candy bar for you. OK?"

OK? What does OK mean? He handed me a candy bar with writing I could not read and a pack of cigarettes.

Sitting across from him, I watched him while he shuffled some papers around. "So you're from Goerlitz and you worked, among other places, in a Konversatoren factory." Surprised, I nodded. "And you were also arrested a week before you and your stepfather escaped from East Germany." Looking at me he said, "Is that right?" I was speechless. My face turned red. Making himself comfortable in his leather chair, he said, "Tell me about the arrest, about the factory and about how you made the condensers. We're interested in your past work."

Sitting in front of that blue uniformed American I asked as politely as possible, "Excuse me. How do you know all that?"

He only smiled, "We know everything." Since there were no secrets, I relaxed and told him what he wanted to know. We talked about living conditions in East Germany under the Russians, with him interrupting with questions. Once in a while, he'd note something in the file in front of him. When he closed the file, I knew the interview was over. He came around the desk, and said, "Thank you for coming, Fraeulein Knebel. You will hear from us again. We have your mother's address from Wittlich on file." With his "Good-bye," I was excused.

When I met Vati in the lobby, I shook my head in disbelief. "Do you know he knew where I worked and knew about my arrest?"

"They knew everything about me too." Vati said.

"Ja, but how do they know all that?"

"Because they have their connections, just like East Germany has over here." I kept shaking my head. Never had I heard of any thing like that before. "He said I would hear from them again. Were you told the same?"

"Yes, after we got to Wittlich."

"I wonder what they want from us."

"Who knows, let's just wait and see."

Soon after we visited the embassies, Frau Ziegler notified me that I was scheduled for a meeting with the youth board the following day at ten o'clock. Her secretary gave me the address, and Vati and I met early the next morning to ride the bus to the nearest stop. We walked a short distance to a big old building that miraculously had survived the bombs, showing only a bit of damage. The room where I was to meet the board looked like a courtroom, but it was not. A long, heavy, ornate wooden table with seven matching high-backed chairs, sat against the far wall, facing into the room. Across from that big, long table was a smaller wooden table with four chairs and in back of that table were rows of chairs all facing the long table. Vati was allowed to join me, and we sat at the small table facing the board's table.

When the solemn faced board members came in through a side door, Vati and I stood up and waited until we were told, "Be seated!" Looking at the board, I saw three woman and four men, each around fifty. A man who sat in the middle spoke up. "Please state your name and where you're from!"

My heart pounding, my knees weak, I jumped up, my chair screeching on the highly polished floor. All eyes on me, I swallowed. My face red, I said, "My name is Gisela Knebel, and I'm from Goerlitz."

"Please stay seated, Fraeulein Knebel."

I tried to look self-assured, but my eyes didn't know where to settle. "Thank you." I sat down.

Then, the questioning began: "How did you come to West Berlin? Why do you want to enter West Germany?" With a tense stomach, my mouth dry, I told the board that life in East Germany was unbearable, with only enough food to barely survive on; that living under the iron rule of Stalin's successor, Nikita Khrushchev, Ulbricht and Pieck the East German leaders was depressing. That to survive I would have to join the communist party. That I felt politically threatened when I refused to join or participate in the communist organizations and their functions.

While I answered the speaker's questions the board members made notes. Then, I was asked about my parents. I told them my father had died in 1945, so I was here with my stepfather, Martin Hentschke. We were asking permission to enter West Germany to be reunited with my mother, his wife, already in West Germany. When I was asked why my mother was already in West Germany, I explained why.

With the members listening, their eyes on me, my heart racing, I tried several times to swallow that lump in my throat, but it wouldn't go down, so I was glad I was allowed to sit during the question and answer period. After what seemed a lifetime of questioning, the speaker looked at his fellow members, and they nodded their heads. Turning to me, he said, "We have concluded our investigation, Fraeulein Knebel. Please stay seated until we return." Their folders rustled closed; their chairs scraped as they stood up. They filed out through the same door they had come in.

Relieved but worried, I looked at Vati. "Do you think they'll send me back to East Germany? Deny me entry to West Germany?"

"I don't think so. I have heard that only in extreme cases have young people been denied entry to West Germany."

Before I could ask another question, the board members, folders under their arms, returned in duck order, while Vati and I stood and waited for the board to be seated.

"Be seated," the speaker said. Then, locking eyes with me, he continued, "Fraeulein Knebel, seldom have we, the board, denied entry to West Germany to a young adult. Therefore, the board unanimously has granted you permanent residency in West Germany."

Plunk, the lump in my throat went down and a wave of happiness went through me. *I made it! I made it!* Trying to keep my excitement under control, to show I was worthy of the freedom given me, I stood up and with a clear voice, I said, "Danke Schoen." Then, set down.

The board members smiled and nodded their heads in return. The speaker continued, "We are aware that you and Herr Hentschke, your stepfather, together have asked for asylum, but we are only responsible for young adults under twenty-one. We recommend that you fly out of West Berlin as soon as possible. But under the circumstances, you have a choice to wait for your stepfather or to fly now, with in a couple of days."

Without hesitation I said, "With the board's permission, I will wait for my stepfather."

The speaker talked to the persons on either side of him. Then, he turned to me and said, "Fraeulein Knebel, we have decided to grant you your request and will note it in your file. We hope Herr Hentschke will be granted permanent residency in West Germany soon, because we want to transfer you out of West Berlin as soon as possible." Then they all stood up, and the speaker said, "This meeting is closed!"

Elated, Vati and I left the building, but not before I hugged him.

Having received permission to enter West Germany, we had to wait only for my stepfather to appear before the board that reviewed his case. Every day Vati came to my camp, and we went for walks. The gatekeeper no longer gave Vati funny looks. Sometimes they'd be in deep conversation. Even Frau Ziegler visited with Vati, and the girls were always glad to see him.

Every day I asked, "Did you hear anything yet?"

"No, not yet."

We'd go on our walks and exchange Mutti's letters. In the first letter, she told us that Tante Elfriede had written, that our apartment had been forcefully opened at seven thirty a.m., the same time we'd arrived in East Berlin's Hauptbahnhof. Had they broken into the apartment an hour earlier, they would've caught us in Koenigs-Wusterhausen, where the train was stopped before entering East Berlin's Hauptbahnhof. Tante Elfriede also wrote that Oma had been at the Bahnhof. Because we had not looked around in the Bahnhof Halle, we had missed her.

When I read that, I felt so guilty that Oma had braved that still dark, icy morning and had made a thirty-minute walk to the Bahnhof to say good-bye once more. It made my heart hurt all over again, made me aware how much I missed her.

In another letter, Mutti wrote she had rented a place for when we got to Wittlich. The people she had rented from were in the process of building their house, but had stopped to fine tune the interior of the house because of finances. Mutti rented the unfinished large bathroom with a small window and an additional room across the hall, for a bedroom. The bathroom would be our kitchen with a stove in place of the future bathtub, with enough space opposite the stove for a table, two chairs and a small couch against the wall where I would sleep. Most of the furnishings belonged to the landlord and some of it had been given to us. Since Mutti didn't have money to pay rent, she was helping *Frau Kohler*, the landlord's wife, with cleaning, cooking, and general housework. *What have we got ourselves into?*

Besides reading Mutti's letters, I enjoyed our walks and window-shopping. However, my well-used East German shoes were falling apart from our daily walks, so I window-shopped at shoe stores. Tapping on the on the window, I'd say, "Look Vati, over there, on the pedestal. See the black patent leather shoes with the buckle on top? I like them. Oh! How about the red ones? Oh! I like the gray suede high heeled ones too!" Eyes shining, I shopped for shoes like a child for toys, forgetting I had no money.

Vati tried to pull me away. "Come on; let's go. You know you can't buy shoes right now. But once you're in West Germany and have a job, then you can buy as many shoes as you want." His words didn't help me much. Whenever girls passed us, I looked at their shoes in envy, ashamed at my worn out East German shoes. The next time Vati visited with Frau Ziegler, he told her about my shoe problem.

"I know of a place where Fraeulein Knebel can get another pair of shoes for free. Come to my office and I'll give you the address." My mind reeled. I heard only, *shoes for free*. In her office Frau Ziegler gave us the address.

I thanked her, then turned to Vati, "Can we go right now?" Having nothing else to do, Vati agreed.

On the way there I could think only that, finally, I would have shoes like the ones I saw in the windows, as pretty as those the other girls were wearing. My face aglow, I hurried, urging Vati to walk faster too, but he warned me, "Don't get your hopes up."

But I wouldn't listen. "Frau Ziegler said, 'shoes for free.'"

"Yes, that is what she said, but you'd better wait and see."

The address Frau Ziegler gave us turned out to be a house with a simple plaque that read "*Heilsarmee*," Salvation Armee. Surprised, I turned to Vati. "What's a Salvation Armee?"

"It's a kind of a religion, I think."

"They have shoes?"

"I don't know, but let's find out."

After we rang the doorbell, an older lady, her dress covered by an apron, opened the door. "You must be Fraeulein Knebel," was her friendly greeting. "Frau Ziegler called, so I've been expecting you. Please come in." Seeing her shiny floor, Vati and I wiped our shoes on the mat by the house door, and walked in. "So you're in need of a pair of shoes." She looked at my feet. "We have shoes and you can select whatever pair you want." I could hardly control my excitement. I pictured shoes, neatly lined on shelves, just waiting for me. She asked us to follow her to the back of the house where she opened a door and turned on the light. "Here are the shoes. You pick whatever kind you like. You'll have to do some searching to find your size and its match, because they're a little scattered. Take all the time you need. If you want me, I'm in the kitchen." Smiling, she left the room.

I looked, and there were shoes! A pyramid of shoes! Discarded old women's shoes heaped in the middle of the room. My shoulders slumped. I wanted to cry. I looked at Vati. "It's not as bad as it looks." No words could ease my disappointment as my eyes roamed over that pyramid. Vati walked over to that pile. "Come on. I'll help you find a decent pair." After endless searching and trying on, we found a pair in good condition, made of light brown leather and suede, with a stocky heel. "They're not bad shoes and pretty sturdy," Vati soothed, "good for the winter weather too."

Looking at my not so modern used shoes, turning my feet this way and that, wondering whose feet they'd been on, I nodded, "I guess you're right."

Just about that time the lady reappeared, smiling brightly. "You found a pair. How nice!" With the shoes on my feet, we thanked the lady with a handshake and left, throwing my East German shoes in the first garbage container we saw. I vowed then, that I would never wear used shoes again.

Not only my old East German shoes marked me but also Frau Ziegler's strict camp cleanliness. Female supervisors worked in shifts so someone was always on duty day and night, when Frau Ziegler was not. Under their supervision, housemaid's daily scrubbed and disinfected our quarters. Once a week they sprayed our bunks, including our opened suitcases, coats and jackets. "I feel like a flea unable to get away from that awful stinking smell," I complained Vati.

"Ja, I know, my clothes smells too." To cover up that smell, I bought a small bottle of 4711 cologne. Made for centuries in Cologne, Germany, Glockengasse 4711. This cologne is a refresher for face, neck, hands, or, sprayed on handkerchiefs. Compared to perfume, it's inexpensive.

"I think you're making it worse," Vati laughed as I doused my coat with 4711. Its scent didn't last long. No matter how much I saturated myself, the strong smell of disinfectant spray always came back. Wherever we went, that aroma of disinfectant flea spray mixed with 4711 followed, a flag fluttering in the breeze, alerting people that we were refugees from behind the *Iron Curtain,* a Western label for East Germany.

With the beginning of the Christmas season, the merchants of West Berlin had begun decorating their windows with magical enchantments for young and old. I'd never seen such Christmas displays. Vati and I went to see the big department store windows decorated like winter wonderlands, with moving dolls, gnomes, teddy bears, toy trains, waving Santa's, and glittering angels with hymnbooks in their hands suspended over each scene. Crowds of children and grownups gathered, moving from window to window. I tried to join them, but I couldn't see, even standing tiptoe. Frustrated, I looked at Vati who stood further back, with a grin that said, "I know something that you don't."

"What?"

Hands in his coat pockets, still smiling, he motioned with his head for me to come to him. Leaning forward, he whispered, "I don't know why you're trying so hard to get near the windows."

"Because I want to see."

"If you just wait a minute, you'll get all windows to yourself." Vati looked like a little boy who had just discovered a big secret.

"How?"

Clearing his throat, as if there wasn't any hurry, he said, "Well, I've been watching, and I notice people keep looking at you; then, they back away."

"They are? Why?"

"Because of your disinfectant and 4711 stink."

"Really?"

"Yes! Really!"

To test it, I placed myself right next to people. Pretty soon, with wrinkled noses, they fled with their children to the next window. Trying not to laugh, I looked at Vati.

Amusement written on his face, Vati said, "See, what did I tell you? All you have to do is wait and you'll have the whole window to yourself." It became a game, as Vati and I moved from window to window. Whenever I saw a crowd of people, I'd stand close and watch as they slowly backed away. Then, I thought how low I had become because at home I would never have gone anywhere with the slightest hint of odor about me.

Not long after this window experience, Vati met with the board and was given permission to enter West Germany to unite the family. Again we packed our small suitcases, this time with smiling faces. After cleaning my bunk, returning the blankets and my eating utensils, I said good-by to Frau Ziegler and thanked her for her care. Then, I met Vati, suitcase in hand, waiting for me. He too shook hands with Frau Ziegler and the gatekeeper. Walking along the outside of the fence made to protect us girls, I thought about the girl who had disappeared, hoping she was somewhere safe. Looking at my stepfather I gave him a soft punch on his upper arm. Surprised, he said, "What was that for?"

Feeling secure as I used to feel with my real father, I answered, "I'm so happy we're leaving and so glad that you're here with me." Arm in arm, carrying our suitcases, we started the next stage of our journey to a holding place near the Tempelhof Airport, where we were to be placed, space available, on flights to West Germany.

Documents of approval in our pockets, Vati and I rode the bus to the stop nearest our destination, then walked until we saw a large, oblong concrete building, cold and uninviting. "What kind of a building is that?"

"Well," Vati said, looking around, "we're near the airport's industrial area, so this building may have been a warehouse, converted to house refugees waiting for flights to West Germany."

"I don't want to go inside! It looks unfriendly"

"We have no choice. It'll be over soon."

"No, it won't! Remember, once we're in West Germany, we have to stay in a camp in Worms before we're allowed to go to Wittlich."

"I remember." My stepfather sounded tired as he walked to the entrance, me trailing behind him.

The gatekeeper, an older man, asked for our names, looked at our documents, then said, "First door on the right, they'll sign you in." Vati and I walked into a dimly lit hallway smelling of disinfectant and knocked on the door marked "*Verwaltung,* Management." On hearing the "Herein," with a "Guten Tag," we entered the brightly lit room, where a middle aged lady sat behind a counter. After her "names, please," she went to a cabinet, pulled out a file, and sat down again. "You're Herr Hentschke and you're Fraeulein Knebel." Standing, we nodded. "Your documents?" We handed them to her. "And your identification, please?" Silently we handed her our West German passes. Looking up as she returned our passes, she said, "We have strict rules here. First, because you're on a space available flying list, you have to be accessible at all times. Your names will be called over the loudspeaker system in the building. When your name is called, you report here. So pay close attention to our announcements and be ready to leave at a moment's notice. Second, if you do leave the building, never do so before noon and always, I repeat, always, sign in and out in this office. Do you understand?" We nodded.

More restrictions, when is this going to end? I looked at Vati but he was listening attentively to the lady. "Herr Hentschke, you and your stepdaughter, Fraeulein Knebel, will be on the second floor, room number twelve. Blankets will be supplied to you next door by one of our housemaids. She'll also inform you about meal times." Closing the folder, she got up, indicating that she was through with us.

We picked up our suitcases and went back into the hallway. "I think we'll drop our suitcases off first; then, we'll go for our blankets," Vati suggested as he walked up the stairs.

"It's cold!" I shivered.

"Yes, it's a cold, drafty concrete building where the wind whistles around corners and in stairwells."

"I hope our room will be warmer." Vati had that "let's-wait-and-see-look" on his face. On the second floor we looked for room twelve and walked in without knocking. Instantly, I turned to walk out, but a hand gripped my arm. Dim, noisy, and stifling, the room was crowded with people, families with young children and, to my horror, men. Their conversation stopped as they looked at us. Still gripping my arm, Vati said, "Guten Tag," and, with eyes following us, walked to the empty bunk that sat between rows of bunks, pulling me behind him. He took my suitcase, laid it on the upper bunk and put his on the lower one. Then, we walked back into the hallway again. There the air, cold but clean, met us, and I took a deep breath. Tears in my eyes, I said, "I can't stay here. I want to go home. Did you see the men? And that horrible smell?"

Vati put his arm around me. "I feel the same way. I hope with any luck we'll soon be gone from here. But in the meantime, I'll make sure you're safe. So come. We need to get blankets and find out about the meal times."

The housemaid, also an older woman—*no young girl would work here*—gave each of us two disinfectant smelling blankets and two towels, telling us not to lose them and to return them when we left. "Lose them?" I asked.

"Yes, lose them," she said, leaving us to decide her meaning. Meals were three times a day with lights out at ten.

"It feels like a jail," I told Vati, when, with blankets and towels, we walked to the room.

After that, Vati and I went to locate the not-so-clean bathrooms and showers at the far end of our floor. "At least they're separated," I muttered. It was a busy place because it was the only one for the second floor. Young children of both sexes ran in and out, their mothers behind them. After the evening meal, when I'd brushed my teeth and washed my face, I decided that I'd only shower when all the others were in their bunks.

Back in the room, I took off my shoes and climbed to the upper bunk and covered myself with the smelly blanket and my coat. Vati asked, "Are you sleeping with your clothes on?"

"I'm not undressing in front of those people and the men!"

"I'll fix that for you. Come down and sit on my bed."

"Why?"

"Just do it."

So I sat inside his bunk and watched as Vati took one of my blankets and hung it from the upper bunk, and hung his blanket on the other side. At the foot of the bed he hung our coats, shielding me from prying eyes on all sides. Every morning and night, Vati built that tent, and I dressed or undressed by sitting inside his bunk while he stationed himself at the foot of the bunk like a guard, daring anyone to come near. When I showered late in the evening, he guarded the bathroom.

In our not very large room were six bunk sets for twelve people sticking out from one wall, with six for another twelve people sticking out from the opposite wall with barely enough room to walk between them. In the tiny space left in the center of the room, littered with occupant's belongings and children's toys, sat a small table with six chairs. I had thought bunking with the girls was bad, but, here, others snoring made sleep nearly impossible. With the door closed at night and no room ventilation, the air was unbearable because of smelly bodies and babies' diapers.

Vati and I spent little time in our room. While we were away, our suitcases were locked and ready, stored under our blankets. Because it was cold, we always wore our coats. We spent time in the day room, where there were newspapers and magazines and we could listen for announcements. Once we were called, but the flight was canceled within the hour, leaving me disappointed. Other days we went for walks, but not before checking that we weren't scheduled for a flight. Then, we had several days with no flights, because Berlin was fogged in. Vati and I still went for a walk. There was no street noise, only unidentifiable muffled sounds from a distance. It was eerily quiet, like being wrapped in damp, cold, milky white cotton, bringing back the memory of the humid steam from the railroad engines rising over the bridge in Kohlfurt. "How come Berlin has such thick fog?"

"That's because of the rivers Spree, Havel, Panke, and the Teltow Canal. They all flow through or around the city, so when the temperature and the atmosphere are right, Berlin is fogged in. I think we better go back, the fog is too dense for us to see."

"We'll never get out of here by Christmas!" I groaned.

In the middle of December, however, our names were called for a flight to Frankfurt, West Germany. On the plane with about one hundred other passengers, I sat next to an attractive, slightly gray-haired gentleman in suit and tie. He didn't seem to be bothered by my disinfectant smell, or else he was too polite to show it. I had an aisle seat and Vati had one a couple rows behind me on the other side so that when I turned, I could see him. The stewardess in a dark blue uniform greeted her passengers as the "fasten seat belts" sign lit up. I turned to Vati, wanting to ask what that meant, but he was sitting too far away, and I didn't want to shout. The gentleman next to me said, "Fraeulein, you have to put on your seatbelt, like so," showing me how with his seatbelt.

"Do I have to?"

"It would be a good idea."

"Why?"

Smiling broadly, showing a perfect set of white teeth, he said, "It's because we're flipping over three times before getting off the ground." Seeing my shocked look, he laughed and patted my hand. "Don't worry. I'm only kidding. But you have to put your seatbelt on."

I turned to Vati, but he was busy talking to someone. So there I was, holding one half of my seatbelt, unable to find the other half. Watching me, my neighbor said, "I think you're sitting on the other half of your belt, Fraeulein."

Red faced, I got up and retrieved the other half. Watching me fumbling with my seatbelt, he leaned over and said, "Here let me help you." As if I were a little girl, he buckled me in. I thanked him with an outward smile. During in the flight, he asked where I was from and where I was going, and, before I knew it, we landed in Frankfurt, West Germany.

"We're here already?"

"Yes, we have landed, and what a nice time I had visiting with you, Fraeulein." With a twinkle in his eyes, he added, "And the pilot didn't even flip us." I smiled at him. The gray haired gentleman and I shook hands, and he wished me luck in the new *Heimat*, the new home.

Once we landed at the Frankfurt Airport, Vati and I rode the bus to catch the train to Worms, a city near Frankfurt where we had to stay at another camp until we were allowed to travel to Wittlich. Before we left for Frankfurt, we were given money for food, the buses, and for the train tickets to Worms. Walking among well-dressed people, Vati and I looked like drifters, unclean and smelly. Our five-weeks of living in a camp, along with the ten days in the cramped quarters before we'd flown out of West Berlin had changed our appearance. My once clean hair was greasy with hardly a curl left from the permanent I'd had at home. My well-worn coat stunk. Now, watching people's reactions to our odor was not fun, but embarrassing. Not only was I wearing old women's shoes, but one of my stockings also had a run. Although it had started above the knee, as we traveled, it, too, had traveled down my leg and spread like a spider. On the bus to the train station, Vati sat in the aisle seat, so my legs weren't exposed. But when we were inside the train station, I felt people's looks that said, "a young girl so unkempt." Ashamed, I walked with my head down. I was glad it was cold on the train because people kept their coats on. By seating myself sideways at the edge of the seat while looking out the window, I could hide my ruined stockings under my coat.

I glanced at Vati across from me. He didn't look much better. I saw men wearing expensive suits and ties. Although Vati wore his suit and tie, his was wrinkled from constant wear, and it needed cleaning. His white shirt had acquired a yellow ring around the collar. Vati didn't seem affected by his shabby appearance, or perhaps he didn't want to show it, thinking it would make me feel worse.

By the time we arrived at our new camp, it was dark. We had been traveling since early morning and were ready to sleep. With the papers we had carried, we were signed in. Then, because the kitchen was closed, we were handed barely warm coffee and a sandwich that we devoured because we were hungry. Then, blankets under our arms, Vati and I went to separate buildings. When I entered my assigned room, it was dark. Only the glow from an outside light enabled me to find a bunk. I quietly laid my suitcase on the upper bunk. Then, I showered, put my stinky nightgown on and went to sleep, not caring about anything or where I was. I wanted only to close my eyes, to forget my hobo appearance and the smell that followed me everywhere.

The next morning when a woman smiled and said, "Guten Morgen, Fraeulein Knebel," I had to think where I was. Slowly I opened my eyes to see whose cheerful voice that was. The woman in front of my bunk said, "I'm *Frau Kuhn*, the camp's housekeeper, and I think it's time for you to get up."

"What time is it?"

"It's past ten and your stepfather is getting worried, wanting to know if you're all right. Generally, we do not allow anyone to sleep late, but you had a long trip yesterday. Tomorrow it's wake up at seven sharp."

Rubbing my face, I said, "I didn't mean to sleep that long. Thank you for calling me, Frau Kuhn."

"Your stepfather is waiting for you in the dayroom and has a sandwich for you. Breakfast is over, and we're getting ready to prepare the noon meal." Then, with a backward glance she walked out and closed the door behind her. From my bunk I looked around the room. It was a small but clean room with four bunks, a closet on one wall with a table and chairs in the center. By the looks of it, the room was not fully occupied because some of the bunks had no blankets or suitcases. Two bunks were made up, the girls gone elsewhere. I hurried through my morning routine. Then, I quickly washed my nightgown and hung it on my bunk to dry. By the time I met Vati in the dayroom, I was in better spirits. Folding his newspaper and smiling Vati said, "Guten Morgen! I thought you were never getting up."

"I didn't know it was so late. I didn't even hear my roommates this morning. How long have you been up?"

"Since six o'clock. I walked all over the compound. It's nice and clean. No barracks, only small brick houses. After you eat your sandwich, we'll walk around."

Vati was right. There were individual small houses, a small yard, a fence and a gatekeeper. "I wonder how long we have to stay here."

"We have an appointment this afternoon with the camp director, *Frau Beck*. I talked to her this morning, but she wants to see both of us this afternoon."

At two o'clock we knocked on Frau Beck's door. At her, "Herein," we entered her office and saw Frau Beck in a fashionable gray middy and high heels. She offered us two chairs in front of her desk, looked at me, and smiled. "And how did you sleep? I was told we had to wake you."

"I was tired. But I didn't mean to sleep so late."

"So, now let's see. A few more forms are needed and a letter from the Buergermeister in Wittlich stating acceptance of a refugee family, meaning you, Herr Hentschke, your wife, and you, Fraeulein Knebel, before we can release you."

"But my mother is already in Wittlich?"

"Yes, she is, but she is here in West Germany with a visiting visa from East Germany. Although she didn't go through camp, she is being processed right along with you as a family unification."

"How long will it be before we hear from Wittlich?" Vati asked.

"About a week, depending on how quick the Buergermeister is in answering our request. In the meantime, you'll stay here."

Vati and I got up. Frau Beck, younger than the camp housekeeper, got up too. "I will send for you as soon as I hear something."

Saying, "Danke Schoen," Vati and I left her office.

"I hope the Buergermeister in Wittlich doesn't take too long to answer. We don't have any money and I need to buy stockings. I can't walk around wearing two different colored stockings."

Looking, Vati said, "That does look funny, and, if I had the money, I'd buy you stockings and me, smokes."

I started thinking. *If only I could earn some money.* "I need a job," I told Vati.

"A job?"

"Yes, a job!" I walked off.

"Where are you going?"

"I'm going to ask Frau Beck for a job." Vati shook his head in disbelief. "Wait for me in the dayroom. I'll be right back!"

When I told Frau Beck that I wanted a job and why, and that it didn't mater what it was, she said, "Check with Frau Kuhn our housekeeper. Sometimes, she needs help in cleaning the buildings. If you don't mind doing that, tell her that I sent you."

"Vielen Dank, Frau Beck. I'll do that right away." I left her office to tell Vati our good fortune. From then on, I scrubbed stairwells and bathrooms and did whatever else Frau Kuhn needed me to do. At the end of the week, I had enough money to buy stockings, chocolate, and smokes for Vati. The stockings I saved for the train trip to Wittlich, wearing odd ones that weren't the same color while I cleaned and scrubbed.

On December 18, 1953, three days before my nephew Stefan was born, Vati and I got off the train in Wittlich. Mutti's first words to us were, "Oh, you two smell something awful!"

Beaming, our ordeal of living like hobos for seven weeks finally ended, my stepfather and I looked at each other and said, "What smell?"

And so a new chapter of our life began, to make a home away from home.

Never did I think my final destination would be halfway around the world—where I was to make *my home* away from home.

Did Oma really foresee my future that day in 1954 in Wittlich?

CLOSING REFLECTION

In January of 1954, my stepfather and I each received a request with train tickets to appear at the American Military Facility in Mannheim, for further investigation. The letter also stated we would receive additional monies for expenses and return train tickets. Vati and I made the two-hour train trip to Mannheim southeast of Wittlich. At the American Military Facility, official German-speaking Americans interviewed us separately. I was asked about the process of making condensers, the factory and the management, the FDJ, communist teachings, the uprising in June of 1953, its aftermath and my arrest.

My stepfather was asked about his border patrol job, his superiors, the uprising, and general living conditions in East Germany. After our interviews, to save the money given to us, Vati and I took the evening train home, wondering why the Americans had wanted us because what we were asked was not top-secret information. But for us the interviews provided extra money we desperately needed.

In the summer of 1954, nine months after our escape, Oma, with a visitor's permit from East Germany, made the daylong train trip from Goerlitz to Wittlich. I was sitting outside with Oma, enjoying the sunshine, when she said, "Someday you'll go far away from here."

I laughed, "Where am I supposed to go, Oma?"

She shook her head and replied in a soft, thoughtful voice, "I really don't know where, but you will go far away and you'll never come back."

Gently I took her hand. "Oma, I'm not going anywhere."

"You will! Just wait!"

That was the last time I saw Oma. A year later in October of 1955, after a short illness, Oma passed away in Goerlitz; her loving heart and busy hands at rest forever. I didn't attend Oma's funeral, because I feared returning to Goerlitz so soon after escaping.

Did Oma really foresee my future that day in 1954 in Wittlich?

Most of my adult life I have lived in America, as a nationalized citizen of the United States, making my life in Germany a distant memory

I began to write my memoir in 2000 at Southwestern Oregon Community College in Coos Bay, Oregon. Then, in 2010, I moved to Washington. There, I continued over Skype with the autobiography class at the community college in Coos Bay. In 2014, after many interruptions, I finished my memoir of Goerlitz, my family, living through WWII, then behind the Iron Curtain, escaping to West Germany, and eventually making America my home.

Often I have wondered what my future would have been had my parents not divorced, had my father not passed away. Or if the Second World War had not destroyed so many innocent lives, uprooted families, spreading them all over the globe.

Never did I think I could or would write a memoir because I never had had English in school. But I did. I learned reading and writing along with my children when they started school in the United States. It was and still is a real challenge for me to write in perfect English, to learn and understand its ins and outs, but it can be done by anyone—if they are willing to do so.

Over the years of writing, my classmates and friends from the autobiography class were the best support anyone could ask for. They encouraged me to write. They critiqued my writing. They gave me advice. They wanted to hear more, so I kept writing.

But my deepest gratitude and appreciation go to *Sally Harrold Ph.D.* I know without her knowledge, her care and interest, my memoir would not be what it is—in fact, it would not exist. Therefore, I want to say *"Thank you, Sally!"* My children and I owe you a multitude of thanks for guiding me from the beginning of writing my memoir to the end.

Last but not least I thank my grandson Henry for his design of the book cover.

Most of all, I want to thank my children for loving and believing in me, encouraging me to continue writing even when dark clouds were on the horizon. They have soothed my homesickness with the love and care we have had for each other all through our lives, and I hope and pray they will continue doing so for each other when I'm gone. There is no one in this world, except God, who will love you more than your family. I'm so thankful for the love of my children. They have taught me to be strong.

For the love of my children, I wrote this memoir, to show them what it was like for their mother to grow up in a war torn Germany.

THE PERSONS IN MY BOOK

My stepmother, whom I never saw again, remarried and passed away in 1974 in Goerlitz.

In 1957, my sister with her family, my mother, and stepfather moved to Mannheim, Germany, where in 1975 my stepfather passed away, my mother in 1986, and my sister in 2001.

My niece Claudia, who was born in Goerlitz, is residing with her husband near Heidelberg, Germany, where they raised two boys.

My cousin Uschi never left Goerlitz. Her husband and she raised three children. Both her husband and she have passed away.

My aunts and uncles also never left Goerlitz and passed away many years ago.

Soon after my escape, Brigitte escaped from East Germany in spring of 1954 and lives near the Bodensee. We are in contact and I visit her whenever I'm in Germany.

Then, Renate escaped from East Germany in fall of 1954 and settled in Cologne. She passed away in 2007. Until her death, we visited whenever I was in Germany.

Since the unification of Germany in 1990, I visited Goerlitz often and renewed old friendships.

My cousin Werner, wedding and birthday partner still lives in Goerlitz. So does Karl-Heinz, my friend, dancing and birthday partner. Both celebrated there 80th birthday.

Erna, my locksmith friend, also, never left Goerlitz. I lodged with her whenever I visited Goerlitz until she passed away in 2009.

Sigrid and Margot, both passed away, early in their lives in Goerlitz: Sigrid at age thirty-six of cancer and Margot at twenty-two after the birth of her first baby.

Over the years I have cherished fond memories of my friends and the good times we shared in a harsh and hopeless environment. They were and always will be part of my life.